Complex Systems Leadership Theory
New Perspectives from Complexity Science on Social and Organizational Effectiveness

A Volume in the *Exploring Organizational Complexity* Series
Volume 1

A Volume in the *Exploring Organizational Complexity* Series
Volume 1

Complex Systems Leadership Theory
New Perspectives from Complexity Science on Social and Organizational Effectiveness

Edited by
James K. Hazy, Jeffrey A. Goldstein and Benyamin B. Lichtenstein

ISCE
Publishing

395 Central Street
Mansfield, MA 02048

Complex Systems Leadership Theory:
New Perspectives from Complexity Science on Social and Organizational Effectiveness
A Volume in the *Exploring Organizational Complexity* Series: Volume 1
Edited by: James K. Hazy, Jeffrey A. Goldstein and Benyamin B. Lichtenstein

Library of Congress Control Number: 2007937000

ISBN13: 978-0-9791688-6-4

Copyright © 2007 ISCE Publishing, 395 Central Street, Mansfield, MA 02048, USA

Printed in the United States of America

Acknowledgements

Like any complex project, the origins of this book are multi-faceted, and its fruition calls for some important acknowledgements.

We begin by thanking Russ Marion and Mary Uhl-Bien for their tireless efforts at integrating complexity science into leadership theory, or more accurately, for applying complexity science in ways that generate a new theory of leadership. Through their inspiration two large-scale conferences emerged, thanks in large part to the two cosponsors: George Washington University and its graduate program in Human and Organizational Learning, and the Center for Creative Leadership in Greensboro, NC. We appreciate the organizational leadership of Margaret Gorman at GW and especially Ellen Van Velsor at CCL for their efforts those events. In both conferences Russ and Mary provided a strong intellectual foundation and an effective social context, through which emerged some powerful ideas and effective partnerships, including the one between the three of us, of which Jim Hazy deserves the most credit for envisioning it at one of the conference events.

Another important step in the creation of a Complex Systems Leadership Theory is the production of two special issues on those themes, and we thank the publishers and special editors of those journals: Russ Marion, Mary Uhl-Bien, and Paul Hanges at *The Leadership Quarterly;* and Kurt Richardson at ISCE Publishing, the publisher of *Emergence: Complexity and Organization (E:CO)*. We also thank the authors who submitted to that special issue; all the papers that were accepted have been reproduced in this volume.

Complexity science shows that such collaborations do not come out of the blue, but are linked to ongoing networks and are sparked by more formalized groups. In particular, we appreciate those who founded and organize the *Society of Chaos Theory in Psychology and the Life Sciences* and its founder Stephen Guastello.

We also want to acknowledge those coauthors and colleagues who have had an important and lasting effect on our work including especially Kevin Dooley and Bill McKelvey, among many others.

Although we've mentioned him above, we more formally want to acknowledge our publisher, ISCE Publishing; in particular we appreciate Kurt Richardson who has been supportive and helpful in every aspect of this endeavor. From the success of the special issue of *E:CO*, through the editing and publishing of the final product we could not have asked for better support.

Finally thanks to you the reader for taking the insights here and using them to further your work and the work of creating a Complex Systems Leadership Theory.

CONTENTS

CONTENTS

CHAPTER ONE
Complex Systems Leadership Theory

PART I: COMPLEXITY, EMERGENCE & LEADERSHIP

CHAPTER TWO
An Emerging Complexity Paradigm in Leadership Research

CHAPTER THREE
Systems and Leadership: Coevolution or Mutual Evolution Towards Complexity?

CHAPTER FOUR
A New Model for Emergence and its Leadership Implications

CHAPTER FIVE
Leadership in the Four Stages of Emergence

CHAPTER SIX
Emergent Leadership:
Getting Beyond Heroes and Scapegoats

CHAPTER SEVEN
Complexity Leadership Theory: An Interactive Perspective on
Leading in Complex Adaptive Systems

CHAPTER EIGHT
Paradigmatic Influence and Leadership:
The Perspectives of Complexity Theory and Bureaucracy Theory

PART II: MATHEMATICAL AND COMPUTATIONAL
MODELING OF LEADERSHIP

CHAPTER NINE
Mathematical and Computational Models of Leadership:
Past and Future

CHAPTER TEN
Toward an Understanding of Membership and Leadership in Youth Organizations: Sudden Changes in Average Participation Due to the Behavior of One Individual

CHAPTER ELEVEN
The Emergence of Effective Leaders: An Experimental and Computational Approach

CHAPTER TWELVE
Leadership Style as an Enabler of Organizational Complex Functioning

CHAPTER THIRTEEN
Bureaucratic Agents: Simulating Organizational Behavior and Hierarchical Decision-Making

CHAPTER FOURTEEN
The Role of Leadership: What Management Science Can Give Back to the Study of Complex Systems

PART III: METHODS, MODELS & METAPHORS

CHAPTER FIFTEEN
A Matrix of Complexity for Leadership:
Fourteen Disciplines of Complex Systems Leadership Theory

CHAPTER SIXTEEN
The Paradox of Complex Organizations: Leadership as Integrative Influence

CHAPTER SEVENTEEN
Leadership and a Computational Model of Organizations

CHAPTER EIGHTEEN
Leadership as the Promise of Simplification

CHAPTER NINETEEN
Generative Leadership: Nurturing Innovation in Complex Systems

CHAPTER TWENTY
Towards Social Complexity View on Conflict, Communication, and Leadership

CHAPTER TWENTY-ONE
Leaders' Detection of Problematic Self-Organized Patterns in the Workplace

CHAPTER ONE
COMPLEX SYSTEMS LEADERSHIP THEORY: AN INTRODUCTION

James K. Hazy, Jeffrey A. Goldstein & Benyamin B. Lichtenstein

James K. Hazy is an Associate Professor, Department of Management, Marketing, and Decision Sciences at the School of Business, Adelphi University, Garden City, NY. His research interests include organizational leadership, leadership effectiveness metrics, complex systems in social science, and computational organizational theory. He has published numerous journal articles, book chapters and proceedings' papers. With over 25 years of senior management experience at AT&T, Ernst & Young, LLP and other firms before entering academia, he received his doctorate with distinguished honors from the George Washington University and MBA in Finance with distinction for the Wharton School of the University of Pennsylvania.

Jeffrey Goldstein, Ph.D. is Full Professor, Department of Management, Marketing, and Decision Sciences at the School of Business, Adelphi University, Garden City, NY. Professor Goldstein is also an Associate Clinical Professor at the Derner Institute for Advanced Psychological Studies at Adelphi. He is co-editor-in-chief of the journal *Emergence: Complexity & Organization*, is a board member of the journal *Nonlinear Dynamics, Psychology, and Life Sciences*, is on the Science Advisory Board of the Plexus Institute, and is a fellow of the Institute for the Study of Coherence and Emergence.

Benyamin B. Lichtenstein is Assistant Professor of Management and Entrepreneurship at the University of Massachusetts, Boston. Dr. Lichtenstein's research expertise focuses on applications of complexity science to leadership, entrepreneurial emergence and transformation, and on collaboration, trust and inter-organizational learning. "Professor Benyamin" as his students call him, has published over 35 papers and chapters and presented several dozen more, including articles in internationally recognized journals such as *Organization Science, Journal of Business Venturing, Human Relations* and *Academy of Management Executive*, where he received the article of the year award in 2000. In addition to his scholarly work, and his executive consulting to entrepreneurs and managers, he finds great joy connecting with his beautiful wife Sasha and their two children, Simeon and Moriah.

Introduction

"We meet here in a new light the old truth that in our description of nature the purpose is not to disclose the real essence of the phenomena but only to track down, so far as it is possible, relations between the manifold aspects of our experience."

Niels Bohr (1934: 18)
Atomic Theory and the Description of Nature.

Explaining "the real essence of the phenomena" that embody *leadership* has been a subject of intense interest almost from the beginning of recorded history. Indeed, a major theme in many of the earliest surviving epics, myths and folk tales involves a hero learning the lessons of leadership through a retelling of his or her successes and failures. In so doing these stories expose in narrative form the multifarious relations among people that are customarily considered to reflect leadership. More recently, many classic studies in social science and management have continued this tradition by focusing on the dynamics of leadership. Yet from all of this intensive study "the essence of the phenomenon" of leadership has not been fully revealed, nor has a general set of principles of effective leadership been accepted. In fact, what we even mean by leadership has in large measure remained obscure.

This volume offers a new and very different approach to exploring leadership, one based on the new sciences of complexity. What we are calling "Complex Systems Leadership Theory" posits that leadership can be enacted through *any interaction* in an organization. Far from being the sole province of managers and executives, we contend leadership is an *emergent* phenomenon within complex systems. As such, exploring the meaning and implications of "emergent" is one of the major issues taken up by the chapters in this book. Through advances in computational modeling and non-linear dynamics, the interactions which generate leadership can be "tracked" in a much more rigorous way, enabling managers to better understand and encourage those dynamics of interaction which prove to have beneficial effects on the organization. Overall, we see a Complex Systems Leadership Theory as the core of a new era in leadership studies; introducing and furthering this new era are the primary goals of the present volume.

This edited volume has arisen out of a growing sense among us, the editors, as well as among our colleagues – especially Russ Marion, Mary Uhl-Bien and Bill McKelvey (Marion & Uhl-Bien, in press; Marion & Uhl-Bien, 2007; Uhl-Bien, Marion & McKelvey, in press), that the field of leadership is in an ideal position to benefit from the insights and methods that complexity science has provided to other academic fields. It is important to note, however, that this volume is significantly different from many other accounts of complexity applied to organizations. Much of the latter have tended to be figurative and loosely conceived, often veering into mere platitudes. In contrast, each of the closely reviewed research papers in this volume employs carefully thought-out approaches based on a deep understanding of the science underlying complexity and complex adaptive systems; each author utilizes this understanding to reveal new insights about leadership. As editors we have selected scholars who bring an accurate and nuanced understanding of complexity science to the study of leadership and management, and we have encouraged (and in some cases enforced) the use of well specified definitions and hypotheses as well as sound scientific modeling for each study in this volume.

The first stage of this effort was a Special Issue, "Complexity and Leadership," in the journal *Emergence: Complexity and Organization* (Issue 8.4, 2006), edited by Jeffrey Goldstein and James K. Hazy. This special issue contained seven papers along with an introduction and a reprinted classical paper as is the custom of *E:CO*. These articles specifically addressed the application of complexity theory to leadership from the perspective of qualitative and quantitative research methods as applied within a reframed conceptual model of the leadership issues being considered.

Due to the success of this Special Issue of *E:CO*, we put out an additional call for papers and invited a small number of well-known researchers to contribute their perspectives to the collection, the result being a much expanded volume that includes the initial papers of the Special Issue as well as fourteen new chapters. The present volume thus represents a much more complete picture of the present state of the emerging paradigm that we are calling "complex systems leadership theory." The contributors to this edited book hail from diverse and interdisciplinary fields including: mathematics, physics, computer science, law, education, philosophy, psychology, sociology, communications, and leadership studies. The wide range of the disciplines involved follows what is now a hallmark of complexity-based research. We are heartened that this interdisciplinary trend continues into applications of complexity to leadership studies.

Key Terms and Definitions
The Need for Clear Definitions

One of the recalcitrant stumbling blocks in leadership research has been a lingering vagueness around the definition of leadership itself, a problem reflected in the following comment by the well-known management scholar James March: "I doubt that 'leadership' is a useful concept for serious scholarship" (March & Contu, 2006: 85). Like other social scientists, March was echoing the belief that leadership as a construct is simply too ill-defined to form the basis for any kind of rigorous scientific inquiry. In contrast, the present book attests to how leadership can in fact be studied rigorously and cogently using new constructs and methods coming out of the sciences of complex systems, through which the processes and outcomes of leadership can be more closely defined and explained. Advances over the last half century have brought new techniques, new modeling strategies, and new constructs for rethinking how human systems evolve and the role of leadership in these evolving systems.

As stated above, most of the previous supposedly "complex systems" approaches to leadership have not engendered a sense that there was more to using complexity than applying general metaphors that were not necessarily rooted in the mathematics or science of dynamical systems theory. Thus, one often heard about the "unpredictability of complex systems" and how leaders had to accordingly be aware of and utilize this growing recognition. The lasting message, though, often devolved into: "Unfortunately, there is really nothing you can do about it." Due to an inability to operationalize complexity metaphors in practical settings, the whole use of complexity often degenerated into nothing more than a short-lived fad (McKelvey, 1999).

In addition, many popular accounts relied on an understanding of complexity as the science of bottom-up emergence – "order out of chaos" if you will, the popular meaning of self-organization. The moral was: simply put together the right conditions and the hoped for result for will "bubble up" or "emerge" on their own, spontaneously and fully-formed as new processes and strategies that dramatically increase the competitive advantage of the firm...! As many managers and scholars soon learned, it doesn't happen that way. Emergence in real organizations requires constant attention, support and resources, and the 'success' of emergence – like successful leadership – depends in large measure on the quality of resources and attention that individuals and managers bring to the process.

One of the ways that the present volume aims to improve on these previous approaches is to provide clear and precise definitions. This is particularly important to do right at the outset since the chapters in this volume represent state-of-the-art research and thinking which may be unfamiliar to some readers. An important prerequisite to the systematic and scientific pursuit of complex systems leadership theory is the use of precisely defined technical terms which we will try to supply without becoming heavy handed in the process. At the same time it was infeasible to maintain complete precision across all chapters; accordingly, there are some differences in usage that the discerning reader will uncover. With this caveat in mind, we define the following terms in the next few pages: complex systems, complex adaptive systems, agents, local rules of interaction, and emergence. This discussion will culminate in a preliminary definition for leadership in complex systems.

Complex Systems and Complex Adaptive Systems

Organizational systems are complex in a technical sense; in customary usage when people say "complex" they usually mean "complicated" in the sense of an intricate and detailed interweaving that one might see in a tangled fishing line. In contrast, the technical meaning of complexity does not refer to how complicated organizations are, but to the type of interactions that occur between their elements. Complexity generally refers to a high degree of systemic interdependence, which, among other things, leads to non-linearity, emergent order creation, and other surprising dynamics. It is these surprising dynamics of emergence and order creation that are the focus of complexity research.

Many authors use the term "complex adaptive system" as a synonym for "complex system." Although the phrase "complex adaptive system" was popularized by the influential Santa Fe Institute, the term appears to have first been used by Buckley (1967) to refer to a class of systems that have a capacity for adapting to a changing environment. In its current Santa Fe Institute-usage, "complex adaptive system" retains the sense of adaptability to a changing environment, and it also includes newly specified mechanisms that describe how such adaptation can occur. Mainly through research into cellular automata, artificial life, and multi-agent simulation models, the Santa Fe Institute brand of complex adaptive systems focuses on the emergence of new capabilities or functionalities that arise out of the interaction of semi-autonomous agents.

However, there are other trends in the study of complex systems that rely less on computational simulations and more on the study of complex phenomena as such self-organization in physical or biological systems (Haken, 1987; Nicolis & Prigogine, 1989). In these studies the systems under analysis are usually simply referred to as "complex systems" rather than as "complex adaptive systems," even though they may exhibit adaptive characteristics – mostly through random variations, recombinatory operations, evolutionary selection, and feedback mechanisms. Non-computational complexity studies thus focus on social systems which are complex in this formal sense. Thus, we propose that complex systems be used in the general case, and that the term "complex adaptive systems" be reserved for studies of systems composed of semi-autonomous agents that recombine into new capabilities as a mechanism of adaptation.

Agents, Local Rules of Interaction and Agent-Based Models

In the study of complex (adaptive) systems, the focus is no longer on discrete components, events, or systems; instead, the heart of the new complexity paradigm is on the interactions and networks that *connect* individual agents or elements. A prime example is the agent-based model where attention is focused on the nature of interactions among agents and how changes in the rules governing those interactions can lead to dramatically different outcomes.

In complexity parlance, agents represent semi-autonomous entities that can interact with other agents and change their behavior ("learn") as a result of those interactions. One can define the agents as any "level" of organization, including for example: traits, individuals, procedures or routines, decision making units, systems, firms, and so on. Agent-based models such as Cellular Automata, *NK* Landscapes, Genetic Algorithms, and Dynamic Network Analysis models, each provides a unique methods for exploring how agent interactions lead to emergent outcomes. A crucial aspect of such agent-based models is how they define the "local rules" governing the interaction among the agents, rules which determine, e.g., how the agents make choices. For instance, each agent must continually decide with which other agents it will engage, and what information and resources it will exchange with them.

Although criticism has been directed at the overly simplified assumptions and interaction rules of agent-based models, this criticism is mitigated by the recognition that any particular outcome is valuable only if it leads to further insight into more appropriate rules and more apt simulations. That is, simulation is not designed to provide *the* answer but offers a method to explore many possible interactions and emergences over time.

Emergence

"Emergence" refers to the coming-into-being of novel, "higher" level structures, patterns, processes, properties, dynamics, and laws, and how this more complex order arises out of the interactions among components (agents) that make up the system itself (Goldstein, 1999). Although sometimes incorrectly invoked as a kind of magical sundering of causality, emergence is actually an outcome of variegated and constructed dynamics generated out of interactions between the "lower level" agents that constitute the system. A key insight of complex systems is that once a novel "higher level" system has emerged, its presence and behavior becomes a salient layer for the exploration of explanatory relationships, perhaps even more so than the level of the components by themselves (Anderson, 1972). Thus, the focus of inquiry in complexity is what emerges out of lower level interaction, and how the laws among these emergent properties, patterns, structures, and entities differ from that of the lower level dynamics.

What is unique in human systems – and what offers the opportunity for unique insights within the complexity field broadly – is that human beings as individuals are at the nexus of emergences at the social level. Emergent properties and patterns must be recognized, navigated and in some way encouraged by individuals if they are to take advantage of coordinated action. Leadership of course is caught up in this nexus, and the unique position we occupy as individuals within social, cultural and economic systems provides a level of visibility into the relations between the manifold aspects of our experience. Thus, we see an opportunity in this research not just for better understand leadership through a better understanding of emergence, but also to better understand emergence through a better understanding of leadership.

The whole notion of emergence with its emphasis on the coming into being of the genuinely novel departs the Aristotelian denigration of novelty as a mere aberration away from an ideal type. In management studies, this Aristotelian disparagement of novelty has been embedded in the emphasis on keeping an equilibrium and maintaining control. In contrast a complexity view of leadership recognizes novelty as the growing edge of healthy adaptive systems, and provides a consistent framework for tracking and understanding how and why novel order emerges in complex systems, including novelty in the dynamics of leadership and organizations.

Emergent order in organizations can also be understood as the result of opposing currents. On the one hand, emergence cannot be "controlled" in a traditional sense; the notion of self-organization is usually invoked within this pole of emergence. Several of the papers in this volume explore the relation between emergence and self-organization. At the same time, and despite the way self-organization has been proclaimed in the popular press, careful complexity research reveals that emergence does not simply happen by itself – it involves tending and encouragement from its component agents as well as from a higher level.

Toward a Definition of Leadership in Complex Systems

With the above definitions as a foundation we can now turn to defining leadership in terms of the sciences of complex systems. We start with the traditional conception that leadership occurs when the behavior of one individual (agent) is influenced or moderated through interaction(s) with other agents. Although we agree that leadership is at least partly about influence, the two concepts are not the same. First, leadership is more than simply bilateral influence. Encouraging or motivating individuals to act, enacting a vision of the future, and engendering a sense of purpose in others are widely considered to be leadership, but these are broader and more sweeping concepts than the term "influence" implies. Second, influence is not always leadership. When a person sees a threatening individual in a dark alley he or she may be influenced to cross the street to avoid confrontation, and sales people routinely influence others to buy, but these interactions do not entail leadership as it is commonly construed. A more precise definition that is consistent with the complexity principles of interaction and emergence is needed.

One of the advantages of the computational analyses described in Part II is that they require precision to code a definition of leadership into the behavior of the agents. Taking these models together, a convenient definition of leadership would be those aspects of agent interactions that change the "local rules" governing the future interactions among agents. Because the system is complex, if leadership in this sense is about changing the local rules of interaction, it also potentially changes the system's overall dynamics and thus opens up new futures for the system.

Based on these models we suggest that *leadership* in complex systems takes place during interactions among agents when those interactions lead to changes in the way agents expect to relate to one another in the future. This change can be due to changes in a perceived purpose, strategy or objective, or to changes in perceived norms as to acceptable choices, behaviors and communication.

Effective leadership occurs when the changes observed in one or more agents (i.e., leadership) leads to increased fitness for that system in its environment. We define fitness in relation to some metric of sustainability, especially in terms of evolutionary selection. Of course, how "effective" leadership is depends on what metric of sustainable performance is chosen, which itself depends on *who* does the choosing. Note that effective leadership is always defined with respect to a particular complex system and its particular fitness metric(s).

By proposing these definitions we are not suggesting that each chapter applies them in just this way. At the same time, the above definition is based on the insights from all the chapters. We encourage readers to track how individual scholars converge and depart from this definition. Over time, these definitions will become more specific and linked to empirical studies of leadership.

Organization of this Volume

In summary we contend that a new theory of leadership is needed which incorporates the principles of complexity while matching common experience – approaches that are theoretically sound and empirically supported. In our attempt to organize this collection of responses to that call, we have separated this edited volume into three sections. Part I develops fundamental conceptual revisions to the construct of leadership that are prompted by key ideas from complexity science such as emergence, emergent leadership, and mutual evolution. Part II then grounds these and other insights through mathematical and computational modeling of leadership dynamics and behavior. Finally, Part III describes various models, metaphors and methods arising in the application of complexity theory to leadership. Each of these sections is described further below.

Part I: Foundations for a Complex Systems Leadership Theory

In a sense, the first set of papers expands on the definitions we've summarized above, thus building up the foundations of a Complex Systems Leadership Theory (CSLT). As one might expect, the concept requiring the most attention is "emergence," which is the topic of two papers in this section. Although emergence, and its cousin self-organization, are perhaps the most closely associated with complexity, they are also among the most widely misused ideas in the field. These chapters take this challenge head-on by generating a specific and operational definition of emergence as a "self-transcending construction" – a semi-autonomous set of processes which includes but transcends its components (Goldstein, 2006). A crucial insight is that emergence is rarely spontaneous in practice, nor do complex administrative entities organize "on their own." Instead, emergence is usually *constructed* out of materials ready-to-hand, with the help of tangible constraints – including managers – who provide the leadership necessary to encourage and support nascent bundles of organized order. Further these self-transcending constructions appear to emerge in a series of stages that define the origins of hierarchical organization out of homogeneous agents, networks, groups, and so on.

This foundation around emergence leads to the question, what are the mechanisms that support emergent order? Even the formulation of the question hints at the answer: a complexity leadership theory does not rely on specific individuals – managers, supervisors, executives or others in hierarchically salient roles – to initiate nor to complete any given emergence process. As we have already said, one of the primary insights of CSLT is that the locus of leadership is in *interaction;* thus, leadership is truly a verb not a noun. Several of the chapters in Part 1 describe in some detail what this means in a tangible sense. For example, seeing leadership as a systems phenomena means there are fewer people to praise or blame for the events in organizations; instead, all employees can be attuned to the qualities and mechanisms that lead to emergent order and to act in ways that help generate those qualities. Furthermore, "finding" the locus of leadership means looking into the "space between" – inquiring into the nature of relationships throughout the organization, and utilizing theoretical and analytic methods that help uncover how certain interactions are leadership while others are not.

Interactive though leadership is, there are formal managers in all organizations, which leads to another key issue brought to the fore in Part I: What can formal leaders do to support the emergence of order in organizations? It turns out that there is plenty to do. By understanding some of the underlying mechanisms that give rise to emergent phenomena, supervisors and managers can marshal the resources and energy needed to enact emergent structures. Furthermore, managing in a 21st Century organization means more than simply encouraging emergence – there are roles and tasks a manager should perform which remain bureaucratic and functional to the core; distinguishing between these and those requires a great deal of skill and aptitude.

Together these concepts lead to a different way of seeing – a new lens – that highlights the dynamical and ever-changing process of leading. This lens borrows from systems theory, from leadership theory, and from complexity science. Several chapters in Part 1 detail the elements of this new lens, comparing it especially to traditional models. Moreover as we said above, ours is one volume of four being published within a 2-year period, composing more than 25 distinct articles in all. The core ideas of all of these studies have been content analyzed by Jennings and Dooley (this volume), using a "centering resonance" analysis (CRA) software technology. Essentially they collected all 35 articles and ran them through a CRA analysis, to identify the central ideas in each essay and build a network of "nodes" that represents the most important ideas linking all the essays. Their chapter summarizes these ideas in a clear and concise way thus providing an unprecedented overview to this nascent field of Complex Systems Leadership Theory. In all, Part I lays the conceptual groundwork for the kinds of scientific hypothesis testing taken-up in Part II.

Part II: Learning about Leadership from Computational Models

Our preliminary definition of leadership focuses on how agents' expectations with respect to relationships with one another changes through interactions. Although this definition is relatively straight forward and simple, it is also very general and therefore not particularly useful for driving research. For a particular research project to progress, the aspects of leadership interactions that are of interest need to be delimited, and hypotheses about how these change agents' expectations about future relations must be clearly specified.

As described earlier, in a complex adaptive system, these changed expectations are typically tracked by examining the rules which guide agent action, and by learning how those rules might change over time. Further, in order to pursue research on these issues, the nature of the agents being studied must be clearly defined and specified, as must the particulars of human interaction that are to be explored. The studies described in Part II begin this process. We prepare the reader for these analyses – which although simplified, are also quite detailed and specific – by describing some of the aspects of human interaction they address.

Perhaps the most primitive dynamic in human interactions is the "first mover" advantage in the leader-follower relationship. When two agents are each confronted with a situation, the one who acts first can make it more difficult for his "competitor" to be successful in the dynamic environment that now includes the enactments of the first mover. The leadership question is: how and when do human interactions in this situation result in changes to the expectations with respect to interaction among agents, i.e., when does leadership imply a shift in future action in a direction other than what was advocated by the first mover?

A related leadership quandary occurs when individual agents either choose to "join" a group that is already pursuing a common objective or not. How and when are these joiners accepted into that group? For example, one model described in this section found that agents who were each acting in their own self-interest could under the right circumstances collectively shift toward a correlated set of actions pursuing a common purpose. Further, this shift occurred in a manner characterized by punctuated change that can be modeled dynamically according to a bifurcation point. These ideas can be summarized in the following proposition: Leadership is observed in a complex system when agent actions or communications lead two or more agents to participate in (or join) a leader/follower dyad or a led-group within the system.

In addition to the attractiveness of a common purpose, agents are also influenced by social pressure to conform that influences each agent's decision to join a group or not. Models described in this book show that gathering and maintaining follower-agents requires agents to enact leadership actions that establish a "bias for joining." According to this framework, leadership is observed when at least one other agent chooses to participate in a program rather than to continue to follow an alternative, even though rational analysis might suggest that the alternative would be to his or her benefit.

Thus far the aspects we have focused on have been bottom up in nature which follows a well-established complexity framework for organizations as being informed by interactions among agents within networks of *heterarchical* ties. This represents a corrective to the traditional top-down, command and control view of leadership. But the real world works in terms of both heterarchy and hierarchy. This is not just a concession to reality: it turns out that hierarchy and the centralized control it establishes may play a crucial role in limiting the potential for complexity catastrophe—a situation where the number and diversity of interactions overwhelms the ability of individuals to cope with them—in a well functioning organization. These ideas are also explored in this volume leading to another proposition of leadership in complex systems: One aspect of effective leadership is establishing structure and control in ways that limit the potential for complexity catastrophe, while also enabling requisite complexity within the system as the environment changes.

Taken together, the chapters in PART II aim at developing models with specific and precise definitions for leadership and agent action, while making up for a lack of computational modeling in the field of leadership (Hazy, *et al.*, this volume). One additional benefit of these models is the high degree of precision they bring to operationalizations of leadership. Although a reader can agree or disagree with the approach, there is no denying that the models are clearly defined and delimited. Models such as these can serve to identify "leaders" out of the patterns observed in the interactions of agents, the dynamics of common strategies adopted by the agents brought about by social influence of the agents on each other ("peer pressure"), and which skills on the part of leader agents are needed to bring about a common strategy.

Part III: What Can Be Said About Real World Problems?

In the final section of the book, we turn to more specific and in some ways more speculative applications of the ideas of complexity science to real world human problems. Although the ultimate goal of Complex Systems Leadership Theory consists in part of practical applications, we realize we are only at an early stage of its development. Indeed, the field is only now reaching a point where such problems can even be articulated in precise terms. As such, the chapters in Part III lean toward practical applications of complexity to human systems, even if they cannot provide fully actionable recommendations. That is, these final chapters represent a sampling of models, metaphors and methods that are currently moving the field forward.

"Model" and "metaphor" here refer to how the complexity pioneer and computer scientist John Holland (1998) describes the inner workings of scientific theories. According to Holland, the use of models in scientific research and theorizing is not just to set the stage for the validation of the correctness of a theory, they also function in at least two other roles. First models provide a demonstration that something is in fact possible, as in John von Neumann's demonstration that a self-reproducing machine was possible (an important landmark on the road to the complexity rich field of artificial life). Second, models suggest ideas about a complex system which serve as guides to where to look for certain phenomena. As Holland says, "the validation of the model is in the cogency and relevance of the ideas they produce" (p. 241). Likewise in our sense, the models in Part III involve the "cogency and relevance" of complexity ideas in the study of leadership, and how these ideas can be constructively applied to human systems in ways that improve the process of leadership and leading.

Similarly, "metaphor" is not being used in the sense of an "anything goes" approach, but rather as a tool of conceptualization which has an inherent logic of rigor all their own. This can be seen for example in Fauconnier and Turner's (2002) explication of the indispensable role of metaphor in problem-solving cognition. For these authors, the making of metaphor is part and parcel of the use of the imagination in both the development of theories and their extension to varied implications. In that regard, Fauconnier and Turner have shown how in the use of metaphor, mapping schemes can be established among meanings that are "flatly literal," figuratively metaphoric, scientifically analogical, even "surrealistically suggestive" (p. 154). Holland has connected his idea of model with that of metaphor, citing the philosopher Max Black who had written, "The metaphor selects, emphasizes, suppresses, and organizes features of the principal subject..." (Black quoted in Holland, 1998: 208). According to Fauconnier and

Turner, "work in a number of fields is converging toward the rehabilitation of imagination as a fundamental scientific topic, since it is the fundamental engine of meaning behind the most ordinary mental events (p. 15).

The title of Part III also includes the term "methods." Although this book is not about methods per se in the specific sense of technique, we are not silent about this crucial component of a Complex Systems Leadership Theory. In one sense, all of Part II is about methods since mathematical and computational modeling involve methods that are unique and perhaps less understood than the analytic methods traditional used by leadership scholars. However, these methods are well established in the fields of complexity science. Likewise, the concepts described in this book present additional methodological challenges if they are to form the foundation of a new science of leadership in human systems. The methodological challenges that derive from non-linearity and mutual causality are not to be underestimated, and so we offer in this last section some examples and methodological suggestions for the reader to ponder.

The models, metaphors and methods in this section reflect a range of approaches authors have taken to grapple with the perplexing questions that a complex systems perspective forces leadership scholars to confront. Questions like: How do human interactions lead to new ideas and innovations? What are the dynamics among individual autonomous agents that lead to the perception that leadership has happened? Can these dynamics be observed? Can their outcome be predicted? How do individual agents recognize and adapt to the presence of these dynamics? If recognized, can agents realistically intervene in these dynamics to turn them to their advantage? What about turning them toward the system's advantage? These deep questions are certainly not completely answered here, but these questions and others like them and the gradual uncovering of relations that begin to answer them, are likely to form the agenda for leadership research over the coming years. That agenda will likely begin with metaphors and models, and end with empirically supported theory and computational models with capacities to predict outcomes with reasonable accuracy. This book reports the progress of scientific advance along these new fronts at present, but again what we are able to report today is just the beginning.

What We Learned from this Project

As we began this project, we found that many of the articles that were submitted and that we reviewed assumed the traditional viewpoint in which leadership rests in a particular person or small group of persons who exercise authority and control. Leadership was thus implicitly defined as directed outward from the leader or leaders with the intent to control or influence others toward the leaders' ends. These papers then brought up complexity science as an alternative viewpoint for gaining insight into that situation and better frame the challenges that leaders face in their decision processes. But the problems being considered were the same old ones and the papers assumed the same old traditional command and control posture but dressed up in new garments.

At the same time, we also noticed papers demonstrating the evolution of something else entirely: complex systems view of leadership could grapple with an entirely different set of problems. In this stream, the questions of interest related to the dynamics of the system and not a superior acting on a subordinate. These new questions like the following began sparking our interest: How does leadership emerge from within the dynamics of a system? To what extent and by what mechanisms does individual agency influence system dynamics? Does collective agency emerge? If so, how does this come about? Was leadership a function of one individual exercising power over another or was more about a dynamic that emerged across groups of people in interaction? What we were seeing therefore were explorations of leadership as a *systemic* event rather than as a personal attribute.

As editors, we found this development quite promising for the field. We elected to follow this thread, to explore its implications more fully, and in the end to collect selected contributions that followed this new way. In other words, for this book we consider leadership to be an intrinsic property emerging out of complex systems of human interaction. Leadership is embedded in those interactions and serves a system level purpose even as it furthers the purposes of those individuals who participate in its function. What that purpose is and how leadership relates to individual agents within the system, to groups of agents, and to the system as a whole are the subjects explored in this book. Taken together, we believe these contributions constitute a new theoretical foundation and research program for an emerging *scientific* theory of leadership in complex systems, one that offers great promise to inform both empirical research and the day to day practice of leadership.

PART I
COMPLEXITY, EMERGENCE AND LEADERSHIP

CHAPTER TWO
AN EMERGING COMPLEXITY PARADIGM IN LEADERSHIP RESEARCH

Peter L. Jennings & Kevin J. Dooley

Complex systems leadership theory (CSLT) is an emerging paradigm that promises to make both the study and practice of leadership more effective by bridging the gap between conventional leadership theory and the complex realities of global organization and management. Using a new form of network text analysis called centering resonance analysis (CRA), this chapter reviews recent "state-of-the-art" academic research and cutting-edge thinking on CSLT to provide an overview of this emerging paradigm. Three overarching themes are identified in the literature: first, the larger social-economic context providing the impetus behind the CSLT paradigm shift; second, a core set of concepts that depart significantly from traditional conceptualizations of leadership; and third, innovative research methods that provide more comprehensive and integrative theoretical insights than traditional research methods. Emergent dynamics are highlighted as the anchor point phenomenon of CSLT along with a triadic formula of core leadership mechanisms. Challenges and future directions for CSLT research are discussed including the need to reconcile bureaucracy and complexity conceptualizations of organization, the need to integrate bottom-up self-organizing concepts of emergence with top-down central organizing concepts of leadership, and the need for more empirical studies that operationalize and test CSLT.

Peter L. Jennings is currently a doctoral student in the Supply Chain Management department at the W.P. Carey School of Business at Arizona State University. His areas of study are complexity and leadership; implementing operations and supply strategy; and leading organizational transformation. Previously, Pete served as an infantry officer in the Marines including tours in both the Gulf and Iraq wars. Additionally, he spent several years in management in the high-tech industry. Pete received an M.B.A from Michigan State University and a B.S. from Miami University.

Kevin J. Dooley is a Professor of Supply Chain Management at Arizona State University. He has published over 100 research articles and coauthored an award winning book, *Organizational Change and Innovation Processes*. He has coauthored two patents concerning Centering Resonance Analysis, a novel form of network text analysis, and is cofounder and CEO of Crawdad Technologies, LLC. He has a Ph.D. in Mechanical Engineering from the University of Illinois.

Introduction

Understanding leadership and making it effective in organizations is a perennial challenge for management that has gained increased urgency. Recent decades testify to a melee of "creative destruction" in which revolutionary technologies and intense global competition have provoked a systemic and continuous struggle for survival. The need to improve performance has stimulated heightened interest in leadership among practitioners and scholars (Conger, 1999). Yet, as 21ˢᵗ century global economy continues to progress, there is a growing recognition that conventional conceptions of leadership are overly simplistic and increasingly ineffective (Lichtenstein, *et al.*, 2006). Complex systems leadership theory (CSLT) is an emerging paradigm that promises to make both the study and practice of leadership more effective by bridging the gap between conventional leadership theory and the complex realities of global organization and management.

In response to this interest, two "special issues" in academic journal have recently been published – Uhl-Bien and Marion (Eds) (2007) "Complexity and Leadership" in the *Leadership Quarterly* and Goldstein and Hazy (2006) *Emergence: Complexity and Organization.* In addition, two edited books are to be published in 2007 – the present volume and Uhl-Bien and Marion's (2007), *Complexity & Leadership, Volume I: Conceptual Foundations.* The steady progress culminating in the recent surge of new publications is exciting for this scholarly community. It evidences that complexity has indeed taken root in the field of leadership. Yet, the linkage between complexity and leadership is still nascent: the assumptions of complexity science require clarification despite much description of relevant theories (Schneider & Somers, 2006), and a major re-conceptualization of leadership based on the principles of complexity science remains incomplete (Plowman & Duchon, in press).

As one step toward clarifying this new paradigm, the current chapter provides an overview of the emerging complex systems leadership field. It divides into four sections. First is a brief description of the context and impetus behind the emergence of CSLT. Then the next two sections provide an analysis of key themes defining the field based on our interpretation of the results from a computerized text analysis of the relevant literature. The text analysis was performed using a network form of text analysis, centering resonance analysis (CRA). In the final section, we discuss the implications and challenges for CSLT.

The Need for a New Leadership Paradigm

Almost as many definitions of leadership exist as theorists who have defined the concept (Bass, 1990: 11). Leadership has been conceived as a matter of personality, as a matter of inducing compliance, as the exercise of influence, as particular behaviors, as a form of persuasion, as a power relation, as an instrument to achieve goals, as an effect of interaction, as the focus of group processes, as a differentiated role, as initiation of structure, and "as many combinations of these definitions" (Bass, 1990: 11). The many dimensions into which leadership has been cast provoked Pfeffer (1977), among others, to note that many of the definitions are ambiguous and blur the distinction between leadership and other influencers of social dynamics. To this end, nearly 50 years ago, Bennis (1959) remarked:

"Of all the hazy and confounding areas in social psychology, leadership theory undoubtedly contends for nomination. And ironically, probably more has been written and less is known about leadership than about any other topic in the behavioural sciences" (pp. 259-260).

Traditional conceptions of leadership are heavily grounded in the premise that leadership is "interpersonal influence" (Marion & Uhl-Bien, 2001: 391). They conceive of leadership as one person or small group of persons (leader/s) who deliberately exert influence over others (followers) in order to achieve a predetermined outcome (Yukl, 1999b). Influence theories are based on an assumption of certainty derived from traditional bureaucratic notions of organization in which the world is knowable, social systems are predictable, and organizational outcomes are deterministic of leader actions and follower responses (Plowman & Duchon, in press). From this perspective, conventional leadership theory assumes direct causal relation between leader(s) influence, follower response and desired organizational outcomes as depicted in Figure 1.

Over the last decade, however, a growing cadre of leading-edge scholars and practitioners have begun to challenge bureaucratic *certainty* assumptions underlying conventional leadership theory. Instead, these scholars argue that *uncertainty* is a better starting point (Plowman & Duchon, in press). In a complex, rapidly changing global business environment the world is not knowable, social systems are inherently unpredictable, and organizational outcomes are not directly deterministic from leader actions. The uncertainty assumptions are based on a "new science" of complexity that grew out of the physical sciences and moved into the social sciences (Marion & Uhl-Bien, 2001: 389). In the simplest terms, complexity science moves away from linear, mechanistic views of the world where simple cause-effect solutions are expected to explain social

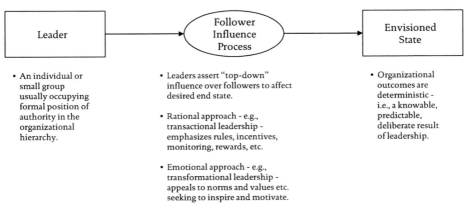

Figure 1 *Simple direct cause-effect model representative of conventional leadership theories.*

phenomena, to a nonlinear, holistic perspective in which complex interactive dynamics explain social phenomena (Dooley, 1997).

Complexity Science and Leadership: Looking for Congruence in a Nascent Field

One way to accelerate development of a field is to identify areas of congruence. We accepted this task and conducted a review of the complex systems leadership literature searching for common themes. To facilitate our study, we employed a new form of network text analysis called centering resonance analysis (CRA; Corman, *et al.*, 2002). CRA is a manifest content analysis approach grounded in centering theory of communicative coherence (Grosz, *et al.*, 1995). Competent authors generate texts that are locally coherent by focusing their statements on conversational "centers" – the words and noun phrases that constitute the subjects and objects of the text (Corman, *et al.*, 2002: 123). Communicators write coherently by creating statements that deploy a stream of words in a semantic structure that comprise a center. The resulting coherence is a fundamental criterion for understandable, relevant communication and provides the basis for CRA (Corman, *et al.*, 2002).

CRA uses linguistic analysis to identify important words in text and links them into a network. Important words are those making up noun phrases, which are potential semantic centers in the texts. Accumulating these words and their links over a set of texts yields a network that represents the aggregate semantic strategy of the author(s). Some words in this network are especially influential due to their location in the structure, tying together many other words and helping organize the whole. Thus, by analyzing the CRA network structure, we can index the structural importance of words and draw inferences about key integrating themes that tie the text(s) together. To the extent that different texts deploy words in the same way, they are said to "resonate"; and the more frequently different texts use the same words in influential positions, the more word resonance they have and the more likely we are to identify common themes that tie the set of texts together (Corman, *et al.*, 2002: 178-9).

We conducted our CRA in three main steps: first, we identified competent authors and an appropriate sampling of texts; second, we constructed the CRA networks using Crawdad Text Analysis System 2.0 (Corman & Dooley, 2006); and third, we analyzed the CRA networks along with a latent content analysis of the texts to identify unifying themes within and across texts. For our sample, we selected academic authors recognized as thought leaders and experts in complexity leadership research. Texts from these authors were selected from the recent series of special issue journals and edited books on complex systems leadership research. Multiple texts from the same author were included, provided the texts were substantively different and not duplicates, i.e. the same text appearing in different sources were omitted. Each of these sources provides a compilation of the "state-of-the-art" academic research and cutting-edge thinking on complexity leadership. Thus, they provided a robust theoretical sampling of expert text upon which to base our analysis (Eisenhardt, 1989; see Appendix A).

After reviewing the texts to gain familiarity with their content and 'cleansing' them of extraneous data, i.e., headers, page numbers, references, embedded graphs and tables, etc., Crawdad text analysis software was used to generate CRA-related data. First, the most influential words and co-words within each paper were identified. This gave us a sense of which words were common across all texts and how each text differed in its content. Second, the texts were automatically clustered using the CRA-based resonance metric. Papers within the same cluster had relatively similar content while papers in different clusters had relatively different content. For each of the three resultant clusters, aggregate CRA networks were created and examined to identify key words and phrases (see Appendix B for sample CRA outputs and analysis). Finally, the papers were re-read with the clustering results in mind. This helped us refine the conceptual framework and labels derived from the manifest analysis and allowed us to create a coherent interpretation, as presented below.

Results: Towards a New Paradigm for Leadership

Our analysis found a great deal of similarity across the authors and texts analyzed from which we were able to develop a good sense of the state of CSLT. A general summary of themes is presented in Figure 2.

As our analysis suggests, three themes characterize CSLT research. First, the literature explicitly recognizes the larger social-economic *context* that is providing much of the impetus behind the complexity and leadership paradigm shift. Second, the literature explicates a core set of leadership *concepts* that depart significantly from traditional conceptualizations and provide a foundation

Overarching Research Questions:

How and why does new order emerge from complex organizational dynamics?

How do leadership mechanisms interact to create and enable emergence?

CONTEXT	CONCEPTS	METHODS

FROM INDUSTRIAL ERA
- Production economy
- Bureaucratic organization
- Central top-down authority
- Control and efficiency

LEADERSHIP
- An emergent phenomenon
- In complex adaptive systems
- Product of individual and collective interactions

WHOLE SYSTEMS
- Holistic approach
- Multi-dimensional analysis
- Combine analytical and empirical techniques

TO KNOWLEDGE ERA
- Information economy
- Networked organization
- Diffuse complex relationships
- Learning and adaptation

DEPARTURES
- Dispelling myths about emergence & leadership
- Reconciling bureaucracy and complexity
- Integrating self- and central organizing

INNOVATIONS
- Emergence as foundation for explanation
- Explicating the process of emergence
- Delineating the mechanisms and patterns of leadership

Figure 2 *A synthesis of findings from Crawdad® computerized text analysis of recent complex systems leadership research.*

for the emerging paradigm. Third, innovative research *methods* from complexity science provide more comprehensive and integrative theoretical insights than traditional research methods. Next, each of these organizing themes is briefly discussed.

Context: From Mechanistic to Complex Adaptive Leadership

Complex theory is not the intellectual hobbyhorse of an eclectic group of leadership scholars. On the contrary, CSLT is grounded in the radically and rapidly changing social-economic realities that are rendering traditional leadership theory and research obsolete. Traditional leadership theories are the artifacts of the 20th century industrial era and the production economy that dominated it (Marion & Uhl-Bien, this volume). CSLT takes for impetus and inspiration, the 21st century information era and the knowledge economy. The implications of this global social-economic paradigm shift are far reaching. It involves no less than a re-conceptualization of the organization from a mechanistic bureaucratic system to a complex adaptive system; order and stability are replaced by complexity and dynamism as dominant characteristics, and adaptation rather than equilibrium are the primary object. Figure 3 highlights the key elements of this re-conceptualization based on a synthesis of concepts, models and terminology from the texts analyzed.

The implications for management and leadership are equally profound, entailing a pendulum shift from central top-down authority emphasizing control and efficiency to diffuse complex relationships emphasizing learning and adaptation (Dooley, *et al.*, 1995). Consequently, management, and specifically leadership, is becoming less about asserting control then about enabling adaptation; it is becoming less role-centric and more relation-centric; influence is no longer primarily direct and top-down, but indirect and multi-directional. Ultimately, leadership is becoming reconceptualized from an elusive trait or behavior embodied in an individual to an interactive event emergent among social relations.

Complexity science entered the lexicon of business organization and management in the 1990s (Anderson, 1999). The late 1990s witnessed a flurry of academic, consulting and practitioner oriented publications in which the ideas of complexity theory were promised to revolutionize strategy, operations, marketing, supply chain, etc. Though the advertised revolution of business practice has not yet materialized, the ideas of complexity theory have become seeded into the various disciplines of business, including leadership (Dooley, in press). Marion and Uhl-Bien's (2001) paper, *Leadership in complex organizations*, was one of the first published formulations of complex systems leadership theory. Since then, the application of complexity to leadership has been diligently cultivated, yielding a promising new leadership paradigm attracting a growing community of scholars.

Concepts: Leadership as an Emergent Phenomenon

The new theory of leadership based on complexity science explores the dynamics of social network behavior, focusing on leadership as the products of interde-

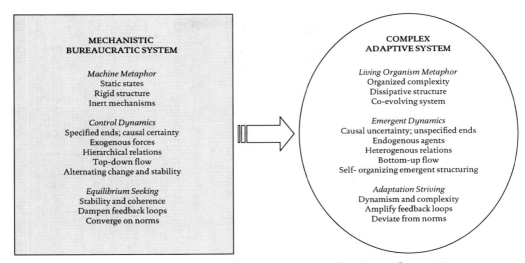

Figure 3 *Key elements in the re-conceptualization of organization for the 21st information era and knowledge economy.*

pendent interaction more than on the products of direct management (Marion & Uhl-Bien, in press). It describes leadership as a complex of entangled functions that, when properly interacting, foster emergent dynamics and enable dynamically adaptive organizations (Marion & Uhl-Bien, in press). "Emergent dynamics" represents the lynchpin in the transition from mechanistic bureaucratic system to complex adaptive systems (Marion & Uhl-Bien, in press).

Emergence is widely recognized in the literature as complexity theory's "anchor point phenomenon" (Chiles, *et al.*, 2004: 502). Though termed variously by different authors who emphasize different aspects of the concept, emergence captures the natural tendency of agents (individuals, groups, departments, etc.) in a social system to interact in complex, dynamic ways – to exchange information, take actions, and continuously respond to feedback. These interactive dynamics produce real change, the creation of novel order and ultimately system-level adaptation (Lichtenstein, *et al.*, 2006).

The importance of emergence becomes more apparent when placed in the context of an integrated complex systems leadership framework. From our interpretations of the papers in this cluster we have assembled an integrated conceptual model that synthesizes the various concepts of leadership in CASs (see Figure 4). Of particular note is the definition of leadership as an emergent behavioral phenomenon that results from the relational interactions of agents in the system. Across the literature we examined there was a consistent "emergent" conceptualization of leadership, though again, terminology varied considerably. In the model, leadership, as an emergent phenomenon, is sparked by tension caused by an "adaptive challenge" and results in an adaptive outcome in which the interactive dynamics of the CAS produce new patterns of behavior and new modes of operating (Lichtenstein, *et al.*, 2006: 4; Marion & Uhl-Bien, 2001, this volume). The model, thus, highlights the central role emergent dynamics plays in producing adaptive outcomes for the organization: emergent dynamics constitute the underlying generative mechanism of leadership and

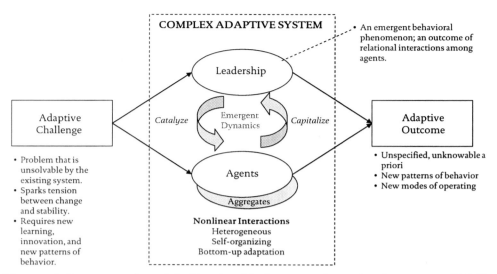

Figure 4 *Conceptual model of leadership in a complex adaptive system (CAS).*

adaptive change in social systems.

    CSLT posits that leaders cannot control emergent dynamics, but they can "catalyze" them by creating the right kind of organizational conditions or fostering certain behaviors or activities (Marion & Uhl-Bien, 2001: 399). For example, leadership catalyzes emergent dynamics by destabilizing existing interactive dynamics, encouraging innovation and making sense of change (Plowman, *et al.*, in press); by creating "pathways of opportunity" (Kilduff, *et al.*, in press); by nurturing innovation (Surie & Hazy, 2006); and by exercising a "participative" rather than "directive" leadership "style" (Schreiber & Carley, 2006: 69). Then, once catalyzed, CSLT posits that leaders may capitalize on emergent dynamics by reinforcing or inhibiting certain changes, creating or dissolving others, in order moderate the tension between change and stability. The ideal is a "coupling pattern" that is not too strong to prohibit change and adaptation but not too weak to provoke chaos (Marion & Uhl-Bien, 2001: 400). This ideal state is often described as "the edge of chaos" (Kauffman, 1993: 220).

    Overall CSLT represents the leadership process as a more limited yet interdependent and interactive process than that suggested by more traditional leadership theories: leaders do not control emergent dynamics; they help to enable and exploit them to a certain extent (Marion & Uhl-Bien, 2001). CSLT scholars debate the degree to which leaders should enable or exploit emergent dynamics. Plowman and Duchon (in press) for example, argue for direct involvement in the process whereas Lord (in press) favors indirect influence of "biasing factors" – e.g. emotions and goals – to avoid micro-managing and excess control. Still other scholars argue the role and importance of traditional leadership concepts – e.g. the need for formal hierarchy, central organization and top-down control as well as the importance of strategic leadership. Notwithstanding the variations of CSLT and the need for further refinement, the power of the paradigm lies in its recognition of a fundamental concept: that *emergence* is the primary generative mechanism of new adaptive orders and the focal phenomenon that leaders seek to enable and exploit.

Methods: Research Innovations

Emergence is an elusive almost enigmatic phenomenon that is difficult to apprehend. Traditional leadership research has failed to penetrate and explicate the complex dynamics inherent in emergence. To explain and understand emergence requires information about how and why it occurs. In other words, the underlying influence processes need to be delineated and analyzed for description and explanation (Woodward, 2003). However, traditional leadership studies tend to be cross-sectional using statistical regression techniques with relatively few comparative statics studies or process oriented studies (Hunt, 1999). Furthermore, Yukl (1999a) notes that most well-known theories of leadership effectiveness were initially formulated using a "two-factor conception" of leadership, e.g., task versus relations-oriented leadership, autocratic versus participative leadership, and leadership versus management, transformational versus transactional, etc. (Yukl, 1999a: 34). Yukl argued that two-factor theories tend to "over simplify a complex phenomenon" and obscure important underlying notions included within the factors (Yukl, 1999a: 34). Because researchers rarely observe the actual "leadership process," a process story or logic must be deduced from existing or new theory to explain why an independent variable exerts a causal influence over a dependent variable (Van De Ven, 1992: 170). Typically, a number of different causal structures will be compatible with a given body of correlational evidence (Woodward, 2003: 106). Almost inevitably, reliance on cross-sectional surveys, two-factor theory and deductive process explanations results in a confounding reductionism (Poole, *et al.*, 2000).

Traditional leadership research has been long pilloried for its fragmentary, unrealistic, trivial and dull nature (Hunt, 1999; Barker, 2001; March, 2006). It is persistently criticized for insufficient description of explanatory processes, an overemphasis on dyadic processes and omission of relevant variables; for constructs that are insufficiently discrete, inadequately defined and measured inconsistently and inaccurately; for insufficient specification of limiting conditions, and a bias toward heroic conceptions of leadership (Yukl, 1999b; Beyer, 1999a, 1999b). As a result, the empirical evidence generated by traditional leadership research entails highly restrictive and unrealistic assumptions while the causal explanations tend to be overstated given ambiguity around the directionality of the relationships. Findings tend to be not only shallow and unilluminating but inherently causally ambiguous and unreliable (Pfeffer, 1977).

Thus, the reality of the traditional leadership research is that it results in uncertainty not clarity; and divergence not consensus – there are simply too many unknowns and exceptions to almost any rule. Rather than empirical certainty, conceptual and methodological ambiguity is endemic in traditional leadership research (Pfeffer, 1977; Beyer, 1999a, 1999b). The fact is that the craft of maneuvering through a complex multi-dimensional intrinsic social phenomenon like emergence may be too subtle and too complex for traditional methods to measure. To this end, Bass (1990: 882), a widely acknowledged authority on traditional leadership, in his chapter on leadership issues for the 21st century, recognized the "possibility of new revolutionary paradigms that can affect both future methods and the content of leadership research":

"Recent developments in the mathematics of dealing with irregularities, reversals in trends, and seemingly chaotic conditions may be applied to modeling the natural discontinuities in leader-follower relationships. The physical sciences may suggest new ways of looking at short-lived phenomena, for example, the emergence of instant leadership in a crisis followed by its equally instant disappearance. The willingness to accept two distinctive ways of dealing with the same phenomenon, as is common in wave and particle physics, may lead leadership theorists to treat simultaneously the leader's and subordinates' different rationales for what is happening. Cause-and-effect analysis may be seen as the exception to mutual interactions between leader and group outcomes. Given the issues that have dominated leadership theory and research in the past several decades, the societal, technological, and organizational changes; and possible new shifts in thinking, a broadening of methodological and substantive issues is to be sought and expected in the field in the near future" (p. 882).

The identification and explication of emergent dynamics as the anchor point phenomenon of CSLT represents just such a breakthrough shift in leadership research to which Bass alluded. It constitutes an opening up and "delving downwards" into the fundamental "organizing relations" that constitute the mystical element and the proverbial 'black box' that scholars have long sought to open in their quest for the universal model for a successful leader (Goldstein, in press). In this respect, it illustrates the promise of more holistic, integrative systems approach to leadership research.

CSLT departs significantly from the traditional research paradigm. Partly because leadership is a continuous social process – a complex, ongoing development involving many actors and many changes unfolding over time. And partly because the variables involved – human motivations such as people's wants and needs, the ambitions of managers and leaders; the nature and interaction of agency and emergent dynamics; the mysteries of creativity, conflict, and power – are too complex and variegated to lend themselves to simplistic explanations or mono-causal analyses (Burns, 2003). CSLT scholars thus require methods that can more fully apprehend how leadership occurs in today's complex knowledge economy (Hazy, in press).

Our review of CSLT literature reveals a progressive employment of robust mathematical and computational models of leadership (Hazy, *et al.*, in press; Hazy, in press-a). Complementing the analytical studies are a series of robust, longitudinal processional case studies leveraging quantitative and qualitative techniques (e.g., Hazy, in press-b; Hazy, in press-c; Chiles, *et al.*, 2004; Plowman, *et al.*, in press). Studies like these address the multi-level dynamics of leadership (Hazy, in press-a) as well as the multi-temporal dynamics that "occur in time and across time" from micro-level conversations to macro-level interactions extending over weeks and months (Dooley & Lichtenstein, in press). In sum, the potential value of these diverse methods is in their departure from the traditional focus on measuring how static leadership variables interrelate to a focus on examining how leadership emerges and manifests itself in and through the multi-dimensional interactive dynamics of complex systems.

Towards a Triadic Model of Complexity Leadership

Complex systems leadership theory represents a significant and substantive departure from conventional leadership theory. Fundamentally, complexity theory moves leadership to a "whole-systems" view and thus away from the more traditional approaches that focus on individual variables and component parts (Goldstein, in press). It seeks to open up the 'black box' of complex interactive dynamics inherent in social systems and illuminate the underlying generative mechanisms of change, innovation, creativity, growth and adaptation. An ongoing challenge for CSLT, however, is reconciling bureaucracy and complexity and integrating bottom-up self-organizing concepts of emergence with top-down central-organizing concepts.

The 21st century may be the era of complexity and emergence, but the industrial era legacy of bureaucracy persists. Despite the social pathologies that are unavoidable and even endemic in bureaucracy, bureaucracy is an inevitable, necessary and even a beneficial aspect of complex multi-agent systems (Spada, in press; Solow & Szmerekovsky, 2006; Boal, in press; Osborn & Hunt, in press; Marion & Uhl-Bien, this volume; Hazy, in press-b; Hazy in press-c). The reality of business organization and management is a complex coexistence of mechanistic bureaucratic systems and complex adaptive systems. Managers thus need modular and malleable conceptions of leadership that enable them to effectively apply theory to the unique and diverse contexts of practice.

CSLT scholars recognize this paradox between bureaucracy and complexity and the tension between theory and practice. The CSLT literature highlights the need to develop a more comprehensive and integrated theory of emergence and has evolved a diversity of perspectives. Some emphasize the bottom-up "self-organizing" component in which the autonomous and ongoing interactions of agents at lower levels in the organizational system produce an adaptive order at a higher system level (Goldstein, this volume). Others combine a top-down "constructional element" – building block operations, e.g., rules, policies, procedures, norms, elements of the formal and informal managerial fabric of the organization that help to construct and constrain the emergent order (Goldstein, this volume). The practical implications of these diverse conceptions for leaders are significant: emergence founded on bottom-up self-organizing suggests a passive-leader role that allows emergence to occur uninhibited; emergence combining top-down constructional operations suggests a more active-leader role setting-up and shaping the conditions and sources for creation of new order (Goldstein, this volume).

Between these polarities, the recent literature reviewed for this study appears to be driving towards a consensus by dispelling myths about emergence and further delineating the dimensions and levels of emergence (Goldstein, this volume; Lichtenstein, this volume; McKelvey & Lichtenstein, this volume). The net finding is that emergence is 'emerging' as a "tangled, mutually causal mixture of bottom-up autonomous organizing and top-down managerial interventions" the combination of which fluctuates and progresses with the size and complexity of the organization (McKelvey & Lichtenstein, this volume). From these additional insights into emergence, CSLT continues to be refined, focusing in on the idea of leadership as a modular and malleable "series of system mechanisms" (Hazy, in press-c).

Hazy (in press-b, citing Hernes, 1998: 74) defines a mechanism as "an assembly of elements producing an effect not inherent in any of them." Mechanisms are dynamically assembled and reassembled as patterns of communication acts and influence relationships among interacting individuals producing particular system level effects. By catalyzing interactions and cooperation among individuals, leadership mechanisms navigate the system as an entity through a changing environment – towards a new order and adaptive outcome. The recent CSLT literature appears to be coalescing around a triad of core "leadership mechanisms" as articulated by Uhl-Bien and Marion's (2007) adaptive, administrative and enabling leadership and by Hazy's (in press-b; in press-c) Leadership Capabilities Model (LCM) that combines convergent, generative and unifying leadership mechanisms with five distinct organizational "leverage points" (Hazy, in press-b). These triadic models integrate top-down central-organizing mechanisms (administrative/converging) with bottom-up self-organizing mechanisms (adaptive/generative) and tie them together with enabling/unifying leadership mechanisms. This triadic formula is thus emerging as the three conceptual legs upon which CSLT will stand and deliver on the promise of making leadership more effective by bridging the gap between conventional leadership theory and the complex realities of global organization and management.

Future Directions for a Complexity Leadership Paradigm

Despite a diverse range of research models and wide number of approaches to complexity and leadership, we believe that two overarching research questions can summarize the *theoretical* challenges that face CSLT scholars. First, how does order in the form of organizational structures, processes, patterns of behavior, etc. emerge from complex organizational dynamics? Second, given an understanding of the first question, what can leaders do to enable emergence that is favorable to the goals of the organization?

As yet there are very few empirical studies that take up these questions. One of the few is Hazy's LCM, which represents one of the first attempts to operationalize and empirically test a comprehensive and integrated CSLT model through 'real world' action research case studies. In so doing, it points towards an important way ahead for CSLT: to further develop and operationalize their analytical and theoretical frameworks through more empirical field studies.

In addition, Lichtenstein, *et al.*, (2006) highlight the following focus areas for CSLT research:

- Expanding the locus of leadership from isolated, role-based actions of individuals to the innovative, contextual interactions that occur across an entire social system;
- Extending current theory and practice by focusing on micro-strategic leadership actions across all organizational levels and across organizational bound-

aries;

- Increasing the relevance and accuracy of leadership theory by exploring how leadership outcomes are based on complex interactions, rather than "independent" variables;

- Highlighting the relational foundations of change in emerging organizational fields, through the idea that leadership occurs in the "spaces between" agents;

- Providing a new and rich foundation for explaining the constructive process of collective action as well as the influential "behaviors" of collective actors;

- Connecting to innovative methodologies that can enrich our understanding of how leadership gets enacted and received in complex environments.

With the above shift in focus, CSLT promises to be much more responsive to the complex adaptive needs of organizations in an increasingly uncertain and unstable, global environment and consequently holds much promise for leadership research and practice.

Appendix A: Sources Used for Centering Resonance Analysis

Source: Book: *Complex Systems Leadership Theory*

Aula, P. and Siira, K. (2007- this volume). "Towards social complexity view on conflict, communication, and leadership," in J.K. Hazy, J.A. Goldstein and B.B. Lichtenstein (eds.), *Complex Systems Leadership Theory*, ISBN 9780979168864.

Dooley, K.J. (2007- this volume). "Leadership and a computational model of organizations," in J.K. Hazy, J.A. Goldstein and B.B. Lichtenstein (eds.), *Complex Systems Leadership Theory*, ISBN 9780979168864.

Goldstein, J.A. (2007- this volume). "A new model for emergence and its leadership implications," in J.K. Hazy, J.A. Goldstein and B.B. Lichtenstein (eds.), *Complex Systems Leadership Theory*, ISBN 9780979168864.

Hazy, J. K., Milhiser, W. and Solow, D. (2007- this volume). "Mathematical & computational models of leadership: Past & future," in J.K. Hazy, J.A. Goldstein and B.B. Lichtenstein (eds.), *Complex Systems Leadership Theory*, ISBN 9780979168864.

Henning, P.B. and Dugan, S. (2007- this volume). "Leaders' detection of problematic self-organization in the workplace," in J.K. Hazy, J.A. Goldstein and B.B. Lichtenstein (eds.), *Complex Systems Leadership Theory*, ISBN 9780979168864.

Lichtenstein, B.B. (2007- this volume). "A matrix of complexity for leadership: 14 disciplines of complex systems leadership theory," in J.K. Hazy, J.A. Goldstein and B.B. Lichtenstein (eds.), *Complex Systems Leadership Theory*, ISBN 9780979168864.

McKelvey, B. and Lichtenstein, B.B. (2007- this volume). "Leadership in the four stages of emergence," in J.K. Hazy, J.A. Goldstein and B.B. Lichtenstein (eds.), *Complex Systems Leadership Theory*, ISBN 9780979168864.

Marion, R. and Uhl-Bien, M. (2007- this volume). "Paradigmatic influence and leadership: The perspectives of complexity theory and bureaucracy theory," in J.K. Hazy, J.A. Goldstein and B.B. Lichtenstein (eds.), *Complex Systems Leadership Theory*, ISBN 9780979168864.

Panzar, C., Hazy, J. K., McKelvey, B., Schwandt, D. R. (2007 - this volume). "The paradox of complex organizations: Leadership as integrative influence," in J.K. Hazy, J.A. Goldstein and B.B. Lichtenstein (eds.), *Complex Systems Leadership Theory*, ISBN 9780979168864.

Plowman, D. A. & Duchon, D. (2007 - this volume). "Emergent leadership: Getting beyond heroes & scapegoats," in J.K. Hazy, J.A. Goldstein and B.B. Lichtenstein (eds.), *Complex Systems Leadership Theory*, ISBN 9780979168864.

Spada, C. (2007 - this volume). "Bureaucratic agents: Simulating organizational behavior and hierarchical decision-making," in J.K. Hazy, J.A. Goldstein and B.B. Lichtenstein (eds.), *Complex Systems Leadership Theory*, ISBN 9780979168864.

Schwandt, D. R. & Szabla D. (2007 - this volume). "Systems and leadership: Coevolution or mutual evolution towards complexity?" in J.K. Hazy, J.A. Goldstein and B.B. Lichtenstein (eds.), *Complex Systems Leadership Theory*, ISBN 9780979168864.

Source: Book: *Complexity and Leadership Volume I: Conceptual Foundations*

Dooley, K. and Lichtenstein, B. (in press). "Research methods for studying the complexity dynamics of leadership," in M. Uhl-Bien and R. Marion (eds.), *Complexity and Leadership Volume I: Conceptual Foundations,* Charlotte, NC: Information Age Publishing.

Goldstein, J. (in press). "Conceptual foundations of complexity science: Development and main constructs," in M. Uhl-Bien and R. Marion (eds.), *Complexity and Leadership Volume I: Conceptual Foundations,* Charlotte, NC: Information Age Publishing.

Hazy, J.K. (in press). "Leadership or luck? The system dynamics of Intel's shift to microprocessors in the 1970s and 1980s," in M. Uhl-Bien and R. Marion (eds.), *Complexity and Leadership Volume I: Conceptual Foundations,* Charlotte, NC: Information Age Publishing.

Hazy, J.K. (in press). "Patterns of leadership: A case study of influence signaling in an entrepreneurial firm," in M. Uhl-Bien and R. Marion (eds.), *Complexity and Leadership Volume I: Conceptual Foundations,* Charlotte, NC: Information Age Publishing.

Kilduff, M., Crossland, C. and Tsai, W. (in press). "Pathways of opportunity in dynamic organizational networks," in M. Uhl-Bien and R. Marion (eds.), *Complexity and Leadership Volume I: Conceptual Foundations,* Charlotte, NC: Information Age Publishing.

Lord, R.G. (in press). "Beyond transactional and transformational leadership: Can leaders still lead when they don't know what to do?" in M. Uhl-Bien and R. Marion (eds.), *Complexity and Leadership Volume I: Conceptual Foundations,* Charlotte, NC: Information Age Publishing.

Plowman, D.A. and Duchon, D. (in press). "Dispelling the myths about leadership: From cybernetics to emergence," in M. Uhl-Bien and R. Marion (eds.), *Complexity and Leadership Volume I: Conceptual Foundations,* Charlotte, NC: Information Age Publishing.

Schwandt, D.R. (in press). "Individual and collective coevolution: Leadership as emergent social structuring," in M. Uhl-Bien and R. Marion (eds.), *Complexity and Leadership Volume I: Conceptual Foundations,* Charlotte, NC: Information Age Publishing.

Schreiber, C. and Carley, K.M. (in press). "Dynamic network leadership: Leading for learning and adaptability," in M. Uhl-Bien and R. Marion (eds.), *Complexity and Leadership Volume I: Conceptual Foundations,* Charlotte, NC: Information Age Publishing.

Uhl-Bien, M. and Marion, R. (in press). "Complexity leadership theory: a leadership model for new and innovative organizational forms," in M. Uhl-Bien and R. Marion (eds.), *Complexity and Leadership Volume I: Conceptual Foundations,* Charlotte, NC: Information Age Publishing.

Vallacher, R.R. and Nowak, A. (in press). "Dynamical social psychology: On complexity and coordination in human experience," in M. Uhl-Bien and R. Marion (eds.), *Complexity and Leadership Volume I: Conceptual Foundations,* Charlotte, NC: Information Age Publishing.

Source: Journal Special Issue: *The Leadership Quarterly* (in press):

Boal, K.B. and Schultz, P.L. (in press). "Storytelling, time, and evolution: The role of strategic leadership in complex adaptive systems," *The Leadership Quarterly*, ISSN 1048-9843.

Guastello. S.J. (in press). "Non-linear dynamics and leadership emergence," *The Leadership Quarterly*, ISSN 1048-9843.

Hazy, J.K. (in press). "Computer models of leadership: Foundations for a new discipline or meaningless diversion?" *The Leadership Quarterly*, ISSN 1048-9843.

Hogue, M. and Lord, R.B. (in press). "A multilevel, complexity theory approach to understanding gender bias in leadership," *The Leadership Quarterly*, ISSN 1048-9843.

Osborn, R.N. and Hunt, J.G. (in press). "Leadership and the choice of order: Complexity and hierarchical perspectives near the edge of chaos," *The Leadership Quarterly*, ISSN 1048-9843.

Plowman, D.A., Baker, L., Beck, T.E., Kulkami, M., Solansky, S. and Travis, D. V. (in press). "The role of leadership in emergent, self-organization," *The Leadership Quarterly*, ISSN 1048-9843.

Uhl-Bien, M., Marion, R. and McKelvey, B. (in press). "Complexity leadership theory: Shifting leadership form the industrial age to the knowledge era," *The Leadership Quarterly*, ISSN 1048-9843.

Source: Journal Special Issue: *Emergence: Complexity & Organization* (E:CO)

Dal Forno, A. and Merlone, U. (2006). "The emergence of effective leaders: An experimental and computational approach," *Emergence: Complexity & Organization,* ISSN 1521-7000, 8(4): 36-51.

Harter, N. (2007). "Leadership as the promise of simplification," *Emergence: Complexity & Organization,* ISSN: 15217000, 8(4): 77-87.

Lichtenstein, B.B., Marion, R., Orton, J. A., Schreiber, C., Seers, A. and Uhl-Bien, M. (2006). "Complexity leadership theory: An interactive perspective on leading in complex adaptive systems," *Emergence: Complexity & Organization,* ISSN 1521-7000, 8(4): 2-12.

Phelps, K.C. and Hubler, A.W. (2006). "Towards an understanding of membership and leadership in youth organizations: Sudden changes in average participation due to the behavior of one individual," *Emergence: Complexity & Organization,* ISSN

1521-7000, 8(4): 28-35.

Schreiber, C. and Carley, K.M. (2006). "Leadership style as an enabler of organizational complex functioning," *Emergence: Complexity & Organization,* ISSN 1521-7000, 8(4): 61-76.

Solow, D. and Szmerekovsky, J. G. (2006). "The role of leadership: what management science can give back to the study of complex systems," *Emergence: Complexity & Organization,* ISSN 1521-7000, 8(4): 52-60.

Surie, G. and Hazy, J. K. (2006). "Generative leadership: Nurturing innovation in complex systems," *Emergence: Complexity & Organization,* ISSN 1521-7000, 8(4): 13-27.

Appendix B: CRA Analysis Sample Outputs

The following sample outputs from our CRA analysis demonstrate how, using *Crawdad®* automated text analysis capability, we proceeded from CRA network analysis to identifying semantic centers, to clustering influential pairs of shared words, and then using these findings with a close re-reading of the texts to develop interpretive themes. The sample outputs below are from the "within source" analysis of the journal special issue *Emergence: Complexity & Organization.* A similar process was used to identify and synthesize themes across the four different sources incorporated in the sample in this study. These analyses and findings guided our synthesis of concepts, models, terminology across authors and texts to produce Figures 2, 3, and 4 and the discussions that accompany them.

Sample CRA Network for E:CO

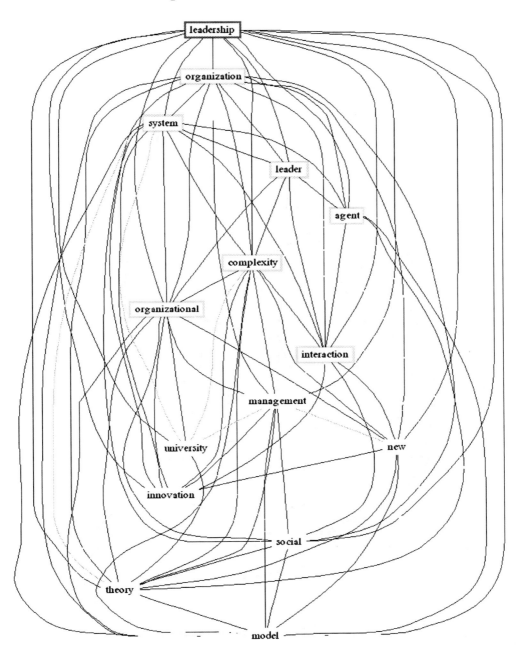

Sample Clusters of Influential Shared Words

Cluster 1: Influential Shared Words

Cluster 2: Influential Shared Words

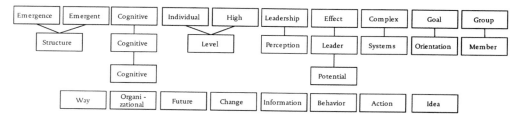

Interpretation of Themes

Special Issue: Complexity Science & Leadership
Leadership as an emergent phenomenon among agents & events
within complex social systems.

- -

Cluster: Leadership Interactions

TITLES
- An interactive perspective on leading in CAS (Practitioner)
- Generative leadership: nurturing innovation in CAS (Practitioner)
- Leadership style as an enabler

THEMES
Leadership
- As emergent phenomenon
Interactions & events
- Result in *innovations* & adaptations
- *Leader* impact on *network*
- *New* theory, technology, perspective

Cluster: Leadership Emergence

TITLES
- Membership & leadership in youth organizations
- Emergence of leaders: computational experimental approach
- The role of leadership
- Complexity and philosophy

THEMES
- Conditions for leader emergence
- Centralized *organization* and the exercise of *control*
- Leader impact on *organization* participation
- Leadership, *order* & simplification
- *Agent*-based modeling

CHAPTER THREE
Systems and Leadership: Coevolution or Mutual Evolution Towards Complexity?

David R. Schwandt & David B. Szabla

This chapter explores the evolution of the discourses concerning the relationship between social systems theory and leadership theory over a 100-year time span. A historical understanding of this relationship informs our present discussion concerning leadership and the complexity sciences because complexity deals with systems. Three aspects of the evolution of the two fields of study are discussed. First, a slow movement has occurred from a reductionary/rational worldview to one of holism and non-rationality. Second, social systems and leadership have always had complexity embedded in their discussions. Finally, the two fields have coevolved through an interaction of content and process. Each of these observations brings understanding to the complex understanding of leadership in the context of social systems.

David R. Schwandt is Professor of Human and Organizational Studies at The George Washington University. His current research centers on organizational issues that relate to collective cognition, complex adaptive systems, and experiments with agent based modeling. His teaching responsibilities include instruction at both the Doctoral and Masters levels in the areas of organizational systems analysis, performance management systems, consultation, international human resource development, organizational learning, managerial and organization cognition, and chaos theory. He has also served on the faculty of The Johns Hopkins University's Applied Behavioral Science Program and the University of Maryland's University College Management Program.

David B. Szabla is an Assistant Professor of Human and Organizational Studies at The George Washington University where he teaches organizational change, organizational learning, organizational culture, and advanced research methods. His research focuses on the content, process, and context of organizational change. Currently, Dr. Szabla is using the complexity sciences as a framework for developing a new model for thinking about and leading organizational change. Dr. Szabla received his masters in Human Resource Education from Boston University and his doctorate in Human and Organizational Studies from The George Washington University.

"Lessons from simple systems of the past can be dangerously misleading as a basis for leadership in an increasingly complex world" (Forrester, 1996: 2).

Introduction

Jay Forrester's quote reflects a real concern for those of us interested in the relationship between leadership and social systems. He goes on to say, "Complex social systems behave in ways quite different from expectations arising from experience with simple systems. But simple systems still form the basis for most principles of leadership" (Forrester, 1996: 2). If we underestimate and/or misunderstand the complexity of the social system, it may lead to unanticipated and possibly negative consequences. Examples of these consequences are apparent in the leadership actions we have seen in the recent past. They have resulted in failures of companies (Enron), failed public policy (immigration and healthcare), and international relationships that have led to war.

Much of this book is concerned with the present and future development of leadership concepts in the context of complex adaptive systems. However, this chapter deals with the past. It is our premise that a better understanding of the historical discourse concerning systems of human interaction (such as organizations, groups, and societies) can provide insights as to the purpose and nature of leadership. The purpose of this chapter is to examine the evolution of the discourse[1] concerning possible evolutionary relationships between systems theory and leadership theory. It is important to understand this relationship because the present complexity discourse is questioning traditional person- and/or position-centered leadership models in the context of adaptive systems (Griffin, 2002; McKelvey, 2002).

An interesting aspect of the historical relationship between leadership and systems theory is that, at first, they seem to have been considered two separate fields of study. With the exception of some social psychologists (Katz & Kahn, 1966; Weick, 1979), many of the approaches to the study of leadership and social systems have been characterized in terms of the age-old arguments concerning the crossing of levels of analysis (e.g., individual, group, organization) in research efforts (Klein, *et al.*, 1999). However, as we point out, the interaction of the two fields was important to their respective development.

Until the advent of complexity science's interest in the social sciences, social systems were the territory of the sociologist, and leadership was the domain of the psychologist. The classic discipline-based arguments and differing worldviews have artificially separated the two fields and created operational falsities that have delimited the potential of both individuals and collectives in their efforts to understand social interaction. Complexity science is now weigh-

1 In using the word *discourse*, we are assuming the basic definition of a formal and orderly expression of thought on a subject - primarily in conversations and writing. However, on a more specific level concerning management, leadership, and systems, we employ Barley and Kunda's (1992) conceptualization of discourse: "Although managerial theories can be assessed as sets of propositions, they may also be treated as rhetorics or ideologies. By an ideology we mean a stream of discourse that promulgates, however unwittingly, a set of assumptions about the nature of the objects with which it deals" (p. 363).

ing in on these ontological and epistemological arguments (evidence the current collection of chapters in this volume) by saying that all levels of analysis and disciplines must be considered simultaneously to understand human interaction and emergent social phenomena.

There may be skepticism concerning the usefulness of a review of this type. However, the cultures we live in, and the histories we live with, provide social (and organizational) interactions with meaningfulness (Weick, 2001). Thus, we believe this chapter will be of value to both those who are interested in complexity science and those who are interested in questions concerning leadership in complex environments. More specifically, discourse influences our actions as researchers and as practitioners (Luhmann, 1995; Taylor & Van Every, 2000). History may or may not foreshadow the future. However, if we are to participate in the complexity discourse, we have a responsibility to at least consider the past. In addition, the evolution of systems theory and leadership concepts has implications for our day-to-day lives. If we assume emergence from human interaction (McKelvey, 2003), we must engage the language and rhetoric of both fields of study simultaneously to understand their meaning.

The chapter begins by presenting a delineation of the discourses concerning the development of social systems and leadership over a period of 100 years. We analyze the changes in discourse over three time segments. The first period, *Work Systems to Cooperative Systems (1900-1940)*, represents the social systems and leadership discourse in a transition from the improvement of work processes to the maintenance of cooperative systems. In the second time period, *Functionally Driven Systems to Interactive Systems (1940-1970),* we examine the shift of the discourse from considering social systems and leadership as functions comprised of actions (behaviors) to a focus on the interactions themselves and their capacity to generate emergent order within the system as it relates to its environment. The discourse in the final time period, *Learning Systems to Complex Systems Theory (1970-2000),* portrays the movement from the role of social systems and leadership in collective learning to a more complex role in knowledge and meaning creation and represents the ending period for our analysis of the development of the two constructs. The discourse from 2000–2007, although rich in substance, represents the early formation of a period of potential consolidation. However, it is too early to derive any rhetorical patterns. The three periods were selected because they represent identifiable shifts in the social systems discourse from an emphasis on mechanics, to an emphasis on function, to a consideration of meaning making (Barley & Kunda, 1992; Eastman & Bailey, 1998). The chapter concludes in an attempt to retrospectively make sense of the relationships between the discourses, their mutual evolution, and implications for our present dialogues.

Social Systems and Leadership Discourse

In this section, first, we provide a review of the definitions of each field of study. Following this discussion, we present separately an overview of each discourse by the time periods stipulated above so that readers can draw their own inferences concerning the relationships between the two fields of study.

Although early nomenclatures vary from today's interpretations, one can ascertain the shifts in ideology and rhetoric. The ideas represent multiple disciplines (management, sociology, social psychology, and complexity) and were chosen as indicative representations of the discourse during a specific period of time. They certainly are not all inclusive, and we are sure that other authors would have picked different examples of the discourse to characterize social systems and/or leadership.

Systems Definitions

The systems concept originated in the realm of the physical or natural sciences (e.g., physics and biology). Its migration to the social sciences entailed the acceptance of a rational and objective worldview that became the basis for social formalism and mechanical applications of systems theory to social research and practice. In general, the core components of the definition of a system have not significantly varied over the 100 years we examine (see Table 1). Each theorist appears to have accepted a general and simplistic definition of a system that included some set of defined elements and a number of relationships between and among the elements. This concept was formalized by Bertalanffy (1956) in his discussion of General Systems Theory as "a set of elements standing in interaction" (p. 3). However, as we will see, what have varied are the nature of the elements and the complexity of their relationships.

The social systems discourse throughout the century has not been as concerned as we might think with leadership per se. It has been more concerned (even preoccupied) with the concepts of survival (goals), causation, and structures (control and power) as descriptions of the relationships between elements of the system. One possible relationship could be a leader role that would include the dynamics of power, goals, and control. However, the leadership role was not seen as the only manifestation of these dynamics. Early social systems theorists saw social structure as any enduring pattern of social arrangements within the collective (usually with the purpose of maintaining stability). Over time the idea of structure as a multitude of relationships has become more dynamic, to include concerns with its purposes, its formation, and its endurance. Social structure can include explicit and implicit mechanisms such as rules, cultural values, norms, and also action-oriented relationships among the elements such as language and traditional acts of leadership.

Leadership Definitions

The origins of the study of leadership started with the examination of the power elite—those leaders thought to have a built-in genius. In the early 1900s, the trait approach explained the notion of "the great man theory of leadership" as people who were born, not made. These initial definitions of leadership depicted leaders as commanding and controlling; later theories described leaders as strategic thinkers, teachers, and stewards (see Table 2). Throughout the century, the image of the leader as an authority figured slowly dissolved into a representation of the leader as a facilitator. The early discourse concentrated on the leader and positioned leaders as apart from the group, directing the behavior of followers.

Source	Characterization
Period One: Work Systems to Cooperative Systems	
Taylor, 1911 Gantt, 1919 Mayo, 1933 Fayol, 1949	Social arrangements (although not considered systems per se) for the purpose of facilitating work (and production) are characterized in formal and recurring processes that involved individuals and groups. Efficiency of the "system" is dependent on its work design, control, administration, and human factors.
Parsons, 1937	Social systems are systems of human actions with characteristics of (1) an end, (2) a situation, analyzable in terms of (a) means and (b) conditions, and (3) at least one selective standard in terms of which the end is related to the situation. These have meaning only in terms of the subjective point of view of the actor.
Barnard, 1938	A cooperative system is a complex of physical, biological, personal, and social components that are in a specific systematic relationship by reason of the core operation of two or more persons for at least one definite end.
Period Two: Functionally Driven Systems to Interactive Systems	
Parsons, 1951 Parsons & Shils, 1952	The social system is made up of relationships of individuals, but it is a system that is organized around the problems inherent in or arising from social interaction. The most general and fundamental property of the system is the interdependence of parts in the existence of determinate relationships among the parts or variables as contrasted with randomness of variability. The system is characterized by the existence of functional prerequisites: environmental adaptation, goal attainment, integration, and latent pattern maintenance.
Wiener, 1954 Boulding, 1956 Bertalanffy, 1962	A system is elements "standing in interaction" characterized by levels of complexity. Each level incorporates all those below it, is open to information, vulnerable to entropy, capable of self-organization and equifinality. "Cybernetics has concerned itself with the study of phenomena which behave as if they had goals. More specifically, it is concerned with the theory of complex interlocking 'chains of causation' from which goal-seeking and self-controlling forms of behavior emerge" (Burrell & Morgan, 1979: 66).

Table 1 *Examples of Systems Discourse Over 100 Years (continued)*

Author	Description
Hall & Fagen, 1956	A system is a complex of elements or components directly or indirectly related in a causal network, such that each component is related to at least some others in a more or less stable way within any particular time. The components may be relatively simple and stable, or complex and changing. They may vary in only one or two properties or take on many different states. The interrelations between them may be mutual or unidirectional, linear, nonlinear or intermittent in varying degrees of causal efficacy or priority.
Katz & Kahn, 1966	All social systems, including organizations, are consistent patterns of activities of a number of individuals. Moreover, these patterned activities are complementary or interdependent with respect to some common output or outcome. They are repeated, relatively enduring, and bounded in space and time. The stability or re-occurrence of activities can be examined in relation to the energetic input into the system, transformation of energies within the system, and the resulting product of energetic output.
Buckley, 1968	Characteristics of complex adaptive systems entail constant interchange with environmental events (acting on and reacting to them), variety in components and interactions, selective criteria that map variations in the system closely to the environment and in arrangement for preserving and or propagating successful mappings.
Klir, 1969	The system is a given time-invariant relation between instantaneous and/or past and/or future values of the external quantities. Every element of the relation may, but need not be, associated with a probability of its oc-currence.

Period Three: Learning Systems to Complex Systems Theory

Author	Description
Miller, 1978	Living systems are a special subset of the set of all possible concrete systems. They all have the following char-acteristics: (a) they are open systems, with significant inputs, throughputs, and outputs of various sorts of matter – energy and information, (b) they maintain a steady state of negative entropy, even though entropic changes occur in them as they do everywhere else.

Table 1 *Examples of Systems Discourse Over 100 Years (continued)*

Giddens, 1979	Social systems are reproduced relationships between actors and collectivities, whereas system integration is achieved through reciprocity between groups or collectivities. Structure of the systems has a dual nature – it influences action and is influenced by action. Structuration "represents conditions governing the continuity or transformation of structures, and therefore the reproduction of the system" (p. 66).
Habermas, 1987	Society is composed of the social system, which refers to the way in which social structures and the functional imperative constrains actions through the media of money and power, and the life world, which refers to the shared meanings and taken-for-granted nature of daily activities. Life world is central to social reproduction. Society is constantly made and remade through these routine practices. The life world refers to communicative actions that relate to the objective world, the social world, and the subjective world.
Bailey, 1994	A system is a bounded set of interrelated components that has an entropy value below the maximum.
Luhmann, 1995	A differentiated system is no longer simply composed of a certain number of parts and the relationships among them, rather, it is composed of a relatively large number of operationally employable system/ environment differences, which each, along different cutting lines, reconstruct the whole system as a unity of subsystems and environment.
Morel & Ramanujam, 1999	Complex systems tend to be made up of a large number of elements that interact with one another. Such interactions are typically associated with the presence of feedback mechanisms in the system. They have emergent properties that are referred to as independently observable in empirically verifiable patterns.
Anderson, 1999	Complex Adaptive Systems (CAS) theory "asks how changes in the agent's decision rules, the interconnections among agents, or the fitness function that agents employ produce different aggregate outcomes" (p. 220).

Table 1 *Examples of Systems Discourse Over 100 Years (continued)*

(See Stogdill, 1974, for a compilation of leadership research history.) By the end of the century, the focus moved to followers and leaders becoming a part of the group. It appears that no single theory dominated the discourse during a specific time period, nor did one theory disappear when a new theory was suggested. For example, group theory became an important topic in the conversation in the 1930s, and although other theories were emphasized at different times thereafter, the principles of group theory never diminished. Finally, most of the theories have a structural-functional perspective and are based on a Western scientific worldview that is hierarchical, linear, and rational. Nonlinear perspectives did not become part of the leadership conversation until the end of the century.

To explore the relations between leadership and social systems in more depth, we will scrutinize each of the three time periods to emphasize the critical progressions of each of the fields of study and to provide insights to the possible influence of each on the other during that time period.

Period One: Work Systems to Cooperative Systems (1900-1940)
Systems Discourse

During this period, the concept of systems began its movement away from the mechanical and formalized reductionary application of systems theory to a functionalist analysis of the social system. The discourse is characterized by the control of production of materials and products and the need to structure a workforce in an industrial age that could provide the labor requirements for a growing population and economy. In this early time frame, economical and societal influence arguments, concerning the rational and formal philosophy, manifested social system's structure as management's control of the work force (Barley & Kunda, 1992). Although these efforts may not represent what we might call today a systems theory approach, they did deal with work elements (people, material, and time) and their relationships to each other (control). Social engineers such as Taylor and Gantt applied rational, linear cause-effect models to human work processes, emulating the formalism found in the world of the natural scientists. Information was data that could be used to measure or facilitate the control of work to achieve efficiency. Although some interpret this social structure as humanistic (Weisbord, 1990)[2], others saw it as suppressing the worker and social progress.

Scientific management, although achieving increases in efficiencies, reached a "social saturation point." The simplistic single cause-effect analysis of the relationship among systems elements (people) was no longer adequate for improvements in productivity and became the seed of worker discontent. This ushered in a concern for a theoretical understanding of human interactions within the system. The writings of Mayo (1933) and the research of Roethlisberger and Dickson (1939) with their Hawthorne studies in 1927 "moved away from the narrowly behavioral and deterministic approach characteristic of sci-

2 This interpretation does have merit in that it treats the control and structure of work as providing a humanistic relief from the exploitation of undereducated and unskilled workers by the industry.

entific management and early industrial psychology and towards a mechanical equilibrium systems model" (Burrell & Morgan, 1979: 132). This shift in the social systems discourse acknowledged the need for a more complex treatment of the system's influence on people, and people's influence on the system.

Toward the end of this time period we find a focus being placed on the nature of the relationships between the elements of the system in order to maintain the system's stability or equilibrium. The elements of the system were no longer just the workers and the work; they became the roles of workers and management in hierarchical structures (Weber, 1930). Parsons (1937), a sociologist, introduced the idea of "a system of actions" in which the unit of analysis was no longer the person, but their actions. These acts were defined in terms of the goals of the action, the situation (context) of the action, and a set of social norms (rules) that linked the goals to the situation and influenced the person's free choice. Parsons theory of action provided a plausible explanation for the relationship between control of the system (through peoples' actions and social norms) and the purpose of the system (to maintain equilibrium or stability)[3].

This early discourse on social systems indicates the beginning of a shift away from the purely objective and reductionary ideology that accompanied the migration of systems theory from the hard sciences to the social sciences. Reductionary thought processes emphasize the reduction of the systems elements to the lowest level of recognition. Such processes emphasize the analytic nature of systems at the expense of synthesis. In response to this reductionary ideology, "human" systems set the stage for an ongoing discourse concerning actors' potential for free choice and their ability to volunteer their participation in the system, thus adding to the complexity of the relationship among system elements. In addition, maintaining the integrity of the system and achieving equilibrium required a social structure that included a focus on the goal of the system in the context of its environment. We see the beginning of an understanding that efficiency was dependent, not only on the rational control processes imposed on elements (people), but also on the mutual action of the elements under social conditions (role definitions) and a set of societal standards that guided the choice of the individuals (norms). This early systems thinking and its analytic orientation promoted leadership as a problem-solving process in organizations that were in "disequilibrium."

Leadership Discourse

The leadership construct also manifested a reductionary approach by attributing salient leadership characteristics to the individual. Leadership thought in the early 1900s was dominated by the "great man"[4] theory. The basic premise of this theory, which originally was postulated by Thomas Carlyle (1907) in his writings on the theory of the hero, was that men are created *not* equal. In an analysis of Carlyle's work, Lehman (1928) construed that "there is no democracy in the realm of the intellect; men have widely differing holds on their envi-

---

3 In fairness to the Parsonian debate - Parsons saw equilibrium only as an "analytical state" rather than an achievable social condition.
4 Unfortunately this time period reflected the use of the male gender as leader.

Source	Characterization
Period One: Work Systems to Cooperative Systems	
1900	Great man theory – leadership is an innate ability – leaders are born, not made
Steward, in Moore, 1927	Leadership is "the ability to impress the will of the leader on those led and induce obedience, respect, loyalty, and cooperation" (p. 124).
Schmidt, 1933	Leadership is defined "as the relation between an individual and a group built around some common interest and behaving in a manner directed or determined by him" (p. 282).
Bogardus, 1934	Leadership is "the interaction between specific traits of one person and other traits of the many, in such a way that the course of action of the many is changed by the one" (p. 3).
Period Two: Functionally Driven Systems to Interactive Systems	
Copeland, 1942	Leadership is "the art of influencing … people by persuasion or example to follow a line of action. It must never be confused with drivership … which is the art of compelling … people by intimidation or force to follow a line of action" (p. 77).
Reuter, 1941	Leadership is "the result of an ability to persuade or direct men, apart from the prestige or power that comes from office or other external circumstances" (p. 133).
Jennings, 1944	Leadership is "a manner of interaction involving behavior by and toward the individual 'lifted' to a leader role by other individuals" (p. 432).
Stogdill, 1955	Leadership is a process of influencing a group toward goal setting and achievement.
Selznick, 1957	"Leadership is a kind of work done to meet the needs of a social situation" (p. 22). "Leadership is not equivalent to office-holding or high prestige or authority or decision-making" (p. 23). "Leadership is dispensable" (p.23).
Seeman, 1960	Leadership is "acts by persons which influence other persons in a shared direction" (p. 127).

Table 2 *Examples of Leadership Discourse Over 100 Years*

Tannenbaum, Weschler, & Massarik, 1961	"We define leadership as interpersonal influence, exercised in situation and directed, through the communication process, toward the attainment of a specified goal or goals. Leadership always involves attempts on the part of a leader (influencer) to affect (influence) the behavior of a follower (influencee) or followers in situation" (p. 24).
Katz & Kahn, 1966	Essence of organizational leadership – "influential increment over and above mechanical compliance with the routine directives of the organization" (p. 528).

Period Three: Learning Systems to Complex Systems Theory

Bass, 1973	"Any or all members can emerge as leaders, depending on how much of the functional roles they enact, the particular patterns of behavior they display in relationship to the task of socio-emotional development and operations of the group" (p. 383).
Boles & Davenport, 1975	Leadership is " a process in which an individual takes initiative to assist a group to move towards the production goals that are acceptable to maintain the group, and to dispose the needs of individuals within the group that compelled them to join it" (p. 117).
Burns, 1978	"Leadership over human beings is exercised when persons with certain motives and purposes mobilize, in competition or conflict with others, institutional, political, psychological, and other resources so as to arouse, engage, and satisfy the motives of followers in order to realize goals mutually held by both leaders and followers" (p. 18).
Bennis & Nanus, 1985	"Leaders lead by pulling rather than pushing; by inspiring rather than ordering; by creating achievable, though challenging expectations and rewarding progress toward them rather than manipulating; by enabling people to use their own initiative and experiences rather than by denying or constraining their experiences and actions" (p. 225).
Senge, 1990	Leaders are designers of living systems; leaders are strategic thinkers; leaders are teachers; leaders are stewards. "They are responsible for building organizations where people continually expand their capacities to understand complexity, clarify vision and improve shared mental models, that is, they are responsible for learning" (p. 340).

Table 2 *Examples of Leadership Discourse Over 100 Years (continued)*

Jacques & Clement, 1990	"Leadership is a process in which one person sets the purpose or direction for one or more persons, and gets them to move along together with him or her and with each other in that direction with competence and full commitment" (p. 4).
Kotter, 1996	Leadership entails (a) establishing direction (developing a vision of the future and the strategies to create it), (b) aligning people (communicating direction in words and deeds to everyone whose cooperation is needed to create the vision), and (c) motivating and inspiring (energizing people to overcome major political, bureaucratic, and resource barriers to change by satisfying basic, but often unfulfilled human needs).
Pearce & Conger, 2003	Leadership is "a dynamic interactive influence process among individuals in groups for which the objective is to lead one another to the achievement of group or organizational goals" (p. 1).

Table 2 *Examples of Leadership Discourse Over 100 Years (continued)*

ronments through complex instrumentality of hand and head and heart" (p. 5). Galton (1871) believed that "man's natural abilities are derived by inheritance, under exactly the same limitations as are the form and physical features of the whole organic world" (p. 1).

Because there was no question about the inequality of men at the time, those investigating leadership focused on unraveling the innate traits of those presumed to be great men. Galton employed the statistical concepts of regression and correlation (which he created) to study human differences and the inheritance of intelligence among famous people. Although the traits identified by early leadership researchers were certainly respectable (e.g., initiative, imagination, faith in others, self-patience), many great men were not necessarily forthright individuals. This was reflected in the definitions of leadership at the time. Leadership was defined as "the ability to impress the will of the leader on those led and induce obedience, respect, loyalty, and cooperation" (Moore, 1927: 124). Bundel (1930) characterized leadership as "the art of inducing others to do what you want them to do" (p. 339). Characterizations of leadership emphasized control and the centralization of power and did not necessarily emphasize making ethical decisions.

In the 1930s, researchers began to question the strength of the great man theory. Cowley (1928) raised an important issue: "Is there any difference between leadership in a particular situation and the ability to be a leader in *several* or perhaps even in *any* situation?" (p. 149). He found that different situations stressed different traits and that to understand traits one must understand various situations. Leadership as a mysterious set of factors resident in some and lacking in others became suspect as researchers began to explore the notion of leadership as a function of the situation. Although the significance of the situation did not take hold at this time, early on researchers saw its importance and the limitations of the great man theory.

The focus on the situation brought an acknowledgement of the group, or those being led, into the conversation. Bogardus (1934), a prominent social-psychologist at the time, brought his trait-and-group theory to the leadership discussion. "Leadership," he wrote, "is interaction between specific traits of one person and other traits of the many, in such a way that the course of action of the many is changed by the one" (p. 3). Tead (1935) defined leadership as "the ability of influencing people to cooperate toward some goal which they come to find desirable" (p. 20). Researchers began to talk about how leaders induce a group to work together to achieve a goal. How groups respond to and interact with leaders became topics researchers began to explore.

With a consideration emerging for those being led, definitions of leadership as the control of many by a single person began to fade. Pigors (1935), who compared leadership with domination, saw leadership as "a process of mutual stimulation which, by the successful interplay of relevant individual differences, controls human energy in the pursuit of a common cause" (p. 16). *The Encyclopedia of the Social Sciences* of 1933 asserted that leadership appears "only where a group follows an individual from free choice and not under command or coercion and, secondly, not in response to blind drives, but on positive and more or less rational grounds" (Schmidt, 1933: 282). The language used to describe leadership started to change. Words and phrases such as "impress," "inducing," and "will of the leader" were replaced with "mutual stimulation," "interplay," "free choice," "influencing," and "cooperate." A new direction in thinking about leadership became apparent by 1940. Leadership was no longer defined as the traits of a single great man, but as a social process that includes both leaders and those being led.

Period Two: Functionally Driven Systems to Interactive Systems (1940-1970)
Systems Discourse

This section continues with the examination of the drift in systems discourse away from a purely objective-reductionary ideology to a functional rationalism that is influenced by subjective judgment. The establishment of a typology of a general systems theory (Boulding, 1956) focused the discourse on the "difference" in the complexity of systems (mechanical, biological, social, etc.). This typology reinforced the difference between open and closed systems, thus escalating the discourse's complexity, not only by accounting for the control of internal relationships, but by including relationships between the system and its environment.

Two streams of the systems discourse provided for the evolution of thinking along different courses. The first stream assumed that it is the internal system's actions that maintain a balance with the system's environment. These actions would provide the system with the capability to adapt to any disturbance in the environment (import needed energy), achieve system's goals, integrate itself (coordinate and control the actions to achieve goals), and maintain a set of cultural patterns to support the values and norms of the collective (Parsons & Shils, 1952). Critical to systems' structure was the functional prerequisite of integration. It comprised acceptable collective norms and actions, coordination, control, and communications. It reflected a rational orientation to systems, but acknowledged the individual cognitive and cathectic (emotional) influences on the actor's orientation to the system.

The second stream of influence on the discourse resulted from the introduction of computational sciences to the understanding of social communications (Wiener, 1948). It emphasized the need for information in the form of feedback so that the system could maintain a homeostasis state. The introduction of "cybernetics" as a conceptual analytical frame focused on the responsiveness of the system to forces in the environment that were responsible for deviations from intended outcomes (as opposed to equilibrium; Buckley, 1967). Important to the achievement of the goal, with respect to the environment, was the maintenance of a variety of actions (Ashby, 1956) within the system that matched the variety, or complexity, of the environment and its behavior. The role of system's structure was to provide for the control of information flow and distribution, the scanning of the environment for required information, the selection of sources of information, and the importation of information as a source of energy to combat entropy (the disordering and eventual death of the system).

Although cybernetic discourse emphasized the rational and analytical nature of information, it also incorporated a role for social control: "For all these forms of behavior, and particularly for the more complicated ones, we must have central decision organs which determine what the machine is to do next on the basis of information fed back to it, which it stores by means analogous to the memory of a living organism" (Wiener, 1954: 33).

Both information and functional social actions provided mechanisms for investigating multiple cause-effect relations, both inside and outside the system (in practice this led to organizational analysis and organizational development interventions). Social system discourse expanded from a focus on work processes to exploring social concerns of power and authority (Buckley, 1967; March & Simon, 1961; Simon, 1947), increasing employee commitment and participation, developing plans for the future, understanding the personalities of the role players (McClelland, 1961), and designing structures (physical and political) of the organization (House, 1971; Likert, 1961a, 1961b). Both of these streams of social systems discourse, although adding complexity to our understanding of systems and moving away from reductionism, still operationally approached multiple causation and interaction from a rational and linear perspective.

The convergence of these paths occurred toward the end of this time period with the incorporation of many of the concepts of cybernetics with social interactions (both subjective and objective) to explain the movement away from stability (homeostasis and equilibrium) and predictability and toward self-regulation (Buckley, 1967). "The internal source of dynamics for the ongoing process is the continuous generation of varying degrees of tension, 'stress' or 'strain' within and between the interacting components; such tension is now being recognized as an inherent and essential characteristic of such systems" (p. 129). This work signaled the discourse's interest in the emergence of new phenomena (such as emergent structures) from the interactions of the individuals in the system. This led to a morphogenic orientation to understanding social systems dynamics, and to an interest in the system's capability to create, distribute, and utilize power. Buckley differentiates power from authority in that "power [is the] control or influence over the actions of others to promote one's goals without their consent, against their 'will', or without their knowledge or understanding," whereas "authority is the direction or control of the behavior of others for the promotion of collective goals, based on some ascertainable form of their knowledgeable consent" (p. 186).

Although Buckley's work did not enter the mainstream of the applied managerial control discourse, it did influence subsequent thinking concerning the sociological understanding of organizations. This is evident in the classical works of Simon (1947) concerning administrative behavior and, later, Cyert and March's (1963) work on the behavioral theory of the firm. The introduction of the concept of complexity and the loss of the perceived ability to control and predict social dynamics provided a critical turning point in the discourse concerning social systems. The emphasis became increased variety as opposed to the suppression, or control, of variety. Wiener anticipated this shift in his classic discourse on cybernetics and human beings: "Those who would organize us according to permanent individual functions and permanent individual restrictions condemned the human race to move at much less than half-steam. They throw away nearly all our human possibilities and by limiting the modes in which we may adapt ourselves to future contingencies, they reduce our chances for a reasonably long existence on this earth" (Wiener, 1954: 52).

Leadership Discourse

During this period, sociologists joined the leadership conversation and group dynamics became a dominant framework through which scholars examined leadership. The notion that leadership is defined by organizational rank was dismissed. Reuter (1941) advanced this insight: "Leadership is the result of an ability to persuade or direct men, apart from the prestige or power that comes from office or other external circumstances" (p. 133). The leadership conversation centered on leader-group relations and group effectiveness. Gibb (1954) asserted that to understand leadership you have to understand the characteristics and mechanisms of groups as "leadership is what leaders do in groups" (p. 882). Leadership became characterized as a dyadic relationship between leaders and followers. Leaders achieved rank, not because of position, birthright or genetics, but because they were able to develop effective relationships through which organizational goals were achieved.

Some researchers stressed the characteristics of the group to such an extent that a leader was conceived as a person not *apart from the group*, but *a part of the group*. Cartwright and Zander (1953) asserted that the concept of leadership contains two important ideas: (a) "any member of a group may be a leader in the sense that he may take actions which serve group functions" (p. 494), and (b) "a given function may be served by many different behaviors" (p. 494). Anyone in a group could be a leader and any function could involve leadership. Leadership became synonymous with the group (Cattell, 1951).

Probably the most significant shift of this time period was the movement away from trait theory and toward behavior theory. What leaders actually do (not their characteristics) started to drive the leadership research agenda. The Ohio State Leadership Studies Program established behavior theory as a way of explaining leadership (Fleishman, 1953). As opposed to psychometric tests that classify those with leadership promise from those who haven't got a chance, researchers were assessing leadership success and the desirable actions of leaders. Researchers found that leadership could be defined by two independent behaviors: *consideration*, or the degree to which the leader acts in a friendly manner toward subordinates, and *initiating structure*, or the degree to which a leader defines and structures his or her role and the roles of the subordinates towards achieving the goals of the group. These findings generated a stream of research that centered on maintaining the equilibrium of the group through the balance of these two leader behaviors. As an example, Berrien (1961) argued that the primary task of the leader was to keep steady group-need satisfactions and formal achievement.

In addition to focusing on leader behaviors, researchers started to investigate the circumstances under which leaders must lead. The work of Cowley in the late 1920s on the *situation* began to resurface. Two theories of leadership emerged: situational theories and contingency theories. The fundamental basis of both theories is the emphasis on the conditions that influence leader behavior and its effectiveness. The primary difference is that situational theories focus on the behaviors a leader should adopt given situational factors, for example, follower behavior. Contingency theories take more into account and include contingent factors about leader capability and other variables in the situation. Situational theories tended to focus on the internal process of the organization, whereas contingency theories were more expansive, including factors outside the organization.

In the late 1960s, Hersey and Blanchard (1977), and others, developed their situational leadership theory, which asserted that task and relationship behaviors were moderated by follower development style and the willingness of followers to perform required tasks. According to this theory, leaders adapt their behavior based on the follower maturity and their competence and motivation. House's (1971) path-goal theory argued that leader behavior was moderated by characteristics of task and environment, and characteristics of subordinates. By the 1980s, Hoy and Miskel (1987) identified four areas of situational leadership: "structural properties of the organization, organizational climate, role characteristics, and subordinate characteristics" (p. 273).

In the late 1960s, researchers no longer focused only on the internal processes of the organization. They also began to deliberate the relationship between the organization and its environment. According to Lawrence and Lorsch (1967), two kinds of leaders were required to deal with the complexity of the environment: (a) routine task leaders (i.e., those who focused on equilibrium), and (b) center of innovation leaders (i.e., those who focused on adaptation). Leadership discourse was progressing from an internal, closed system focus to an external, open system focus. The adaptive-reactive theory of leadership behavior (Osborn & Hunt, 1975) epitomized this shift of leadership thought. With this theory, leadership behavior was explained as both adapting to the externally determined macro variables and reacting to internally determined micro variables. By 1970, leadership theory now involved leader behavior *and* the many factors of the systems and sub-systems both internal and external to the organization.

Period Three: Learning Systems to Complex Systems Theory (1970-2000)

Systems Discourse

This time period did not see an end of functionalism, rather it saw its augmentation with concepts of information control, knowledge utilization (rational contingent decision-making, strategic thinking, and eventually organizational learning), and a reemphasis of the individual's interpretive influence on social systems' structures. Early movements of process improvement employing reductionism and rational cause-effect analysis were moderated by the realization that knowledge is dependent not only on information and context but also on the self. This meant that meaning was interpretive; therefore, knowledge was interpretive and sensemaking in organizations had to consider individual free choice and collective values supported by a relativistic culture (Schein, 1992; Weick & Roberts, 1993).

Social systems discourse incorporated three major concepts that again moved away from the psychological security of reductionism: self-generation, learning, and complexity. Self-generation reflected the realization that social structure was emergent and regenerative[5] stemming from reciprocal and ongoing social interactions. This neo-functionalism "reject[ed] mechanistic views of the social world in which structures are seen as imposed upon people. Instead, people are portrayed as active agents - their behavior being constrained, but not determined" (Baert, 1998: 4). Giddens's (1979, 1984) theory of structuration described the dual nature of social structure - guiding the actions of the agents, and the actions of the agents altering the structure. Social systems became self-sustaining through language and communicative actions (Habermas, 1987). These concepts led to the reconsideration of social structure as not simply a response to external forces, but as self-organizing and structurally determined (Mingers, 1989). "Both internal and external actions can trigger [system] changes. The internal structure determines what changes can occur (only those which maintain autopoeisis), and thus which environmental interactions will trigger changes in the system" (Bailey, 1994: 304). Communication was no longer seen as being constituted by the control of information flow, feedback, and the correction of deviation. It included the concept of language (Luhmann, 1995) and conversation as a source of emergent structure (Taylor & Van Every, 2000) in efforts to reduce entropy (or disorder).

The second stream of social systems discourse emanated from the conceptualization of social systems as, not only having goals of production, but also being driven by goals of knowledge creation through learning (Crossan, *et al.*, 1999; Schwandt & Marquardt, 2000; Senge, 1994; Senge & Sterman, 1992). To create knowledge, those exerting actions of control must relinquish to those providing operational flexibility and experimentation. In this discourse, in which neg-entropy (or energy) is critical to the system's survival (Bailey, 1994), cybernetics is joined with social action in valuing information as knowledge. The movement from the concept of exploitation only to the need for exploitation and exploration (March, 1991) changed the nature of control within the system. This discourse also led to a reaffirmation[6] of the importance of intangible values and basic assumptions that are stored in the culture of the social system and are used to regenerate the system (morphogenesis) and its knowledge creation capability (Archer, 1988; Schein, 1992).

The third stream of social system discourse may mark the ending of the century's struggle with social control through reductionism. This discourse reflects a merger of cybernetics, organizational learning, complexity science, and the dynamics of social interaction. Emergent social structure from interactions in complex systems is the subject of this book, thus, the discourse continues and it is too premature (and dangerous) to draw any historical generalizations from

5 These concepts picked up where Buckley (1968) left off with his complex systems approach.

6 We use the term reaffirmation because Parsons foreshadowed its importance in his cybernetic hierarchy scheme of social systems (Parsons & Shils, 1952).

a work in progress. However, we can say that the direction of the discourse appears to continue in a retreat from only reductive, rational, and objective forms of social structure.

Emergence and tension have become major concepts in understanding structure and leadership. Emergence can be thought of as the evolution and recombination of interactions into new actions (Anderson 1999). It is a reflection of Giddens's structuration theory in that it assumes that structure is multifaceted and is ever changing itself. The concept of emergence supports the "morphogenetic or structure-building" processes encountered with feedback of information that is not deviation reducing, but deviation amplifying (Maruyama, 1963).

The social tension of interaction, both among actors, and the actors and their culture, characterizes the new systems discourse (McKelvey, 2002). The concept of social tension of interaction, although defined differently in different disciplines, refers to "manifestations under conditions of felt blockages, [that are] ever present in one form or another throughout the socio-cultural system - sometimes as diffuse, socially unstructured strivings, frustrations, enthusiasms, aggressions, neurotic or normative deviation; sometimes as clustered and minimally structured crowd or quasi-group processes, normatively constructive as well as destructive; and sometimes as socio-culturally structured creativity and production, conflict and competition, or upheaval and destruction" (Buckley, 1967: 51).

It appears that modern social systems discourse, in conjunction with the complexity sciences, will pursue this self-organizing concept as the foundation of systems structuring processes (Prigogine & Stengers, 1984), will study its nonlinear creative capability (Goldstein, 1994), and will "combat these examples [objectivism and reductionism] of obsolescence through non equilibrium analysis, through emphasis on feedback, through emphasis on individual action and control, through emphasis on subjectivity (not all systems theorists will agree with this), through emphasis on operationalization, as for example through the methods of contemporary information theory - not to mention utilization of the computerized models - and through the use of concepts from the field such as artificial intelligence" (Bailey, 1994: 74).

Leadership Discourse

During this period, the amount of leadership discourse increased. Topical theories were extended. Fresh theories and research methods emerged. Old and new theories were combined into new theoretical frameworks to uncover the nature of a phenomenon that was both important and perplexing to researchers. Hollander and Julian (1969) introduced a transactional approach into the leadership conversation asserting that leadership "involves an exchange or transaction between leaders and followers in which the leader both gives something and gets something" (p. 388). Leadership began to be characterized as a dyadic, two-way process in which leaders gave themselves as resources to help attain group goals, and in return they received status and legitimacy from groups. Jacobs (1970) embraced the transactional slant and using social exchange theory introduced the idea of stable group leadership. He viewed groups in organizations as energy systems that could be tapped by supervisors to attain organizational goals. However, the amount of energy expended by groups depended on specific social exchange principles between leaders and followers, fair and equitable exchanges, agreed upon goals, positive rather than coercive means, and group success. Group members needed to experience achievement in order for leaders to retain their influence. Leadership became known "as a process, not a person" (Hollander, 1978: 4) that "involves an ongoing transaction between leaders and followers" (p. 12). The discourse began to represent followers as exerting their own power through their evaluations of leaders. Whether or not leaders remained in influential positions depended on how followers assessed leader performance.

Toward the end of the 1970s, the discourse expanded to include input from other disciplines. Paige (1977) took a multidisciplinary approach to explore the concepts of leadership. His "multivariate, multidimensional linkage approach" identified specific predictors of political leadership patterns such as personality, role, organization, task, values, and setting. Burns (1978) pointed out the importance of transactional leadership, but also discussed the value of leaders and followers working together toward mutual benefit. He is best known for his contribution of transformational leadership, which "looks for motives in followers, seeks to satisfy higher needs, and engages the full person of the follower" (p. 4). Kracke (1978), an anthropologist, asserted that leadership is a social phenomenon that is rooted in the inner motives of leaders and followers - what he refers to as the "interplay of personalities" (p. 252). His findings supported the notion that leadership is a key element of social structure formation.

During the economic unrest of the 70s and 80s, scholars extended the research that Lawrence and Lorsch started in the late 1960s that depicted the dual role of leadership (i.e., (a) manager of internal systems and (b) manager of organizational interface with environmental systems). Researchers moved their studies from inside to outside organizations, and the notion of "strategic leadership" emerged. The tactical ability to manage the environmental cross points of organizations was now a critical aspect of leadership. Potts and Behr (1987) posited that leadership entailed confronting issues such as anticipating change in the environment and acting quickly, establishing alliances, taking risks to improve competitive position, and keeping an eye on the future. Strategic leadership brought a renewed emphasis on trait theory. Clinical approaches were used to build new representations of leadership that included interest in extraordinary risk takers (Levinson & Rosenthal, 1984), eminent decision-makers (Donaldson & Lorsch, 1983), and distinguished change agents (Tichy & Devanna, 1986).

The idea that leaders needed to be strategic thinkers refocused research from a behavior orientation to a cognitive orientation. Jacques and Clement (1990) brought "cognitive power" and Senge (1990) brought "systems thinking" to the leadership discussion. Effective leadership required a shift of mind in which leaders perceived the whole system and reasoned and made judgments based on the interrelationships between system components both inside and outside the organization. "Seeing systems" became a critical cognitive ability for leaders.

Toward the end of this period, leadership discourse migrated from an exchange between leaders and followers to leadership as dynamic interactions of lateral influence among peer members of a group. In the late 1980s, the notion that leadership is shared among members of a group became evident with the advent of what researchers called organizational leadership. Organizational leadership theories contended that leadership was a characteristic of the entire organization, in which "leader roles overlapped, complemented each other, and shifted from time to time and from person to person" (Barnes & Kriger, 1986: 16). A more inclusive concept of leadership became fully apparent.

At the end of the century, the notion of shared leadership was unmistakable. Researchers began to use the complexity sciences to explore leadership (Griffin, 2002; Stacey, *et al.*, 2000). They found that conventional leadership thought did not accommodate a new division of labor that was interdependent and dispersed. Leadership was being talked about as a phenomenon that emerged from and was embodied in the interactions of participants. The research was intense and several leadership conceptualizations based on this new framework emerged, including *shared leadership*, which was defined as "a dynamic interactive influence process among individuals in groups for which the objective is to lead one another to the achievement of group or organizational goals" (Pearce & Conger, 2003: 1), and *distributed leadership*, which was characterized by the criterion of "conjoint agency" (Gronn, 2003).

Discussion

We began this chapter by asking what has been the nature of the relationship between social systems discourse and that of leadership over a 100 year period. We felt that a historical understanding of this relationship could inform our present discourse concerning leadership and complexity science because complexity deals with systems. This section will attempt to make sense of the interactions of the discourses discussed above and draw some implications for going forward.

In general, the discourse in leadership and social systems both reflect a slow, but sure, movement away from reductionism to a concern for a more holistic and subjective concern for the nature of social interactions. Figure 1 reflects the major theoretical discourses over time. In the first period, we see a movement away from the conceptualization of social systems as mechanical in nature and the leader's actions being considered as one of the possible control mechanisms for achieving system efficiency. As individual members of the system sought more autonomy and free choice, leadership became a means of motivation and facilitation of those humans as elements of the system. This acknowledgement of the autonomy of the actors began the journey away from structural determinism to a complex change orientation for both fields of study.

In the second period, social system's thought focused on the need for collective-functional actions and the flow of information to ascertain system stability, or homeostasis, in an ever-changing environment. At the same time, leadership discourse focused on the leader as a role that required behaviors that contributed, not only to internal integration of actors' actions, but also to the

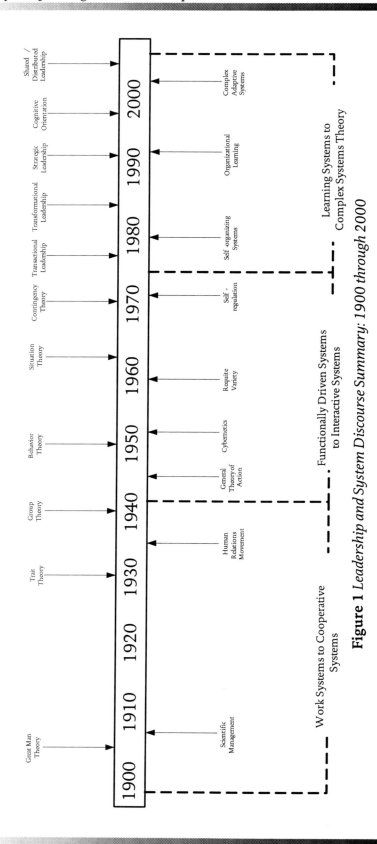

Figure 1 *Leadership and System Discourse Summary: 1900 through 2000*

formulation of strategic goals in relationship to the environment to achieve the system's survival.

The third period continued the drift toward complexity through the realization that predictions based on concepts of social systems were difficult at best and that new directions emerged from the dynamics of agent interactions. Concerns with information and its control gave way to processes of knowledge creation and the elevation of the importance of *meaning* to both the system and individuals. The leadership role expanded from integration to setting strategic direction, knowledge management, and "systems thinking."

This evolution of systems and leadership discourses is in line with Eastman and Bailey (1998) and their treatment of the evolution of managerial discourse from one of "fact" to one of "value partisan." Their explanation that the progression of managerial discourse has moved from concepts of formal reductionism to a more interpretive, constructionist view based on relative human values is supported by our analysis of the more narrow discourse of systems and leadership. Both fields of study have relinquished their dependence on the reductional nature of social interaction. Systems study moved from efficiency and effectively chemical relationships to information flow, multiple causation, and self-generation. At the same time, conceptually, leadership moved from personal traits to motivational behaviors, cognition, and emergent interactions that are governed by a value orientation. This move away from reductionism has been accompanied by the addition of levels of complexity and less predictive capability for both fields of study. One of the major implications for this movement away from reductionism is the necessity to find an approach to incorporate both subjective and objective interactions of agents within the system, simultaneously.

During our examination of the discourses, it became apparent that complexity is not a new phenomenon to either field of study. Its acknowledgement and naming is new. Both fields have understated complexity in favor of a rational worldview. The elements of complexity have been embedded in systems discourse from the beginning. However, when the complexity of interaction was felt, the response was to suppress it in the discourse, or to try to explain it using rational models of systems and leadership behavior. Thus, the idea of "the autonomy of actors" versus the control of the system was addressed through the incorporation of the concept of manipulation of the individual's commitment to the system through mechanisms of "involvement" (usually dependent on reward systems and the actions of leadership). Consequently, the complexity of the interaction was minimized by the current theories of the time or the discourse itself. For example, linear cause-effect relationships such as behavioral motivational theory were developed in controlled environments and promoted as a condition-response mode of management. These theories, and their simplicity, failed when they were implemented in complex linear environments (e.g., pay for performance programs).

This lack of acknowledgement of the complex nature of human interaction in social systems may also have been due to a lack of language that was flexible enough to handle the concepts and the psychological impact of confronting the idea of our inability to predict. The rational worldview that has dominated psychology, management sciences, economics, and organizational theory reinforces a "control and predictive" language as part of the defense of their paradigms (Kuhn, 1961). This Kuhnian dynamic has implications for the theoretical convergence that is occurring around complexity, social systems, and leadership. If we begin to use terms such as complexity leadership without a full understanding of the dynamics of social interaction and its accompanying emergence, we may lose the opportunity to fully realize the unstructured potential of complex systems. We must provide bridges in our language so that people in the system are not intimidated by the complexity, or see it as only another laboratory-developed idea that falters in real-time application. We must be vigilant as to our understanding of the language we use to describe each of these fields of study.

To more specifically address the question of the relationship between the two discourses, it is very difficult to state definitively any cause-effect relationship over such a large time span. At first glance, it appears that leadership (control or influence) is a component, or means, for social system to control its elements. Also it appears that the evolution of leadership lagged the development of the conceptualization of systems. For example, one could consider the move to humanitarian leadership (circa 1930) as a response to the over-controlling concepts of scientific management. During the 1950s to 1960s, the leader's actions to influence motivation were in response to the theorized functional need for the system to obtain more commitment of its elements through "participation and alignment of their goals with that of the system." These arguments are quite plausible and have implications for the way in which people are seen as agents in systems as leadership and social systems coevolve.

However, we could also make the argument that systems theorists altered their conception of normative influence based on their understanding of the leader's operational actions of incorporating positive feedback as a means to increasing individual motivation. Or, we could argue that leadership's acknowledgement of the importance of cultural values was in response to the lack of success with process improvement (circa 1990s). This complex lead-lag relationship in the discourses has led us to suggest that even though the two streams seemed disconnected over much of this period, the relationship between the discourses was coevolutionary rather than sequential or independent.

The move from the rational to the non-rational, the objective to the subjective, and from fact to value has been a result of the dynamic interaction of the two fields over time. Systems has benefited from reports of leadership research (motivation, communications, transformation, etc.) and the leadership discourse has benefited from systems theory (information flow, importance of environment, knowledge sharing). The interaction of the two discourses has itself been more complex than one might think.

The nature of leadership, because of its pragmatic orientation, is more immediately dependent on feedback from practice (or operationalization) than the concepts of social systems. This does not mean that systems theory is not pragmatic; it means that its discourse is less accessible and therefore seen as more abstract. The theoretical development of social systems discourse is dependent on the knowledge obtained from leadership practice. In turn, leadership practice is dependent on its theoretical knowledge of social systems. Thus, the coevolution of leadership and systems is not only a function of their changing contents but also of their theory-practice exchange process. The implication of this coevolutionary relationship becomes important as we move forward in our development of complexity theory and its relationship to human systems and their emergent structures. We must always provide a healthy coevolutionary bridge between theory and practice to maintain integrity and validity of the new science.

Conclusion

The above discussion has emphasized three aspects of the evolution of the leadership and social systems discourse. A slow movement has occurred from a reductionary/rational worldview to one of holism and non-rationality. Social systems and leadership have always had complexity embedded in their discourse, however, it was not acknowledged. The two fields have actually coevolved through an interaction of content and theory-practice processes. Each of these observations has implications for our field as we bring this understanding to the complex nature of leadership in the context of social systems. First, for a well-educated and free society, the emphasis on person-centered leadership can be reduced to deal with increasing complexity. Second, to achieve this reductionism in our reliance on a person-centered leadership model, we must understand more about the evolution of societal norms and values that reinforce our dependence (structuration).

If we are to take full advantage of the convergence of multidisciplinary thought and further our understanding of the nature of complex social change, we must pursue paths of inquiry that challenge the single focus of the person-role, or leadership types. We must broaden our perspectives to include a more distributed concept of human interactions, we must add specificity to our models of social interactions, and we must continue to relate our theoretical and simulated models to the practices of human interaction.

We may now be ready to understand that the next phase of development, both for people interested in complexity and people interested in leadership, may be in the direction of a more human cognitive orientation to influence. Today, emergent structure is the primary focus of the discourse in complex systems theory and is equated with the system's capability to exist. There is no assumption of systems homeostasis, equilibrium, or stability. Structure stems from the diversity of thought and interaction and is not expected to provide predictability. Although leadership is seen as a type of interaction, it is being redefined. However, in our enthusiasm to move forward, we must remember that our discourse shapes our actions. For example, as we read the contents of this book, we should think critically about the theories and patterns presented. We must ask the question, What are we asking people in their social systems to believe and to implement? This retrospective has allowed us to see those patterns, which may not be apparent while we're in the actual act of discourse. In some respects, we're playing out what Giddens said about language being the essence of society. How we speak is what we are.

CHAPTER FOUR
A NEW MODEL FOR EMERGENCE AND ITS LEADERSHIP IMPLICATIONS

Jeffrey A. Goldstein

Emergence is one of the major concepts from complexity science which has been influencing recent leadership studies. Emergence, though, is typically understood in terms of self-organization with the latter connoting a sense of passivity in the face of some kind of interruption, dismantling, or absence of hierarchical control in complex systems. These connotations of self-organization have, accordingly, biased applications of the idea of emergence since emergence has been almost exclusively discussed in terms of self-organization. That is why it is quite common to hear suggestions that leaders pull back or loosen their hierarchical imposed control in order to purportedly encourage the self-organization of emergent novel patterns. I unhinge the unfortunate alliance between emergence and self-organization by taking a careful look how emergence is actually described in the scientific and mathematical literature. I reveal how the idea of emergence has been encumbered by several bits of "folklore" and conceptual snares. Emergence is simply not a passive process that somehow magically occurs spontaneously, but is instead the outcome of a set of varied constraints and constructional process. To remedy the self-organizational picture of emergence plaguing leadership applications of the latter notion, a wider, more inclusive and more accurate model of emergence is developed based on the idea of "self-transcending constructions." This idea is developed to provide a new understanding of emergence in terms of specifically defined constructional operations which bring about novel order with novel properties. To better grasp the advantages of the new model of emergence, it is applied to several critical philosophy of science issues evoked by the idea of emergence. Leadership implications are discussed in relation to each of these applications of the new model of emergence.

Jeffrey Goldstein, Ph.D. is Full Professor, Department of Management, Marketing, and Decision Sciences at the School of Business, Adelphi University, Garden City, NY. Professor Goldstein is also an Associate Clinical Professor at the Derner Institute for Advanced Psychological Studies at Adelphi. He is co-editor-in-chief of the journal *Emergence: Complexity and Organization*, is a board member of the journal *Nonlinear Dynamics, Psychology, and Life Sciences*, is on the Science Advisory Board of the Plexus Institute, and is a fellow of the Institute for the Study of Coherence and Emergence.

Emergence, Organizations, and Leadership

Emergence stands out among a wide set of intriguing phenomena within complexity science as particularly salient for organizational and leadership studies because of its departure from classical and traditional categories. As Laughlin, (1996), a Nobel Prize winning physicist, has recently asserted, we are now leaving the Age of Reductionism and entering the Age of Emergence. Emergence can be observed among quite diverse types of systems including, to name just a few, computational simulations known as artificial life (Adami, 1998; Langton, 1986, 1996), neural networks (Marinaro & Tagiaferri, 2002), evolving dynamical systems in mathematics (Martelli, 1999), "dissipative structures" observed in the physical laboratory (Nicolis, 1989), phase transitions in solid state physics (Laughlin, 2005), and social systems about which more will be said below.

Emergence has recently surfaced as an important construct in studies of organizational dynamics and leadership (Goldstein, 1999; Chiles, *et. al.*, 2004; Guastello, 2002; Marion & Uhl-Bien, 2001; and others). Most of these organizational studies, though, share a theoretical presumption pervasive in the literature: that emergence takes place by means of supposedly "self-organizing" processes, a phrase connoting such descriptors as *spontaneous, taking place without leadership command and control*, and *inner-driven* in the sense that the new order which emerges is not imposed but is supposed to spontaneously come out of a system's own internal capabilities. Without a doubt, this use of the idea of self-organization in organizational studies has provided a much needed corrective to the hoary belief that novel order within a system must be the result of an imposition from outside. This corrective in turn has led to an equally revolutionary perspective in leadership studies whereby novel, emergent order in an organization can arise in lieu of a leader's control. As a result, various new research agendas are now following through on the ground broken by initial applications of self-organizing systems to organizations (Buckle, 2003).

This same revolutionary point of view offered by the idea of self-organization, though, has tended to slant organizational applications of emergence towards the positing of a kind of *passivity* in the role of leaders since self-organizing processes are putatively those that result from a *loosening* or *pulling back* of active interventions on the part of leaders. Allusions to this kind of passivity on the part of leaders can be detected in just about every article or book (too numerous to cite here) promulgating complexity, self-organization, and emergence in relation to leadership. Two often told tales regarding self-organization demonstrate this sort of passivity. The first involves how the 25,000 restaurants in New York City receive their necessary food supplies every day without the need of a centralized and hierarchical command and control authority directing the supply chain – that is, the food distribution system is presumed to be self-organizing. This tale emphasizes the lack of leadership intervention in the food distribution network. The second tale refers to the manner by which the internet functions and grows without a centralized command and control leadership function dictating which new web sites are to be established and how these sites will be linked to existing ones. In both cases self-organization is posed as a set of processes defined as *contra* leader control.

This paper questions these implications for leadership by rethinking the understanding of emergence in general, and in organizations in particular, by way of self-organization. In its stead, a new model of emergence is offered, one that includes the advances made by the idea of self-organization, but takes these advances up into a wider and more general understanding of emergence. It is claimed that this new model of emergence corresponds more closely to actual research into emergent systems where the idea of self-organization was first proposed. The origins of this new model as well as its key elements will be presented. Then the new model will be applied to certain issues in the philosophy of science prompted by the idea of emergence, not for the sake of mere philosophical argumentation but rather to set the stage, in the case of each issue, for applications of the new model to the role of leaders in fostering organizational emergence.

Applications of Emergence to Organizations

In one of the most significant usages of the idea of emergence for understanding organizational dynamics, Chiles, *et. al.* (2004) examined "organizational collectives" involving country music that have sprang up over the last century in and around the town of Branson, Missouri. These emergent collectives have become so successful as to attract over 6 million visitors annually (in contrast to the Grand Canyon which only gets 4 million visitors). Building on earlier work of MacIntosh and MacLean (1999), Chiles, *et al.* utilized a "dissipative structure" model of emergence stemming from the Far-from-equilibrium Thermodynamics School founded by Prigogine (Nicolis & Prigogine, 1989). In that school, "dissipative structures" refer to the coherent and stable new structures emerging by means of supposedly self-organizing processes taking place at critical thresholds of certain control parameters.

This model of Chiles, *et al.* is composed of four basic elements:

1. Spontaneous fluctuations which initiate and form the seeds of the new emergent order;
2. Positive feedbacks which amplify the fluctuations of #1;
3. Coordinating mechanisms that stabilize the new order;
4. Recombinations of existing resources that help construct the new order.

An important aspect of this "dissipative structure" model is the claim that by its "self-organizing logic" the "organizational collectives" are a set of "hodge podge configurations" of components that are neither "planned," "controlled," nor "created" through "human design" (p. 510). This "self-organizing logic" is one of the key elements of those organizational uses of emergence that will be challenged in this paper.

Another example of a "dissipative structure" model of emergence applied to organizations can be found in Maguire's (2002) conceptualization of emergent structures as "resolving" an "adaptive tension" that is supposed to build-up in complex systems. Here, Maguire is following the thermodynamic origin of the idea of "dissipative structures" of which more will be said later on. Maguire provides a list of examples of "emergent social networks" including: dyadic or triadic communication channels; informal or formal teams, groups, or other "network configurations of individuals;" networks across groups; and so forth. We see here a telling hierarchy of emergent phenomena being formed, an idea we'll encounter again below. But a conceptual trap lurks here, since such a hierarchy seems to indicate that emergence is a process of induction up the hierarchy, i.e., induction over individuals to form a class, induction over classes to form a higher class of classes, induction over classes of classes to form a class of classes of classes and so forth up the ladder. This, however, serves to conflate emergence with some kinds of logical operations, a problem that we'll be coming back to below.

Emergence also plays a role in Marion's and Uhl-Bien's (2001) wider study of the implications of complexity theory in general for leadership. Marion and Uhl-Bien point to the spontaneous emergence of group structures at different sizes and scales which, borrowing from Holland's (1995, 1998) work on computational emergence, they refer to as "aggregates" and "meta-aggregates." Similar to the study of Chiles, Meyer, and Hench, Marion and Uhl-Bien talk about emergence taking place through "self-organizing" processes operating in a "bottom -up" fashion and consisting of three primary elements: randomness (which can be said to correspond to the fluctuations element of the model described above); nonlinearity (corresponding to feedback in the above model); and correlation (corresponding to #'s 3 and 4 above). The close connection between these two models is not surprising since both employ an understanding of emergence which relies on the notion of self-organizing systems that was largely shaped by Prigogine's approach.

Basing itself on the mathematical field of nonlinear dynamical systems theory (NDS), Guastello (2002) has approached emergent phenomena in organizations through numerous empirical studies relying on the NDS constructs of bifurcations and attractors. Crucial to Guastello's work has been "emergent leadership," a type of "informal" leadership emerging in leaderless groups. Much of Guastello's research in this area confirms findings such as those by Pillai (1996) and Kolb (1997) on how and why leadership roles tends to emerge in leaderless groups during particular situations, e.g., crises. In particular, Guastello has found emergent leadership taking place in the presence of "chaos" as measured in time series data of variables measured in leaderless groups. Guastello, like the other authors above, also understands the ensuing leader emergence out of "chaos" as a process self-organization.

The author of this paper had also earlier employed a self-organizational model as a basis for a theory and practice of organizational change centering on the leader as change agent (Goldstein, 1994). Later, however, focusing on both emergent leadership as well as on what were labeled "emergent networks, I (Goldstein, 1997, 1999, 2000) have sketched out the main ingredients of emergence in general as well as those philosophy science issues prompted by the idea of emergence in order to be in a better conceptual position to suggest how emergence might be applied to organizations. To illustrate the intersection between emergent leadership and emergent networks, I pointed to a classic study of Murnigan and Conlon (1991) on successful and unsuccessful string quartets in England. The way successful quartets were organized in terms of the interaction among the four members was observed to be a function not of an imposition on the part of an official management structure but rather emerged out of the string quartet's actual practicing their music. That is, a self-organizing network of leadership among the four players emerged to deal with the issues of effective strategies and work processes, conflict resolution methods, and leadership roles. So even here, self-organization was the key.

Self-organization therefore has remained a common ingredient among most cases of applying emergence to organizations, with leaders relying on self-organization as the driver by which emergence is believed to take place, particularly in situations marked, for one reason or another, by the absence of formal leadership. It is to this idea and the model I am proposing to replace it that we now turn.

Emergence: An Idea Freighted with Heavy Conceptual Baggage

For all the revolutionary promise that has been offered by applications of emergence to organizations and leadership, it must at the same time be recognized that emergence has remained an elusive and somewhat enigmatic concept due to two main types of conceptual baggage which have accompanied the idea. The first involves sundry bits of "folklore" which have grown up around the idea while the second concerns the varied conceptual snares awaiting in a host of philosophy of science issues that have been prompted by it. "Folklore" in this sense refers to the various conceptual associations and cognate presumptions that have become attached to the idea of emergence as it has been developing since its inception in 1875, about which more will be described later on in the paper. The word "folklore" is being used intentionally in order to indicate that much of the associations hanging onto the idea of emergence are based more on *popular interpretations* of research findings than in the findings themselves. "Conceptual snares," on the other hand, refers to the many puzzling theoretical issues that the idea of emergence has provoked during the same period of time.

A close reading of emergentist literature reveals that different traditions and different contexts have put different spins on what emergence entails and implies. As Peirce (Taylor, In press) once put it, in science and mathematics metaphysics leaks-in at every joint. Such leakage is only compounded in the case of emergence because it has so often been weighted with some very heavy metaphysical baggage indeed. Since to not address these troublesome aspects issues would only serve to forestall the usefulness of applications, it is my contention that before emergence can be efficaciously applied in the study of leadership, it must first be disentangled from both the "folklore" and the conceptual snares accompanying it.

The three examples of "folklore" that will be described below include three interrelated notions: the first is that complex, orderly dynamics emerge suddenly and *en masse* out of far simpler or random ones; the second is the idea that emergence brings about order "for free," an idea promulgated primarily by Kauffman (1995); and, most importantly for the purpose of this paper, the third concerns the close tie-in between emergence and so-called "self-organizing" processes. More time will be spent going over the last one in particular since it has the most important repercussions for leadership applications as will be explained below.

In terms of the varied conceptual snares surrounding emergence, the focus will be on such philosophy of sciences issues as the nature of causality in emergent systems, the idea of emergent levels, the ontological status of emergent phenomena, and related issues. Because much of the bothersome aspects of these issues stem from the bits of "folklore" attached to conceptualizations of the idea of emergence, they are a good place to place to start. This will in turn set the stage for developing a new model of emergence that is less attached to the "folklore" and more attuned to actual research into emergence. Once this model has been elaborated, then we can carefully inspect each issue from the philosophy of science in order to clarify the nature of emergence according to the new model presented here and thus allow for a more satisfactory application of it to leadership research and practice.

Complexity from Simplicity and "Order for Free"

The first bit of "folklore" that has attached itself to the idea of emergence is the belief that the complexity exhibited in emergent order comes directly and spontaneously out of far simpler or even random dynamics in a manner not unlike that of the mythological Athena springing directly out of the head of Zeus. This belief is implicit in the self-organizational description of processes leading to emergent order as working from the "bottom-up" with the "bottom" understood in terms of far less complex or even random states. Thus, in the early days of chaos theory it was often touted that the amazing complexity of technical "chaos" came forth seemingly suddenly and immediately out of much simpler rules or equations. This idea can even be seen in the title of May's (1976) vastly influential early exploration of chaotic dynamics: "Simple mathematical models with very complicated dynamics." Indeed, for the original explorers of the fantastic realms of chaotic systems, it was the emergence of complex phenomena out of seemingly simple systems which captured the attention of mathematicians and scientists and led to a great plethora of research into chaos.

But just because an effect is startlingly novel with respect to its causes doesn't necessarily entail there are not a host of intermediate means by which the novelty ensues (Goldstein, 1996).

Indeed, a close study of the evolution of the logistic equation which has become something of an emblem of chaos theory, demonstrates that many mathematical operations are taking place before actual "chaos" can be demonstrated, including, to name a few: a host of iterative processes; criticalization of parameters; bifurcations; and so forth. The point is that "chaos" simply does not just emerge spontaneously and immediately from simple equations. Rather, a great deal of complexifying (Casti, 1994) operations must go into the transition from simple to complex.

Similarly, there are multifarious sources of nascent order and sundry "complexifying" operations found in the emergence of novel order in the physical laboratory of so-called self-organizing systems. This research has demonstrated that the emergence of new order is like what Turing (1952) said about emergent order in biological morphogenesis: "Most of an organism most of the time is developing from one pattern to another not from homogeneity into a pattern" (quoted in Kelso, 1995: 3). In a similar vein, Bateson (1969) once offered the following suggestion in response to the ancient Greek focus on the idea of substance: "From where I sit it looks as if most of the behavioral scientists... tried to hook up their stuff to the wrong half of the fundamentals of science. That is, they followed the Ionians in asking questions about substance 'What is it made of? How much of it is there?' They should have followed the Pythagoreans in asking about forms and patterns." Likewise, what is being proposed here is that the key to understanding emergence order is not to assume an emergence straight away out of disorder but rather to ask a series of questions about the transformation of order from disorder: How do novel emergent patterns relate to previous patterns in the system? How exactly are these extant patterns transformed? What in the new patterns is novel and what is a carryover from earlier states of the system? What processes and operations are utilized to build-up toward complex order? We'll be coming back to questions like these when the idea of self-organization is discussed in more depth.

The second representative of "folklore" surrounding emergence, and as we'll see below one related to the first, concerns Kauffman's (1995) influential concept of "order for free," his appellation for the emergent patterns observed in his electronic Boolean networks, a form of artificial life. The claim that emergent order is "for free," in my estimation, must have caught on mainly due to the considerable reputation of its progenitor since even a brief inspection reveals that in Kauffman's electronic networks emergent order is any thing but free. That this bit of "folklore" is closely related to the notion of self-organization can be seen in this passage from Kauffman (1995: 25):"... most of the beautiful order seen in ontogeny is spontaneous, a natural expression of the stunning self-organization that abounds in very complex regulatory networks... Order, vast and generative, arises naturally..."

Kauffman's obviously metaphysical concept of emergence needs a bit of unpacking which will require some technical considerations having to do with the nature of Kauffman's electronic networks. The main reason why Kauffman concluded that the order observed in his networks was "for free" had to do with his claim that such order arose out of the randomly assigned rules by which his networks operate. These rules are similar to those found in the logic of computational processes, i.e., the "and," "or," and "and/or" gates. If the rules are assigned randomly and order ensues then this would seem to imply there was no preset design causing the resulting order, hence it was "for free." Yet, as Kauffman (1995) himself has admitted, "...if the network has more than $K = 2$ inputs per light bulb, then certain *biases* in the Boolean rules, captured by the P parameter, *can be adjusted* to ensure order" (p. 103; emphases added). "Biases" here refer to just those rules, i.e., the "or" and the "and" rules, which serve to generate and propagate redundant order through the networks. Kauffman calls such biased rules "canalyzing" for they serve to channel order into "canals" of redundancy, in other words, they operate as constraining factors about which more will be discussed below.

Closer scrutiny and thought, however, reveals that Kauffman has glossed over just how crucial these biases are in the bringing about of emergent order since it is only the biased rules, not the unbiased ones, which channel the electric current to generate redundant order. To be sure, the identification of this bias as a bias had to wait until after the run of a simulation because the rules were indeed assigned randomly. But the important point to note is that, whether the biases were known beforehand or only afterwards, the emergent order *only* ensued when the biased rules are operative. This implies that it must be the built-in bias of the rules that constructs the ensuing order, not some "free," supposedly spontaneous self-organizing activity of the network. Indeed, to conceive of Kauffman's emergent order as really "free" in the self-organizing sense is to also believe that an unusual and persisting "come-out" run of sevens in a casino game of craps is "for free." Such would certainly not be the conclusion of pit bosses overseeing craps table. These sentinels against dishonest gaming would instead infer that the dice were loaded. Like Kauffman's biased rules, loaded dice are *constructed* to produce a redundant pattern more often than the laws of probabilities would allow. Again, it doesn't matter if it is not discovered until after the dice are thrown whether or not the dice are in fact loaded – loaded dice will always be biased to generate redundancies in congruence with how they are loaded. Similarly, In Kauffman's networks, the order which emerges is constructed to do so since the biased rules operating networks are biased toward redundancies.

Furthermore, the focus on "order for free" neglects the critical role of the "containers" involved in self-organizing systems. In this context for example, Berg and his associates (Berge, et al.,1984) found that in the Benard convection, a typical example of the "dissipative structure" model of emergence, the distance separating two neighboring currents was on the order of the vertical height of the container. Similarly, the number of convection rolls can be curtailed by reducing the ratio of horizontal dimension to vertical height. In a similar vein, Weiss (1987) found that instabilities in the thermal boundaries of liquid systems similar to the Benard system lead to more complicated kinds of convection. Kauffman (1995) himself pointed to this source of emergent structure with his positing of a type of necessary "compartmentalization" as membranes form molecules into gel-like structures which then concentrate organic molecules inside and exchange them across their boundaries. Furthermore, citing similar research, Kauffman suggested that "compartmentalization" could amplify order generating process. These facts suggest that a crucial source of emergent order, rather than being free or coming purely from self-organizing process, comes in part from the specific order of the containers in which emergence takes place. It is important to note that the order making-up the container functions as one of the sources of nascent order that then undergoes varied constructional operations in order to result in later emergent structures. The significance and "costs" of this sort of nascent order in complex systems is usually overlooked when emergent order is thought as spontaneous and immediate or when it is thought of as "for free."

An enthusiasm for "order for free" also shows up on the part of organizational proponents of emergence and self-organization who link it to a dismantling of the normal command and control hierarchy. Certainly, there may be times when such a strategy may confer benefits on an organization, but there are other times that this can be a strategy for disaster. For example, there was a great deal of self-organizing going on in Yugoslavia after the death of Tito and his centralized authoritarian government. Indeed, a search through *Sociofile* of that era reveals many articles on self-organization in social systems written in Serbo-Croatian! But was this emergent "order for free" a beneficial outcome for the various ethnic groups in the region? Holding to the presumption that emergent order is "for free" not only has the unfortunate effect of neglecting very important determining conditions of emergent order, it also neglects that emerging order may not be beneficial at all, both of which are things leaders cannot afford to overlook!

Moving Beyond Self-Organization

The third piece of "folklore" that has grown-up around emergence and the one most important for our purposes because of both its widespread influence and the implications for leadership drawn from it involves the explicit conceptual entanglement of emergence with self-organization. This close association goes back to the schools of Prigogine (Nicolis & Prigogine, 1989; Prigogine & Stengers, 1984) and Haken (1981, 1987) both of which put the onus of the emergence of new order in physical systems on self-organizing processes. It was from the Prigogine school in particular that the "dissipative structure" model of emergence achieved prominence. Prigogine, to underscore the difference of his research with phase transitional order occurring at the lowering of temperature, described the order emerging in self-organizing systems when temperature was increased as a "dissipative structure," cleverly juxtaposing two terms usually kept apart in thermodynamics circles: "dissipative" and "structure." "Dissipative" customarily refers to the loss of energy taking place during the transmutation of one kind of energy to another, for example, the loss of heat seen in steam engines, a phenomenon crucial in the very formulation of the Second Law of Thermodynamics and its central idea of entropy increase. Since an increase of entropy was eventually understood as a disintegrating tendency, "dissipative" then carried connotations diametrically opposite to those of the building-up of "structure" since the latter denoted some kind of endurance over time. For this reason "dissipative structures" are often described as steady states, thus connoting something that is in a dynamic, rather than static equilibrium, or to use an analogy, like a vortex where its shape or organization remains intact although its water molecules are in constant flux. By bringing these contrary terms together, Prigogine was calling attention to how in a "dissipative structure" heat transfer is not correlated with the dissolution of order, but is actually the source of new order. Incidentally, one of Haken's (1987) terms for "dissipative structures" has been "partly structured" again referring to the constant flux of energy and matter passing through them.

According to Prigogine as well as Haken, emergent order comes about through self-organizing processes and it is this wedding of the two that has found its way into the model of emergence utilized by studies described above. In this model the "self" of "self-organizing" connotes such properties as "innate," "unplanned," "spontaneous," and only taking place in "uncontrolled (read: "leaderless") situations. Remember that Chiles, *et al.* even describe their investigation as guided by a "self-organizing logic" neither "planned," "controlled," nor "created" through "human design. With such a "logic" underpinning emergence, the role of leaders is prescribed to be primarily a matter of keeping hierarchical control mechanisms from interfering with what is naturally and spontaneously emerging in a "bottom-up" direction.

It must be recognized, however, that this setting-up of a too close alliance between emergence and self-organization is simply not borne-out by a close inspection of how emergent order in the laboratory actually comes about in each instance when it does. Although it appears that self-organizing processes may play a role, a wider and more general conceptualization of emergent order is needed that can include the varied and special types of constructional operations involved in the emergence of new order. The term "constructional," it should be noted, neither entails that "external constructors" are required nor that such constructional operations correspond to traditional "top-down" associations. Rather, if emergent order is about novel *structures, then it is* con-*struct*ional operations which bring about new structures. Although one might expect that the "organizing" of "self-organizing" would point to such structure building, structure *per se* and processes involved in the building-up of structure have actually gotten short shrift in self-organizational research. This neglect is due, in part, to the "folklore" described above, namely, the suppositions that complex emergent order arise in *toto* directly and "for free" out of simplicity or randomness, both of which imply the absence of intermediate constructional operations. In contrast to these bits of "folklore," *constructional* operations call attention to the diverse sources of order already existing in the complex system, nascent order which is transformed during processes of emergence in a manner echoing Turing's above quoted remark about patterns evolving out of previous patterns.

As a matter of fact, it turns out that that the notion of construction as such was intimately tied into emergence right at the beginning of contemporary *neo*-emergentist research when Anderson (1972), a winner of the Nobel Prize in physics, offered his "Constructionist Hypothesis" as a response to arch reductionism rampant among particle physicists. This hypothesis proposed that although it might be possible to reduce nature to certain simple, fundamental laws, this did not then entail a similar ability for re-*constructing* the universe from these simple laws since each new level of complexity involved the emergence of entirely new properties and laws not appearing at the lower levels. That is, each new level of complexity would exhibit the construction of new structures with new properties that transcend lower level characteristics and dynamics.

Two representative examples from research in complex systems, ones that, paradoxically enough have been prime sources for the close connection between emergence and self-organization, illustrate the key role of constructional operations in the emergence of new order. The first has to do with the production of laser light which Haken's (1981) Synergetics School has put forward as an exemplar of self-organization. A close examination of how laser light actually comes about reveals that the emergent coherence characterizing lasers is expedited only through the most strenuous of *non*-self-organizational processes including, among others (see Haken, 1981; Nicolis & Prigogine, 1989; Strogatz, 2003):

- Because atoms only generate light when they fall to their lowest energy ground state, they must be first "lifted up" through a huge investment of energy from outside the system;
- A "resonant cavity" must be constructed such as a long glass tube filled by an appropriate gas or a solid, e.g., a ruby rod;
- Mirrors must be constructed at both ends of the resonant cavity, with one mirror being slightly less than 100 % reflective so that light can escape at this end.

To this list of constraints and constructional operations necessary for the generation of "self-organizing" lasers can be added the fact that even top researchers in the field admit that lasers can be "persuaded" to oscillate in a single mode only with the utmost of imposed manipulations and with great difficulty (Anderson and Stein, 1987).

It is because of these kinds of powerful constraining and constructional factors that Haken (1981) has described the order of self-organizing systems as an "enslavement" of system variables to an order parameter driving the system. Constructed and constrained "enslavement," though, hardly conforms to the connotations of self-organizing processes described above. In response to the argument that because of all these constraints and constructional operations, lasers should not be presented as an appropriate exemplar of self-organizing processes, it turns out that Prigogine who had been less interested in lasers and more in the Benard system with its hexagonal convection cells as well as the Belousov-Zhabotinsky reaction with its spiral waves of colors, once qualified what he meant by the "self-" of "self-organization" with the phrase "*constrained situated dependentness*" (emphasis added; Lissack, 2000). In addition, the Prigogine School consistently uses language likes "constraints", "invasion," and "domination (see Prigogine & Stengers, 1984; Nicolis & Prigogine, 1989).

It might be asked at this juncture why the phrase "self-organization" with all of its associations of being unconstrained and unconstructed was ever used in the first place in these lines of research. In my opinion, this probably had to do with two things. The first was Turing's use of the term which influenced Prigogine early on in his research (Dupuy, 2000). By the way, this early use of "self-organization" was criticized at the time as self-contradictory by Ashby (1962), a leading early cybernetician. The second probable reason why the term "self-organization" was employed had to do with the way emergent structures were maintained by way of cross- and self-referential feedback. This was illustrated in Haken's (1981) appeal to Escher's famous drawing of two hands drawing themselves out of a piece of paper as what happens analogously in self-organizing systems. Self-organization then connoted this kind of self-referentiality.

Be that as it may, one of the contentions being broached in this paper is that the concept of self-organization as typically interpreted is simply not up to par when it comes to the emergence of novel order. Although one would have supposed that the "organizing" part of "self-organizing" would draw attention to structure building in process, most appeals to self-organization focus on just one action and one outcome, namely that process which leads to one particular "dissipative structure" at one particular critical parameter threshold (Prigogine & Stengers, 1984). However, the type of "dissipative structures" customarily studied by advocates of self-organization are not necessary the most prevalent or interesting in their implications. For example, Klimontovich (2001) points out that the more interesting and complex emergence characterizing the transition from laminar to turbulent flow occurs at higher temperatures than that for "dissipative structures."

A review of studies interested in applying self-organization to leadership demonstrates that they simply don't pay a whole lot of attention to exactly how structure is constructed as well as how structure is changed as further constructional operations take place. Yet, if, as McKelvey (2001) has put it, complexity in organizations is about *order creation*, then a main issue for the application of self-organization to leadership would have to be the role of leaders in the generation of novel order, an issue which has not been of great importance in approaches relying on the self-organization model. In the latter new order only comes about when normative control mechanism have been interrupted which implies a passive role for leaders.

The Self-Transcending Construction of Emergent Order

As stated above, self-organizing processes in organizations have been customarily associated with some kind of lacuna in leadership control as well as the presumption that new, emergent order self-organizes out of what is either low or totally lacking in order (Goldstein, 2001, 2002, 2004). Yet, since emergence is more sufficiently understood as more in line with varied constructional operations, the model which guides organizational appliers of emergence needs to be accordingly revised. To be sure, self-organization as such will play an important role in this revised model. Nevertheless I suggest a wider and more general conceptualization of emergence in terms of what I am calling "self-transcending constructions" (STCs) which place attention on how pre-existing order is transformed into emergent order. STCs incorporate self-organizing process but also include many additional constructional operations. The "self-" and "transcendence" of "self-transcending" refer to how emergent order *arises out of* yet *transcends* lower level and antecedent conditions. This dual nature of STCs is congruent with the actual phenomenology of emergence in whatever context it has been explored since although emergent phenomena may be radically novel with respect to what they are generated out of, they are not magical appearances out of the blue but rather build on lower level components. Hence, self-transcendence includes the two fundamental requirements for emergence: building blocks and a simultaneous transcendence of the same building blocks. In other words, emergent order consists of a continuing build-up of structures along with an ongoing shifting and merging of structures with one another to generate new structures.

Since STCs must be powerful enough to bring about radically novel emergent phenomena, the constructional operations involved must be *special* kinds of constructions. That is, if emergence is to live up to its claim of amounting to something surpassing ordinary change, STCs must consist in processes that possess the potency of self-transcendence, i.e., transcending the very same lower level antecedent conditions out of which the higher emergent level is constructed. Such a potency is represented in the radical novelty operators represented in the mathematical formalism of STCs laid-out in Appendix I, in particular, the mapping and negation operators indicated by the bold-face type in Definition 2 and Definition 4.iv. It is important to recognize that this formalism follows a very different "logic" than the self-organizing "logic" described previously by Chiles, Meyer, and Hench, a logic that will be described in more detail below.

To the extent the idea of emergence shows promise for leadership studies, it will be more on the mark to consider emergence from the wider perspective of self-transcending constructions and their unique logic which includes but is wider and more general than self-organizing processes alone. To foreshadow for a moment, whereas leadership applications founded on the model of emergence following the "logic" of self-organizing processes tend to place leaders in a passive role in which they allow or get out of the way so that such processes may take place, leadership applications founded on the viewpoint of STCs suggest a more active role of leaders in setting-up and shaping the conditions and sources for the self-transcending construction of emergent order. This more capacious model provides room for self-organizing processes but it also opens up the organizational arena of leadership to functions having to do with constraining, channeling and structuring what is to emerge, not in the older sense of command and control but more in line with what research into emergence is revealing.

One of the unfortunate consequences stemming from the over-emphasis on self-organizing processes as the key to emergence has been the driving of a conceptual wedge between the supposedly spontaneous, inner-directed processes of self-organization and those otherwise constructional in nature. This wedge has served to put self-organization on the side of what's natural and spontaneous over against the other side which characterizes construction as what is unnatural, a result of artifice and design. In point of fact, though, self-transcending constructional activity can be as natural as self-organization is supposed to be, a fact attested by such natural constructional phenomena, to mention just a few, as bone growth, turtle shells, beaver dams, bird nests, hurricanes, ant hills, termite cones, protein assemblies, and so forth. Indeed, one can find in evolutionary biological literature more and more references to naturally occurring constructional activities (see, e.g., Odling-Smee, *et al.*, 2003). Constructional operations can be seen even in mathematical situations where randomness is thought to hold sway, e.g., the field of random graph theory (Barabási, 2002) which has been proving so important in the complexity-related fields of network theory including social network theory (see, e.g., Kilduff & Tsai, 2003). In random graph theory the assignation of nodes and links may be random, nevertheless the nodes and linkages themselves have to be somehow constructed in order to produce such emergent phenomena as "giant clusters."

Since emergent order is not sufficiently captured by pointing to either its putative spontaneity or its quality of being "for free," but rather comes about through intermediate steps by means of constructional operations, a self-transcending constructional approach to emergence places explanatory attention on the sources of emergent order and how seminal order is transmuted during processes of emergence. An analogy is the construction of a dam by a beaver where the sources of the construction may include the topography of the creek bed and bank, the available sticks, twigs, and leaves, the beaver's ability to manipulate the former, and so forth. Also, it is important to note that construction in this sense doesn't necessarily entail an external constructor because novel order can arise out of the interaction of elements which are already ordered to some nascent extent. Another example is how the internal organization of a cell is constructed out of a complex interaction of self-regulatory feedback loops, protein folding, multimolecular modularization, and other spatial and temporal constraining operations in tandem with genetic information (see Moss, 2003). To be sure, the models of emergence offered by both Chiles, Meyer, and Hench as well as Marion and Uhl-Bien, do include certain aspects of such constructional activities, e.g., feedback, correlations, but even with these, there is the sense that leaders tend to allow them to happen rather than playing an active role in their construction.

Another source of order crucial to self-transcending constructions is the "containers" in which emergence takes place (see the research of Berge, *et al.*, 1984 and Weiss, 1987 mentioned above), a fact mostly ignored by organizational applications of self-organization. For instance, the manner by which biased rules constrain Kauffman's networks towards emergent order is related to how the shape of their actual physical containers biases the emergent order observed in dissipative structures. The critical role of containers suggest that a crucial source of emergent order, rather than being free or coming purely from self-organizing process, is the specific order "contained" in the containers within which emergence takes place.

Since it is clearly not enough to simply posit that emergent order self-organizes itself into existence, emergence requires a set of constructional elements, building block type operations which may have been mentioned in passing in this or that applications involving the self-organization approach but have not received the attention they deserve. These constructional operations will include:

1. Already present, nascent order that is transformed through the means of order building operations, e.g., Kauffman's canalyzing rules, ordering constraints inside and outside the laboratory, the orderliness of the "containers" within which emergence takes place;

2. Recombination strategies which serve to expand and complexify the nascent order, e.g., Holland's (1994) genetic operators, recombination mentioned in MacIntosh and MacLean (1999), Romanelli (1991) and so forth. Such operations are closely related to analogous forms of recombination found in creative process (see Baughman & Mumford, 1996);

3. Randomization methods which will be more fully described below in the section on the purported unpredictability of emergence.

The Conceptual Background of Self-Transcending Constructions

In order to appreciate exactly how the new model of emergence based on the scheme of self-transcending constructions differs from that of the self-organizational one, I would like to trace its development out of several important strands in complexity theory and earlier systems perspectives. This discussion will necessarily have to be at times technical but this is necessary in order to enable a better understanding of how this new model of emergence entails a different view of the role of leadership. As there is not enough space here to go into great detail (see Goldstein, Forthcoming), here I will focus only on just eight such strands numerically demarcated according on the "whale" diagram in Figure 1. The unnumbered influences are more well-known as trends in the self-organizational picture of emergence and are de-emphasized here, e.g., , both the Synergetics School of Haken and the Far-from-equilibrium Thermodynamics School of Prigogine are left unnumbered since they are the source of the "self-organizing/ dissipative structure" model.

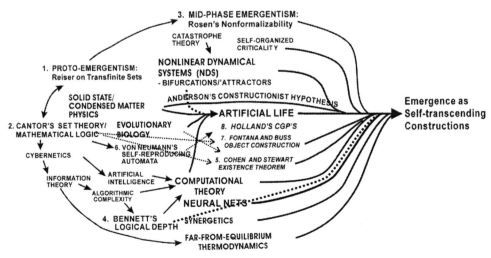

Figure 1 *Conceptual Background of Self-transcending Constructions*

The first inklings of what I later termed STCs is Reiser's (1935) description of emergent wholes using an analogy from transfinite set theory (marked #1 in Figure 1): "Just as assertions about the properties of finite classes cannot be made to apply to transfinite aggregates, so in a similar way, the peculiar non-additive properties of an emergent whole (gestalt) cannot be predicated of the constituent parts" (p. 63). Reiser's pointing to transfinite sets was an appeal to source #2, Cantor's (see Tiles, 1989) theorems on transfinite sets ("aggregate" is Reiser's translation of the German "Menge" which today is usually translated as "set" and in the sense mentioned above by Marion and Uhl-Bien). According to Cantor's work, transfinite sets were not arrived at by any kind of piecemeal addition of the parts of which they are composed. Instead, Cantor used a special mathematical construction, an operation which was later disparagingly called a "self-transcending construction" by Kaufmann (1978), an eminent Austrian philosopher of mathematics and one time member of the influential "Vienna Circle." Kaufmann used the expression "self-transcending construction" in order to point out what he took as the absurdity of Cantor's constructional operations (represented in the mathematical formalism of STCs found in Appendix I), that is, the impossibility of a construction able to transcend itself (technically, in this case, the impossibility of a higher infinite cardinality to come out of a lower one). But rather than accepting this as a pejorative expression, it struck me that the phrase "self-transcending construction" fit very aptly the way emergent phenomena are produced out of yet transcend lower level components.

There is another reason for discussing Cantor's STC here having to do with its indirect but critical role in later approaches to emergence, particularly through the employment of Cantor's specific self-transcending construction in the later limitative theorems in mathematical logic formulated in 1931 by Gödel (1962) and then in 1937 by Turing (1937). In this regard, Rosen (1996) later claimed, listed as #3 in the diagram, that emergence was essentially unformalizability to any specific model, the latter understood in the mathematical logical sense of a domain where every proposition from a formal system is true. Rosen contended that emergent phenomena were neither predictable nor deducible from that from which they emerged – in other words, could be said to transcend any perspective derived from lower level dynamics alone. This claim relates to the point made by Laughlin (2005) that emergent phenomena are in principle *insensitive* to lower level dynamics.

The second influence of the STC of Cantor besides that on Gödel and Turing was in the development of a complexity metric, *logical depth*, #4, devised by Bennett (1986), a complexity oriented physicist and computer scientist. Bennett came up with logical depth as an improvement over the earlier metric of algorithmic complexity (Chaitin, 2001) since the latter reaches a maximum in a totally random system whereas logical depth reaches its zenith with emergent systems whose order is complex yet not random. Bennett has explained how logical depth could be said to use a variant of the same Cantorian self-transcending construction. Here we can see self-transcending constructions informing the development of a measure for emergent order.

The Cantorian STC shows up indirectly yet again in Cohen's and Stewart's (1994), "Existence Theorem for Emergence" labeled #5, which applies a Turing-like conjecture to "prove" that emergent phenomena cannot be expressed except in intractably long deductive chains emanating from their lower level or antecedent conditions. In a related analogy, Cohen and Stewart talk of the "Ant Country" borrowed from the "ant" cellular automaton developed by Langton (Gale, 1993) who showed how a very simple set of rules on a local level can lead to the emergence of patterns at a more global level. In Cohen's and Stewart's reworking, if one came across the emergent, higher level patterns without knowing how they were produced, it would be impossible to trace them backwards to their source in initial conditions and simple rules. Thus the "Ant Country" analogy illustrates how a purely reductionist strategy will inevitably come-up against such a pleroma of entangled complexities that the study of emergent phenomena would require a new kind of theory which would have to consist of some kind of transcendence of lower level specificities.

Yet another source of the idea of self-transcending constructions as a model for emergence comes out of the work of von Neumann (von Neumann & Burks, 1966), #6, on self-reproducing automata which has served as the progenitor for the type of computational emergence found in artificial life. Von Neumann's formalism for his self-reproducing automata was deeply influenced by the work of Turing and Gödel. An organizational application of it can be found in Luksha (2005) who has used von Neumann's model for understanding the evolution of firms, mapping specific organizational elements onto von Neumann's formal classes of automata. Certain artificial life simulations like Conway's Game of Life have been proven to possess a capacity for being a universal Turing machine (Reitman, 1993). It must be noted that the computational emergence observed in artificial life are made possible by various STCs through a concatenation of recursive and innovation-generating operations, e.g., Holland's genetic operators, Lindenmayer systems, and similar mathematical processes (Langton, 1996).

One influential species of artificial life that both rests more directly on the work of Turing and Gödel involving their Cantorian underpinnings as well as adopts a constructional perspective is the "object construction" theory of computational emergence put forward by Fontana and Buss (1994), marked # 7, which utilizes a proof-theoretical foundation derived from the limitative theorems in mathematical logic. With their computationally emergent formulation of chemistry, Fontana and Buss emphasize the *structure* of emergent phenomena and the *constructional* operations leading to that structure as more pertinent than the phase space conceptualizations of attractors found in nonlinear dynamical systems.

This list of sources for the idea of a self-transcending construction could be continued but for now we'll end it with Holland's (1994, 1998), #8, computational model of emergence based on his recursive scheme of "constrained generating procedures" (CGPs) which are a type of self-transcending constructions. According to this scheme, it is the interaction between networks of linked "mechanisms," similar to subroutines in a computer program, which generate emergent order. In this way, each CGP is similar to a building-block, and the interaction and combination of different CGPs at one level lead to emergent structures at higher levels. Moreover, and this ties directly to Cantor's self-transcending construction, to further his project Holland has called for the development of a new mathematics for emergence that possesses the ability for changing its "cardinality," a technical matter in mathematics the full exposition of which would take us too far a field except to note that such a change in cardinality was critical to the self-transcending construction of Cantor in his proof of transfinite sets. Indeed, a change in cardinality is equivalent to self-transcendence of a previous frame of reference. Moreover, like Holland's recursive formalism, self-transcending constructions posses the capacity for being applied repeatedly in order to produce ever more novel outcomes.

Whereas a model based on self-organization would tend to emphasize how emergent order happens on its own when controlling mechanisms are relaxed, a model of emergence based on self-transcending constructions instead emphasizes a host of structuring operations. This in turn indicates that leadership in emergent systems would be better understood according to the constructional roles of expediting, linking people and projects, shaping, and other constructional ways of facilitating the emergence of novel structures.

Self-Transcending Constructions and Philosophy Science Issues Prompted by Emergence

Now that the self-transcending constructional model for emergence has been somewhat fleshed-out, we can reinterpret those philosophy of science issues which have been troublesome for the idea of emergence in general (Goldstein, 2000). This will help in setting the stage for applying emergence to leadership since the reworking of each issue will help clarify how leaders can be involved in STCs in their organizations in a manner that goes beyond mere self-organizing processes.

Beyond Bottom-up Descriptions of Emergent Order

The first issue prompted by emergence concerns its role in scientific explanations. Typically emergence is appealed to when the dynamics of the system being investigated appear better understood through focus on higher level, across-system *organization* than through its parts or the properties of parts alone (Bechtel & Richardson, 1993). Explanations involving the construct of emergence also claim that the emergent level properties of the organization are neither predictable from, deducible from, nor reducible to the lower level of parts alone. It is in this sense that Laughlin (2005) can contend that not only the emergent phenomena themselves but the scientific laws operative at the emergent level are *insensitive* to the lower level.

In fact, a closer look at the use of emergence in explanations reveals that it functions not so much as an explanation as a *description* pointing to the patterns, structures, or properties that are exhibited on the macro-level. That is, explanatory appeals to emergence act like *indexical markers* pointing to not only the higher, emergent level but also the need to investigate what operations are taking place which have the potency of bringing about the qualities exhibited by emergent level entities. This can be seen even in the "dissipative structure" model of emergence, (see Nicolis, 1989; Prigogine & Stengers, 1984) which shifts attention to the appropriate macro-level from which further investigation and theory building may proceed. In other words, emergence, by pointing to the emergent level entities and properties, elicits a search for the special, higher-level laws which elucidate the emergent phenomena. This implies that the construct of emergence functions as a foundation on which to build an explanation and not the terminus of an explanation. Complexity research holds the promise of developing the necessary tools, methods, and constructs that can render intelligible the higher emergent level as well as the processes powerful enough for generating it.

This also implies that the study of complex systems requires both emergentist *and* reductionist inquiry. In this regard, Wimsatt (1972, 1976, 1994, 1997) has pushed for reductionist strategies of inquiry in order to find out as much as possible concerning higher level features from the properties of lower ones, as well as a concomitant emergentist strategy in the reverse direction to gain as much insight as possible about emergent level from the laws and dynamics appropriate to that level. Likewise, Simon (quoted in Wimsatt, 1972: 174) once put forward a methodological principle that has since then become something of a working guideline among complexity theorists, "... in the face of complexity, an in-principle reductionist may be at the same time a pragmatic holist." In this way, reductionism and emergentism are complementary. Similarly, Clark (1996), a philosopher of neuroscience, has remarked that to contrast emergentist explanations with reductionistic ones is to invite a misunderstanding of emergence by suggesting that emergentist accounts are silent about how order arises. The truth, however, about research into emergence is that how order is constructed during the process of emergence is very much on the agenda.

Take, for example, "dissipative structures" which are thought to be maintained by feedback flows within a system and between a system and its environment(s), e.g., Benard convection cells are kept together by a continual pumping of energy into the system in which they are exhibited. When it comes to organizational examples of emergence, the self-organizational picture would have it that such "dissipative structures" are being maintained by "bottom-up" flows but this leaves researchers in a quandary as to what in turn might be maintaining such "bottom-up" flows. It is not enough to simply say these flows result from the criticalization of certain parameters, i.e., some sort of cranking-up of a parameter which thereby "pushes" the system through different orderly regimes. Instead, inquiry needs to focus on exactly how structure changes via constructional operations acting upon already extant order.

Accordingly, in contrast to the idea of self-organization which tends to remain mute as to exactly how higher level organization is built-up from "bottom-up" processes, one of the advantages of the idea of self-transcending constructions is that it has as it primary focal point the varied sources of order and constructional operations which are involved in the onset of emergent order. Again, this implies that unlike the conceptual lacuna found in the self-organization picture as to how the emergence of order actually arises and the concomitant passive role for leaders suggested by this lacuna, the self-transcending constructional approach offers leaders diverse proposals for active roles in the constructional operations constituting emergence.

The Ontological Status of Emergent Phenomena

Are emergent phenomena part of the real "furniture of the world"? Or are they merely a function of the limitations of our epistemological/cognitive apparatus? Or perhaps the term is just a provisional marker in the sense that it is only useful until a more adequate micro-level explanation comes along? Such questions have been debated vigorously ever since the idea of emergence was first broached. Even in the contemporary world of complexity theory, these issues are contested. For example, Holland (1998) has proffered a distinction between authentically emergent phenomena and what he calls "serendipitous novelty" such as the play of light on leaves in a breeze. Along a similar vein, Crutchfield (1993), a well-know complexity-oriented physicist, has pointed out that emergent patterns detected by scientists are often assumed to be there through assumptions implicit in the statistics used in detection. Since the presumption of newness in the emergent pattern is usually referred outside the system to some observer who anticipates the structures via a fixed palette of possible regularities, Crutchfield has proposed instead defining computational emergence according to its "intrinsic computational capacity." However, defining emergence in terms of an intrinsic computational capacity raises all sorts of scientific and philosophical concerns such as Searle's (1994) contention that since computational capacity always contains an implicit external connection, it cannot be totally an intrinsic property. Although "intrinsic computational capacity" may not be directly pertinent to non-computational instances of emergence such as emergence in organizations, the core of Crutchfield's proposal is relevant to how emergent patterns, structures, and properties must possess some kind of potency in effecting the world around them or they fade into irrelevance as being mere epiphenomena.

The provisionality side of this debate, though, has a direct relevance to the model of emergence according to self-transcending constructions, namely, the correspondence between provisionality and self-transcendence. First, consider that the provisionality claim holds that once a better theory supplants the current one, appeals to emergence will no longer be necessary since this better theory will be able to predict, deduce and reduce emergent phenomena to micro-level processes (see, e.g., Henle, 1942). Similarly, according to Hempel and Oppenheim (1948), since emergence can only be defined with respect to a specific theory, and since theories are always developing, the construct of emergence will eventually be discarded when a better theory supercedes the current one which has emergence within it. Not only did the coiner of the term "emergent," Lewes (1975) himself incline in this direction, other influential early emergentists like Morgan (Stephan, 1992) thought the provisional nature of emergence did not so much count as evidence against its ontological status as supporting it instead since science always dealt with things of which it did not yet have perfect knowledge.

But understanding emergence in terms of self-transcending constructions incorporates the issue of provisionality right into its inner workings since emergent phenomena are defined as precisely those that are always provisional in respect to pre-existing theories, models, laws, and principles. That is, self-transcending constructions insure that emergent phenomena are defined as that which transcends pre-existing theories, models, laws, representations, and structures. This implies that provisionality of theory becomes provisionality of the actual emergence phenomenon. This was at the heart of at least two of the above described clues forming the conceptual background of STCs, notably, Rosen's (1996) argument for the unformalizability of emergence and Cohen's and Stewart's (1994) Turing-type of conjecture on the existence of emergence. From a leadership perspective, the provisionality of emergent phenomena can be seen as a good thing since provisionality as such entails there must be a great degree of fluidity of emergent structures, each one surpassing the previous ones, not just vertically but horizontally in the organization in an unending development of novel modes of organizing. If leaders were being guided by a purely self-organizational model of emergence in which the leader's disposition is passive to self-organizing "flows," what's to keep emergent structures from settling down in consonance with a state of group conformity which by definition is intransigent to change (see Buckle Henning & Dugan in this Volume)? On the other hand, leaders guided by the self-transcending constructional model of emergence in which provisionality is a feature of emergent structures themselves, would be actively engaged in the self-transcending construction of ever new emergent structures offering better and better adaptation. The STC model of emergence accordingly celebrates the provisional status of emergent order since the point is to insure that organizations remain adaptable through the ongoing supersession of existing structures.

The Type of Coherence Characterizing Emergent Phenomena

Another philosophy of science issue involving emergence concerns the nature of the coherence characterizing emergent phenomena, one of their salient defining properties. In computational emergence this property of coherence is exhibited in the varied structures which arise and then hold together across the lattice of cells in Conway's Game of Life, e.g., "gliders," "spaceships," B heptominos," and "R pentominos" (Poundstone, 1985). Coherence is also a quality of the "dissipative structures" of self-organizational research which demonstrate an across-system correlation that "overpowers" local forces and thereby holds together over time even though the lower level components are in a state of constant flux (Nicolis, 1989). It is this property of coherence which is behind the characterization of emergents as being "more than the sum of the parts," a feature which follows mathematically from a complex system's nonlinearity. Coherence is also related to the issue of the ontological status of emergent phenomena since it is one of the properties responsible for emergents having some degree of causal efficacy (see Schroder, 1998; Sperry, 1986).

There is a critical question, however, as to exactly what kind of coherence emergent phenomena are thought to possess. In the "dissipative structure" model, emergents posses an extreme cohesive type of coherence evident, e.g., in Haken's use of the term "enslavement," mentioned above, to describe the relation of variables to the overarching order parameter representing a system's self-organizing dynamics. Although some of his students have held the term "enslavement" to have been merely a poor choice of words on Haken's part, in my opinion, this term is actually quite appropriate for characterizing the coherent order of something like lasers where all the rays are focused in the same direction. But is this the kind of coherence appropriate for "organized collectivities," "emergent networks," and so on? I believe this is more than a semantical issue stemming from translating from the realm of physical to social systems but instead goes to the heart of the kind of coherence emergents are expected to have.

Organizational researchers have for many years recognized just how rife with pressures toward compliance and conformity organizations are, even to the point of Haken's variety of "enslaved" coherence. A great deal of research in the social-psychology of group interaction has repeatedly demonstrated how shared norms, over-arching goals, and homogeneity among participants in terms of their backgrounds, perceptions, attitudes, and feelings can lead to what Hogg (1992) calls normative and informational influences for conformity. While the first kind of influence includes a seeking-after acceptance and the consequent compliant behaviors to bring about that acceptance, the second is an intentional need to agree in order to get something done. Along the same lines, Sinclair (1999) has called attention to how a "tyranny" resulting from team ideology can enforce compliance to conformity. In a system thought to exhibit only self-organizing processes, what's to keep social interaction from reaching this kind of "enslaved" conformity? Why should a "bottom-up" driven self-organizing process not pull social actors into an "attractor" characterized by conformity and compliance? Nothing would hinder this being a possible outcome in a situation where leaders simply allow or provide "room" for self-organization to take place.

What the idea of self-transcending constructions can offer here instead is a different approach to the coherence of emergent phenomena, one which aims more toward a kind of *nonconformist integration* that follows what Mitchell (2004) has called the "integrative pluralistic" metaphysics underlying complexity theory. This perspective reflects a condition in which heterogeneous elements are allowed to express their individual differences while, at the same, time operating as a unity (on the power of difference and diversity in organizations see Page, 2007). STCs enable this nonconformist integration through their special logic of following and negation (see Appendix One), the negation insuring against mere conformity by negating any kind of conflation into rigid conformity. Along similar lines, I (1994) earlier proposed a method of group process called *difference questioning* which involves this operation of negation since every attempt to conformity is negated through the asking of questions that differentiate the perspectives, attitudes, ideas, and opinions of each group member.

This difference-enhancing characteristic of STCs corresponds to research in group dynamics finding that creative outcomes demand *non*conformity. In this regard, Van Dyne and Saavedra (1996) have demonstrated that rather than the homogeneity found in a Haken-like "enslaved" conformity, creativity in terms of divergent thinking and originality increases when a marked minority influence is allowed in a work group. Similarly, Jackson, *et al.* (1995) found that group heterogeneity in terms of a mix of personalities, gender, attitudes, and background of experience was positively related to the creativity and the decision-making effectiveness of teams. Moreover, Bantel and Jackson (1989) found that innovation in the banking industry was positively associated with diversity in team composition. Because it is probable that, left on their own, social groups succumb all too easily to pressures for conformity, by following the STC model of emergence, leaders would play an active role in not letting this happen. What is needed, is a paradoxically sounding "non-consensus coherence." This is an area of research where a great deal more needs to be done in inquiring how leaders can foster such kinds of emergent organizational structures, e.g., investigating specifically what kinds of connectivities, rules, and process variables determine degrees of nonconformity, creativity, adaptability and so on.

The Nature of Emergent Levels

Since the early days of emergentist thought, emergent phenomena have been understood as manifesting on a "higher" *macro*-level out of "lower," *micro*-level components. Emergent Evolutionists, for example, conceived evolution as a series of discontinuous emergences of new qualitative levels of reality (Blitz, 1992). This level distinction is also central to modern complexity theory as seen, e.g., by Langton (Lewin, 1992) conceiving of a global, emergent level "up here" made-up of the interactions of components "down here," and Bedau (1997) describing emergent phenomena as being "autonomous" with respect to the underlying processes leading to them. This same level differentiation is also found in the dynamical systems approach (Diner, *et al.*, 1986).

Wimsatt (1974, 1994, 1997) describes the notion of a level in a complex system as that which houses entities with comparable size, rates of change, patterns, and dynamical properties. Accordingly, a level consists of entities and their relations that hang together more strongly with one another on the same level than they do with other units and relations on other levels. The richness of emergent phenomena therefore are thought to require a set of functional laws congruent with their own level (see Bunge, 2003; Emmech, *et al.*, 1998; Gillett, 1998). That's why emergence entails an ontological commitment to level pluralism and not the ontological level monism underlying overly rigid reductionist points of view, a good example of which can be found in Pepper (1926).

Although they are often conflated, it is important to distinguish *level* in the emergent sense with the idea of *scale*. This is a distinction to which not enough attention is paid on the part of complexity aficionados especially in the aftermath of finding power law signatures in data that indicates scaling dynamics, in particular, evidence of self-similarity. But because what's transcended in the higher emergent level by means of STCs are the rules, laws, and principles operative at the lower level, this implies a type of *scale variance* and not scale invariance. Indeed, emergent structures and properties need to be considered as *self-dissimilar* at different levels (Wolpert & Macready, 2000). Similarly, I (2002) have written of the *singular* nature of emergent levels since, unlike scale invariance, the idea of the novelty characterizing emergent levels does not square with the notion of scale invariance.

For similar reasons, processes of emergence cannot be reduced to those consonant with an ascension up a "nested" hierarchy (O'Neill, *et al.*, 1986) where each new level is merely a wider class that is inclusive of the lower ones. If emergence were equivalent to that kind of logical operation, there would really be nothing new about the higher level and its properties. Rather, in accord with Anderson's (1972) aforementioned emergentist Constructionist Hypothesis, it is because each level is radically novel with respect to lower ones that STCs must be powerful to lead to phenomena with unique laws distinct from those operative at lower levels. If the emergent level were not novel with respect to the lower level from which it is composed, it wouldn't require a set of new laws.

In addition to the distinctiveness among levels in emergent systems, there is at the same time an ongoing interaction among them resulting in what can be called a "confoundedness" of the emergent level (Goldstein, 2002). In this context, it is important to recognize that one of the hallmarks of emergent levels being special and not just a designation of a different scale self-similar to other scales is that the novel emergent level *takes-up* the lower level into a new configuration. This is quite different than conceiving emergence as constituted by a crisp process of class inclusion as one moves up the hierarchy, i.e., first individuals, then a class of individuals, then classes of classes, then classes of classes of classes, and so on.

Moreover, it is with respect to level interaction that Hofstadter (1979) has written of "tangled hierarchies" and Wimsatt (1994) of "causal thickets" which increase the difficulty of localizing an entity on any one level unambiguously. Also, this is why it is often the case that the interplay between the level of parts and that of organization is what yields the highest explanatory payoff (Lewin, 1992). This also corresponds to what McShea (2000) has proposed takes place in emergent hierarchies in biological organisms: as functionality arises at higher emergent levels, the number of different subpart types decreases since functions are shared, that is, the higher emergent level represents a *mixing-up* of what was previously separate at the lower level. In other words, the higher emergent level transcends the category distinctions operative at the lower level.

This, of course, makes the study of emergence in complex systems a much messier matter than either presuming the self-similarity of scale invariance or holding that emergent levels are crisply distinct in relation to each other. This also means that in organizational applications of the construct of emergence there will be many opportunities to get confused about what is happening on what level. But this kind of confusion can be taken as a good sign, one that leaders can take advantage of since it means one is getting closer to the real emergent phenomena. The implications for leaders are twofold. First, properties at lower levels would not necessarily be appropriate at higher emergent levels. Thus, talk about somehow making organizations self-similar on different levels would just not be to the point. Second, leaders consequently would be placed in the role of fostering interaction among levels rather than assuming their role is to simply allow self-organization to putatively proceed spontaneously.

Emergence and Causality

From its inception onward, the idea of emergence has engendered no small amount of conceptual mischief through seeming to imply some kind of causal breach. Because of the pervasiveness of this issue, more attention will be given in this section than the previous ones. Indeed, the idea of a causal breach is a by-product of all three items of "folklore" discussed above since they all seem to give the impression that something is gotten for nothing. Such an interpretation also appears to follow from the use of emergence as a bulwark against what was perceived as overly mechanistic or reductionistic explanatory strategies, a use of emergence found all the way back in the original definition of "emergent" in 1875 by the American/English philosopher G.H. Lewes (1875) to distinguish causal process: "...although each effect is the resultant of its components, we cannot always trace the steps of the process, so as to see in the product the mode of operation of each factor. In the latter case, I propose to call the effect an *emergent*. It arises out of the combined agencies, but in a form which does not display the agents in action... the emergent cannot be reduced either to their sum or their difference" (pp. 368-369; emphasis added). The very fact that "emergent" was defined by way of untraceability, irreducibility, and as being more than a summation of causal factors leading to it, inevitably led to the sense that somehow emergence was sundering the causal chain.

It was along such lines of thought that Morgan (1923), a proponent of early emergentist thought, avowed that emergent novelty necessitated a distinction between "causality" and "causation": "causality" referring to the causal nexus of natural processes and "causation" alluding to a breach in natural processes afforded by emergent novelty. "Causation," according to Morgan would allow for a place for the inclusion of divinity in the natural world. However murky Morgan's distinction appears, it does point to the way in which emergence pushes us up against traditional notions of causality.

It is not a far cry from these early speculations of the implications of emergence on our notion of causality to similar ideas in today's complexity theory. Thus, Stacey (1996), a pioneer in applying complexity to organizational theory, has contended "Causal links between specific actions and specific organizational outcomes over the long term disappear in the complexity of the interaction between people in an organization, and between them and people in other organizations that constitute the environment" (p. 187). Although, Stacey was not averring that complex systems are *a*causal but rather that their causal links are obscured, such a caution frequently is overlooked in popular accounts of complex systems, some of which have made a big impact on how chaos and complexity theories should be applied to organizations. There is a close conceptual link between the sentiment expressed in Stacey's comment and Cohen's and Stewart's (1997) aforementioned "Existence Theorem for Emergence" which, by positing an intractably long deductive sequence between emergent cause and effect, was one of the clues described above leading to the conceptualization of emergence according to self-transcending constructions.

Another reason for the association of emergence with disruptions in the causal chain comes from the representation of emergence through the use of mathematical constructs coming out of nonlinear dynamical systems theory, especially that of phase space, bifurcation, and attractors. The deep insights into complex system behavior that have accrued by a geometric and topological investigation of attractor patterns in phase space have led certain enthusiasts of this approach to claim (Kellert, 1993: 104-105): "... the mechanisms responsible for unpredictable behavior, but that *these are not causal processes*. Instead, these mechanisms are best understood as geometrical..." (emphasis added). Newman (1996) has demonstrated the connection of emergence with the idea of an attractor, in particular strange attractors in chaotic systems: being in the basin of a strange attractor is an emergent property it is neither deducible from, predictable from, nor reducible to antecedent conditions or factors. Abraham (1987) discussed the same phenomena from a more technical mathematical vantage point: "An attractor functions as a symbol when it is viewed through an output projection map [map of a system by concentration of some variable into a finite dimension state space] by a slow observer. If the dynamic along the attractor is too fast to be recorded by the slow-reading observer, he may then recognize the attractor only by its averaged attributes, fractal dimension, power spectrum, and so on, but fail to recognize the trajectory along the attractor as a deterministic system" (p. 606; his emphasis). Similarly, Crutchfield (1994) has pointed how emergent structure is "not directly described by the defining constraints and instantaneous forces that control a system...not directly specified by the equations of motion...[and] cannot be explicitly represented in the initial and boundary conditions" (p. 1). Consequently, the radical novelty of emergent phenomena can appear quite enigmatic.

Yet another reason for the belief in a causal breach has to do with how discrepant the outcome of emergence is with respect to antecedent conditions, a discrepancy that early emergentists described as an incommensurability. For example, Bergson (1911), whose ideas on "creative evolution" were of great important to early emerentists, wrote, "organic evolution resembles the evolution of a consciousness, in which the past presses against the present and causes the *upspringing* of a new form of consciousness, *incommensurable* with its antecedents " (pp. 27-28; emphasis added). And, Lewes (1875) in a continuation of his definition of emergence stated above asserted a similar thing "... the emergent is unlike its components in so far as these are *incommensurable*, and it cannot be reduced either to their sum or their difference" (pp. 368-369; emphasis added).

However, it must be noted that conceiving an outcome as incommensurable with the input would only require a breach of causality to those who cannot imagine processes powerful enough to bring about emergent outcomes from lower level building blocks. The idea of self-transcending constructions was developed exactly to talk about such processes that transcend lower levels and antecedent conditions even though they are built out of the latter. Such a thing is possible because STCs exploit operations such as recombination and randomness. Indeed, these are one of the key findings coming out of the study of computational emergence where higher level patterns result from intentional recombination and randomization. An example is Holland's (1998) CGPs model of emergence modeled on his genetic algorithms in which crossover (recombination) and mutation operations are taken from the theory of evolution. These operations are formalized by the "following" and "negation" sides of the logic self-transcending constructions mentioned earlier. Because self-organization implies that such things happen spontaneously and "for free," it tends to neglect exactly how this incommensurability can be caused to happen. But a leader following the new model of emergence being expressed in this paper would focus on ways of following and then negating past and lower level conditions as the organization gropes its way toward innovative solutions to its challenges.

The Unpredictability of Emergent Phenomena

Yet another philosophy science issue, one closely related to that of causality, has to do with the purported unpredictability customarily thought of as a defining characteristic of emergent phenomena. This includes chaos theory's startling discovery of deterministic processes that could lead to, contrary to received wisdom, dynamics as effectively unpredictable as stochastic ones (Abraham, 1987). This notion of unpredictability has been transferred over to emergence when the scheme of bifurcation into new attractors has been used to codify emergence. There is also the unpredictability resulting from the formal non-analyticity (unsolvability) of the nonlinear equations used to represent complex and emergent systems. The latter introduces a degree of unpredictability that even in principle will not completely yield to further probing. Furthermore, there is unpredictability of "dissipative structures" in Prigogine's (Nicolis & Prigogine, 1989) approach arising from amplification of random fluctuations. To the degree that fluctuations are random and thereby unpredictable, then to that degree emergent order is supposedly unpredictable.

Randomness indeed appears to play an important role in a complex system's adaptability. As Allen and McGlade (1985) state, in order to learn about the world around them, it may be the random departures of systems from norm-seeking, average behavior which are decisive. Or, as Nicolis and Prigogine (1989) have put it, a system under the influence of random occurrences coming from its unpredictable environment may develop temporary structures or processes suitable for novel occasions as they may arise. Nicolis has evidence that permanent and rigid structures or processes in a system which is interacting with an unpredictable environment will bring the system to a less than optimal condition whereas, a system which has a high rate of unpredictable explorations (i.e., able to be influenced by the random occurrences of its unpredictable environment) can develop temporary structures or processes suitable for any occasion that may arise. By the way, notice the emphasis on *temporary* structures, an emphasis not associated with the self-organizational view of emergence.

Because of its reliance on the "dissipative structure" model of Prigogine, unpredictability has also been a major tenet of the self-organizational picture of emergence. Moreover, in that self-organizing processes are supposed to happen on their own, spontaneously, and neither directed, conditioned, nor guided, it is believed they cannot be known ahead of time (in other words, the ostensive property of emergent phenomena listed at the beginning of this article).

Self-organization's utilization of chance fluctuations can be found in all of the applications of emergence to organizations described at the beginning of this paper.

A critical question, though, arises here concerning exactly how unpredictability and randomness are to be dealt with by leaders. In the self-organization approach, cognizant of the putative unpredictability of the novel order emerging from self-organization, leaders allow self-organization to proceed as it takes advantage of fluctuations in a "bottom-up" fashion. That is, the self-organization model would have it that unpredictability is the last word on emergent systems. But this is borne out neither by research into self-organizing physical systems nor in the computational emergence found in the field of artificial life. For example in research into "dissipative structures" it is predictable in the sense that given the right container, and the right liquid, and the right process of heating, the remarkable Benard convection cells will emerge, and their patterns will be quite similar to those observed in previous experiments. Furthermore, the only thing totally unpredictable in the Benard system is the directionality of each hexagonal convection cell since this directionality hinges on which specific random currents become amplified (see Nicolis & Prigogine, 1989).

Predictability also shows up in the *Game of Life* (see Poundstone, 1985), an exemplar of computational emergence, where the presence of two emergent patterns called "t-tetraminos" in close proximity to one another can be used to predict the later emergence of another pattern, the "pentadecathelon." At first, this predictability was unknown so the "pentadecathelon" was presumed to be an unpredictable emergent, but now that a correlation has been established between the "t-tetramino" and the "pentadecathelon," the latter has become much more predictable, a progress in prediction that will continue as more and more outcomes of the Game and Life are catalogued and studied. As more is put into taxonomies and typologies of emergent phenomena, such classification schemes will aid in the discovery of repeating patterns and thereby greater predictability. Even in chaotic systems, which are touted as full-blown unpredictable, there is a great deal of predictability due to the attractors of the system which serve to delimit the possible states of the system (Goldstein, 1997b). For example, although the exact temperature next July 4 in New York City is unpredictable, that it will be hot is indeed predictable.

Moreover, as stated above, much of the order found in emergent phenomena derives from the order inherent in the "containers" of the self-organizing processes. Both knowledge of the order of the pre-existing "containers" plus the actual construction of such "containers" on the part of leaders, therefore, can help in predicting the type of order that will be found in the ensuing emergent processes. Indeed, experiments on how changing the order of containers changes the resulting emergents will no doubt increase the predictability of emergence. Additionally, another reason that emergent structures are not completely unpredictable involves the presence of "generic forms" towards which emergence converges as described by Goodwin (1994). No doubt an interesting area of organizational research will be concerned with analogous organizational "generic forms."

Leaders can work with the "containers" which constrain the direction and shape of emergent order brought about via self-transcending constructions. Juarrero's (1999) insights into constraints are pertinent here: constraints have to do with the relational properties parts acquire by virtue of being united into wholes. She gives the example of how the tibia's connection to the knee constrains the movement possibilities of the lower leg. Moreover, constraints need not only serve to reduce a system's degrees of freedom since, as Juarrero suggests, constraints can also open up a system to new possibilities by moving it away from pure chance, e.g., the necessarily constrained alphabet of English simultaneously constrains and opens up possibilities for what words can be meaningfully constructed. Indeed, Guerin and Kunkle (2004) have shown how constraints emerge in agent-based models. Similarly, leaders can "play" with various "containers" and constraints to see which kinds of outcomes emerge. For example, "containers" can be firmed-up and loosened (see Goldstein, 1994). These "containers" can be psychological (e.g., a sense of safety), social (e.g., rules of interaction), cultural (e.g., rituals and stories), technological (e.g., computer networks), even physical (e.g., the actual physical attributes of the workplace). Moreover, leaders can actively work with these "containers" in conjunction with their staffs in a more directive way than a pure self-organizational model would allow.

In the self-transcending constructional approach to emergence, the issue of unpredictability versus predictability can lead to other active interventions on the part of leaders. First, rather than waiting for self-organization to spontaneously happen in the face of random fluctuations, processes involving randomization can be fostered. This can be modeled on creativity techniques which set up opportunities to take advantage of randomness (Gordon, 1961; and more recently, Finke, et al., 1996). Indeed, randomization can lead to the kind of divergent thinking which research has shown can be a critical factor to be taken advantage of by leaders early on in the problem-solving cycle (Vincent, et al., 2002). Indeed, as studies of innovation in science demonstrate, the incorporation of randomness seems to be a necessary component, at some stage, in the process of organization innovation.

Conclusion: The Future of Emergence and Leadership Studies

The self-organization picture of emergence would have it that the emergence of order occurs within the context of social interaction by means of the spontaneous amplification of random fluctuations when leader-dictated control mechanisms are dismantled. The order that emerges is considered "for free" because of the spontaneity of the amplification, the random nature of the fluctuations, and the lack of leadership design. It is because of the last factor that the self-organizational model of emergence implies a sort of passivity on the part of leaders. Indeed, a typical guideline coming out of this picture is that leader's may be directive in terms of setting a goal or vision for the organization or work group, but when it comes to the exact way of accomplishing this goal they should be passive in letting self-organization take place.

However, this passive role of leaders doesn't seem to be one associated with high quality outcomes. Thus, Peterson (1997) found that a much more active role was correlated with quality results: a leader's directiveness in relation to task group process was predictive of quality outcomes whereas outcome directiveness was associated with a much smaller and less coherent array of group outcomes. Interaction among the social group by itself is simply not enough to make the emergence of novel structures likely. Instead, it must be interaction which is encouraged, constrained, shaped, and undergoing self-transcending constructional operations which has the possibility of ushering forth novel patterns, structures, dynamics, patterns, and properties.

Furthermore, since the course of self-organization follows from the occurrence of random fluctuations, then in a strictly self-organizational model the ensuing emergence of order would itself be largely random in terms of its effects. When it comes to adaptability of an organization to its environment, a random search among new possibilities of organizational functioning is not the most effective means toward adaptation to its environment. As Kauffman (1995) has proposed random searches can get trapped at very low peaks in the adaptive fitness landscape, a way of visualizing the success potential of different possibilities of novel emergent order and properties. Moreover, in a random search the rate of improvement will be inevitably slow so that adaptation to the highest peak becomes virtually impossible. Furthermore, when a search is merely random with no clues about upward trends, the only way to find the highest pinnacle is to search the whole space. This can be seen in biological as well as technological evolution since they both consist of processes that attempt to optimize systems riddled with conflicting constraints (Kauffman & Macready, 1995).

These remarks on adaptation appear to suggest that waiting around for random searches by way of self-organizing processes is not the best strategy to take in regard to organization's functioning, structure, and work processes. Instead, Maquire (1997) suggests that the search for improvements in the latter amounts to a *design* problem since it is a matter of understanding diverse options among various combinations of organizational processes to construct a strategy. The idea of "design" is counter, though, to the above mentioned cleaving of self-organization as a natural, spontaneous occurrence from construction, artifice and design. As a matter of fact, one adaptive but designed strategy may be a "foolish" one (Kauffman, 1995) which oddly enough goes back down from peaks where the search may be trapped. A foolish adaptation then may be advantageous since it frees up those modifications trapped on lower valued short peaks. But how is a model of emergence strictly following the self-organizational picture to come up with a foolish walk down a fitness peak?

Organizational leaders need to move from a passive to an active role in the emergence of new organizational forms and it is the self-transcending constructional approach to emergence that can be of assistance here. By indicating the role of "design" in such a move, the point is not to predict so much as to explore possible scenarios. The leader's role here is to recognize, identify, foster, sift, provide, shape, and constrain resources of order to be used for emergent modifications. To be sure, sometimes random searches are what's called-for, sometimes what is required is the seemingly foolish move of going down a hill, and there are, of course, many other seemingly practices that may be called-for (on the variety of diverse methods available, see Page, 2007). It is not at all likely that these latter alternatives can be facilitated by self-organization as customarily understood.

What's necessary for future research is how organizational emergence can be guided toward granting greater adaptability to organizations. Since randomness alone doesn't supply the answer, there will be a need for assessing the varied constructed approaches that are possible. Since the model of emergence according to self-transcending constructions includes as one important element self-organizing processes, it does involve some degree of randomization but this random element is combined with all manner of order construction operations. However, in the face of all of these suggestions for design and construction, it must be also remarked that what is being offered here is not to be taken as a call for a return to command and control leadership. The self-transcending constructional approach to emergence instead calls on leaders to a play an active role in the building up of novel structures with novel properties. What research needs to determine in more detail is what exactly what this active role involves. An additional research item concerns the above mentioned generic forms in organizations: Do organizations like biological organisms possess such forms? How are they identified? What can leaders do in relation to them?

Finally, amid all the hoopla surrounding both self-organization and emergence, it is often assumed they are necessarily good things, that is, that systems exhibiting them are significantly better off in certain ways, or, at least, what is problematic in these systems is markedly ameliorated. But as the point made above concerning Yugoslavia tried to get at, emergent structures may form around pre-existing fault lines of unwanted infrastructures. Dismantling control mechanisms and thereby encouraging self-organization and emergence, therefore, doesn't necessarily mean you're going to have a better state of affairs than you had before. The self-transcending constructional approach to emergence therefore prompts much more research into what factors lead to beneficial and not destructive emergent organizational forms.

Appendix One: Formalism for Self-transcending Constructions

(Modified from Simmons, 1990, in order to render a definition of an example of a self-transcending construction)

Cantor's specific STC can be formalized as an anti-diagonal sequence constructed as follows: an array constituted by a side D_1 which is a vertical list of elements from a denumerable set and a top, D_2, which is a horizontal list of natural numbers ($\mathbb{N}$):

Definition 1: Let R be a 3-place relation and, D_1 and D_2 be sets. Then R is an array on D_1 and $D_2 \leftrightarrow_{df} \forall x \forall y \ (x \in D_1 \ \& \ y \in D_2 \rightarrow \exists ! z Rxyz)$.

Definition 2: F is a diagonal on D_1 and $D_2 \leftrightarrow_{df}$ is a bijection $D_1 \rightarrow D_2$.

Definition 3: Let R be an array on D_1 and D_2, and let F be a diagonal on D_1 and D_2. Then G is the value of the diagonal F in $R \leftrightarrow_{df} \forall x \forall y \ (Gxyz \leftrightarrow Fxy \ \& \ Rxyz)$.

Definition 4: Let R be an array F a diagonal, Stc is an anti-diagonal of F in $R \leftrightarrow_{df}$

iv. $\forall x \forall y (\exists z Stcxyz \rightarrow Fxy)$
v. $\forall x \forall y \forall z \forall z' \ (Stcxyz \ \& \ Stcxyz' \rightarrow z=z')$
vi. $\forall x \forall y \forall z \ (Stcxyz \rightarrow z \in$ Range $\mathbb{R})$
vii. $\forall x \forall y \forall z \ (Stcxyz \rightarrow \neg \ Gxyz)$.

     A generalization of Cantor's anti-diagonal construction would need to retain a way to recursively map elements one to one in order to create some sequence and at the same time a way to introduce a innovation operation during this mapping so that a radically new sequence is constructed.
     The logic of *following* and *negating* by which STCs operate can be depicted as follows:

1. *Following* is illustrated in Definition 2 as the diagonal on D_1 and D_2, a mapping function which can be considered a *following* of the intersections of the already existing lists D_1 and D_2, which is continued through Definition 3 and 4 (the latter where it is *followed* in generating the anti-diagonal). Moreover, we are considering *all* ($\forall x \forall y \forall z$) the items on the diagonal.
2. Negating is depicted in definition 4 where we can see the radical novelty operation of the anti-diagonal construction by means of negation $\neg$, an operation which generates the radical novelty innovation from the realm of the natural numbers $\mathbb{N}$ originally presumed over to the real numbers $\mathbb{R}$ signified in Definition 4.iii.
3. What is transcended, consequently, is the isomorphism between D_1 and D_2 which is signified by the bijection $D_1 \rightarrow D_2$ in Definition 2.

CHAPTER FIVE
LEADERSHIP IN THE FOUR STAGES OF EMERGENCE

Bill McKelvey & Benyamin B. Lichtenstein

Current complexity researchers leave unanswered a key question about emergence, namely: does the process of "self-organization" really operate by itself? In other words, do large complex organizations actually self-organize "all the way up" into a multi-layered nested hierarchy? And if not, to what degree or at what point is leadership necessary to support the supposedly automatic organizing process of emergence? We take an empirical approach to the question, by reviewing nearly 300 CAS simulation models that focus on how agents self-organize based on a small number of rules. Our assessment yields a crucial finding: CAS models show (only) four stages of self-organizing emergent behavior: emergent networks, emergent groups, emergent hierarchy, and emergent coordination complexity. Even within these four stages – and certainly beyond them – leadership actions are absolutely necessary in order to achieve the complex organizations we find in the 21st century landscape. We conclude with implications for theory and practice.

Bill McKelvey, who received his Ph.D., from MIT in 1967, is Professor of Strategic Organizing and Complexity Science at the UCLA Anderson School. His book, Organizational Systematics (1982) remains a definitive treatment of organizational taxonomy and evolution. He chaired the building committee that produced the $110,000,000 Anderson Complex. He directed over 170 field study teams on strategic improvements to client firms. In 1997 he initiated the founding of UCLA's Center for Human Complex Systems & Computational Social Science. McKelvey has coedited *Variations in Organization Science* (1999) and special issues of *Emergence* (now *E:CO*) and JIT. He has 55 papers on complexity science applied to organizations and management.

Benyamin B. Lichtenstein is Assistant Professor of Management and Entrepreneurship at the University of Massachusetts, Boston. Dr. Lichtenstein's research expertise focuses on applications of complexity science to leadership, entrepreneurial emergence and transformation, and on collaboration, trust and inter-organizational learning. "Professor Benyamin" as his students call him, has published over 35 papers and chapters and presented several dozen more, including articles in internationally recognized journals such as *Organization Science, Journal of Business Venturing, Human Relations* and *Academy of Management Executive,* where he received the article of the year award in 2000. In addition to his scholarly work, and his executive consulting to entrepreneurs and managers, he finds great joy connecting with his beautiful wife Sasha and their two children, Simeon and Moriah.

Introduction

Complexity science has been heralded as a new paradigm in management – a powerful set of methods for explaining non-linear, emergent behavior in organizations (McKelvey, 1997; Anderson, et al., 1999). Complexity studies of emergence have extended our understanding of many organizational phenomena, including innovation (Cheng & Van de Ven, 1996; Saviotti & Mani, 1998; Rivkin, 2000, 2001); entrepreneurship (Stevenson & Harmeling, 1990; McKelvey, 2004; Lichtenstein, et al., 2007), organizational learning (Carley & Svoboda, 1996; Carley & Hill, 2001), organization design (Garud, et al., 2006; Siggelkow & Rivkin, 2006), and strategic adaptation and organizational evolution (McKelvey, 1999; Morel & Ramanujam, 1999; Gavetti & Levinthal, 2000), among many others.

In the field of leadership there is a long history of explanations for emergent order in groups and organizations (e.g., Weber, 1924; Roethlisberger & Dixon, 1939; Sayles, 1957 – see Table 1 below). Thus, it makes sense that leadership scholars have also been exploring how complexity science can help explain and support emergent behavior in dynamic organizations (Marion & Uhl-Bein, 2001; Uhl-Bein, et al., 2007; Hazy, Millhiser & Solow, this volume). Given the need for ongoing innovation in many organizations, and given the increasing amount of information that most knowledge workers possess, scholars of Complex Systems Leadership Theory argue that leadership should not be "held" in a particular role or within a particular person. Instead, leadership is more accurately seen as a process embedded within each and every interaction throughout the organization (Lichtenstein, et al., 2006b – in this volume). Complexity science, with its emphasis on interactions and the role of interactions on emergence, provides an ideal method and theory for explaining how a "decentralized" and "relational" leadership can lead to greater levels of innovation, adaptability, and emergent behavior (Uhl-Bein, et al., 2007).

Some leading edge work on complexity leadership suggests that managers and supervisors do well by creating the conditions within which emergence can flourish (e.g., Plowman, et al., 2007; Hazy, et al., in this volume). According to this "traditional" complexity notion, heterogeneous agents, interacting according to a small number of simple rules, will create new regimes of order on their own through "self-organization" dynamics that are inherent in these complexity conditions. Following this argument to its logical extreme, by embedding the capacity for emergent behavior within the culture, processes and interaction dynamics of the organization, agents in a company could essentially self-organize all the way up – levels upon levels upon levels – without the need for a central controller (e.g., CEO) or strategic directorate; this claim was originally suggested by Anderson (1999). With the right conditions in place, emergent behavior across all organization members could effectively "lead" a company by maximizing innovation, adaptability, and knowledge sharing.

Other complexity leadership scholars have suggested that a combination of bottom-up and top-down dynamics are necessary in complex organizations (Uhl-Bein, et al., 2007), while Goldstein (this volume) makes a compelling argument against the longstanding belief (what he terms "folklore") that bottom-up self-organization can generate any order at all without significant enabling and constraint factors, i.e., managerial influence. This debate is especially important to leadership theory, for each of the two approaches comes with a stream of implications around whether, how, and when leaders should enact formal organizational policies and processes to encourage innovation and emergence, versus a more passive notion of leadership in which everyone is encouraged to "self-organize" their way to success.

One way to grapple with this question is to review the empirical evidence around bottom-up emergence in organizations. Our hope is that the results of many complexity-based models should help reveal insights about how complex an organization could actually become if its agent-members, through their on-going interactions, were allowed to generate emergent structures and increasing levels of aggregation _on their own_, i.e., without the benefit of additional control through formal leaders. The question we ask is: how large and how complex could such a "self-organized" organization become?

Complexity science does provide an answer to this question, and the answer is not what we originally expected. The purpose of this chapter is to review complexity studies of emergent behavior based on the existing simulation research and on thick, qualitative research studies, to organize and assess what we currently know about the potential for bottom-up emergence to generate complex organizations. Based on our analysis, a maximum of _four levels of order_ could ever emerge without top-town leadership influence – these we call four "stages" of emergence (Lichtenstein & McKelvey, 2005). Beyond that, an increasing number of specific leadership activities are necessary in order to support the development of complicated and complex organizations that form the societal landscape of the 21st century.

Levels of Emergence? Findings from Complexity
Methods for Studying Emergence

Management scholarship has revealed an extremely wide range of emergent phenomena, starting with classic studies on the emergence of bureaucracy and hierarchy (e.g., Weber, 1924/1947), the division of labor (Babbage, 1832), and the emergence of the "invisible hand" of the market. Early organization studies identified the emergence of groups and group norms (e.g., Roethlisberger & Dixon, 1939; Homans, 1950; Trist & Bamforth, 1951; Gross, 1953; Roy, 1954). Over time, the study of emergence has expanded to include multiple contexts and levels of organizing; a summary of examples is given in Table 1. Unfortunately, this quagmire of emergent phenomena makes it nearly impossible to identify common patterns or processes of emergence.

A powerful approach for identifying common patterns of emergence is the use of agent-based computational models (Kauffman, 1969, 1993; Holland, 1975, 1995, 1998; Wolfram, 1983, 1994, 2001). Computational experiments allow investigators to play out the nuances of emergence across many heterogeneous agents, at various degrees of interactiveness, at various structural levels, and over time. Computational models are "...particularly effective in the 'sweet spot' between theory-creating research using ... inductive multiple case studies

MANAGEMENT STUDY OF EMERGENCE	REFERENCE *(Listed Chronologically)*
Emergent Division of Labor	Babbage, 1832
Emergence of Hierarchy and Bureaucracy	Weber, 1924/1947
Emergent Groups and Group Norms	Roethlisberger & Dixon, 1939; Homans, 1950; Trist & Bamforth, 1951; Gross, 1953; Roy, 1954
Emergent Social Control	Breed, 1955
Emergent Coordination	Sayles, 1957
Emergence of Staff Units	Golembiewski, 1961
Emergent Collaboration	Dutton & Walton, 1965
Self-Organization of Internal Control Structures	Weick, 1977
Emergence of Internal Corporate Ventures	Burgelman, 1983
Creation and Development of Organizational Routines	Pentland, 1992
Regions of Emergent Complexity in Innovation Projects	Brown & Eisenhardt, 1997
Emergence of New Management Logics	Dijksterhuis, *et al.*, 1999
Emergence of New Organizational Configurations	Lichtenstein, 2000; Lichtenstein, Dooley & Lumpkin, 2006a
Emergence of Nascent Firms	Lichtenstein, *et al.*, 2007
Coevolutionary Emergence of Institutions and Industries	Chiles, *et al.*, 2004; Jones, 2001; Maguire, *et al.*,, 2004

Table 1 *Selected Studies of Emergence in Organizations*

and formal modeling, and theory-testing research using multivariate, statistical analysis" (Davis, *et al.*, 2007: 481). Computational models have also been valuable for leadership scholars exploring the dynamics of leadership emergence from a complexity perspective (e.g., Surie & Hazy, 2006; Hazy, 2007; Hazy, *et al.*, in this volume). For these reasons we draw primarily on computational models to identify a parsimonious set of emergent types. We add richness to our review by referencing narrative exemplars at each level of emergence.

To date well over 300 computational modeling experiments relevant to organizations have been published (for example, see Ferber 1999; Gilbert & Troitzsch, 1999; Ilgen & Hulin, 2000; Masuch, 1990; Warglien & Masuch, 1996; Prietula, *et al.*, 1998; Sorenson, 2002; Davis, *et al.*, 2007; Hazy, *et al.*, *in this volume*). Through our familiarity with over two-thirds of these, we suggest that complexity studies of emergence can be organized into four streams of research. We find that these streams represent four "levels" of emergence (Bar-Yam, 2004; Lichtenstein & McKelvey, 2005). Although our analysis necessarily oversimplifies specific research findings, it does lead to a parsimonious understanding of emergence in terms of a small number of categories (levels) that are common to organization and management theory. Further, the evidence suggests that these four levels of emergence build one on the other, leading to the added insight that there are four distinct *stages* of emergence which are revealed through complexity experiments. We name these stages *Networks, Groups, Hierarchies*, and *Complex Coordination Structures*; each one represents one of four levels or stages of emergence. These stages are summarized in Table 2; each level/stage is presented in the sub-sections that follow.

Networks
Groups
Hierarchies
Complex Coordination structures

LEVEL 1 EMERGENCE: Complexity Streams that Model Emergent Networks

The complexity research showing Level 1 emergence focuses on how network-level properties come into being through the interactions across moderately heterogeneous agents; very little "leadership" is implied.

Self-organized Criticality. In this classic complexity model, unpolished grains of sand (heterogeneous agents) are dropped onto a sandpile. Once the sandpile reaches a requisite size (based on the diameter of its base) the pile is disrupted by an ongoing series of "punctuated avalanches." A power law explains the distribution of avalanches, with the implication that very large system changes are rare but to be expected (Bak & Chen, 1991). Additional analysis shows that this phenomenon of self-organized criticality explains the dynamics behind earthquakes, species extinctions, and stock-market behavior (Casti, 1994; Bak, 1996; Krugman, 1996; Mandelbrot & Hudson, 2004). Bak's work on self-organized criticality (scalability) is an important element of complexity science (Brock, 2000); however, since there is neither hierarchy nor properties associated with the self-organized criticality, his model reaches only the first level of emergence.

The Edge of Chaos: Defining a Region of Emergence. The next two approaches are based on cellular automata (CA) models, which examine the interactions of mildly heterogeneous agents in a two-dimensional grid (network). Agents self-organize to produce some macro effect, such as improved fitness relative to the imposed environmental selection context. Simple though they are, CA models reveal the non-directed organization of cellular agents into emergent and stable patterns of order which are not programmed into the computational experiment.

Early complexity studies at the Santa Fe Institute found a specific class of dynamic order in CA models – labeled "the edge of chaos" – that leads to self-organization and order creation (Langton, 1985). Researchers have used the "edge of chaos" metaphor to explain a diverse series of business processes, including changes in innovation projects (Dubinskas, 1994), organizing dynamics in product development projects (Brown & Eisenhardt, 1997), leadership in complex organizations (Marion, 1999), and new approaches to strategic adaptation (Pascale, *et al.*, 1999). McKelvey (2001) discusses ways in which managers may enlarge the region of emergence and improve the probability that self-organizing behavior will occur. Although the "edge of chaos" idea cannot distinguish

EMERGENCE LEVEL	Analytic or Modeling Approach	Exemplar Complexity Studies	Exemplar Applications in Management
1. Emergent Networks	Self-organized criticality	Bak & Chen, 1991	Krugman, 1996
	Edge of Chaos	Langton, 1985	Brown & Eisenhardt, 1997
	NK Landscape	Kauffman, 1993	Levinthal, 1997; Rivkin 2000
2. Emergent Groups	Micro-Sociology	Schelling, 1978	
	Coevolutionary games	Axelrod & Bennett, 1993	Axelrod, 1997
	Global System Properties	Krugman, 1996	
	Genetic Algorithms	Holland, 1995	Axelrod & Cohen, 2000
	Simulated Coordination		Paul, *et al*, 1996 Crowston, 1996
	Multi-Agent Learning	Carley, 1991; 1996	Carley & Hill 2001
3. Emergent Hierarchy	Emergent societies	Epstein & Axtell, 1996	
4. Emergent Coordination Complexity	Carley's ORGAHEAD simulation		Carley, 1999; Carley & Lee, 1998

Table 2 *Analysis of Complexity Studies at Successive Levels of Emergence*

different types of emergent structure, it does focus on the conditions that create the region (not an edge) of self-organization. Without this region, complexity science is not possible. Therefore, we put "edge" models in Level 1.

Tunable NK Landscapes: Emergent Fitness. Kauffman's (1993) *NK* Fitness Landscape model simulates a coevolutionary process in which both the individual agents, *N = the number of agents*, and the level of interdependency between them, *K = density of agent interactions*, are modeled over time. As individual agents change, they affect all other agents, thus altering some aspects of the nearest-neighbor landscape. It turns out that the degree of order in the overall landscape crucially depends on the level of *K,* the degree of system-wide interdependence, that is, complexity (Kauffman, 1993).

The *NK* model is the one most frequently applied to organizations; Maguire, *et al.* (2006) list twenty-four applications; *NK*-based studies on innovation continue to published at a rapid rate (e.g., Siggelkow & Rivkin, 2006; Sorenson, *et al.*, 2006). Researchers have applied the *NK* model to business settings by exploring what level of connectedness will bring an entire system to a higher level of fitness without locking it into a "catastrophe" of interdependence (Levinthal, 1997; Rivkin, 2000). Moderate levels of interconnection can be achieved by:

- Modularization of the production process (Levinthal & Warglien, 1999);
- Keeping internal value chain interdependencies to levels just below opponents' (McKelvey, 1999), or;
- Adopting strategies based on the industry-wide level of firm interdependence (Baum, 1999).

In an empirical test of the *NK* application to innovation, Fleming and Sorenson (2001: 1025) show "invention can be maximized by working with a large number of components that interact to an intermediate degree."

There is not actually very much emergence, per se, in the *NK* model. For the most part, self-organization is limited to agent connections (networks) with nearest neighbors. For example, when Kauffman studies the effects of species of varying size, *S,* he does so by changing *S* as a control parameter, not by allowing the size of *S* (groups) to emerge from agent interactions. In this respect most *NK* models represent a sophisticated example of Level 1 Emergence, with the capability of advancing into Level 2 Emergence. According to recent reviews (Carley, 2002; Eisenhardt & Bhatia, 2002; Sorenson, 2002), the vast majority of complexity studies utilize *NK* models and other computational experiments to show how emergent networks materialize within and across complex adaptive systems.

Narrative Studies of Level 1 Emergence. In an early and insightful study of emergent practices in a dynamic work group, Weick (1977) shows how the "strike" by Apollo 13 astronauts was a self-organized process through which the agents wrested control from their managers and, thereby, became more efficient and effective in their tasks. The emergent property of positive performance has been linked to the self-organization of groups (Smith & Comer, 1994), and to self-organized change in high-growth ventures (Lichtenstein, 2000). In general, there are very few thick-description narrative studies of *just* network formations.

LEVEL 2 EMERGENCE: Emergent Groups

It is one thing to describe the emergence of properties within a given organizational level, as all of the foregoing studies do. However, it is quite another thing to show the emergence of a new *level* of order with its own interdependent, adaptive agents (Salthe, 1985; Kelso, 1995). Level 2 emergence studies are of this type. Note that these studies do not assume any "leadership" nor influence, *per se*, from a central controller, nor is there a structure or context that emerges separate from the agents themselves. Instead the models show how interactions among agents generate emergent order in the form of semi-autonomous groups within the simulation.

Cellular Automata Studies of Emergent Groups. Schelling's (1978) micro-sociology of racial behavior uses a CA spatial model to explain how agents with similar interests become grouped together in a physical space. Though simple, it is the classic modeling of emergence resulting in the formation of groups of self-organizing agents. Axelrod and Bennett (1993) use a "spin-glass" type CA landscape model to study group formation; applying the model to 1939 data, they accurately predict the political alliance formation of all but one nation during WWII. In another complexity extension of his previous work in game theory, Axelrod and Bennett (1993) study group formation as a result of extortion behavior, again showing how a very few simple agent rules lead to emergent behaviors that produces semi-autonomous groups. Finally, economist Krugman (1996) uses a simple CA application of spatial modeling, to ask why "edge cities" form, and whether their distribution can be explained through a power law. He finds that randomly dispersed business activities will always evolve into highly ordered "edge cities" that are ontologically distinct from their component businesses – a result that falls under Level 2 emergence and supports Simon's (1955) "lumping/clumping" theory explaining the power-law distribution of city sizes in the U.S.

Holland's Genetic Algorithms – Rule Changing. An important advance in modeling emergence occurs through the use of genetic algorithms (GAs), invented by Holland (1975, 1995). GAs allow agents to learn and change over time by changing the rules governing their behavior. Whereas CA models are limited (methodologically) to very few rules (usually one or two), GAs allow agents to have many rules (Macy & Skvoretz, 1998). New agent formations can have varying numbers of rules from each prior agent form, thus allowing the increased evolutionary fitness of complex processes such as decision-making and learning, along with recombinations of diverse skills. As agents in horizontal networks coevolve toward improved adaptive capability, differentiated groups emerge; soon thereafter group norms also solidify.

GAs have been applied in a range of models. For example, Paul, *et al.*

(1996) examine the adaptation of emergent financial trading firms (groups), in which firms may activate or deactivate their agents, or form combinations of seemingly better performing agents from prior periods. In an efficient market performance climate with a 50% probability of success, their model firms beat the market 60% of the time. Separately, Crowston's (1996) GA model examines whether coordination - although necessary to accomplish interdependent tasks - is costly in terms of time. His results show that organizations and/or their employee agents do in fact minimize coordination costs by organizing in particular ways. Both of these simulations model the behavior of agents and groups of agents, thus they exemplify Level 2 emergence.

Multi-Agent Learning Models. Carley and her colleagues have produced some of the more sophisticated models to date in computational modeling, which combine elements of CA, GA, and neural networks. In her CONSTRUCT (1991) and CONSTRUCT-O models (Carley & Hill, 2001), simulated agents have a position or role in a social network and a mental model consisting of knowledge about other agents. Agents communicate and learn from others with similar types of knowledge. CONSTRUCT-O allows for the rapid formation of subgroups and the emergence of culture, which, when it crystallizes, supervenes to alter agent coevolution and search for improved performance. These models show the emergence of communication networks (Level 1) and the formation of stable hierarchical groups (Level 2); they also show how higher levels of order supervene to influence lower-level behavior. Supervenience, the mechanism by which higher-level components intervene to alter the behavior of their lower-level components, has been called a crucial characteristic of emergence (Klee, 1984; Blitz, 1992). As such, these are sophisticated examples of Level 2 emergence.

Narrative Studies of Level 2 Emergence. One of the best-known narrative complexity studies is Brown and Eisenhardt's (1997, 1998) examination of how organizing structures form and interact in high-velocity (far-from-equilibrium) environments. Although their analysis draws extensively from the "edge-of-chaos" metaphor (Level 1 Emergence), they also provide examples of how project groups become ontologically distinct from the agents that compose them, thus linking their application to Level 2 emergence. Separately, in a longitudinal study of new venture creation dynamics, Lichtenstein, *et al.* (2006a) identify an "emergence event" as the nearly simultaneous emergence of three distinct (new) modes of entrepreneurial organizing. Specifically the entrepreneur's shift in tactical organizing generated a shift in strategic organizing, which resulted in the emergence of a new vision (identity) of the nascent venture; this three-level process provides a link to Level 3 emergence.

LEVEL 3 EMERGENCE: Emergent Hierarchical Complexity

With Level 3 models there is enough internal emergence to draw on the more formal definition of emergence as "qualitative novelty," which recognizes that for a property or structure to be emergent it should be "different in kind" from its components; thus, a different discipline (and different language) is necessary to investigate the new level (Bechtel & Richardson, 1992). A good example of this formal definition is seen in "strategy emergence." At one level the components of an emergent strategy are generated through individual- and group-level interactions; however, the accumulative (performance) impact of these innovations can only be defined in terms of corporate strategy, competitive advantage, and dynamic environmental adaptiveness, which reference a "higher" organizational level (Quinn, 1992; Teece, *et al.*, 1997). The result is a formal hierarchy that includes three distinct and interdependent levels of activity – agents, groups, and organizational dynamics.

Epstein and Axtell's Sugarscape: Emergent Societies. Quite possibly the most famous example of "bottom-up" agent-based modeling is Epstein and Axtell's *Growing Artificial Societies* (1996). They boil their agent behavior down to a single rule: "Look around as far as your vision permits, find the spot with the most sugar, go there and eat the sugar" (p. 6). Agents search on a CA landscape and come to hold genetic-identity-culture identification tags according to a GA. This model not only builds social networks (Level 1), but also higher-level groups emerge (Level 2). These groups develop cultural properties; once cultures form they can supervene and alter the behavior and groupings of agents (Level 3). The Sugarscape intrasystem elements include agents, emergent groups, higher-level groupings, emergent culture, multiple causalities, along with environmental resources and constraints.

As mentioned above, Carley's CONSTRUCT and CONSTRUCT-O models come close to being Level 3 studies. Further, her ORGAHEAD model (Carley, 1990, 1999) is a highly sophisticated Level 3 study, which we also place in Level 4 emergence and, thus, describe below.

Narrative Studies of Level 3 Emergence. A good example of Level 3 emergence is Zohar and Borkman's (1997) examination of Alcoholics Anonymous [AA] from a self-organization perspective. Their analysis shows how individuals in need of support (i.e., agents driven by adaptive tension) use bottom-up organizing to develop semi-autonomous AA groupings (meetings). These independent groups are then organized into regional, national, and international volunteer centers that provide information and resources to the meetings. In addition to their process description of emergent multi-level order, their analysis of mechanisms that provide a balance of control and increased growth provides a useful link to Level 4 emergence. Although neither of these models purports to need a leader or leadership in a formal sense, the AA organization does rely on emergent leaders who coordinate speakers for the local meetings, and help design programs and policies at the regional, national, and international level.

LEVEL 4 EMERGENCE: Emergent Coordination Complexity

Once multilevel hierarchies form, causal flows become far more complicated; new coordinating structures and regulation processes must emerge to maintain adaptive capability. Like the 3-body problem in physics, the uncertainty produced makes it impossible to identify where in the system a particular causal force originates and where it has its most pronounced effects (Lindblom, 1959; Chaisson, 2001). As such, Level 4 emergence may never stabilize; the multi-layered system is constantly in flux (Tsoukas & Chia, 2002). Thus, although there is a critical need for leadership throughout the system, the role of leadership is diffuse and hard to pin down.

Carley's ORGAHEAD *Model.* Carley's (1990, 1999a) four-level simulation consists of small groups of interacting workers (agents) led by an executive team that develops firm-level strategy based on environmental inputs. Groups that emerge in this model control who agents will interact with, learn from, and so on, thereby altering subsequent coevolutionary emergence. Also, the emergent culture alters the knowledge-creation strategies of agents. In these ways Carley's model fits into Level 4 emergence, but just barely.

Mostly, the Level 4 set is empty of computational experiments. Essentially, it has been nearly impossible to develop a computational model whose agents create four distinct levels of hierarchical order on their own, i.e., without influence or order-creation processes being programmed into the simulation. Of course, many simulations have explored leadership and organizational dynamics within multi-leveled entities, but virtually all of these assume (i.e., program in) a specific agent and/or top management team with capabilities that are beyond those of member agents.

Organizational and Regional Emergence. A rigorous, Level 4 narrative study analyzed the origin and development of the Musical Theater industry in Branson, Missouri (Chiles, *et al.*, 2004). The authors show how the emergence and dramatic growth of the area was caused by non-linear interactions between local agents (retirees, tourists, and musicians), agent groups and organizations (local businesses, banks, theaters), government institutions (transportation, statewide recreation and water management boards), and national events (e.g., significant changes in the Nashville music industry, and a key "60-Minutes" news report).

This study is rich with allusions to the role of leadership through interactions across all the system levels. For example, agent groups played an important role in initiating large-scale government projects that spurred tourism and created more demand to grow the local economy. Likewise, cultural norms – both tacit and explicit – played a crucial role in defining what musical entertainment was "appropriate," which both enabled and constrained the emergence of the musical theater industry. Many more examples could be identified. As we reach these more far-reaching levels, leadership becomes an increasingly significant part of the emergence process.

Leadership Across the Stages of Emergence
The Role of Interactive Leadership Throughout the System

Our framework can be summarized as follows: By far the most frequent type of emergence appears as networks, our Level 1 emergence. Some of these emergent network configurations lead to the emergence of groups and group norms – our Level 2. In certain cases, groups differentiate to more advantageously draw in environmental resources. This results in the beginnings of hierarchy (Massie, 1965; Salthe, 1993). This Stage 3 emergence solidifies the definition of "qualitative novelty" – an emergent property is defined as "different in kind" from its components (Blitz, 1992; Crutchfield, 1994; Goldstein, 2000). Finally, a few hierarchies grow on their own to become larger, i.e., large enough that new kinds of more complex coordinating structures and regulation processes must emerge if adaptive capability and efficiency are to be maintained.

Complexity researchers working computationally and via narrative studies have, therefore, found that heterogeneous agents, operating according to a specific set of rules, conditions, and enablers, can – on their own so to speak – generate up to four levels of order. Essentially the first two stages – emergent networks and emergent groups – require in some cases very little leadership beyond the rule-following efforts of agents (programmed into) the system. Of course, the importance of leadership at even these simplest of levels has been confirmed by numerous studies, including three key papers in this volume: Hazy, Millhiser & Solow; Phelps & Hubler, and Dal Forno & Merlone.

In contrast, level 3 and level 4 already require some formal leadership to emerge, albeit leadership that need not be embodied within a particular person, nor a formalize direction coming from "outside" the system itself. But it appears that some distinction in terms of resources or attributes is mostly necessary in order to create hierarchies (level 3) or complex coordination systems (level 4), although in some instances even this degree of hierarchical complexity may emerge on its own.

...and the Role of Specific Leaders who are Managers

It is easy to recognize, however, that more than four stages of emergence do occur in large real-world organizations. Managers and other agents influence the development of large-scale organizations, through the emergence of increasing hierarchical or strategic levels (Uhl-Bein, *et al.*, 2007). Any number of organization theorists have recognized that 21st century multi-national corporations are necessarily composed of upwards of 7 or 8 hierarchical levels, each one commanding a degree of leadership control (e.g., Jacques, 1989).

Once these larger and more sophisticated stages are taken into account it becomes clear that that emergence in organizations is more likely a "quasi-natural" event (McKelvey, 1997), i.e., each instance of emergence is a tangled, mutually causal mixture of bottom-up autonomous organizing and top-down managerial interventions. Likewise, many if not most real-world narratives are about emergent networks and groups – primarily emerging against official, formal bureaucratic objectives (see Table 1). But beyond those first few stages, our analysis of the complexity research to date suggests that emergence doesn't seem to happen without considerable supervenience, i.e., "top-down" initiative. If it did, we would see empirical studies (based on simulation or on qualitative techniques) detailing emergent phenomenon that are more complex than Emergent Coordination Complexity. There are good simulation-based studies that show the dynamics of very complex systems, e.g., Hall's (1976) study of the Saturday Evening Post, and Hazy's (2007) model of Intel. However, as we've shown, empirical research showing the spontaneous up-building of four or more hierarchical levels of order simply does not exist.

One key implication of this finding is that absent the aid of higher-level managers, the emergence produced solely by autonomous agents tails off at around Stage 3, maximally Stage 4. Later stages seem more influenced by formal managers, in conjunction with bottom-up agent effects (e.g., Hazy, 2007). Thus, large complex organizations may only be possible due to leadership given by managers with legitimate power and access to significant resources including financial capital, social capital, reward and referent power, and so on. Complexity researchers have found that what can be managed are the systemic conditions that support self-organizing effects within firms (Uhl-Bien, *et al.*, 2007; McKelvey, 2001, 2007). These scholars show how traditional "control oriented leadership" can be reshaped into a "complexity leadership style" that focuses on "enabling" activities that generate the "simple rules" and contextual conditions within which emergent self-organized order is likely to emerge (Marion & Uhl-Bien, 2001; Uhl-Bien, *et al.*, 2007). Drawing from a wide variety of complexity-based research, many managerial approaches have been suggested that support emergent leadership and successful self-organized behavior (Goldstein, 1994; Brown & Eisenhardt, 1998; Pascale, *et al.*, 1999; Lichtenstein, 2000; Wood, 2000; Marion & Uhl-Bein, 2001; Colbert, 2004).

Although these practical approaches to organizing complexity may be helpful, they do not hide the apparent oxymoron of effectively "managing" natural emergence – bottom-up self-organization processes – through top-down "enabling" interventions. Classical and modern leadership theory recommends that managers use leadership and organizing skills that are quite the opposite of what is needed to efficaciously "steer" firms in dynamical, complex environments (Massie, 1965; Marion & Uhl-Bein, 2001; Uhl-Bien, *et al.*, 2007). We can't overestimate that leaders of modern complex organizations face a fundamental uncertainty and ambiguity generated by organized anarchy, requisite variety, mutual causality, and so on (Thomas, *et al.*, 2005).

This is an important point that requires some explanation. Essentially we are making a significant break from the common complexity-inspired belief that organizations self-organize "all the way up," i.e., across all levels of the hierarchy. In contrast, our review of the empirical literature on emergence shows that such bottom-up organizing is highly common in Stage 1 emergence; less and less common in generating Stage 2 and Stage 3 emergence, and is almost non-existent in Stage 4 emergence (and on up). We can explain this apparent rapid drop-off of self-organizing behavior at higher levels of emergence by referencing two key elements of our framework – adaptive tension and coordination mechanisms. Specifically the massive, highly complex diversified firms that dominate the 21ˢᵗ century landscape do require a highly skilled degree of top-down management in order to access the huge level of adaptive tensions and the remarkable coordination involved in maintaining such firms in complex dynamical environments.

Conclusion

The leadership literature presently focuses mainly on the idea that it takes visionary, charismatic leaders to bring about necessary transformative changes, given a chaotic context and "two-sided" organizations (Bennis, 1996). On the other hand, this same charismatic leadership style produces agent homogeneity rather than heterogeneity, with the result that strong leadership undermines the basic ingredient of emergence. The consequence of this, as Bennis and O'Toole (2000) have recently observed, is that we see increased "churning" at the CEO level – increasing turnover which they attribute it to organizational flattening, globalization, new technologies, and mega-mergers.

Complexity science provides a both-and response to this challenge, by showing how emergence in organizations requires a combination of leadership styles (Uhl-Bien, *et al.*, 2007), including:

- Generating the conditions for "bottom-up," agent-initiated organizing;
- Managing resources and making large-scale strategic moves through "top-down" managerial leadership, and;
- Facilitating the interaction of these two poles, to "…manage the coordination rhythms between top-down, hierarchical dynamics and emergent complex adaptive systems" (Uhl-Bein, *et al.*, 2007).

How, then, does a leader facilitate this interaction? How does anyone within the organization find the balance between agency and emergence, and learn when to enact either one, or both? What is the secret to becoming a truly generative leader? How can emergent, interactive leadership at all levels be encouraged and facilitated? Which contingencies should be leveraged in order to spark further levels of emergence that create world-class organizations?

These are core questions in a Complex Systems Leadership Theory, and they are the focus of the chapters in this volume. Whereas many practitioners and some academics say they have the "answer," in fact the answers are themselves emerging through an adaptive learning process that reflects the science of complexity. Our goal in the present essay is to emphasize one emerging edge of this learning: emergence requires far more than an aggregation of "bottom-up" interactions which are "allowed" by a passive, laissez-faire leader. Thus, the literal notion of "self-organizing" may be valid for only the initial levels or stages of emergence, and even then the emergence of networks and groups requires a good deal of effort by forward-thinking individuals (leaders) within the system (Goldstein, this volume). As organizing becomes more developed – as further stages build on previous ones – a highly complex combination of leadership moves is required to nurture agent-based innovation, to channel increased resources to the emerging levels, and to adroitly manage the interaction between top-down and bottom-up organizing. Our hope is that this essay takes a small step toward understanding and enacting this subtle and exciting dynamic of leadership.

CHAPTER SIX
EMERGENT LEADERSHIP:
GETTING BEYOND HEROES AND SCAPEGOATS

Donde Ashmos Plowman & Dennis Duchon

Conventional views of leadership often hold leaders responsible for bringing about transformational change and creating positive organizational futures, for being heroes. When change efforts fail, or futures unfold differently than planned, leaders quickly become the scapegoats, blamed for unsuccessful organizational outcomes. Most traditional views of leadership reflect the continued dominance of a rational, mechanistic model of organizations that places heavy emphasis on a leader's ability to predict and control outcomes. A complex systems view of organizations offers the potential for re-conceptualizing the notion of leadership from that of a role or person to an emergent behavior, which is possible when organizations area designed for emergence. In this chapter we present four properties of leadership for emergence – distributing intelligence, fostering conversation, sustaining tension and looking for patterns.

Donde Ashmos Plowman is the Flaskerud Professor of Strategic Management at The University of Tennessee. She received her Ph.D. from The University of Texas at Austin. Her publications have appeared in *Academy of Management Journal*, *Academy of Management Review*, *The Leadership Quarterly*, *Decision Sciences*, *Journal of Management Studies*, and *Health Services Research*, among others. Her current research interests include organizational change, leadership, decision making, interpretation, and participation in complex adaptive systems.

Dennis Duchon is the Stokely Professor of Human Resources at The University of Tennessee. He received his Ph.D. from the University of Houston. His publications have appeared in *Journal of Applied Psychology*, *Organizational Behavior and Human Decision Processes*, *Journal of Management*, *MIS Quarterly*, *Journal of Management Studies*, and *The Leadership Quarterly* among others. His research interests include decision making in organizations, work motivation, leadership, and complexity science.

Introduction

In spite of the organizational literature's near obsession with the topic of leadership, it remains elusive. Critics argue that we have highly romanticized what it is that leaders do, preferring to think of them as *heroes* (Meindl, *et al.*, 1985) who should be able to control organizational futures and devise optimal solutions to organizational problems. When leaders fail, or futures unfold differently than planned, leaders often become the *scapegoats*. These larger-than-life organizational figures, then, assume either the credit or the blame for organizational outcomes. Other critics suggest that leadership is a social myth, needed to reinforce social beliefs about the necessity of hierarchy (Gemmill & Oakley, 1992). Scholars like Bennis (1989) have gone so far as to say that leadership is a social hoax invented to maintain the status quo in organizations. While these arguments illustrate some of the frustrations with conceptualizations of leadership, we suggest that a broader problem, namely, the continued dominance of a rational, mechanistic (Newtonian) model of organizations has contributed to the disappointing condition of leadership research. In this paper, we suggest that a complex systems view of organizations offers the potential for re-conceptualizing the notion of leadership.

Conventional views of leadership, even criticisms of conventional views of leadership such as those cited above, are largely based on assumptions of organizations as rational, mechanistic systems in which cause and effect are tightly linked, such that process outcomes are predictable, and the linear pathways towards desired futures can be known. Unexpected events are often attributed to a failure in control mechanisms. Disruption is seen as a failure in leadership. When the future unfolds differently than planned, leaders are viewed as out of control or as having failed to envision or articulate the right future. It is no wonder that researchers have been frustrated. This frustration can be eliminated through a complexity view of organizations, in which emergent self-organization is a theoretical anchor point. A complexity science leadership theory offers a new conceptualization of leadership – one in which leadership is a *behavior* not a role, a *process* not a person.

In this paper, we argue that organizations are complex systems, whose properties of non-linearity, far from equilibrium conditions, and emergence, require a theoretical re-conceptualization of leadership. In fact, given conventional views of leadership, each of these properties creates a unique leadership dilemma. We present a view of leadership as *emergent behavior* that many different people can assume across different situations, and occurs most effectively when organizations are d*esigned for emergence* rather than for specific outcomes. This stands in stark contrast to the conventional literature on leadership that continues to focus on leadership as a role occupied by a person with transformational duties and abilities. In the traditional view leaders use organizational design in hopes of ensuring "fit" and achieving a priori specified behavioral and performance outcomes.

We draw on three literatures to develop the arguments in this paper. First, the complexity science literature orients this discussion to the unique characteristics of organizations as complex systems, each of which creates a leadership dilemma, and necessitates a re-conceptualization of leadership. Second, we briefly review the increasingly popular literature on transformational leadership as an example of a dominant model of leadership that is incompatible with the features of complex systems. Specifically, when leadership is viewed as a role or person, expected to "transform" the organization, the organization pursues the dream of a hero who quickly becomes a scapegoat when things go bad. Given our assertion that leadership is about designing organizations for emergence, a third literature that informs this work is the literature on organizational design. Our review of that literature suggests that organizational scholars often treat organizational design as a mechanism for achieving fit and/or behavioral and performance outcomes, and ignore the reality that cause-effect relationships in complex systems are impossible to know. These three bodies of literature help ground our work but also reveal theoretical inconsistencies that a revised picture of leadership can address – one which focuses on emergent behavior, and in particular, designing for emergence. We identify four aspects of designing for emergence, each of which contributes to the ongoing emergence of leadership in organizations.

Complexity Dilemmas for Conventional Leadership

Numerous interdependent agents that operate simultaneously and follow local rules or principles to guide behavior make up complex systems. These agents adapt by changing their rules as experience and knowledge accumulate, without the control of a central coordinator (Chiles, *et al.*, 2004). In organizations, agents are autonomous individuals or groups that can act simultaneously without explicit coordination or central communication (Anderson, 1999). A central feature of a complex system is its ability to *learn* from the numerous interactions that are occurring and *adapt*. Thus, as they learn, complex systems are constantly shifting, adapting and re-generating temporal patterns. As complexity scholars continue to point out, this view of organizations – as complex systems – is dramatically different from the traditional view of organizations as rational systems whose structure, rules, and authority are intended to create stability, and in which any major adaptation is directed from the top of the organization. Although it is often referred to as open systems thinking, this traditional view of organizations depicts organizations as faced with uncertainty but "needing determinateness and certainty" (Thompson, 1967: 10). And most often, the expectation is that leaders will be the ones to bring about the needed certainty.

The notion that organizations are complex systems, whose specific characteristics necessitate an alternative view of leadership, ground the view of leadership presented in this paper. Three distinguishing properties of complex systems are important to consider and provide a conceptual framework for considering leadership in complex organizations: (1) non-linearity, (2) far-from-equilibrium conditions, and (3) emergent self-organization. Each of these properties provides a particular dilemma or challenge to managers who are accustomed to defining their role as a leader in conventional terms. While additional properties characterize complex systems, these three present the most direct challenges to traditional conceptualizations of leadership.

First, as complex systems, organizations are made up of individuals who are connected to each other through a web of feedback (Stacey, 1992, 1995), creating a dynamic set of non-linear interactions (Capra, 1996; Wheatley, 1999). *Nonlinearity* means there is no direct relation between the strength of a cause and the consequence of the effect. Popular notions of leadership characterize leaders as those who, armed with knowledge of cause and effect, envision the organization's future and guide others toward that future (Kotter, 1996). Yet, organizations are not easily guided to pre-specified futures because they are made up of individuals and groups who are connected and whose behaviors can be unpredictable.

For example, when disruption occurs in organizations, people talk, concern or interest mounts and connections among individuals and groups tighten. These tightened connections make it easier for information or gossip or ideas to amplify and move through the system quickly, enhancing the possibility that small changes can escalate and become radical in ways that were neither intended nor predicted (Plowman, *et al.*, 2007). Thus, for organizations, uncertainty and unpredictability are not just functions of changing external conditions, but also come from inside organizations, yet beyond the control of managers. Ongoing interactions among a network of organizational actors can produce unpredictable results that 'leaders' are unable to influence. Extensive use of control systems in most organizations is intended to ensure that envisioned solutions (effects) to existing problems (causes) are working. Yet, nonlinear interactions can often occur far from an assumed stable pattern, far from the eye of control systems, making surprise likely. The prominence of nonlinear interactions in organizations creates the following leadership dilemma: *Leaders are often responsible for bringing about change in organizations yet non-linear interactions can amplify small adaptations outside the control or knowledge of the leader, unleashing changes never intended by the organization's leaders, and perhaps counter to leaders' intentions.*

Second, when organizations are provoked by either an unforeseen opportunity or threat, they move *away from equilibrium*, towards instability (Nicolis, 1989; Pascale, 1999; Prigogine & Stengers, 1984). The 'far-from-equilibrium' characteristic creates another challenge for conventional leaders who often assume that disorder and conflict are indicators of failed leadership. When organizations move away from stability and towards disequilibrium into the "region of complexity," (Maguire & McKelvey, 1999), they experience adaptive tensions that make possible opportunities for new order through emergent self-organization. In fact, research suggests that organizational disequilibrium and disorder often give rise to innovation and creativity (Anderson, 1999; McKelvey, 1999).

Of course, being far-from-equilibrium can also provoke conflict and confusion. Traditional views of organizations characterize conflict as a problematic condition, a "breakdown" (March & Simon, 1958), that needs to be reduced, eliminated or overcome (Andrade, *et al.*, 2007; Rahim, 2002); and leaders are expected to bring about the reduction. Thus, the far-from-equilibrium inclination of complex systems creates the following dilemma for conventional leadership: *Leaders are responsible for reducing conflict and creating order in organizations, yet disequilibrium is the source of most novelty and innovation in organizations.*

Third, the property of *emergent self-organization* is considered by some to be complexity theory's "anchor point phenomenon" (Chiles, *et al.*, 2004: 502). According to Goldstein (1999) emergent phenomena are novel, coherent, and observable at a macro level; they occur over time, and are recognizable. In organizations emergence occurs at lower levels in the organization when people exchange information, take actions, and continuously adapt to feedback about others' actions. Because the organization is a system of nested systems (Ashmos & Huber, 1987), other parts of the organization react, enabling responses to bubble up and provide system level order without the imposition of an overall plan by a central authority (Chiles, *et al.*, 2004). Yet leaders are traditionally viewed as the central authority, responsible for crafting overall plans and making them happen through resources allocations and structural arrangements. Thus, the property of emergent self-organization creates the following leadership dilemma: *Leaders are responsible for creating organizational structures that bring about desired outcomes, yet people and groups in organizations will self-organize in spite of organizational blueprints.*

As we have pointed out, these three properties – non-linearity, far-from-equilibrium conditions, and emergence – characterize complex systems and create unique dilemmas for traditional leaders. In fact, conventional views of leadership are *in*compatible with the view of organizations as complex systems. Thus, we argue for an alternative view of leadership in which leadership is better understood as an emergent process and therefore must involve designing for emergence.

Leadership as Role – Hero or Scapegoat

For decades organization scientists have bemoaned both the elusive nature of leadership (Bennis, 1959) and the plethora of definitions generated by researchers (Stogdill, 1974), yet they continued to pursue leadership as an important management topic. Leadership is generally viewed as the intentional influence by one person over others to direct them toward achievement of pre-determined organizational goals (Yukl, 2006). More often than not leadership is viewed as a role, occupied by a person who has authority (or influence) over others. Popular prescriptions for successful leadership include those of Kotter (1996), for example, who directs leaders to bring about organizational change by (1) developing a vision of the future, (2) communicating the vision, and (3) motivating others to attain the vision. Kotter's (1996) prescription for leaders, like that of many academic and popular writers, assumes knowledge of essential cause-effect relationships in organizations. From this perspective successful leaders know what causes can bring about the desired effects, and they are capable of communicating that message to others who become inspired by it. Leadership giants such as Lee Iacocca, Sam Walton, or Jack Welch are viewed as heroes of mythical proportion, whose insight, charisma, and solution set were what brought about major organizational transformations. Yet for every Jack Welch and Sam Walton there are others like former Department of Defense Secretary Don Runsfeld or former Viacom CEO Tom Feston whose insight, charisma and solution set were blamed for organizational failures, thus earning them the title of scapegoat.

A central premise of this paper is that when leadership is viewed as a person who occupies a role, the theoretical conversation assumes a "dispositional" frame, that is, there is something about the *person* that enables effective cause-effect linkages in organizations. In spite of the many weaknesses of a dispositional approach to organizational research (Davis-Blake & Pfeffer, 1989), the leadership literature, which years ago moved away from a focus on personal traits, continues to focus on dispositions.

For example, transformational leadership focuses on the traits of the leader, particularly his/her ability to "inspire" organizational success. Nearly two decades ago Peter Senge (1990) captured the attention of many with his book, *The Fifth Discipline,* where he challenged conventional views of leadership. He wrote, "At its heart, the traditional view of leadership is based on assumptions of people's powerlessness, their lack of personal vision and inability to master the forces of change, deficits which can only be remedied by a few great leaders" (1990: 340). While Senge called for a new vision of leadership that would foster learning in organizations, much of the popular and academic leadership literature continues the search for leaders as "captain(s) of the cavalry leading the charge to rescue the settlers from the attacking Indians" (1990: 340). Senge's call, however, has for the most part gone unheeded as both practitioners and scholars continue to seek organizational redemption in the form of a Messiah. For example, in the last ten years nearly 60% of the articles on leadership in *Academy of Management Journal* focused on transformational leadership. See Table 1 for a summary.

One interpretation of Table 1 is that in spite of the literature's affection for transformational leadership, there is not much to show for it. First of all, due to poor samples and non-generalizable methods, most studies hardly provide convincing samples for testing theory about transformational leadership. More importantly, evidenced in the table are researchers' continued beliefs that cause-effect relationships are knowable, that transformational leadership must cause something to happen or is affected by yet other specifiable variables that can be observed. For ten years, in studies in which transformational leadership was the independent variable, there is no evidence of any effect on organizational performance. The only exception we can identify is the study by Waldman, *et al.* (2001) who found that the interaction of transformational leadership and environmental uncertainty explained modest financial performance. Yet, even these results are somewhat questionable given that there was a 25% turnover rate among their informants from the beginning of the study. In the remaining studies in which transformational leadership was the dependent variable, we see modest evidence that it explains why some, but not all, followers are productive in brainstorming, and that under certain conditions it is associated with how people perceive their jobs or their willingness to recognize emotion. These results suggest that researchers continue to believe that charismatic leaders will be heroes, but in fact, it is just as likely, if not more so, that they will experience failures as organizational conditions and circumstances change.

Almost thirty years ago Kerr & Jermier (1978) demonstrated that many of the kinds of cause-effect relationships pursued in empirical leadership studies could be explained by "substitutes for leadership." Yet, in the organizational literature we continue to want to believe that people in roles of leadership cause certain kinds of things to happen and other kinds of things not to happen, even if those relationships fail to turn up in empirical studies.

Scholars are not alone in characterizing leaders either as heroes or scapegoats. We recently conducted a review of the popular business press and found further evidence of our assertion that leadership is often viewed as a role, occupied by a person, who either becomes a hero when things go well, or in most cases, becomes the scapegoat when things do not go so well. For example, during the month of October 2006 *Business Week* published 130 articles that focused on the CEO or other top executive's leadership abilities. Of those articles, 22% focused on the heroic efforts of the executive, 36% lodged blame for company problems on the executive and 42% assigned neither credit nor blame.

Looking for leadership within a few formal roles, looking for individuals with transformative powers, and looking for heroes or scapegoats has produced little that explains influence in complex systems where agents engage in mutual influence and adaptation. Thus, we turn from leadership as a role to an alternative view – leadership as emergent behavior.

Leadership as Emergent Behavior

Traditional views of leadership assume that people at the top of the organization fill the leadership role – the CEO, the top management team, the individuals with the authority to command and control the actions of others. Yet, *the essence of leadership is influence*, and influence can occur anywhere at anytime in a system, particularly outside the formal boundaries of hierarchical roles. The existence of such "informal" systems of leadership has been noted by scholars (Kickul & Neuman, 2000; Wheelan & Johnston, 1996), but there is little research on the characteristics and behaviors of informal leadership. We contend that a complex systems approach to understanding organizations not only explains the existence of informal leadership systems, but also can argue their value.

Influence processes are like air; necessary for survival, but invisible and taken for granted. In complex systems, mutual influence and adaptation among agents are necessary for survival, but so commonplace as to be invisible. The agents are in continual interaction exchanging information, learning, and adapting their behavior in locally coherent ways. Every contact, every exchange of information presents an opportunity for influence, and, therefore, leadership. While these everyday contacts may seem routine, they can be significant because no two contacts are the same. The agents in the system learn, recognize the meaning of a given exchange, adjust their own behavior, and the system continues to function smoothly. Yet, it is not the same system. Mutual influence and adjustment processes have altered not just the behavior of the system, but also the system's capacity to learn. As the agents adjust to new information, they

Authors	Dependent Variable	Independent Variable	Results	Method and Sample
Agle, Nagarajan, Sonnenfeld & Srinivasan (2006)	Organizational Performance	Charisma	No relationship	Field study: Executives from 128 US corporations
Bono, & Judge (2003)	Follower tendency to set self-concordant goals	Transformational leadership	Mixed results between field study and lab study	Field study: 247 leaders and 954 followers in 1 organization; Lab experiment: 162 undergraduate students
Jung, & Avolio (1999)	Transaction leadership style; Transformational leadership style	Individualist brainstorming; Collectivists brainstorming	Collectivists with transformational leader generated more ideas; individualists with transactional leaders generated more ideas.	Lab experiment: 347 undergraduate students
Waldman, D. Ramirez, G., House, R. & Puranam (2001)	Financial performance	Charismatic leadership; Transactional leadership; Environmental uncertainty	No main effect for charismatic leadership and financial performance; modest effect for interaction of charisma and uncertainty; (substantial turnover among CEO's in the sample)	Field study: leaders from 48 Fortune 500
Piccolo & Colquit (2006)	Transformational leadership	Follower perception of job characteristics	Transformational leadership affects how followers perceive job characteristics particularly when followers perceive high leader-member exchange	Field study: 217 individuals from multiple firms and their supervisors

Dvir, Eden, Avolio, & Shamir (2002)	Follower development; follower performance	Transformational leadership	Leaders who received training in transformation leadership had more positive impact on direct follower development, but not performance and more positive impact on indirect followers' performance but not development, than did control group leaders	Field experiment: 54 military leaders, 90 direct followers, 724 indirect followers in Israel Defense Forces
Yammarino, Dubinsky, Comer & Jolson (1997)	Subordinate commitment, performance and female leaders' effectiveness in dyads	Transformational leadership; contingent reward leadership	Both leadership styles related to subordinate commitment, performance, and female leaders' effectiveness.	Field study: 15 female superiors and 30 (male and female) subordinates
Rubin, Munz, & Bommer (2005)	Transformation Leadership	Emotion Recognition; extraversion	Emotion recognition and extraversion associated with transformational leadership behavior	Field study: 234 managers and 1400 subordinates in 1 organization
Shin & Zhou (2003)	Follower creativity	Transformational leadership	Intrinsic motivation mediates relationship between transformational leadership and follower creativity	Field study: 290 subordinates and 77 supervisors

Table 1 *Transformational Leadership Studies*[1]

1 The review of literature reported in this table is based on a ten-year review of studies published in the *Academy of Management Journal*. This list is not intended to represent all the empirical research on transformational leadership. Rather, it illustrates the type of empirical work that has been done in the last ten years in the journal which "aspires to be the 'journal of choice' for the best empirical work examining multiple areas of management" (*Academy of Management Journal* editors, 2005: 732–737).

expand their own behavioral repertoire, which, in effect, expands the behavioral repertoire of the system itself. Thus, leadership processes occur continuously, and they are changing the system and the system's capabilities. While the changes may seem small, they can become amplified once they emerge (Plowman, *et al.*, 2007a). But, more importantly, these leadership processes are not directed or controlled by a person occupying a role. Rather, they are part of the organization's very being: leadership processes can emerge anywhere in the system at any time.

Recognizing the emergent quality of leadership processes requires moving away from traditional role/person/controlling approaches to leadership. For example, Marion & Uhl-Bien (2001) call for "complex leaders" who *enable* rather than control future desired states. The word "enabling" means that managers (the hierarchy is not likely to disappear anytime soon) look for ways to encourage emergent behavior rather than control behavior presumed to be necessary to satisfy central coordination requirements. In this vein, Regine & Lewin (2000) dispel the leadership myths of autonomy, control, and omniscience in their call for "paradoxical leadership" where *allowing* replaces controlling, invisibility replaces visibility, and not knowing replaces knowing.

Harnessing the power of emergent leadership processes means developing a capacity to accept that solutions to difficult adaptive challenges may not be found in the repertoire of the people in the formal roles of leadership, but instead may exist in the repertoire of the system. Solutions to adaptive problems can emerge if intelligence has been distributed through the organization, if conversation flows freely, if rules don't stifle the judgments and discretion of people throughout the system, and if attention is focused on the difficulty at hand. Leadership is about designing systems for emergence.

Properties of a Leadership for Emergence

Almost thirty years ago Peter Senge (1990) laid out a view of learning organizations, that called for a shift of mind towards systems thinking and he argued that leaders need to pay attention to organizational design and create structures and rules that enhance organizational learning. We build on his idea of "leader as designer" and begin our discussion of designing for emergence with a brief look at the organizational design literature in the last twenty years.

In a review of articles published in *Administrative Science Quarterly, Academy of Management Journal, Academy of Management Review, Strategic Management Journal* and *Journal of Management* over a twenty-one year period, we identified 53 papers that focus on organizational design or organizational structure, and the leadership assumptions in each paper. The articles fall into three broad categories depending on how authors conceptualized organizational design. In these studies organizational design was viewed as a mechanism for: (1) achieving "fit" between an organization and it's environment and/or its strategy, (2) achieving behavioral outcomes such as subordinate attitudes or approaches to information sharing and decision making, or (3) achieving performance outcomes such as goal achievement or financial outcome. See Table 2 for summary. These distinctions are important because they imply a leadership metaphor for each that emphasizes unique leadership tasks, and assumed leader knowledge. For example if organization design is intended to achieve "fit," the implied leadership metaphor is one of "strategic engineer." As strategic engineer, the leader is responsible for matching strategy, structure and environmental conditions and presumes knowledge of cause and effect linkages between strategy and structure. If, however, organizational design is a mechanism for achieving behavioral outcomes, the implied leadership metaphor is "social engineer," in which the major leadership task is to specify desired human behaviors that need to be altered, and then identify which aspects of structure will lead to the desired behavioral outcome. In this role, the leader is presumed to know the cause-effect linkages between a particular structural dimension and some specific aspect of human behavior, such as motivation, commitment, etc. The third category of research is about organizational design as a mechanism for achieving performance outcomes and the implied leadership metaphor is "economic engineer." In this situation, the leader's major task is to specify desired performance goals and alter the structural dimensions that affect the specific performance goal. The leader is presumed to know the cause and effect linkages between the elements of organizational structure and specific financial indicators.

What our review of the organizational design literature shows is the research community's continued pursuit of complex relationships such as organizational design, organizational strategy, human behavior, and organizational effectiveness through assumptions of simple, linear relationships. These assumptions also have implications for how leadership is viewed and what the leader's major tasks are. When the leader is expected to function as some kind of engineer, whether strategic, social, or economic, it assumes that cause-effect linkages can be known, that solutions can be developed in advance of problems, and that followers can be "motivated." Given the (un)likelihood of all of this, a different approach is needed: designing for emergence (Garud, et al., 2006). Rather than thinking about organizational design as a mechanism for achieving fit, behavior, or performance outcomes, it is more useful to see organizational design as a mechanism for *enabling emergence*. Adopting a complex systems view means seeing leadership processes as enabling, not engineering. Designing for emergence provides organizations with the capacity to use the intelligence that is distributed throughout the system, and develop novel responses to the challenges which organizations face. Designing for emergence includes the responses elaborated below, each of which addresses one of the dilemmas presented by conventional views of leadership: distributing intelligence, fostering conversation/enriching connections, sustaining tension, and looking for patterns. The responses and managerial activities described in Table 3, in part, grew out of an empirical study of emergent, radical change (Plowman, et al., 2007) and a study of leadership in emergent, self-organization (Plowman, et al., forthcoming) as well as ideas suggested by Marion & Uhl-Bien (2001). A summary of these responses and associated managerial activities is presented in Table 3.

Organizational Design Metaphor	Articles in last 20 years	Leadership Metaphor	Leadership Task	Assumed Leader Knowledge
Designing for Fit	14	Leader as strategic engineer	Match strategy, structure and environmental conditions	Cause effect between strategy and structure
Designing For Performance Outcomes	15	Leader as economic engineer	Specify performance goal alter structural dimension that affects that goal	Cause effect between design dimension and financial indicators
Designing for behavioral Outcomes	24	Leader as social engineer	Specify desired behaviors to be altered and alter structural dimension that affects the desired human behavior	Cause effect between design dimension and human behavior such as motivation, commitment, etc.

Table 2 *Summary of Organizational Design Literature*[1]

1 The literature summary provided in this table is based on a review of articles with a focus on organizational design or organizational structure published between 1985 and 2006 in *Administrative Science Quarterly, Academy of Management Journal, Academy of management Review, Strategic Management Journal* and *Journal of Management*.

Conventional 'Leadership as Engineer' Dilemma	Designing an Emergent Response	Managerial Activity Enabling Emergence
Leaders are often responsible for bringing about change in organizations yet non-linear interactions can amplify small adaptations outside the control or knowledge of the leader, unleashing changes never intended by the organization's leaders, and perhaps counter to leaders' intentions.	Distributing Intelligence	Make data widely available; openness and accessibility are values; no censoring; few secrets; unleash information
	Fostering conversations/ enriching connections	Break down functional silos; cross-functional teams; straight talk; enable transparency; put people together; manage conversations
Leaders are responsible for reducing conflict and creating order in organizations, yet disequilibrium is the source of most novelty and innovation in organizations.	Sustaining Tension	Confront conflict; use adversity to grow; encourage experimentation; use failures as opportunity to learn; endure irritants.
Leaders are responsible for creating organizational structures that bring about desired outcomes, yet people and groups in organizations will self-organize in spite of organizational blueprints.	Looking for Patterns	Adopt holistic view; avoid quick judgments; think in terms of energy, not roles; not forcing; patience

Table 3 *Properties of a Leadership for Emergence, Not Engineering*

Designing for Emergence
Distributing Intelligence

Designing for emergence means focusing on learning, and because information is the essential fuel for learning, emergent design devotes effort to providing large fuel stocks (information stocks) that are readily available and widely distributed. All the system's agents need access to information so that their actions are not only locally coherent, but also benefit the larger system. This cannot be accomplished if information is possessed and stockpiled by only a few.

Traditional views of organizations often see information as a commodity that is transferred from one place to another as directed by the organization's leaders (Wheatley, 1999). This view of information gives rise to the common notion that "information is power," encouraging information hoarding and secrecy. In complex systems, information is seen to posses a dynamic quality such that its value and utility change as the system learns and adapts. Agents attach meaning to information as it is processed and interpreted, as it becomes "intelligence." This intelligence needs to be widely distributed, not hoarded, so that system agents can learn how their local actions affect the larger system. Thus, as intelligence is distributed and used, more learning can take place. Learning, in turn, injects new information and intelligence back into the system. In a sense, then, information is a fuel that grows more plentiful as it is used - the more it is used, the faster it can grow.

Distributing intelligence enables not just learning, but rather the kind of learning that allows system agents to be both self-aware and system-aware. Distributing intelligence enables the entire system to develop a knowledge of conditions, which, in turn, positions the system to change itself in ways that a single intelligence (i.e., one leader) could never image. How does a leader deal with unplanned change? Essentially, the leader prepares the system to deal with it by allowing system agents access to data and information that they can use to make functionally coherent adaptations. The leader does not determine what information is relevant; the system's agents determine this for themselves.

It is important to note that there is a "cost" associated with distributing intelligence because such a response likely will create redundancies in the system as agents and groups learn similar things and develop similar capabilities. Traditional views of organizations consider such redundancies inefficient, and traditional approaches to organizing strive mightily to eliminate inefficiency. However, consider, for example, that the divisional/product form of organization builds in redundancy in order to achieve flexibility and adaptability. Adaptability through redundancy is the preferred outcome for two reasons. First, redundancy ensures that an injury to one part of the system will not cause total collapse because the knowledge/capability of the injured part is possessed by other parts of the system and thus restorable. Second, redundancy creates potentially greater power in the system as a whole. It is possible that local agents identify similar opportunities and begin to self-organize around that opportunity. As the opportunity becomes more real, more possible, the system will find itself better able to take advantage of the opportunity because multiple local agents have prepared themselves, without central direction and control.

In designing for emergence, an important step is distributing intelligence, which involves making information widely available to everyone. Openness and accessibility becomes a value in organizations designed for emergence because information is the lifeblood of organizations, the energy that enables innovation and new ideas. Thus managers who design for emergence do not censor information; rather they unleash it into the organization knowing that some of it will create disequilibrium, a necessary condition for organization growth and learning (Garud, *et al.*, 2006).

Fostering Conversation/Enriching Connections

Communication networks are viewed by some to be the centerpiece of what it means to be an organization (Boden, 1997; Dooley, , *et al.*, 2003; Gronn, 1983). As Pascale, *et al.* put it, (2000: 186) "organizations are networks of conversations – via memos, e-mail, reports, procedures, talking out loud, and thinking to oneself." Organizations designed for emergence, encourage "talk," and foster conversation. In traditional organizations, the leaders (those in authority) determine and orchestrate what they believe to be the necessary and appropriate conversations. Because conventional views of leadership assume that leaders possess or can acquire information necessary for decision making, and they can devise appropriate solutions to problems, rarely is there opportunity for front-line managers to converse with top managers.

Conversation puts the distributed intelligence into play; it is how agents make sense of what is going on around them. Cohen, *et al.*, (1972: 25) describe organizations as a "set of procedures for argumentation and interpretation" and Weick (1995) notes the important role of talk, discourse and conversation for sensemaking in organizations and argues that "people talk in order to see what they think" (Weick, 1995: 184). Lots of talking, rampant conversation, is messy, from a conventional view of organizations. It is time consuming and it generates conflict. Unbridled conversation keeps equilibrium at bay, which may be why traditional views of organizations that value efficiency and control, find rampant conversation problematic. However, for complex systems, conversation is both a critical source and conduit for the energy that keeps the system alive.

By fostering conversations, the leader is letting go of "message control." Fostering conversations means taking advantage of non-linear interactions in a way that will accelerate, not block, the transmission of useful information. For example, the leader will not be solely responsible for scripting messages. Rather, the transparent availability of information will enable system agents to learn faster and more effectively because they can talk openly (and knowledgeably) about both success and failure in terms that make sense locally.

Fostering conversations also helps build the kinds of connections and relationships that further enhance awareness and learning. Organizations are networks of people both strongly and weakly connected to others in the network. Conventional views of organizations concentrate on connections in the vertical hierarchy, and in practice, this leads to system silos that operate in relative isolation. When managers design for emergence they enable a network that has rich connections both vertically and horizontally. The term "rich" refers to the *number* of nodes connected in the network (its density), and the *quality* of the connections, that is the amount of intelligence that passes among the nodes (its depth). Rich connections – lots of nodes and quality connections among the nodes - enable the effective distribution of intelligence, accelerate learning, and are the medium for conversations.

In an organizational system, nodes are people and groups, but they can also be events – such as staff meetings or town hall meetings where managers hold conversations with front line workers. The more different nodes there are the greater the likelihood that multiple perspectives will shape information, strengthening intelligence, and fostering self-organization. The quality of connections among nodes is enhanced and strengthened when people spend time together and develop emotional involvement and mutually responsive relationships. Strong connections occur when people trust each other and are free to share information, ideas, and concerns. However, if the strong connections occur among only a few vertical nodes, repetitive and stable behavior occurs, minimizing the chances of self-organization. Designing for emergence means paying attention to how many nodes there are and the quality and strength of connections among the nodes.

Fostering conversations and enabling strong, rich connections is an important part of designing for emergence. In a practical sense, this suggests seeking out opportunities to put people (agents) together. For example, using cross-functional teams to solve problems makes more sense than having one or two leaders strategize in private. The conversations and connections made possible by formal teams or even informal socializing can enable system learning. It is through talking that people become open to new information, the ideas of others and the possibility of changing what they believe and think. Thus, for organizations to change and renew themselves, it requires managers who take seriously the business of conversation and connections, who see their jobs as one CEO described it as - "managing conversations."[1]

Sustaining Tension

Designing for emergence means sustaining tension across the system: creating the tension of paradox (McKelvey, 2004). Systems learn and adapt effectively when they address the tensions created by contradictory or countervailing forces. Countervailing forces place into relief the advantages and disadvantages of different forms of adaptation, and the seeming contradictions create tension and irritation. The system is motivated to relieve the tension. In other words, the system is motivated to learn about the irritation and seek a successful adaptation. Tension is necessary for change and growth and although it is a source of discomfort, it is an asset that needs to be sustained.

Conventional approaches to organizing, however, seek to routinize behavior, ensuring stability and predictability. Over time, this numbs the system to both its environment and itself: it becomes detached from environmental de-

---

1 This comment is attributed to Lew Platt, former CEO of Hewlett-Packard, by Pascale, *et al.* (2000: 202).

mands, and it is numb to its own internal contradictions. Numb systems do not learn effectively. The conditions for tension exist, but can't be felt, so there is little motivation to change. The conventional system does not change because, in large part, it does not feel the tension necessary for change.

Designing for emergence means sustaining tension by embracing paradox. Embracing paradox involves seeking out both the comfort of stability and discomfort of instability; encouraging both efficiency and trial and error; developing both agility and power, speed and deliberateness. Tension in an organization is sustained through the paradox of using centralized structures (appropriate for elements of the organization where there is certainty) and decentralized structures (necessary for elements of the organization where there is uncertainty) at the same time. Such tension helps keep the organization alert to effective adaptation. Consider the paradox created by teams in organizations. A well-functioning team is autonomous, utilizes free exchange of ideas, and can dream up ideas that can help organizations made smart adaptive responses to environmental challenges. Yet the autonomous team cannot be free to do just anything. Rather, it must function coherently within a larger system. Managing teams effectively means addressing the tension created by the paradoxes of freedom and cooperation, creativity and coherence, system challenge and system discipline.

Designing for emergence is essentially about designing for learning, and learning requires confronting the unknown and dealing with what is new and different. Such an encounter can be unsettling, uncomfortable, and difficult. A system may have trouble choosing or motivating itself to be uncomfortable. A disturbance such as a failed decision, or a conflict, however, will trigger the kind of discomfort that can be the first step to new learning. A disturbance can trigger learning only if the system, paradoxically, views the disturbance as an opportunity for learning, and not as a problem or threat.

We noted earlier that conventional approaches to leadership require the leader to reduce conflict (tension or disturbance) and restore "order." Conventional approaches to design see disturbance as something that is counterproductive; disturbance is a distraction that produces inefficiencies and conflicts. From a traditional view, disturbance is a management failure (Barley & Kunda, 1992; Barnard, 1968) and must therefore be eliminated, or, better, designed completely out of the system. Essentially, conventional systems are thus designed not to learn. In contrast, designing for emergence requires accepting disturbances as opportunities for learning and growth. Accepting disturbance is a way to sustain tension in the system and, paradoxically, tension is good because it forces the system and its agents to pay attention and learn.

Organizations designed for emergence will be characterized by adaptive tensions, by the presence of conflict, and the recognition of adversity. Rather than sweep conflict or disappointments under the rug, managers who design for emergence, try to use adversity to learn and grow. Sustaining tension occurs when managers encourage experimentation, allow for failures and then openly examine them, as well as endure what conventional leaders might see as irritants. Jack Welch is famous for his "work-out sessions" in which lower level employees aired their concerns about specific problems in a public setting and managers were required to listen and then act on the solutions devised by the work-out group. Using such public settings for identifying and solving operational problems built needed tension into the organization.

Looking for Patterns

Coherent action at both the local level and the system level requires effective pattern recognition and sensemaking. As Smircich & Stubbart (1986: 730) argue "People make sense of their situation by engaging in an interpretive process that forms the basis for their organized behavior." The language, stories, and metaphors in organizations can form patterns that contain meaning about what is happening to people, what they value, and what they need. At a more strategic level identifying external/environmental patterns creates opportunities for identifying emerging markets, while identifying internal system patterns creates opportunities for identifying emerging capabilities. In either case early pattern recognition provides an advantage. Designing for emergence involves being able to identify and attach meaning to patterns. Essentially designing for emergence means enabling, not blocking, the system's impulse to self-organize because self-organizing is an exercise in pattern formation and recognition.

Organizations that are experiencing continuous change (Weick & Quinn, 1999: 366), that is, "a pattern of endless modifications in work practice and social practice" are ripe for pattern recognition. Pattern recognition involves giving shape and meaning to emerging modifications. Plowman, *et al.* (2007b) found that a critical function of leadership in emergent change is being able to recognize patterns in lots of local adaptations and giving meaning to the patterns through the use of language and symbols.

Conventional views of leadership suggest that most change is intended and leaders are responsible for creating change. Designing for emergence recognizes that much change is unintended, that small changes can escalate, amplify and turn into something quite large. In complex systems, where autonomous agents are interacting with each other and making local adaptations, patterns in those local adaptations can provide powerful new meaning for the organization. Pattern recognition requires adopting a large or holistic frame. Contrast this with the traditional view of organizations that adopts a reductionist frame when problem solving. A reductionist frame has the problem solver examine individual parts or pieces of the problem, assuming that fixing a piece fixes the whole. Fixing individual pieces does not require recognizing patterns. Complexity science however, encourages looking to the whole system, where recurring behaviors, themes, and patterns provide meaning.

In organizations designed for emergence, leaders and managers look for patterns in the activities and events that are happening around them. Looking for patterns requires patience, and a willingness to "sit in the unfamiliar seat of not knowing" (Wheatley, 1999: 6). Managers who look for patterns are slow to judge and label events. Instead, they are keen observers of where the energy in the system is coming from, what event is attracting people's attention. Looking for patterns requires the manager to step back, using time and distance to allow shapes to emerge that can then be harnessed into productive change. Looking for patterns means seeking emergent order by observing energy sources, not roles, and then channeling that energy in productive ways.

Summary and Conclusions

In spite of its many definitions and the stops and starts with the topic of leadership, it remains important. We have argued that rather than continue to conceptualize leadership as a role occupied by a person, who is sought after as a potential hero and often realized as a scapegoat, complexity science offers a way out of the conceptual dilemma. The characteristics of complex systems are incompatible with traditional notions of leadership that emphasize the ability to predict, plan, and control organizational futures. Complex systems, are made up of thinking, adapting human beings, capable of learning and novelty. With every contact between people or groups in organizations, with every exchange of information there is the opportunity for influence, and therefore leadership. The ongoing mutual adaptations that occur in complex systems are the makings of learning and leadership – continuously, and throughout the organization. When organizations are designed for emergence rather than for fit, or for specific outcomes, intelligence is widely distributed, conversations multiply, rich connections among people abound, tension drives innovations, and patterns embody meaning that help guide the organization.

CHAPTER SEVEN
COMPLEXITY LEADERSHIP THEORY: AN INTERACTIVE PERSPECTIVE ON LEADING IN COMPLEX ADAPTIVE SYSTEMS

Benyamin B. Lichtenstein, Mary Uhl-Bien, Russ Marion, Anson Seers, James Douglas Orton & Craig Schreiber

Traditional, hierarchical views of leadership are less and less useful given the complexities of our modern world. Leadership theory must transition to new perspectives that account for the complex adaptive needs of organizations. In this paper, we propose that leadership (as opposed to leaders) can be seen as a complex dynamic process that emerges in the interactive "spaces between" people and ideas. That is, leadership is a dynamic that transcends the capabilities of individuals alone; it is the product of interaction, tension, and exchange rules governing changes in perceptions and understanding. We label this a dynamic of adaptive leadership, and we show how this dynamic provides important insights about the nature of leadership and its outcomes in organizational fields. We define a leadership event as a perceived segment of action whose meaning is created by the interactions of actors involved in producing it, and we present a set of innovative methods for capturing and analyzing these contextually driven processes. We provide theoretical and practical implications of these ideas for organizational behavior and organization and management theory.

Benyamin B. Lichtenstein, Ph.D. (Boston College, 1998) is Assistant Professor of Management and Entrepreneurship at the University of Massachusetts, Boston. He has helped grow entrepreneurship programs at the University of Hartford, Syracuse University, and most recently at U-Mass Boston. Dr. Lichtenstein's research expertise focuses on applications of complexity science to leadership, entrepreneurial emergence and transformation, and collaboration, trust, and inter-organizational learning. "Professor Benyamin," as his students call him, has published over 40 papers and chapters and presented several dozen more, including articles in internationally recognized journals such as *Organization Science, Journal of Business Venturing, Entrepreneurship Theory and Practice, Human Relations,* and the *Academy of Management Executive,* where he received the "Article of the Year" award in 2000. He regularly provides consulting support for entrepreneurial firms and large companies. In addition to his professional work, he finds his greatest joy these days connecting with his beautiful wife Sasha and their two young children, Simeon and Moriah.

Mary Uhl-Bien, Ph.D. (University of Cincinnati, 1991) is the Howard Hawks Chair in Business Ethics and Leadership and the Associate Director of the Gallup Leadership Institute at the University of Nebraska-Lincoln. She has published articles on leadership (e.g., relational leadership theory, leader–member exchange, social exchange, and complexity leadership) in leading national and international journals, including *Academy of Management Journal, Journal of Applied Psychology, Journal of Management, Human Relations*, and *The Leadership Quarterly*. She is Senior Editor of the Leadership Horizons Series published by Information Age Publishing, and serves on the editorial boards of *The Leadership Quarterly* and the *Academy of Management Journal*. She has consulted with organizations including State Farm Insurance, Walt Disney World, the U.S. Fish & Wildlife Service, British Petroleum, and the General Accounting Office.

Russ Marion (Clemson University) is author of *The Edge of Organization* (1999), *Leadership in Education* (2001), and *Leadership in Complex Organizations* (The Leadership Quarterly). Marion is currently coeditor of a special edition on Complexity Leadership for *The Leadership Quarterly*, and is coeditor of a volume of *Leadership Horizons: The Series*. He co-organized workshops on complexity leadership at the Center for Creative Leadership and at George Washington University. Marion has presented on complexity leadership at the India Institute of Technology, the Institute for Management Development in Switzerland, and in workshops on destructing complex movements at the US Department of Defense.

Anson Seers is currently a Professor of Management at Virginia Commonwealth University School of Business, and holds a Ph.D. degree in business administration from the University of Cincinnati. His research publications have focused on work roles and working relationships, encompassing topics such as leader–member exchange relationships, team–member exchange relationships, emergent leadership, role conflict and role ambiguity, team and organizational commitment, work team effectiveness, and task force pacing. Dr. Seers is a Fellow and Past President of the Southern Management Association.

Doug Orton studies strategic organizational leadership processes in the U.S. national security community and other loosely coupled networks. After completing his dissertation at University of Michigan (Karl Weick was the chair), Doug taught at HEC Paris for six years. On September 10, 2001, Doug started co-teaching a course on crisis management to 65 Pentagon officers in Arlington, Virginia, and continues to try to bridge the business strategy and national security communities. He has conducted long-term studies of the microstrategic leadership actions of four of the 18 national security advisers from 1953-2007: McGeorge Bundy, Brent Scowcroft, Condoleezza Rice, and Stephen Hadley.

Craig Schreiber recently earned his Ph.D. in Computation, Organizations and Society from Carnegie Mellon University. He was a member of the Center for Computational Analysis of Social and Organizational Systems (CASOS) at the Institute for Software Research International in the School of Computer Science. He is currently a research associate for the National Research Council. Previously he has worked on research projects sponsored by the National Science Foundation, NASA, the Office of Naval Research and Army Research Labs. His interests include strategic management, organization and management theory, leadership, influence and power, organizational structure, organizational performance, organizational risk, organizational learning, knowledge management, information technology, computational organization science, social network analysis, dynamic network analysis, and model validation.

Introduction

As twenty-first-century management continues to emphasize decentralized organizing structures and co-evolutionary ecologies of firms, institutions, and markets, there is a growing recognition that traditional top-down theories of leadership are at best overly simplistic (Osborn, *et al.*, 2002). That is, leading-edge theorists and the leaders they inform are questioning the assumption that the essence of leadership rests within the character or the characteristic behaviors of effective supervisors (Seers, 2004). Worse, the notion that a leader exogenously "acts on" organizations in order to achieve the leader's objectives may be misguided in the presence of the insight that organizations are highly complex and nonlinear (Meyer, *et al.*, 2005). There is also a growing realization that effective leadership does not necessarily reside within the leader's symbolic, motivational, or charismatic actions.

If leadership is not "in" a leader or "done by" a leader, however, how are we to insightfully conceive exactly what constitutes leadership and from where it originates? A novel approach for answering these questions is grounded in complexity science, namely the notion that *leadership is an emergent event*, an *outcome of* relational interactions among agents. In this view, leadership is more than a skill, an exchange, or a symbol – leadership *emerges through* dynamic interactions (Bradbury & Lichtenstein, 2000). "Complexity leadership theory" investigates the role of leadership in expediting those processes in organizations through which interdependent actions among many individuals combine into a collective venture (Drath, 2001; Meyer, *et al.*, 2005).

Founding the approach of this paper on complexity theory *per se* moves us to a whole-systems view and thus away from the more traditional approaches that focus on variables and component parts. Instead, we will focus on:

- Expanding the locus of leadership from the isolated, role-based actions of individuals to the innovative, contextual interactions that occur across an entire social system;

- Extending current theory and practice by focusing on micro-strategic leadership actions across all organizational levels and across organizational boundaries;

- Increasing the relevance and accuracy of leadership theory by exploring how leadership outcomes are based on complex interactions, rather than "independent" variables;

- Highlighting the relational foundations of change in emerging organizational fields, through the idea that leadership occurs in the "spaces between" agents;

- Providing a new and rich foundation for explaining the constructive process of collective action as well as the influential "behaviors" of collective actors;

- Connecting to innovative methodologies that can enrich our understanding of how leadership gets enacted and received in complex environments.

Toward a New Era in Leadership: Complexity Leadership Theory

Leadership study, indeed society in general, is infatuated with leaders – people who occupy some elevated status or position and to whom we often ascribe some form of "greatness" (Gronn, 2002). The Western mindset about leaders seems ruled by assumptions that leaders have some innate capacity to plan futures, arrive at rational and correct decisions (Bluedorn, 2002), and control social outcomes (Meindl, *et al.*, 1985).

A new mindset is beginning to emerge, however, which recognizes that social processes are too complex and "messy" to be attributed to a single individual or pre-planned streams of events (Finkelstein, 2002; Marion and Uhl-Bien, 2001). As Finkelstein (2002: 77) put it:

"I understand that as researchers we need to simplify very complex processes to study them carefully, but what are we left with when we remove the messiness, the back-and-forth, the reality?"

Although the complexity leadership approach redirects emphasis away from the individual as leader, it does not in any way diminish the importance of leadership as an organizational phenomenon; rather, it recognizes that leadership transcends the individual by being fundamentally a system phenomenon (Marion & Uhl-Bien, 2001, 2003; Uhl-Bien, *et al.*, 2004; Hazy, 2006). Drawing from complexity science (Marion, 1999), complexity leadership theory offers a new perspective for leadership research by considering leadership within the framework of the idea of a complex adaptive system (CAS). In such systems, relationships are not primarily defined hierarchically, as they are in bureaucratic systems, but rather by *interactions* among heterogeneous agents and across agent networks.

A CAS is comprised of agents, individuals as well as groups of individuals, who "resonate" through sharing common interests, knowledge and/or goals due to their history of interaction and sharing of worldviews. Agents respond to both external pressures (from environment or from other CAS or agents, e.g., leaders) and internal pressures that are generated as the agents struggle with interdependency and resulting conflicting constraints (e.g., when the needs of one agent conflict with those of another). These tensions, when spread across a network of interactive and interdependent agents, generate *system-wide* emergent learnings, capabilities, innovations, and adaptability. Importantly, such elaborations are products of *interactions among agents*, rather than being "caused" by the specific acts of individuals described as leaders.

A complex systems perspective introduces a new leadership "logic" to leadership theory and research by understanding leadership in terms of an *emergent event* rather than a person. A complexity view suggests a form of "distributed" leadership (Brown & Gioia, 2002; Gronn, 2002) that does not lie in a person but rather in an interactive dynamic, within which any particular person will participate as leader or a follower at different times and for different purposes. It is not limited to a formal managerial role, but rather emerges in the systemic interactions between heterogeneous agents (Marion and Uhl-Bien, 2001, 2003). Therefore, complexity leadership includes a descriptive analysis examining the conditions and dynamic processes of these interactions and the emergent phenomena that they call forth:

"There is a growing sense that effective organization change has its own dynamic, a process that cannot simply follow strategic shifts and that is longer and subtler than can be managed by any single leader. It is generated by the insights of many people trying to improve the whole, and it accumulates, as it were, over long periods" (Heckscher, 1994: 24).

In other words, "leaders" in the *formal* sense can enable the conditions within which the process occurs, but they are not the direct source of change.

A key contribution of a complexity leadership theory is that it provides an integrative theoretical framework for explaining interactive dynamics that have been acknowledged by a variety of emerging leadership theories, e.g., shared leadership (Pearce & Conger, 2003), collective leadership (Weick & Roberts, 1993), distributed leadership (Gronn, 2002), relational leadership (Drath, 2001; Uhl-Bien, 2007), adaptive leadership (Linsky & Heifetz, 2002; Uhl-Bien, *et al.*, 2004), and leadership as an emergent organizational meta-capability (Hazy, 2004, 2006).

Specifying the Interactive Nature of Leadership in Events

Adaptive leadership is defined for this paper as an interactive event in which knowledge, action preferences, and behaviors change, thereby provoking an organization to become more adaptive. This definition focuses on change, as many definitions of leadership already do (Bryman, 1996), but also distinguishes between leadership (as a product of interactive dynamics) and leaders (people who influence this process). As such, adaptive leadership does not mean getting followers to follow the leader's wishes; rather, leadership occurs when interacting agents generate adaptive outcomes. According to this definition, leadership can occur anywhere within a social system. It need not be authority or position based, but is instead a complex interactive dynamic sparked by adaptive challenges. Individuals act as leaders in this dynamic when they mobilize people to seize new opportunities and tackle tough problems. As the situation changes, different people may act as leaders by leveraging their differing skills and experience.

An excellent starting place for developing a model of adaptive leadership in events can be found in the work of Mead (1932, 1934, 1938), who brought to the fore the neglected dimension of inter-subjectivity in the establishment of both individual and collective behavior. For Mead, the very notion of self (identity) becomes intimately connected to the identity of agents (objects and individuals) with which one interacts in a social structure. Allport (1954, 1962, 1967) builds on this idea by conceptualizing social structure as an ongoing *cycle* of events. Events are the observable nodes in these cycles; multiple cycles may interact directly or they may be tangential. Allport's theory provides a powerful precedent to complexity science in affirming that longitudinal analyses of inter-action events should replace cross-sectional frameworks that purport to examine how single variables "cause" some dependent (pre-assigned) outcome.

Weick's (1979) social psychology of organizing modernizes Allport's analysis. Weick argues that the basic unit of organization is the "double inter-act" of interdependent behaviors between individuals. He also emphasized that "events in organizations are held together and regulated by dense, circular, lengthy strands of causality perceived by members" (Weick, 1979: 13).

Recently, Cilliers (1998) applied a complexity, postmodern lens by connecting these earlier ideas on intersubjectivity to Giddens's (1984) partly cognitive model of structuration. An event is thus a bracketing of ongoing interactions to create meaning. Following this reasoning, we propose a new definition for an event, namely a perceived segment of action for which meaning relates to *interactions* among actors. All of the actors need not play equivalent roles in the action, but all of the roles are interrelated. Another way to say this is that meaning emerges in the "spaces between" people rather than in the acts of individuals *per se* (Buber, 1970). "In essence... [Buber's work] points to the relational perspective that self and others are not separable... but are, rather, coevolving..." (Bradbury & Lichtenstein, 2000: 551). In a similar way, Drath (2001: 136) proposed that:

"people construct reality through their interactions within worldviews... [They do it] when they explain things to one another, tell each other stories, create models and theories... and in general when they interact through thought, word, and action."

Accordingly, leadership events are not constructed by the actions of single individuals; rather, they emerge through the interactions between agents over time.

Drivers of Adaptive Leadership
Collective Identity Formation as a Driver of Adaptive Leadership

According to most complexity researchers, agent interactions are governed by rules and mechanisms for changing rules. One fundamental form of rule change occurs when interactions in leadership events produce a new identity (e.g., Gioia, *et al.*, 2000). According to the adaptive leadership perspective, this identify formation occurs over time, as participants together define "who we are" and what we are doing through our interactions. In this way, the emergence of a social object occurs through the "in-forming" of a joint social identity. Importantly, such social objects arise jointly, through the mutual interactions of its participant creators. This driver of collective identity formation can be forgotten as soon as the participants create a common-sense conception of a formal leader "out there," with themselves holding complementary follower roles (Kahneman & Tversky, 1972). By this account, complexity leadership theory suggests that participants need to be made aware of this dual process of identity creation and projection, in order to take back ownership of their role in the identity-formation process.

Complexity leadership theory's conception of interactive events offers the potential for specifying the construction process of collective action, and thus collective actors (Seers & Wilkerson, 2005). Note how different this conception is from traditional models of leadership, and from most complexity models of agent rule following. Most simulation researchers suggest that agents are governed by a selfish rule (Bonabeau & Meyer, 2001). For example, Nowak, *et al.*, (1995) show cellular automata simulations in which selfish behaviors of agents may, under certain circumstances, generate cooperative behaviors across an interactive system. In contrast, complexity leadership theory develops a more nuanced view of how rules are used and how they can change through interactions over time.

Tension as a Driver of Adaptive Leadership

A second driver of innovation in adaptive leadership events occurs when the interactions between agents spark tension that leads to adaptive change. According to complexity leadership theory, when agents interact they may experience tension in the form of pressures on and challenges to their personal knowledge base (Carley & Hill, 2001). Such challenges to agent schema can, under the right enabling conditions, foster realignment of agents' cognitive maps to resonate better with the new information. That is, agents realign their schema in order to accommodate and thus mitigate disagreement (Kauffman, 1993; Marion & Uhl-Bien, 2001).

These tension-related accommodations often generate completely new information; that is, ideas, innovations, and frameworks emerge that are unanticipated given the information currently available (Uhl-Bien, *et al.*, 2007). Therein lay the seeds of adaptive leadership: Agent interactions can generate tension through which novel information can emerge; when those new ideas lead to positive change, adaptive leadership has occurred. In this case, the tension that arises in agent interactions can function as a core driver for change in adaptive leadership. Adaptive leadership then may take advantage of such tension as a driver through which interacting agents (people, ideas, etc.) address complex challenges in ways that produce new patterns of cognition and behavior. But how do we measure these dynamics, and how can we expand our understanding of leadership in events such that formal leaders can help create the conditions for adaptive leadership and complexity leadership?

Measuring the Space Between: Methods for Exploring and Analyzing Leadership Events

Given our interest in exploring the events that generate leadership, we have identified several methods that can be used to measure and analyze specific leadership events over time, as well as the interrelationships that enact them. Specifically we are interested in "episodes" of leadership, and on the interactions that are bracketed into those events. Since interactive dynamics are processes that take place over time, we need methods that attend to the longitudinal and dynamic nature of interactive events and the relationships that construct them.

Focusing on events as the prime unit of analysis means more than applying new methods in order to analyze cross-sectional data on individual characteristics. Instead, measuring "the space between" involves:

- Identifying and bracketing the events, episodes, and interactions of interest;
- Capturing these events or interactions as data in a systematic way;
- Gathering individual/agent level data that describe interaction cues received over time;
- Modeling these data in ways that highlight their longitudinal and relational qualities;
- Analyzing these data in terms of their relational qualities and longitudinal dynamics.

Identifying and bracketing events need not be complicated, depending on the nature of the organizing processes one is examining. A paradigmatic case is Barley's (1986) examination of interactions between radiologists and technicians during a period of dramatic technological change. In that case, the context of these interactions was defined (bracketed) by a radiological procedure, which in our case would be the event within its nexus of relationships. Less common, but no less interesting, is the research on organizational meetings or special events, in which the crucial episodes are defined *a priori* by the research interest, and the bracketing of these processes is structurally produced and distinguished by the organizational members themselves.

Capturing events and interactions systematically may result from the in-depth exploration of organizing processes. For example, management researchers have recognized the important role that temporal events play in making progress (Brown & Eisenhardt, 1997) and catalyzing changes (Gersick, 1994) in dynamic contexts. In those two studies, the researchers were able to identify temporal and event-based transitions that structured the development of the project/venture being studied. A more formal approach was taken by Lichtenstein *et al.* (2006) in their discovery of an "emergence event" within a nascent entrepreneurial venture. Using grounded theory (Strauss & Corbin, 1993), they coded bi-weekly interview data into four categories, then transformed these codes into a quantitative format (Van de Ven & Poole, 1990). Next, they analyzed each of the time series' using quality control methods, which highlighted a dramatic change in one variable (Dooley & Van de Ven, 1999). *Post-hoc* heuristic tests confirmed the presence of two distinct "epochs" (events) within these data. The interview corresponding to the specific change point was more deeply examined; it became the nexus of a series of changes that were explained as interdependent aspects of an emergence event.

Gathering individual/agent level data about the members' interdependencies and the interaction cues that they receive over time (traditionally, the cues that "lead them") is necessary for exploring how leadership events diffuse through "the space between" the participants to influence a population. These data can be gathered through observation and surveys in the laboratory (Guastello, *et al.*, 2005) or in the field (Schreiber & Carley, 2005). To fully understand leadership events, however, it is also necessary to know how these leadership cues or triggers are perceived by the individual agents who must make particular choices or take specific actions (Hazy, 2006). Because events unfold over time, the data set must be longitudinal, to capture how these qualities change over time, as well as cross-sectional, to understand agents' perceptions and qualities at specific moments in time. Accessing and gathering this type of data is challenging; fortunately, software tools and other techniques enable detailed data gathering at regular intervals in organizations (www.leadershipscience.com; Amabile, *et al.*, 2005). Once gathered, the data can be used as inputs to computational models as described below or for other quantitative, qualitative, or mixed method analytic techniques.

Modeling data in ways that highlight their longitudinal and relational qualities enables exploration of the complex and interrelated dynamics inherent in leadership events. A recent survey of computer modeling approaches in leadership research (Hazy, 2007) identified several different techniques that have been used for this, including system dynamics modeling (Davis, 2005; Hazy, 2004; Jacobsen & House, 2001), discrete event simulation (Jiang & Burton, 2002), agent-based modeling (Black & Oliver, 2004; Black, *et al.*, 2006; Carley & Ren, 2001), network modeling such as the NK Model (Solow & Leenawong, 2003), and dynamical network analysis (Schreiber & Carley, 2004a, 2005a). These techniques can be used to explore the nonlinear relationships resident in the data and to better understand the analytical implications of theory. Based on these synthetic results, computational analysis can pose research questions and identify hypotheses for empirical studies that might have otherwise gone unnoticed.

In addition, computational modeling can be used to answer questions that are normative or plausible. Plausible questions ask "what might be" and explore or go beyond what has transpired (Burton, 2003). Computational models are particularly useful in respect to research on organizational complexity, as real-world complex adaptive systems do not lend themselves to controlled experimentation. Through simulation, we can explore the complex effects of explanatory variables in a systematic way.

Analyzing data with a focus on their dynamics and interdependence is also a critical element of research that explores a complexity science perspective on leadership. Nonlinear dynamical relationships inherent in the data create new challenges in data analysis. In addition to the variables that have been measured in traditional research, such as individual traits or behaviors, new metrics must be identified that more fully capture the system dynamics. This is a work in progress and offers opportunities for methodological research. In addition, new analytical techniques must be developed.

One such technique for rigorously understanding these relational dynamics is dynamic network analysis. The new dynamic network analysis methodology combines techniques of social network analysis with multi-agent simulations (Carley, 2003). Dynamic network analysis represents sociotechnical systems in terms of the complex relational qualities that characterize the interdependencies of the system (Krackhardt & Carley, 1998). Also, dynamic network analysis models dynamic changes resulting from natural evolutionary processes such as learning (Carley & Hill, 2001) and strategic intervention processes such as altering the set of individuals within a group (Schreiber & Carley, 2004b). Through the use of dynamic network analysis, the contextual nature of the network and emergent structure and behavior, including leadership events, can be analyzed as well as the effects of emergence on outcomes such as performance, innovation, and adaptability.

In addition, non-simulation methods are being perfected for developing rigorous longitudinal analysis of critical events in emergence over time. An exemplar is the study of events leading to the emergence of the Branson, Missouri community (Chiles, *et al.*, 2004). Their data analysis methods (see pp. 504-506) include grounded theory, pattern matching, visual mapping, narrative techniques, temporal bracketing, and quantification using an event count model analyzed through a Poisson regression. This approach resulted in the identification of four specific eras of emergence punctuated by a carefully defined series of events; moreover, the researchers were able to generalize from these events four drivers of organizational emergence – fluctuation dynamics, positive feedback dynamics, stabilization dynamics, and recombination dynamics – which may be applicable as elements of adaptive leadership and complexity leadership.

Conclusions: Implications for Organization Science

By looking for leadership as emerging endogenously within interactions while being embedded within organizations, so-called leaders are not assumed to be directing collective action. There is no linear cause-and-effect relationship to discover. Instead, "leadership" becomes a term that is descriptive of certain social forces at play among actors, which may include a formal leader. This view is consistent with Giddens's (1984) duality of structure in that social structures produce and in some sense lead collective action, while at the same time being reproduced by those actions over time. By considering "leadership action" from an endogenous, time-dependent perspective, we are better able to integrate the time dimension of social systems into organization theory, revealing a unique method for addressing Radcliffe-Brown's (1952) challenge to sociological theory: "How do new types of social structure come into existence?" (cited in Burrell & Morgan, 1979: 56).

Complexity leadership theory begins to address this issue by arguing that certain interactions in a social network will have a nonlinear influence on future interactions within the network. As such, leadership actions may be seen as "field"-level effects that potentially catalyze the emergence of new firms (Uhl-Bien, *et al.*, 2007), proto-institutions (Maguire, *et al.*, 2004) or organizational fields (Chiles, *et al.*, 2004). "Field" is being used here in a cognate sense to that found in physics; that is, a matrix underlying a social grouping whose influence reaches to all the actors within that "field."

Another application for complexity leadership theory focuses on how leadership events may occur within and/or give rise to emergent nodes in a social network. Such an approach presents a unique addition to research on networks, by exploring how and when certain nodes may be highly leveraged within a collective social system. Moreover, by exploring influential nodes in terms of leadership outcomes – rather than in terms of the individualized roles these nodes might represent – complexity leadership theory may offer a new way to explain the role of individual action in the enactment of structures of constraint and opportunity (Ibarra, *et al.*, 2005: 359).

Complexity leadership theory also reflects a new approach to understanding dynamic organizational capabilities, including innovation, strategic alliance making, and merger and acquisition capabilities (Teece, *et al.*, 1997; Eisenhardt & Martin, 2000). Teece (2005) has argued that the next horizon of management research is how to manage and lead an organization's dynamic capabilities. In our view, leadership is the emergent result of interacting individuals such that behavior and resource elements of the organization come together in useful ways – a frame that can be formalized in terms of dynamic organizational capabilities and routines. Such a link between leadership and organizational capabilities has recently been explored through computational modeling (Hazy, 2006).

Such framing reflects the growing use of computational modeling in organization theory (Carley& Prietula, 1994; Carley & Svoboda, 1996; Levinthal & Warglien, 1999; March, 1991; March & Olsen, 1976) and the use of complementary modeling techniques in leadership research (Hazy, 2006). Of particular note is the use of Kaufmann's (1993) NK model in organizational contexts (Levinthal, 2001; Levinthal & Warglien, 1999) to explore strategic choices and top management team dynamics. Although that approach has been focused around strategic search, innovation, and learning (e.g., Rivkin, 2000, 2001; Siggelkow, 2001, 2002), Siggelkow and Rivkin's (2005) approach comes close to modeling the microdynamics of leadership.

Moreover, complexity leadership theory accepts the juxtaposition of order and apparent chaotic change as an essential characteristic of social environments; in this way a complexity framework for leadership is fully integrated within the social psychology of organizing (Weick, 1979; Weick, *et al.*, 2005). Similarly, by framing leadership as emergent and thus endogenous, it can be usefully explored from both the interpretivist and the functionalist traditions of organizational analysis (Burrell & Morgan, 1979).

Complexity leadership theory also offers an important middle ground between computational analyses of individual agents, and the structures that emerge through their interactions. It explores the actions and events that catalyze emergent structures, and by reducing dependence on the individual the new theory expands our explanations about the origin and directionality of transformative change.

The practical and managerial implications of complexity leadership theory are legion; we offer here just a few initial suggestions. By focusing on how leadership may occur in any interaction, this new perspective dramatically expands the potential for creativity, influence, and positive change in an organization. More than simplistic notions of empowerment, this approach encourages all members to *be* leaders – to "own" their leadership within each interaction, potentially evoking a much broader array of responses from everyone in an organization. Complexity leadership theory provides a clear and unambiguous pathway for driving responsibility downward, sparking self-organization and innovation, and making the firm much more responsive and adaptive at the boundaries. In turn, significant pressure is taken off formal leaders, allowing them to attend more directly to identifying strategic opportunities, developing unique alliances, and bridging gaps across the organizational hierarchy.

Complexity leadership theory generates new managerial strategies, including the use of tension to create adaptive change; that is, when lower-level tensions are induced in the organization to produce adaptive change that addresses the complex challenges facing the organization (Uhl-Bien, *et al.*, 2007). Goldstein (1994) first showed how internal tension, carefully introduced, could help spark transformative change; Uhl-Bien *et al.* (2007) convincingly argue that Jack Welch was a consistent user of management by tension during his tenure at GE. Many more practical suggestions may be garnered through this approach.

Making interactions and relationships primary creates a new avenue for improving ethical and behavioral standards in an organization, for it is much easier to identify a set of appropriate rules for interactions between individuals than it is for someone (who?) to distinguish between appropriate and inappropriate leadership behaviors. Complexity leadership theory also provides a pathway for respecting diversity, not only through its formal emphasis on heterogeneity, but also because cultural respect is much easier to cultivate through one-on-one interactions than it is to consistently enact through one-to-many leadership exchanges.

In conclusion, Scott's (2004) reflections on the nature of emerging organizational trends argue for increased attention to the relationships through which organizational activity is conducted. Whereas leadership research has been focused on durable, distinctive properties of entities, a complexity-inspired model of leadership in events presents an alternative conceptual framework, based in relationships, complex interactions, and influences that occur in the "space between" individuals. As such, it reflects the complexity of the real world, increases the relevance of our leadership theories, and provides new insights for students, researchers, and managers in the complex world of business.

CHAPTER EIGHT
PARADIGMATIC INFLUENCE AND LEADERSHIP: THE PERSPECTIVES OF COMPLEXITY THEORY AND BUREAUCRACY THEORY

Russ Marion & Mary Uhl-Bien

Traditional leadership developed from a bureaucracy paradigm established in the Industrial Age. Complexity leadership, in contrast, has emerged out of the new science of complex behavior and offers a quite different perspective. In this paper, we compare traditional and complexity leadership. We describe the complexity leadership framework and show how the three functions of complexity leadership – adaptive leadership, enabling leadership, and administrative leadership – differ from traditional leadership conceptualizations. We conclude by offering complexity leadership as a more appropriate framework for meeting the needs for adaptability and responsiveness in the knowledge era.

Russ Marion, Professor, Department of Leadership, Counseling, and Human and Organizational Development, Clemson University, is author of *The Edge of Organization* (1999), *Leadership in Education* (2001), and *Leadership in Complex Organizations* (*The Leadership Quarterly*). Marion is currently coeditor of a special edition on *Complexity Leadership* for *The Leadership Quarterly*, and is coeditor of a volume of *Leadership Horizons: The Series*. He co-organized workshops on complexity leadership at the Center for Creative Leadership and at George Washington University. Marion has presented on complexity leadership at the India Institute of Technology, the Institute for Management Development in Switzerland, and in workshops on destructing complex movements at the US Department of Defense.

Mary Uhl-Bien, who received her Ph.D. from the University of Cincinnati in 1991, is the Howard Hawks Chair in Business Ethics and Leadership and the Associate Director of the Gallup Leadership Institute at the University of Nebraska-Lincoln. She has published articles on leadership (e.g., relational leadership theory, leader-member exchange, social exchange, and complexity leadership) in leading national and international journals including *Academy of Management Journal*, *Journal of Applied Psychology*, *Journal of Management*, *Human Relations*, and *The Leadership Quarterly*. She is Senior Editor of the *Leadership Horizons Series* published by Information Age Publishing, and serves on the editorial boards of *The Leadership Quarterly*, and the *Academy of Management Journal*. She has consulted with organizations including State Farm Insurance, Walt Disney World, The U.S. Fish and Wildlife Service, British Petroleum and the General Accounting Office.

Introduction

Traditional leadership theories of the 20th century have been heavily influenced by the bureaucratic paradigm and by the production economy that dominated that century. These theories have, for the most part, assumed that leadership is actions of individuals based on top-down decision-making and authority (Fiedler, 1967; Jacobs & Jaques, 1990), formal (managerial) positions, centralization of goals, separation of planning and doing (Barnard, 1938; Taylor, 1911), alignment of individual preferences with organizational goals (Berson & Avolio, 2004; Stogdill, 1950), homogeneity of outlook (Berson & Avolio, 2004), and human relations approaches to motivate and avoid conflict (Graen & Uhl-Bien, 1995). Further, despite numerous acknowledgements in the literature of the separation of leadership and management, much of the leadership literature has, in theory and in methodology, failed to make such distinctions (Bedeian & Hunt, 2006).

A new theory of leadership based on complexity science, called Complexity Leadership Theory (Marion & Uhl-Bien, 2001; Uhl-Bien, *et al.*, in press), is premised on uniquely different assumptions, and its perceptions of leadership are dramatically different from traditional perspectives. Complexity Leadership Theory explores the dynamics of social network behavior, focusing on leadership as the products of interdependent interaction more than on the products of direct management (Marion & Uhl-Bien, 2001; Uhl-Bien, *et al.*, in press). It describes leadership as a complex of entangled functions that, when properly interacting, foster emergent dynamics and enable dynamically adaptive organizations.

In this paper we will discuss what is meant by complexity leadership and describe leaders' roles in the development of learning, adaptive, and creative – complex – organizations. We begin by outlining how traditional leadership assumptions have been influenced by their embeddedness in the bureaucratic paradigm. We explain that traditional leadership was focused by the needs of a production economy and therefore developed primarily to foster efficiency and alignment for productivity and performance. We then show how complexity leadership – grounded in complexity science – offers a very different perspective; one that focuses not on alignment and control but on heterogeneity and unpredictability. We discuss key differences between administrative functions in complexity and in traditional leadership (relative to vision, control, change and coordination) that reflect the divergent paradigms in which the two leadership approaches are based. We conclude by reiterating the value of complexity leadership theory as a means to incorporate complexity concepts into bureaucratic organizational structures to generate learning, creativity, and adaptability appropriate for the knowledge era (Uhl-Bien, *et al.*, in press).

Leadership Shaped by Traditional Paradigmatic Assumptions

Differences between traditional and complexity leadership can be described in terms of the paradigmatic influences (Kuhn, 1970) and economic needs that shaped them. Traditional leadership models were developed under an Industrial Age economy and were shaped by a bureaucracy paradigm, or set of bureaucratic principles assumed to be true and complete (see Kuhn, 1970 for discussion). The leadership worldview of these models valued alignment of preferences and control around a manager-led vision in order to accomplish productivity and performance. It valued positive human relations outcomes (e.g., satisfaction, commitment, trust) because such outcomes contributed to goal alignment and performance. This leadership worldview is one of efficient productivity in stable, predictable work environments.

Complexity leadership models address a different economic need and are based on different paradigmatic assumptions. The economic needs addressed by complexity leadership are products of (among other things) globalization, rapid change, the decline of production-based manufacturing in the so called industrialized nations and the rise of knowledge based organizations (Boisot, 1998), hyper-competitiveness, and rapid communication capabilities. Knowledge era leadership values rapid learning, innovation and adaptability outcomes within a structure that optimizes the analytical capacity of the organization. It is concerned with structuring and organizing conditions that enable the spontaneous (as opposed to planned) emergence of outcomes.

The Assumptions of the Bureaucratic Paradigm

Because it was developed in the Industrial Age, the paradigmatic heart (the assumptions that shaped organizational form and behavior) of 20th century traditional leadership models is bureaucracy. Weber (1947) warned that once a society adopts the bureaucratic model, it will not escape it. We propose that this has validity not because bureaucracy itself imposes an iron cage but rather because society imposes the cage on itself. It does this by embracing the reality defined by the bureaucracy paradigm, and once embraced, the society can perceive no alternative.

The core of Weber's bureaucratic form is the separation of the person from the office (Heckscher & Donnellon, 1994). The other well-known characteristics, such as hierarchical chain of command, meritocracy, and rules-based decision making, all derive from the separation of person and office notion. Separation means that authority is defined by the position and not by the personality. To accomplish this separation, every position within an organization should be clearly and succinctly defined "in terms of duties and methods" (Heckscher & Dennellon, 1994: 19). This enables a system in which binding decisions are generated; such decisions would not be the possible, according to the bureaucratic assumption, in systems where authority is indeterminate or overlapping.

This seemingly innocuous principle has many significant implications for the way we understand organization and leadership, so much so that it can be considered a paradigmatic (hence largely unchallenged) assumption. The primary implication is that positional authority and leadership are one and the same (e.g., Bedeian's first letter in Bedeian & Hunt, 2006). That is, leadership is ascribed to authority and position regardless of the behaviors that actually occur in that position. For example, we recognize the presence of both good and bad behaviors in given positions, but bad leadership – which likely is not leadership at all – is still called leadership. Management behaviors are likewise given the label leadership, a fact that was at the core of Bedeian and Hunt's (2006) exchange. Further, leadership behaviors expressed outside of authority and position is recognized as "leadership potential" when in fact it is leadership itself – it is just leadership without the mantle of position and authority.

The generalized assumption that leadership is a function of position also suggests that leadership is the property of the person who occupies that position. The possibility that leadership can be vested in group dynamics, an argument we will proffer in this paper, is not on the radar screen in traditional leadership theory (with the exception of newly emerging work on shared leadership approaches; cf. Pearce & Conger, 2003). This association of persons with leadership can be seen or inferred in nearly all definitions of leader or leadership. Northouse (2007), for example, claims that "Leadership is a process whereby an *individual* [italic added] influences a group of individuals to achieve a common goal" (p. 3). Fiedler (1967) argued that a leader is, "The *individual* [italic added] in the group given the task of directing and coordinating task-relevant group activities" (p. 8). Moreover, leaders and leadership are presumed to be interchangeable – leadership as a process is rarely perceived independently of leaders (i.e., individuals). By failing to clearly distinguish these roles, traditional leadership implicitly suggests that only individuals in authority roles express leadership, or that anyone who expresses leadership is, *de facto*, a leader with authority. The interchangeability of these concepts would seem self evident, but we argue (subsequently) that leadership can be expressed outside of formal roles and authority.

Another characteristic of the bureaucratic principle, the separation of planning and doing, has very long history. Taylor (1911) explicitly crafted this separation in his notion of floor management. The bureaucracy paradigm requires that role responsibilities be carefully specified, and consequently planning and doing tend to gravitate to different functional positions. The implications for leadership are that leaders plan and subordinates do.

As alluded earlier, bureaucratic assumptions also contribute to problems in traditional leadership research of the difficulty in separating management and leadership. As described by Hunt (Bedeian & Hunt, 2006), "the directing function is remarkably close to what is often meant by leading. Thus, leading or leadership is seen as one, but only one, important aspect of management" (p. 193). That management and leadership are confused or indistinguishable, we argue, is consistent with a relationship between bureaucratic leadership and the management of *rules and regulations* to enforce role specialization. In the "ideal form" of bureaucracy, rules ensure coordinated activity and prevent conflict (Gouldner, 1954). Leadership has little obvious function, then, except to assure the smooth functioning of those rules (which is really management).

Because bureaucracies do not achieve the ideal of a pure formal structure based on rules (see, for example, Gouldner, 1954), managerial oversight becomes necessary to deal with tendencies among workers to work around rules, to minimize rather than maximize effort when rules specify minimum requirements, and to respond to client requests with responses that do not fit well with rules. These unplanned situations create conflict, and directors/leaders deal with this conflict by further increasing supervision (Gouldner, 1954) and by seeking to reestablish the harmonious functioning of rules. Hence, Hunt's observation that leading is remarkably close to directing is quite accurate.

The result of this, in combination with the central notion of hierarchy of authority in bureaucracies, generates a view of leadership as a top-down phenomenon in which plans, strategies, and decisions emanate from authoritarian levels in the system and are carried out in the lower levels. This notion of *top-down leadership* is a central force that is rather firmly entrenched in traditional leadership literature. It is implicit in definitions such as Jacobs and Jaques' (1990) view that "Leadership is a process of giving purpose (meaningful direction) to collective effort, and causing willing effort to be expended to achieve purpose" (p. 281). It is also evident in literature which addresses broad distances between hierarchical levels and subordinates, such as the strategic leadership literature (see Canella & Monroe, 1997).

Traditional Leadership Conceptualizations

Consistent with this top-down view, a prime role of leaders in traditional conceptualizations is to influence people to embrace or achieve a common goal (Bryman, 1996). Stogdill (1950) classically articulated this principle when he stated that: "Leadership may be considered as the process (act) of influencing the activities of an organized group in its efforts toward goal setting and goal achievement" (p. 3). This observation may also be seen in a more recent statement by Berson and Avolio (2004: 626):

"A core responsibility for organizational leaders is to direct followers towards achieving organizational purposes by articulating the organization's mission, vision, strategy, and goals (Zaccaro & Klimoski, 2001). Leaders at all levels are responsible for the dissemination of strategic organizational goals, as well as for convincing their constituents to effectively implement those goals."

The influence of bureaucracy on traditional leadership conceptualizations can also be seen in the partitioning and restriction of heterogeneity. As noted above, each function in a bureaucracy is carefully described around a limited set of behaviors, thus any given person's input to decision making is restricted to the job specification for which he or she is responsible. Heckscher and Donnellon (1994) describe this as a "waste of intelligence" (p. 20) in organizations, and suggest that the only place in a bureaucracy in which intelligence is fully utilized is in the upper echelons. From a complexity perspective, we refer to this as a homogenization of skills, preferences, and worldviews. Bureaucratic compartmentalization means that all activities are focused on a coordinated, centralized goal structure (the top-down principle described above) – everyone is "on the same page," so to speak, and diversity, or heterogeneity, is suppressed. Moreover, it manifests in a "preference for harmony" and desire for unified actions around common goals. This has led scholars and practitioners to place considerable premium on the leader's capacity to settle disputes and motivate unified action. Leadership even tends to smooth over conflicts that might be useful for the organization – what Jehn (1997) and others call task-related conflicts, or heterogeneous ideas about how to best deal with tasks.

Bureaucracy's paradigmatic influence, then, has resulted in traditional leadership conceptualizations that leadership is positional, individual, and top-down. This view of leadership is (perhaps unwittingly) mired in assumptions of the separation of planning and doing, the centralization of goals, in aligning individuals with those goals, and homogeneity of outlook and purpose. Because of this, traditional leadership has not concerned itself with separating leadership from management (Bedeian & Hunt, 2006) and has been dominated by a "human relations" model that focuses on managers using consideration and support to motivate action and suppress conflicts (see Table 1). As we will suggest below, these assumptions limit the applicability of traditional leadership for the knowledge era.

The Complexity Paradigm of Leadership
Paradigmatic Assumptions of Complexity Theory

Complexity theory offers paradigmatic assumptions that lead to dramatically different views of leadership. Complexity theory is the study of self-reinforcing interdependent interaction among adaptive entities and how such interaction creates creativity, learning, adaptability, and change (Arthur, 1989; Bak, 1996; Coveney, 2003; Holland, 1995; Kauffman, 1993). According to complexity theory, innovative organizational behaviors are impelled more by interactive dynamics across an organization than by leadership action. Complexity envisions organizations as social networks, or complex adaptive systems (CAS), composed of a diversity of adapting agents that recurrently (Cilliers, 1998) interact with, and mutually affect, one another, and in so doing generate novel behavior for the system as a whole (Regine & Lewin, 2000). Leadership's role is not to create that novel behavior but to foster conditions that enable it.

A basic assumption of complexity theory is that the problems facing many organizations (particularly in the knowledge era) are too complex and under-specified to be solved by rational thinking (an observation that was articulated for complexity theory by Kauffman, 1993, but which has roots in Simon's, 1957, notion of satisficing). Based on this logic, complexity theory suggests that networks of interacting, competing problem solvers and innovators are superior to centralized decision makers at knowledge development and clarification (see also Souder, 1987). Ideas compete within such networks; conflicting constraints are negotiated; knowledge is subject to rich cross-currents of criticism and alternatives; and different pieces of knowledge are subject to aggregation forces that re-combine local ideas at increasingly higher levels of sophistication. Complexity theorists refer to this as "emergence," defined as "instability inspired

Bureaucratic Paradigm Traditional Leadership	Complexity Paradigm Administrative Leadership	Complexity Paradigm Enabling Leadership	Complexity Paradigm Adaptive Leadership
Positional (leadership occurs in managerial roles)	Positional (administrative leadership occurs in managerial roles)	Enabling leadership can occur in or outside of managerial roles	Informal (adaptive leadership does not require formal managerial role or positional authority)
Individual (associated with individuals in formal, managerial positions)	Individual (associated with individuals in administrative or managerial positions)	Individual (associated with individuals acting in managerial or non-managerial roles)	Collective and distributed (emerges within and from complex interactive dynamics)
Top-down	Top-down but recognizes bottom-up and emergent	Top-down and emergent	Informal and emergent (e.g., bottom-up)
Aligns individual with organizational goals Homogeneity of outlook and purpose	Allows flexibility with such things as indeterminate vision Does not require homogeneity; allows emergent coordination	Embraces and fosters diverse thinking Enables heterogeneity of outlook and purpose	Thrives on diverse perspectives Emanates from heterogeneity of outlook and purpose
Management is equated with leadership (focus is managerial leadership)	Administrative leadership is a managerial leadership function that addresses bureaucratic needs of complex organizations	Enabling leadership is an entangled function between complex systems and administrative structure	Adaptive leadership is an emergent change process that can occur anywhere; it is not a managerial form of leadership
Human Relations Focus: Managerial leaders engage in interpersonal relationships to motivate behavior aligned with goals	Complex Organization Focus: Administrative leaders recognize the importance of complex systems and do not impinge on them with policy	Complex Systems Focus: Enabling leaders foster conditions for complex dynamics and manage interface between bureaucratic and complex systems	Complex Dynamics Focus: Adaptive leadership is a collective, interactive change dynamic oriented to innovation and adaptation

Table 1 *Comparison of Leadership Shaped by Bureaucratic Paradigm and by Complexity Paradigm*

... generation of overall characteristics that do not reduce to a linear composition of the interacting parts" (Sengupta, 200: 338). Holland (1998) defines it more simply as "much coming from little" (p.1).

A variation on this idea is suggested by Ashby (1960), who observed that a successful system responds to variety with an equal degree of variety. Complexity theorists propose that the variety with which innovation-based organizations must deal is too complex to be codified and plotted; if it were plot-able, then it could be effectively resolved with leader rationality. Rather, the complex variety that these systems face demands an equally complex, learning and variety absorbing system (as opposed to the variety reducing strategies of traditional theories; Boisot, 1998): That is, it demands a complex network. McKelvey (in press) refers to such systems as distributed intelligences (DI) networks to suggest a neural-like, interdependent network of intelligent agents.

Leaders (and managers) cannot directly plan and execute variety-absorbing (adaptive) distributed intelligence networks that are equal to the demands of complex environments. Blueprints for networks that can resolve complex problems posed by given environments, and which can also adapt to shifts in those environments, are beyond rational construction. Rather, they create conditions that allow complex networks to emerge and evolve (Marion & Uhl-Bien, 2001). Leaders and managers stimulate interaction and interdependency, they manage the resources needed by the network, and they help negotiate external support networks. Given sufficient structural conditions, resources, and decision-making latitude, the networks themselves mold to the problems they face (what Boisot, 1998, referred to as variety absorbing). If leaders/managers guide such development too closely, either by mandate or by selling a vision, they limit the requisite variety that makes adaptive network dynamics effective.

Complexity perspectives, then, fundamentally change the way we consider leadership. In contrast to traditional top-down, managerially-controlled perspectives of organizational processes (i.e., bureaucracy), complexity theory views organizing as an informal dynamic that is generated through interactive bonding among interdependent, need-seeking individuals, each of which are driven by their local (bounded) assessments of social and organizational events (Marion & Uhl-Bien, 2001). Complex systems thrive on the challenge of conflicting constraints and diverse pressures; thus complexity leadership fosters complex systems in organizations by enabling diversity rather than promoting leader-brokered consensus.

Complexity Leadership Theory

The implications of complexity for leadership are conceptualized in a new leadership framework called Complexity Leadership Theory (Uhl-Bien, et al., in press). This framework incorporates complexity concepts of adaptability and interactive networks into bureaucratic structures by acknowledging both formal (bureaucratic) and informal (complex systems) dynamics of leadership in organizations. Complexity leadership recognizes that bureaucracy is inevitable – and useful – in organizations but that we need new ways of thinking about how leadership can and should function within bureaucratic structures to meet the needs for adaptability and responsiveness in the knowledge era.

It does this by positing three types of leadership, each representing different functions: administrative leadership represents the need to manage the bureaucratic requirements of the organization, and enabling and adaptive leadership reflect the need to enable complex interactive dynamics (e.g., complex adaptive systems) that generate creativity and adaptability for the organization. In particular, adaptive leadership is a collective (and distributed) form of leadership that emanates from complex dynamics and draws upon the combined expertise of organizational members to generate adaptive outcomes (innovation, creativity, and learning) for the organization. Administrative leadership is a managerial form of leadership that addresses the bureaucratic functions of the organization while not stifling the complex dynamics capable of producing adaptive change. Enabling leadership acts in the interface between the other two: It works to foster conditions conducive to the complex interactive dynamics of adaptive leadership and manages the administrative-to-adaptive and innovation-to-organization interfaces.

Each of these forms of leadership, and their implications relative to traditional conceptualizations, are described further below. We begin with adaptive leadership, which is the most counter to traditional thinking because it represents a distributed, informal, and emergent form of leadership grounded in complex dynamics. We then describe enabling and administrative leadership and their functions relative to the needs of adaptive leadership. In the discussion of administrative, we describe how key functions of administrative leadership (vision, control, change, coordination) differ in complexity leadership theory from more traditional conceptualizations of leadership grounded in the bureaucratic paradigm.

Adaptive Leadership. Adaptive leadership reflects the interactive nature of leadership processes; it is not based in hierarchy but instead in the interactive dynamics that occur among people, and among people and contexts. Adaptive leadership refers to change that emerges from the interactive dynamics of two or more agents. To be considered leadership, this change must be characterized by impact (possessing effect beyond the generative source) and significance (possessing relevance to problems at hand). Adaptive leadership is not the property of any given individual; rather it is expressed by the complex interactive dynamic itself. Human volition of individuals is certainly important, but this form of leadership is truly a social *process.*

Because of its nature, adaptive leadership is not positional but can, instead, occur anywhere (e.g., in the board room or on the shop floor). It is a product of emergent dynamics (complexity theorists prefer the term bottom-up dynamics, but that smacks too much of hierarchy so we instead use the term emergent). Adaptive leadership thrives on heterogeneity of preferences, needs, worldviews, skills, and goals, for heterogeneity provides diversity necessary for adaptive leadership to generate learning, creativity, and adaptability.

Complex dynamics are capable of producing learning, adaptability, and creativity. They accomplish this because multiple, heterogeneous preferences interact, diverge, converge, elaborate, and transform within a dynamic social and ideational "soup." This, perhaps more than anything, underscores how complexity leadership differs from traditional leadership. Traditional leadership (grounded in bureaucracy) is focused on the reliable production of commodities; it requires predictive stability and commonly focused effort to accomplish efficient production. Traditional leadership works to assure predictability by motivating centrally aligned and hierarchically defined goal oriented behaviors. Complexity leadership seeks to produce new, emergent, and innovative products; thus it seeks to capitalize on the knowledge invested in organizational members. Its strategy is to maximize the capacity of its knowledge capital by fostering productive interactive dynamics (i.e., adaptive leadership).

A comparison of traditional and adaptive leadership is provided in Table 1. As illustrated in this table, adaptive leadership is seemingly the opposite of traditional leadership. Specifically, it is non-positional, a product of interaction and not of individuals, informal (bottom-up), decentralized, embraces heterogeneity, separate from management, and oriented to change rather than efficiency and control.

Enabling Leadership. Enabling leadership serves two roles: It fosters conditions that enable the emergence of complexity dynamics, or adaptive leadership, within an organization; and it mediates the relationship between the administrative structure (bureaucratic system) and the complex interactive dynamics of adaptive leadership (complex adaptive system). It does this by trying to assure a healthy administrative ambiance for the complexity dynamic while simultaneously trying to assure that the complexity dynamic serves the goals and mission created by administrative leadership.

Enabling leadership fosters emergence by bringing together the enabling conditions (mechanisms and contexts) necessary for adaptive leadership to emerge (Uhl-Bien, *et al.*, in press). These conditions include interaction, interdependencies (i.e., one person's preference achievement dependent on the actions of others), simple adaptive rules (e.g., rules that force interdependency), adaptive tension (i.e., pressures to act), and flow of information and resources (e.g., rewarding creativity with additional funding; Bonabeau & Meyer, 2001). Enabling leadership mediates the relationship between administrative and adaptive leadership in two ways: It manages the organizational conditions in which adaptive leadership exists (administrative-to-adaptive interface), and it helps disseminate innovative products of adaptive leadership upward and through the formal managerial system (innovation-to-organization interface).

In the former (administrative-to-adaptive), it engages in managerial activities that foster rather than suppress complexity dynamics. For example, enabling leaders work to promote behavior that advances strategic goals by structuring conditions such as missions, physical conditions, crises, personal conflicts, and external threats in ways that support creative adaptive behaviors. This includes managing resources (money, supplies, information, personnel, etc.) that support adaptive leadership and allowing these resources to follow emergent ideas (e.g., Dougherty & Hardy, 1996). They keep administrative leadership from stifling adaptive functions by dealing with crises that threaten to derail adaptive leadership (Mumford, *et al.*, in press) and by protecting the creative process from forces (e.g., boards or directors, other administrators, environmental pressures) that would limit the capacity of the organization or its subsystems to engage in creativity, learning, and adaptation. Enabling leaders also promote missions that are not so specific they restrict the creative process (i.e., missions that are sufficiently flexible to change with changing conditions), and discourage non-useful adaptations (those not conducive to mission).

In the second role (innovation-to-organization interface) enabling leaders use their power to facilitate, orchestrate, and share innovative ideas and outcomes throughout the organization (Dougherty & Hardy, 1996). For example, they champion creative ideas by demonstrating personal commitment to the idea, promoting the idea through informal networks, and willingly risk their position and reputation to ensure its success (Howell & Boies, 2004). They also establish and maintain contact with top management to keep them informed and enthusiastic about projects. In this way they serve to move outputs of adaptive leadership through the bureaucratic pitfalls of the administrative levels.

A comparison of traditional leadership and enabling leadership are illustrated in Table 1. As the table reveals, there is some overlap in that enabling leadership could occur in managerial positions, is often associated with individuals, is at times top-down, and may be seen as a managerial function. It differs from traditional leadership, however, in that it does not *have* to occur in a managerial position – it can be engaged in by non-managers and can be informal rather than top-down. It also differs in that enabling leadership recognizes the value of heterogeneous goals, so does not seek to quell emergent dynamics by forcing alignment with pre-specified centralized goals. Moreover, it goes beyond the more limited focus of traditional leadership on human relations and instead recognizes the importance of fostering complex dynamics and conditions in organizations (which may at times seem counterintuitive relative to human relations emphases, see Heifetz & Laurie, 2001).

Administrative Leadership. Administrative leadership is managerial leadership that occurs in formal, hierarchical roles and is responsible for such things as organizational strategy, resource acquisition and allocation, policy making, and general management. It is related to traditional, bureaucratic leadership as developed earlier, but with some differences (see Table 1). In the complexity leadership framework, administrative leadership works to adapt its behaviors to the needs of the complex dynamic (and vice versa). Administrative leadership acknowledges the interdependence between its traditional functions and that of adaptive leadership; it understands, for example, that adaptive, emergent response to and decision making about localized conditions is an important element of organizational strategy (Marion & Uhl-Bien, 2007). It recognizes that complex dynamics – the capacity for adaptability and creativity – are important to its own decision-making functioning, and strives to act in a more "complex" manner (i.e., valuing and supportive of complex dynamics in organizations). It does this by differently managing issues of vision, control, change and coordination (see Table 2).

Vision. Whereas traditional leadership often exerts control by aligning individual preferences around a strong organizational vision, complexity leadership adopts an approach of "indeterminate" vision (Marion & Uhl-Bien, 2007) – complexity leadership theory distinguishes between vision that projects a determinate future and that which enables an indeterminate one. Determinate futures are (a) expansions of current reality (e.g., to improve the firm's product), or (b) fulfillment of leader-endorsed deviation from the norm (e.g., to develop a marketable product based on recent technological advances in the firm's market). Determinate visions unfold an existing or a recently derived reality; typically, they are rather specific about the desired outcome.

From Boisot's (1998) perspective, determinate visions convert the probable into the marketable. They seek to control the future and the worker's commitment to that future. Determinate visions are appropriate for productivity and performance outcomes, and because of this they are useful for traditional leadership grounded in the bureaucratic paradigm. Their goal is to lead workers to embrace an organizational vision, and the commitment to that vision controls behaviors and outcomes. By colonizing individual behaviors with an organization-endorsed vision, traditional leaders create a climate of consensus and order, or homogeneity.

Indeterminate visions are appropriate for complexity leadership and the knowledge era because they focus on more entrepreneurial knowledge production and innovation. They enable a future that cannot be clearly foreseen or defined. They seek to influence organizational dynamics in ways that foster learning, creativity, and adaptability. The indeterminate visions used by administrative leaders in complexity leadership enable networks that maximize creative potential and encourage interaction among ideas. Examples can be seen in Capital One and Nordstrom. In 1995, an upstart Capital One exhorted its workers to "move fast to exploit [opportunities] and move on when they fade" (Bonabeau & Meyer, 2001: 113). Nordstrom encourages its people to "present your own ideas. Your buyers have a great deal of autonomy, and are encouraged to seek out and promote new fashion directions at all times ... and we encourage you to share your concerns, suggestions and ideas" (Pfeffer, 2005: 99).

Moreover, complexity leadership theory values heterogeneity rather than homogeneity of focus. Therefore, administrative leaders in complex organizations allow for multiple, locally derived visions rather than a few consensus-based visions. Multiple visions within the context of networks of interdependency create conflicting constraints, and bottom-up negotiations of these constraints lead to elaboration of organizational purpose and higher order innovation, learning, and adaptability (Goldstein, 1994; Kauffman, 1993, 1995; Marion, 1999; Smith & Comer, 1994), fitness (Lichtenstein, 2000), and organizational growth (Petzinger, 1999).

Control. In traditional leadership, control lies with the leader/manager. In complexity perspectives, significant control is imbedded in interactive dynamics of the system. Therefore, complexity leadership works to build structures that foster emergent control (interdependency, adaptive rules, etc.). That is, it reorients

	Traditional Leadership	**Complexity Leadership**
General Role	Administrative leaders play central role in organizational effectiveness, with top leaders predominating. Activities revolve around direction provided by hierarchical leaders and those with formal authority.	Administrative leaders recognize that organizational effectiveness is a function of complex network activity (adaptive leadership) effectively intertwined with bureaucratic structure (enabling), and develop structures and systems that foster distributed leadership, heterogeneity and emergence.
Vision	Administrative leaders provide centralized direction to achieve high level production in accordance with strategic goals of organization. Management of alignment and meaning.	Administrative leaders provide indeterminate vision that fosters creativity, learning, and adaptability. Heterogeneous and dispersed visions are valued and supported.
Control	Administrative leaders control by transforming attitudes around core strategic vision. Managers supervise to drive task performance and accountability for results.	Control lies within complex interactive dynamics and not in bureaucracy. Administrative leaders structure control into decentralized systems to assure divergence of perspective, foster conflicting constraints, create adaptive tension, and stimulate informal problem solving.
Change	Change is incremental movement that moves the system away from status quo. Future view is expressed as vision by top leader—view pre-exists and defines the movement.	Change is created *by* the movement; it emerges nonlinearly out of the interactive dynamics that create the movement and is not pre-defined. Administrative leaders do not attempt to overly control change through top-down policy and directives or controlled, incremental behaviors.
Coordination	Centralized to ensure alignment with strategic direction; leave room for empowerment/ participation to allow autonomy and personalization within the vision. This fosters motivation and commitment and allows for appropriate adjustments to task structure/design.	Coordination of adaptive functions is decentralized (bottom-up or informal) to foster emergence, innovation, and adaptability.

Table 2 *Comparison of Administrative Functions in Traditional Leadership Theory versus Complexity Leadership Theory*

its traditional top-down approach away from bureaucratic thinking and toward complexity thinking. In the complexity leadership framework, adaptive leadership is disassociated to large extent from traditional top-down control structures (Stacey, *et al.*, 2000; Streatfield, 2001).

In traditional leadership, control can only be seen as top down and related to leader preferences – this is a fundamental bureaucratic assumption. If one stays in the bureaucratic framework, there is no alternative to hierarchical control and accountability. It is for this reason that attempts to move toward empowerment in the managerial literature have failed: In the bureaucratic paradigm control always lies with hierarchical leaders, so there is no possibility for attaining true empowerment within this paradigmatic framework.

Complexity sees control very differently; in the complexity paradigm, control is embedded within the complex, interactive dynamic. Control lies within an array of subtle and complex coordinating tools, such as tension, interdependency among agent preferences and work productivity, conflicting constraints, simple rules, and need. In complexity leadership, therefore, administrative leaders build control into processes and structures rather than organizing for top-down control. For example, Microsoft organizes their programming teams for autonomous decision making, yet enforces adaptive rules requiring periodic interdependency (Cusumano, 2001). It is these interdependencies emanating from simple rules (different programmers' codes must work together seamlessly) that foster coordinated action. Nordstrom encourages its people to respond autonomously and with good judgment to their environments (Pfeffer, 2005); it is the caveat to make good decisions that keep employees accountable. Bonabeau and Meyer (2001) report that Jim Donahey, former CEO of Capital One, governed his organization with four simple adaptive rules (instead of command and control bureaucracy):

1. Always align IT activities with the company (that is, keep the company's overall goal in mind);
2. Use good economic judgment (spend the money like its your own);
3. Be flexible (don't box yourself into one thought pattern);
4. Have empathy for others in the organization (when people ask you to do something you don't agree with, put yourself in their shoes (p. 111).

Control, then, is intelligently constructed to be emergent rather than top down.

In sum, while traditional leadership argues the potency of unified, determinate focus and vision for achieving productivity and performance, complexity leadership argues the potency of heterogeneity and diffuse control, coupled with indeterminate vision, for achieving innovation and adaptability. Administrative leadership based on the complexity theory recognizes that by remaining in the bureaucratic paradigm, approaches such as shared leadership will never reach their full potential for producing a distributed form of leadership because the control assumptions of hierarchy and authority will always get in the way. Administrative leadership, then, advocates "non-control" strategies that traditional leadership would reject. They do so because they realize the need to find ways of controlling organizations without compromising the flexibility and speed required in a knowledge economy.

Change. Both complexity and traditional leadership are oriented to change but there are key differences in how they define change. Traditional leadership theorists tend to perceive change as incremental movement toward a leader-defined view that moves the system away from status quo (Fiol, *et al.*, 1999). The future view is expressed as a vision by the traditional leader (e.g., the "I had a dream" speech of Martin Luther King), and followers are attracted to the vision by the actions of that leader. The view, then, pre-exists and defines the movement.

In complexity leadership theory, change is created *by* the movement, particularly at the adaptive leadership level. It emerges out of the interactive dynamics that create the movement (it is not pre-defined). It is product of restive dynamics among networked agents and groups, the convergence and divergence of ideas, and the formation or collapse of initiatives and of structures for performing those initiatives. Complex change is nonlinear rather than gradual, meaning that it is often sudden and seemingly unrelated to its causes.

For administrative leaders, complexity leadership means the focus is on creating structures that allow new and surprising innovation and adaptability to emerge. It is leading a "complex" (adaptive and emergent) rather than "bureaucratic" (control-oriented) organization. Administrative leaders in the complexity framework recognize the unpredictable and unfolding nature of change, and therefore stifle their control preferences in dealing with change. They do not attempt to overly control change through top-down policy and directives or controlled, incremental behaviors; nor do not rely on vision-led change or change "programs." Rather, they design and protect organizational structures and systems that foster continuous change through healthy adaptive dynamics. They think systemically in terms of movements and interactive behaviors; they learn to recognize the patterns of complexity so they can work to interact effectively with these patterns of complex dynamics; and they promote learning-enabled organizations and big picture (systems) thinking (Senge, 1990) by sharing of information and creating dynamic, networked interaction.

Coordination. Complexity theory counter-intuitively observes that informal, emergent (i.e., bottom-up) coordination strategies can often be preferable to top-down, carefully controlled coordination – particularly in highly complex situations. There is a growing body of simulated and organizational research in the complexity literature that demonstrates the potency of complex, bottom-up, informal systems in solving seemingly intractable problems, problems that defy the efforts of intelligent rationality (Bonabeau & Meyer, 2001; Carley, 1997, 1999; Lin & Pai, 2000; Souder, 1987). Bonabeau and Meyer (2001), for example, have used bottom-up strategies to address efficiency problems in product delivery businesses and in airline industry cargo routing procedures. Souder (1987) found that organizations that structure for extensive and frequent interaction with multiple channels and diffused coordination are effective at dealing with unfamiliar tasks.

Thus in complexity leadership theory, administrative leaders realize that distributed coordination can offer them competitive advantage (Marion & Uhl-Bien, 2007). They recognize that leadership which guides and controls knowledge searches compromises bottom-up flexibility and limits the organization's ability to find solutions to difficult problems. That is, they recognize that top-down, bureaucratic coordination strategies, the same coordination strategies that Weber (1947) said would become inevitable in modern society, may very well retard their ability to survive and thrive in a hypercompetitive, fast paced, knowledge-oriented environment.

Summary and Conclusions

In this chapter we present a view of traditional and complexity leadership as grounded in very different paradigms – traditional in bureaucracy and complexity in complexity systems theory. We suggest that the paradigmatic influences of these two approaches lend themselves to vastly different contexts: Traditional leadership is appropriate to efficiency and control contexts (Industrial Age) and complexity leadership is appropriate for innovation and knowledge contexts (knowledge era).

Complexity leadership fits into a new, emerging genre of leadership research that moves us away from conventional thinking (Gordon, 2002; Gronn, 2002; Surie & Hazy, 2007; McKelvey, in press; Parry, 1998; Plowman, *et al.*, in press; Schneider & Somers, 2006). It draws from complexity sciences and, because of this, is not grounded in the human relations and managerial leadership models that dominate much of conventional leadership research. We see this as a step beyond traditional leadership models, and one that may help advance theoretical and practical understanding in ways that cannot be considered by the bureaucratic paradigm.

Specifically, complexity leadership moves leadership to a next level of evolution – it takes us from the era of leadership as *influence and meaning* to an era of leadership as *emergence*. Complexity theory allows us to focus on generative processes of adaptive leadership and on the administrative and enabling leaders' functions in creating and enabling conditions that promote these generative processes. Like traditional leadership, it recognizes the need for growth and profitability, but it adds a dimension beyond simply directing these outcomes. It explains the *dynamics* that produce adaptive outcomes through which growth and profitability may be realized. It suggests that leadership theory needs to recognize not only manager-led transformations but also organizationally-generated adaptations and innovation. It does this by acknowledging not only the formal (bureaucratic/administrative) functions of management but also the informal (complexity) dynamics of emergent *adaptive* leadership.

Bureaucratic and complex adaptive systems are intimately intertwined in any given organization. They are entangled by function (some departments may be production-oriented while others are knowledge-oriented, for example), within functions (departments may be generally oriented toward missions but specifically free to pursue initiatives and critique authority), and by individuals (certain individuals might be encouraged, because of their skills and disposition, to explore and create while others are encouraged toward consensual behavior). This suggests that organizations should manage this entanglement to tailor strategies to the situation and to enable complex behavior within vision-oriented systems to foster complex adaptive behavior within knowledge-producing systems. Complexity leadership also implies a different function of administrative leaders in complex organizations. It suggests roles that appreciate emergent change, more subtle control and coordination strategies, and the potency of indeterminate vision for maintaining flexible organizations.

In sum, complexity leadership provides a perspective grounded in the physical sciences rather than the social sciences (and human relations models). It moves us away from a focus on the hierarchical, managerial leader to a view of leadership as the management (and creation) of emergence. Yukl (1999) describes an alternative perspective to traditional leadership models as one that defines leadership as a shared process of enhancing the collective and individual capacity of people to accomplish their roles effectively. Complexity leadership advocates and elaborates upon just such a collective process of leadership.

PART II
MATHEMATICAL AND COMPUTATIONAL MODELING OF LEADERSHIP

CHAPTER NINE
MATHEMATICAL AND COMPUTATIONAL MODELS OF LEADERSHIP: PAST AND FUTURE

James K. Hazy, William P. Millhiser & Daniel Solow

This chapter explores the approaches, results and research potential of various mathematical and computer modeling techniques that have been applied to leadership research. First, each technique that has been used to date is described as background so that the reader can appreciate their strengths and limitations. Next, each of the studies and applications that have appeared to date is briefly described providing a complete, albeit high-level, sense of progress in the field. As is described, the research has touched several levels of analysis, including individuals, dyads, groups, and the organization itself. Finally, the potential of these methods and their contribution to a new paradigm in leadership research are discussed.

James K. Hazy is an Associate Professor, Department of Management, Marketing, and Decision Sciences at the School of Business, Adelphi University, Garden City, NY. His research interests include organizational leadership, leadership effectiveness metrics, complex systems in social science, and computational organizational theory. He has published numerous journal articles, book chapters and proceedings' papers. With over 25 years of senior management experience at AT&T, Ernst & Young, LLP and other firms before entering academia, he received his doctorate with distinguished honors from the George Washington University and MBA in Finance with distinction for the Wharton School of the University of Pennsylvania.

Will Millhiser is an Assistant Professor in the Department of Management at the City University of New York's Baruch College. Prior to this, he held a visiting appointment at Case Western Reserve University where he received a PhD in Operations Research. In addition to studying interdependence in human organizations, other research interests include capacity and revenue management in various manufacturing and service operations as well as the optimal control of queuing systems. In an earlier life, Will was an industrial engineer (BS, Lehigh University) who worked at AT&T Corporation during the "golden" (pre-Internet) age of long-distance telecommunications. He lives with his wife Camila in New York City's Chelsea district.

Daniel Solow is Associate Professor of Operations, Department of Operations, Weatherhead School of Management at Case Western University in Cleveland Ohio. Professor Solow has a PhD in Operations Research from Stanford University, and his research interests focus on using mathematical models, analysis and computer simulations to study how properties emerge in complex adaptive systems with applications to teams and leadership in organizations. He also conducts research in linear, combinatorial and nonlinear optimization.

Introduction

Mathematical and computational modeling has become increasingly popular in many of the social sciences: economics, sociology, ecology, and management. Although some promising inroads have been made, surprising little has been done thus far in leadership research. We think this will change. As we explore in this chapter, the field of complexity science has provided new tools and theoretical foundations. The studies described in these pages give us confidence that a robust field of mathematical and computational leadership theory will emerge to support the broader field of complex systems leadership explored in this volume.

To begin, we provide an overview of the mathematical and computational theory that is used to support leadership research. Next, drawing upon work done previously by one of the authors (Hazy, 2007a), we briefly describe studies that have appeared to date, including those in this volume. The results are then synthesized into a discussion of how this developing field may ultimately contribute to the emerging theory of leadership in complex systems.

Terminology from the study of complex systems is used throughout the chapter. In that regard, a complex system is considered as a collection of individual "agents." The agents represent the individual components of the complex system and might typically be thought of as individuals in a business organization. However, the term "agents" should be interpreted here in the broadest sense – for example, the agents in a model of corporate decision making are the individual decisions that must be made; the agents in the Internet are computers; the agents in the brain are neurons, and so on. Whatever the agents are, it is their highly nonlinear interactions in a multi-leveled evolving environment that result in observed system behavior. Here, however, we distinguish between "interactions" that have the *potential* to alter the agents' behavior and "interdependencies" that *actually* change behaviors. That is, when agents are interdependent, their actions depend on, and are changed by, those of other agents in the system.

Background On Methods and Theoretical Foundations

The idea that organizations can be treated as open systems has its roots in system theory (von Bertalanffy, 1950) and the approach of modeling organizations using computers goes back to Simon (1957, 1962) and Cyert and March (1963). Since then, many studies looked at organizations using these methods, but their use in leadership research has only begun in the last two decades. Below is a brief discussion of the mathematical and computational theories and methods that have been used in the study of leadership. In a later section, we describe how these general methods have been applied in specific studies.

Game Theory Models

Game theory models are mathematical models used to identify the "best" sequence of strategies available to a collection of "players," such as individuals working together in an organization. Early in the 1990s, game theory researchers built upon prior theory (Rapoport, 1967) to explore the mathematics underlying the coordination of strategies among players in multi-player, multi-trial games (Calvert, 1992). In exploring these game-theory situations, emergent leader-follower dynamics became an area of focus. Researchers labeled the first mover as "the leader" in a particular multi-player game (e.g., the "battle of the sexes" or "the leadership game"). This game is characterized as having an advantage for the player who makes the first move (Calvert, 1992; Colomer, 1995; Rapoport, 1967) and who, in so doing, chooses to act as "the leader." This application of game theory to leadership provides theoretical support for many of the computational models described subsequently in this chapter.

Another type of leader-follower model used to study leadership is referred to as a "Stackelberg" game (see Fudenberg & Tirole, 1991) and works as follows. For any given strategy chosen by the leader, one determines – analytically or computationally – the best response strategy by each of the other players (often called the "followers"), who are maximizing their own individual objective functions. The leader then uses these known optimal follower responses to identify the strategy that maximizes the leader's personal objective function. A specific example of such a game follows in the section *Leadership and Central Control*.

System Dynamics Modeling

One of the oldest techniques used to study non-linear systems is dynamical systems theory. Forrester (1987) showed that organizational phenomena can be analyzed at the systems level using techniques borrowed from the study of the natural sciences. With system dynamics models, a collection of numerical values, denoted here by S_t, are used to describe the "state" of the system at time t. For example, the state at time t could include the number of individuals in the system and the degree to which each individual influences each other individual. It is then necessary to specify the "system dynamics," that is, how S_t changes over time.

When working in continuous time, ordinary and partial differential equations are used to model the instantaneous rate of change of the state at time t. Then, given some initial conditions at, say, time $t = 0$, the solution to these equations – whether in closed-form or with numerical methods – provides a method for determining the state at any given future time.

In contrast, when the model involves discrete time periods, a transition function or a set of difference equations specifies how to obtain the state S_{t+1} at the next time period $t + 1$, given S_t. For example, if the state at time t is represented by a single positive integer, then the following is an example of a closed-form transition function (the system dynamics) that specifies how to obtain the state at the next time period:

$$S_{t+1} = \begin{cases} S_t/2 & \text{if } S_t \text{ is even} \\ 3S_t+1 & \text{if } S_t \text{ is odd} \end{cases} \tag{1}$$

Given the state of the system at the initial time $t = 0$, the system dynamics are then used to see how the state evolves over time. For instance, in the foregoing example, if the system starts with $S_0 = 5$ then, using equation (1), the states of the system are $S_1 = 3(5) + 1 = 16$, $S_2 = 16 / 2 = 8$, $S_3 = 8 / 2 = 4$, $S_4 = 4 / 2 = 2$, $S_5 = 2 / 2 = 1$, and so on. Even though the system dynamics are *deterministic*, that is, the state S_{t+1} of the system at time $t + 1$ is completely determined by the state at time t, it is not clear what the state is going to be in the distant future. For example, it has been conjectured that starting with any positive integer at time 0 and using the system dynamics in equation (1), there is a future time t at which the system will be in state 1, that is, there is a time t such that $S_t = 1$. To date, mathematicians have not been able to prove this conjecture (see Solow (2000) for a discussion of this particular dynamical system). Important questions about dynamical systems include the following:

- What happens to the sequence of states of the system over time? For example, do they approach a limiting state or set of states, collectively called *attractors*?

- How sensitive is the system to initial conditions and parameters, that is, if the initial conditions or system parameters are changed slightly, does the behavior of the system change radically or remain pretty much the same?

System dynamics modeling has been shown to be useful for diagnostic purposes and has been used to explore why things often go wrong in complex systems (Dorner, 1996; Sterman, 2000).

The *NK* Model and the Performance Landscape

The *NK* model (Kauffman & Levin, 1987; Kauffman, 1993) was developed to study the effects of interdependencies in the evolution of genes in the chromosome and has subsequently been used to study a variety

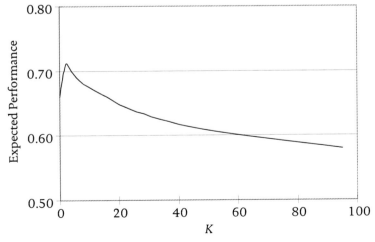

Figure 1 *The expected performance of local maxima for various levels of interaction K in the NK model when N = 96.*

of organizational problems (see Sorenson, 2002; Chang & Harrington, 2006 for surveys), including leadership, as discussed subsequently here. The primary question that the *NK* model addresses is how system performance varies with the number of interdependencies among the agents in a complex system. A brief description of that model with its primary results is given now; a more detailed description is in the appendix to this chapter.

In a general setting of the *NK* model, a complex system is viewed as a collection of *N* agents. However, for each of the *N* positions in the system, it is assumed that there are two agents, numbered 0 and 1, available for each position, with the understanding that the two agents available for one position are different from the two agents available for every other position. A complex system is obtained by choosing one of the two available agents for each position i = 1, ..., *N* and is represented as an *N*-vector $\mathbf{x} = (x_1, ..., x_N)$, in which $x_i = 0$ means that agent 0 is chosen for position i and $x_i = 1$ means that agent 1 is chosen for position i. Once a system is formed, the chosen agents interact in complex ways that ultimately determine how well the system performs. The performance of system $\mathbf{x}$ is modeled as a real number $p(\mathbf{x})$ between 0 and 1, with numbers closer to 1 indicating better performance. In determining $p(\mathbf{x})$, it is assumed that each position i contributes some amount, denoted $p_i(\mathbf{x})$, to the overall performance. Then $p(\mathbf{x})$ is taken to be the average of the performance contributions of the individual agents:

$$p(\mathbf{x}) = [p_1(\mathbf{x}) + ... + p_N(\mathbf{x})] / N \qquad (2)$$

The primary contribution of the *NK* model is the inclusion of a controllable *interdependency parameter K* whose value represents the number of other agents in the system that affects the performance contribution of each agent (see the appendix for details). For a fixed value of *K* between 0 and *N* − 1, the performance contribution of each agent is generated as a uniform random number between 0 and 1. For given values of *N* and *K*, the collection of all 2^N system configurations that can be formed, together with their performances as computed by using equation (2) and choosing random numbers from a uniform 0 - 1 distribution as the value for each individual contribution, constitute the *performance landscape*. The objective is to find the system $\mathbf{x}$ whose performance is best, that is, whose performance $p(\mathbf{x})$ is the largest. This goal, while not achieved in general, is approached by starting with an arbitrary initial system $\mathbf{x}$ and generating a sequence of systems – each of which has better performance than its predecessor system – by replacing the agent in exactly one position of the system, until no further improvement can be obtained by a single replacement in any of the *N* positions. The final system thus obtained is referred to as a *local maximum system*.

Through analysis and computer simulations, Kauffman was able to determine how the performance of a local maximum system varies with the amount of interdependence. As shown in Figure 1, those results indicate that, for large *N*, and for small non-zero values of the interdependence parameter *K*, the expected performance of a local maximum system exceeds the performance of the system when the agents have no interdependence ($K = 0$), which works out to be 2/3. But then, as K increases further beyond a value of peak performance, the expected performance of a local maximum system decreases toward 1/2, in what Kauffman refers to as the *complexity catastrophe*. A formal explanation of the causes of the complexity catastrophe, as well as ways to attenuate it, are presented in Solow, *et al.* (1999b). Many modifications and extensions to the *NK* model are found in Solow, *et al.* (1999a) and Solow, *et al.* (2000).

Each application of the *NK* model involves interpreting the system, the agents and the performance contributions in the context of a specific problem. For example, in one application, a system **x** consists of an organizational team consisting of *N* interdependent individuals (the agents) in which $p_i(\mathbf{x})$ is the performance of individual *i* on team **x** when that individual's performance depends on *K* other individuals on the team.

Network Models

A *network* consists of a finite collection of circles, called *nodes*, that represent physical items in a problem, together with a collection of lines, called *arcs*, each of which connects selected pairs of nodes to indicate a relationship between the objects represented by those nodes. As an example, the *NK* model can be thought of as a network in which there is one node for each of the *N* agents and each agent *i* (node) is connected by *K* arcs to the *K* other agents (nodes) that affect the performance of agent *i*. In addition, a numerical value of interest can be associated with each node and/or arc. Using the above example, in the network representation of the *NK* model, associated with each agent (node) is a performance contribution. Given such a network, one can ask a variety of questions of interest, and the goal is to provide efficient analytical or algorithmic solutions. One application to leadership, as described here in the section *Leader-follower dynamics with many agents,* is a network model that shows that when agents receive advice from other agents, aggregates of agents can form and follow the influence of a single agent (the "leader") when they make individual decisions.

Computational Organization Theory: Agent-Based Modeling

In the mid 1990s, computational organization science (Carley & Prietula, 1994) began to emerge. This theoretical formalism built upon Simon's (1976) notion of bounded rationality provided an organization-science context for agent-based modeling in organizational settings (Carley, 1992). Although not originally used in leadership research, it has been shown in the years since that, when collections of agents perform specific tasks, those agents who find themselves overwhelmed by copious interactions at the center of the activity can exhibit behaviors that might be considered leadership (Carley & Ren, 2001).

Agent-based modeling is a type of discrete simulation that does not rely on a model with an underlying equation, but can nonetheless be represented formally. In agent-based simulation, the individual entities (e.g., workers, managers, or decision-making units) are represented directly rather than by their density or concentration. The agents are modeled to possess an internal state and a set of behaviors, or rules, that determine how the agent's state is updated from

Researcher(s)	Year	Modeling technique	Theoretical basis	Key modeling results
Micro leadership: The leader-follower relationship				
Vroom & Jago Vroom	1988 2000	Expert system	Contingent leadership	Normative software-based decision support tool to help managers determine a leadership strategy, depending upon the situation
Calvert	1992	Not computer based	Game theory	Explored the role of coordinated action in multiplayer, multi-round games
Hubler & Pines	1994	Agent-based model	Non-linear dynamical systems control theory	When two agents each attempt to predict and actively train the environment, a stable leader-follower situation emerges as optimal for each
Colomer	1995	Not computer based	Game theory	Exploring the "leader game," a variation of the "battle of the sexes" game, demonstrates that acting first causes de-facto leader-follower behaviors to occur
Phelps & Hubler	2006	Agent-based Model	Non-linear dynamical systems control theory	With multiple agents, when the benefits of cooperation to a single agent interact with a peer pressure parameter, a state change occurs from self-interested agent behavior to cooperative behavior.
Meso-leadership: Individuals in collectives, groups and teams				
Carley & Ren	2001	Agent-based modeling and networks	Computational organization theory	Examined the conditions within organizational networks whereby heterogeneous agent situations might enable leader-follower relationships to emerge
Schreiber & Carley	2004 2005 2006	Agent-based modeling and dynamic network analysis	Computational organization theory	Found differences in team network configuration and performance outcomes when different leader style (directive versus participative) was used by the agent in the facilitator or leader-role
Anghel, Toroczkai, Bassler & Korniss	2003	Agent-based modeling and networks	Game theory social network theory	Examined the emergence of scale-free advice networks that enable a small number of agents to influence the decision of many agents in the aggregate
Dal Forno & Merlone	2006	Lab experiment & Agent-based Model	Team/groups	Demonstrated differential success of leadership styles due to sorting of followers among teams based upon different attitudes and behaviors of team leaders.

Author(s)	Year	Model	Theory	Description
Solow, Leenawong; Solow, Piderit, Burnetas & Leenawong	2003 2005	NK model	Mathematics and random network theory	Explored how leadership can improve performance and counteract interaction catastrophes in teams
Rivkin & Siggelkow; Siggelkow & Rivkin	2003 2005 2006	NK model/ agent-based modeling	Top management teams and organizational design	The activity of a vertical hierarchy, how decisions are decomposed, incentives, abilities and communication flows—all influence potential performance of a top management team; what is best varies depending upon the needs of stability and the search
Black & Oliver; Black, King & Oliver; Black, Oliver, Howell & King	2004 2005 2006	Agent-based model	Context-for-learning	Examined how leader agents with different leadership profiles affect the learning of groups; group level feedback to individual learning also examined.
Jiang & Burton	2002	Discrete event simulation	Contingency theory	The right match between leader expertise and team objectives positively affects outcomes
Macro-leadership: Organization level				
Solow & Szmerekovsky	2006	NK Model and Agent-based model	Mathematics and random network theory	Examines the relative benefits of centralized versus decentralized control/leadership depending upon conditions in the environment.
Jacobson & House	2001	System dynamics	Charismatic leadership theory	Modeled followers identifying with, adopting, and committing to a vision, and then abandoning it as bureaucracy takes hold
Hazy	2003 2004a 2004c 2005 in press	System dynamics	Complex adaptive systems, organizational capabilities and resource-based view.	Modeled the functional demands of a leadership process on a non-linear dynamical social system; showed how leadership activities function to influence the adaptation of an organizational system in its exploitation and exploration of a changing environment
Davis	2005	System dynamics	Routinization of charisma theory (Trice & Beyer, 1993)	Modeled five elements involved in the routinization of charisma
Spada	2007	Agent-based Model	Model of Bureaucracy and Meritocracy	Modeled agents in an ideal bureaucracy to determine the potential for the emergence of a meritocracy and agent mobility up and down the hierarchy based upon performance

Table 1 *A Typology of Computer Models of Leadership*

one time-step to the next, usually based on how the agent interacts with other agents. Agent models that use a genetic algorithm (Holland, 1995) or some other learning process can change their rules over time and thus adapt to a changing environment. Sophisticated models with several types of agents, including ones with nested functions, are sometimes called "multi-agent models." When agents and their network connections are tracked and analyzed, the approach can be called *dynamic network analysis*, a technique that is described in detail elsewhere in this volume (Schreiber & Carley, 2006).

Hybrid Modeling

Because each of the above techniques offers distinct perspectives, increasingly, two or more approaches are combined into hybrid models. For example, the combination of a genetic algorithm (Holland, 1995) and an agent-based model was described above. In addition, *NK* and other network models have been combined with agent-based models to explore organizational design (Carley & Ren, 2001; Rivkin & Siggelkow, 2003). Yet another hybrid model was created by Hubler and Pines (1994), in which they developed an agent-based model that shows, with a non-linear dynamical system, the "first mover" advantage in the leader-follower relationship. These models and others are described in the next section. As modeling becomes more widely used in leadership research, hybrid models that use combinations of the approaches described here, as well as other possible techniques like neural network modeling, are expected to become more common.

Models Published to Date

Although many aspects of human organizations have been studied using computational methods, the field of leadership and management has received much less attention (Hazy, 2007b). This may be because, until recently, the leadership field has focused almost exclusively on individual and dyadic processes in an effort to understand and improve leadership in organizations (i.e., competencies or behaviors of individuals as they influence one another). Because related research questions include issues of individual and collective cognition, interpretation, and nuanced communication, their exploration is not easily addressed through computer modeling. Some progress has been made, however. Models of leadership that have been developed to date are described below and are summarized in Table 1.

Expert Systems as Decision Support for Managers

The earliest research that linked leadership and computing involved the development of an expert system to provide advice on leadership decisions (Vroom & Jago, 1988). This work built upon original research by Vroom and Yetton (1973) that was used to develop a knowledge base. However, this earliest leadership software implementation was designed not to study leadership, but rather to help leaders choose courses of action in particular situations. Burton and Obel (2002) also developed a knowledge base and expert system that recommends leadership action for a given situation. Although the decision support system

(DSS) approach to computer modeling continues, it is outside the scope of this article.

The Leader-Follower Relationship

If computational modeling is to become a useful approach for leadership research, it is essential to understand the critical relationship between individuals (i.e., agents) and how these interactions approximate the leader-follower relationship in human interaction systems. Relevant pioneering computer models follow.

A Two-Agent Leader-Follower Model

In the earliest computer model to describe the intricate interdependencies between leaders and followers, Hubler and Pines (1994) simulated an environment wherein agents attempt to predict and influence the state of the environment. They found that a natural cooperative association, called a *leader-follower relationship,* develops between two agents when both attempt to predict the environment.

For purposes of the Hubler and Pines (1994) model, the environment is assumed to change over time along a simple logistics map. To build their models, the agents draw upon past experience, build an analytical model of the environment and predict its state at the next time step. After that time step, agents compare their predictions to experience and attempt to improve their models.

An agent can also attempt to change the environment in an effort to make it more predictable by emitting a control signal into the environment. If that signal is of sufficient power and of sufficiently similar dynamics (i.e., what the authors call *goal dynamics*) to the environment, the environment will resonate with the signal and adopt its state, called the *entrained* state. Entrainment is not always successful. Success depends upon the interplay between the specific dynamics of the environment and the goal dynamics of the control signal. As an agent's signal becomes more complex, the potential for the environment to become entrained to the signal increases. Thus, for each agent acting alone, becoming active and emitting a complex or even chaotic control signal is the best strategy for the agent to improve its prediction performance. Since the agent controls the environmental state, the agent can predict that state.

When two or more agents are embedded in the same environment, the situation is more complicated, although models with more than two agents were not discussed. With two agents, there are essentially three possibilities: both agents can be passive, each trying independently and passively to predict the environment; one can be passive and the other active, the latter emitting a control signal; or both can be active and compete with one another to entrain the environment according to each agent's individual control signal. During any given simulation, the period when both are passive is relatively short because eventually one agent, the first mover, will attempt to actively control the environment. Whichever goes first (i.e., called the *leader*), the other is then in an environment that includes the perturbations initiated by the leader. The second agent can thus either choose to remain passive (and thus try to predict the entrained environment) or can become active.

If the second agent becomes active, that agent attempts to overwhelm the training signal of the first in an effort to force the environment to resonate with its signal. What ensues can lead to an inefficient competitive dynamic that hurts both agents' prediction accuracy. When both are active, the agent who attempts to entrain the environment with more complex goal dynamics captures the environment and maintains the role of signal emitter or "leader." This remains true as long as the goal dynamics are not chaotic. Thus, the two agents adjust the relevant parameter in their respective signals to trade control with increasingly complex goal dynamics. In so doing, they "lead" the system through multiple bifurcations to the point where the system is about to bifurcate and converge toward a "strange" structural attractor (Allen & Strathern, 2003). In other words, they lead the system to what might be called "the edge of chaos." When both agents are active, the most stable leader-follower relationship is the one in which the ultimate leader agent emits a signal with goal dynamics "at the edge of chaos." The follower agent is thus unable to take control, returns to a passive, follower state and learns to predict the environment as entrained by the leader agent. Of course, this relatively stable situation can change if the environment changes.

Phelps and Hubler (2006, 2007 - this volume) extended this idea to multiple agents and explored the dynamics wherein individual agents choose to "join" a group that is pursuing a common strategy or program of action. In these models they found a bifurcation point occurred - a relatively rapid change from a condition where agents acted in their own narrow self interest to one where the agents cooperated in a common purpose - after a time delay, when even a single agent had a reason to cooperate and where there was sufficient peer pressure to participate.

These studies demonstrate the possible interaction dynamics that may account for the phase shift from individual agents acting independently to one where agent actions are highly correlated around a program of action. These results will help researchers identify when they are observing "leadership" among agents.

Although these results are abstract, they have important implications for leadership theory. First, with respect to predicting the environment, a stable leader-follower relationship has a fitness advantage vis-à-vis inter-agent competition in complex environments. Second, this research provides evidence that organizing patterns among agents might experience a type of natural stability with conditions just before the edge of chaos, an assertion made by other authors (Kauffman, 1995). Finally, it supports the notion that a level of inherent fitness advantage exists for agents who are susceptible to influence from other agents, a trait Simon (1990) called *docility*. Cooperation is a more efficient arrangement than continually competing for control of an environment that is perceived to be complex. Once formed, collectives of cooperating individuals that follow a common program of action as described by Phelps and Hubler (2006; 2007 - this volume) form a relatively stable state for the system.

Leader Agents in Defined Task Environments

In an effort to advance computational modeling in organization science, Carley, Prietula and their colleagues began modeling organizations with agents who interact in ways that are consistent with organization theory. They called their approach *computational organization theory* (Carley & Gasser, 1999; Carley & Prietula, 1994). In this tradition, Carley and Svoboda (1996) modeled organizational learning and adaptation at two levels of analysis: the individual agent and the organization. In their formulation, organization-level adaptation is assumed to reflect leadership decisions that implement "restructuring strategies" (p. 141), but leadership was not explicitly modeled.

Later, these models included network theory. An approach called Meta-Matrix formalism more fully described the relationships among agents, tasks, knowledge, and resources, and specified the dynamics of organizing, organization designs, and performance (Carley & Krackhardt, 1999; Carley & Ren, 2001; Carley, et al., 2000a; Krackhardt, 1994; Krackhardt & Carley, 1998). In a series of studies (Carley, 1997; Carley & Krackhardt, 1999; Carley & Ren, 2001; Carley, et al., 2000a; Carley, et al., 2000b), the researchers showed that certain agents in important, central network positions were likely to develop certain leader-like characteristics, as described below.

Using their agent-based models, Carley and colleagues explored organizational designs in various task environments (Carley, 1992; Carley & Prietula, 1994; Carley & Ren, 2001; Carley & Svoboda, 1996; Katz & Kahn, 1978). Their objective was to determine which designs led to optimal performance and which were optimized for adaptation (Carley & Ren, 2001; Carley et al., 2000a; Krackhardt, 1994; Krackhardt & Carley, 1998). Not surprisingly, they found the optimal design for each model to be quite different. In this context, one rather complex metric, called *cognitive demand*, takes into account the centrality of the agent (i.e., the number of tasks, resources, and other agent interactions that agents must navigate in order to perform a role). This measure, it was argued, is a predictor of emergent leadership in agents because agents in these roles are likely to shed connections (e.g., by assigning tasks), and thus alter the structure of the network.

More generally, these results (Carley & Ren, 2001; Carley, et al., 2000a) follow from the emergence of positional heterogeneity among agents; in particular, heterogeneity with respect to the cognitive demand metric among various agents. The authors described empirical results that imply that agents with high cognitive demand would begin to assign tasks, resources, and agent interactions to others in an effort to maintain approximate parity in work load, and to minimize bottlenecks. To the extent this type of delegation is perceived to be an indicator of a leader-follower relationship among agents, this research provides a context for the emergence of these leadership actions among heterogeneous agents.

To explore these questions further, Schreiber and Carley (2004, 2005, 2006, 2007 - this volume) tested the idea that different styles used by the leader agent in these high cognitive demand locations might result in observable differences in the resulting dynamic network structure and performance outcomes.

In their model, the researchers used observed data from NASA teams. They defined two groups of leader agents: those who acted with a directive leadership style and those who acted with a participative leadership style. The simulation was run, and the resulting network configuration and outcomes were observed over time.

Schreiber and Carley (2004, 2005, 2006, 2007 - this volume) found that, when the leader agent was designated as participative, additional highly centralized nodes within the team resulted. This was in contrast with a directive leader-agent, in whose team only the leader agent was highly centralized. Furthermore, they found that, for the specific situation modeled, a participative leadership style outperformed a directive leadership style, even when the knowledge sets of the leader agents were equivalent. These results imply a possible relationship between the nature of the leader-follower interaction, the observable network structure that emerges, and the performance outcomes for the team.

The approaches described in this section make the assumption that a defined set of tasks to be accomplished exists, and that leadership is determined exogenously and embodied as an assigned role. A complexity-science perspective would suggest that it is more likely that "leadership" is a result of agent interactions, an artifact that is interpreted by the agents as "leadership." Even with the simplifying assumption of an assigned "formal" leader, however, these agent models shed light on the dynamics of human systems, and thus make a significant contribution.

Leader-Follower Dynamics With Many Agents

An important area of study is the emergence and subsequent persistence of leader agents among groups of individuals. What is it that enables one agent to recruit followers and sustain a group of loyal members over time? Dal Forno and Merlone (2006; 2007 - this volume) address this problem in an agent based model that uses laboratory data to explore why some agents effectively recruit and retain followers.

How Leaders Recruit and Maintain Followers: The Dal Forno and Merlone (2006; 2007 - this volume) simulation looked at leader agents that exhibited different categories of behaviors. To determine what leader and follower characteristics lead to persistent leader-led groups, they explored how a collection of heterogeneous agents organized groups around agents with different leadership characteristics, based upon data gathered in laboratory experiments.

In particular, leaders were modeled to distribute resources in three ways: They are "fair" if they distribute rewards according to an even formula, "heuristic" if they distribute rewards such that followers receive less that an even share, or "competitive" if they start out with the heuristic reward distribution but adjust reward distribution according to their success at collecting followers, giving out less reward to followers as the group gets bigger. Followers could be either "obedient" or "free riders" and would choose their leaders based upon their attitude toward the leader which changed according to experience. Certain leaders could punish followers who acted as free riders. The results of their analysis are contingent on the specifics. In general, they specified situations where followers collect around a small number of leaders, in fact sometimes a single leader, in a persistent configuration. As one example, a "punishing fair leader" tended to become the sole leader when competing with other "fair leaders" who do not punish free riders. The punishing fair leader is more productive and therefore can successfully recruit and retain followers.

The Emergence of Hierarchy: Rather than focus on a defined set of tasks, agent-based modeling has also been used in conjunction with game theory and social network theory in simulation. Anghel, *et al.* (2004) showed that, when playing the minority game (described below), if agents are allowed to receive advice from other agents, aggregates of agents can emerge and follow the influence of a single agent as they make individual decisions. This is relevant because it may provide the backdrop wherein micro-states of leader-follow interactions aggregate to create system level effects.

In their model, Anghel, *et al.* (2004) assumed a substrate wherein the underlying social network was characterized by a *small-world* social network (Barabasi, 2002; Granovetter, 1973). Small-world networks have the characteristic that each agent tends to have many dense network ties with a relatively small local group. These local networks are then connected by relatively few longer, but weaker, ties. In this model, agents in a social network engaged in the multi-player minority game, commonly used to model financial markets in game theory research. This game is played when many agents each choose between two alternatives (e.g., heads or tails). Once the choices are tabulated, the agents in the minority win. This simulates a bidding process wherein the agent is choosing to buy or sell a security. By being in the minority (e.g., a seller), the agent gains a pricing advantage because there are more buyers than sellers, and thus the seller gains a higher price. In the Anghel, *et al.* model, agents can choose to follow another agent's advice. To make such decisions, agents can track the performance of the agents from whom they might take advice.

Anghel, *et al.* (2004) found that, unlike the underlying small-world social network, the advice network that develops is scale-free, namely, the advice of a small number of agents drives almost all of the decisions taken by other agents. Scale-free networks often arise when agents can choose their connections based upon experience and have the characteristic of conforming to power laws in which there are relatively few agents who have the most connections in the network, some agents who have slightly fewer connections, and so on, with the bulk of the agents having very few connections. An example of a power-law distribution is wealth distribution in a country where relatively few people have great wealth and a large number have little wealth. Other examples of scale-free networks include the World Wide Web and collaboration networks among academic researchers (Barabasi, 2002).

These results are potentially important for three reasons. First, they bring together game theory, network theory, and notions about leadership in the context of agent-based modeling. Second, they provide insights about the meso-level effects that might enable individual agents, or leaders, to leverage their unique position in a network to influence aggregates of agents to enable action in concert. Finally, they hint at persistent aggregates of agents in a system context that can potentially be studied in their own right. These aggregates may, for example, provide selection advantages as hierarchical components of the system within an "architecture of complexity" (Simon, 1962), and thus provide a mechanism wherein system level processes could support the functional demands placed upon the leadership process by the social system.

Leadership, Bureaucracy and Meritocracy: As organizations become larger they also become increasingly complicated as well as complex. Most collections of individuals that are of interest to researchers and practitioners are actually groups embedded within a larger organization or organizations. These large organizations and their subordinate groups have traditionally been understood in the context of bureaucracies (Weber, 1958). As such, a complex systems theory of leadership cannot ignore the reality of bureaucratic life; it must include it within a complex systems framework.

Later in this volume, Spada explores this potentiality using a simple model in which self-interested agents act within the context of a bureaucracy while following the basic precepts of the complex adaptive systems paradigm. In the model, agents that are initially homogeneous come to utilize heterogeneous reasoning skills depending upon their position in the hierarchy, some positions requiring higher level reasoning than others. The bureaucracy evolves as agents achieve levels of hierarchy based upon their performance, and this in turn relates to their highest level of reasoning skills. In other words, what is modeled would appear to be a meritocracy that Weber (1958) suggested would result from an ideal bureaucracy. In his model, Spada looked at the reality of agent mobility across levels of hierarchy within such a bureaucratic system and found structural limitations even to this ideal formulation of a bureaucracy. Indeed, he found that agent mobility across levels declines over time. In the future, when models such as this are connected to empirical data, the effectiveness of real world bureaucracies may be improved through a better understanding of leadership in complex systems.

Work Groups and Teams: How Leaders Impact Teams

Beyond the dynamics of leader-follower interactions, researchers are interested in the ways in which variations in a designated team leader's characteristics and behavior affect team performance. In the last few years, several models have been developed to explore this question.

Leader Expertise and Team Performance

Jiang and Burton (2002) developed a discrete event simulation model to explore the assumptions of contingency theory with respect to different levels of various factors that influence team performance. In the model, Jiang and Burton examined a specific team and the effect of nine combinations of factors (e.g., the level of the leader's expertise) on the performance of the team.

The group under study, a team charged with trading global fixed income securities, had a well-defined task. The nature of the leader's expertise was assumed to dominate other leadership traits. Specifically, the authors hypothesized that, if the leader's expertise fit with the team's task, performance would be high; if the leader's expertise conflicted with the team's task, performance would be impaired. Two other contingency factors were considered to determine fit: variations across a flat versus a hierarchical team structure, and various combinations of communications techniques across a continuum of computer-aided communications and face-to-face communications.

Jiang and Burton (2002) found a relationship between the leader's expertise and the team's performance. Furthermore, they compared the alternative combinations with the one used most often by investment banks (e.g., a hierarchical organization with high levels of face-to-face communication and a leader with "medium" expertise.) Their simulation suggests that higher performing structural alternatives exist.

Cooperation, Motivation and Team Performance

Solow and Leenawong (2003) and Solow, *et al.* (2005) extended Kauffman's *NK* model (1993) to explore how what might be called "motivational" and "cooperational" leadership skills might improve team performance.

The NK Model and Team Replacement: In their models, as in the *NK* model described previously, Solow and Leenawong (2003) and Solow, *et al.* (2005) assume that a team consists of *N* job positions. For each position, it is necessary to choose one of two available qualified individuals (the "agents") who are then interdependent on *K* other members of the team. Following the *NK* model, each individual contributes some amount to team performance, which is computed as the average of the individual contributions. Unlike the *NK* model, however, these individual contributions are not simply generated as random numbers. Rather, each individual has a range of *possible* contribution values. The *actual* contribution within this range is then determined by the leader, based either on the leader's motivational skill (Solow, *et al.*, 2005) or ability to instill cooperation among workers (Solow and Leenawong, 2003). With these performance contributions, teams evolve through the one-replacement heuristic (see the appendix) in which a sequence of teams, each with better performance than that of its predecessor team, is generated by replacing the individual in one position of the current team (Solow, *et al.* 2002). The new team becomes the current team as long as such a replacement results in improved performance. Details of how individual performance is computed and the resulting managerial implications from both the motivational and cooperational leadership models are now described.

The Impact of Motivational Leadership: In Solow, *et al.* (2005), the role of motivational leadership is modeled by first assuming that each team member x_i can contribute to performance anywhere within a range $[a_i, b_i]$, where $0 \le a_i \le b_i \le 1$. The lower bound a_i and upper bound b_i are generated as the minimum and maximum, respectively, of two random numbers drawn from a uniform distribution from 0 to 1 and whose values depend on the K individuals whom affect the performance of x_i, as in the *NK* model. The actual performance of x_i within the range $[a_i, b_i]$ then depends on the working relationship between that individual and the leader. This relationship is modeled as a real number r_i with $0 \leq r_i \leq 1$, in which values closer to 1 indicate a better relationship with the leader. The actual performance of individual x_i, namely $p_i(\mathbf{x})$, is then computed as follows:

$$p_i(\mathbf{x}) = (1 - r_i)\, a_i + r_i\, b_i \qquad (3)$$

Observe that when $r_i = 0$, the relationship with the leader is poor and, from equation (3), $p_i(\mathbf{x}) = a_i$, indicating that individual x_i is unmotivated and performs at the lowest possible level. At the other extreme, if $r_i = 1$, the relationship with the leader is good and equation (3) yields $p_i(\mathbf{x}) = b_i$, indicating that individual x_i has been motivated to perform at the highest possible level.

The authors show that if these relationships are generated uniformly between 0 and 1, then the performance of the team is the same as if there were no leader. Thus, they develop a method for generating relationships that are based on the motivational skill μ and standard deviation σ of the skill of the leader. As the skill of the leader increases from 0, relationships are, on average, closer to 1. In their model, the standard deviation reflects the consistency of the leader's relationship with the team members. For example, if $\sigma = 0$, then the leader has the same relationship with each team member. As σ increases, the leader's relationships vary more and more from one person to the next.

This model shows the expected result that, as the skill of the leader increases, all else being equal, the average performance of a local maximum team increases. Also, as in the *NK* model, this motivation leadership model suffers from the complexity catastrophe of decreasing performance associated with increasing levels of interdependence among team members. However, through the use of mathematical analysis and computer simulations, the following new insights into the role of motivational leadership on team performance are obtained from this model. First, choosing the best leader from a group that has no particular motivational skill can improve performance of small (but not large) teams. Second, skillful leaders are more likely to improve team performance than controlling the amount of worker interdependence. Finally, higher variability of motivational skill is beneficial to performance when the leader has a low skill level. This benefit decreases as the amount of interdependence among members of the team increases. In contrast, for leaders with higher skill, having higher variability in that skill is detrimental to performance, regardless of the amount of interdependence" (Solow, et al., 2005: 6). Millhiser and Solow (2007) subsequently explored when teams grow too large for effective motivation from leaders.

The Impact of Cooperational Leadership: In Solow and Leenawong (2003), three different models of cooperational leadership are provided although only one is described here. Like their work on motivational leadership, this cooperational model starts by first assuming that each team member x_i can contribute to performance anywhere with a range $[a_i, b_i]$, where $0 \le a_i \le b_i \le 1$. The lower bound a_i and upper bound b_i are generated as the minimum and maximum, respectively, of two uniform 0 - 1 random numbers; however, unlike their motivational leadership model, these bounds depend only on the individual x_i. The actual performance of x_i then depends on the working relationship between that individual and the K individuals on whom the performance of x_i depends. This relationship is modeled as a real number r_i with $0 \le r_i \le 1$, in which values closer to 1 indicate a better relationship with the K co-workers. The value for this relationship r_i is generated using random numbers that depend not only on x_i and the K coworkers but also on the skill μ and standard deviation σ of the leader in achieving cooperation among them. In other words, when one of the K coworkers on whom agent x_i depends is replaced, the performance-contribution range a_i to b_i does not change, but the relationship r_i between x_i and the leader does. Once the value of r_i is determined, the performance of individual x_i, namely $p_i(\mathbf{x})$, is then computed using equation (3) as in the motivational model.

Through mathematical analysis and computer simulations, the authors show that if the leader has no cooperational skill ($\mu = 0$), then the performance of the team is the same as if there were no leader at all. Also, as in the *NK* model, this model suffers from the complexity catastrophe of decreasing team performance associated increasing levels of interdependence among team members. However, as the cooperational skill of the leader increases, not only does the average performance of a local maximum team increase, but also the complexity catastrophe is attenuated. That is, a leader skilled in achieving cooperation can handle more interdependence among workers before performance deteriorates.

Taken together, the results from these models offer insights into certain aspects of team leadership. This approach captures how the motivational and cooperational skill level of leaders and the variance in the leader's application of those skills affect team performance. In addition to skilled leaders improving team performance, through these models, we learn that a role of leaders may be, in part, to minimize the otherwise detrimental effects of the complexity catastrophe. Without such modeling, these dynamics might remain hidden. However, these models are static and do not incorporate learning dynamics and how leadership reacts to change as exploration and experimentation add knowledge to the system (Allen & Strathern, 2003).

Leader's Learning Orientation and Team Context-for-Learning
Black, Oliver, Howell and King.(2006) used agent-based models to explore how leader types and group skill level interact to affect team learning. In particular, they were interested in a metric called *context-for-learning* (CFL; Black, King & Oliver, 2005). Their approach took a step beyond individual and dyadic effects. The model included a downward feedback effect, from the group level to each agent's CFL metric. In a related study, Black and Oliver (2004) looked at active versus passive leadership styles as influencers of CFL.

In these models, three types of agents were defined: the leader, the followers, and the group. The leader and the follower agents were each modeled to learn from their experiences during each time step. Their learning was determined based upon their current CFL competencies. These competencies were carried in each agent's profile and included discipline, stretch, trust, and support. The group or team was also an agent and had a CFL profile. This was calculated to be the aggregate of the group members' and leader's CFL metrics. The group level CFL also influenced the learning of followers in the group in a downward feedback loop that approximated the influence of the peer group on individual learning.

Followers also learned directly from the leader if (a) followers paid attention to the leader's behavior, and (b) the skill with which the leader exhibited appropriate behaviors as defined in the model was sufficient. Thus, the skill of the leader at executing these appropriate behaviors became a factor that influenced all of the agents' growth in the CFL metric.

Leaders were assigned scores in eight leader roles (Denison, *et al.*, 1995): aggressive achiever, abrasive coordinator, chaotic adapter, conceptual producer, drowning workaholic, extreme unproductive, master manager and peaceful team builder. Various profiles of leader skills for these roles were used in the model. The leader agent learned from experience to improve skills, but only learned in the role for which that agent had the most expertise.

Finally, the team or group, itself an agent, was assumed to learn as the group members learned. The leader's positional power and the followers' expertise power were used to apply weights when the aggregate measure for group CFL was calculated. The developmental path of the group CFL metric (the value of the metric over time) was the outcome measured in the simulation experiments described below.

The researchers (Black & Oliver, 2004; Black, *et al.*, 2006) described several findings. As was expected, different leader role profiles resulted in different group level developmental paths. Also as expected, the leader roles assumed to be more effective (e.g., Master Manager) resulted in superior rates of group development. This was true for all groups simulated, regardless of the level of group expertise. Interestingly, the variation in developmental paths across different leader roles was more pronounced when the group began with low expertise.

In summary, these results imply that the leader-group combination determines the developmental path, and that the rate of development is influenced by both the leader profile and the composition of the group.

Leadership, Centralized Control and the Top Management Team
The Question of Centralized Versus Decentralized Control

Much organizational (and systems) research has focused on centralized versus decentralized control. Consider the literatures of decentralized systems in control theory (Sandell, *et al.*,1978; Jamshidi, 1997), manufacturing (Lasdon & Schoeffler, 1966; Sethi, *et al.*, 2002), supply chain management (Bernstein & Federgruen, 2003; 2005; Bernstein & DeCroix, 2004), business strategy (Rivkin & Siggelkow, 2003), and organizational design (Malone, 1987; Malone & Smith, 1988; Siggelkow & Rivkin, 2005).

Such work has led Solow and Szmerekovsky (2007) to ask how much central control a leader should exert in a complex system. To gain insights into this question, they build a Stackelberg game-theoretic model to determine conditions under which complex systems benefit from small, moderate, and large amounts of central control. In their model, a complex system consists of a group of n agents together with a leader. The action chosen by each agent i under the influence of the leader is represented as a real number, x_i. Their collective actions, denoted by $\mathbf{x} = (x_1, ..., x_n)$, in turn affect system performance, which is represented by the real number $p^+(\mathbf{x})$, in which larger values denote better system performance. The amount of control exerted by the leader is modeled as a real number $\lambda \geq 0$, with $\lambda = 0$ corresponding to no control and increasing values of λ corresponding to increasing amounts of control. The effect of the leader exerting an amount of control λ is to impose restrictions on the actions available to agents. Within the set of restricted actions, each agent i chooses the action that maximizes that agent's personal utility function, $f_i(x)$. The resulting agent actions are represented by $\mathbf{x}(\lambda) = (x_1(\lambda), ..., x_n(\lambda))$. Thus, exerting an amount λ of control causes the agents to perform actions they might not choose to do. To account for resulting agent dissatisfaction, Solow and Szmerekovsky define overall system performance as $p(\mathbf{x}) = p^+(\mathbf{x}) - p^-(\mathbf{x})$, in which $p^-(\mathbf{x})$ is the amount of dissatisfaction associated with forcing the agents to perform the actions $\mathbf{x}$ instead of the actions the agents would choose when left alone with no control. The objective is for the leader to determine the optimal amount of control λ to exert so that the resulting agents' actions, $\mathbf{x}(\lambda)$, maximize the system performance $p(\mathbf{x}(\lambda))$.

This problem can be solved in the context of a leader-follower game. Suppose that the leader moves first by choosing some fixed amount of control λ. Given λ and a specific form of the agents' utility functions $f_i(x)$, it is sometimes possible to compute analytically the agents' (that is, the followers') actions $\mathbf{x}(\lambda)$ that maximize their utility functions. For a specific analytical form of the system performance function, those actions result in the system performance being $p(\mathbf{x}(\lambda))$. Finally, given the expression for $p(\mathbf{x}(\lambda))$, it is then possible to find the value of λ that maximizes $p(\mathbf{x}(\lambda))$.

When analytical solutions to their game are not available, Solow and Szmerekovsky use computer simulations to obtain insights such as, strong central control is optimal for systems in which coordination of the agents is needed for successful performance (for example, in the military during a war). Another of their results is that system performance can improve when the agents' goals conflict with the leader's perception of system goals in that compromise can lead to good results for the system. They also show that more skillful leaders can have fewer satisfied agents than less skillful leaders. This is because a more skillful leader may exert high levels of control to achieve what the leader correctly knows is good for the system, resulting in more dissatisfied agents than a less skilled leader who does not exert as much control over the agents.

The Special Case of the Top Management Team

A special workgroup or team, the top management team (TMT), is of critical importance to research in strategy and organizational science (Hambrick & Mason,

1984). In many ways the TMT epitomizes the centralization/decentralization question for many organizations. Only recently has the top management team been the subject of computer modeling. As mentioned earlier, in their model of the micro and macro effects of organizational learning, Carley and Svoboda (1996) described organization level leadership decisions as "restructuring strategies" (p. 141). Others (Rivkin & Siggelkow, 2003; Siggelkow & Rivkin, 2005; 2006) have continued in this direction by using agent-based modeling and the analytical techniques introduced with the *NK* model to explore structuring decisions in top management teams. Although the Rivkin and Siggelkow models are not about leadership per se, they explore the dynamics of decision making in a team context at the top of an organization; as such, they are relevant to a discussion of leadership models in organizations.

Rivkin and Siggelkow (2002; 2003) explored decisions in organizations regarding the strength and characteristics of vertical hierarchy, incentives, decomposition of decisions into departments, patterns of interdependence, and the cognitive abilities of managers. All five of these variables were explored simultaneously using a computational modeling approach. Their models (Rivkin & Siggelkow, 2002, 2003; Siggelkow & Rivkin, 2005, 2006) defined a simple hierarchy: a CEO and two subordinate managers. In their studies, each subordinate manager oversaw a subset of the organization's N interdependent decisions. At each time step, as the model ran, the subordinate managers decided whether to change any decisions under their purview and then made recommendations to the CEO. The CEO reviewed the recommendations from each subordinate and accepted the ones that best supported the overall firm. The CEO could also choose to overrule those decisions that did not support the overall firm. With this basic structure, by varying parameters, specific models of firms could be made to differ in several ways. For example, the flow of information to the CEO agent could affect that person's ability to choose whether to overrule a particular decision; incentives at the subordinate level could likewise be made to influence both decisions and the flow of information within the three-person team. How decisions were organized and decomposed among the subordinates and the cognitive abilities of the subordinates and the CEO could also be varied to influence results. One of the virtues of computer modeling is that all of these factors can be studied together, so that the complex dynamics that ensue can be explored.

In analyzing a large number of possible scenarios, Rivkin and Siggelkow (2003) found results that, as they said, "bound conventional wisdom" (p. 292). For example, they found that, as would be expected, an active vertical hierarchy could become overloaded and slow down the decision-making process. However, in situations where the interdependence of decisions was especially significant, the benefits of active management could outweigh this cost. At the same time, however, when information flows are poor and decision interdependence is high, an active hierarchy can limit long-term performance by eliminating the incubation of local alternatives that might be beneficial to the firm in the long term. As another example, their modeling confirmed that, when decisions can be decomposed completely, hierarchy has no benefits.

This research explores the dynamics of decision making at the top of a hierarchy, where presumably decisions taken affect the nature, direction and accomplishments of the organization.

Related research into the organizational design under which effective leadership occurs include Qian (1994) who explored how the amount of leadership control at various levels of a hierarchy and wages of leaders vs. subordinates lead to particular hierarchical structures. More recently, Hart and Moore (2005) provided support for why leaders should be "coordinators" (not specialists), and why pyramidal organization designs may be optimal. This research explores to the leadership of organizations to a degree. Next, we turn to research that directly addresses organization level leadership.

Leadership of Organizations

For simulating the processes and mechanisms that lead organizations in their ongoing performance and adaptation, to date, system dynamics (Sterman, 2000) has been the method of choice. This deterministic method deals analytically with large-scale features of organizations, such as the sorting of the organization's members among factions (Jacobsen & House, 2001); the growth of a descriptive factor, such as an organization's "administrative apparatus" (Davis, 2005); or an organization's success at appropriating economic rent from the environment and accumulating slack resources (Hazy, 2004a, 2004c). The models described below import dynamical systems theory to explore the evolution of emergent structures in organizations and relate the dynamics of these structures to the functional needs of the system as it sustains itself as a distinct entity within the environment.

The Charismatic Leadership Process

Jacobsen and House (2001) used system dynamics modeling (Sterman, 2000) to analyze the process of charismatic leadership in organizations. Data sets from six different charismatic leadership projects were replicated using a model and the authors' computational results supported the theory described. Specifically, Jacobsen and House (2001) described six phases in the charismatic leadership process:

1. Identification: An aspiring leader recognizes a distressed constituency, formulates a vision, and promises the constituency a better future;

2. Activity arousal: The charismatic leader challenges the constituency to bring about change;

3. Commitment: The leader demonstrates personal commitment and moves a select set of others to likewise demonstrate strong commitment to the cause. These committed elite form a significant constituency;

4. Disenchantment: The routinization of activities surrounding the cause may influence some constituents to lose their identification with the vision;

5. Depersonalization: Fewer followers are internally motivated, so different rewards are used. Some followers are likely to resent this standardization;

6. Alienation: Bureaucratization leads some to be alienated from the social structure and perhaps even from the vision. Some may leave the cause.

This six-phase charismatic leadership process is simulated by modeling an organization as a personnel-sorting algorithm. The constituency is sorted into four categories, as follows: (a) those who accept the status quo; (b) those who identify with the leader's message, but are not yet active; (c) those who are active followers; and (d) the highly committed elite. The charismatic leadership process is assumed to move people through the above buckets. The flow among the buckets is influenced by the characteristics of the leader, the status quo situation, and the emerging new vision espoused by the charismatic leader.

Using this simulation model, Jacobsen and House (2001) were able to duplicate longitudinal data collected for six leaders, each of whom was generally considered to possess charisma. For example, the dataset included information on John F. Kennedy, Lee Iacocca, and Adolf Hitler. The overall match between the simulation and the dataset exceeded 75%, providing further support for decades of charismatic leadership theory and research. The dynamics modeled related to followers' identification with and commitment to a new leadership vision over time. As such, the simulation explored the mechanism wherein leadership identifies a new vision and then catalyzes action in a new direction.

Routinization of Charisma

One aspect of the charismatic leadership process, routinization, was explored further by Davis (2005). Also using system dynamics modeling, Davis explored Trice and Beyer's (1993) theory of the routinization of charisma. This simulation model looked at how charismatic leadership develops within an organization, and how, once it develops, it is routinized within the organization's social structure (Giddens, 1984, 1993).

In his computer simulation model, Davis (2005) specified the relationships between various levels of Trice and Beyer's (1993) five elements of charisma (i.e., followers, successes, crises, solutions proposed and the leader's traits, and the level of charisma that emerged). Also modeled were levels for five elements of routinization: administrative apparatus, rites and ceremonies, continuity, a successor and traditions, and how these influenced the degree to which charisma was routinized. To support the validity of the model, the stylized facts from a case study were duplicated.

Davis (2005) used the simulation to test a series of hypotheses implied by Trice and Beyer's (1993) theory. He found support for roughly half, demonstrating the usefulness of computer models in determining the analytical adequacy of conceptual models with respect to theory. The simulation also clarified some contradictions and inconsistencies in published theory. For example, through simulation, he found that, by modeling interaction among the variables that represented the elements of charisma multiplicatively rather than additively (i.e., by making interactions non-linear), the model more robustly duplicated case data. This non-linear formulation implied that all of the factors must be present to some degree for charisma to develop. Likewise, when followers were modeled as being attracted to the leader's vision, rather than to the leader personally (again testing an inconsistency in the published theory), the results approximated the case. With respect to the routinization, as expected, the Davis model showed that routinization of charisma requires that some solutions are implemented successfully.

The above two models explored the analytical adequacy and consistency of the body of theory (McKelvey, 1999), in particular charismatic leadership theory. How organized systems sustain themselves through leadership processes is another important area that has been explored through simulation.

The Functional Demands of Organizational Leadership

None of the approaches described thus far say anything about how the organization relates to the environment or its prospects for survival. The development and configuration of organizational capabilities, and how leadership influences these processes to improve the organization's prospects for prosperity and survival (i.e., the leadership of organizations) was modeled by Hazy (2004a, 2004c) using system dynamics (Sterman, 2000).

Considering Katz and Kahn's (1978) definition of organizational leadership (i.e., that leadership is the "influential increment" over routine directives of the organization), Hazy's (2004a) model explored the potential effects that the process of organizational leadership has on an organization's potential to survive and to adapt in a changing environment. The model specified the mechanisms of this influential increment. It took as its basis the resource-based view of the firm (Barney, 1991; Peteraf, 1993) as interpreted within the context of evolutionary economics and the dynamics of organizational capabilities (Dosi, *et al.*, 2000; Makadok, 2001; Nelson & Winter, 1982; Teece & Pisano, 1994). Stylized facts from three published case studies were duplicated to offer support for the validity of the model.

The model (Hazy, 2004a) was used to explore how leadership activities support an organization's performance and adaptation. It assumed that leadership processes bias the underlying dynamics of rent approbation from the environment into the firm, the flow of information about the organization and the environment, and the flow of excess or slack resources (Cyert & March, 1963; Nohria & Gulati, 1996) within the system. Taken together, these leadership activities serve to determine and predict the state of the organization and the environment and to match the organization's capabilities to perceived opportunities, present and future. The influential increment of leadership is thus modeled as an organizational meta-capability, subject to the same evolutionary selection pressures as other organizational capabilities (Dosi, *et al.*, 2000).

The results from Hazy's (2004a, 2006) simulation showed that leadership activities that serve to increase the rate of rent approbation for the system by exploiting known rent-producing sources in the environment (i.e., activities such as motivating individuals to perform or enabling the system's convergence to an ultimate state of efficiency or effectiveness) are necessary to sustain the system. This is because these activities enable the system to maintain a basis of resources (i.e., profits) that supports the members' continued participation in the organized activity. Many of these activities might be called managerial or trans-actional leadership as they clarify task relationships, assign accountabilities and distribute rewards (Bass, 1985; Bass, 1990; Sashkin & Sashkin, 2003). On the other hand, when an organization's environment changes so that known oppor-tunities or markets decline in their rent-producing capacity, leadership activities that search or explore for potentially new sources of rent and generate variety and diversity within the system also become necessary for an organization to survive. Allen and Strathern (2003) demonstrate the importance of actions like these that increase micro-diversity in the system. As changes or variations in the system are selected and retained within the system's structure, their theory says, the system accumulates knowledge about the environment and itself. This knowledge can be used for adaptation because diversity generating activities like exploration increase the options available to the organization in the future. Thus, Hazy's model supports analytically a theory of leadership within open systems (Katz & Kahn, 1978), composed of evolving organizational capabilities (Dosi, *et al.*, 2000; Nelson & Winter, 1982; Teece, *et al.*, 1997), and in which leadership activities form an organizational capability that biases evolutionary processes. When an organization possesses this leadership capability and thus is (a) able to gather and process information about the environment and about the system itself, and is (b) able to, based upon that information, bias system processes to predict and influence the system's environment, it is better able to sustain itself and survive over time. Thus, leadership enables the organization to sustain itself as a separate entity, or as described by Maturana and Varela (1998), as a "unity" distinct from its environment (i.e., a distinct open system), and more specifi-cally, as a complex adaptive system (Hazy, 2003, 2004a, 2004b, 2004c, 2005). Similar to the charismatic leadership process described above, leadership is thus modeled as a key element of the organizing processes in human interaction sys-tems.

This research is potentially significant because it provides a framework from which to consider and evaluate the interaction of organizational leader-ship processes and individual leadership activities in the context of an underly-ing rent-producing complex adaptive system. Thus, the functional demands on leadership as a system process can be specified, and hypotheses about the effec-tiveness of the leadership process can be considered. In this way, the complete picture of leadership as an influential increment – from the many leader-follow-er micro-interactions to the aggregates of self-organizing meso-structures (e.g., groups or teams) to the mechanisms that coordinate decisions and actions for the organization as a whole – can truly come into focus.

The Future of Mathematical and Computational Modeling of Leadership

This chapter has summarized much of the work that has been done in mod-eling leadership in and of organizations and has shown the benefits of mathematical analysis and computer simulations. As we have described, leadership has been modeled at the individual and dyadic level (Hubler & Pines, 1994), the team level (Solow & Leenawong, 2003; Solow, *et al.*, 2005), and at the organizational level (Rivkin & Siggelkow, 2003; Hazy, 2004a; in press). So where does this type of research go from here?

It is, of course, possible to continue modeling leadership of organizations in much the same way as was described here. For examples, other chapters in this volume describe models that explore the emergence of leaders in groups (Phelps & Hubler, 2006), the ability of individual leaders to recruit and maintain followers (Dal Forno & Merlone, 2006), the impact of leader style on organizational networks (Schreiber & Carley, 2006), and the potential for emergent meritocracy in bureaucratic organizations (Spada, 2007). In addition, several complexity leadership theories described in the volume may also be amenable to mathematical or computational modeling. See, for example, Panzer, *et al.* (this volume), Uhl-Bien, *et al.* (2004) and Surie and Hazy (2006). Other research opportunities in this direction include modeling the span of control, leadership compensation, leadership attribution and leadership turnover. While these subjects have been studied by various economic and organizational scholars (e.g., Keren & Levhari, 1979; Weber, *et al.*, 2001), it appears that little computational work has yet been done in the complexity sciences.

Of note, however, is the realization that thus far, each research group has, for the most part, used a distinctly different mathematical and computational formalism to frame the definitions of leadership and distinct models to perform their simulations. A continuing challenge for the field, therefore, is defining a basis for a cumulative science of leadership in complex systems. This is not to say that a canonical platform is needed or even desirable at this time, but its absence remains an impediment to broad collaboration in the field, the reproducibility of results and ultimately to cumulative knowledge. We are hopeful that this discussion, and the chapters that follow in this volume, will provide a basis upon which future researchers can begin to build such a platform; however, the reader is warned that attempts to create a unified theory of complex systems have, so far, been unsuccessful.

More generally, the field should strive to create common definitions and terms for leadership, followership and their interdependencies. For example, one can consider all the various roles of leaders – as identified in (Luthans, *et al.*, 1988) and summarized in (Solow & Szmerekovsky, 2006) – to see which ones are amenable to mathematical and computer modeling. Such research would identify factors that might help leaders perform their roles better. Alternatively, data from empirical studies, for example on transformational and transactional leadership (Bass, 1985) and charismatic leadership (Conger & Kanungo, 1994), could be used to define and then model the agent characteristics that influence leader-follower dyad effectiveness.

Other aspects of organizational life associated with leadership, such as strategic decision making and sense making might also be modeled. For example, Rivkin and Sigglekow (2003) have modeled the leader as a decision maker. Other aspects of decision making might also be modeled, such as deciding how and when to allocate scarce resources to achieve a goal or how to plan and implement a strategy or vision for an organization. The organizational level influences of leadership on the above processes has been modeled (Hazy, 2004a), but much more needs to be done to uncover the relevant interactions of individual agents within the organizational "black box". More challenging work in this area might be to model simultaneously two (or more) roles of a leader or of shared leadership among multiple agents to gain insights into how these roles interact, what tradeoffs arise between these roles, the interaction on individual agents enacting them, and the network structure that defines the organization's social capital.

Yet another area with research opportunities is to create models for studying the emergence of leadership, that is, how and why leadership arises. Three such papers are included in this volume (Dal Forno & Merlone, 2006; Spada, 2007; Phelps & Hubler, 2006). Dal Forno and Merlone (2006), for example, use a computer model to identify conditions under which individuals emerge as effective leaders. Another possibility is to go back further in time and see if it is possible to provide a mathematical justification for the evolutionary emergence of leadership in early human groups (demonstrate a genetic basis, perhaps). Then, extending the concept of leadership from a single individual to a collection of managers, it might be possible to show the emergence of a hierarchical structure consisting of a CEO and various levels of management. In this volume, Spada (2007) looks at the emergence of hierarchy in bureaucracies.

Most of the work cited in this chapter uses ideas from complex systems theory to study leadership in organizations. In a later chapter in this volume, Solow and Szmerekovsky (2006) suggest that another approach is to reverse the direction and apply knowledge about organizational leadership to leadership of complex systems in general. For example, the work of Solow and Szmerekovsky (2007), discussed here in the section *Leadership and Central Control*, attempts to address the issue of how much central control is beneficial to the performance of a complex system. Are there other aspects of organizational leadership that can be transferred to the study of general complex system?

Perhaps the most important area for research using mathematical and computational models is combining them with empirical research. There are two aspects of this. On one hand, there is a need to validate these models through empirical studies. For example, with the exception of Sorenson (1997), despite its broad application in developing "thought experiments" within organization theory, little empirical evidence has been presented to support the complexity catastrophe in the NK model nor the fact that a small amount of interdependency among agents in a complex organizational system is better than no interdependence at all. On the other hand, these models have implications that can be used to generate propositions and hypotheses about real world organizations (Hazy, in press). These could be studied with empirical methods, both qualitative and quantitative. While some of the models presented here are based on empirical results, the field would benefit from greater emphasis on mathematical and computational research that is supported by, informed by and used to motivate empirical studies.

From what has been presented here, it appears that modelers in the field of leadership research will not be out of business anytime soon. We remain optimistic and strongly believe that mathematical and computational modelers will be full partners in the development of the emerging theory of leadership in complex systems.

Appendix: Detailed Description of the *NK* Model

Recall, from the section *The NK Model and the Performance Landscape*, that in a general setting of the *NK* model, a complex system is viewed as a collection of *N* agents and that for each of the *N* positions in the system, it is necessary to choose one of two available agents, numbered 0 and 1, with the understanding that the two agents available for one position are different from the two agents available for every other position. Each such complex system is represented as an *N*-vector $\mathbf{x} = (x_1, \ldots , x_N)$, in which $x_i = 0$ means that agent 0 is chosen for position *i* and $x_i = 1$ means that agent 1 is chosen for position *i*.

Once a system is formed, the chosen agents depend on each other in complex ways that ultimately determine how well the system performs. The performance of system $\mathbf{x}$, namely $p(\mathbf{x})$, is modeled as a real number between 0 and 1, with numbers closer to 1 indicating better performance. In determining $p(\mathbf{x})$, it is assumed that each position *i* contributes some amount, denoted by $p_i(\mathbf{x})$, to the overall performance and $p(\mathbf{x})$ is taken to be the average of the performance contributions of the individual agents, as was given in equation (2).

Determining the performance contributions of the individual agents in a real-world setting is often difficult, if not impossible, due in part to their complex interdependencies and the inability to isolate each agent's contribution. To avoid this challenge, performance contributions in the *NK* model are generated randomly. While any distribution on [0, 1] can be used, without an a priori reason for choosing a specific one, the uniform distribution is used. To illustrate, consider a system consisting of *N* = 3 agents. For each of the two available agents for a given position of the system, a uniform 0 - 1 random number is generated to represent what that agent's contribution would be, as summarized the following table:

Agent	Position		
	1	2	3
0	0.4	0.8	0.2
1	0.5	0.6	0.7

Table A.1 *Table of Random Performance Contributions*

Table A.1 is used to generate the performance contributions for any system. For example, consider the system $\mathbf{x} = (1, 0, 1)$. Because agent 1 is chosen for position 1, the associated performance contribution obtained from Table A.1 is 0.5. Likewise, Table A.1 indicates that agent 0 in position 2 contributes 0.8 and agent 1 in position 3 contributes 0.7. Consequently, the performance of the system using equation (2) is:

$$p(\mathbf{x}) = [p_1(\mathbf{x}) + p_2(\mathbf{x}) + p_3(\mathbf{x})] / 3 = (0.5 + 0.8 + 0.7) / 3 = 2/3.$$

In the foregoing example, each agent's performance contribution is independent of each other agent. The main contribution of the *NK* model is the inclusion of a controllable *interdependence parameter K*, whose value means that each agent's contribution depends on K other agents in the system ($0 \leq K \leq N - 1$). For simplicity, it is assumed here that the K agents to the right of the agent in position i, wrapping around if necessary, affect the contribution of agent x_i. Thus, if $K = 1$ in the foregoing numerical example, then the contribution of agent x_1 depends on x_1 and x_2, the contribution of agent x_2 depends on x_2 and x_3, and the contribution of agent x_3 depends on x_3 and x_1. In this case, a random number table such as the following is used to determine individual agent contributions:

	Position		
Agents	1	2	3
00	0.3	0.4	0.9
01	0.5	0.6	0.4
10	0.1	0.7	0.8
11	0.8	0.2	0.5

Table A.2 *Table of Random Performance Contributions when K = 1.*

For example, consider the system $\mathbf{x} = (1, 0, 1)$ with $K = 1$. Because the contribution of agent 1 in position 1 also depends on agent 0 in position 2, the associated performance contribution of 0.1 is obtained from the row labeled 10 in column 1 of Table A.2. Likewise, Table A.2 indicates that the contribution of agent 0 in position 2, which also depends on agent 1 in position 3, is 0.6. Finally, the contribution of agent 1 in position 3 also depends on agent 1 in position 1 and, from the row labeled 11 in Table A.2, is 0.5. Consequently, the performance of the system $\mathbf{x} = (1, 0, 1)$ using equation (2) is:

$$p(\mathbf{x}) = [p_1(\mathbf{x}) + p_2(\mathbf{x}) + p_3(\mathbf{x})] / 3 = (0.1 + 0.6 + 0.5) / 3 = 0.4.$$

This scheme for generating agent contributions extends to any value of the interdependence parameter K between 0 and $N-1$, but the corresponding table of random numbers requires 2^{K+1} rows. In any event, the larger the value of K, the more interdependencies there are among the agents. Thus, when $K = 0$, each agent contributes independently of every other agent. At the other extreme, when $K = N-1$, the contribution of each agent depends on all of the other $N-1$ agents in the system.

The NK model *performance landscape* consists of given values for N, K, and the table of random performance contributions for the agents. Of the 2^N possible systems that can be formed by choosing different agents for each of the N positions, the objective is to find a system $\mathbf{x}^*$ that has the best performance, as defined by equation (1).

As shown in Solow, *et al.* (2000), finding the best system in the NK model is NP-hard. This means that for large systems, in practice, it is not possible to find the best configuration. Instead, one attempts to find a system whose performance, though not necessarily optimal, is hopefully good. In the biological setting, Kauffman (1993) suggested a heuristic based on mutation. In the context of a complex system, the heuristic proceeds as follows. Starting with an initial system **x**, a new system, **x**´, is created by considering what happens if the agent in position i of **x** is replaced with the other available agent for that position, resulting in a *one-replacement neighbor of* **x**. The new system is retained only if the performance of **x**´ is better than that of **x**, that is, if $p(\mathbf{x}´) > p(\mathbf{x})$. Repeating this replacement process results in a sequence of systems, each with better performance than its predecessor, until obtaining a *local maximum system* – that is, a system whose performance is at least as good as all its one-replacement neighbors.

The primary results of the *NK* model relating how the values of N and K affect the performance of a local maximum system are discussed in the section *The NK Model and the Performance Landscape.*

CHAPTER TEN

TOWARD AN UNDERSTANDING OF MEMBERSHIP AND LEADERSHIP IN YOUTH ORGANIZATIONS: SUDDEN CHANGES IN AVERAGE PARTICIPATION DUE TO THE BEHAVIOR OF ONE INDIVIDUAL

Kirstin C. Phelps & Alfred W. Hubler

Peer pressure can induce sudden, unexpected changes in the behavior of a group. With agent-based simulations, we study the impact of one individual on the behavior of a social network of people. We find that an individual with the largest benefit dominates the group behavior. If that individual happens to have a leadership role, the impact is particularly strong. The model suggests that even if the average benefit for the group changes slowly, the average participation changes suddenly but with a delay. The delay is shorter if the network is subject to large, unpredictable outside influences. Further, we find that incentives that target leaders are more effective than unspecific incentives. We discuss applications of the model to the dynamics of membership in an agricultural youth organization.

Kirstin C. Phelps (MS, Agricultural Education, UIUC, 2006) is the Program Manager of the Illinois Leadership® Center at the University of Illinois, Urbana-Champaign. She designs, develops, and implements student leadership workshops; oversees the development and implementation of leadership retreats called i-programs; and advises and consults students and registered student organizations regarding organizational leadership issues and effectiveness.

Alfred W. Hubler (PhD, Physics, Technical University of Munich, Germany, 1987) is Associate Professor of Physics at the University of Illinois at Urbana-Champaign. He is the director of the Center for Complex Systems Research at the UIUC (www.ccsr.uiuc.edu) and the executive editor of the journal *Complexity*. He has been a pioneer in several important recent developments in nonlinear science research, including the modeling and control of chaos, the resonant coupling of nonlinear oscillators, and the resonant stimulation of nonlinear oscillators. Hubler was the very first to recognize that seemingly erratic, random motions associated with deterministic chaos could, in fact, be controlled, and that "chaotic" systems could be steered with less effort than systems undergoing more regular motion. Another ground-breaking discovery was Hubler's observation that nonlinear dynamical systems react most sensitively to a forcing function that complements their natural motion. This may lead to a new generation of spectroscopic instruments.

Introduction

In recent years, the youth agricultural organizations FFA and 4-H have both faced declining enrollment and membership (Hoover & Scanlon, 1991; Talbert & Balschweid, 2004). This may in turn have widespread effects on local, state, and national chapters and programs through potential losses in chapter funding, lowered teacher salaries due to reduced responsibilities, fewer new position openings, and decreased support and maintenance to current programs (Hoover & Scanlon, 1991). Previous studies on enrollment and retention issues in FFA and 4-H have shown that contributing factors for not joining agricultural youth programs include peer influence, lack of time or money, and lack of student interest, as well as a negative image of the organizations and/or the agricultural industry (Croom & Flowers, 2001; Hoover & Scanlon, 1991; Stoller & Knobloch, 2005; Talbert & Balschweid, 2004).

While image has long been adduced as a key factor in reduced participation in agricultural youth programs, other factors may also be significant. Larson and Seepersad (2003), in investigating the different ways in which American adolescents spend their leisure time, found that 40–60 percent of high-school students are employed part time, an average much higher than found in other countries. The amount of time spent working after school results in less time that the students could dedicate to other pursuits (Larson & Seepersad, 2003). On average, 40-50 percent of boys' and girls' daily time is considered free time; the other half is dedicated to chores, jobs, and schoolwork. Of the proposed free time, unsupervised free time is thought to be the riskiest time when adolescents may engage in delinquent behaviors (Riggs & Greenberg, 2004; Roffman, *et al.*, 2001). In comparison, adolescents may choose to utilize their free time to participate in the over 400 national, or tens of thousands of local, structured youth programs (Larson & Seepersad, 2003). Agricultural youth programs are just one option among many school, community, religious, and sport-based youth activities, and therefore must compete for members. Regardless of the type or purpose of youth organizations, the question of how to recruit and retain members remains of high importance.

An additional challenge facing agricultural youth programs is the changing student demographic. The original purpose of agricultural youth organizations such as FFA and 4-H was to establish a place for agriculture in public schools and provide learning experiences that would improve farming techniques and practices (Brown, 2002). For much of the history of the FFA, the "typical" demographics of agricultural students, and subsequent FFA members, were white males from a farming background. In 1989, however, recommendations to change the image of the FFA to one appealing to all students interested in agriculture were implemented and have expanded today's FFA members to include a mix of youth from various upbringings, ethnicities, and gender (Hoover and Scanlon, 1991). However, while a study on minority enrollment in Ohio 4-H programs reported that minority youth have a faster growth rate than non-minority youth and account for one-third of the total youth in America, minority membership in agricultural youth organizations has continued to decline (Cano & Bankston, 1992; U.S. Census Bureau, 2002; Wakefield, 2003). In general, agricultural youth organizations are finding it harder and harder to recruit and retain a diverse range of students, whether due to competition on time, interest in the subject matter, or other factors.

Several attempts have been made to model the emergence and evolution of non-profit organizations with agent-based models: Smith (2004) suggested using complexity theory to model the evolution of sports organizations in Australia; Moldoveanu (2004) introduced a quantitative agent-based model to study the complexity in organizations, and Fioretti and Visser (2004) added a theory of decision making to such models. While the above models do describe complex structures in organizations, much less attention has been given to the dynamics of organizational change (McKelvey, 2004). However, recently agent-based models have been used to illustrate that a sequence of symmetry breakings from the largest to the smallest scales leads to phenomena that are typically described with the phrase "the whole is more than the sum of the parts" (Hubler, 2005). Also, physical implementations of agent-based systems shows the growth of emergent, fractally structured hierarchies (Jun & Hubler, 2005).

In this paper we use an agent-based model to study the dynamics of participation in an organization, particularly with regard to the impact of youths possessing leadership skills. We assume that all agents are subject to peer pressure, with the amount of peer pressure being a system parameter. Furthermore, we assume that youths with leadership skills can generate a larger degree of peer pressure. First, we study populations with no pronounced leaders and determine the participation and appreciation of the organization as a function of incentives. Incentives can be described as the factors that may lead to participation or non-participation. Such factors may include marketing, peer participation, role-modeling behaviors, and suggestions from trusted sources. We do not differentiate between the incentives given by family, teachers, and counselors, but consider only the total amount of incentives. However, we do consider the fact that the individuals have different personal situations and therefore have different barriers for participating. Then we study the impact of leadership among the youth. Finally, we explore a situation where the incentives are slowly increased or decreased to determine effects on participation.

An Agent-Based Model of a Social Network

Participation in a youth organization is considered to be a function of the leadership skills of the youth and peer pressure. We consider a group of M agents. We model the level of participation of each agent in the youth organization during the nth business cycle. We assume that the rate at which the participation increases depends on the current participation and the peer pressure. The participation during the next business cycle is proportional to the participation in the current business cycle, where the proportionality constant is called appreciation. Peer pressure increases the participation as well. Further, we assume that the participation is subject to some random fluctuations.

The peer pressure depends on the participation levels of the other agents and increases exponentially with the difference in leadership skills between the agents. A leader is a person who acts as a role model for other youth. The quantity

S measures the strength of the interactions between the agents. For $S = 1/(M–1)$ peer pressures in the network are very high. In contrast, for $S=0$ this model describes a group of individualists who do not respond to peer pressure. Hence S is a measure of the peer pressure in the system. Further, we assume that the appreciation decreases when the participation reaches 100%, due to time constraints, money constraints, and so on. We use the logistic map to model such diminishing returns.

The personal situation of each agent is considered to be slightly different. For instance, a student from a farming background may see more value and relevance to participation in an agricultural youth organization than a student from a non-farming background. Also, for each agent there is a different barrier to participation in the organization. Positive experiences and the quality of the program contribute to the appreciation of the organization, which is also increased by incentives. Hence we assume that the appreciation during the current business cycles is proportional to the appreciation in the previous business cycle. It is also affected by the participation, the personal situation of the agent, and the net effect of incentives provided by the youth organization, teachers, parents, and other advocates.

Average-Quality Youth Groups with No Strong Leaders

First we study the consequences of peer pressure in an average-quality youth program with no strong leaders. If the net incentive is small, only the agent with the smallest barrier develops a positive attitude in which the agent's participation and appreciation of the program approach a stable fixed point; that is, over time the participation of the agent approaches a constant value.

If the incentive is smaller than the smallest barrier, the limiting appreciation of all agents is zero. Consequently, none of the agents will participate. However, if the incentive is between the lowest barrier and the second lowest barrier, then the limiting appreciation of that agent is greater than zero. Nevertheless, the participation of the agents is still zero. Only if the benefit, which is the difference between the incentive and the lowest barrier, exceeds a certain threshold will a bifurcation occurs; that is, in the following situations:

- If the peer pressure S is large, then the limiting participation of all agents jumps from zero to 100%.

- If the peer pressure S is small, then the limiting participation of all agents increases gradually to 100%.

Despite the fact that the appreciation of the other agents is zero, they start to participate due to the peer pressure. Figure 1 shows the limiting participation versus the benefit of the agent with the smallest barrier and versus the peer pressure for a network $M = 10$ agents for the agent with the smallest barrier (a) and the other agents (b). If the incentive is less than the threshold indicated by the continuous blue line, then the limiting participation is zero for all agents. If the peer pressure exceeds the threshold, indicated by the dashed line, then the participation of all agents is equal to one.

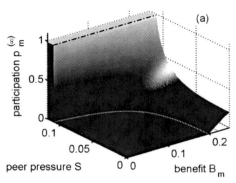
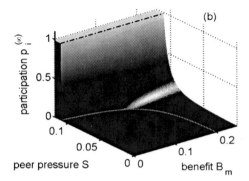

Figure 1 *The participation of the agent with the smallest barrier (a) and the other agents (b), versus the benefit of the agent with the smallest barrier and versus the peer pressure. Only if the benefit for at least one agent exceeds a threshold (blue line) do the agents participate. The threshold is smaller for larger peer pressure. If the peer pressure is very large (beyond dashed line) then the participation of all agents is 100% if at least one agent has a benefit from participating.*

Figure 2 shows the time dependence of a system with 10 agents with random barriers. The peer pressure is high, but below the threshold. For this set of barriers, agent 6 has the lowest barrier. For this parameter set agent 6 is the only agent that has a positive benefit. Figure 2 shows that agent 6 is the only agent that develops a positive appreciation. The top curve is the participation of the agent with the lowest barrier; the lower curves are the participation levels of all other agents. The dashed lines are the theoretical values (see mathematical appendix).

Average-Quality Youth Groups with Strong Leaders

Next, we consider the impact of leadership. We consider a system where the agent with the smallest barrier is also a strong leader, and the system is an average-quality youth program.

If the incentive is smaller than the smallest barrier, then the benefit is negative for all agents, and the limiting appreciation of all agents is zero as well. However, if the incentive is between the lowest barrier and the second lowest barrier, then one agent has a positive benefit and the fixed point appreciation of that agent is greater than zero, whereas the appreciation level of the other agents is still zero. In the following we will consider this case. Since that agent is the only agent with non-zero appreciation, we treat it separately from the other agents.

Figure 3 shows the time dependence of the participation and the appreciation of a system with ten agents where the parameters are the same. The exception being that agent 6 has a large leadership level. Agent 6 is the only agent which develops an appreciation. The limiting participation of agent 6 does not depend on leadership skills as long as the participation of the other agents is less than one, but the limiting participation of the other agents do increase if the leadership of agent 6 increases. The lower curve is the participation of the agent

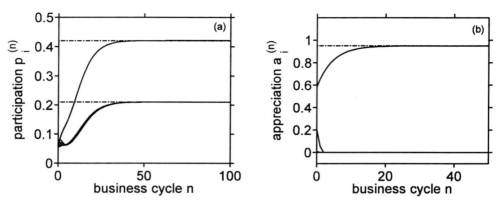

Figure 2 *The participation and appreciation of the organization versus time. The top curve is the participation of the agent with the lowest barrier; the lower curves are the participation levels of all other agents. The other agents do not appreciate the organization but participate somewhat because of peer pressure.*

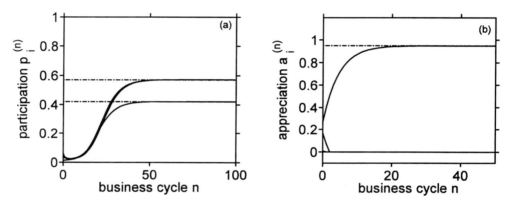

Figure 3 *The participation and appreciation versus time for a system with a strong leader. The lower curve is the participation of the leader, the upper curves are the participation levels of all other agents. The other agents participate more than the leader, due to peer pressure, despite the fact that they do not appreciate the organization. The dashed lines are the theoretical values.*

with the lowest barrier; the upper curves are the participation levels of all other agents. The dashed lines are the theoretical values.

Systems with Slowly Changing Incentives

Next, we consider the situation where the incentives are changing slowly, and determine the average level of participation. Figure 4 shows a numerical simulation of a social system where the net incentive increases very slowly, starting from zero. All other parameters are as in Figure 2. We find that the average participation changes suddenly. As soon as the agent with the lowest barrier starts to participate, a second-order phase transition occurs. This phase transition may be less pronounced if the system is less social; that is, if the peer pressure is small.

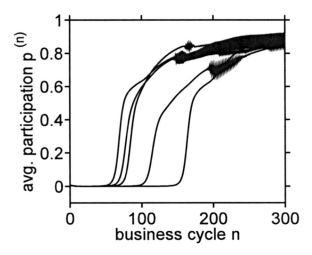

Figure 4 *The average participation versus time for five different sets of agents. Despite the fact that the incentives grow at a constant rate, the average participation changes suddenly and at a different time. Even if the benefit exceeds the threshold for participation, it takes a long time before this translates into a significant participation and noise determines when the participation grows rapidly. If there is a large amount of noise in the participation dynamics, these delays are much shorter.*

We find that the participation starts to grow if the benefits of one of the agents are positive. However, if the noise level is small, it may take many time steps before the growth in participation becomes noticeable. For small noise levels there is a significant delay between the time when the limiting participation becomes positive and the time when the participation is actually significantly different from zero. This means that the participation may stay zero for a long time, unless a youth participates accidentally in the youth organization. We conclude that the larger the accidental participation, the faster the growth of the youth organization. Even if the potential for growth is there, the organization may not grow unless there are significant accidental fluctuations in participation.

Discussion

We studied the impact of one individual on the behavior of a social network of people. We found that peer pressure can induce sudden unexpected changes in the behavior of a group. Figure 1 shows that the participation stays zero unless the benefits exceed a threshold, the threshold being some individual level of an agent's participation. Figure 4 shows that these sudden changes may occur after a long delay. The length of the delay depends on the noise in the system. Further, we find that the individual with the largest benefit dominates the group behavior. If that individual happens to have a leadership role, the impact is particularly strong. In addition, we find that incentives targeting leaders are more effective than unspecific incentives. Since youth organizations are typically organized in small local groups, we expect these groups to grow suddenly if incentives target youths who are likely to participate and have leadership skills. Similarly, we expect these groups to disappear suddenly unless incentives target such youths. We expect both the growth and disappearance of these local groups to occur rather unexpectedly long after the incentives have changed.

Acknowledgments

This material is based on work supported by the National Science Foundation Grant No. NSF PHY 01-40179 and NSF DMS 03-25939 ITR. A.H. thanks the Santa Fe Institute for support.

Mathematical Appendix

We consider a group of M agents. We model the level of participation of agent i in the youth organization during the nth business cycle, where $n = 0, 1, \ldots$. The participation of agent i during the next business cycle is a function of the current participation and the peer pressure, the *participation dynamics* is assumed to be $p_i^{(n+1)} = b_i^{(n)} p_i^{(n)} + P_i^{(n)} + r^{(n)}$, *where* $i = 1, 2, \ldots, M$. $p_i^{(n)}$ is the level of participation of agent i in the youth organization during the nth business cycle. $b_i^{(n)}$ is the appreciation factor of that agent. $P_i^{(n)}$ is the peer pressure on agent i. The level of participation is between 0% and 100%, i.e., $0 \le p_i^{(n)} \le 1$. We assume that the participation is subject to some random fluctuations. This is modeled by the term $r^{(n)}$. $r^{(n)}$ are small random numbers that are equally disrupted between $-r$ and r, i.e., where $0 \le r \le 1$. The following equations states that the *peer pressure* on agent i at time step n from other agents depends on the participation levels of the other agents and increases exponentially with the difference in leadership skills between the agents; $P_i^{(n)} = S p_1^{(n)} exp(L_1 - L_i) + S p_2^{(n)} exp(L_2 - L_i) + \ldots + S p_{i-1}^{(n)} exp(L_{i-1} - L_i) + S p_{i+1}^{(n)} exp(L_{i+1} - L_i) + \ldots + S p_M^{(n)} exp(L_M - L_i)$, where L_i is a positive number that measures the leadership skills of an agent i. The quantity S measures the strength of the interactions between the agents, where $0 \le S < 1/(M-1)$. For $S = 1/(M-1)$ peer pressures in the network are very high. Hence S is a measure of peer pressures in the network. We use the logistic map to model *diminishing returns*: $b_i^{(n)} = a_i^{(n)} (100\% - p_i^{(n)})$, where $a_i^{(n)}$ is the appreciation of agent i at small participation levels. The quantity s_i describes how much the personal situation of an individual affects the appreciation of the organization. We introduce a measure for the barriers to participation in the organization, $s_i = r_i s$, where $s > 0$ is the spread of the barriers and r_i is a random number between 0 and 1, i.e., $0 \le r_i \le 1$. s is a measure for the diversity of the group.

We use the following equation to model the *dynamics of the appreciation*: $a_i^{(n+1)} = \lambda a_i^{(n)} + q p_i^{(n)} + f - s_i$, where f is the net effect of incentives provided by the youth organization, teachers, parents, and other advocates. f describes those aspects of the appreciation that do not depend on participation in the organization, including advertisements. In contrast, the term $q p_i^{(n)}$ describes the impact on the appreciation due to participating in the program. q is a measure of the quality of the program, compared to other youth programs. $q = 1$ means that the quality is high, and $q = -1$ means that the quality is low, whereas $q = 0$ means that the quality of the program is similar to other youth programs. The quantity λ describes the impact of past experiences, where $0 \le \lambda \le 1$. $\lambda = 1$ means that memories have a strong impact on the current level of appreciation, whereas $\lambda = 0$ means that memories have no impact on the current level of appreciation. $a_i^{(n)}$ is assumed to be within the parameter range of the logistic map, i.e., $0 \le a_i^{(n)} \le 4$.

To model an average-quality youth program with no strong leaders we set $q = 0$ and $L_i = 0$ for all i. If the incentive f is small, only the agent with the smallest barrier develops a positive attitude and the participation and appreciation of the agents approach a stable fixed point, i.e., over time the participation of the agents approaches a constant value. In the following, m is the subscript of the agent with the minimum barrier, i.e., $s_m \le s_i$ for $i \ne m$. If the incentive is smaller than the smallest barrier, i.e., $f < s_m$, the fixed point appreciation of all agents is zero, i.e., $a_i = 0$ for all i. Consequently none of the agents participates, i.e., $p_i^{(\infty)} = 0$ for all i. However, if the incentive f is between the lowest barrier and the second-lowest barrier s_{m2}, i.e., $s_m < f < s_{m2}$, then the fixed point appreciation of agent m is greater than zero, $a_i^{(\infty)} = B_m/(1-\lambda)$ for $i = m$ otherwise, and $a_i^{(\infty)} = 0$, where $B_i = f - s_i$ is the benefit. The participation of the agents is still zero, i.e., $p_i^{(\infty)} = 0$ for all agents. Only if the benefit B_m exceeds a certain threshold B_c then a bifurcation occurs: the fixed point at zero becomes unstable and another fixed point becomes stable. The threshold incentive is $B_c = (1-\lambda)(1+S-MS)(1+S)/(1+2S-MS)$. This means that if $B_c \le B_m \le B_{m2}$ then the limiting participation of agent m is $p_i^{(\infty)} = 100\%$ if the peer pressure S is larger than $S_c = 1/(M-1)$ and $p_i^{(\infty)} = 1 - (1+S-MS)(1+S)/(a_m(1+2S-MS))$ for small peer pressure, i.e., $S < S_c$. And for the other agents, $i \ne m$, the limiting participation of the agent is $p_i^{(\infty)} = 100\%$ as well, if the peer pressure S is larger than S_c and $p_i^{(\infty)} = 1 - p_m^{(\infty)}S/(1+2S-MS)$ for small peer pressure, i.e., $S < S_c$. Hence if the peer pressure is greater than the threshold S_c then the limiting participation of all agents jumps from zero to 100% when the benefits exceed the critical value B_c. If the peer pressure is greater than the threshold S_c then the limiting participation of all agents increases gradually to 100% as soon as the benefits exceed B_c appreciation. Despite the fact that the appreciation of the other agents is zero, they start to participate due to the peer pressure from agent 6. The limiting values of the simulation for the participation and the appreciation of the agents are in excellent agreement with the theoretical values (see Figure 1). Figure 2 shows the time dependence of a system with 10 agents with random barriers, $s_1 = 0.76, s_2 = 0.92, s_3 = 0.89, s_4 = 0.41, s_5 = 0.35, s_6 = 0.11, s_7 = 0.64, s_8 = 0.36, s_9 = 0.49, s_{10} = 0.73$, the incentive $f = 0.3$, and memory $\lambda = 0.8$. The peer pressure is high but below S_c, i.e., $S = 0.1 < S_c$. For this set of barriers, agent 6 has the lowest barrier, i.e., $m = 6$. For this parameter set agent 6 is the only agent who has a positive benefit, i.e., $B_m > 0$, whereas $B_i < 0$ if $i \ne m$. Figure 2 shows that agent 6 is the only agent who develops a positive appreciation.

To model a system where the agent with the smallest barrier is a strong leader as well, we set $L_m = 1$ and $L_i = 0$ for $i \ne m$, and an average-quality youth program, i.e., $q = 0$. The dynamics of the participation is $p_i^{(n+1)} = a_i^{(n)} p_i^{(n)} (1 - p_i^{(n)}) + P_i^{(n)}$, and the dynamics of the appreciation is $a_i^{(n+1)} = \lambda a_i^{(n)} + B_i$. We find that the limiting value of the appreciation is $a_i^{(\infty)} = B_i/(1-\lambda)$ if $B_i > 0$ and $a_i^{(\infty)} = 0$ otherwise.

If the incentive is smaller than the smallest barrier s_m, i.e., $f < s_m$, then the benefit is negative for all agents, i.e., $B_i \le 0$ for all i, and the fixed point appreciation of all agents is zero too, i.e., $a_i^{(\infty)} = 0$ for all agents. However, if the incentive f is between the lowest barrier and the second lowest barrier s_{m2}, i.e., $s_m < f < s_{m2}$, then agent m has a positive benefit $B_m > 0$ and the fixed point appreciation of agent m is greater than zero, whereas the appreciation level of the other agents is still zero. In the following we will consider this case. Since agent m is the only agent with non-zero appreciation, we treat agent m separately from the other agents. Since the other agents have the same equation, we make the assumption that their fixed point values are the same and equal to the fixed point values of the agent with the second-smallest barrier m_2. With the constraint $0 \le p_i^{(\infty)} \le 1$ we find $p_m^{(\infty)} = 0$, if $0 \le B_m \le B_c$; $p_m^{(\infty)} = 1 - (1 + S - M S)(1+S)/(a_m^{(\infty)} (1 + 2 S - M S))$, if $B_c \le B_m \le B_d$ and $S \le S_c$; $p_m^{(\infty)} = (a_m^{(\infty)} - 1 + ((a_m^{(\infty)} - 1)^2 + 4 a_m^{(\infty)} S (M-1) e^{-Lm})^{1/2})/(2 a_m^{(\infty)})$ if $S \le S_c$; and $p_m^{(\infty)} = 1$ otherwise. The condition $p_{m2}^{(\infty)} = p_m^{(\infty)} (S e^{Lm})/(1 + 2 S - M S) \le 1$ is true if $B_m \le B_d$ where $B_d = (e^{Lm}(1-\lambda)S(1+S)(1-(M-1)S))/((1-(M-2)S)(1-(M-2+e^{Lm})S))$. The condition $p_m^{(\infty)} \ge 0$ means $1 - ((1 + S - M S)(1+S))/(a_m^{(\infty)} (1 + 2 S - M S)) \ge 0$. This is true if $B_m \ge B_c$ where $B_c = (1-\lambda)(1 + S - M S)(1 + S)/(1 + 2S - M S)$. The condition $p_m^{(\infty)} \le 1$ means $1 - ((1 + S - M S)(1+S))/(a_m^{(\infty)}(1 + 2 S - M S)) \le 1$. This is true if $S \le S_c$ where $S_c = 1/(M-1)$. With these equations we obtain for the participation of all agents, except for agent m: $p_i^{(\infty)} = 0$, if $0 \le B_m \le B_c$; $p_i^{(\infty)} = (S e^{Lm})/(1 + 2 S - M S)(1 - ((1 + S - M S)(1+S))/(a_m^{(\infty)} (1 + 2 S - M S)))$, if $B_c \le B_m \le B_d$ and $S \le S_c$; $p_i^{(\infty)} = 1$ otherwise. The dashed lines in Figure 3 are determined with this formula.

To model the situation where the incentives are changing slowly, we set $f = f^{(0)} + n \lambda f$. We determine the average level of participation $p^{(n)} = (p_1^{(n)} + p_2^{(n)} + \ldots + p_M^{(n)})/M$.

Figure 4 shows a numerical simulation of a social system for $f^{(0)} = 0\$$ and $\Delta f = 0.0007$. All other parameters are as in Figure 2. The parameters are $S=0.1$, $M=10$, and $s=1$.

CHAPTER ELEVEN
THE EMERGENCE OF EFFECTIVE LEADERS: AN EXPERIMENTAL AND COMPUTATIONAL APPROACH

Arianna Dal Forno & Ugo Merlone

This chapter presents a study of leadership using a method of computational modeling by exploiting the analysis of data and behaviors gathered in a human subject experiment. We incorporate some of the observed behaviors in agents' schemata and build an agent-based model. Analyzing the different interactions, we can examine under what conditions individuals may emerge as effective leaders.

Arianna Dal Forno, Ph.D. (University of Trieste, 2001) is post-doctoral fellow at the department of Applied Mathematics at University of Turin. Her main research interests are mathematical modeling of organizations and the microstructure of market architectures. She has been visiting post-doctoral fellow at Harvard University. Her most recent publications have been in the *Journal of Economic Interaction and Coordination, Journal of Artificial Societies and Social Simulation, Nonlinear Dynamics, Psychology, and Life Sciences*, and *Decisions in Economics and Finance*.

Ugo Merlone, Ph.D. (University of Trieste, 1998) is associate professor of Applied Mathematics at the University of Turin. His main research interests are mathematical modeling of organizations and bounded rationality agents' interaction dynamics. He has published several papers in peer-reviewed journals and has been visiting scholar at University of Arizona, London School of Economics, and Harvard University. Further details are available from http://web.econ.unito.it/merloneugo/.

Introduction

A recent study using *Econlit* shows 172 contributions from 2002 to 2006 with the word "leadership" in the title, while *Psychinfo* has 1,290 contributions on leadership. *The Journal of Applied Psychology* alone contained 27 papers on leadership in the same period. As Bennis (1959) put it almost a half-century ago,

"Of all the hazy and confounding areas in social psychology, leadership theory undoubtedly contends for nomination. And ironically, probably more has been written and less is known about leadership than about any other topic in the behavioral sciences."

Recently, Schneider and Somers (2006) examine some interesting implications of the complexity theory for leadership research. In fact, complexity theory has become a subject appreciated in the field of organization science[1]. In particular, according to Anderson (1999), complexity has become a central construct in the vocabulary of organization scientists, and looking back it does not seem to have been just a fad (McKelvey, 1999).

Computational techniques, including simulation, have played an important role in the study of complex systems. More recently simulation has been used to analyze leadership as well (see review in Hazy, forthcoming). Dal Forno and Merlone (2005) have investigated the effect of behavioral components when selecting co-workers in teams with no supervisor. Their results suggest that, in order to foster larger group formation, the presence of individuals acting as aggregators of knowledge is necessary. These individuals are called *social leaders* because while their role is cardinal in establishing the pace of task accomplishment, they have no formal authority in relation to the other team members.

In this chapter we continue the previous study of group aggregation, but, in order to study under what conditions some individuals may emerge as effective leaders, we explicitly assume the presence of formal leaders. The theoretical model we propose was used in a human subject experiment; by analyzing the data and the behaviors we observed during the experiment, we performed an agent-based simulation and studied under what conditions the effective leaders may emerge. The approach we follow is the one outlined in Dal Forno and Merlone (2004), where data and observations gathered while performing classroom experiments with human subjects are used to model bounded rationality agents. The theory we build is a "grounded theory" in the sense of Strauss and Corbin (1998); that is, a theory that is derived from data systematically gathered and analyzed through the research process.

The reasons for choosing the computational approach are several. First, modeling simple building blocks with many interactions may be a way to make a complex system understandable, as suggested in Anderson (1999); the drawback of this approach is that the system becomes analytically intractable (von

---

1 See *Organization Science*, special issue Application of Complexity Theory to Organization Science (ISSN 10477039, 10(3, May–Jun 1999); for an updated description of different contributions see http://www.complexity andpolicy.org/references.htm.

Bertalanffy, 1969), so it is natural to resort to simulation. Secondly, computational techniques are proving to be an important tool for analyzing organizations as complex systems (Carley & Prietula, 1994; Carley, 2002). Moreover, the comparison of human subject experiment results with simulations allows us to shed some light on the emergence of effective leaders in terms of team performance, free riding, and distributive inequity.

The Model

Both the agent-based simulations and the classroom experiment we performed consider the same interaction model. First, we assume that there is a population of n individuals who are asked to participate in a project producing some quantity of a good that will be sold at unitary price[2]. In order to be productive a project needs one leader and, at least, one follower. The number m of productive projects (and, consequently, the number of leaders) might be at least one (a single group), but not more than $[n/2]$, i.e., the floor of $n/2$. Efforts to produce the good are provided by followers; within each group P_k ($k = 1,...,m$), each follower provides a non-negative individual effort e_{ik} ($i = 1, ..., n(k)$, where $n(k)$ is the number of followers in group P_k. The good production function $f_k = f_k(e_{1k}, ..., e_{n(k),k})$ depends on the joint efforts of the team members belonging to the same group. Followers bear an individual cost with the same cost function $c(e_{ik})$, which depends on the effort exerted. Leaders do not provide any effort – ex ante, for each turn, they provide a sharing rule that is a profit percentage α_{ik} to be attributed to each follower. The undistributed profit is accrued to the leader. Concerning information, while followers cannot observe the profit percentages α_{ik}, leaders cannot discriminate actual efforts exerted by subordinates.

The socially optimal payment plan is then α^*_k for all followers of group P_k, so that all the members, leader included, will get the same profit. See the appendix for the socially optimal plan derivation and the functional forms used in the experiments.

It is worth noticing that the functions considered increase with the number of participants; as a consequence, when assuming no free riders, one expects the formation of a unique large group. Furthermore, it is easy to see that a pure strategy regarding a Nash Equilibrium for the one-shot game consists of a null payment plan by the leader and all the followers exerting no effort. Finally, it must be observed that, when the leader decides to share the profit equally, this policy results in the followers' underpayment.

The Classroom Experiment

The purpose of the experiment was to observe the behavior of human subjects in the situation cognate to the theoretical model. In particular, we were interested in observing the effectiveness of the policies adopted by leaders. For this reason we considered two roles: leaders and followers. We collected the data from two undergraduate populations at the University of Turin. The first population (population A) included about 65 individuals (first-year

2 We assume that price is fixed and that the market can absorb any quantity of the good.

undergraduates in the Math class of Business Administration). The second one (population B) included about 67 individuals (first-year undergraduates in the Math class of Information and Business Relations).

The experiment was run in 22 weekly sessions with population A and 12 with population B[3]. One week before the first session, subjects were given the instructions for the experiment, together with an example (both are available from the authors on request), and a short explanatory discussion took place.

Since motivating subjects in experiments is a well-known problem, we encouraged our students in the following way. Subjects would receive up to one mark in addition to whatever their grade would be in the final exam of the Math class (the maximum available grade is 30/30 and the pass grade is 18/30). In addition, we asked subjects to provide written explanations for their choices after each session of the experiment. Subjects were also told that the actual incentive depended on their ranked performance in the experiment (incentive = ranked performance[4] normalized in the range [0,1]).

At the end of the experiments the subjects filled in a questionnaire in order for the researchers to infer more than from the mere data of the experiment[5]. In particular, we considered the following points. The first is about the rationale for their *effort*, the only objective economic incentive in the experiment. The second point is about *role tasks*. We were interested in understanding which tasks were directly or indirectly implied in the role that the subjects had. The third point is about *role selection* within the groups. This allowed us to observe the different ways in which a leader was chosen. Then we considered the *free rider issue*[6] and how this was dealt with, as the experiment design allows for the emergence of free riders. In fact, we were interested both in observing the direct reactions of other followers and the leader due to their presence in a group, and also in understanding how the leaders' behavior could be perceived and evaluated by the other followers.

Finally, even if the interaction dynamics moved towards a smaller and smaller number of groups, as predicted by the model, we eventually observed a resistance against the idea itself of the *formation of a single group*, which was something more than friction to change group. In fact, for both populations, when it was clear that the members of the larger group would obtain a higher profit, it would have been rational for the subjects to join the larger group and try to free ride, making minimum effort. Nevertheless, some subjects stayed together in the same small group, exhibiting a sort of team loyalty. It is worth

---

3 The different numbers of sessions in the two population depend on the different schedules of the courses.

4 The ranking of performance may have consequences for strategies. While this may be relevant (see Dal Forno and Merlone, 2001), both our subjects' behavior and their written motivations suggest that they did not seem aware of this issue.

5 In fact the subjects also completed Bass and Avolio's Multifactor Leadership Questionnaire (MLQ; Form 5X-Short), but the results were of little help for the purposes of our research.

6 The free rider problem occurs in situations of collective action where individuals have incentives to behave counterproductively to the social welfare; see Olson (1965) for an analytical generalization.

Effort	Pop. A	Pop. B	Total
Suggested by leader	78.95%	87.93%	83.48%
Suggested by other followers	3.51%	8.62%	6.09%
Randomly	5.26%	0.00%	2.61%
Personal strategy	7.02%	1.72%	4.35%
First randomly, then following leader's directive	1.75%	0.00%	0.87%
First personal strategy, then following leader's directive	1.75%	0.00%	0.87%
Free riding because in a non-organized group	1.75%	0.00%	0.87%
First randomly, then personal strategy	0.00%	1.72%	0.87%

Table 1 *Effort Exerted by Followers*

observing that at the beginning of the experiment subjects did not exhibit behaviors such as team identity and team loyalty, since the subjects were freshmen and their knowledge of each other was minimal. By contrast, some of these behaviors emerged later on during the experiment.

The different tables report the answers that the subjects gave when filling in the final questionnaire; for each population, percentages are computed for the actual number of subjects who answered the relative item.

Table 1 describes how effort was determined by subjects in each population; on the whole, it is clear that the effort to be exerted was suggested mainly by the leader of the group, independently of the population. In a few cases this was done randomly. By examining the different populations and carefully reading the written motivation that each subject provided at the end of each session, we can see that when the effort was not suggested by leaders, followers in population A were more involved in finding personal strategies than those in population B, where the effort was preferably suggested by some other followers. Only population A exhibits one free rider and some random choices. So, what could be the motivation for this different behavior? It must be observed that in population A, a group adopted a system of rotating leadership. In our opinion, this is very important in terms of the discussion about leadership, because members of this group were the only ones who experienced disorganization and instability. In fact, they are the ones who either exerted random effort, or tried to find personal strategies as well as free riding.

Tables 2 and 3 present a list of *tasks* that, in our opinion, could have been part of either the follower's or the leader's role, even if we were not quite sure how to divide them. For this reason, it is interesting to see and compare them both. First of all, a particular comment is due to the perceived necessity of increasing group size. To this end, we found that, for both populations, the most frequent task of followers was recruiting members in order to increase the size of the group. Nevertheless, the two populations are different in terms of the frequency, 36.62% in population A and 57.63% in population B. The reason is that this task was delegated by leaders, because, in this way it would be accomplished in an easier and more effective manner (higher probability of finding a new member). Other common leaders' tasks were, obviously, deciding payments to

Leader's tasks	Pop. A	Pop. B	Total
Invite people to join the group	34.09%	21.43%	29.17%
Keep people in the group	11.36%	7.14%	9.72%
Decide efforts	18.18%	35.71%	25.00%
Decide payments	31.82%	28.57%	30.56%
Defend the position of the leader	2.27%	3.57%	2.78%
Explain the importance of being a large group	2.27%	0.00%	1.39%
Explain computation to followers	0.00%	3.57%	1.39%

Table 2 *Leader's Tasks*

Follower's tasks	Pop. A	Pop. B	Total
Invite people to join the group	36.62%	57.63%	46.15%
Keep people in the group	16.90%	8.47%	13.08%
Decide efforts	11.27%	10.17%	10.77%
Decide payments	4.23%	1.69%	3.08%
Support the leader	25.35%	16.95%	21.54%
Spread the effort decided by the leader to other members of the group	2.82%	0.00%	1.54%
Count the number of members in the group	1.41%	0.00%	0.77%
Check if all members exerted the right effort	1.41%	0.00%	0.77%
Convince other followers to behave loyally	0.00%	3.39%	1.54%
Detect any disparity within the group	0.00%	1.69%	0.77%

Table 3 *Follower's Tasks*

Selection of leaders	Pop. A	Pop. B	Total
Casually	42.86%	27.27%	37.50%
Self-proposing	14.29%	45.45%	25.00%
By election	42.86%	27.27%	37.50%

Table 4 *Procedure to Select Leaders*

be given to followers and, as we have already observed in Table 1, the effort to be made. For population A leaders, deciding payments was almost as frequent as recruiting.

Even if the experimental setting did not ask leaders to delegate tasks to followers, some tasks were actually delegated. These could be, as subjects' comments suggest, of an administrative kind: for instance helping the leader to check the number of people in the group, and informing them all about the effort to be exerted at any time. Other tasks consisted of monitoring: making sure that all the members behaved loyally, that they made the effort recommended by the leader, and so on. This was rather unexpected as, in the interaction, leaders were not meant to delegate part of their job to followers. In this sense some of our human subjects showed the emergence of delegation and peer pressure (Kandel & Lazear, 1992).

Concerning the way *leaders* were selected within the groups, we can see in Table 4 that population B had a considerable number of people proposing themselves as candidate to the position. On the contrary, in population A leaders were either elected by others in the same group, or selected by a rotation mechanism.

The reasons for never being a leader (Table 5) were mainly due to a personal decision, especially in population A. On the other hand, in population B we cannot ignore that the former presence of a good leader, with a well-established good reputation, restrained in many cases the emergence of potential new leaders. In this sense this phenomenon cannot be considered just a mere lack of opportunity. This seemed so valid a motivation that nobody could find starting and leading new groups profitable enough or, at least, it was not so wise to change roles within the groups. The analysis of some further comments allow us to understand also that, behind personal decision of unwillingness to be a leader, there was mainly a sense of incompetence in performing that role.

Finally, we were interested in the motivation that led some leaders to quit. The results are shown in Table 6. In both populations the main reason was sub-optimal performance. This called for the election of new leaders within the same groups, but more often to a change of groups and therefore of role. Notice that both populations also exhibit cases where leaders gave up their role because of unhappiness with their followers' performance.

Let us consider now how *free riders* were perceived by subjects. First of all, while in population A only 5.26% of the subjects reported their presence in the groups, in population B this figure went up to 20%. The latter population observed also that these people were sometimes ostracized or more often penalized by leaders. Subjects in this population were aware that more and more control of followers' behavior was needed. Leaders of population A mainly rejected free riders so that they were almost banned (recall that, according to Table 3, monitoring other followers' effort was a delegated task), whereas in population B they could still be part of large groups but were penalized by receiving no payment in the following session. This is why the presence of free riders was more evident among followers in population B than in population A.

It was puzzling that, while in both populations the number of leaders reduced during the experiment (namely, only three groups remained in population A and two in population B), they did not collapse into a single group at the end. A possible explanation comes from the presence of different forces contrasting its formation. The different reasons we could find are reported in Table 7.

For both populations the number of subjects who did not join the larger group was limited. According to the questionnaire, the main reason was the hope of getting a higher profit in future, despite the fact that at the final sessions of the experiment everybody was aware that the profit function was increasing with respect to the number of team members. Another common reason was the

Never been a leader	Pop. A	Pop. B	Total
My own decision	97.14%	73.47%	83.33%
Others' decision	0.00%	4.08%	2.38%
Lack of opportunity	0.00%	4.08%	2.38%
There was already a good leader	2.86%	16.33%	10.71%
Common decision of selecting different leader	0.00%	2.04%	1.19%

Table 5 *Motivation produced by subjects who never played the leader's role*

Leader resignation	Pop. A	Pop. B	Total
Turnover due to non-optimal performance	33.33%	22.22%	29.63%
Change group due to sub-optimal performance	50.00%	66.67%	55.56%
Incompetence or lack of followers	5.56%	11.11%	7.41%
Try the follower role	11.11%	0.00%	7.41%

Table 6 *Motivation produced by leaders who quit their role before the end of the game*

Not a unique group	Pop. A	Pop. B	Total
Hope for better future performance	58.62%	57.41%	58.04%
Distrust other leaders	8.62%	0.00%	4.46%
Challenge the idea	8.62%	0.00%	4.46%
Remain independent	10.34%	3.70%	7.14%
Pride	0.00%	22.22%	10.71%
Rivalry between leaders	0.00%	7.41%	3.57%
Some people were not accepted in the largest group	3.45%	0.00%	1.79%
To avoid coordination problems in a large group	3.45%	3.70%	3.57%
Lack of social interaction with subjects in the largest group	6.90%	5.56%	6.25%

Table 7 *Reasons for not having had a single group at the end of the experiment*

desire to remain independent from the largest group, which was perceived as a dictatorship, where followers simply executed the leader's orders and therefore lost their individuality.

In Figures 1 and 2 we present the evolution in terms of size of the preeminent groups in each population; for both populations the size of the largest group increases while the others remain stable. We discarded information about short-lived teams that appear only in the transient phase of the experiment. In population A only, a minor group willing to join the largest was rejected by its leader, because some members of this team were suspected of free riding. It must be noted that in these cases the leader always punished free riders by promptly removing them from the group. On the other hand, only in population B was

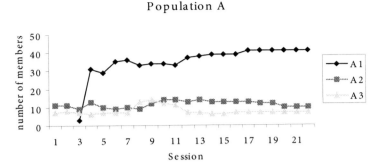

Figure 1 *Number of members in pre-eminent population A groups*

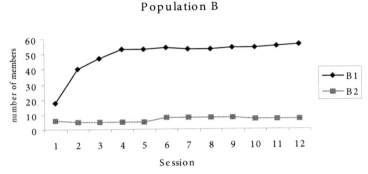

Figure 2 *Number of members in pre-eminent population B groups*

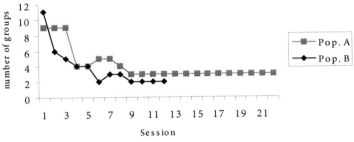

Figure 3 *Number of groups over time*

there also a feeling that the individuals in the minor groups would never agree to join the bigger group because of their pride.

For both populations the number of groups over time follow a common pattern, decreasing over time (see Figure 3). Comparing the two populations' data, it seems that the different time schedule of the two experiments was of little relevance, as for population A after session 12 everything remains stable.

Both quantitative and qualitative observations allowed us to select behaviors and model the interaction between artificial agents in our simulations, as presented in the following section.

Modeling the Interaction

A s from the human subject experiment, several aspects must be considered when modeling a population of artificial agents interacting according to the model we consider. Even the simple interaction we considered presents many elements of complexity theory such as nonlinear interactions (sharing policies influence individual behaviors, which in turn influence future policies), path dependency (free riding at the beginning is likely to frame the climate in the groups), and adaptation (subjects changed their strategies over time).

To keep the analysis manageable we decided to focus on simple features, even if this could result in leaving out some of the behaviors that we observed in the human subject experiments. On the other hand, given the complexity of interactions implicit in our model, considering all the aspects could have resulted in an unmanageable model. In particular, we assumed that agents decide their behavior according to some intrinsic characteristics and attitudes toward the others.

Attitudes toward other agents can be positive, indifferent or negative[7]. At the end of time t, agent i's attitude A_{ij} toward agent j is updated according to the formula:

$$A_{ij}^{t+1} = \delta A_{ij}^t + P_i\left(O_j^t\right) \tag{1}$$

where δ is a decay factor and $P_i\left(O_j^t\right)$ is the effect, in terms of attitude change, when agent i observes either agent j performing action O at time t or the consequences of this action.

When evaluating leaders, agents may consider distributive justice, the number of followers or a combination of both. When evaluating their followers, leaders compare expected and actual individual profit in order to determine free riding. Finally, followers may evaluate co-workers in a similar way; that is, in terms of free riding.

The approach we follow in modeling our agents is similar to the *theory of reasoned action* by Fishbein and Ajzen (1975, 1981), which provides a model of the psychological processes that mediate observed relations between attitudes and behaviors. Nevertheless, some important differences arise. For instance, while Fishbein and Ajzen consider attitudes toward behaviors, we consider attitudes toward targets; furthermore, we do not explicitly consider the subjective norm – that is, what significant others think that the subject should do. While incorporating the theory of reasoned action in our artificial agent is not difficult, the resulting model would be much more complicated and butt up against Occam's razor. Furthermore, since in our model agents may be interested in profit that, under some conditions, depends on the number of followers in the group, considering the others is not ruled out.

In the current implementation the artificial agents are heterogeneous with respect to both the effect on attitude $P_i\left(O_j^t\right)$ and the behaviors that they

---

7 This is consistent with the social psychology literature; see for instance Petty and Cacioppo (1996: 7).

adopt as a function of attitude. In this sense, another important factor that we consider is the probability of changing leaders. We assume that followers have a sort of inertia. This is modeled via the probability of changing leaders conditionally to the attitude changes and it is grounded on subjects' behavior that we observed in the experiments.

Specifically, while in the first round followers choose the leader to whom they have the highest attitude, in the following rounds, when an attitude reversal occurs, they change leader according to a *responsiveness probability*. Since agents are arranged on a rectangular grid, which is similar to the human subjects' disposition in the classroom, in the first round attitudes are computed considering the distance between them: the lower the distance, the higher the attitude. This particular choice represents a step forward in the computer modeling approaches to leadership since, as Hazy (forthcoming) observes, usually research assumes that "aggregates, or teams, have already been organized and that, for simplicity, an agent is in the leader role." In the following iterations the follower's decisions are modeled according to the attitude updating and responsiveness probability as described above.

In the attitude updating process (1) two addenda are considered. While for all agents the decay factor δ applies, we assume that the second addendum $P_i(O'_j)$ is taken into account only under some circumstances. In fact, considering a sort of social visibility, we assume that all the agents update their attitude toward the leaders observing the consequences of leaders' actions, and that the attitude toward each follower is updated only by its own leader and co-workers. In order to evaluate other agents' actions some parameters are computed. Specifically, we consider the number of components in each group, the individual profit, and the group profit; these parameters are used to evaluate inequity.

In terms of motivation, inequity seems to be an important factor (see for instance Adams, 1965). Since in the human subject experiments we could observe both free riders and different retribution policies devised by the leaders in order to deal with free riders, we consider agents' perceived inequity. In our case, to keep the analysis simple, we assign an inequity value to each agent without considering how single agents evaluate each other. This approach allows simplification of the behavioral classes in terms of agent decision.

Inequity is defined differently depending on the role of the agents. For a leader, we consider the individual profit of each follower and its inequity value is defined as the difference between maximum profit and minimum profit. By contrast, for a follower the inequity is defined as the difference between the group profit and the aggregate profit if all the followers in the same group obtained the follower's profit. When updating attitudes, leaders are ranked according to their inequity and the attitude toward each of them is decremented proportionally.

Given the form of the interaction, not all of the parameters are directly observable by the entire population: followers observe only leaders and co-workers, while leaders observe their own followers and other leaders. As a consequence, since the leaders cannot observe directly the effort that each follower exerts, they can only infer whether a follower is free riding by comparing the follower's expected to actual profit. By contrast, followers can update their attitude toward co-workers (i.e., the same leader's followers) simply by interpersonal profit comparison. Another possibility for ranking leaders is to consider the number of followers. In the simulations we report we did not use this approach since it would have given excessive importance to the initial configuration.

The leadership styles we consider are the following:

- *Fair leader*: this rewards the agents according to formula (2) in the mathematical appendix; this way, as we can see in the appendix, all the agents and the leader obtain the same profit;
- *Heuristic leader*: this rewards each member of the team according to the $1/(n+1)$ scheme; the results of this sharing scheme are that the agents are underpaid;
- *Competitive leader*: this starts with the $1/(n+1)$ scheme and increases the share given to the followers when another group has more followers; vice versa, this class of behavior also decreases the given share whenever its group is the bigger.

Some of the leaders may decide to react to free riders by punishing those followers who in the previous round did not make the suggested effort. As a consequence, three further classes of behavior must be considered:

- Punishing fair leader;
- Punishing heuristic leader;
- Punishing competitive leader.

The follower's styles we consider are:

- *Obedient*: exerts the effort that the leader prescribed;
- *Free rider*: exerts a fraction of the effort that the leader prescribed.

In order to analyze how the different behaviors interacted and the convergence results, we have developed a simulation platform where populations consisting of different heterogeneous agents could be examined. After the population is generated according to the parameters specified by the user, the system evolves in discrete rounds. The activities performed in each round correspond to those in a session of the classroom experiment. Specifically, after the leaders are determined, each of the remaining agents chooses a single leader according to its attitudes toward the leaders. Then, leaders who turn out to have no followers have to find a leader. The careful reader will observe that this step is not just a technical point, rather it is related to different contributions in leadership literature (Kelly, 1988; Kouzes & Posner, 1989; Collinson, 2006). Next, each leader determines efforts and shares according to the relevant behavioral class and attitudes. Suggested efforts are communicated to followers, who will decide what their actual effort will be. This particular modeling decision was suggested

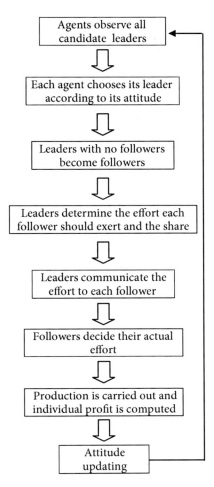

Figure 4 *Scheme of a simulation round*

by the evidence of human subjects' behavior, as reported in Table 1. Production is determined and all state variables are computed. Finally, according to the variables that each agent observes, attitudes are updated. The activities are displayed in Figure 4.

Computational Experiments

I n this section we examine the results of the computational experiments that we performed when considering different leadership styles. Specifically, we test and analyze under what conditions a particular leadership style can emerge from the others. In our framework leaders are able to emerge when they can keep their leadership role; for this reason we measure how often a particular leader can keep their followers for the whole simulation. In order to understand different components of behavior, we study how the different styles performed when competing with each other, under different conditions. Conditions depend on the initial number of leaders (from 2 to 10) and on the responsiveness parameter (from 80% to 100%). For each situation we performed 100 simula-

	Background leader population		
	Fair leaders	**Heuristic leaders**	**Competitive leaders**
Fair leader		Experiment 1	Experiment 2
Heuristic leader	Experiment 5		Experiment 6
Competitive leader	Experiment 4	Experiment 3	

Table 8 *Experiments testing different leadership behaviors*

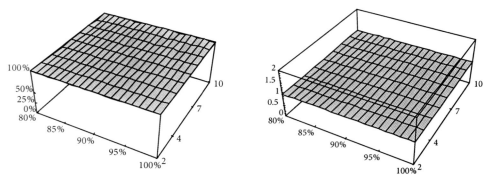

Figure 5 *Percentage of permanence (left) and final number of leaders (right) for a Fair leader vs. Heuristic leaders*

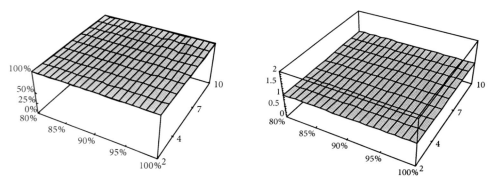

Figure 6 *Percentage of permanence (left) and final number of leaders (right) for a Fair leader vs. Competitive leaders*

tions and in each of them we considered the system configuration after 1,000 iterations.

Finally, it must be noted that, when followers update attitudes toward leaders according to the number of people in their group, the dynamics is rather trivial and depends on the initial configuration. Since this would be inconsistent to what we observed in the classroom experiment, we consider only inequity.

The first series of experiments is summarized in Table 8, where in the first column we indicate which kind of leader we test, and the background leader population is listed in the second row.

For each computational experiment the results are summarized by two graphs. For both the x-axis represents the responsiveness probability in the range

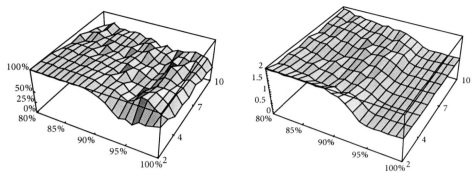

Figure 7 *Percentage of permanence (left) and final number of leaders (right) for a Competitive leader vs. Heuristic leaders*

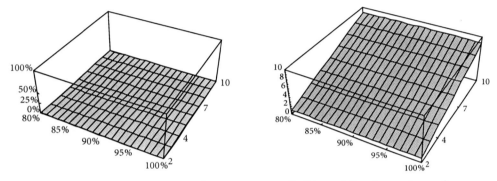

Figure 8 *Percentage of permanence (left) and final number of leaders (right) for a Competitive leader vs. Fair leaders*

80%–100% and the y-axis represents the initial number of leaders, varying from 2 to 10. The first graph in each couple gives the percentage of times in which the tested leader still keeps their role at the end of the simulation. The second graph gives the final number of leaders at the end of the simulation. When for some values of the responsiveness probability and a given initial number of leaders the permanence percentage is close to 100% and the number of final leaders is one, this means that this kind of leader emerges over the others. By contrast, all other configurations show situations in which the leader does not emerge or, even worse, loses their role.

In the first two experiments we consider a Fair leader respectively in a Heuristic (Figure 5) and a Competitive (Figure 6) leader population.

In both cases the Fair leader is likely to emerge when followers are sensitive to inequity only. This is confirmed by our simulations, as almost 100% of times the Fair leader is the only remaining leader. Our results are robust in terms of responsiveness probability and number of leaders. Furthermore, for these cases the standard deviation is low: for both experiments it is in the range [0.0000–0.0291].

For the third experiment results are different; see Figure 7. While we expected something similar to the two previous cases, this did not happen. In fact, we can observe that when the responsiveness probability is lower than 95%, the

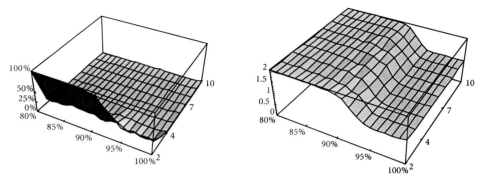

Figure 9 *Percentage of permanence (left) and final number of leaders (right) for a Heuristic leader vs. Competitive leaders*

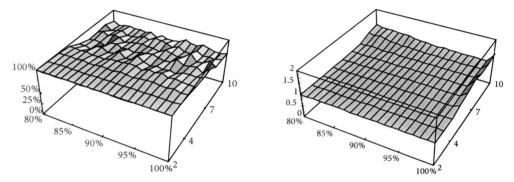

Figure 10 *Percentage of permanence of Punishing Fair leader (left) and final number of leaders (right) for Fair leaders*

number of expected leaders at the end of the simulation is greater than one. Furthermore, the Competitive leader is more likely to lose their role when the initial number of leaders is greater than 4 or the responsiveness is greater than 89%. Finally, when we remain with one single leader (Figure 7 right) the most favorable situation for the Competitive leader is the one with a responsiveness parameter of about 97% (Figure 7 left). It is extremely interesting that, in this case, the prevalence of a single leader does not give guarantees about the prevalence of the potentially fairest leader. These results exhibit much more variance for both the percentage of permanence and final number of leaders, since standard deviation is in the range [0.0000–0.2500]. While in experiment 2 the turbulence caused by the Competitive leaders is somewhat tamed by the Fair leader, in this case the turbulence of the adapting process of the Competitive leader is not controlled by other leaders.

Finally, we tested how leaders with behaviors more likely to increase inequity could lose their role when competing with other leaders. We expected leaders less prone to distributive justice to lose all of their followers, and this was confirmed by our findings. In fact, the results of both Experiments 4 and 5 are quite similar as when respectively a Competitive or a Heuristic leader is competing with Fair leaders they lose all their followers and the only remaining leaders are the Fair ones. This is well illustrated in Figure 8 (the results for Heuristic

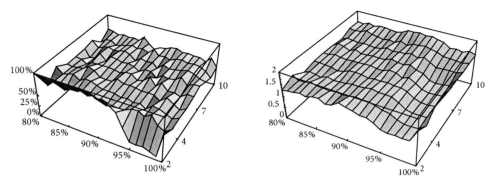

Figure 11 *Percentage of permanence of Punishing Heuristic leader (left) and final number of leaders (right) for Heuristic leaders*

leader vs. Fair leaders are identical). These results, together with the results of Experiments 1 and 2, show the emergence of Fair leaders. This is consistent with the human subject experiment, where in both populations fair leaders could attract more followers.

Furthermore, it must be noted that these results do not depend on the responsiveness of the agents. Also standard deviation is very low for the percentage of permanence in both the experiments (respectively in the range [0.0000–0.1800] and 0.000), while for the number of leaders standard deviation is larger (respectively, in the range [0.0000–0.0196] and [0.0000–0.2011]); this can depend on the initial configuration where some leaders may end up with no followers.

Comparing Experiments 1, 2, 4 and 5 we can observe that, while in the first two cases final production is more efficient since agents end up with one single leader, for Experiments 4 and 5 the agents end up fragmented in several lower-production teams. This could suggest that, in this case, too many fair leaders could be counterproductive for the collective welfare.

Finally, when considering a Heuristic leader competing with Competitive leaders results are different, especially in terms of the final number of leaders. Comparing the percentage of permanence and the final number of leaders in Figure 9, it is clear that the Heuristic leader keeps their role only when the number of initial leaders is very low and the responsiveness is not larger than 90%; in no case, as expected, do they remain the only leader, since at least one competitive leader keeps some follower. In all the other cases they lose their leadership role. Another important aspect is the number of leaders at the end. In order to end with one single leader the responsiveness parameter should be larger than 95%; this is in accordance with what we observed when only Competitive leaders were considered. Variance is greater than in experiments 4 and 5, since for both the percentage of permanence and the final number of leaders standard deviation is now in the range [0.0000–0.2491].

The other series of experiments we performed is related to free riders. Interpreting the data gathered during the human subject experiments, some of the subjects did not exert the effort suggested by the leader. As a consequence, we could observe the leader's reactions in the following rounds. Given our empirical evidence and the importance in the literature of free riding (Albanese and Van Fleet, 1985), we performed some experiments.

To examine the effects on the population we assume the presence of a single free-rider follower[8] exerting only 90% of the suggested effort. Since effort is not observable but payoffs are, in order to identify free riders, leaders may compare for each follower the expected individual payoff to the actual payoff. As in previous experiments, we consider homogeneous leaders with the exception of one punishing leader. Again, we are interested in determining under what conditions the punishing leader can emerge.

In the first experiment we consider a Fair leaders population; that is, one Punishing Fair leader among Fair leaders. From the results summarized in Figure 10 we can observe that, with this sort of leader, usually one single leader maintains its role. Furthermore, one observes immediately that the Punishing leader maintains their role, especially when the initial number of leaders is small.

When considering Heuristic or Competitive leaders the situation is similar but quite different from the previous experiment (Figure 11 for Heuristic leader; Competitive leader graphical results are similar and are therefore omitted).

In both cases the average number of leaders is smaller than two, so it is rather likely that one single leader maintains their role. In both cases, when the responsiveness is immediate (100%) or around 90%, it is less likely that any single leader remains. This different behavior depending on a single variable may confirm the complexity of the system and probably is due to the delays[9] introduced by the attitude change process. This effect is quite evident when considering only two initial leaders: while if responsiveness is smaller than 90% the punishing leader emerges, for larger responsiveness values the punishing leaders lose their followers. For all the free rider experiments the standard deviation of results is large; that is, in the range [0.0000–0.2500] and [0.0000–0.2956].

A final consideration is in order when considering the number of leaders in equilibrium. As we pointed out earlier, it is quite evident that the larger the group, the higher the profit. Even if in our simulations the agents were only sensitive to inequity, in most of the cases the equilibrium consists of one or at most two single leaders. As a consequence, it seems that by trying to minimize inequity the agents end up by maximizing the aggregate profit. This, however, does not happen when too many fair leaders are present.

Discussion and Further Research

The different results we were able to observe, both in the human experiments and the simulations, are a further confirmation of the indispensable significance of interactional complexity in organizations. The simulation proved to be extremely important in analyzing the system behavior when

---

8 We also performed simulations when considering more than one free rider and the results are quite similar.

9 For the critical role of delays in dynamics the reader may refer to Sterman (2000), para. 5.2.5.

some variables have been fixed; this would have been impossible when considering only human subjects, as many uncontrollable factors determine their decisions. In our approach we were interested in finding out under what conditions we could observe different leaders emerge. At the beginning of the interactions, both in the human subject experiments and the computer simulation, leadership roles seemed to be distributed to the agents. In fact, in the human subject experiments the number and composition of initial groups and leaders seemed to be the result of the subjects' physical positioning during the experiment, and this was in some way replicated in the computer simulations. So the question was to understand on what basis only a few of them could *emerge* and survive during the repeated interaction. These leaders emerged in the sense that they could "keep followers." This point is interesting, because it links some aspects of leadership described in the academic literature (Collinson, 2006) and also popular books (O'Toole, 1999) to empirical evidence.

Also comparing the results we obtained with the human subject experiments to the simulations provides some interesting suggestions, since in both cases Fair leaders could emerge.

The interaction we used in the human subjects represented many of the elements of complexity theory *per se*. The computational model we present retains some of these elements. For example, with some classes of leaders we can observe different final outcomes for small variations of the parameters; namely, the responsiveness probability and the initial number of leaders. This was particularly evident when considering either free riders or leadership styles different from Fair. In particular, while in the absence of free riders the only perceived inequity is about leaders' distributive fairness, in a population with free riders further inequity is perceived. Both kinds of inequity cause some turbulence, which, under certain conditions, does not allow the emergence of the fittest leader.

Furthermore, the fact that in human subject experiments we do not end with a single final leader, in contrast to what happens in the computer simulations with high values of the responsiveness probability, may suggest that the human subject responsiveness is not immediate.

In addition, if we assume that in the human subject experiments emerging leaders were those with larger groups, we can observe that the computer simulations (Experiments 1, 2, 4, and 5) are consistent with the empirical evidence, as in both emerging leaders have the larger groups.

As a final point, recall that the underlying theoretical model leads toward a single final group, because of the higher individual profits. We did not implement agents having the maximization profit as an objective; rather, following evidence in human subject experiments, we chose to model sensitiveness to inequity. Yet, inequity minimization led eventually mainly to the maximization of aggregate profit, when not too many Fair leaders were present.

The results of both the human subject experiment and the computer simulation showed how leadership emergence is a complex phenomenon, where many aspects and variables interact. While we could shed light on some aspects of leadership, some other aspects need further analysis. For example, it would be interesting to replicate the experiment with smaller groups in order to assess the importance of group size. Furthermore, it would be interesting to compare the experimental results when considering subjects different from students. Comparing different composition groups could provide interesting insights in terms of behavior. Another limitation is the relatively simple behaviors that were modeled in the computer simulations. While on one hand they allow us to observe the emergence of different styles of behavior in relatively homogeneous groups, more heterogeneous groups need to be studied. In particular, several other behaviors that we found in the human subjects need to be implemented in the computer simulations.

An important issue is the modeling of the leaders' emergence; in other words, it would be interesting to inquire under what conditions an agent may decide to become a leader. One interesting way could be to consider attitude and, for instance, assume that when attitude toward existing leaders falls under a certain value, an agent could decide to become a leader itself.

Another interesting direction is to explore the dynamical aspects of the sociomatrix implicitly defined by agents' attitudes. In fact, while Schreiber and Carley (2004, 2005) study heterogeneity in the network that connects each agent to other agents' resources, it would be interesting, following Proposition 3 in Hazy (forthcoming), to study persistence positions in the network induced by agents' attitudes.

Finally, our approach in modeling agents was grounded on the human subject experiments' result; it would be also interesting to model agents starting from a polar approach, for example incorporating the Fishbein and Ajzen (1975, 1981) theory of reasoned action. By contrasting those results to the ones we describe here, it could be possible to compare the two approaches and the underlying models.

Acknowledgments

We are grateful to Chiara Ghislieri for helpful suggestions; we acknowledge the editors and two anonymous reviewers for their constructive comments; usual caveats apply.

Mathematical Appendix
Social Optimal Plan

Individual profit π_{ik} is:

$$\pi_{ik} = \alpha_{ik} f_k\left(e_{1k},\dots, e_{n(k),k}\right) - c\left(e_{ik}\right) , \quad i = 1,\dots, n(k) , \quad k = 1,\dots m$$

while group P_k leader's profit is

$$\pi_{lk} = \left(1 - \sum_{i=1}^{n(k)} \alpha_{ik}\right) f_k\left(e_{1k},\dots, e_{n(k),k}\right)$$

In order to maximize group aggregate profit, a social planner chooses followers' efforts by solving the program with nonnegativity constraint

$$e_{ik}^*(\alpha_{ik}) = \underset{e_{ik}}{\operatorname{argmax}} \sum_{i=1}^{n(k)} \left[\alpha_{ik} f_k\left(e_{1k},\dots, e_{n(k),k}\right) - c\left(e_{ik}\right)\right] + \left(1 - \sum_{i=1}^{n(k)} \alpha_{ik}\right) f_k\left(e_{1k},\dots, e_{n(k),k}\right)$$

As the objective function is symmetric across agents, we can drop the index i in the optimal solution and denote f_k^* the optimal production of group P_k. At the same time, a fair payment plan can be solved by the equity condition (due to symmetry we have $\alpha_{ik} = \alpha_k$ for all i):

$$\pi_{ik} = \pi_{lk} \quad \forall i = 1,\dots, n(k) \iff \alpha_k f_k^* - c\left(e_k^*\right) = \left(1 - n(k)\alpha_k\right) f_k^* \qquad (2)$$

Production and Cost Functions Used in the Experiments

In order to keep our results comparable, the same functions were used both for the human subject experiment and the artificial simulations. They are:

$$f_k\left(e_{1k},\dots, e_{n(k),k}\right) = \left(\sum_{i=1}^{n(k)} e_{ik}\right)^{3/2} , \quad c\left(e_{ik}\right) = e_{ik}^2 \quad \forall i = 1,\dots, n(k) , \quad \forall k = 1,\dots, m$$

We can immediately compute the socially optimal individual effort and the fair sharing plan.

$$e_k^* = \frac{9}{16} n(k) ; \quad \alpha_k^* = \frac{3/4 + n(k)}{n(k)\left[1 + n(k)\right]} , \quad \forall k = 1,\dots, m$$

With this scheme it is easy to compute leader's and followers' optimal profit

$$\pi_k^* = \alpha_k^*\left[n(k) e_k^*\right]^{3/2} - e_k^{*2} = \frac{27n(k)^3}{256\left[n(k)+1\right]} = \left[1 - n(k)\alpha_k^*\right]\left[n(k) e_k^*\right]^{3/2} = \pi_{lk}^* \quad \forall k + 1,\dots, m$$

CHAPTER TWELVE
LEADERSHIP STYLE AS AN ENABLER OF ORGANIZATIONAL COMPLEX FUNCTIONING

Craig Schreiber & Kathleen M. Carley

The postmodern organization has a design paradox in which leaders are concerned with efficiency and control as well as complex functioning. Traditional leadership theory has limited applicability to postmodern organizations as it is mainly focused on efficiency and control. As a result, a new theory of leadership that recognizes the design paradox has been proposed: complexity leadership theory. This theory conceptualizes the integration of formal leadership roles with complex functioning. Our particular focus is on leadership style and its effect as an enabler of complex functioning. We introduce dynamic network analysis, a new methodology for modeling and analyzing organizations as complex adaptive networks. Dynamic network analysis is a methodology that quantifies complexity leadership theory. Data was collected from a real-world network organization and dynamic network analysis was used to explore the effects of leadership style as an enabler of complex functioning. Results and implications are discussed in relation to leadership theory and practice.

Craig Schreiber recently earned his Ph.D. in Computation, Organizations and Society from Carnegie Mellon University. He was a member of the Center for Computational Analysis of Social and Organizational Systems (CASOS) at the Institute for Software Research International in the School of Computer Science. He is currently a research associate for the National Research Council. Previously he has worked on research projects sponsored by the National Science Foundation, NASA, the Office of Naval Research and Army Research Labs. His interests include strategic management, organization and management theory, leadership, influence and power, organizational structure, organizational performance, organizational risk, organizational learning, knowledge management, information technology, computational organization science, social network analysis, dynamic network analysis, and model validation.

Kathleen M. Carley is a professor at the Institute for Software Research International in the School of Computer Science at Carnegie Mellon University. She is the director of the center for Computational Analysis of Social and Organizational Systems (CASOS) (http://www.casos.cs.cmu.edu/), a university-wide interdisciplinary center that brings together network analysis, computer science, and organization science, and has an associated NSF-funded training program for Ph.D. students. She carries out research that combines cognitive science, dynamic social networks, text processing, organizations, social and computer science in a variety of theoretical and applied venues. Her specific research areas are computational social and organization theory; dynamic social networks; multi-agent network models; group, organizational, and social adaptation and evolution; statistical models for dynamic network analysis and evolution; computational text analysis; and the impact of telecommunication technologies on communication and information diffusion within and among groups. She is the lead developer of ORGAHEAD (http://www.casos.cs.cmu.edu/projects/OrgAhead/), a tool for examining organizational adaptation, Construct (http://www.casos.cs.cmu.edu/projects/construct/), a computational model of the coevolution of people and social networks, DyNet (http://www.casos.cs.cmu.edu/projects/DyNet/), a computational model for network destabilization, BioWar (http://www.casos.cs.cmu.edu/projects/biowar/), a city-scale multi-agent network model of weaponized biological attacks, ORA (http://www.casos.cs.cmu.edu/projects/ora/), a tool for the statistical analysis of social network data and AutoMap (http://www.casos.cs.cmu.edu/projects/automap/), which are computational tools for automated text analysis.

Introduction

Postmodern organizations have a design paradox where they simultaneously maintain a bureaucratic nature and complex functioning (McGrath, 2001). Complex functioning is the coevolution of human and social capital that results from the interdependent interactions among autonomous agents with diverse knowledge. Complex functioning produces learning and adaptation, both of which are needed for effective response in highly volatile environments (McKelvey, under review). Accordingly, postmodern organizations must have efficiency yet learn and adapt; have control yet be responsive; and have centralized vision yet be autonomously decentralized.

Due to this, the nature of leadership has changed and traditional leadership theory has limited applicability in the modern era. Traditional leadership theory mainly studied bureaucratic contexts that focused on leading for efficiency and control (Streatfield, 2001; Zaccaro & Klimoski, 2001). Postmodern organizations must now balance leading for efficiency and control with leading for learning and adaptability. As a consequence of this paradox, traditional leadership theory only speaks to part of the overall nature of leadership. The complexity theory approach to leadership, as is argued in this special issue, speaks to the learning and adaptive nature of leadership – leading for organizational complex functioning.

Our interest is in exploring how traditional leadership roles integrate with leading for learning and adaptability. In particular, we focus on the interaction of formal leadership style with the complex functioning of the informal network. Leadership style is defined by how decisions are made in the organization. We use the directive/participative leadership style delineation as described by Tannenbaum and Schmidt (1958). Directive leadership is a style in which the leader makes and declares decisions without consulting subordinates. Participative leadership is a style in which the leader consults subordinates before making decisions.

Leadership style may be important to complex functioning because differences in how decisions are made within the organization could affect the coevolution of human and social capital. For instance, directive and participative styles of decision making are theorized to have an affect on information flows in an organization (Anthony, 1978). From a structural perspective, these different leadership styles imply different information flows within the organization. For example, information needed for decision making would flow into a directive leader and, in contrast, out from a participative leader. As such, the different information flows could lead to different coevolutions of human and social capital.

In this research, we collected social network data on a real-world organization that had two different leaders. We modeled the organization as a complex adaptive system using a multi-agent network model. The leadership styles of each formal leader were represented in the model and the effects of the respective leadership styles on the complex functioning of the informal network were examined. In this way, we synthesized traditional leadership roles with a complexity science approach to explore the phenomena.

The next section of this paper gives the background to traditional and postmodern leadership. This is followed by the conceptual framework used in this study, complexity leadership theory. The research question is subsequently described and dynamic network analysis, the computational methodology used to explore the research question, is explained. Next, the virtual experiment design is described and followed by the presentation and discussion of results. Lastly, the conclusion provides both theoretical and normative implications of the study.

Background
Traditional Leadership Theory

Prior research has explained leadership using trait (Argyris, 1953; Stogdill, 1948), behavioral (Blake & Mouton, 1994; Tannenbaum & Schmidt, 1958), situational (Hersey & Blanchard, 1977; Vroom & Yetton, 1973), transformational (Bass, 1985; Burns, 1978) and leader–member exchange (Graen & Scandura, 1987) approaches. The above approaches focus on topics such as leading members to produce efficiently and effectively (Zaccaro & Klimoski, 2001), motivating members to successful goal attainment (House and Mitchell, 1974), inspiring members to vision commitment (Yammarino, 1994) and developing quality leader–member relationships that improve organizational outcomes (Graen, 2003).

Although each of these approaches views leadership from a different angle, they also form a single dominant paradigm. This paradigm is about the influence that leaders have on followers, with the goal of getting the follower to achieve some objective. The influence of a leader is due to a personal characteristic, behavior or skill. As such, this paradigm mostly emits a top-down view of leadership that is concerned with the influence of a single, "heroic" leader.

In addition, the research within this paradigm was predominantly conducted in bureaucratic organizations (Zaccaro & Klimoski, 2001) with the focus being on centralized power and formal leadership within hierarchical structures. As a consequence, traditional leadership theory's main concern is leading for efficiency and control within a relatively stable context.

A New Era of Leadership

In contrast, the context of the postmodern knowledge economy is characterized by uncertainty and turbulence. This new, dynamic context is driven by technological revolution and economic globalization (Hitt, 1998), resulting in rapid and continuous change, diminished product lifecycles and the need to turn large amounts of data into useable information (Ireland & Hitt, 1999). Organizations now have to increase the rate at which they learn (Bettis & Hitt, 1995; Child & McGrath, 2001) in order to survive in this environment.

Accordingly, there has been a switch in organizational core competency. Intellectual assets are now the core competency of organizations (Nonaka & Takeuchi, 1995; Prusak, 1996) rather than capital and labor assets, which were the core competencies of organizations in the industrial era (Stewart, 1997). Faster, productive learning provides an organization with the flexibility and mental agility to quickly identify and exploit emergent opportunities in the ever-changing environment (Ireland & Hitt, 1999).

Along with this new economic context and change in organizational core competency has come the recognition that previous standard practices of leadership offer limited insight for dealing with the challenges of postmodern organizations: challenges such as adapting to rapid change and enabling faster learning (Davenport, 2001; Hitt, *et al.*, 1998; Streatfield, 2001). Again, standard leadership practices have dealt more with efficiency and control rather than adaptive change and learning. Therefore, a new leadership mindset has developed that realizes the different paradigm that postmodern organizational leaders face. The following quotes exemplify this new paradigm:

"Increasingly, networked and globalized thinking will be essential for coping with the accelerating pace of change" (Heinrich von Pierer quoted in Ireland and Hitt, 1999: 47).

"The problem facing almost all leaders in the future will be how to develop their organization's social architecture so that it actually generates intellectual capital" (Bennis, 1997: 87).

"John Browne, CEO of British Petroleum Company, believes that the top manager must stimulate the organization rather than control it" (Ireland & Hitt, 1999: 47).

This new mindset recognizes several characteristics of leading for adaptive change and learning in the new era. First, collective change agents are the competitive source of adaptive response and learning. Tapping the collective intelligence of the organization's citizenry allows for a quicker response to change. This moves the paradigm away from the single "heroic" leader who has all the strategic answers to one where the responsibility for learning and reasoning about strategic change falls onto the collective organization.

Second, collective intelligence is the combination of both human and social capital. Developing human capital has long been recognized as an advantage (Becker, 1975), but having an adaptable social structure that can respond to changes and connect human capital in various ways is seen as just as important for sustaining competitive advantage (Baker, 1992). The rise in organic or network forms of organization demonstrates the importance of the social network. Therefore, organizations need to create conditions or cultures that simultaneously stimulate the development of human and social capital.

Third, organizations need to be stimulated, not controlled. Creative change occurs by way of interactions among an organization's citizenry (Bennis & Biederman, 1997). These interactions are what generate collective intelligence. Top-down, command-and-control style leadership can stifle the development of collective intelligence by limiting the development of human and social capital (Bennis, 1997; McKelvey, under review). Quick, adaptive interaction patterns cannot be prescribed by fiat. They are stimulated by conditions such as an accepted and strong learning culture.

Conceptual Framework: Complexity Leadership Theory

Realizing that traditional leadership theory has limited ability to explore and understand postmodern leadership, some theorists are using complexity theory as a new science approach to explaining leadership processes (Marion & Uhl-Bien, 2001; McKelvey, under review; Regine & Lewin, 2000; Wheatley, 1999). The premise is that complexity theory will help explain some of the emergent change processes that are now prevalent in organizations but yet defy explanation when current theories are used (Smith, 2004).

One such theory that uses complexity science and matches the new mindset extremely well is complexity leadership theory (Uhl-Bien, *et al.*, 2004). This new theory recognizes that adaptive change and learning result from the collective action response of agents who are interdependently interacting at the nexus of diverse knowledge. It further recognizes that while organizations need to stimulate emergent collective action, they also have a bureaucratic nature and a need to efficiently control organizational outcomes for exploitation. This is known as the organizational design paradox (Child & McGrath, 2001). Therefore, Uhl-Bien *et al.* (2004) have proposed that postmodern leadership is composed of three separate but entangled roles that accommodate the paradox: managerial leadership, adaptive leadership and enabling leadership (see Figure 1).

Managerial leadership is the traditional notion of formal leadership roles with top-down control and strategic planning. Leadership style is a behavior that is associated with formal leadership roles. *Adaptive leadership* is leadership that occurs within the interdependent interactions of emergent collective action and that helps produce emergent outcomes such as learning and adaptation. Adaptive leadership is important to the complex functioning of the network. *Enabling leadership* has two roles. First, it creates conditions that stimulate emergent collective action and adaptive leadership. Second, it channels productive emergent outcomes originating in the collective action response back up to managerial leadership for strategic planning and exploitation.

The focus of complexity leadership theory is on enabling leadership and adaptive leadership. This is due to the need for understanding the new leadership paradigm. Enabling leadership creates conditions that foster complex functioning and the enactment of adaptive leadership within the informal network. It creates these conditions by injecting tensions into the organization, which induce interactions and create interdependencies among the agents. The combination of interactions and interdependency is needed for complex functioning and the production of emergent outcomes. Interactions facilitate knowledge flow and interdependency stimulates learning by pressuring agents to act on knowledge.

The heart of the complex functioning process is the coevolution of human and social capital[1] (Carley & Hill, 2001; McKelvey, under review) – the production of collective intelligence that occurs through an emergent collective action response. This process is akin to the neural network theory of how the

---

1 Carley and Hill (2001) use the term dual-level learning where the organizational system learns at both the individual agent level and the structural level, but it is the same concept.

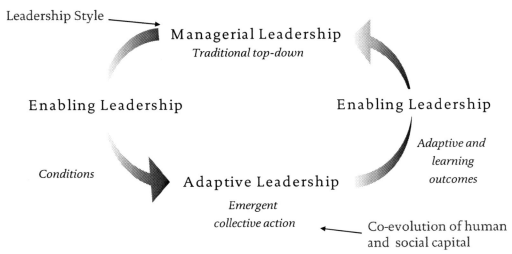

Figure 1 *The three entangled leadership roles of complexity leadership theory*

brain functions and learns. Neural networks learn by neurons making dynamic connections to themselves through synaptic links. Organizations learn by human capital components making dynamic connections to themselves through social capital relations. Human capital appreciation accumulates energy in the form of knowledge. Energy flow in the informal network is knowledge flow through social interactions that are actuated by tensions originating in the conditions created by enabling leadership. These social interactions are fluid and can change in response to changes in knowledge and tension. Change in social interactions can affect where in the network knowledge accumulates and builds on itself, and therefore where learning and adaptation occur. Analyzing the coevolution of human and social capital can give us insights into the effects of enabling conditions for producing productive learning and adaptive outcomes.

Adaptive leadership occurs within the complex functioning process. Adaptive leaders are those who are particularly influential in facilitating interactions and knowledge flows (Uhl-Bien, *et al.*, 2004); that is, complex functioning. In other words, adaptive leaders are those who shape the overall communication structure and help advance the coevolution of human and social capital. Adaptive leaders are not necessarily formal leaders. Adaptive leaders emerge due to the organization's learning and adaptive needs. Anyone in the informal network can emerge as an adaptive leader. In addition, adaptive leadership can be enacted by several agents simultaneously during a distinct event or over time. Therefore, adaptive leadership can also be distributed (Gronn, 2002) and/or shared (Pierce & Conger, 2003) leadership.

Research Question: Leadership Style as an Enabler of Complex Functioning: Synthesizing Traditional Leadership Roles with Complexity

The question we ask is: Does leadership style have varying effects as an enabler of complex functioning? Leadership style, as shown in Figure 1, is a behavior within the managerial leadership role. According to Uhl-Bien and colleagues (2004), a formal leader is in a particularly advantageous spot for performing enabling leadership due to their authority position. Therefore, studying the behavioral differences of formal leaders and the associated effects on complex functioning is appropriate. What we are exploring is whether the decision-making behavior of a formal leader, which is enacted in the managerial leadership role, can also act as enabling leadership and affect the coevolution of human and social capital.

Within the traditional paradigm, leadership style is a behavior that has been well studied. Several dichotomous distinctions have been used to describe leadership style, including directive/participative (Tannenbaum & Schmidt, 1958), authoritative/democratic (Lewin & Lippitt, 1938), consideration/initiating structure (Fleishman, 1953) and task/relational orientation (Hersey & Blanchard, 1977). While all of these distinctions have a concern for how decisions are made, the directive/participative distinction is mainly focused on this behavior. In addition, as previously noted, the directive/participative distinction has been theorized to affect the flow of information within an organization (Miller and Monge, 1986). More specifically, participative leadership is theorized to increase the flow and use of pertinent information (Anthony, 1978; Frost *et al.*, 1974). Information flow is also an important factor in the coevolutionary process (Carley & Hill, 2001; Uhl-Bien, *et al.*, 2004). If the directive/participative distinctions lead to differential effects on information flow then they may also lead to different coevolutions of human and social capital. The directive/participative distinction, therefore, is the distinction that is used in this study.

Prior research has shown that directive/participative leadership has effects on employee satisfaction and performance (Miller & Monge, 1986). To date, there are no studies of the effects of leadership style on network structure and complex functioning.

Methodology
Computational Modeling

We needed to analyze the coevolution of human and social capital in order to study the effects of leadership style on organizational complex functioning. Computational modeling was used to explore the research question for two main reasons. First, the data collected in the field was cross-sectional. Computational modeling affords the ability to evolve empirical networks through simulation and thereby overcome the limitations of cross-sectional data (Schreiber & Carley, 2004a). Second, the coevolution of human and social capital is inherently computational and complex. It is computational in that it involves information-driven activities. It is complex in that it involves not only information-processing factors but also social and cognitive factors. The coevolution of human and social capital is a property of complex adaptive systems.

Computational modeling is an appropriate methodology for analyzing organizations as complex adaptive systems (Carley & Gasser, 1999), especially within the complex context of the postmodern knowledge economy (Hazy, in press).

Several recent efforts have used various computational modeling techniques to explore leadership from a complexity science perspective (Hazy, in press). For example, Vroom and Jago (1988) used an expert system; Anghel *et al.* (2004) and Hubler and Pines (1994) used a multi-agent model; Schreiber and Carley (2004b, 2005) used dynamic network analysis; Solow *et al.* (2005) used an *NK* model; and Hazy (2004a, 2004b) as well as Jacobson and House (2001) used system dynamics models.

The dynamic network analysis technique was chosen for two reasons. First, dynamic network analysis has been formally described and used as a methodology for quantifying complexity leadership theory (Schreiber, 2006). The methodology uses a bottom-up modeling approach that represents, captures and analyzes the complex interactions among agents in the informal network. Second, out of all of the techniques, only dynamic network analysis allows for the quantification and exploration of the coevolution of human and social capital at multiple levels of analysis. The analysis in this work required the longitudinal representation of the knowledge network and the social network at both the node and graph levels. Changes in social capital are analyzed at the graph (organizational) level, and human capital and adaptive leaders are analyzed at the node (individual) level.

Dynamic network analysis, as explained in the next section, not only represents complex network structure by way of the MetaMatrix but also represents coevolutionary network dynamics through the use of multi-agent simulation (Carley, 2003). This technique allows for longitudinal reasoning about the effects of leadership style on dynamic network structure.

Dynamic Network Analysis

Dynamic network analysis is a methodology for modeling and analyzing the complex relational qualities and longitudinal dynamics of organizational systems. The techniques of social network analysis and multi-agent simulation are combined in this methodological approach: social network analysis to analyze complex relational qualities and multi-agent simulation to reason about longitudinal dynamics.

In dynamic network analysis, the MetaMatrix framework (Carley, 1999a, 2002; Krackhardt & Carley, 1998) is used to represent organizations as systems of complex relations that are multi-mode and multi-plex (see Figure 2). Multi-mode refers to the various entity classes that are within an organization such as people, knowledge, tasks, and resources. Multi-plex refers to the various types of relations between the entity classes such as communication, knowledge acquisition, task assignment, and resource allocation. Any unique combination of

	People / Agents	Knowledge / Resources	Tasks / Events	Groups / Organizations
People / Agents	Social Network	Knowledge Network / Resource Network	Assignment Network / Attendance Network	Affiliation Network / Membership Network
Knowledge / Resources		Information Network / Substitutes Network	Needs Network	Core Capabilities
Tasks / Events			Precedence Ordering	Institutional Relation
Groups / Organizations				Inter-organizational Network / Inter-group Network

Figure 2 *Illustrative MetaMatrix*

two entity classes and a relation makes a network in the MetaMatrix.

Representing relations between networks is just as important as representing relations within each network, as changes in one network can affect changes in other networks. For instance, human and social capital coevolve because the social network and knowledge network are intricately related. As agents interact in the social network, they can learn knowledge or create new knowledge and this changes the knowledge network. Likewise, changes in the knowledge network can affect future instances of the social network, as changes in knowledge and understanding will influence who an agent subsequently interacts with. Representing organizations as a multi-mode, multi-plex system of networks captures more of the complex interdependencies inherent in the system.

Multi-agent network models simulate organizations as complex adaptive systems of individual cognitive agents who can take action, learn, and alter their networks. The particular multi-agent network model we use for reasoning about organizational complex functioning is Construct (Carley, 1990, 1991, 1999b; Carley & Hill, 2001; Schreiber & Carley, 2004a, 2004b, 2005; Schreiber, *et al.*, 2004).

Agents in Construct are defined as information processing units, which interact and communicate based on well-known social and cognitive processes. Theoretical foundations of these processes in Construct are homophily (Lazarsfeld & Merton, 1978), proximity interactions (Festinger, 1950), double interact (Weick, 1969), structuration (Giddens, 1984) social information processing (Salancik & Pfeffer, 1978), and situated learning (Lave & Wenger, 1991). Natural evolutionary processes of the organizational system, such as learning and network alteration, are based on these theories of social and cognitive processes.

To understand the emergent organizational dynamics we need to reason about basic network evolutionary and strategic intervention processes. Multi-agent network models such as Construct allow for reasoning about these processes. For instance, we can reason about a given set of relations in the Meta-Matrix and how these networks constrain or enable behavior such as emergent collective action and adaptive leadership. We can also reason about the co-evolution of multiple networks, such as the human and social capital networks that generate collective intelligence. The focus is on interactions and processes, not outcomes. System-level outcomes such as collective intelligence emerge due to bottom-up interactions and processes.

Data

MetaMatrix data was collected on Team X at NASA's Jet Propulsion Laboratory. Team X is a first-phase conceptual design team that designs spacecraft for non-human space flight missions. The team for this particular design session was composed of 19 members with one formal leader and the rest of the team being a network organization.

Network organizations are forms of organizing characterized by flexible structures that are horizontal in nature (Miles & Snow, 1986; Nohria, 1992). These forms of organizing are advantageous for organizational adaptation and learning in rapidly changing environments (Hitt, *et al.*, 1998; Powell, 1990).

Team X is designed to be a network organization due to the specific design task that is performed (Wall, 1999). The design task is exemplary of knowledge work in that it is data intensive, intellective and integrative with an innovative product outcome. In addition, the NASA faster, better, cheaper initiative (Mc-Curdy, 2001) influenced the conception of the design task and the team is under extreme time pressure to complete the design. Designing a complex spacecraft requires the team to deal with many unexpected exceptions. So, the team needs to have the ability to form dynamic relations in order to solve problems quickly. These dynamic relations are emergent collective action responses that provide collective intelligence for faster learning and for dealing with change.

Network organizations are ideal for studying the dynamics of the informal network, such as the coevolution of human and social capital, because the informal network is usually more pronounced in these organizations. This by no means limits the findings of this research to only network organizations, as informal networks are within all organizations.

Team X used two different formal leaders during this particular design session, with the change in leadership occurring midstream. Each leader had opposite styles of decision-making behavior[2]. Leader 1 had a directive leadership style and centralized decisions more. Leader 2 had a participative leadership style and decentralized decisions more. The team was co-located in a single room and, from a qualitative perspective, had a distinct feel and noticeably different behaviors under each leader.

The MetaMatrix data was collected via survey and interviews. Only one data collection period was obtained due to the inability to interrupt the design process, but data was collected on both leaders.

---

2 The extreme difference in leadership styles was verified through observation and interviews.

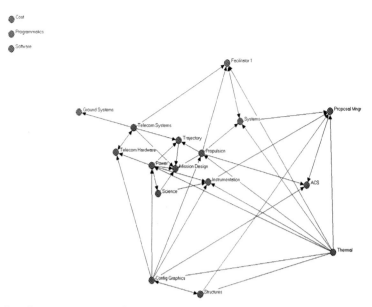

Figure 3 *The directive, centralized style of Leader 1 (task dependency network)*

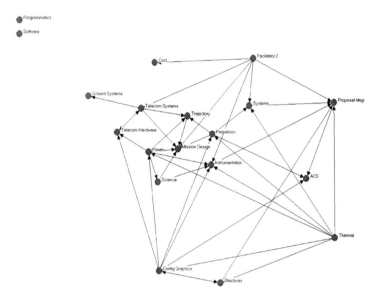

Figure 4 *The participative, decentralized style of
Leader 2 (task dependency network)*

Examination of the task dependency network for Team X also indicated a difference in leadership style (see Figures 3 and 4). The task dependency network is a digraph where the tasks of agent i depend on input from agent j. Figure 3 indicates that Leader 1 centralizes decisions, as the ties are directed in toward the leader node. Leader 1 used tighter control over the design task and coordination. Figure 4 indicates that Leader 2 decentralizes decisions, as ties are directed out to other team member nodes. Leader 2 used looser control of the design task and coordination.

The limitation of one data collection period precluded the empirical study of human and social capital coevolution for each leader. Consequently, we used multi-agent network simulation to evolve the Team X networks under the influence of each leader.

Experimental Design

Using the MetaMatrix data with the distinct delineation of each leadership style, directive and participative, we produced a representation of Team X under each leader. These representations were separately used to initialize Construct and a virtual experiment was run to test the effect of each leader's style on complex functioning. The virtual experiment also included conditions where the knowledge base of each leader was used with the other leader's distinct leadership style representation to ensure that any significant effects were not due to the particular knowledge base of each leader (instead of leadership style). The knowledge base is the specific knowledge that each leader possesses. In other words, it is the ego knowledge network for each leader.

The virtual experiment was run for 150 time periods and the results were averaged over 100 Monte Carlo runs. Output obtained from the model was in terms of performance from agent learning (human capital) and interaction networks (social capital) over time.

Performance from agent learning is represented by the task-relevant knowledge measure in Construct. This measure is the amount of task-relevant knowledge that each agent has, expressed as a percentage of the total amount of task-relevant knowledge that is knowable. Agents perform more accurately with higher levels of task-relevant knowledge. The overall performance measure is an average over all the agents in the organization. Each agent has task-relevant knowledge that is initialized using the empirical knowledge network from the MetaMatrix. An agent can learn additional task-relevant knowledge through interactions with other agents.

Social capital is measured by the graph density and clustering coefficient measures. Graph density is the number of existing relations over the total number of possible relations, and the clustering coefficient is the average density of all ego networks in the graph. Each of these measures is an indicator of social capital at the organizational level of analysis.

In addition, we identified adaptive leaders: individual agents who are central to shaping the overall communication structure of the organization and who therefore facilitate complex functioning. Betweenness centrality was calculated on the simulated interaction networks to identify the adaptive leaders. Betweenness centrality is the normalized percentage of shortest paths that pass through an individual agent. In essence, it measures the degree of influence an agent has in the communication flow of the informal network. This measure is appropriate for identifying adaptive leaders for the simulated team, since agents in Construct are not withholding knowledge or using their network position as a brokering advantage.

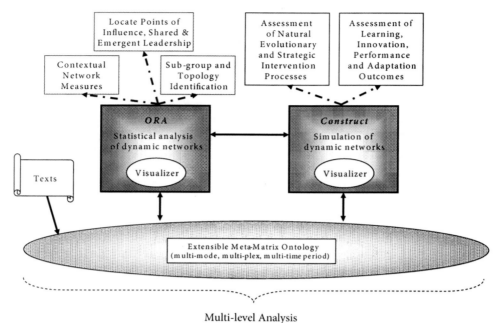

Figure 5 *CMU dynamic network analysis tools for reasoning about complex adaptive systems*

Tool Chain

We used the CMU dynamic network analysis tool chain to analyze and reason about the effects of leadership style on the complex functioning of Team X. The specific tools used in this research are depicted in Figure 5 and consist of:

- DyNetML, an XML-based interchange language for representing MetaMatrix relational data (Tsvetovat, *et al.*, 2004);

- ORA, a statistical tool for the analysis of dynamic network data (Carley & Kamneva, 2004; Carley & Reminga, 2004);

- Construct, a multi-agent network simulation model for reasoning about network change (Schreiber, *et al.*, 2004);

- Social Insight, network visualization tool

Results and Discussion

Figure 6 shows the ending performance results of the virtual experiment. Clearly, the team under the influence of the participative leadership style performs better and the performance difference is not due to any distinction in the knowledge base of the leaders. In other words, any disparity in expertise between the leaders did not significantly affect the outcome measure. What is underlying the difference in performance is an increase in overall human capital. Human capital in the simulated team increased by 63 percent under participative leadership compared to an increase of 59 percent under directive leadership. The higher level of learning resulted in higher performance as agents in the model attained

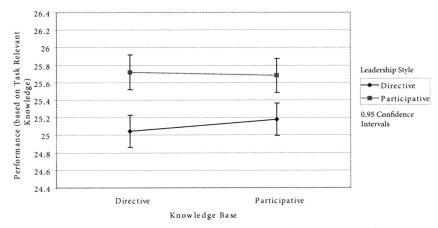

Figure 6 *Aggregate human capital performance analysis (based on agent learning)*

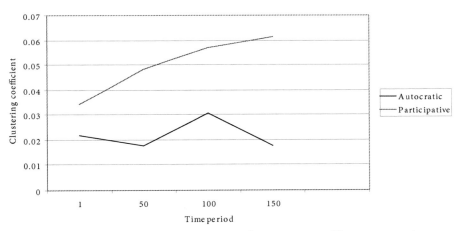

Figure 7 *Social capital measure: Clustering coefficient over time*

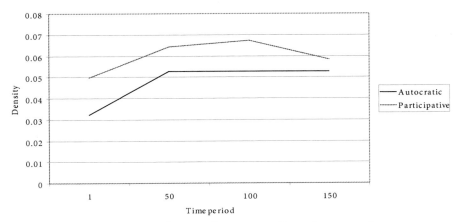

Figure 8 *Social capital measure: Density over time*

more task-relevant knowledge and were therefore more accurate in performing the task.

With a difference in human capital evolution established, we now turn to graph-level measures of social capital over time. Figure 7 shows the clustering coefficient and Figure 8 shows the graph density. Both of these measures reveal consistently higher levels of social capital in the simulated team under participative leadership. The increased evolution of social capital under participative leadership contributed to higher learning by facilitating knowledge flows among the agents.

The difference in the coevolution of human and social capital under the distinct leadership styles is due to a couple of reasons. First, there are differences in information flow due to the leadership style: the directive and participative leaders acted as a sink and a source respectively. In the case of the directive leader, information flowed along fewer paths and toward a central point, as the influence of this leader was to gain knowledge for centralized decisions. The case of the participative leader was different, however. The participative leader acted as a source and pushed information into the team for decentralized decisions. Information flowed along more paths, which not only induced more interactions but also increased interdependencies through a subsequent heterogeneous distribution of knowledge. As heterogeneous knowledge increased in the team, agents searching for information were interdependent with a larger number of other agents. In other words, they could find the information they needed from multiple others rather than just a few, as was the case under directive leadership. Heterogeneous information represents variety in the organization and variety is necessary for increasing organizational learning (Hazy, 2004a, 2006; Hazy & Tivnan, 2004).

Second, the level of emergent adaptive leadership in the informal network varied. Table 1 shows the top three agents in betweenness centrality across all time periods under directive leadership and participative leadership. There is a higher degree of betweenness centrality among the top agents under participative leadership. This result is also obtained at the graph level, as betweenness centrality for the overall team under the directive leadership style is 0.0125, and under the participative leadership style is 0.0187. The participative leadership style enabled conditions that allowed for greater levels of adaptive leadership, mainly through increased interactions and interdependencies. This higher level of adaptive leadership enhanced information flow and facilitated the complex functioning of the informal network.

Directive leadership	Participative leadership
Telecom S (0.0374)	Leader 2 (0.0883)
Thermal (0.0335)	Proposal Mgr (0.0478)
Propulsion (0.0308)	Telecom S (0.0448)

Table 1 *Top three adaptive leaders under each leadership style based on betweenness centrality (in parentheses)*

In addition, these results suggest that agents will be conduits of adaptive leadership to a greater or lesser degree depending on the conditions. For instance, decentralized decisions created tensions that increased interactions and interdependencies among the agents. The agents under this condition, on average, enacted higher levels of adaptive leadership. In contrast, centralized decisions led to a condition with less interactive tensions and lower levels of adaptive leadership.

Another interesting result is the difference in the specific agents who were adaptive leaders. Only one of the agents is an adaptive leader under both leadership styles. This suggests that agents in the informal network will serve different roles – such as leader, peer, and subordinate – depending on the conditions. This includes formal leaders, as they are also embedded in the complex functioning of the informal network. We would like to note that we are not predicting exactly who will be an adaptive leader and at what level through this analysis. What we are saying is that there will most likely be a difference in who is an adaptive leader and at what level given different conditions.

Conclusion

The postmodern era entails an organizational design paradox and a new paradigm of leadership. The needs of organizations are now centered on knowledge work to produce faster learning and adaptive responses in an environment that is characterized by high-velocity change. Standard leadership practices are less effective in the new era as they have traditionally focused on efficiency and control (Zaccaro & Klimoski, 2001) whereas learning and adaptation are vital to survival in this new volatile economy (McKelvey, under review). Yet, efficiency and control are still needed in order to effectively exploit organizational outcomes for gain.

Realizing that there is a need for a leadership theory that addresses the challenges of postmodern organizations, Uhl-Bien *et al.* (2004) have proposed complexity leadership theory. This theory recognizes the organization design paradox and the simultaneous need for leading for efficiency and control and leading for learning and adaptability.

Our interest is in the paradoxical integration of traditional leadership roles with leading for learning and adaptability. In particular, we explored the effects of formal leadership style on the complex functioning of the informal network. This question was explored because the directive/participative leadership styles are theorized to have an effect on organizational information flows (Anthony, 1978) and information flows are also important to organizational complex functioning (Carley & Hill, 2001). This meant that leadership style may affect organizational complex functioning.

Our results suggest that participative-style leadership enables conditions that stimulate higher levels of human and social capital coevolution. This was due to an increase in knowledge flows that induced more interactions and created more interdependencies among the agents. Along with this, our results suggest that participative leadership allows for higher levels of emergent adaptive leadership. Adaptive leaders were central agents who were influential in facilitating interactions and knowledge flows, thereby advancing the co-evolution of human and social capital. In addition, who emerges as an adaptive leader can vary depending on the conditions in the organization. Different agents emerged as adaptive leaders when under the influence of the two distinct leadership styles. These leadership styles induced different levels of tension in the form of knowledge flows.

There is an auxiliary result of this research that is worth mentioning. This is that a change in leadership can lead to unintended structural changes. The only thing that was different for the initial networks in each condition was the leader and their connections. The initial network structure of the members was exactly the same. Yet, two very different member networks resulted over time as a consequence of differential information flows. This means that leadership style has second-order effects in the network. Each leader had no more than six direct connections, but nodes indirectly connected to the leader were also affected.

There are some practical implications that come from this research. The most obvious is that a participative style of leadership stimulates interactions and interdependencies. This leads to higher levels of complex functioning as well as productive learning and adaptive outcomes. However, a more important implication is that such outcomes are achieved by managing tensions that induce interactions and create interdependencies. Complex functioning is a process that results from tensions. It is not controlled or managed by objectives. In fact, traditional top-down control methods, such as centralized decision making, can limit the emergent collective action and slow down the coevolution of human and social capital, thus lessening productive outcomes. Other practices besides leadership style can create tensions in an organization and stimulate the process of complex functioning. For instance, self-forming teams enable interactions and heterogeneous workgroups inject interdependencies.

Nevertheless, tensions do need to be managed. Self-organizing processes have the advantage of quick adaptation and learning, but these processes can also self-define their evolutionary path. The complex self-organized process of complex functioning could stray into counter-productive directions (Uhl-Bien, *et al.*, 2004) such as over-socialization, negative conflict, or strategic goal incongruence. Strategic interventions may need to be invoked that guide the adaptive process in productive directions. For instance, reassigning personnel or reframing problem definitions may reduce negative conflict and restore productive interactions.

In conclusion, the practical main points are that complex functioning is stimulated by tension, complexity leadership is a process that manages tensions, and complexity leaders recognize that the postmodern organization is a complex adaptive system.

Acknowledgments

The research reported herein was supported by NASA Grant No. NAG-2-1569 and Contract No. NNA04AA14C, and the National Science Foundation NSF Grant No. 0452487. Additional support was provided by the NSF IGERT

9972762 for research and training in CASOS and by the center for Computational Analysis of Social and Organizational Systems at Carnegie Mellon University. The views and conclusions contained in this document are those of the authors and should not be interpreted as representing the official policies, either expressed or implied, of NASA, the National Science Foundation or the U.S. government.

CHAPTER THIRTEEN
Bureaucratic Agents: Simulating Organizational Behavior and Hierarchical Decision-Making

Cosimo Spada

The bureaucracy is the predominant organizational model in modern human societies. In its ideal form, the bureaucracy is based on hierarchy, meritocracy, impersonality, voluntary (self-interested) participation, and rational, rule-based authority. Thus, a high position in the bureaucratic hierarchy corresponds to power and authority over lower positions, and the hierarchy is constantly changed by meritocratic mechanisms that delegate power to the most competent decision-makers. Participation in the bureaucracy's activities is encouraged by utilitarian incentives, not forced by coercive measures or persuaded by social pressure, so the bureaucracy relies on its members' self-interest. The bureaucracy's rules are impersonal (i.e., equality before the law) and explicit (supposed to be known by the bureaucracy's members). In this chapter, the bureaucratic organizational model is introduced in a multi-agent system, where agents are confronted with tasks of varying cooperative difficulty. The bureaucratic agents' efficiency in solving these tasks is compared with the performance of unorganized agents. Simulation results indicate that the applied bureaucratic model, after some fine-tuning, succeeds in improving agent cooperation. Furthermore, an analysis of the social dynamics in the agent society shows that social mobility decreases even though the agent society has entered a stable stage, suggesting that the emerging power structure between agents is self-perpetuating.

Cosimo Spada is currently a system developer at Visma Proceedo AB, in Stockholm, Sweden. He has an MSc in Computer and Systems Sciences, Stockholm University, with focus on multi-agent design, and a BA in History of Science and Ideas, Uppsala University with focus on the history of political sciences. He has previously published a paper on Sweden's neutrality policy in the leading Swedish Journal of History of Science, Lychnos ("Institutions of Neutrality", Lychnos, 2003).

Concepts
The Micro-Macro Link

Asociety, as any complex system, is more than the sum of its parts. Seldom are collective behaviors in organizations or societies mere extrapolations of individual behavior. When analyzing societies, whether human or artificial, one usually makes a basic methodological choice between the micro- and the macro-perspectives. Thus, one inquiry can be: How do micro-level events relate to macro-level events? Although the different approaches should be possible to combine, in practice they are often in conflict. From a typical micro-perspective, individual choices determine macro-behavior. In other words, macro-structures are explained in terms of individual interactions. From a typical macro-perspective, on the other hand, individual actions must be analyzed in light of macro-structures; an individual action cannot be fully explained without understanding the actor's social context, i.e., its macro-structure. So how does one make the choice?

The steps between extreme individualism (i.e., when one focuses completely on the micro-perspective) and extreme collectivism (i.e., when one focuses on the macro-perspective) can be described in terms of the relation between micro-level and macro-level events and how they are causally related in a temporal perspective. In other words, the question is: *Events at what level are causally succeeded by events at what other level?* As shown in Figure 1, there are five fundamental steps between the two extremes.

At the individualistic extreme, every micro-level event is caused by some other micro-level event. Macro-level events are basically irrelevant; they are merely by-products of individual interaction. At the next step, micro-events can lead to interesting macro-level phenomena; although macro-level events might influence micro-level events, the former are still treated as proxies for micro-level interactions. The middle position accepts both micro-level events and macro-level events as equally important, allowing all kinds of interactions (micro-to-macro and macro-to-micro) to be equally possible. In the fourth position macro-structures determine micro-behavior; individuals might affect macro-events but only because they are guided by macro-structures which act as proxies for macro-to-macro interaction. The fifth and most radical collectivistic position exclusively accepts macro-to-macro interactions; micro-events are mere derivations from macro-level events.

From a multi-agent engineering point of view, the second position above is by far the most accessible approach. Sawyer (2003: 340) argues: "Artificial societies represent a pure form of methodological individualism; they provide explanations of social phenomena in terms of individuals and their interactions." This position was also the one the 18th century economist Adam Smith adopted

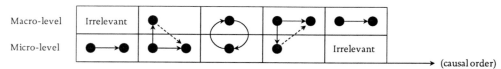

Figure 1 *Five Types of Micro-Macro Relations*

when he examined how individual self-interest on the ideal free market can combine to produce a collectively beneficial macro-behavior – "It is not from the benevolence of the butcher, the brewer or the baker that we expect our dinner, but from their regard to their own interest", reads an often-quoted passage (Smith, 2000: 15). However, there are plenty of macro-outcomes that are a lot less beneficial to the individuals than the free market even when the individuals are perfectly rational. Although rational action is predictable, aggregates of many rational actors might be neither rational nor predictable – a rational micro-behavior often conspires to produce unexpected and non-rational outcomes. At this point, a definition of "rational macro-behavior" should be made – it is used here to describe *a macro-phenomenon that is desirable (rational) at micro-level*, i.e., a macro-behavior that avoids interfering with, and possibly even promotes, the micro-goals. A macro-behavior is only rational insofar as it increases the expected utility at micro-level.

The Tragedy of the Commons

The well-known dilemma of the *Tragedy of the Commons* exemplifies this issue, with serious implications for its participants (Schelling, 1978; Jensen & Lesser 2002). In this dilemma, a common grazing ground gets overused by villagers and their cattle until it is finally destroyed, even though the villagers that cause the destruction are 1) acting rationally, 2) aware of what is happening to the common, and 3) see the destruction of the common as contrary to their goals, i.e., it is non-rational. The basic ingredients of the dilemma are simple. Suppose that all individual villagers want to keep their cattle as well fed as possible and that access to the common is free and unregulated; then they will, of course, want to keep as many of their animals on the common as they can. The common's grazing capacity is limited, so the average grazing utility (or amount of food) for every single animal kept on the common will decrease as the number of animals increase. However, the villagers will still want to put as many of their cattle as possible on the common, because no matter how low the average grazing utility gets, it will still be higher than no grazing utility at all. Thus, until the common is destroyed, it is rational to put all of one's animals there, even though it is this rational behavior that is causing the non-rational destruction. The "tragedy" is that the destruction of the common will happen even if the villagers are aware of what is happening. To remove one's animals from the common in order to save it will benefit everyone – except the one whose animals are removed. In short, there are no incentives to remove one's animals until the common is completely worthless.

These situations represent an interesting special class of micro-to-macro relations where micro-level rationality is transformed to macro-level non-rationality. Even though the typical software agent is at a much lower cognitive level than humans, social dilemmas have been examined in multi-agent system research as well. Jensen and Lesser (2002) call the *Tragedy of the Commons* an example of "social pathologies" of multi-agent systems. They define such pathologies as "a system behavior in which two or more agents interact such that improvements in local performance do not improve system performance" (p.

2). These pathologies are emergent, i.e., not obvious in the properties of the individual agent – if they were, the agents themselves would not be rational; and the pathology would be personal and not social.

Multi-agent systems frequently exhibit this kind of suboptimal behavior that springs from locally self-interested behavior. It can even be argued that a multi-agent system with fully optimal behavior – i.e., when there is no locally self-interested behavior that interferes with the global goal – is not really a multi-agent system but a decentralised object-oriented architecture. Global optimality is obtained through global control, but global control over a multi-agent system is not consistent with the maxim that "objects do it for free, agents do it because they want to" (Wooldridge 2002: 26). Therefore, if social pathology is defined as *suboptimal macro-behavior resulting from locally beneficial actions*, then it is clear that social pathologies are unavoidable, and even endemic in multi-agent systems. There is no way to completely prevent all social pathologies without turning the agents into objects, and the multi-agent system into an ordinary object-oriented system. Wiping out all social pathologies would be the equivalent of introducing a harsh totalitarian rule. Anarchy is not the only alternative to totalitarianism, however; fortunately, there are many benign forms of government in between. Likewise, while it is futile to try to eliminate social pathologies completely, they can successfully be counteracted without turning the agents into objects.

Returning to the Tragedy of the Commons, the best solution to the farmers' tragedy would probably be to regulate access to the common in some way. In general, to avoid such harmful macro-outcomes, to improve cooperation and to solve conflicts of interest between members in a society, some kind of organizational structure is commonly introduced. The predominant form of organization in modern human societies is the bureaucracy, and these societies themselves are often based on bureaucratic principles. Thus, we turn to a discussion of bureaucracy in its ideal and computational forms.

Max Weber's Ideal Bureaucracy

When Max Weber in the early 20th century formulated his theories about different kinds of organizations and power, the bureaucracy had already begun to emerge as an efficient and performance-improving kind of organization. Weber's theoretical description of the ideal bureaucracy is a useful blueprint for how any hierarchical and rational form of organization is intended to work, even in a multi-agent system. Weber's ideal bureaucracy functions through the use of rational legal authority; it is impersonal, voluntary and strictly hierarchical, and each level in the hierarchy (each "office") has a clearly defined sphere of competence and responsibilities. All authority is regulated by formal, abstract rules, and there is a system of control and discipline, which constantly oversees that everything is going by the rules. Officials employed in the hierarchy are paid, and are appointed after having been tested for proper qualifications. The most important features of Weber's ideal bureaucracy (Weber, 1947) are:

- **Hierarchy.** A bureaucracy is a hierarchy, and a high position in the hierarchy corresponds with power and authority over lower positions. A high position is also directly or indirectly associated with high rewards, e.g., a high salary.

- **Meritocracy.** Weber clearly emphasizes the necessity of a meritocratic mechanism in a bureaucracy, which should have a system of promotion according to achievement, where promotion means rising in the hierarchy and obtaining the benefits associated with a higher position.

- **Control through formal rules.** Decision-making, authority, and other issues of organizational order are regulated through formal, abstract, and explicit rules. Members of the bureaucracy are expected to know these rules, and to act and interact in accordance with them.

- **Impersonality.** A member's identity is irrelevant. Only the rank and the position in the bureaucracy matters. This holds in all interactions between members of the bureaucracy.

- **Voluntary (or profit-driven) employment.** The bureaucracy's members are voluntary members, employed as long as they want to. Employees are encouraged to seek promotion as higher positions in the bureaucracy lead to more power and profit. Thus, the bureaucracy expects, and even hopes, that members are acting in a self-interested manner. (Why bureaucracies want its members to be self-interested is discussed in the next subsection.)

The power privileges granted by the hierarchy are strictly utilitarian (neither coercive nor social), i.e., only use the bureaucracy's reward system, and never extend outside of the organization. In fact, members of the bureaucracy typically have the alternative of leaving the bureaucracy altogether. Likewise, engaging in the meritocratic pursuit of promotion is a voluntary activity. Furthermore, the bureaucracy both expects its members to be a heterogeneous group – if all agents were identical, both the hierarchy and the meritocracy would be difficult to sustain – and increases the agents' heterogeneity by delegating power and creating a division of labor. Finally, it should be noted that a bureaucratic organization when applied to a society as a whole is a prerequisite of Popper's definition of the "open society" (Popper, 1966). In bureaucratic organizations the society is "open" in the sense that the rule of the society (or organization) is within reach of the individual agents through, e.g., democratic elections or other meritocratic procedures. This means that the fate of society lies in the hands of the society's members. It is open and dynamic in contrast to the closed nature of dictatorial or tribal societies.

Different Kinds of Power

In a hierarchical organization, the higher levels have some form of power over the lower levels. Amitai Etzioni has made a very influential distinction between three basic kinds of power: coercive, utilitarian, and normative-social power (Etzioni, 1964). Coercive power is exercised through the use, or threat of use, of physical sanctions (e.g., physical punishment); utilitarian power through material sanctions (e.g., material rewards or fines); and normative-social power through symbolic sanctions (e.g., symbols of prestige, appreciation, love).

The use of coercive, "forcing", power tends to be the strongest but most alienating kind of power, while normative-social, "convincing", power tends to be the least alienating but potentially weakest kind of power. This puts the utilitarian power in the middle. A bureaucratic organization is based on utilitarian power, the ideal bureaucracy exclusively so; both coercive and normative power are in conflict with the principle of voluntary or profit-driven participation and in part with the principle of meritocracy as well. While in a real, human bureaucracy both hard (forcing) and soft (convincing) power might be used in some situations, its use is not required in principle. The ideal bureaucracy appeals solely to the individual's self-interest, i.e., it does not make a collective utility measure available to the individual agent. Its use of utilitarian power creates a desired macro-behavior (organizational cooperation) by influencing the micro-motives (making it profitable to work in the organization). Because the bureaucracy relies on the individual's self-interest, it prefers rational and self-interested members. Only with such members can the bureaucracy influence its members to work as desired. The meritocratic mechanism, in particular, exploits this individual self-interest; when the best-working and most competent members are given higher rewards and rise in the hierarchy, all the bureaucracy's members are encouraged to work better and increase their competence.

Because the bureaucracy relies on utilitarian power, it expects its subjects to be rational utility-maximizers, e.g., they should prefer high wages to low wages. Therefore, a benign selfishness is a prerequisite for utilitarian power, and consequently for bureaucratic organizations in general. Individuals who strive for higher wages are easier to coordinate and predict than individuals who do not care about wages or promotion. From a bureaucratic point of view then, rational action is more predictable than non-rational action. According to the most common interpretation, rational actions are actions that maximize the individual's utility, i.e., are in greatest accordance with the individual's goals (whichever these goals may be – egoistic or altruistic, short-term or long-term, et cetera). According to Russell and Norvig (1995), the "ideal rational agent should do whatever action is expected to maximize its performance measure" (p. 33). In Game Theory, the rational player is likewise described as someone who "maximizes" his or hers utilitarian gains; for example, Luce and Raiffa (1957) postulates that the rational player "will choose the [alternative] which yields the more preferred outcome, […] in terms of the utility function he will attempt to maximize expected utility"(p. 50); Schelling (1960) defines rational player behavior as "a calculating, value-maximizing strategy of decision" (p. 17); and Rapoport (1961) states that in games, "the objective of a 'rational' individual is to maximize the utility expectation accruing to him consistently with the constraints of the situation" (p. 122).

A perfectly rational, self-interested behavior is the behavior of the fictional *Homo oeconomicus*. The *Homo oeconomicus* is not a recent conceptual invention; the 19th-century philosopher J. S. Mill used it explicitly (Mainzer, 1997), but already Adam Smith based his macroeconomic theories on the concept of the individual that solely pursues its own self-interest. The concept has survived less because of its descriptive qualities (few, if any, human beings act as the ideal *Homo oeconomicus*) and more because of its good heuristics. The *Homo oeconomicus* acts in a calculable and therefore predictable way, whereas a non-rational actor acts in an incalculable and therefore unpredictable way. In short, rational action is predictable action. When it is stated that the *Homo oeconomicus* maximizes his or her utility, nothing has been said about the nature of this utility.

A Proposed Typology for Bureaucratic Agents

The bureaucracy is, fundamentally, a control structure. As such, it has different levels of decision-making that are qualitatively different. These levels are related to the agents' social and cognitive capabilities. Verhagen (2000a) proposes a model for social and cognitive agents, comprised of four different stages, in part based on an agent typology conceived by Conte and Castelfranchi (1995). At the lowest level of this model one finds pure reactivity, and each subsequent level of superior reasoning capabilities is a superset of the preceding level. Thus, all agents are at least reactive. At the second level, the agents are "plan autonomous", which means that the agents can independently decide how to achieve a certain goal, compare and evaluate plans, but cannot reason about the goal itself. At the third level, agents are "goal autonomous" and thus able to reason about goals, to compare, to modify, and to change them. However, agents at the third level cannot reason about the value system that determines whether a goal is a good goal, i.e., they cannot reason about the norms that determine the value of goals. At the fourth level agents are "norm autonomous" and can, consequently, question the very norm system that evaluates goals. In other words, they can change the definition of what a "good goal" is.

This model, however, does not have an explicit formulation of the different levels of decision-making. Such a formulation is necessary for modeling the control and power relationships in a decision-making hierarchy. The 19th century military theorist Carl von Clausewitz (2004) explored different levels of military decision-making – perhaps most known for his grim comment that war is a continuation of politics with other means, he is probably the most important thinker to formalize the modern fundamental difference between tactics and strategy. According to Clausewitz, the highest level of power struggle is the political level; tactics is the employment of military forces in battle, and strategy is the employment of battles to obtain the war's political goals. Thus, political goals determine the strategic goals, which in turn determine the tactical goals. Stripped of the military context, the result is a decision-making hierarchy, applicable not only to warfare, but to all kinds of social reasoning and planning. Building on the Verhagen (2000a) typology, this paper proposes an agent typology that focuses on the decision-making capabilities of the agents:

I. **Reactivity.** Reactivity is the minimum requirement of any agent. An agent that does not even have reactive capabilities is so unfit for agent life that it is either a dead agent or not an agent at all (i.e., an object).

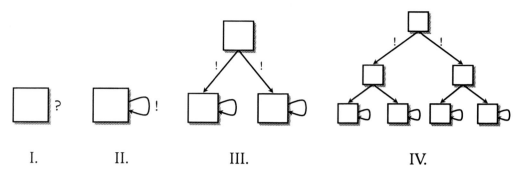

I.   II.   III.   IV.

Figure 2 *Agent Typology for Bureaucratic Agents*

II. **Tactical Reasoning.** At the tactical level, the organization's member reasons about the smallest agent unit, such as itself, and what it can do on its own to achieve its goals. It compares different plans with respect to how well the plans promote its goals. For example, it might evaluate the different plans in terms of utility, choosing the plan with the highest expected utility yield. It does not bother with calculations about other's actions; neither does it try to influence others. Because of their narrow scope, tactical decisions are the most easily computed.

III. **Strategic Reasoning.** At the strategic level, the organization's member not only reasons about what it can do on its own to achieve its goals; it also tries to influence the goals of other members. Thus, the strategic agent reasons about and tries to impose its will on agent units that are multiples of the smallest unit, i.e., it will try to influence the behavior of other agents. It reasons about parallel, mutually reinforcing or interfering goals, and it compares, evaluates and tries to coordinate different goals, both goals of its own and of others. It follows from this that strategic decisions are more complex than tactical ones.

IV. **Political Reasoning.** At the political level, the organization's member reasons about the entire society or organization; i.e., it reasons about all other members. The political agent thus tries to influence all other agents in the whole society or organization to choose goals that the political agent approves of. It does this by questioning and influencing the very norm system that guides the whole society or organization, and which determines whether a goal is a good goal or not. Consequently, the political member can reason about several different norm systems, or different political systems, and political decisions thus constitute the most complex kind of decisions in the bureaucratic organization.

Experiments
Related Research

Sawyer (2003) argues that there are two general approaches in multi-agent research: Simulation (agent-based modeling) and equation-based modeling (e.g., Game Theory); according to him, both approaches have their advantages and drawbacks. The relation between the two approaches can be conflicting; one such example is game theorist Ken Binmore's critique of Robert Axelrod's *Iterated Prisoner's Dilemma* simulations (Binmore. 1999; Axelrod. 1984, 1997). Binmore argues that Axelrod's simulations are not creating any real insights into the prisoner's dilemma; he is just looking at the consequences without really understanding them. This critique could in some respects be directed towards all simulation-based studies; on the other hand, in the realm of multi-agent interactions, Game Theory might well be too exact. Most important, however, is that whereas Game Theory focuses on finding static game equilibriums (i.e., optimal solutions to finite games), simulation provides an accessible way to explore dynamic effects in infinite games of interaction. Still, many basic game theoretic concepts, such as zero-sum/non-zero-sum games and the qualitative difference between 2-person and n-person games, are highly relevant in simulation-based research.

The bureaucratic model developed in this paper is an agent-based modeling implementation of organizational theories mostly developed before computer simulations became possible. The experimental procedures, however, relate to many of the earlier established computational research programs described in Hazy, Millhiser and Solow (2007, this volume), even though they have not always been used here. Applying network models to the bureaucratic model, for example, would be very interesting, as bureaucracies are usually treated as pyramidal organizations; the connectedness between agents in a bureaucracy is not explored here, but it would be interesting to contrast a bureaucratic model with a "Small-Worlds" network structure, for example. Another possibility that is not tried here is to introduce genetic algorithms or processes of generational shift in the bureaucratic model. Research done on the spreading of norms is also relevant; for example, in Boman (1999), "social awareness" is created among utility-maximizing agents by introducing a collective utility measure; in Verhagen (2000a, 2000b), agents are endowed with an ability for subjectively approximating the collective utility measure and updating it through feedback from other agents; in Axelrod (1997), norms are supplemented with meta-norms that punish agents that do not enforce the norms. In the bureaucratic model, such norm-establishing reasoning takes place at the political level; therefore, the spreading of norms is an important part of the bureaucratic model, although (as is discussed later) the political decision-making level has not been implemented in the simulations. Introduced in a bureaucratic model, the modeling of norm spreading would, together with the meritocratic process, translate to a testing of leadership styles, such as the ones described in Hazy, Millhiser and Solow (2007, this volume).

The experimental environment of this paper resembles one of the better-known spatial agent testbeds, Tileworld. Originally a simple computer game, it was turned into an experimental environment in 1990 to investigate reasoning in agents (Lees, 2002). In the original Tileworld testbed, agents populate a 2-dimensional world full of spontaneously appearing and disappearing tiles and holes; the agents' task is to push the tiles into the holes, for which they are rewarded with points. Many new features have since been added to the Tileworld environment to extend its applicability, such as fuel maintenance. Tileworld and similar testbeds have been criticized for pretending to be more reliable than they actually are (Lees, 2002). A poorly designed testbed will produce results that are valid only for that particular testbed. Even a well-designed testbed will, if used for the wrong experiments, produce misleading results; a testbed that works equally well for all different kinds of experiments is unlikely. Making the testbed more "realistic" (and complex) by adding features such as fuel maintenance will not necessarily make it produce more valid results; fuel levels might in some circumstances be irrelevant and therefore obscure the results. In fact, a testbed probably benefits from being as simple as possible without being trivial, because then it will share its basic features with other more complex environments.

Experimental Setup

The point of a bureaucracy is, among other things, to make cooperation more efficient, but a badly constructed bureaucracy can of course create exactly the opposite – impaired cooperation. On the other hand, one could spend an unlimited amount of time fine-tuning an organization to perfection. Therefore, no interesting, falsifiable hypotheses are formulated here – introducing a bureaucratic organization might improve agent cooperation, but only if effort were made to fine-tune it, so a hypothesis that states that all bureaucracies improve cooperation would be obviously false and a hypothesis stating that bureaucracies *can* improve cooperation would simply not be falsifiable.

The experimental application tests how well a group of agents is able to solve cooperative tasks in a 2-dimensional world that is randomly dotted with obstacles (inaccessible areas) and interesting objects. The tasks are of varying difficulty, such as exploration and object-search, and the performance of bureaucratic agents is measured against the performance of unorganized agents. The agents populating the experimental environment move around freely; they gather information about the world, and store the information in a knowledge base accessible to all agents. Information in the knowledge base is used to determine the rewards due to the agents for their work, thus functioning as the agents' employer for the purposes of the simulation. An umpire performs the function of monitoring and calculating the bureaucratic power relationships between the agents, in effect functioning as the law (with the agents as law-enforcers). The result is an ideal mini-society, with hard-working and (mostly) law-abiding agents, striving to maximize their utility rewards from the knowledge base, while not getting in trouble with the law.

The Environment

The physical world of the bureaucratic agents experimental application resembles an old-fashioned computer game. It is a 2-dimensional surface, dotted with non-traversable obstacles; the obstacles are randomly distributed, and the individual size, shape, and placement of each obstacle are randomly determined as well. The world is partitioned in a grid, where each cell represents a discrete location that can either be accessible or inaccessible, and if accessible, can contain either one agent or one object. Two agents cannot simultaneously occupy the same location, so a cell that contains an agent is temporarily inaccessible. In the second scenario, the world contains objects that are of special interest to the agents. These objects are "repaired" when two agents cooperate to repair it, so an agent who finds an object sticks around until another agent comes for help.

The Knowledge Base and the Umpire

Both the Knowledge Base (KB) and the Umpire are parts of the complex adaptive system within which the agents interact. They are not pro-active agents in themselves, but are functions of the system. The KB functions as the agents' employer in a limited sense, that is, the KB is the system function upon which the agents depend for their rewards. When agents have mapped an unknown part of the terrain or repaired an object, their results are recorded in the KB, which simulates an organizational memory store for future access by all agents. For simplicity, these data are used to determine the utility points each agent receives as reward for its effort as calculated in the payoff function. Once explored, unknown terrain will thus cease to be unknown and will no longer be a possible source of reward for the agents. Therefore, the agents are, in their pursuit of utility points, competing for access to unknown terrain and interesting objects. When an agent does not know where to go next, it accesses the KB for information about the geographically nearest unexplored spot or object. Viewed as an employer, then, the KB practices a complete laissez-faire attitude towards its employees – it does not provide any organizational decisions or cooperational advice.

The system's Umpire function keeps constant track of all the agents' accumulated rewards. Through this data, the Umpire calculates and provides information to the agents about the current state of the decision-making hierarchy. The agents use this information to determine their current position in the hierarchy. The meritocratic rule is simple – the higher the amount of accumulated rewards, the higher the position in the hierarchy. The Umpire also provides information about two things that are critical to the agent cooperation in the organization: each agent's jurisdictional area and, in the case of the agent having acquired an elevated position in the bureaucracy, the agent's subordinates. Superior agents – agents that have acquired decision-making privileges over other agents – will calculate and issue orders to subordinate agents that are within the superior agent's jurisdiction. Agents that have received orders will suffer a light punishment if they disobey. This punishment takes the form of a "fine" that decreases the reward the agent would otherwise receive from the KB. However, keeping in line with the bureaucratic principle of voluntary participation in the organization, an agent will never receive negative rewards, as that would make a self-interested agent considering leaving the organization altogether. Furthermore, an agent might choose to disobey a particular order if it has been given several contradictory orders from superiors that have overlapping jurisdictions, or if the local benefit of disobeying an order outweighs the punishment (see below for further discussion on how the agent makes its choice).

The hierarchy is configurable by the (human) application user by modifying two parameters: hierarchy width and hierarchy depth. The former determines the number of agents at each hierarchical level, and the latter the number of hierarchical levels. Therefore, the total number of agents is a function of the hierarchy structure. A bureaucracy with a hierarchy width of three and hierarchy depth of three, for example, will have one agent at the top decision-making level, three agents at the second level, and nine at the third and lowest level.

The Agent

All agents are created equal, so the agent group will in principle be almost completely homogeneous, but as the simulation starts, it will instantly become heterogeneous. The agent's behavior is described in terms of the agent typology described earlier (see the section on different levels of decision-making). These decision-making "faculties" are arranged in a subsumption hierarchy, as pioneered by Brooks (1990). This means that lower levels (such as the reactive layer) produce behavior that takes precedence over higher layers (such as the tactical and strategic layers). The agent group's heterogeneity springs from the bureaucracy's division of labor in superior agents (agents that have both tactical and strategic decision-making privileges) and subordinate agents (agents that only make tactical decisions). In other words, all agents have the same cognitive potential, but only the agents that have an elevated position in the bureaucracy will use it to its full extent.

Agent Behavior: Reactive Layer

The reactive layer distinguishes between accessible and inaccessible terrain, and understands that accessible terrain that is occupied by another agent is temporarily inaccessible, so this layer simply helps the agent understanding which actions are possible.

Agent Behavior: Tactical Layer

This is the home of the agent's *Homo oeconomicus*. At the tactical level, the agent calculates how it should move to reach as many unexplored cells as possible (thereby maximizing its utility profits). At each point, the agent has nine possible courses of action to choose from. It can move in all directions – vertically, horizontally, and diagonally – and it can remain in the same location. The agent is able to explore the terrain only in its immediate vicinity, which means that it will record information of all cells that are adjacent to the cell where it is standing. Because the agent is rewarded when exploring unknown terrain, the individual agent will at every point compute from which position it can expect to examine the largest amount of unknown area, i.e., the largest number of unknown cells. The agent is rewarded a much larger utility amount if it repairs an item; therefore, an agent who encounters an item will stick around and wait for help. As the agents have no capability of such a high-level reasoning act as predicting the future, they will wait indefinitely until another agent comes by to help. Thus, when all agents are waiting for another agent to help, a deadlock situation has arisen.

The agent switches between three different "mindsets" that determine how the agent will want to move. The simple state diagram in Figure 3 shows the transition between the three states.

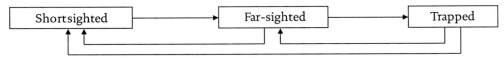

Figure 3 *Three Agent Mind States*

As long as there are unexplored cells in the immediate vicinity, the agent will continue to act and reason in a short sighted, "greedy" way. Eventually, however, the agent will be in a situation where there are no adjacent cells from which it is possible to examine any unknown cells. When this happens, the agent will switch to far-sighted reasoning. If the world is not completely explored, some unexplored spots or some objects that are not yet repaired will exist somewhere. The agent will consult the KB for information about the nearest such spot or object, and make it its current long-term goal. To reach the goal, the agent will at each move compute how it can get closer to the goal. As long as there are no obstacles between the agent and the goal, the agent will just move in a straight line towards the goal. If the reactive layer senses that some obstacle is in the way, however, the agent switches to "trapped" reasoning, and will try to round the obstacle. It will follow the obstacle either around its left or right edge until it assumes the obstacle has been rounded at which point it will return to normal far-sighted behavior, i.e., moving ever closer to the goal.

Agent Behavior: Strategic Layer

If all agents were merely tactical, no bureaucratic organization would exist, as tactical agents only reason about their own actions and never try to impose their will on other agents. Therefore, the strategic layer is the location for all the bureaucratic, meritocratic mechanisms; the bureaucracy manifests itself in the agents' *orders* to each other, or more specifically, how superior agents send orders to subordinate agents. As all order-issuing actions are in the strategic layer, the organization becomes a very well defined part of the agents' cognitive layers: it lies completely in the strategic layer, so the lowest-ranked agents that lack subordinates are, in effect, incapable of strategic actions.

After having received information of the current subordinates, the strategic reasoning layer goes through four main parts.

- First, the agent decides whether it has found an interesting object. If it has, it will send orders to the nearest of its subordinates to come for assistance.

- Second, it examines whether any of its immediate subordinates (agents whose rank is exactly one level below) has found an object. If so, the agent orders other subordinates who have not found objects to assist the subordinate agent.

- Third, the agent surveys its jurisdictional area, splits it in four sections and determines which of these that still contain unexplored terrain. Then it makes sure at least one subordinate is occupied in the partially unexplored sections.

- Fourth, the agent makes sure that its subordinates all have available subordinates of their own. In other words, it searches for sub-subordinates that seem to be unsupervised and orders them into the jurisdictions of its direct subordinates. This is the only time the decision-making function reaches further than a single hierarchical level. The point of this last step is to ensure that there is a necessary redundancy in the strategic orders, if the agent's subordinates are having difficulties executing orders (e.g., trapped behind an obstacle).

Agent Behavior: Political Level

As will be discussed later, the higher the level of decision-making, the harder the decisions are to compute. The experimental application created for this paper has not implemented a political reasoning level for the agents; it is a deliberate limitation that has to do with the complexity of computing political decisions. Such a high reasoning level would typically assume (and have the capability to modify) the Umpire and the KB functions, and it would be able to dynamically change settings and parameters now set by the human application user, e.g., hierarchy structure, utility rewards and punishments, i.e., the decrease in reward following the disobedience of an order. (The implications of introducing a political level are discussed further in the concluding section.)

Implementation of the Bureaucracy

As the implementation of the different decision-making levels and the utilitarian power employed in the organization should be clear, it might be helpful to describe how the bureaucratic principles are implemented. Note that the bureaucracy manifests itself solely in agents' actions and orders to other actions, so the bureaucratic principles are always actualized as locally operating rules in local agent interaction.

The hierarchy of the agent bureaucracy is configurable through setting two basic hierarchy parameters: "hierarchy width" which determines the number of subordinates at each hierarchical level, and "hierarchy depth" which determines the number of hierarchical levels. In all runs, both the hierarchy width and depth were set to 3. This results in a total number of 13 agents (1 agent at the top level, 3 agents at the middle level, and 9 agents at the bottom level).

Hierarchy

The hierarchy manifests itself in the division of agents in different decision-making levels, where agents in higher positions in the bureaucracy have power over agents in lower positions. Agents do not need to know the numbers of levels above them or under them, as long as they have some supervisors and some subordinates.

Meritocracy

The goal of the meritocracy, the "rule of the merited", is to ensure that the most competent individuals are given most power, so that the strategic decisions made for the organization will be competent. Therefore, the meritocratic mechanism clearly has *organizational* competence, and not just any competence, in mind when it wants to reward competent individuals. "Organizational competence" is operationally best defined as "capability of making competent decisions". The concrete ingredients of a competent decision are, of course, closely linked to the actual environment the organization acts in. Adjusting the definition of merit is one of the things that has to be done when fine-tuning the bureaucratic organization; if the definition of merit is a bad one, decision-making agents will make incompetent decisions and the organization will suffer. One way to measure the quality of the working definition of merit is to substitute the meritocratic mechanism with a randomized hierarchy and determine whether the randomized hierarchy performs better – if it does, the definition of merit should be improved; if it does not, the definition of merit seems to be putting competent decision-makers in power.

In the experimental application, merit is connected to the number of utility points, which usually means that agents that have gone further into unexplored terrain will be seen as merited. These agents might not be competent in the normal sense of the word, but because they will be deeper into unknown terrain, they are supposed to be in *a place to make more competent decisions* which gives them organizational competence as defined above.

Control through Formal Rules

Members of a bureaucracy are supposed to be aware of the organization's rules; a formulation better suited for software agents would be that members of the agent bureaucracy should be *including the anticipated consequences of the relevant organizational rules in their reasoning*. They do this by anticipating the punishments from disobeying orders when comparing action alternatives.

Impersonality

In the bureaucracy, a member's identity is irrelevant. Thus, the rules never consider an agent's identity; instead, the agent's position or "office" in the bureaucracy determines all interactions.

Voluntary (or Profit-Driven) Employment

The agents are not hard-wired to obey orders, but they often choose to do so as disobedience result in lower utility rewards. On the other hand, agents are hard-wired to be utility-maximizers. That the agents are hard-coded to maximize their utility does not weaken the principle of voluntary employment, however. The concept of being a utility-maximizer has a strong tautological element, once a utility measure has been established. The utility measure is based on an individual preference scale; because individuals (unsurprisingly) will prefer to act in accordance with their preferences, being a utility-maximizer is to prefer to act to gain what one prefers. Note that this does not mean that the agents have perfect information; they are perfectly rational only in the sense that they always choose the action with the highest expected utility yield, but they have very limited information and very limited capacities to analyze future courses of actions.

Experimental Scenarios

The agents are confronted with two different scenarios – one with a task of limited cooperational difficulty ("Exploration"), and another with a cooperatively more demanding task ("Repair"). In "Exploration", the agents have to map an unexplored area; in "Repair", the agents in addition to mapping the area have to cooperate to repair objects randomly placed in the environment. In the first scenario, the goal is to explore the world as fast and efficiently as possible, so performance is measured in the total number of moves needed to explore the whole world. In the second scenario, the goal is to avoid the deadlock that arises when all agents are waiting for some other agent to come for repair assistance; therefore, performance is measured in a simple failure/success ratio. Both scenarios are tested in one unorganized and one bureaucratic agent group.

Simulation Procedures

Every time the experimental application is launched, a randomized terrain is created; consequently, the complexity of the terrain varies widely. Therefore, to make the measurements as valid as possible, the application first creates a new randomized terrain and lets the bureaucratic agents solve the given task, and then runs the simulation again in the exact same environment, but this time with unorganized agents. This means that each simulation in practice consists of two runs where the two agent groups are pitted against one another to see which of the agent groups is better at solving the given task in the particular terrain. Each environmental setting is tested in 50 simulations, or 100 runs. In addition, a limited test that tries to isolate and measure the beneficial effects of the meritocratic mechanisms is done in one of the environmental settings of scenario 1 (Exploration). This test is done by running the simulations in a special setting where the agents are organized in a static hierarchy, defined as the case where rank is randomly assigned to the agents and never updated. Potentially, this test run makes it possible to distinguish the benefits of a hierarchy per se from the added benefits of ensuring (by way of meritocracy) the competence of the top ranks in the hierarchy.

The simulations are logged; all agent actions, all events, all orders sent between agents, all hierarchy changes and all agents' accumulated utility are stored in simple text files for analysis. Furthermore, these logs can be used by the experimental application to replay, pause and rewind any of the simulations.

Results

In the "Exploration" scenario, bureaucratic agents performed better than unorganized agents in 86 per cent of the cases; bureaucratic agents on average needed 1390 moves to complete the task, whereas non-bureaucratic agents needed 1617 moves. Limited tests were conducted in environments with other settings, such as a larger area or more obstacles, and in these settings the performance differences were smaller, so the bureaucracy seems to be in need of some organizational fine-tuning. Generally, the bureaucracy performed best in environments where the number of obstacles was at a medium level. In addition, it seems like a large number of agents in a comparatively small environment favored unorganized agents. The attempt, mentioned above, to isolate the beneficial effects of the meritocracy from those that come from the hierarchy showed, however, that the bureaucracy with meritocratic mechanisms performed better than an agent organization with a randomly assigned, static hierarchy, in 64 per cent of the cases, so the meritocratic mechanism is helping the bureaucracy improve efficiency.

In the cooperatively more demanding "Repair" scenario, the performance differences between unorganized and bureaucratic agents were larger (see Figure 4). This suggests that the bureaucratic organization was of greater use when the agents needed to cooperate directly, than when their cooperation was of a more indirect nature.

Developmental Stages of the Bureaucratic Agents Society

Because the agent bureaucracy primarily manifests itself through the decisions and orders the strategic agents make, the number of orders sent during the simulations is a good measure of societal activity. Figure 5 shows the number of orders that are sent each percent (in terms of agent moves) of simulations. For example, during the first 2-3 percent of the average simulation, orders will peak to around 95 per cent of the absolute maximum number of orders issued during the whole simulation (of course, in any *individual* simulation, the absolute peak would be 100 per cent). Imagine a simulation that takes 1500 agent moves. During the first 15 moves (the first per cent of the simulation), the rate of orders increases rapidly, and in the interval of 31-45 moves (3 per cent through the simulation) the rate in this example peaks at 50 orders being sent during this particular interval of the simulation.

If this simulation follows the average development depicted in the chart in Figure 5, the number of orders sent every 15 agent moves will decrease to

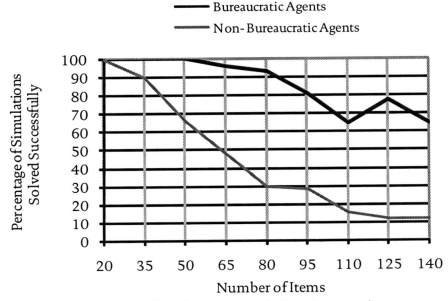

Figure 4 *Failure/success ratio in Repair scenario*

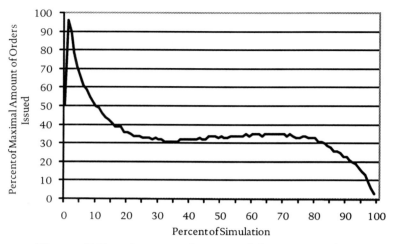

Figure 5 *Developmental stages of the agent society*

about 25 orders (or 50 percent of the maximum rate) after 150 agent moves (or at 10 percent through the simulation). It will fall further to 15-17 orders (i.e., 30-34 percent of the maximum rate) after 300 agent moves (i.e., at 20 percent through the simulation). This rate of 15-17 orders every 15 agent moves will be stable until around 80 percent through the simulation, when the rate will start to approach zero. (The chart includes order-issuing statistics from 550 simulations.)

Figure 5 indicates that there are three developmental stages in the typical Bureaucratic Agent society, stages that are unrelated to any system-level design but emerging from agent interaction:

1. *Emergence.* During the first 20 percent of the average simulation, a very large amount of orders are sent between agents in what could be likened to a formation or emergence of a society structure. In this stage, the bureaucracy could be characterized as somewhat confused, with agents having conflicting strategic goals, thus often issuing contradictory orders to other agents. At this stage then, the power relationships do not work as intended, and agents are often disobeyed.

2. *Normal-State Society.* The extraordinary levels of orders decrease rapidly, and at 20 per cent of the average simulation, these levels stabilize around 30-35 per cent of the maximum amount of orders. The agent society enters a comparably uniform state. In this stage, the bureaucracy could be characterized as harmonious – the bureaucracy works well, and conflicting goals and contradictory orders are uncommon. This could be called the bureaucracy's and the society's *normal state* – the power relationships work as intended and agents are seldom disobeyed.

3. *Decline.* At 80 per cent of the simulation, as the end of the task is getting nearer, the bureaucracy will become increasingly unnecessary. Agents will no more have to send orders to other agents, as the need for strategic de-

cisions has disappeared and tactical decision-making has become sufficient for solving the task. This final state of decline is due solely to the fact that the solving of the task is near, and in a simulation without an infinite task, this state might not appear at all.

Development of the Meritocracy

Figure 6 shows the number of agents changing rank to a higher or lower level, i.e., the social mobility, during the average simulation. As before, this is measured in percent of the maximum level of social mobility.

It is clear that the levels of social mobility decrease rapidly and steadily throughout the average simulation. In the beginning, the top rank is obtainable by all agents, while it becomes considerably harder to achieve a higher rank as the simulation proceeds. This social immobility is also unrelated to any system level design but an emergent phenomenon produced by agent interaction.

Meritocracy can only exist if there is at least some social mobility; when social mobility has disappeared, all meritocratic mechanisms have become superfluous. Meritocracy is probably at its best when there is compromise between stability and mobility. Where this middle-way between stability and mobility is situated depends on the organization, of course, but it is worrying for the meritocracy that social mobility seems to be approaching zero.

Meritocratic Petrifaction in Normal State Society

Figure 7 shows the development of societal activity and social mobility during normal-state society, i.e., between 20 and 80 per cent of the average simulation. It is clear that while the bureaucracy has become relatively stable at around 35 per cent, social mobility continues to decrease steadily, from circa 30 per cent to 0-5 per cent. It approaches very low levels, down to a few percent of the social

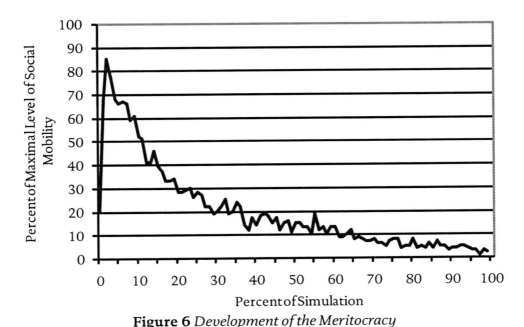

Figure 6 *Development of the Meritocracy*

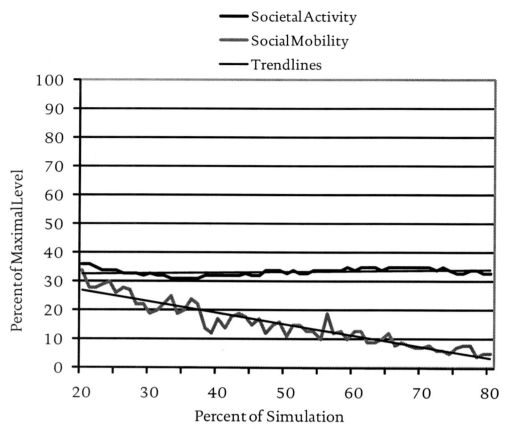

Figure 7 *Decline of social mobility in normal-state society*

mobility in the initial stages of the simulation. This suggests that the bureaucracy has become a self-perpetuating power structure. In other words, the power structure created by the meritocracy seems to have become an increasingly rigid structure less and less subject to meritocratic mechanisms. Thus, the meritocracy is in effect wiping itself out. This is not necessarily a bad thing, if interpreted as a consolidation of a benign power structure. However, if social mobility disappears altogether, the meritocracy has in effect disappeared as well.

Discussion

An observation from the experiments that is hard to quantify statistically is that both performance results and bureaucratic structure vary widely when the basic settings (environment size, obstacle frequency) are the same, and even in cases when agents are deployed in the exact same environment. This is a strong indication that history is crucial to how the individual simulation evolves, a common characteristic of complex systems dynamics; small differences at the start of the simulation propagate and rapidly create large differences between different simulations. In spite of this strong system instability, however, the simulations display a transient state of structured non-equilibrium manifested in what was called "normal-state society", a seemingly stable state in a system that is strongly out of equilibrium. The normal-state society is perhaps the most notable emergent system characteristic to be extracted from the simulation data; it does not spring from any deliberate pre-designed system characteristic, and was not hypothesized before running the simulations.

A Bureaucratic Organization Can Improve Efficiency

The general conclusion that can be drawn from the results is that a bureaucratic organizational model can be configured to produce efficiency-improving results in a multi-agent system, and can effectively make individual agents cooperate without any recurring intervention from a human coordinator. This organization can be constructed as a part of the agents' cognitive mechanisms, so that a hierarchical structure emerges in a group of agents. This agent group is initially homogeneous, but becomes heterogeneous as the organizational mechanisms create a successful division of labor. It is also possible to construct a self-supporting mechanism for dynamical reorganizations in this hierarchy, i.e., a meritocratic hierarchy.

As in Weber's model of the ideal bureaucracy, the agents are motivated by self-interest, by the personal rewards they get from engaging in the organization. The agents are not hard-coded to obey every order they get, but are only hard-coded to be utility-maximizers. In this particular sense then, they are being perfectly rational, always choosing the action with the highest expected utility yield. However, it would not be correct to describe them as being perfectly rational in a general sense as they have far from perfect information (i.e., ability to interpret the environment and other agents' actions). For example, they are definitely not good at calculating possible future events, and their ability to coordinate other agents is clearly in need of some improvements – unorganized agents manage to perform better than the bureaucratic agents in several of the simulations. Of course, the agents are not sophisticated enough to question their pursuit of utilitarian rewards. The principal difference between utilitarian power (the one that guides the agents) and coercive power remains, however. The agents are not forced, but *paid* (or persuaded) to obey.

Another general conclusion is that the higher you get on the decision-making ladder, the harder it becomes to calculate good orders. In other words, strategic decisions are harder to make than tactical decisions. This is unsurprising, considering the fact that strategic decisions have to coordinate several tactical actions. From this it follows that political decisions will be even harder to make, as they not only have to coordinate several tactical and strategic actions but also create guidelines for making strategic decisions.

Petrifaction of the Meritocracy: Power Creates Power

One of the most striking results of the development of the bureaucratic agent society is the steady decline of social mobility in an otherwise stable society. In effect, this decline means that the meritocratic mechanisms are activated increasingly seldom; to an ever-lessening extent are agents' merits enough to rise in rank. The meritocracy is creating a power structure that is self-perpetuating, so meritocracy is giving way to something resembling a new aristocracy. The problem is how the meritocracy interacts with another of the bureaucratic organization's components – the hierarchy. For a meritocracy to work there must be some privileges associated with higher positions in the hierarchy. Otherwise, there would be no incentives to work harder and seek promotion.

The hierarchy's privileges often come in the form of more power and higher utility rewards. Those privileges are petrifying the meritocracy, because individuals with power will (if they have the self-interest that bureaucracies expect from its members) use their power to keep their power. For example, in the bureaucratic agents society, a superior agent A is relatively free to explore the world in the personally most profitable way, but while doing this, A will order its subordinate agents B and C to act in a way that does not hinder A's plans. Consequently, A may sometimes oppose the striving for power of agents B and C, and because A has more power than them, A will often prevail (but not always – its power over B and C will typically be far from absolute, and interaction in a bureaucracy is typically not a zero-sum game). As long as A is making competent decisions, its tendency to hold on to its power can be good for the system as a whole, but when A starts making incompetent decisions, a new social pathology has been created – this time by the organization that was supposed to counteract social pathologies. In effect then, the meritocracy has calcified into an incompetent aristocracy. (Ironically, the original Greek meaning of "aristocracy" is in fact "rule of the best", in other words, *rule of the most merited*; but that has evolved into meaning "rule of the noble", in other words, *rule of the most powerful*.)

If the above reasoning is correct, then petrifying tendencies can exist (to some extent) in all meritocracies. This is a problem, because whereas incompetent rule in a well-functioning meritocracy is quickly replaced with competent rule, incompetent rule in a petrified, non-changing hierarchy will remain incompetent. Therefore, a good meritocracy should have mechanisms to keep these petrifying tendencies in check. The best way of doing this is to keep social mobility at a healthy level, for example by trying to retain a general equality of opportunity for all agents, limiting the number of "terms" any agent can hold the highest positions in the bureaucracy, or making sure that the power differences never grow too large.

Problems and Advantages of Hierarchies

Hierarchical structures have both inherent advantages and potential drawbacks. One of the problems decision-making hierarchies can produce is the problem of incompetent decision-makers using hierarchy to preserve their power as discussed earlier. Furthermore, an inflexible hierarchy might be inefficient in delegating power (e.g., not delegating it to the agents best suited to deal with the task) and inefficient in communicating information. As has been discussed, a way to deal with some of these problems is to introduce meritocracy. The question, then, is to determine what to define as "meritable" behavior. One way to test if the definition of merit is appropriate – i.e., if the meritocratic mechanisms lead to more competent strategic decision-making – is to compare the results from a meritocratic bureaucracy with a randomized hierarchy. If there are no performance differences between the meritocratic bureaucracy and the randomized one, all organizational benefits can probably be ascribed to the hierarchical decision-making per se, and the organizational definition of 'competence' is probably incomplete or incorrect.

The basic advantage of all decision-making hierarchies is that, in order to make the actors act in a concerted fashion, it creates a superior source of coordination (Milgram, 1974). By doing so, the hierarchic control structure cuts through the Gordian knot – in which all agents must negotiate mutual agreements for all actions – to mitigate non-productive conflict. Agents in a non-hierarchical agent group that try to coordinate their own actions by figuring out the plans of others, clearly need rather sophisticated cognitive mechanisms. Furthermore, to succeed they will have to retain a large number of plans, both their own and those of others, and attempt to predict highly complex outcomes. Such agents will probably want to take into consideration the plans of *all* nearby agents, and will probably have to calculate the other agents' probable plans of action for more than just a few steps into the future. Because all agents' plans are influenced by other agents' assumptions about other agents, it is easy to see that without a decision-making hierarchy, one arrives to an infinite regress where agents are making guesses about other agents' guesses.

Furthermore, a hierarchy can lessen the need for calculating possible future world states. If agents have to reason about what they think that other agents are about to do, they must calculate several steps into the future. As shown in, e.g., Scheutz and Schermerhorn (2003), predictive agents are not at all impossible to design. In fact, their results show that predictive capabilities can greatly improve performance in both reactive and deliberative agents. However, there are environments where prediction is difficult and thus uncertain. In such environments, prediction might be too risky to be a valuable or even safe source of advice. In a hierarchy then, instead of having the individual agents trying to coordinate their actions with other agents by making complicated guesses about other agents' intentions and possible future states, a superior agent tells them how to act. The difficult task of calculating other agents' probable actions is replaced by a much easier task: simply tell them what to do.

Conclusion: Political Agents?

What does the interaction between the local micro-level and the organizational macro-level look like? As noted before, strategic decisions are harder to make than tactical decisions, and political decisions are even harder. In this paper, the political decision-making level has not been reached; the agents are not cognitively advanced enough to practice political reasoning. Even if the political decision-making level had been implemented, though, it is hard to see how a genuine macro-to-micro interaction could exist in a multi-agent system in the same way as in a cognitively sophisticated human society. As mentioned earlier, it is argued by Sawyer (2003) that multi-agent systems by necessity must apply a methodological individualism; you have to start by designing the agents. This does not mean that multi-agent macro-behaviors are mere extrapolations of individual behavior, only that the individual is always the *primus motor*, and that the macro-level essentially must act as a proxy for micro-to-micro interaction.

While the notion of genuine macro-to-micro interaction seems elusive in multi-agent systems, a step towards agents comprehending and influencing the macro-level is to make them capable of political decision-making (as defined earlier). In the context of the experimental setup described, this would mean that agents would take over some or all the functions performed by the Umpire and the KB in this simulation, and make the organizational rules open for debate. Assume, then, that more than two top-level agents with powers to modify the organization's rule set were allowed. One "benevolent" agent might grant its subordinates a large amount of freedom and pay them well for their work, while another "malevolent" agent might terrorize its subordinates by sending out harsh orders and taxing them severely. The two top agents, the benevolent and the malevolent, would in effect have conflicting world-views (however trivial).

Different leadership styles might be allowed in the simulation; for example, some agents might prefer a large amount of direct subordinates where other would be happy with few subordinates; some agents might be very harsh when punishing their subordinates and strict in the supervision of them, while others might be very laissez-faire minded towards their subordinates, etc. Agents could also tax their subordinates in order to get a share of their subordinates' success, thus reaping the potential benefits of their leadership style. An interesting experiment would be one where agents with different organizational "personalities" started interacting in an environment that allowed for meritocratic power climbing. Then, in a population of agents with many different organizational personalities, it might be possible to see different political currents emerge, as the meritocratic process gives power to agents with different, competing views of how a good bureaucratic organization is constructed.

CHAPTER FOURTEEN
THE ROLE OF LEADERSHIP: WHAT MANAGEMENT SCIENCE CAN GIVE BACK TO THE STUDY OF COMPLEX SYSTEMS

Daniel Solow & Joseph G. Szmerekovsky

In recent times, the study of complex systems and complex-systems thinking has influenced research and approaches to research in business. While business has benefited from this influence, this paper suggests that ideas from the study of management can, and should, be applied to the study of complex systems. In particular, much of the complex-system literature is oriented around self-organization, in which individual agents in a system organize themselves, with no external influence, in such a way as to produce interesting and useful emergent system behaviors. In most business organizations, however, central organization plays a significant role in the organization's performance. It is suggested here through numerous examples and a naïve mathematical model that the study of complex systems could benefit from examining the role and impact of central organization, and leadership in particular.

Daniel Solow is Associate Professor of Operations, Department of Operations, Weatherhead School of Management at Case Western Reserve University in Cleveland, Ohio. Professor Solow has a Ph.D. in Operations Research from Stanford University. His research interests focus on the use of mathematical models, analysis, and computer simulations to study how properties emerge in complex adaptive systems, with applications to teams and leadership in organizations. He also conducts research in linear, combinatorial, and nonlinear optimization.

Joseph G. Szmerekovsky is Assistant Professor of Management, Department of Management, Marketing and Finance, College of Business, North Dakota State University in Fargo, North Dakota. Professor Szmerekovsky has a Ph.D. in Operations Research from Case Western Reserve University. His research interests include project management, complex systems, supply chain management, and scheduling. His research has appeared or is scheduled to appear in *Management Science, Complexity, Naval Research Logistics*, and *European Journal of Operational Research*.

Introduction

Complex systems are systems consisting of interacting agents. Such systems are ubiquitous, arising in the biological, social and physical sciences. Examples include human society with interacting people; an ecosystem of interacting species; the solar system in which the planets and the sun interact through gravity; a bee colony; the human brain consisting of interacting neurons; a business organization consisting of workers and managers; a financial market of buyers and sellers; the human body consisting of interacting cells; the military; and the internet with interacting computers.

While in recent times researchers have borrowed ideas, methodologies, and mathematical models from the complex systems literature to study business problems (discussed in more detail below), the thesis here is that complex-systems researchers can benefit significantly from some of the ideas, methodologies, and mathematical models used in business research. Specifically, much of the study of complex systems has been based on the fascinating property of *self-organization*, in which individual agents in a complex system organize themselves, with no external influence, in such a way as to produce interesting and useful emergent system behaviors. Self-organization has been used to explain behavior in many socioeconomic systems including market economies (Ruzavin, 1994; Markose, 2005), politics (Rhee, 2000), entrepreneurship (Nicholls-Nixon, 2005), innovation projects (Harkema, 2003), and task-specialization (Solow & Szmerekovsky, 2005). Self-organization has also been observed in both biological systems (Bonabeau & Meyer, 2001; Capra, 2005) and physical systems (Richardson, 2005). In business organizations, however, central organization, with leadership in particular, plays a significant role in the organization's performance (see later).

While many complex systems may initially arise from self-organization (e.g., the planets, the World Wide Web, and perhaps even biological organisms), as many of these systems evolve it is the emergence of some sort of centralized organization that allows for high levels of performance that might not have been achieved otherwise. An obvious example is human society, which may have started out more in a self-organizing mode but has since evolved hierarchical governmental structures involving central control that account, to a large degree, for social successes over the years. Other examples of complex systems whose performance is due in large part to central organization include the human body, controlled by the brain and the nervous system, and the solar system, in which leadership is embodied in the role of the sun.

To the extent, then, that the behavior of certain complex systems is affected greatly by central organization, our understanding of the behavior of these systems should include the study of how central organization and leadership affect system performance. For instance, it is commonly accepted that one role of central organization is to exert control over the agents of a complex system. But *how much* control should be exercised to achieve optimal system performance; or, in other words, under what conditions do systems benefit from different amounts of central control? There are systems that function well with little or no central control (such as the internet), while other systems require high levels of central control to achieve good performance (such as the military or the solar system as controlled by the gravitational force of the sun), and still other systems that function best with intermediate levels of control (the human body, for example). The answers to these questions have practical implications. For example, how much control should the Federal Reserve board exercise in the form of interest rates? To what degree should the federal government control the price of heating oil and natural gas? To be sure, these are very difficult, maybe even intractable questions. However, mathematical models are presented later in this paper and in the appendix to indicate that indeed there are mathematical conditions under which optimal performance of a complex system can be achieved with no central control, other conditions under which intermediate levels of control are best, and still other conditions under which the system requires full control for optimal performance.

The Impact of Complex Systems Research on Business Research

Because the behavior of a complex system generally results from *interaction* among the agents (and not from any single agent), a complex-systems approach is to study the system as a whole, atte3mpting to understand how agent interaction affects the system (rather than to take a "reductionist" approach of studying the individual agents). This kind of "holistic" approach also arises in the study of business organizations, a prominent example being the *supply chain*, consisting of suppliers, manufacturers, retailers, and customers. Rather than studying each individual player in the supply chain in isolation, supply chain management requires studying how the constituents interact with order quantities and sales through demand uncertainties and prices (see, for example, Mantrala & Raman, 1999; Munson & Rosenblatt, 2001; and Kolay, *et al.*, 2004).

Another example of holistic complex-systems thinking in business research is in the realization that the actions and decisions in one functional area affect the performance of other functional areas. Thus, rather than using the reductionist approach of studying each functional area separately – as was often done in the past – much recent research in business includes the interaction of two or more functional areas. Kaeter (1993) describes the business world's transition from specialized "silo" structures to more general cross-functional team structures. Current theory suggests the use of cross-functional teams in a variety of areas to improve organizational performance. These areas are as diverse as in-store IT development (Rowen, 2006), business partnerships (Boedeker & Hughes, 2005), safety enhancement (Smith, 2005), new product development (Fredericks, 2005; Mosey, 2005), and global-sourcing (Gopal, *et al.*, 2004). However, these improvements are not automatic. For example, Webber (2002) indicates the importance of trust in improving cross-functional team performance, and Rowe (2004) identifies the role of accounting procedures and team structure in eliminating free-riders in cross-functional teams. In addition, Mohamed, *et al.* (2004) recommend combining cross-functionality and knowledge management to achieve superior results.

Other examples where complex-systems approaches have influenced research in business include the *NK* model, which was initially developed by Kauffman and Levin (1987) and Kauffman (1993) to study the impact of interactions among genes on chromosome evolution by way of the notion of a *fitness landscape* and has been used in the study of business organizations since the mid-1990s (Levinthal, 1997; Levinthal & Warglien, 1999; McKelvey, 1999). Rivkin (2000) suggests that firms can use a fitness landscape to prevent competitors from copying successful business strategies. Another application of the *NK* model arises in the study of an organizational team consisting of interacting workers (Rivkin & Siggelkow, 2002). Solow, *et al.* (2002) use the *NK* model to provide managerial insights on how worker interaction affects the performance of various worker-replacement policies.

How Business Research Can Influence Complex-Systems Research

While much of the foregoing business literature borrows from the complex-systems approach, business research can provide ideas that have an equally valuable impact on the study of complex systems. One such example, as mentioned in the introduction, is the impact of leadership on organizations, for which there is a large and rich literature that we briefly summarize into four categories (Luthans, *et al.*, 1988):

- Traditional management activities, such as planning (Kotter, 1982; Bennis & Townsend, 1995; Chemers, 1997), decision making (Mintzberg, 1973; Kotter, 1982), and controlling (Kotter, 1982; Bennis & Townsend, 1995; Chemers, 1997);

- Human resource management activities, such as motivating/reinforcing (Fiedler, 1967; Mintzberg, 1973; Kotter, 1982; Manz & Sims, 1989; Cole, 1996; Chemers, 1997), disciplining/punishing (Mintzberg, 1973), seeking cooperation and managing conflict (Mintzberg, 1973; Kotter, 1982), staffing and training/development (Mintzberg, 1973);

- Communication activities, such as exchanging information (Mintzberg, 1973; Kotter, 1982; Chemers, 1997) and handling paperwork (Mintzberg, 1973);

- Networking activities, such as interacting with outsiders (Mintzberg, 1973) and socializing/politicking (Kotter, 1982).

Some business researchers who have borrowed ideas from the complex-systems literature have realized the need to include some of the foregoing leadership roles in their work. For example, when studying teams, Solow and Leenawong (2003) and Solow, *et al.* (2005) modify the *NK* model to include a leader and show how the effects of cooperational and motivational leadership, in addition to worker interactions, affect team performance. In a different direction, Rivkin and Siggelkow (2003) extend the *NK* model to capture management's decision-making role. Their paper considers two department managers and a

CEO, where decisions made in each department affect other decisions throughout the firm. Insights are provided into how managerial ability, incentives, interaction, and the way decisions are assigned have impacts on firm performance.

The thesis presented here is that the study of complex systems would benefit significantly by considering how leadership affects system performance. Thus, a careful analysis of the foregoing leadership roles is needed to identify which ones apply to other complex systems; or better yet, to broad collections of complex systems. For example, consider the role of a leader as one who exerts control on the individuals in the organization. By "control" is meant any of the direct and indirect means by which a central authority seeks to achieve enhanced performance by changing the behavior of the individuals. This change in behavior can be realized, for example, in an authoritarian manner by issuing rules, orders, and regulations (as in bureaucratic control); in a motivating manner by providing directives and incentives (Eisenhardt, 1989; Fama, 1980; Jensen & Meckling, 1976); in a cooperative manner by achieving coordination among the agents (Lee, 2001); or in a passive-responsive manner by exerting influence only when the system is not behaving within specified limits.

The concept of control applies to many complex systems. For example, governments control their populations through laws and regulations; the brain and central nervous system control the human body through bio-feedback loops; the sun's gravitational field controls the orbits of the planets in our solar system. Thus, as mentioned in the introduction, an interesting and important question is how much central control is good for complex systems; or, more accurately, under what conditions do complex systems benefit from low, intermediate, and high levels of central control? While no specific answers are provided here, a model is presented to show that there are mathematical conditions under which optimal performance of a complex system is achieved with no central control, other conditions under which partial levels of control are best, and still other conditions under which the system requires full control for optimal performance.

A Mathematical Framework for Studying Central Control

To study the effects of different amounts of central control, a complex system is represented as a group of n agents together with a leader. The effort of each agent i under the influence of the leader is assumed to result in a real number, x_i. These efforts are collectively denoted by $x = (x_1, \dots, x_n)$ and are called the *agents' outputs*. System performance depends on the agents' outputs and is represented by the real number $p(x)$, with larger values of $p(x)$ denoting better system performance.

The key issue is how the leader's control affects system performance. To that end, control is assumed to change the agents' behaviors, which, in this model, are represented by the agents' outputs. Thus, control by the leader changes the agents' outputs, which in turn change system performance.

When the leader has direct and immediate influence on the individual agents, it is possible and reasonable for the leader to exert a different amount of control on each agent. This would be the case, for example, with the manager of a department in a business organization or with a platoon leader in the army. However, when the leader has less immediate contact with the agents (for example, the CEO of a large corporation or the Secretary of Defense for the military), it is impractical (or unfair) for the leader to set different amounts of control for each agent. In this case, the leader's control, in theory, affects all agents equally. This latter situation is modeled here by the assumption that the control by the leader on each agent is the same. As such, the amount of control is denoted by a real number $\lambda \geq 0$, in which $\lambda = 0$ corresponds to no control and $\lambda = 1$ to full control, with increasing values of λ corresponding to increasing amounts of control. A small value for λ might reflect a system in which the agents require little supervision or oversight, such as the internet or the faculty at a university. In contrast, a value for λ close to 1 might correspond to detailed regulations that are aggressively enforced through constant supervision of the agents, such as in the military.

When left on their own with no control from the leader ($\lambda = 0$), each agent i has no restrictions and is therefore allowed to choose its own output, which is represented by the real number $x_i(0)$. The specific way in which the agent chooses this output value is not important in the model proposed here. Thus, $\boldsymbol{x}(0) = (x_1(0), \dots, x_n(0))$ represents the collective outputs of the agents when there is no control and the associated system performance is $p(\boldsymbol{x}(0))$.

As the leader exerts more control by increasing the value of λ, the effect is to change the agents' behaviors and hence their outputs from $\boldsymbol{x}(0)$ to new values denoted by $\boldsymbol{x}(\lambda) = (x_1(\lambda), \dots, x_n(\lambda))$. An important question is how the values of $\boldsymbol{x}(\lambda)$ are determined in that regard. It is assumed that the leader has an *a priori* estimate of the agents' output values, say, $\boldsymbol{x}(1) = (x_1(1), \dots, x_n(1))$, that would, in the leader's opinion, provide maximum system performance. Note that one measure of the skill of the leader is how close the leader's values of $\boldsymbol{x}(1)$ are to the actual agent outputs that result in optimal system performance. In any event, an obvious question to ask is: If the leader believes that the output values $\boldsymbol{x}(1)$ are best for system performance, then why should the leader not exert full control? One answer is because the leader does not know the performance function explicitly, for example in a nascent business. Therefore, by exerting full control, the leader may find that the outputs $\boldsymbol{x}(1)$ do not result in the best system performance. Thus, the leader needs to determine the optimal amount of control λ to exert so that the agents' outputs, $\boldsymbol{x}(\lambda)$, maximize the system performance $p(\boldsymbol{x}(\lambda))$. In order to analyze this optimization problem, it is necessary to know how the agents' outputs, $\boldsymbol{x}(\lambda)$, vary as the amount of control λ varies and also the specific form of $p(\boldsymbol{x})$; that is, how the performance of the system varies as the agents' outputs vary.

Analytical Results From a Specific Form of the General Model

Specific forms are now given for how the agents' outputs, $\boldsymbol{x}(\lambda)$, change as a function of the amount of control and for how system performance, $p(\boldsymbol{x})$, changes as the agents' outputs change. Keep in mind that the forms proposed here are not meant to be realistic or to reflect any specific complex system. Rather, the proposed forms of $\boldsymbol{x}(\lambda)$ and $p(\boldsymbol{x})$ are used to show that there are mathematical conditions under which optimal system performance is achieved with no control, other conditions under which the system performs best with an intermediate amount of control, and still other conditions for which it is best to exert full control. To simplify the model, the system is assumed here to consist of a leader and a single agent (and is extended in the appendix to include n agents).

Turning first to how the amount of control λ affects the agent's output, as the leader increases control from 0 to 1, the agent's output is assumed to change in a linear way from $x(0)$ (the outputs chosen by the agent under no control) to $x(1)$ (the agent's output deemed best by the leader). That is, for any amount of control $0 \leq \lambda \leq 1$, the output of the agent is given mathematically as $x(\lambda) = (1 - \lambda)x(0) + \lambda x(1)$.

Turning to the performance function, a quadratic form is assumed; that is, when the output of the agent is x, the system achieves the performance $p(x) = qx^2$, where q is a given negative number. Observe that the maximum possible system performance is $p(x) = 0$ and is achieved when the agent's output is $x = 0$. The value of q represents how fast system performance deteriorates as the agent's output deviates from its optimal value of 0.

Having specified both $x(\lambda)$ and $p(x)$, the goal of the leader is to determine the optimal amount of control – that is, the value of λ – that solves the following problem:

Max: $\qquad p(x(\lambda)) = q\, x(\lambda)^2$ $\qquad\qquad\qquad\qquad$ (1)

Subject to: $\qquad x(\lambda) = (1 - \lambda)x(0) + \lambda x(1)$
$\qquad\qquad\qquad 0 \leq \lambda \leq 1$

Because of the specific form chosen for $p(x)$ and the fact that q is negative, it is possible to solve the optimization problem in (1) by setting the derivative of $p(x(\lambda))$ with respect to λ equal to 0 and solving for λ. Details of doing so are given in the appendix, but the result is that the solution, λ^*, to the optimization problem is given in the following cases.

Case 1: No control ($\lambda^* = 0$).
The optimal solution to (1) is $\lambda^* = 0$ if and only if $x(0)x(1) \geq x(0)^2$.

Case 2: Full control ($\lambda^* = 1$).
The optimal solution is $\lambda^* = 1$ if and only if,
$x(1)^2 \leq x(0)x(1)$.

Case 3: Partial control ($0 < \lambda^* < 1$).
Finally, $0 < \lambda^* < 1$ if and only if $x(0)^2 > x(0)x(1)$ and $x(1)^2 > x(0)x(1)$.

While the foregoing mathematical model is not realistic, it is possible to conjecture conditions under which real-world systems benefit from differing amounts of control. For instance, it is likely that a system will benefit from low levels of control when the agents' choices of outputs under low control are closely aligned with those outputs that result in good system performance. One such example is the faculty at a university who, when left alone, generally choose actions that result in good performance for the university. Another circumstance in which low levels of control are likely to be best is when the survival of the individual agents depends on the survival of the system, as in early human civilizations where self-organizing behavior, more than leadership, resulted in the survival of the species. A final circumstance under which systems might benefit from low levels of control is when enforcing the leader's will on the agents would result in outputs that degrade rather than improve system performance. Though much speculation is often made as to when this situation occurs, no general scheme is proposed here.

A condition on real-world systems under which exerting a large amount of control is likely to be beneficial occurs when the agents' self-chosen outputs under no control conflict with the performance and survival of the system. One such example is a prison. The prisoners would like to escape the prison, whereas the goal of the prison system is their continued incarceration. Other conditions under which high levels of central control might be beneficial are when the leader has accurate knowledge of the agents' outputs that indeed are good for the system, and small deviations from those outputs result in poor system performance. One example of such a system is the classic assembly line, where the leader knows what each worker should do to get the job done and so exerts a lot of control by specifying what, when, and how tasks should be done. Further, should a single member of the line fail in his or her duties, the final product will prove defective and/or the assembly line may be forced to shut down. Hence, it is necessary and beneficial for central control to be enforced on assembly lines. Even some more modern manufacturing methods such as just in time (JIT) and statistical process control (SPC) require regimented control of the system agents. Employing these methods requires a clear target for each agent. Determining such targets requires experience of which behaviors result in good system performance. Hence, "full control" is likely to be beneficial in very stable environments where system needs do not change significantly over time.

As we have seen, low and high levels of control are beneficial if the system is volatile or stable, is in danger of extinction unless the agents choose appropriate outputs, or if the leader's knowledge of the system is extremely poor or accurate. Moderate levels of control might be appropriate under less severe conditions. For example, if the system is facing rapid change then it is not always clear what agent outputs will be optimal for system performance and if the system is not on the edge of collapse, agents will likely pursue their own interests along with the system's interests. Under these circumstances "full control" is not appropriate because the leader's knowledge of the outputs that are best for the system is not complete. Instead, the leader must depend in part on the agents to determine what is best for the system. However, if "no control" is used, the agents could easily abuse their freedom at the expense of the system or otherwise choose outputs that do not result in good system performance. Hence, some level of "partial control" will prove best. This situation occurs in such areas as entrepreneurship, venture capitalism, new product development, and emerging markets. A similar scenario arises when the success of a system requires inputs from agents with diverse areas of expertise. The leader is not likely to be an expert in all areas and hence cannot exercise "full control," but must depend partially on the agents to determine their own inputs. Of course, "no control" is again an unsatisfactory option. This situation occurs with many contemporary management structures, including cross-functional teams, matrix structures, project management, and organic structures.

A model has been presented for which there are conditions under which it is optimal for the leader to exert no control ($\lambda^* = 0$), partial control ($0 < \lambda^* < 1$), and full control ($\lambda^* = 1$) over the agents. However, this model has many deficiencies. For example, no mention has been made of how the agents determine their preferred input levels. A model that overcomes these deficiencies and allows the agents to choose their outputs based on their own individual utility functions is presented in Solow and Szmerekovsky (2006).

Conclusion

While the study of complex systems and complex-systems thinking has influenced research and approaches to research in business, the reverse appears not to have taken place to any significant degree. Recognizing that central organization and leadership have a substantial impact on business organizations, it has been argued that there are potential benefits to be gained by considering the role played by central organization and leadership in general complex systems. Consideration of numerous examples has shown that there are many complex systems whose extraordinary performance is attributable, in large part, to central control exerted by a leader. A simple (but non-realistic) model has been presented here to illustrate that there are mathematical conditions under which optimal performance of a complex system is achieved with no central control, other conditions under which intermediate levels of control are best, and still other conditions under which the system requires full control for optimal performance

In the authors' opinion, this model is the tip of an iceberg that represents the wealth of results and insights that can be realized from research in complex systems that takes into account the role, value, and importance of central organization and leadership. For example, one interesting question is to understand under what conditions complex systems benefit from each different type of central control (authoritarian, motivational, cooperational, and passive-responsive). Another direction is to investigate the extent to which leadership roles other than control, as identified in this paper, affect the performance of complex systems in general. No central organization is needed to conduct this research, but the authors are grateful to the central organization of the editors that led to this edited volume.

Mathematical appendix

The model given in (1) above is now generalized to include n agents. To that end, when the leader increases control from 0 to 1, the output of each agent i is assumed to change in a linear way from $x_i(0)$ (the output chosen by that agent under no control) to $x_i(1)$ (the agent output deemed best by the leader). That is, for any amount of control $0 \le \lambda \le 1$:

$$x_i(\lambda) = (1 - \lambda)x_i(0) + \lambda x_i(1),$$

or equivalently, using vectors,

$$\boldsymbol{x}(\lambda) = (1-\lambda)\boldsymbol{x}(0) + \lambda \, \boldsymbol{x}(1). \tag{2}$$

Turning to the performance function, a quadratic form is assumed; that is, when the outputs of the agent are $\boldsymbol{x}$, the system achieves the following level of performance:

$$p(\boldsymbol{x}) = \boldsymbol{x}^T Q \boldsymbol{x}, \tag{3}$$

where Q is a given ($n \times n$) negative semidefinite symmetric matrix. Observe that the maximum value of $p(\boldsymbol{x})$ in (3) is 0 and is achieved when the agents' outputs are all 0; that is, when $\boldsymbol{x} = (0, ..., 0)$. The values of Q represent the way – that is, how fast – system performance deteriorates as the agents' outputs deviate from their optimal values of 0.

Having specified both $\boldsymbol{x}(\lambda)$ and $p(\boldsymbol{x})$, the goal of the leader is to determine the optimal amount of control – that is, the value of λ – that solves the following problem:

Max $\qquad p(\boldsymbol{x}(\lambda)) = \boldsymbol{x}(\lambda)^T Q \, \boldsymbol{x}(\lambda)$ $\qquad\qquad\qquad$ (4)

Subject to $\qquad \boldsymbol{x}(\lambda) = (1 - \lambda)\boldsymbol{x}(0) + \lambda\boldsymbol{x}(1)$
$\qquad\qquad\qquad 0 \le \lambda \le 1$

Because of the specific form chosen for $p(\boldsymbol{x})$ in (3) and the fact that Q is negative semidefinite (and hence $p(\boldsymbol{x}(\lambda))$ is concave in λ), it is possible to solve the optimization problem in (4) by setting the derivative of $p(\boldsymbol{x}(\lambda))$ with respect to λ equal to 0 and solving for λ. To that end, notationally letting $\boldsymbol{y} = \boldsymbol{x}(0)$ and $\boldsymbol{z} = \boldsymbol{x}(1)$, for $\boldsymbol{x}(\lambda) = (1-\lambda)\boldsymbol{y} + \lambda\boldsymbol{z}$, it follows from (3) that

$$\begin{aligned}
p(\boldsymbol{x}(\lambda)) &= [(1-\lambda)\boldsymbol{y} + \lambda\boldsymbol{z}]^T Q[(1-\lambda)\boldsymbol{y} + \lambda\boldsymbol{z}] \\
&= (1-\lambda)^2 \boldsymbol{y}^T Q\boldsymbol{y} + 2\lambda(1-\lambda)\boldsymbol{y}^T Q\boldsymbol{z} + \lambda^2 \boldsymbol{z}^T Q\boldsymbol{z} \\
&= (\boldsymbol{y}^T Q\boldsymbol{y} - 2\boldsymbol{y}^T Q\boldsymbol{z} + \boldsymbol{z}^T Q\boldsymbol{z})\lambda^2 + (2\boldsymbol{y}^T Q\boldsymbol{z} - 2\boldsymbol{y}^T Q\boldsymbol{y})\lambda + \boldsymbol{y}^T Q\boldsymbol{y}.
\end{aligned}$$

Letting,

$$\begin{aligned}
a &= \boldsymbol{y}^T Q\boldsymbol{y} - 2\,\boldsymbol{y}^T Q\boldsymbol{z} + \boldsymbol{z}^T Q\boldsymbol{z} = \boldsymbol{y} - \boldsymbol{z}^T Q\,(\boldsymbol{y} - \boldsymbol{z}), \\
b &= 2\,\boldsymbol{y}^T Q\boldsymbol{z} - 2\,\boldsymbol{y}^T Q\boldsymbol{y} = 2(\boldsymbol{y}^T Q\boldsymbol{z} - \boldsymbol{y}^T Q\boldsymbol{y}), \\
c &= \boldsymbol{y}^T Q\boldsymbol{y}, \\
f(\lambda) &= p(\boldsymbol{x}(\lambda)),
\end{aligned}$$

it follows that,

$$f(\lambda) = a\lambda^2 + b\lambda + c \text{ and} \qquad (5)$$
$$f'(\lambda) = 2a\lambda + b \qquad (6)$$

The solution, λ^*, to the optimization problem in (4) for the foregoing special form of $f'(\lambda)$ in (5) and $f'(\lambda)$ in (6) is given in the following cases.

Case 1: No control ($\lambda^* = 0$). It is easy to prove that the optimal solution to (4) is $\lambda^* = 0$ if and only if $f'(0) \leq 0$; that is, if and only if $f'(0) = b = 2(\boldsymbol{y}^T\boldsymbol{Qz} - \boldsymbol{y}^T\boldsymbol{Qy}) \leq 0$; that is, $\boldsymbol{y}^T\boldsymbol{Qz} \leq \boldsymbol{y}^T\boldsymbol{Qy}$.

Case 2: Full control ($\lambda^* = 1$). Likewise, the optimal solution to (4) is $\lambda^* = 1$ if and only if $f'(1) \geq 0$, that is, if and only if $f'(1) = 2a + b = 2(\boldsymbol{z}^T\boldsymbol{Qz} - \boldsymbol{y}^T\boldsymbol{Qz}) \geq 0$; that is, $\boldsymbol{z}^T\boldsymbol{Qz} \geq \boldsymbol{y}^T\boldsymbol{Qz}$.

Case 3: Partial control ($0 < \lambda^* < 1$). Finally, if $f'(0) > 0$ and $f'(1) < 0$, the optimal solution to (4) is the value of λ^* for which $f'(\lambda^*) = 0$, that is,

$$\lambda^* = -b / 2a = (\boldsymbol{y}^T\boldsymbol{Qy} - \boldsymbol{y}^T\boldsymbol{Qz}) / (\boldsymbol{y}^T\boldsymbol{Qy} - 2\boldsymbol{y}^T\boldsymbol{Qz} + \boldsymbol{z}^T\boldsymbol{Qz}),$$

with $0 < \lambda^* < 1$ if and only if $0 < b < -2a$; that is, if and only if $\boldsymbol{y}^T\boldsymbol{Qz} > \boldsymbol{y}^T\boldsymbol{Qy}$ and $\boldsymbol{z}^T\boldsymbol{Qz} < \boldsymbol{y}^T\boldsymbol{Qz}$.

PART III
METHODS, MODELS AND METAPHORS

CHAPTER FIFTEEN
A MATRIX OF COMPLEXITY FOR LEADERSHIP: FOURTEEN DISCIPLINES OF COMPLEX SYSTEMS LEADERSHIP THEORY[1]

Benyamin B. Lichtenstein

This volume confirms the truism that complexity is a science composed of many (competing) disciplines or methods, each of which reflecting a particular orientation as well as a specific set of assumptions. Through a review of complexity surveys, I explore the nature of complexity science and the different ways it explains emergence, which I believe is the core contribution of complexity for management. After a comprehensive definition of emergence, I identify two dimensions of emergence: The first reflects the type of emergence being studied: (a) the discovery of emergence, (b) the modeling of emergence, and (c) intrinsic emergence. The second dimension reflects the levels of emergence being explored: (1) emergent patterns within one system level; (2) emergent dynamics within a system, i.e., two levels; and (3) principles of emergence, comprising three or more levels). Together these two dimensions generate a typology – the matrix – which can distinguish 14 distinct complexity approaches. I then show how each of these disciplines can uniquely contribute to a Complex Science Leadership Theory. Finally I argue that the more self-conscious we can be about the nature of complexity research, the more likely it is that complexity will strengthen our academic scholarship, and increase the likelihood of creating together a theory of complexity for management.

Benyamin B. Lichtenstein is Assistant Professor of Management and Entrepreneurship at the University of Massachusetts, Boston. Dr. Lichtenstein's research expertise focuses on applications of complexity science to leadership, entrepreneurial emergence and transformation, and on collaboration, trust and inter-organizational learning. "Professor Benyamin" as his students call him, has published over 35 papers and chapters and presented several dozen more, including articles in internationally recognized journals such as *Organization*

1 Over the years (about eight!) this chapter benefited from very useful comments by Phil Anderson, Janice Black, Kathleen Carley, Kevin Dooley, Robert Drazin, Bob Farias, Bill McKelvey, and Olav Sorenson, among others. Jeff Goldstein provided very useful comments to this and other drafts, which, along with the encouragement of Jim Hazy, have also been extremely helpful. I am indebted to participants of the 2000 Academy of Management symposium, "Bringing Complexity to Bear on Organizations" (organized by Alan Meyer) for their perceptive feedback. Research leading to the development of this paper was generously funded by the Center for Entrepreneurial Leadership Inc., and the Ewing Marion Kauffman Foundation, as well as by the Irwin Foundation. The contents of this publication are solely the responsibility of the author.

Science, Journal of Business Venturing, Human Relations and *Academy of Management Executive*, where he received the article of the year award in 2000. In addition to his scholarly work, and his executive consulting to entrepreneurs and managers, he finds great joy connecting with his beautiful wife Sasha and their two children, Simeon and Moriah.

Introduction

For some time, scholars have suggested that complexity research can play an important role in management theory generally (Simon, 1962; Schieve & Allen, 1982; Ulrich & Probst, 1984; Weick, 1977; Anderson, 1999; McKelvey, 1999a), and more specifically in explaining the dynamics of organizational change and adaptation (Zeleny, 1981; Bigelow, 1982; Goldstein, 1986; Nonaka, 1988; Smith & Gemmill, 1991; Carley & Prietula, 1994). Complexity-inspired research papers have appeared in virtually all of the top journals in management, reflecting an increasing ability for researchers to integrate the insights from these methods into mainstream organization theory (McKelvey, 2004b; Siggelkow & Rivkin, 2006; Plowman, *et al.*, 2007 - this volume).

Leadership scholars have also been recognizing the potential value of complexity frameworks for exploring and explaining the interactive, generative, and emergent nature of leadership properties and processes (Guastello, 1998; Marion & Uhl-Bien, 2001; Uhl-Bien, Marion, & McKelvey, 2007). Complexity models and methods may be particularly valuable for studying the multi-level properties, multi-directional causalities, non-linearities, positive feedbacks, and path dependent processes that are increasingly important in explaining leadership in dynamic contexts (Lichtenstein, *et al.*, 2007; Plowman, *et al.*, 2007 - this volume). Additionally, complexity provides a framework for understanding adaptive order, innovation and emergence, issues that are becoming more central to leadership scholarship (Rivkin, 2000; Garud, *et al.*, 2006; Plowman, *et al.*, 2007). These prospects have led to two recent special issues on Leadership and Complexity Theory, in *The Leadership Quarterly*, and *Emergence: Complexity & Organization*, as well as two edited books – the present volume, and a companion volume edited by Uhl-Bien and Marion (in press).

One challenge with this stream of research is that it draws on a diverse range of models and wide number of approaches which, though different in many ways, all seem to fall under the banner of "complexity." This confusion is increased when more popular and 'metaphorical' accounts of complexity are added to the mix (see Maguire & McKelvey, 1999). Early enthusiasm about complexity sparked a proliferation of popular managerial articles and books that utilize complexity models to explain everything from strategy formation (Bienhocker, 1999; Stacy, 1992) to management practice (Lissack & Roos, 1999; Wheatley & Kellner-Rogers, 1996); from product development (Brown & Eisenhardt, 1998) to organizational development (Goldstein, 1994). This diversity in topic and in method is matched by differing expectations about how complexity should be understood. Some authors think of complexity as a science (Dent, 1999), others see it as a theory (Anderson, 1999), and others consider it "collection of results, models, and methods" (Cohen, 1999: 375). Some place its origin in the European research of Ilya Prigogine (McKelvey, 2004a), others argue that complexity was formulated by scholars from the Santa Fe Institute (Waldrop, 1992); some mark its beginnings in the mathematics of deterministic chaos (Gleick, 1987; Kauffman, 1993), while others locate its source in cybernetics, dynamic systems modeling, and so on (Capra, 1996; Goldstein, 2000).

What is the essence of this diverse stream of complexity research, and should complexity be utilized to study leadership? More specifically, how can the multiple approaches to complexity be organized into a framework that would allow leadership scholars to match the right approach with the particular question they are asking (Davis, *et al.*, 2007)? In this brief review article I will offer one answer to these questions. I start by affirming the idea that "emergence" is the core issue which integrates the research being placed under the complexity banner (McKelvey, 2004). Next I outline two dimensions that can help organize the range of methods being utilized by complexity researchers. One dimension reflects the type of emergence being studied, and the other dimension reflects the levels of emergence being explored. Together these dimensions generate a typology – the matrix – that distinguishes 14 distinct complexity approaches. I then show how each of these approaches can support the development and testing of a complexity-based leadership theory. Finally I argue that the more self-conscious we can be about the nature of complexity research, the more likely it is that complexity will strengthen our academic scholarship, rather than continue to degenerate into a fad (McKelvey, 1999a).

Brief History and a Definition of Complexity Research

Research underlying what is being called "complexity" has existed for many decades. Its origins according to some complexity scholars are in Prigogine's research on "dissipative structures," which explains how regimes of order come into being and retain their form amidst a constant dissipation of energy and resources (Prigogine, 1955; Prigogine & Stengers, 1984; Lichtenstein, 2000a). This idea became popularized in the 1960s and 1970s as general systems theory (von Bertalanffy, 1968; Miller, 1978) and open systems (Kast & Rosenzweig, 1972), whose applications were foundational to organization science (Lawrence & Lorsch, 1967; Thompson, 1967; cf. Ashmos & Huber, 1987).

During this same early period researchers in a wide variety of fields were experimenting with non-linear models of dynamic systems. Several major schools of thought were born of these explorations, including: cybernetics (Weiner, 1948/1961), system dynamics (Forrester, 1961; Maruyama, 1963), computational genetic algorithms (Neumann, 1966), complex adaptive systems (Holland, 1975), deterministic chaos theory (May, 1976), catastrophe theory (Zeeman, 1977), synergetics (Haken, 1977), autopoiesis (Maturana & Varela, 1980), and fractals (Mandelbrot, 1983). With Gleick's (1987) best-selling book many of these approaches became known as "chaos" theories. Some years later Lewin (1992) and Waldrop (1992) described a new synthesis of these models, based on research coming out of the Santa Fe Institute. At that point, "complexity" became the buzz word, referring to a well-received set of studies using computational agents (Cowan, *et al.*, 1994; Holland, 1995; Kauffman, 1993), cellular automata (Axelrod & Bennett, 1993; Krugman, 1996) and other agent-based simulations (Carley, 1995, 1999) to understand emergence in new ways. (See Goldstein, 1999, 2000 for a complementary overview of the origins and elaboration of complexity.)

Each complexity theorist tends to specialize in one or two disciplinary methods for studying complex dynamical systems – this explains why complexity research appears so diverse. A key goal of this article is to connect and begin to integrate these various approaches, with an eye toward developing a more comprehensive and useful leadership theory based on complex systems. An overview of the breadth of these disciplinary approaches is presented in Table 1. The table is based on classic and recent overviews and summary accounts by Gleick (1987), Lewin (1992), Waldrop (1992), Casti (1994), Cowan, *et al.*, (1994), Goerner (1994), Guastello (1995), Capra (1996), Elliott & Kiel (1996), Dooley (1997), Eve, Horsfall & Lee (1997), Anderson, *et al.*, (1999); Goldstein (1999; 2000), Marion (1999), McKelvey (1999a, 1999b, 2004a, 2004b), and Davis, *et al.* (2007); among others. Undoubtedly some scholars will disagree with the categorizations and brief descriptions of these disciplinary approaches; this list should properly be thought of as an evolving framework (a complex adaptive system) that will change based on feedback from readers like yourself. Nevertheless, this table does provide a starting point for bounding complexity research.

The goal of this paper is not to provide yet another introduction to each of the disciplines – the summaries that were used to develop Table 1 do an excellent job of accomplishing this task. Instead, our goal is to identify the essence of these research streams, and organize them in a way that can support researchers in testing a complex systems leadership theory. Each of these 14 disciplines of complexity explores the conditions, properties, or processes of emergence in dynamic, complex systems, and they do it in different ways. Before describing these ways, I provide one definition of emergence.

At its essence, complexity researchers are providing new ways to understand *how and why order emerges* (Lichtenstein, 2000b; McKelvey, 2001, 2004a). Formally, emergence has been defined in terms of "qualitative novelty" (Blitz, 1992; Newman, 1996; Popper, 1926); emergence scholars focus on the creation of coherent structures in a dynamic system (Goldstein, 1999, 2000; Holland, 1994). When these emergent structures are different 'in kind' from the elements that compose them – when a new "level" of order has come into being, or a pattern of activity can be discerned that in some way *transcends but includes* the elements of the system, emergence can be said to have occurred. Thus, emergence is a process by which "...patterns or global-level structures arise from interactive local-level processes... [The] combination of elements with one another brings with it something that was not there before" (Mead, 1932: 641; in Mihata, 1997: 31).

Leaders routinely put enormous effort into supporting the emergence of higher-order structures in their organizations, and identifying and amplifying self-organizing patterns or structures that shift the nature of the organization in some way (Buckle-Hennings & Dugan, this volume). In addition, leaders themselves sometimes become identified through emergent processes (Guastello, 1998), and emergent events are often catalyzed by leadership activities originating from throughout the organization, including from senior managers (Plowman, *et al.*, 2007). These dynamics and efforts have been understood and

Research Stream	Insights from Theory	Managerial Insights from Theory	Management References
Deterministic Chaos Theory	Emergent order (attractors) can be identified in data that appears random. Dynamic systems are highly sensitive to initial conditions (i.e. Butterfly effect).	Strange attractors are "basins of attraction" toward which organizational behaviors tend. These attractors can be statistically identified in time series data. Changes in attractors may imply learning and/or organizational transformation.	Kiel, 1994; Thietart & Forgues, 1995; Cheng & Van de Ven, 1996
Catastrophe Theory	Transformative change can be qualitatively modeled to show how incremental change across one parameter (variable) creates "catastrophic" (punctuated) changes across another.	Transformative organizational change can occur incrementally or in a punctuation. Re-analysis of behavioral data using non-linear catastrophe models explains up to 400% more variance than the same data analyzed using linear regression models.	Bigelow, 1982; Guastello, 1995; Gresov, *et al.*, 1993
System Dynamics	Positive/negative feedback loops can be mapped, allowing for a systematic experimentation of dynamic conditions in very complex systems.	Multi-level dynamic interactions across systems can be modeled, showing how and why unexpected behavior occurs in complex systems. These models can be used to find "leverage" points that avoid unintended effects.	Hall, 1976; Sastry, 1997; Rudolph & Repenning, 2002
Self-Organized Criticality	Certain dynamic systems evolve to a state in which all changes are related through a single power-law.	Specific strategies and organizational processes can generate dynamic structuring at the "edge of chaos." This dynamic strategy/structure supports high innovation and creativity in organizations.	Bak & Chen, 1991;
Fractals	Natural systems exhibit self-similarity across scales, whose dimensionality can be measured using a mathematical mapping technique.	Organizations exhibit self-similar behavior and/or values across levels (e.g., individual, group, company-wide.)	Zimmerman & Hurst, 1990
Power Laws	Certain processes repeat themselves across many scales; these repetitions can be identified through their unique signature (power law).	Many seemingly distinct organizational phenomena are inherently related to each other through a single set of underlying causal dynamics.	Carneiro, 1970; Stanley, *et al.*, 1996

Cellular Automata	The physical closeness/distance of agents significantly affects the dynamics of their evolution.	Macro-level structures are determined in part by spatial qualities of a field including e.g. density, proximity, and size.	Shelling, 1971; Lomi & Larson, 1996.
NK Landscapes	Organisms and environment co-evolve. The "fitness" of an organism depends on the overall fitness of its environment, and vice versa.	An organization and its market environment co-evolve. The "fitness" of an organization depends on its environmental influence, and vice versa. Value chain relationships can be effectively modeled, and new value chain strategies generated, using this approach.	McKelvey, 1999b; Levinthal & Warglein, 1999; Fleming & Sorenson, 2001
Genetic Algorithms	Programmed entities (cellular automata) display complex emergent patterns as they evolve toward a critical value.	Strategic moves are constrained by the decisions/behaviors of one's immediate neighbors; these constraints generate emergent patterns in computer simulations.	Axelrod, 1984; 1987; Krugman, 1996, Holland, 1995; Axelrod & Cohen, 2000.
Agent-Based Simulations / Multi-Agent Learning Models	Multiple algorithms can be linked in a single model, allowing researchers to explore complex phenomena.	Organizational adaptation and learning evolve through optimal moves which are constrained and made possible by agent qualities (e.g. knowledge) and local conditions (e.g. dynamism) that change over time.	Carley, 1990; 1999; Carley & Svoboda, 1996; Epstein & Axtell, 1996.
Autogenesis/ Autopoiesis	Some dissipative structures can self-generate and self-replicate their internal order. Autogenic systems (like "mind" are self-organized and display emergent behavior.	Organizing processes self-replicate their internal order, based on a deep structure that generates rules and more visible operations. Rule creating and rule following behavior is an emergent, self-organized process.	Pantzar & Csanyi, 1991; Drazin & Sandelands, 1992
Dissipative Structures	New levels of order can spontaneously emerge in non-equilibrium situations, through a self-amplifying process sparked by fluctuations, resulting in greater system capacity.	Groups and organizational systems can generate new order or maintain themselves at a high degree of order by dissipating large amounts of energy, information, and resources.	Smith, 1986; Wicken, 1986; Adams, 1988; Lichtenstein, 2000.
Emergent Evolution	Evolution is a self-organizing process that creates new forms, which then undergo natural selection processes. The universe has experienced an increase in complexity across evolution.	Organizational coevolution is a combination of variation-selection-retention and non-linear adaptation. Long-term development involves multiple transforms, that can be achieved through action learning and managerial capacity and development.	Leifer, 1989; White, et al., 1997;

Table 1 *Summary of Complexity Disciplines for Understanding Emergence*

explained in a variety of different ways (e.g., Lichtenstein, *et al.,* 2007; Hazy, Millhiser & Solow, this volume; Goldstein, this volume). Why this variety? Beyond the obvious recognition that each research study explores slightly different phenomena using a different base of data, in each case the choice of complexity method itself comes with a set of assumptions that enable and constrain the insights which may be gained.

As Davis, *et al.,* (2007: 285) expressed for a limited subset of complexity models: "In fact, the choice of simulation approach may be closer to choosing a theoretical framework ... because of its framing of research questions, key assumptions, and theoretical logic." Thus, one goal is to provide a framework for understanding the breadth of choices fully available to leadership scholars who are developing your own study of Complex Systems Leadership Theory.

Two Dimensions of Emergence

Each of the complexity disciplines listed in Table 1 explores and explains emergence in ways that crucially depend on a series of assumptions and goals which usually are unexamined. These fourteen disciplines reflect the entire spectrum of approaches that in any way refer to "complexity." Furthermore, rather than simply a listing of models, I aim to differentiate the 14 complexity disciplines according to (1) the type of emergence they produce (Crutchfield, 1994), and (2) levels or units of emergence they can capture. These two dimensions together generate a typology of emergence disciplines (see Table 2), which can help leadership scholars find the appropriate method for theory building and empirical testing. This typology is what I mean by a matrix of complexity.

Three Types of Emergence

The first dimension is presented by Crutchfield (1994), who distinguishes complexity theories according to the aspect or quality of emergence each seeks to explain: the *discovery of emergence*, the *modeling of emergence*, or *intrinsic emergence*. The first type refers to the *discovery* that something new has appeared in a complex system. This something could be a pattern, a degree of order, or a structure. Fractal analysis or deterministic chaos theory fit into this category, for they both have been used to *discover* order across multiple scales or in apparently random time series. Chaos theory has been used to identify periods of nonlinear interaction across a set of common factors in the early stages of two innovation ventures (Cheng & Van de Ven, 1996), and the distributions of work behavior in public service organizations (Kiel, 1994). The discovery of order at this level is in the eye of an observer: "Surely, the system state doesn't know its behavior is unpredictable" (Crutchfield, 1994: 517). Thus, theories at this level usually involve post-hoc analysis of time series that are "objectively" separate from the researcher.

The second type refers to the *modeling* of emergence, in which computational or mathematical systems are developed to represent system emergence. This level refers to research streams that have deduced rules or heuristics from simple systems and used them to develop modeling contexts in which order

	Emergent Patterns within One System Level	Emergent Dynamics within a System (two levels)	Principles of Emergence (three or more levels)
Discovery of Order:	Deterministic Chaos Theory	Catastrophe Theory System Dynamics Self-Organized Criticality	Fractal analysis Power Laws
Modeling Emergent Order:	Cellular Automata NK Landscapes	Genetic Algorithms	Agent-Based Modeling
Intrinsic Emergence:	Autopoiesis/ Autogenesis	Dissipative Structures	Multi-Agent Learning Models Emergent Evolution

Table 2 *The Matrix of Complexity: A Typology of Complexity Disciplines*

emerges over time. For example, Kauffman's (1993) "NK landscapes" have been used to model the order that can emerge in coevolutionary niches (Baum, 1999) or through firm strategies (Rivkin, 2000). Using different computational methods, system dynamics has been used to model the unexpected outcomes of strategic decisions in complex systems (Hall, 1976) and of theoretical assumptions in complex theories (Sastry, 1997). Other examples of this level include self-organized criticality, which has been used to model the behavior of stock markets (Bak, 1996), and catastrophe theory, which has been used to model discontinuities in organizational behavior (Guastello, 1995), strategic change (Gresov, *et al.*, 1993) and organizational transformation (Bigelow, 1982; Brown, 1995). In this context, theorists are more involved in the emergence process, as they identify rules and mathematical relationships that are used to (computationally) recreate emergent processes in complex systems.

Crutchfield's final type is *"intrinsic emergence,"* in which the increased capabilities generated by the system's emergence can be capitalized on by the system itself, lending additional functionality to the system (1994: 518). In a sense, rather than a description of or model about emergence, in intrinsic emergence the "observer" is a part of the system, and thus "has the requisite information processing capability with which to take advantage of the emergent patterns." Behavioral descriptions of "dissipative structures" (Smith & Gemmill, 1991; Browning, *et al.*, 1995; Leifer, 1989; Lichtenstein, 2000a) fall into this category, as do a class of agent-based modeling approaches in which agents fundamentally extend their behavioral capabilities by learning over time (Gell-Mann, 1994; Macready & Meyer, 1999; Carley & Svoboda, 1996).

Three Levels of Emergence

The second dimension refers to the *levels of emergence* that each method can usefully capture. The notion of "levels" has a long history in systems theory, where early researches identified a relatively coherent and common set of nested hierarchical levels that composed organisms, organizations, and societies e.g., von Bertalanffy (1968); Boulding (1978); Miller (1978); Salthe (1985). Management scholars have long recognized the importance of levels of analysis in describing organizations (Kast & Rosenzweig, 1972; Rosen, 1974; Ashmos & Huber, 1987), and in grappling with the challenges of doing multi-level research (Rousseau, 1985; Dansereau, *et al.*, 1999; Davidsson & Wiklund, 2001). These challenges have led to limitations in our understanding of emergence; in entrepreneurship, for example, where emergence is recognized to be a central topic area, less than 0.05% of top tier articles over a 10-year period utilized both multi-level and non-retrospective longitudinal designs (Chandler & Lyon, 2001).

Examining more than a single level of analysis is implicit in the long-standing definition of emergence as "qualitative novelty," which refers to a shift in kind or type. This is exemplified in Mead's early characterization of emergence in terms of "...patterns or global-level structures [that] arise from interactive local-level processes" (Mead, 1932 in Mihata, 1997: 31). Based on this definition, the minimal exploration of emergence is the observation of a *pattern within* a single level of system interactions. For example, management researchers have used deterministic chaos theory to identify emerging order within organizational change processes (Dooley & Van de Ven, 1999) and organizational procedures (Kiel, 1994). Likewise, catastrophe theory has been used to identify change points and the dynamics of hysteresis in organizational transformations of all kinds (Bigelow, 1982; Guastello, 1995; Guastello, 1998). Similarly, computational studies using cellular automata and *NK* landscapes have detailed the processes whereby a new system-wide order emerges out of agent interactions, leading to intriguing findings around innovation systems (Fleming & Sorenson, 2001), economic geography (Sorenson & Audia, 2000), and strategic learning (Garud & Van de Ven, 2002; Siggelkow, *et al.*, 2006). Many other examples are provided in the summaries by Sorenson (2002) and Maguire and his colleagues (Maguire, *et al.*, 2006).

A different set of methods highlight the novel dynamics that can arise out the interactions of agents in a system, thus focusing on *two levels of system activity*. More than an emergent pattern or structure that can be discerned within a system, these disciplines describe how and when a new dynamic or level of order "arises" out of a system's lower-level components. For example, synergetics (Haken, 1977) offers a unique framework for examining "self-organized" patterns of activity that arise through the "enslavement" of system components to a higher-order resonance (Haken, 1984; Bushev, 1994). Separately, genetic algorithms are a tool for modeling the evolutionary learning of a system through unique combinations of system elements (traits) that generate a new dynamic within the system itself (Holland, 1998). In a different way, dissipative structures has been used to explain the emergence of new, coherent structures in a system (Leifer, 1989) which can transform its functionality and organizing capacity (Nonaka, 1994; Lichtenstein, 2000a).

Third, some complexity methods have been able to capture *multiple levels of activity,* which allow researchers to understand some of the underlying mechanisms of emergence in organizations. For example, power law analyses have shown how a systemic process or dynamic can generate multiple interdependent levels of order across organizations (Stanley, *et al.*, 1996) and throughout social systems (Carniero, 1970). Agent-based modeling explains how agent interactions develop these interdependent levels of emergent order (Malerba, *et al.*, 1999), and some multi-agent leaning models provide evidence that three or more levels of emergent hierarchy can self-organize given the right conditions (Carley, 1990, 1999; cf. McKelvey & Lichtenstein, this volume). Finally emergent evolution shows how self-organized evolutionary processes can explain the breadth of development in biological (Weber & Depew, 1990) and social systems (Adams, 1988; Chiles, *et al.*, 2004); and even more significantly, how the self-organization of a system is in some measure a reflection of the capacities of the leaders within that system (Wilber, 2001; Rooke & Torbert, 2005).

These two dimensions provide a matrix of complexity approaches, each of which can be classified as one of the "sciences" of complexity (Cohen, 1999). Next, I briefly suggest how each of these streams of complexity can be used to explore the dynamics of leadership from a complex systems perspective.

Complexity Models for Leadership

Advances in complexity science may help provide a much needed theoretical footing for leadership research. Many of the key processes in leadership - emergent processes, adaptation on multiple levels, dynamic feedback loops, mutually causal flows of knowledge across boundaries - are at the core of several complexity disciplines. More importantly, the essential outcome of Complex Systems Leadership Theory - enacting adaptive change through the interactions within and between all levels of organizational and environmental interaction - can be framed in terms of emergence, i.e., the coming-into-being of "macro patterns that depend on [continuously] shifting micro patterns" (Holland, 1998: 7). Emergence is a multi-dimensional feature and quality of systems; each discipline of complexity provides a unique view on the dynamics that reflect or generate emergent processes.

Discovering Order
Deterministic Chaos Theory

The new models of Complex Systems Leadership Theory focus on how leadership is enacted thorough interactions across an organizational system (Marion & Uhl-Bien, 2001). In most cases these interactions reflect and generate patterns of activity – a configuration of behaviors or models that are coherent over time (Dooley & Van de Ven, 1999). Although these patterns may appear stochastic on the surface, in fact they may be highly structured if mathematically complicated emergent processes which can only be discerned using tools like deterministic chaos theory (Baker & Gollub, 1996; Sulis & Combs, 1996). In a formal sense, mathematical tools like Lyapunov exponents, embedding dimensions and attractor reconstructions allow skilled researchers to rigorously identify these patterns amidst time series with at least 50 distinct data points (Guastello, 1995). Leadership scholars could use this framework to distinguish and detect even subtle patterns of interaction within a range of organizational interactions (e.g., Buckle-Henning & Dugan, this volume); or to identify specific bifurcation points in a significant system-wide shift of activity regimes (Cheng & Van de Ven, 1996). In an informal sense, leadership and organizational researchers have developed a metaphorical understanding of "complex attractor" as a configuration of activity over time (Marion, 1999). Identifying such configurations and tracking how they change may provide insight into how system-wide interactions influence changes in organizational behavior, while also reflecting path dependency and historical embeddedness leadership properties in the firm.

Catastrophe Theory

A different set of mathematical tools is helpful in explaining the transitions between one regime of stability (order) and a second or third regime, particularly when the shift from the one to the other is non-incremental. Thom (1975) and Zeeman (1977) developed a series of equations now known as *catastrophe theory* (Guastello, 1995), which describe system-wide, "catastrophic changes" in organizational behavior (Bigelow, 1982) and strategic design (Gresov, Haveman, & Oliva, 1993). Guastello (1998) used a four-dimensional model from catastrophe theory to describe three types of leaders that emerged in a series of four-person task groups; his "swallowtail" equation resulted in an R^2 of .9993 (with all variables significant at the .05 level). These results were replicated in a cross-cultural test using the same experimental conditions and a similar sample (Zaror & Guastello, 2000), suggesting that the emergence of leadership qualities may be a quality of the internal dynamics of the system itself, rather than due solely to environmental or contextual cues. Catastrophe is thus an excellent approach for identifying the rapid or discontinuous emergence of leadership qualities in a range of situations.

System Dynamics

A critical part of explaining interactions between and across levels is the feedback loops that are involved. "The goal of leadership inquiry is understanding how the structure of direct interactions and feedback within organization-environment systems give rise to their dynamic behavior" (Baum & Singh, 1994: 380). These bi-directional influencing processes are a central property of leadership research, and *system dynamics* provides a powerful means for modeling the non-linearities of these positive feedback systems. System dynamics forces researchers to carefully identify each feedback process within an entire system (Sastry, 1997); the rule-based computational model can reveal hidden interdependencies and emergent characteristics that are not tractable using linear thinking (Hall, 1976). The value of system dynamics for leadership is illustrated in Rudolph and Repenning's (2002) analysis of system-wide forces – in this case an accumulation of non-normal events – that can overwhelm the processing capacity of even the most effective groups and their leaders.

Self-Organized Criticality

A different approach for modeling a dynamic system that evolves to a adaptive but stable state was developed by Bak and Chen (1991; Bak, 1996). The paradigm for their model is the well-known "sandpile" consisting of a stream of sand (representing any ongoing input to the system) dropping onto a plate with fixed diameter (representing a specific capacity that the system can reach). Once the sandpile has reached a specific size it will remain dynamically in a predictable range, exhibiting mostly small changes (avalanches) interspersed with a few large-scale transformative shifts (Bak, 1996). For example, Gunz, Lichtenstein & Long (2002) studied vacancy chains in three organizations and found that, as predicted by the model of *self-organized criticality [SOC]*, the size and frequency of vacancy chains followed the signature form of a power law (Bak & Chen, 1991). In this self-organized state large scale transformative changes are rare but normal (Gunz, *et al.*, 2002); thus leadership scholars could utilize *SOC* as a diagnostic tool for identifying how close an interaction system is to reaching that dynamic, self-organized state, and how the system might be "tuned" through shifts in the system conditions (i.e., in the 'diameter' of the sandpile).

Fractals

Just as SOC identifies patterns of behavior within a system, *fractal* mathematics allows for a careful mapping of subtle similarities across multiple system levels (Mandelbrot, 1983). These tools offer a framework for studying "self-similarity across scales" – patterns and dynamics that repeat themselves in specific ways as one extends outward from simple to increasingly encompassing systems. This approach has been used, for example, for exploring how change occurs in similar ways at the individual-, group-, departmental- and whole-organizational-level of analysis (Zimmerman & Hurst, 1993); and more recently for determining the efficacy of a company's information technology by exploring the "continued coherence" between organizational activities and IT capabilities across levels (Dhillon & Fabian, 2005). Such an approach is ideal for identifying which arenas in an organization display the characteristics of complex leadership versus areas that are less vibrant in those qualities, providing a unique tool for diagnosis and follow-up of new leadership programs.

Power Laws

A more formal approach for examining cross-level patterns of interaction is based on a simple but powerful premise: certain generative mechanisms of self-organization are scale-free, i.e., they operate across multiple orders of magnitude or system levels (McKelvey & Andriani, 2005). These scale-free dynamics can be readily discerned (and predicted) by charting their outcomes according to a simple formula which is described by an inverse power law (McKelvey, 2006). For example, Stanley and his colleagues (Stanley, *et al.*, 1996) find that a single scaling law accounts for the relationship between growth rates and internal structure of U.S. manufacturing companies between 1975 and 1991, across more than seven orders of magnitude (i.e., from companies with 10 employees to those with more than 100,000!). Similarly, Carneiro (1987)found a distinct generative mechanism that accounts for the growth dynamics of native villages regardless of size or region. Power laws thus reflect generative dynamics at multiple levels, a key quality of CSLT (Lichtenstein, *et al.*, 2007).

Modeling Emergent Order

Over the past two decades several sophisticated computational methods have developed that allow researchers to develop dynamic models of emergence processes and test them in highly controlled and repeatable ways. These models include a small number of specific research streams: cellular automata (Krugman, 1996), NK landscape models (Kauffman, 1993), Genetic Algorithms (Holland, 1995), and combinations of several approaches found in agent-based modeling (Carley, 1999; Malerba, *et al.*, 1999). Research studies within each stream encompass a range of capability, e.g., some genetic algorithm studies show the emergence of one new level of order from agent interactions, while others suggest the emergence of two or more levels of order. On average, however – and for the sake of simplicity – these streams may be provisionally categorized within in a specific cell[2].

Cellular Automata

Early computational approaches explored what happens when a set of agents situated in a linear or a 2-dimensional matrix evolves based on the decisions of its (nearest) neighbors (e.g., Schelling, 1978). It turns out that even small initial differences in preferences or traits tend to aggregate, leading to a consistent degree of order across the system. Although technically this order is expressed as a visible pattern within the system, some advanced applications have interpreted this emergent pattern to represent a new level. For example, economist Krugman (1996) uses a simple CA application of spatial modeling, to ask why "edge cities" form, and whether their distribution can be explained through a power law. He finds that randomly dispersed business activities will always evolve into highly ordered edge cities that are ontologically distinct from their component businesses. Axelrod and Bennett (1993), using a "spin-glass" type CA landscape model to study group formation; applying the model to 1939 data, they accurately predict the political alliance formation of all but one nation during WWII.

This approach could augment leadership research by examining the relationship between individual agent moves (e.g., initiating a project) and the responses of that agent's immediate neighbors. Such studies might find how local reactions to emergent change processes can either catalyze or inhibit a good idea from diffusing successfully, and thus how the quality of emergent leadership crucially depends on spatial effects as much as internal networks, power dynamics, and so on.

NK Landscapes

By specifying two additional parameters to the basic cellular automata computational system, Kauffman (1993) developed a dynamic modeling tool that shows how internal structures can emerge in a system through the adaptive changes of

---

2 You may disagree, and I welcome your expertise and interaction on these specifics (please e-mail me at benymain.bml@gmail.com.) The more learning we can do together the more likely we all will gain success in our efforts to build a science of complexity for leadership and management.

its component agents. In this approach each cell is an agent with N traits or attributes that can change over time. At every time step each agent draws from its nearby neighbors a combination of attributes which appear to be most adaptive in the local neighborhood. Overall, agents' attributes are interdependent (K), such that the higher the K the more a change in one attribute will effect changes in other attributes. After a short number of iterations an internal structure emerges in the landscape, reflecting those combinations of attributes that are most and least adaptive relative to all others. As 'everyone' knows, the degree of order in the overall landscape crucially depends on the level of K, the degree of interdependence across the system (Kauffman, 1993). The general insight is that some measure of connectedness brings the entire system to a higher level of fitness and adaptability, but too much interconnection can lock the system into a "catastrophe" of interdependence (Sorenson, 1997; McKelvey, 1999c).

One exemplary use of the NK model for studying Type 1 emergence is Fleming and Sorenson's (2001) study of technological invention. Treating invention as a re-combination of existing components in a given field, they show that the usefulness of an invention (measured as the 6-year citation count) "... can be maximized by working with a large number of components that interact to an intermediate degree" (Fleming & Sorenson, 2001: 1025). Other management scholars have utilized the NK model to study the adaptiveness of strategies in a dynamic industry (McKelvey, 1999; Sorenson, 1997), the corporate performance contribution of cognitive vs. experiential learning (Gavetti & Levinthal, 2000; Gavetti, et al., 2005) and the ways that organizational design and decision-making effect organizational outcomes (Rivkin & Siggelkow, 2003; Siggelkow & Rivkin, 2005).

There is not actually very much emergence, per se, in the NK model (Lichtenstein & McKelvey, 2005). For the most part, self-organization is limited to agent connections (networks) with nearest neighbors. In this respect most NK models detail how patterns emerge within a specific system; Level 1 Emergence, with the capability of advancing into Level 2 Emergence. According to recent reviews (Eisenhardt & Bhatia, 2002; Maguire, et al., 2006), the vast majority of complexity studies utilize NK models and other computational experiments to show how emergent networks materialize within and across complex adaptive systems. At the same time, complexity leadership scholars can gain insight into the optimal combination of qualities (number and degree of interdependence) that could generate an ecology of innovation in a firm (Surie & Hazy, 2007), or to explore which and how many specific leadership "moves" (micro-processes or interventions) lead to successful organizational changes.

Genetic Algorithms

An important advance in modeling emergence occurs through the use of genetic algorithms, invented by Holland (1975, 1995). In the computational models identified up to here, agents have the capacity to change their attributes over time – they can learn (Carley & Hill, 2000), innovate new products (Fleming & Sorenson, 2001), and develop new strategies (Gavetti, et al., 2005;) – yet they necessarily interact according to rules that are programmed into the system. In contrast, genetic algorithms (GAs) allow agents with multiple rules to change the rule strings governing their behavior (Macy & Skvoretz, 1998). As agents in horizontal networks coevolve toward improved adaptive capability, differentiated groups emerge; soon thereafter group norms also solidify. Holland (1998: 190-191) describes how aggregates of new rules can represent "macro-laws" at a higher "level" of order:

"Just what is a new level in a CGP? The answer turns on one of the basic properties of a CGP: the possibility of combining mechanisms to make a more complex mechanism... [T]he resulting composite [is a] subassembly that can be used to form still more complex mechanisms... We have moved up one level of description."

GAs have been applied in a range of models. For example, Paul, *et al.* (1996) examine the adaptation of emergent financial trading firms (groups) and find combinations of increasingly better performing agents across prior periods. Crowston's (1996) GA model shows that organizations and/or their employee agents can minimize coordination costs by organizing in particular ways. GA models can show how emergent behaviors of agents adapts and changes in a coevolving context (Holland, 1998). Here, agent moves (i.e., changes) are leadership moves, thus allowing leadership scholars to explore how, in complex systems, "...agents adapt by changing their rules as experience accumulates" (Holland, 1995: 10). In addition, "each change of strategy by a worker alters the context in which the next change will be tried and evaluated. When multiple populations of agents are adapting to each other, the result is a leadership process" (Axelrod & Cohen, 2000: 8). Equally important, GA models can help define interaction process that hold across levels, which may allow researchers to identify similar patterns acting in macroevolution and in microevolution (Axelrod & Cohen, 2000).

Agent-Based Learning Models and Multi-Agent Learning Models
Carley and her colleagues have produced some of the more sophisticated models to date in computational modeling, which combine elements of CA, GA, and neural networks. In her CONSTRUCT (1991) and CONSTRUCT-O models (Carley & Hill, 2001), simulated agents have a position or role in a social network and a mental model consisting of knowledge about other agents. Agents communicate and learn from others with similar types of knowledge. CONSTRUCT-O allows for the rapid formation of subgroups and the emergence of culture, which, when it crystallizes, supervenes to alter agent coevolution and search for improved performance. These models show the emergence of communication networks (one level) and the formation of stable hierarchical groups (2 levels); they also show how higher levels of order "supervene" to influence lower-level behavior. Supervenience, the mechanism by which higher-level components intervene to alter the behavior of their lower-level components, has been called a crucial characteristic of emergence (Klee, 1984; Blitz, 1992).

Quite possibly the most famous example of "bottom-up" agent-based modeling is Epstein and Axtell's *Growing Artificial Societies* (1996). They boil their agent behavior down to a single rule: "Look around as far as your vision permits, find the spot with the most sugar, go there and eat the sugar" (p. 6). Agents search on a CA landscape and come to hold genetic-identity-culture identification tags according to a GA. This model not only builds social networks (one level), but also higher-level groups emerge (2 levels). These groups develop cultural properties that can supervene to alter the behavior and groupings of agents (three levels). Another sophisticated agent model is Carley's (1990, 1999) complex ORGAHEAD *Model*. This simulation consists of small groups of interacting workers (agents) led by an executive team that develops firm-level strategy based on environmental inputs. Groups that emerge in this model control who agents will interact with, learn from, and so on, thereby altering subsequent co-evolutionary emergence. Also, the emergent culture alters the knowledge-creation strategies of agents. In these ways Carley's model reflects three levels of order. Each of these, and many others, provide intriguing examples of how agent moves (leadership) at one level affect the structure and context for further moves (learning and leadership) at higher levels.

Intrinsic Emergence

In contrast to the computational and mathematical approaches described thus far, the disciplines which explore intrinsic emergence are from philosophical biology (Autopoiesis), thermodynamic chemistry (dissipative structures) and evolutionary theory (emergent evolution). Insofar as these disciplines are rigorously applied to organizations and management they exhibit the features of intrinsic emergence, i.e., their physical expression (realization) of emergence is not a model of something else, but itself generates a new level (or pattern) of tangible system order in real time.

Autogenesis/Autopoiesis

Deep structures and resource flows are at the heart of *autogenesis* and *Autopoiesis*. Both of these theories focus on how an autonomous system – an agent – produces its internal structures through a regenerative organizing process. The original theory, Autopoiesis (Maturana & Valera, 1980), explained how and why we experience ourselves as autonomous beings even though we are inextricably linked to an external environment. Their argument, which results in a unique material definition of life, is based on the concept of "structural coupling," the internal mechanism that couples (links) behavioral actions to information that (appears to) derive from the environment. This approach was drawn out in the social sciences through autogenesis (Csanyi & Kampis, 1985; Panzar & Csanyi, 1991), which explores identity-making processes in which an agent's core values and schemas define the rules that formulate emergent structures (Drazin & Sandelands, 1992) and social structures (Kickert, 1993). This autogenesis/autopoiesis approach is valuable for its conceptualization of the mutual causality – structural coupling – of resource flows and environmental potentials (Swenson, 1992; Swenson, 1997); understanding these flows provides the capability for accessing further regimes of resources, for example in the form of knowledge, opportunity, and competitive advantage.

Autopoiesis provides a useful model for understanding how one's leadership is a reflection of one's own internal perceptions and sense-making. In particular, the theory helps explain why our interpretations of the world and those powerfully felt impulses to make change based on those interpretations, are driven by internal patterns and psychological structures as much as by external events (Manz & Neck, 2004). In common parlance, Autopoiesis provides the theoretical underpinning for the well-known dictum: "believing is seeing" (Weick, 1979). This effect is crucial in the context of pattern recognition (Buckle-Henning & Dugin, this volume) and a systems view of leadership, for it helps identify how patterns that a leader perceives are in some ways also reflected in the perceiver. Disentangling this bias can highlight subtle elements of the pattern, with positive effects for getting at the heart of system's dynamics.

Dissipative Structures

Perhaps the best known and most utilized non-computational complexity model is drawn from Prigogine's Nobel-Prize winning work on how order is spontaneously created in far-from-equilibrium systems (Prigogine 1955; Prigogine & Glansdorf, 1971). According to their theory of *dissipative structures* (Prigogine & Stengers, 1984), when increasing resource flows cause a focal system to shift from near-equilibrium to far-from-equilibrium dynamics, a new level of macro-structures can spontaneously form in the focal system (Bénard, 1901; Prigogine, 1955; Nicolis & Prigogine, 1989). In a formal sense, these "macro-structures" increase the capacity of the system to dissipate resources (heat); according to one set of experiments, the new level of order expands the system's processing capacity by several orders of magnitude (Swenson, 1989, 1991).

Swenson himself was an entrepreneur who created a successful small business that was one of the first to commercially produce and sell a new kind of cereal in the 1960s: Granola. Swenson's understanding of how dissipative structures can generate and explain organizational growth is comparable to many researchers who have applied the dissipative structures model to entrepreneurship (Binks & Vale, 1990; Foster, 2000), innovation (Dosi & Fagiolo, 1998; Saviotti & Mani, 1998), group dynamics (Smith, 1986; Smith & Comer, 1994), and economics in general (Georgescu-Roegen, 1971; De Vany, 1996). In management this approach has been used to explain the emergence of order in high-growth entrepreneurial ventures (Lichtenstein, 2000a); the emergence of a new dominant logic for strategy (Bettis & Prahalad, 1995), transformative change in strategy (Garud, *et al.*, 2002; MacIntosh & MacLean, 1999) and organization (Goldstein, 1994; Leifer, 1989), the emergence of industry-level collaborative ventures (Browning, *et al.*, 1995), the emergence of sustainable economic regions (Chiles, *et al.*, 2004), and so on.

A dissipative structures model is well suited for studying emergent order in leadership. On one level, the conditions that spark order creation in dissipative structures (Smith & Gemmill, 1991) are strongly connected to the conditions that spark adaptive and emergent leadership from a complexity perspective (Marion, *et al.*, 2001; Surie & Hazy, this volume, Plowman & Duchon, this volume). Furthermore, studies have shown that periods of internal order creation that often accompany innovation and rapid growth may be facilitated by a broader view of interaction-based leadership that is supported by a Complex Systems Leadership Theory (e.g., Garud & Karnøe, 2003; Lichtenstein & Jones, 2004). Even more broadly, the kind of systemic approach to leading that is the foundation of a complexity-inspired leadership is also at the core of dissipative structures (Artigiani, 1987; Goldstein, 1986). Using this approach to explore how to lead systemically as well as how to let the system lead would contribute to the dissipative structures model as much as to complexity leadership.

Emergent Evolution

Emergent Evolution is perhaps the least known stream in complexity science, but it offers perhaps the most profound implications for leadership, change, and social integration of all the complexity models. At its core, the theory of emergent evolution theory argues that biological and social evolution are best represented as an ongoing emergence of increasingly complex layers of macro-systems, each layer providing important gains in the system's capacity to operate effectively in it's environment. *Emergent evolution* provides the only complete account of evolutionary dynamics that compares with traditional neo-Darwinism (see Depew & Weber, 1985; Depew & Weber, 1995), and it is the only one that can successfully integrate physical, biological, social and cultural evolution through a single mechanism. This account was first written by Jantsch (1980); deeper explanations and contributions to this stream have continued to the present in Wicken, (1986), Lazslo (1987), Adams (1988), Weber, *et al.*'s important compilation in (1990), Swenson (1992), Coren, (1998), Chaisson, (2001), and others.

In the context of leadership, this approach makes the strong claim that organizational development is a reflection of one's internal development – internal and the external processes of change are inextricably linked (Wilber, 1995, 2001). Management authors have also made this claim, albeit from a slightly different theoretical framework (e.g., Bartunek, *et al.*, 1983; Senge, 1990; Torbert, 1991; 2004). In my view, leadership is represented by the emergence of new levels of order, whose development increases the potential for others to grow and change as well (Fisher, *et al.*, 2003). As such, leadership involves the influence of internal factors as much as external ones, and progresses in an overall direction of increased information, communication, trust, interdependence, and managerial development (Torbert, 1991; Wilber, 1995; 1998; Lichtenstein, 2000c). This optimistic yet challenging framework is also expressed in a few of the managerial applications of leadership and complexity (e.g., McMaster, 1995; Jaworski, 1998; Petzinger, 1999).

Conclusion

Developing a Complex Systems Theory of Leadership is conceptually challenging; at least we now have a set of analytic tools that can significantly improve ability to understand and explain how leadership emerges in interactions. The purpose of this essay has been to make more clear the distinct benefits of using these tools, and equally important, to highlight the vast array of disciplines that are at our disposal in the process. Unfortunately management scholars seem to hold a relatively limited view as to this range of options, as Davis, *et al.* (2007) inadvertently made clear. The more options, the more likely a researcher will choose the model which best analyzes their research questions.

In fact, there is more at stake than which discipline to use. Leadership is a rich and nuanced phenomena, and a new era of leadership will require a combination of in-depth, richly qualitative studies along with precisely operationalized quantitative and simulation-based methods. As other complexity scholars have argued, the fullest interpretations and meanings from complexity may only be realized when mathematical modeling is a complement to case study analyses which use careful operationalizations and analogical reasoning (Lichtenstein, 2000d; McKelvey, 1999b; Sorenson, 1997). Only through this combination of qualitative and quantitative is a Complex Systems Theory of Leadership likely to reach its potential.

Unfortunately such a multi-disciplinary approach is not well developed yet; complexity research is framed by many as a purely mathematical or computational endeavor. This bias is cited by Morel and Ramanujam (1999: 289) who conclude their article by saying, "Application of complex systems theory to organization theory must rely on mathematically proven or computationally justified facts... Whenever dynamics is involved, there is no good alternative to mathematical modeling." However, this approach of theory-model development leaves out the complementary aspect of model-phenomenon testing (McKelvey, 2002). As McKelvey has shown, both of these activities are interdependent and necessary in order to generate an overall theory that is epistemically realistic while retaining high face validity (McKelvey, 1999a). This argument certainly holds in leadership research, which involves subtle internal processes and arenas that do not necessarily resolve into easily operational decisions.

For these reasons, I am advocating for a multi-disciplinary approach to complexity, one that would include both the mathematical modelers and the qualitative researchers and all those in between. Furthermore, using the arguments from path dependence, by institutionalizing an openness to multi-disciplinary work at this stage of paradigm development, we create an opportunity for unexpected approaches and collaborations to emerge over time. As a result I believe a matrix of complexity will increase the chances that our insights about complexity leadership will become more than another fad, offering a significant contribution to academic scholars and management practitioners throughout the world.

CHAPTER SIXTEEN
THE PARADOX OF COMPLEX ORGANIZATIONS: LEADERSHIP AS INTEGRATIVE INFLUENCE

Carmen Panzar, James K. Hazy, Bill McKelvey & David R. Schwandt

The paradox of organizations that operate in complex environments is that they need to combine centralized control for exploitation of resources with bottom–up autonomy for innovation and adaptation. We argue that negotiating this paradox requires a model of leadership that allows for both control and autonomy, often at the same time. Considering organizations as complex adaptive systems, we propose an Integrative Leadership model where traditional leadership (exercised by the formal leader) coexists and coevolves with emergent leadership (exercised by various organizational members) and shared leadership (exercised by groups). Integrative Leadership reflects dynamically fluctuating influence patterns over time as agents try to adapt to the requirements of the tasks and the complexity of the environment. Although we build our model at the work team level, it also has applicability to cross–functional as well as middle and top management teams. We suggest a set of propositions for future research to explore the dynamics of Integrative Leadership and its dependency on individual characteristics, task requirements, and the complexity of the environment. We conclude by reviewing the implications of the model to leadership theory and practice.

Carmen Panzar is currently the Director of Corporate Center Leadership Development for Citigroup and is a doctoral student with The George Washington University, Executive Leadership Program. Carmen worked in various leadership development positions with Fortune 50 companies, including Chase and Citigroup, and she was the Executive Director of the British Romanian Management Consulting and Training Foundation supporting organizational restructuring in Eastern Europe. As a practitioner Carmen became interested in the organizational development and leadership development fields and presented several related communications at ASTD and ISPI international conferences. Carmen's research interests include: leadership in teams, complex systems in social science, computational organization theory, and organizational capabilities. Carmen received a MSc OD with distinction from University of Hertfordshire, UK and is currently finalizing her doctoral dissertation with GWU.

James K. Hazy is an Associate Professor, Department of Management, Marketing, and Decision Sciences at the School of Business, Adelphi University, Garden City, NY. His research interests include organizational leadership, leadership effectiveness metrics, complex systems in social science, and computational organizational theory. He has published numerous journal articles, book chapters and proceedings' papers. With over 25 years of senior management experience at AT&T, Ernst & Young, LLP and other firms before entering academia, he received his doctorate with distinguished honors from the George Washington University and MBA in Finance with distinction for the Wharton School of the University of Pennsylvania.

Bill McKelvey, who received his Ph.D., from MIT in 1967, is Professor of Strategic Organizing and Complexity Science at the UCLA Anderson School. His book, Organizational Systematics (1982) remains a definitive treatment of organizational taxonomy and evolution. He chaired the building committee that produced the $110,000,000 Anderson Complex. He directed over 170 field study teams on strategic improvements to client firms. In 1997 he initiated the founding of UCLA's Center for Human Complex Systems & Computational Social Science. McKelvey has co-edited Variations in Organization Science (1999) and special issues of Emergence (now E:CO) and JIT. He has 55 papers on complexity science applied to organizations and management.

David R. Schwandt is Professor of Human and Organizational Studies at The George Washington University. His current research centers on organizational issues that relate to collective cognition, complex adaptive systems, and experiments with agent based modeling. His teaching responsibilities include instruction at both the Doctoral and Masters levels in the areas of organizational systems analysis, performance management systems, consultation, international human resource development, organizational learning, managerial and organization cognition, and chaos theory. He has also served on the faculty of The Johns Hopkins University's Applied Behavioral Science Program and the University of Maryland's University College Management Program.

"There are two kinds of truth. There are superficial truths, the opposite of which are obviously wrong. But there are also profound truths, whose opposites are equally right." – attributed to Niels Bohr

Introduction

The paradox of organizations operating in complex environments is that they need both top-down, centralized control for efficient exploitation of resources and markets coupled with bottom-up autonomy to innovate and effectively adapt to their changing competitive environment. They do this by acting as a unified entity but also by capitalizing on employee heterogeneity. Following March's (1991) discussion of the importance of exploration and exploitation, several authors have contributed to the ongoing dialog concerning the dilemma between control and autonomy in complex environments (Stacey, *et al.*, 2000; Stacey, 2003; Lichtenstein, *et al.*, 2006). They conclude that leadership is a process resulting from micro-dynamic interactions, or what Wiley (1988) described as the self (individual agent) and the interactions between agents that enable the organization to survive in its environment (Hazy, in press).

The purpose of this chapter is to address this paradoxical relationship and to propose a more complete model of leadership. We posit that leadership must be understood as a nonlinear mechanism within the system in which individual agents – both acting as individuals and as groups – engage in a search process across several potential patterns of communication and influence that are described later in the chapter. When conducting this search, the agents in the system adjust system "parameters", for example local rules of interactions or norms, resulting in different leadership dynamics, each with specific effects with respect to how cooperative activities are organized. These approaches are tested for fitness in the environment with respect to how well they appear to reduce *adaptive tension*[1] by matching the internal dynamics of the system with the changing needs of the environment. For simplicity, we shorten the above description of the leadership process to *"dynamical search"* in the pages that follow. We build our leadership model at the level of work teams as an exemplar of a more general dynamic. Our approach describes the process whereby autonomous agents – for example, individuals on a team or decision making entities such as business units – form together into a collective enterprise through the combined, nonlinear workings of agent autonomy, local rules of interaction and a broader signaling network. Together these constitute the mechanisms of leadership in organizations (Hazy, 2007).

The adaptive tensions (McKelvey, in press) created by discrepancies between the requirements in the environment and the actual resources of the organization may lead to an organizational response in the form of an emergent

---

1 Adaptive tension is a contextually imposed energy differential (McKelvey, in press), arising from the disequilibrium between two adjacent systems or "fields" due to different concentration of resources, such as information, knowledge, capital, market, and potential. The disequilibrium is one of the origins of order creation (Prigogine & Stengers, 1984).

overall strategic direction that cascades down the organization in the form of team goals or assigned tasks. To address the complexity of their task environment, agents and their interactions reconfigure themselves by continuously creating new and unpredictable forms of emerging order (Holland, 1998). At the core of this emergent order are the changing power and influence relationships between agents that reflect the continuous evolution of leadership mechanisms as dynamic processes of social structuring.

Tension-caused changes in power and influence relationships stimulate a dynamical search among three potentially appropriate leadership responses. First, the *formal leader or leaders*, if there are any, act as "linking pins" (Likert, 1961) among teams and levels of hierarchy. They provide new information from the internal system and the external team environment, and constrain agents' interactions. They provide long run coherence and focus on the efficient exploitation of existing competitive advantages. Second, dynamical search also originates from the complexity of the tasks being performed (Boisot & Child, 1999). The higher the complexity of the task (measured as skills, information, and interdependencies) the more team members will tend to temporarily concentrate around a particular individual as the leader for a specific task. This produces an *emergent leader* (Hollander, 1961) – a role taken by different agents as tasks change. Third, team norms, which exist "to the extent that individuals usually act in a certain way, and are often punished when seen not to be acting in this way" (Axelrod, 1997: 47), shape the interactions between agents through a process of collective influence, defined in the literature as *shared leadership* (Pearce & Sims, 2000).

Our integrative model of leadership assumes dynamically fluctuating influence patterns over time as the agents involved engage in dynamical search among the above leadership states – influences that are a function of inter–agent dynamics, organizational adaptation and competitive performance in a changing competitive context – requires a paradigm shift in the study of leadership, integrating the collective and the individual level of analysis in order to allow focusing on the cross level recursive patterns of interactions, while maintaining functional invariance across the level of analysis (Schwandt, in press). Our conceptualization of leadership moves away from the focus only on the formal leader and followers, and posits leadership as a process mechanism unfolding between multiple agents in a changing environment under pressure to survive and compete efficaciously.

Our understanding of micro-dynamics among agents builds from Gidden's (1979) classic work on his "*structuration theory*". But micro-dynamics to what end? We argue that to survive and prosper, organizations and firms have to conform to the demands of the so-called "*1st Principles*" of efficacious adaptation (McKelvey, 2004). Two of these have already been mentioned: adaptive tension and dynamical search. Our integrative theory describes how the dynamical search across formal, emergent, and shared leadership approaches combines to resolve and/or take advantage of the potentially conflicting or constructive interactions between the demands of the internal task environment and external competitive context and the structuration process of the embedded social system of agents at various levels of an organization. By doing so our theory offers three distinct contributions:

1. Defines complexity leadership as resulting from the dynamical search across three more specific foci of leadership influence: formal, emergent, and shared leadership;

2. Takes an approach that holds leadership accountable to adaptive demands – the 1st Principles – imposed by the external competitive environment;

3. Takes advantage of Giddens's (1979) structuration theory as an overarching framework within which to embed our discussion of micro-dynamic power and influence behaviors within organizational social systems.

We begin with a brief review of current thinking about complexity leadership. Next we present our model of integrative leadership theory. We follow this with four propositions that integrate the three types of leadership in the context of structuration theory and 1st Principles.

Leadership and Complexity Contributions

Stacey, Griffin, and Shaw (2000) point out that although most authors using complexity science in relationship to organizations emphasize the importance of interactions and relationships, many of the complexity leadership theories tend to revert to the focus on the individual leader and how she/he can influence interactions, for instance by acting at the deep structures level – values and basic assumptions (MacIntosh & MacLean, 1999). Stacey (2003) takes this argument further by discussing how most leadership theorists while acknowledging the paradoxes raised by complexity theory attempt to eliminate them by taking a systems view of human organizations, where the leader is considered an objective observer who can influence relationships by rational choice.

Many studies using the complexity worldview focus on either organizational or individual leadership by discussing leadership as an organizational meta-capability (Hazy, 2005; Winter, 2005), the top management team's impact on organizational adaptation through "restructuring strategies" (Carley & Svoboda, 1996), or strategies for the individual leader (Mackey, *et al.*, 2006); even the studies focusing on team leadership take the approach of understanding the leader's impact on team performance (Jiang & Burton, 2002; Guastello, Craven, *et al.*, 2005).

The focus on just top management or behaviors of leaders is not sufficient to explain the behavior of an organization. In a complexity worldview the researcher has to look at the whole system and its leadership (Osborn, *et al.*, 2002). We learn from complexity theory that higher level organizational behaviors are determined by local interactions (Cilliers, 1998; Anderson, 1999) and their dependencies on individual agents' preferences (Dooley, 1997). Therefore, research that focuses on the work-team level where distributed leadership occurs (Gronn, 2002) in the process of team members' interactions is a likely first step in uncovering the mechanisms of leadership as a process in complex systems.

While recognizing that "leaders do not create the system but rather are created by it, through a process of aggregation and emergence" (Marion & Uhl-Bien, 2003: 60), some theorists identify specific leadership roles (Surie & Hazy, 2006; Uhl-Bien, *et al.*, 2007) shaping agents' interactions, and although they state that these roles could be played by both formal leaders and individual agents, they tend to associate leadership roles with particular hierarchical levels in the organization, considering formal leaders to be central in influencing and enabling bottom up emergence.

Stacey, *et al.* (2000; Stacey, 2003) posits leadership as a "complex responsive process" calls for a focus on human interactions, constituted by communicative acts, and involving agent freedom of choice in a context of both enabling and constraining interactions. His view of leadership as a self-organizing process of agents' relationships realized through communicative acts moves away from the focus on the individual agent and his ability to control the evolution of the social system.

Stacey (1995) argues that organizations operating under internal and external complexity conditions are attracted by a state of bounded instability where rich patterns of interactions at the local level produce new forms of global order continuously emerging. It is the number and diversity of random interconnections that determine the variety of behaviors in the system. Based on these observations Stacey concludes that the focus of research needs to be shifted towards understanding the group dynamics determining the organizational direction and outcome. He cites Bion (1961) when calling researchers' attention to the "notion of leadership which is located not simply in one person but shifts from person to person according to task needs or the emotional states of groups of people operating in informal networks." (Stacey, 1995: 492).

Similarly, Lichtenstein, *et al.* (2006) propose to shift the study of leadership from an individual–foci to contextual interactions occurring within the social system, thereby focusing on micro-strategic leadership actions shaped by collective influence. These leadership theorists recognize the nature of the leadership construct as a recursive organizational process depending on agents' interactions (or the "space between").

The researchers studying complexity leadership have thus far contributed to the field by starting to ask questions about the appropriateness of traditional leadership. Some of these authors continue to support traditional leadership constructs in a "new" complex environment. Several authors researching complexity leadership start from recognizing that leadership is a result of interactions, although they regard leaders as objective observers capable of influencing agents' interactions towards desired patterns. Recent contributions propose a new approach to leadership considering it as a process emerging from contextual interactions (see Plowman, *et al.*, in this volume).

Thus far, complexity leadership theorists have not explored the specific dynamics of agent level interactions, the way these are impacted by the particulars of context – like, for example, agent heterogeneity, interaction history and the environment – and the resulting system level effects. They try to explain system level properties by the properties of individual parts of the system, particularly the "formal leader" and his intent, rather than focusing on interactions. In other words, researchers have not yet explained the mechanistic effects of leadership in teams (Hernes, 1998). It is our contention that the field can benefit from extending these works to a more "dynamic" emerging model of leadership that relies on not only the interactions of team members (agents), but also incorporates a larger dependence on context and information flow. Table 1 compares and contrasts the most influential theoretical contributions in complexity leadership, highlighting the key aspects in their conceptualization.

Integrative Leadership Model

In our model we highlight the dynamic nature of leadership in teams, characterizing leadership as a social structuring process emerging from within the power and influence relationships between individual team members and perhaps others. Its structure changes dynamically during the search. Sometimes it fluctuates predictably between formal, emergent, and shared leadership, sometimes it progresses unpredictably through many possible configurations, and sometimes it stabilizes on focused interaction around a single, formal leader.

Other authors have described an oscillating mechanism between different forms of leadership (Uhl-Bien, *et al.*, 2007), in particular, between what they have called managerial leadership, what others might call "management", and what they call adaptive leadership, what might be thought of as "leading change." The search we are describing is quite different, however, and occurs at a more finely grained level of analysis. We are focusing within the team and looking at the micro-dynamics of changing configuration patterns of agent-to-agent influence relationships among team members and between team members and agents in the environment. Sometimes, the configuration might be quite stable (Guastello, *et al.*, 2005). Under other conditions, however, the complexity of these influence relationships can lead to unpredictable outcomes as new order emerges. The dynamics we are describing are distinct from seeking to understand leadership as a balancing act performed by certain agents as they strive to simultaneously promote performance and adaptation. One additional difference is that, in our analysis we also recognize the importance of collective norms manifested through collective influence, the impact of the tasks being performed, and the changing environment. We thus advance a holistic approach to leadership as an emergent process in organizations.

In our integrative leadership model the focus is on work team level interactions. The selection of work teams for our discussion is appropriate as all the seven principles of efficacious adaptation (McKelvey, 2004) operating in complex systems can be observed. The principles of efficacious adaptation define the causal drivers for emergence, explaining why some structures have adaptive success while others don't. These drivers are: Adaptive Tension, Variation Rates, Requisite Variety, Near Decomposability, Causal Complexity, Mutual Causality, and Causal Rhythm. Each of these principles has been recognized as driving the creation of order in organisms and organizations by various theoretical and research contributions. McKelvey argues: "The ability of agents to create viable

Leadership Theory / Theorists	Complexity View of Leadership	Focus	Key Concepts
Dissipative Processes Management McIntosh & MacLean (1999)	*Leader centered.*	Macro/ organizational	**Leadership concentrated in formal leader** Leaders control organizational interactions through deep structures. In a state of non-equilibrium organizational transformation is achieved by alignment to deep structures, leaders create non-equilibrium to modify deep structures
Leadership as Metacapability Hazy (2005, 2007)	*Process focus*	Macro/ organizational	Leadership as resource & information processing mechanisms • Leadership distributes organizational resources towards exploitation or exploration • Defines convergent, generative, and unifying leadership mechanisms that perform different functions
Complexity Leadership Marion & Uhl-Bien (2001) Uhl-Bien, et al. (2007)	*Leaders as objective observers shape interactions*	Organizational and team level	Leadership as the interplay of three forms enabled by formal leader: • Leaders play various roles: managerial leadership, adaptive leadership, enabling leadership, • Formal leaders use tensions to induce adaptive change • The formal leader is balancing managerial and enabling leadership roles • Team members emerge as adaptive leaders if enabled by the formal leader.
Generative Leadership Surie & Hazy (2006)	*Leaders as objective observers are embedded in the system and intervene to enable bottom up emergence.*	Organizational and team level	Leadership influences the context of interactions: • Describes 5 aspects of this leadership mechanism: interaction experiencing, interaction aligning, interaction partitioning, interaction leveraging, interaction speed. • Leaders influence agents' interactions
Complex Responsive Processes Stacey, et al. (2000) Stacey (2003)	*Leadership as a relating process of agents' communicative acts*	No distinction between micro and macro	Leadership as acts of agents' communication: • Agents jointly act to transform their environments through acts of communications • Agents' communications are power-relating, both enabling and constraining actions • Interactions are reflective of agents' freedom, however repetitive forms of interactions curtail freedom
Adaptive Leadership Lichtenstein, et al. (2006)	*Contextual leadership embedded in interactions.*	Organizational and team level	Leadership as events (space between agents): • Event is defined as action for which meaning relates to interactions among agents • Collective identity, and endogenous tensions as drivers of adaptive actions

Table 1 *Complexity Leadership Contributions*

emergent structures capable of efficacious adaptation in changing environments, comprised by scarce resources and aggressive competitors, is pursued within the confluence of these [principles]" (McKelvey, 2004: 1). The model of integrative leadership considers the seven principles as they apply in work teams, creating the conditions for emerging structures, the evolution of cooperation (Nowak, 2006) and a dynamic process of leadership.

In Figure 1 we depict the following considerations setting the foundation of integrative leadership processes:

- Leadership is a process emerging from agents' relating power relationships (Stacey, 2003) continuously coevolving within the team. The collective and the individual level of analysis cannot be separated. They are integrated in our model;

- The formal leader is regarded as one of many agents engaged in interactions, moving away from the leader centered theories. Leadership emerges from micro-dynamics;

- Human systems are driven by both free choice and constraints (Stacey, 1995). The outcomes of agents' interactions depend upon the constraints imposed by the task system (Boisot & Child, 1999), agents' attributes, and prior histories;

- The team is regarded as a complex adaptive system (Holland, 1975; Anderson, 1999; Dooley, 1997; Meyer, et al., 2005), constituted of agents likewise regarded as complex adaptive systems.

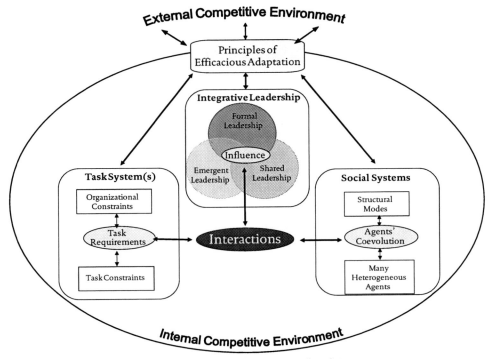

Figure 1 *Integrative Leadership*

The complexity of human systems can be described along cognitive and relationship complexity (Boisot & Child, 1999). Our model takes a holistic approach by considering both cognitive and relationship variables that describe the process of leadership: agents' heterogeneity (influence power/reputation, agents' attributes, agents' histories), task complexity (skills requirements, interdependencies), and environmental complexity (information complexity and rate of change).

Agents in a team are interconnected and interdependent as they complete the task requirements, and they coevolve with one another and with the systems of which they are a part. Agents' interaction configurations are changing continuously between formal, emergent and shared leadership depending upon the initial and changing conditions both on the team and in the environment. If the model is to incorporate the potentials of all three of these dynamical *attractors*[2] – formal leadership, emergent leadership and shared leadership – simultaneously, the model must address the centrality of interactions in social systems, the dynamics of power and influence relationships between agents, and the emergence of structure within the social system. Leadership emerges as a dynamic process of search from among these patterns of interactions over time.

Interactions Within and Between Task and Social Systems

The focus on interactions is not new. Mead's (1938) social act involves the cooperation of more than one individual, whose object defined by the act is a social object. Alfred Schutz (cited in Grathoff, 1978) also argued that social actions should be analyzed by making a distinction between the isolated actor occupied with handling a tool versus acting with others and for others, motivated by others and motivating them. An actor may be understood by "analyzing the modifications which occur through mutual correlation and inter-subjective adjustments" (Grathoff, 1978: 27). Luhmann (1984) explains that the components of social systems are not the actors, but rather *communicative acts,* representing the basis upon which social system's unity is established. In other words, an actor is defined by the communicative acts with other actors. These early theorists emphasized the importance of interactions in performing common tasks as well as the coevolution of actors through interactions.

Task Requirements: Task Environment and Agents' Interactions
According to Simon (1981) the complexity of human behavior depends on the task environment. Many organization theories, however, lack a detailed model of the task (Carley & Prietula, 1994). Boisot and Child (1999) propose the *I-Space* to link the complexity of tasks to the interactions of the agents in relation-

---

2 Nonlinear systems, where relationships between time–dependent variables are nonlinear (Thiétart & Forgues, 1995), tend to settle down over time converging to one of four patterns called attractors: stable equilibrium (point attractor) which is independent of time, a simple oscillating cycle (oscillating attractor) where the system periodically comes back to its previous state, a quasi–periodic attractor, or a chaotic cycle known as strange attractor (Barton, 1994).

ship to the task. They extend Perrow's (1970) two dimensional framework of task complexity (codification and abstraction) linking it to the level of diffusion or interactions required among agents to share information about the task. The higher the codification and abstraction of the task, the fewer interactions will be necessary for sharing information about it. Alternatively, with higher task complexity (skills and amount of information required for performing it) more interactions between agents will be required.

March (1991) argues that teams address complex tasks in changing environments by collaboratively using their knowledge. They combine the skills and knowledge of several individuals in a process of exploration to generate adequate responses to adaptive tensions.

Agents' Coevolution: Heterogeneity and Interactions

In terms of having the required skills and information, besides being able to perform tasks, agents can be described by other attributes linked to their intrinsic motivation and self-efficacy (Bandura, 1989) and their need to establish relationships with other agents. In order to reduce uncertainty in their task environment, agents may seek social support from their friends (Albrecht & Adelman, 1984) or from people they like. This increases the number of interactions between agents beyond those related to performing the tasks themselves. Individuals high on the Positive Affect personality trait tend to show pro–social behaviors in a group setting (George, 1991). Therefore these agents tend to increase their interactions with other agents. The concentration of interactions between agents also depends on some agents' influence over other agents or their perceived power or reputation (French & Raven, 1960).

Through coevolution agents lose their heterogeneity at some rate, slowly moving toward "groupthink" (Janis, 1972). The only way this can be avoided is for agents to have continuous contact with agents outside their immediate team or group, or for new members to join. Maintaining appropriate agent heterogeneity is a key task for complexity leaders (Mackey, *et al.*, 2006).

Dynamics Underlying Integrative Leadership

In this section we discuss influence processes giving rise to dynamical search amongst formal, emergent, and shared leadership. We begin with a discussion of circular organizing and then turn to emergent structure processes.

Social Power Fluctuation: Control and Autonomy

Traditional leadership thinking relies on vertical communications and well defined hierarchical structures. It proves necessary in organizations with large numbers of people to preserve unambiguous accountability (Jaques & Clement, 1991). However, it may also have negative implications on the quality of decisions, employee motivation, and ultimately productivity. Integrative leadership shifts the focus of social power execution to mechanisms of influence within autonomous work groups and self-managed teams (Manz & Sims, 1980) that are characterized by lateral communications, temporary forms of organizing, and heterarchical rather than hierarchical structures (Ouchi, 1981). These forms of control rely on spontaneous communication and informal cooperation, and the formation of commitment to group objectives (Stacey, 1995).

For smaller groups of people distributed control or self-determination appears to be essential in dealing with open-ended, dynamical situations in which new problems and issues are frequently uncovered. On the other hand, centralized control may be more effective in large groups of people under predictable and stable context (Stacey, 1995; Solow & Szmerekovsky, 2006). While most theories tend to see these two forms of control as inconsistent and incompatible alternatives, our model recognizes the value of understanding their complementarity and suggests practical ways to integrate them based on the idea of circularity of power (Ackoff, 1989, Nonaka, 1994, Romme, 1999). Circularity can be broadly defined as the ability of the team to switch between lateral and hierarchical processes (Romme, 1999).

Nonaka (1994) defines circularity as the capacity to produce and process information continuously in a circular process through "middle-up-down" management, in which all members of the organization work together horizontally and vertically. Teams play a central role in this kind of organization, with middle managers serving as team leaders at the intersection of vertical and horizontal flows of information. Ackoff's (1989) circular organizing is based on three rules: 1) the absence of an ultimate authority, 2) the participation (direct or through representation) of all members in decisions affecting them, and 3) full authority over decisions not affecting others. Romme's (1999) concept of circular organizing is based on the double linking pin (Likert, 1961) between hierarchical levels through the formal manager and a representative nominated by the team as equal participants in "decision circles", as observed in several European organizations.

Romme's circular organizing proposes two modes of power setting the foundation for more recent theorizing showing that adaptive organizations solve the control–autonomy dilemma by irregular fluctuations in structure between hierarchy and heterarchy (Thomas, *et al.*, 2005).

Emergence of Structure

The dynamics of search across control and autonomy can be further understood using Giddens's (1979) structuration theory which positions leadership as a process, acknowledging that the organization is as much a structural outcome of action as a vehicle for it, and that leadership does play a structuring role. What is called "field structuration theory" (Giddens, 1979; DiMaggio & Powell, 1983) refers to field-building processes wherein social actors construct patterns of interactions, information sharing, and shared governance (Meyer, *et al.*, 2005). They help the understanding of complexity leadership beyond Romme's (1999) circularity of power by factoring in the influence of individual agents and collective agents. In the framework of structuration theory, leadership emerges as recursive patterns of interactions between team members as they interact along the three dimensions of structure or modalities: (1) the creation of meaning (*signification*) through communication within the social structure, (2) the *domination* or exercise of power relationships allowing for distribution and recreation of resources, and (3) the *legitimation* of team structure by establishing and conforming to norms.

For Giddens (1979), leadership is manifested through the "domination" modality of structuration and is conceptualized as a phenomenon of intended action, exercised as interactions of power having a transformative capacity. In contrast, our integrative leadership model takes a much broader definition of leadership and suggests that *all three of Giddens's modalities of structure are realized through leadership.* The power of influence, we posit, shapes social interactions and is exercised by various agents, resulting in the coexistence of the different types of leadership referenced in the literature, in particular, *formal leadership* (Bass, 1985), *emergent leadership* (Hollander, 1961), and *shared leadership* (Pearce & Sims, 2000).

The formal leader, as a manifestation of institutional domination, has *legitimate power* to distribute information, tasks, and resources; however, in the process of a transformation of resources, tensions between task requirements and the skills of team members determine the flow of influence power (French & Raven, 1960) within the team. Leadership emerges through influential acts of organizing (Gronn, 2002), by structuring interactions and through relationships. Various team members emerge as leaders through their interactions during work practices when they accumulate greater influence over the team based of their *expert power* (skills and knowledge/information required by the task), or because of their *referent power* based on their reputation and their individual attributes. The structuration process is dynamic: as tasks and team membership change, the interactions change and different leaders emerge, thereby causing interactions to concentrate around different *emergent leaders* who are the attractors in the dynamical system of communication acts in certain situations at certain times. The process is dynamic as the team searches for a successful organizing approach in the environment.

The interactions of agents are both constrained by the collective norms and involved in creating the norms, a fact that reflects the legitimation of the structure. Giddens's structuration patterns of acceptable norms emerge in the recursive process of interactions through the legitimation of norms by multiple agents exercising collective influence or *shared leadership*. Norms are enforced through the manifestation of *coercive* or *reward power* (French & Raven, 1960) by the formal leader, emergent leaders or the collective. Individual interactions are motivated by the level of alignment between individual and team norms; individual free-choice plays a vital role in the evolution of the system (Stacey, 1995), thereby influencing the team accepted norms.

The media for agents' interactions are communicative acts, conferring meaning or signification to norms, tasks, and the distribution of resources, and allowing for the creation of a domain of consensuality (Maturana, 1988). Focusing social analysis on communicative acts is compatible with Giddens's structuration theory as has been described by conversation analysis researchers such as Taylor and Van Every (2000). For these researchers it is generalized language that enables coordinated action across time and space. Recent studies on the evolution of cooperation show that language is an important element needed to spread information about agents' reputation. It fosters the cooperation between agents by indirect reciprocity (Nowak, 2006), when cooperation is possible even in the case of asymmetrical interactions (agents may not meet again) based on the reputation built through other people's observations of behaviors and communications. Collective and individual influences are intertwined in the process of signification.

In light of Giddens's structuration theory leadership emerges as a dynamic process based on team members' interdependent influence, where the control versus autonomy dilemma is addressed by a continuous dynamical search across three forms of power: authority, individual influence, and collective dominance. In Table 2 we compare our Integrative Leadership theory with the more specialized formal, emergent, and shared leadership constructs as each relates to organization requirements for leadership, such as: influence, structuring, control, communication, and work environment (context).

Integrative Leadership Propositions

We have argued that complexity leadership is best regarded as a process reflecting the dynamical search across different influence power relationships (French & Raven, 1960) among agents engaged in interactions within organizations and subject to the changing impositions of their competitive context (Uhl-Bien, *et al.*, 2004). Leadership dynamics may also reflect unpredictable changes in agents' preferences. Our *"integrative leadership"* at any given time, then, unfolds as a function of a nonlinear, temporary dominance of one of the three narrower kinds of leadership we discussed earlier: formal, emergent, and shared.

The propositions we present below are based on the application of the 1st Principles of efficacious adaptation (McKelvey, 2004). These are the adaptive demands that shape leadership dynamics by influencing organizational micro-processes so as to continually and dynamically re–configure agent interactions to meet environmental demands for improved effectiveness. These demands result from differences between the needs of the environment and an organization's resources and capabilities.

Leadership as Dynamically Integrated Influence

When the discrepancy between the contextual requirements in the external competitive environment – or managerial perceptions of these requirements – and the actual resources of a team to perform the tasks reaches a certain threshold of adaptive tensions (Prigogine & Stengers, 1984), the team may destabilize and produce creative responses that have the potential to increase the order within the system as a whole (Arikan, 2007). Team interactions are determined by these adaptive tensions through the recursive process of structuration (Giddens, 1979) leading to a dynamical search across collective and individual leadership influence modes (formal or informal).

In their interactions, agents may be interconnected, but each agent has an agenda, and each agenda provides a causal push to organizational action which, given nonlinear dynamical search, can potentially lead to unpredictable

Control Type / Dimensions	Formal Leadership (Authoritarian Domination)	Emergent Leadership (Influential Domination)	Shared Leadership (Self-Determination)	Integrative Leadership (Inter-dependent Influence)
Theoretical Framework	Transformational and Transactional Leadership (Bass, 1985; Sashkin & Sashkin, 2003)	Emerging Leadership (Hollander, 1961; Lewin & Regine, 2003) Influence Power (French & Raven, 1960)	Self-managed teams (Manz & Sims, 1980)	Complexity Theory applied to organizations (Stacey, 1995) Principles of efficacious adaptation operating at team level (McKelvey, 2004)
Definition	The capacity of one participant to carry out his/her will, even under the resistance of other people	The recognition of one team member as the leader for a situation.	The capacity to act autonomously (as an individual or as a group)	Ability to switch between formal, emergent, and shared leadership based on the task and environment demands.
Authority/ Influence	Authority/Position based influence	Influence based on skills and knowledge of the individual and his/her acceptance by the team.	There is no ultimate authority, influence is shared among participants.	Influence irregularly oscillates between the formal leader, several emergent individuals (emergent leaders), and the collective
Organizational Structure	Hierarchy: vertical sequence of layers of accountability	Hierarchy: informal based on individual's accepted accountability, vertical hierarchy exists in parallel	Heterarchy: cooperation based on equivalence and mutual adjustment	Formal and informal hierarchy along with heterarchy coexist and coevolve
Control	Top-down control	Individual accountability	Collective self-regulation	Collective self-regulation (policy making), and individual accountability (for operations)
Communication	Vertical communication	Vertical and horizontal communication	Horizontal communication	Multi-directional communication, up, down, and lateral
Context	A large number of people in a predictable, rather stable context	A relative small number of people fluctuating between different attractors	A relative small number of people in an open-ended dynamic context.	Can deal with complex and unpredictable contexts.

Table 2 *Leadership as an Integrative Construct*

outcomes. According to the principle of *causal complexity* (Lindblom, 1959) these conditions can lead to the emergence of new causal dynamics – up, down, horizontal, nonlinear, etc. The internal tension between the agendas and attributes (e.g., motivations) of individual agents and the collective action necessary to resolve the adaptive tension determines the level of each agent's participation and role in the interaction dynamics. Our emphasis on dynamical search stems from the early works of Dumont (1966) and Dupuy (1992) and the "irregular oscillation" approach of Thomas, *et al.* (2005) for handling the causal dynamics of various influence dualities in complex systems such as organizations.

Proposition 1: *Leadership is a dynamical search process emerging over time from patterns of agents' interactions:*

- *The system of interacting agents searches among three dynamical basins of attraction[3] that characterizes the system's communication and influence state – formal leadership, emergent leadership, and shared leadership – as a function of agents' influence power relationships;*

- *These dynamics are determined by the changes in the environment, the requirements of the tasks to be performed, agents' attributes and prior history.*

Teams Self–Organizing to Meet Task Requirements

As team members focus on completing emergent or assigned tasks, a process of *structuration* (Giddens, 1979) can occur when task or reward interdependencies require communication acts and coordinated action. Agents respond by establishing mutually acceptable work practices, which are then replicated in the future without negotiation, or modified with negotiation as required by circumstances. These emergent structures are based on cooperation to address the complexity of the task as agents collectively solve the problems or address the opportunities that arise during exploration (March, 1991). By combining their skills and knowledge agents can negotiate a program of action that may serve to reduce adaptive tension. Mutual cooperation is realized through a mechanism of indirect reciprocity based on each agent's individual reputation for continuing to cooperate (Nowak, 2006). To synchronize action, the cooperation strategy is propagated throughout the team through a signaling network (Holland, 2001; Hazy, 2006) of correlated communication acts that are orchestrated from a common script like, for example, a mission statement, project plan or an agreed upon deadline.

While the formal leader allocates tasks and resources to team members, new leaders emerge in response to adaptive tensions as the group dynamically searches for an operating strategy. Leader agents use their relative influence over others to rally team members to participate in the task. They do this based on their *referent power* (or reputation) and their *expert power* (skills and knowledge), as described by French and Raven (1960). During the interactions that are necessary to perform the tasks, agents engage into individual and collective

---

3 The collection of trajectories that flow into a particular attractor is called basin of attraction (Kauffman, 1995)

learning (March, 1991). Accomplishing all of this faster than the competition is essential to efficacious adaptation. The applicable 1ˢᵗ Principle is Fisher's (1930) *rate of variation*. As the title of a recent book goes, *It is not the BIG that eat the SMALL... It's the FAST that eat the SLOW* (Jennings & Haughton, 2001). Individuals learning faster than others during the process of adaptation become focal points in the emerging basin of attraction as they each accumulate timely *expert power* and in the process are seen as emergent leaders. Therefore, the patterns of interactions within the team, overall, are dependent upon the rate of learning within each agent and within the collective.

As learning occurs, communicative acts dynamically converge toward a *strange attractor*[4] within which communication acts concentrate around the emerging leaders as foci. Tasks requiring high interdependencies between agents lead to the diffusion of leadership among team members. The greater the extent of organization–wide interdependence, the greater the density of overall leadership capabilities (Gronn, 2002).

Proposition 2: *In performing identified or assigned tasks, agent interactions dynamically search among potential emergent leaders – those individuals whose changing reputations and thus influence are perceived to represent the best potential fit to "lead" the group as it addresses the changing task requirements and environmental context:*

- *Agents emerge as leaders based on their history, skills and perceived knowledge relevant to the task, their reputations, and the agents' internal attributes (e.g., intrinsic motivation and self efficacy);*
- *The dynamics of emergent leadership are a function of task interdependencies, reward interdependence and the frequency of new tasks assigned to the team.*

Teams Dealing with Complexity

As the environment is changing, teams have to continuously adapt. Within teams, agents' interact in the process of *signification* (Giddens, 1979), focusing on understanding and reacting to the complex environment by creating and sharing mental models and communicating through symbols and meaning. However, in complex adaptive systems, agents only act on information that is available in their immediate environments (Anderson, 1999; Cilliers, 1998; Thiétart & Forgues, 1995). Although lower-level agents are in closer touch with changing technologies, market tastes and supplier capabilities, they must also rely on the integrative organizational information channeled through others including formal management. Agents in these positions can act as formal leaders obtaining, processing, and disambiguating information to and from the world outside the team or organizations – either in the environment or the larger organizations – in order to orient the team or organization within its environment and learn from its experience (Daft & Weick, 1984; Nonaka, 1994; Likert, 1961). The formal

---

4 The pattern of a strange attractor is contained within a strange shaped surface, however the trajectory is unpredictable being dependable on initial conditions (Thiétart & Forgues, 1995).

leader channels the information, playing a linking pin role with other layers in the organization, and in doing so represents a *basin of attraction* for agents' communicative acts.

The team also obtains information about the complex environment through agents' local interactions with the environment. Whereas Thompson (1967) argued that top managers absorb external complexity and uncertainty so that lower-level personnel can work in more machine-like environments, (Mélèse, 1991) offered an opposite viewpoint that it is better for lower-level personnel to absorb complexity so that top managers have more time for longer range thinking. The absorption of complexity is facilitated by modular work teams, where complex work-tasks and processes are "decomposed" into semi-autonomous hierarchical subsystems allowing teams to have a fluid structure with agents reconfiguring based on task requirements. This meets the demands of Simon's (1962) principle of *near decomposability* – overall adaptation fares better if components (modules) are nearly autonomous and can, thus, adapt locally and quickly to local perturbations. This process is described as "partitioning" in adaptive or generative leadership terms by Surie and Hazy (2006) as an organization's agents improvise to address the challenges and opportunities in the environment that are creating adaptive tension.

The local absorption of complexity is facilitated by agents' heterogeneity which provides for a wide set of skills and knowledge, in accordance with the principle of *requisite variety* (Ashby, 1956), which McKelvey and Boisot (forthcoming) update to *requisite complexity*. Human systems are different from those that otherwise occur in nature because of unique aspects like language and communication. Stacey (2003) emphasizes the importance of conversation and socially constructed meaning. As such, teams absorb information about the environment through a process of collective sensemaking (Weick, 1985), during which team members analyze the implications of the new information on team processes and norms. The collective, in its role of creating shared meaning, represents another basin of attraction for agents' communicative acts as the group settles into a mutually-reinforced, consensus-based interpretation of events and of intended action.

Proposition 3: *The changing environment requires a team to engage in a sensemaking process, a dynamical search across interaction patterns among agents that tend towards two basins of attraction: formal leadership, in its function as an interface with the larger organization and thus as a source of "official" interpretations of events, and shared leadership in its function as facilitator of collective meaning and consensus understanding and action derived from individual experiences:*

- *The search between basins of attraction is a function of initial (and changing) conditions: team diversity (skills and knowledge available in the team), the environment and the formal versus collective power differential;*

- *The dynamics of interaction patterns across basins of attraction and of convergence within them are determined by the complexity of the information and its rate of change.*

Agents' Coevolution

Teams exist in a dynamic environment where the network of interactions creates a context, or morphological field (Goodwin, 1994), within which agents coevolve amongst each other and with respect to the changing environmental context according to the principle of *mutual causality* (Maruyama, 1963). As early as 1950s, Homans (1958) noted the coevolution of team member attitudes and group norms. Norms are at the center of the "reciprocal influence" in Giddens's structuration theory, meaning that the reaction of each party in a process of interaction depends on the contingency responses of the other(s). Norms have to be sustained at every moment by the interactions and must undergo a process of *legitimation* (Giddens, 1979) by the team. New recruits align their language, beliefs and practices to the organizational/team norms through socialization (March, 1991). In this process, existing team members also get the norms reinforced, thereby allowing the realization of the maintenance goals of the team (Scott, 1998). The outcomes of the process of socialization depend on agents' internal attributes.

The enforcement of norms emerging from coevolving agent teams is realized through *coercive* and *reward power* exercised by the formal leader, emergent leaders and the collective. During the completion of tasks, conflicts may arise in the process of resource coordination. The resolution of conflicts involves both the application of team norms and the adjudication of events through centers of relative power and influence, represented by either formal or emergent leaders. As conflicts surface, agents' interactions fluctuate among formal, emergent, and shared leadership attractors. Interactions centering around singular centers of influence such as formal leaders, on the one hand, and interactions dampening noise that might disturb emergent and/or shared leadership on the other, may signify conflicts inherent in centralized versus decentralized decision making and control (Vroom, 2000).

We have featured the notion of dynamical search throughout our paper. Here, the variance in rate, size, and timing of fluctuations that result is determined by the intensity of conflicts, the relative influence of individuals engaged in conflict, and the maturity of the team, as measured according to its ability to decide and mediate its operating rules. As McKenzie and van Winkelen (2003) note, the build-up of one side of a duality such as control vs. autonomy, or formal vs. emergent vs. shared leadership automatically stimulates the building up of the opposing option.

Proposition 4: *The internal tensions arising from conflicts over resources or agents' power differentials are addressed through the application of team norms and the formal leadership influence. The poles establish a dynamical search across patterns of agents' interactions between opposing basins of attraction: those concentrated around singular (either formal or emergent) and shared leadership:*

- *Agent learning of team norms through socialization depends upon each agent's internal attributes and history.*

- *The dynamics of search are determined by the relative depth and definition of the basins of attraction characterizing formal and shared leadership within the team and are a function of team maturity and team history.*

Conclusions

The application of complexity science to organization studies addresses the limitations of traditional approaches (Maguire, *et al.*, 2006), focusing on interactions when the environment is changing quickly and organizations exist in Prigogine's "*far-from-equilibrium*" state (Prigogine & Stengers, 1984). Moreover, complexity science methods and models apply across levels of analysis. Our understanding of emerging organizational processes hinges on a better understanding of the nonlinear micro-dynamics of organizational processes that foster adaptation.

The theory we present here advances the field by proposing a process view of "*integrative leadership*" as dynamical search among patterns of communication and influence that explains the mechanism through which reciprocal cooperation emerges, evolves, and adapts in human social systems. Although we base our model on the operation of work teams, integrative leadership can operate at multiple organizational levels, as the same dynamics may be seen among agents at various levels within an organization – from the dyadic interactions of coworkers engaged in an assigned task to the development and implementation of a corporate-wide strategy or even inter-agency interactions within a government's domestic policy organizations. Our theory of integrative leadership is set in the context of Giddens's structuration theory (1979) of social system dynamics, organization task systems and McKelvey's (2004) 1st Principles of efficacious adaptation. Integrative leadership emerges from the dynamical search across influence structures of formal, emergent, and shared leadership in response to agent micro-dynamics and the external environmental competitive context.

Our leadership theory recognizes paradox as fundamental to organizational realities. Leadership is formed by individual and group influence on relationships and forms agents' relationships at the same time, while evolving in both predictable and unpredictable ways. Leadership paradox cannot be resolved by management, it is endlessly transformed in the realities of agents' interactions.

From a *theoretical perspective* our model provides a new approach to leadership, which is seen as a process emerging in social interactions and influenced by all social actors, formal leader and team members alike. Much of leadership research focuses on the dyadic influence between leader and follower. Collective processes and reciprocal influence have been largely neglected. The traditional approach to leadership does not appropriately address the complexity of current organizational and economic environments. A paradigm shift is required to explain leadership as a dynamic process where several forms of leadership (formal, emergent, shared) coexist and coevolve. Our model promotes the study of leadership as a team process conditioned by other team processes, e.g., team sensemaking, team learning, and linking team processes with team attributes, such as team diversity, team maturity, and team history.

From a *research perspective*, our model offers a rich agenda for future research. It calls for cross–level research methodologies, and a holistic integration of variables (agents' attributes, task attributes, and context, or environment). The seminal work of Carley and Prietula (1994) in their development of a computational organization science research, known as ACTS theory, set the basis for computer simulations. In this theory organizations are viewed as "collections of intelligent agents who are cognitively restricted, task oriented, and socially situated (Carley & Prietula, 1994: 56). Our model's alignment with ACTS theory makes the model appropriate for computer simulations to study the dynamics of leadership over time. The propositions implied by our theory can be tested in specific industries, organizations, or teams and potentially extended through simulation.

Our new explanation of leadership as a nonlinear dynamical process has vital implications in *practice*. Gerard Endenburg, the founder and promoter of "circular organizing" in *Endenburg Elektrotechniek* in the 70s-90s timeframe "was amazed by how little the social sciences had to say about designing and shaping organizational structures, whereas the technical sciences proved to be quite useful" (Romme, 1999: 810). Many organization theorists, when discussing implications for practice, tend to identify specific "*Monday morning*" prescriptions that will make the organizations more effective. From a complexity perspective, predefined linear prescriptions do not necessarily lead to effectiveness in a nonlinear world – the dynamical interactions of heterogeneous agents responding to unpredictably changing external complexity often produce unpredictable outcomes. Instead, practice can best benefit by freeing agents from formulaic thinking – effective leadership is more complex than simply top-down control or bottom-up emergent influence.

CHAPTER SEVENTEEN
LEADERSHIP AND A COMPUTATIONAL MODEL OF ORGANIZATIONS

Kevin J. Dooley

This chapter examines the question: if organizations can be thought of as computational systems, what would the implication to leadership be? In such a system, leadership is common and recipricol. The computational perspective highlights two rarely discussed leadership topics. First, the firm's computational capacity is literally determined by how people allocate their attention. Managerial leaders need to set the conditions for psychological flow in order to maximize the value of this attentional resource. Second, managerial leaders must create a sequence of attentional resources and facilitate coordination of timing between agents.

Kevin Dooley is a Professor of Supply Chain Management and a Dean's Council of 100 Distinguished Scholars at Arizona State University. He has published over 100 research articles and coauthored an award winning book, Organizational Change and Innovation Processes. He has coauthored two patents concerning Centering Resonance Analysis, a novel form of network text analysis, and is cofounder and CEO of Crawdad Technologies, LLC. He has a Ph.D. in Mechanical Engineering from the University of Illinois.

Introduction

Since 1945, scientists such as Norbert Weiner, Edward Fredkin, and Stuart Kauffman have explored the connection between information and nature (Kurzweil, 2005). Fractal models of growth in physical and social systems demonstrate that a system's final organization can be the result of simple, recursive computations. Modern biological research highlights the link between information encoded in DNA and RNA and biological growth and evolution. Stephen Wolfram summarizes this position in *A New Kind of Science* (2002): "all processes, whether produced by human effort or occur spontaneously in nature, can be viewed as computations" (p. 715).

A computational model of an organization posits that agents in the organization communicate and interact with one another according to simple rules, and that work is achieved in the organization through agents' activities, or "computations" (Choi, *et al.*, 2001). In a typical system where there is more work to be done than time to do it, an agent's choice of what to "compute" can be seen as equivalent as their decision as to how to allocate their attention. If we accept this model, what does this imply about the management and leading of business organizations? In other words, if an organization is a collection of computational sequences, what is the role of a leader? What special role do managerial leaders have in the computational organization?

A Computational Model of an Organization

The foundation for a computational model of an organization is the computation performed by any single individual. The human brain is estimated to have a computational capacity of approximately 10^{16} calculations per second, although a significant portion of this is reserved for automated functions (Kurzweil, 2005). If a person belongs to an organization, the organization may be considered to be renting that person's computational capacity. The organization may also use technology to substitute for human processing, but the outcome is the same – the organization's collective computational capacity defines how much work it can do.

In reality, a person's information processing capacity is engaged through a process of attention, thus renting a person's computational capacity is equivalent to renting their attention. Consider an "activity" to be a related set of computations that take place continuous in time. While people can work on several conscious tasks at once, they typically only engage in one work-related activity at a time, because of attentional constraints (Shapiro, 2001). Thus saying that an organization of a given size has a certain computational capacity is the same as saying it has a limited capability to perform activities to completion within a given time frame (Figure 1). Here the segments associated with each column represent an activity being done for a specified amount of time. Figure 1 is essentially equivalent to a Gantt chart, except applied at a very microscopic level.

Why does the organization need computational capacity? As a complex system, the organization uses computation to improve its fitness. In common language, the business organization produces outcomes in the form of tangible and intangible assets which help the organization sustain and provide return to

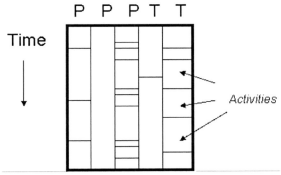

Figure 1 *Organization as Activities Over Time*

owners. In order to achieve any particular outcome, a certain amount of total computation is required, distributed to one or more activities. This required amount of computation can be completed in two ways: by having significant computational capacity (e.g., more people or technology units), or by allowing more time for the computations to be completed. Because attention and thus computational capacity has a finite upper limit, it means that the amount (and type) of computational resources available at any given time define what activities can be done, and thus what outcomes can be achieved.

We cannot assume however that a person will always "pay attention" in a manner which improves organizational fitness. Rather we must assume that individuals will behave in a manner which improves their own (personal) fitness. If the goals of individual agents are not well aligned with the goals of the organizational owners, the organization will not benefit as greatly from agent activity. To the extent that an activity simultaneously improves both the individual's and organization's fitness, organizational outcomes are more likely to be achieved, the organization is more likely to sustain, and agents are more likely to remain a part of the organization (Dooley, 1997). The more complete model is shown in Figure 2.

The model depicts the following process logic:

1. At any given time the organization is defined by its computational resources, comprised from people and technology;

2. At any given time, a person or technology attends to a set of computations, i.e., an activity;

3. Bundles of activities performed over time yield tangible and intangible outcomes that alter both individual agent and organizational fitness. Feedback loops that enable continuous learning can be considered a special type of activity.

The model can be conceptualized as complex system consisting of three different types of sequences: resource, activity, and organizational fitness. A sequence of resources create computationally capacity which is allocated to multiple, parallel sequences of activities. These activities in turn change the current state of the organization, and thus its fitness (Figure 3).

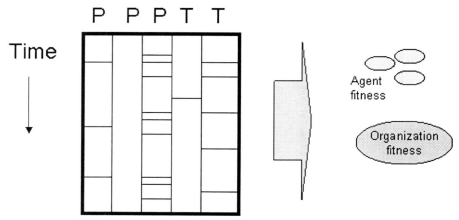

Figure 2 *The Computational Organization*

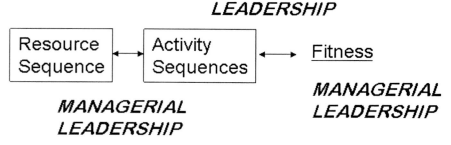

Figure 3 *Leadership in the Computational Organization*

Leadership in the Computational Organization

In a purposeful system such as a business organization, there is a desire to understand and influence these sequences so that fitness is improved over time. This requires us to know which activity sequences are likely to improve fitness, and which resource sequence will properly support the desired activity sequences. This process model can be used to suggest a definition of leadership and managerial leadership that is not dependent on either positional authority or personality attributes, but rather one rooted in activity, sensemaking, and influence:

- *Leaders* enact an action sequence that positively benefits organizational fitness, and influence others to enact action sequences that positively benefit organizational fitness.
- *Managerial leaders* are leaders who also (a) create a sequence of resources that support the desired activity sequences, (b) create conditions of "flow" for themselves and others, and (c) define a set of goals that make the concept of organizational fitness tangible and comprehensible.

First and foremost, leadership starts with one's own actions. A leader learns which outcomes are required or likely to improve organizational fitness and takes action to that end. At best, a non-leader is compliant to actions that improve organizational fitness; at worst a non-leader may engage in action that is counter to organizational fitness. Conversely, a leader consciously extracts personal fitness (satisfaction) from organizational fitness, and may even take action that is personally harmful but useful for others, or the organization. In managing their own activity sequence, a leader is heedful and pays attention to what they are doing; leaders learn to become more efficient in their own activities so as to be able to provide better computationally efficiency for meeting desired outcome sequences. A leader is able to take conflicting or constrained requirements and makes decisions and trade-offs that benefit organizational fitness as best possible. Simply, leaders need to be competent in their own work.

Second, leaders influence others to take action that benefits organizational fitness. This is not to imply that all forms of influence are the same; some make provide short-term benefit but long-term risk. For example, a manager or peer may use fear to influence someone else's near-term behavior, but because this is negative to the person's own fitness there will eventually be negative side effects (e.g., non-compliance, lack of innovation, decreased computational capacity) and thus lowered organizational fitness. Thus influence is not always leadership, but leadership always concerns influence.

Note that leadership in the computational organization is both common and reciprocal. Any person who acts in a way that benefits the organization and influences others to do so is a leader. Further, because influence is often bi-directional, it means that leadership is bi-directional – the teacher leads the student, and the student in turns leads the teacher. Finally, the model suggests that while opportunities for leadership may be enhanced by organizational position, leadership is in no way constrained or defined by organizational position.

However, there are decisions to be made in the computational organization that some leaders make and others do not, so I define managerial leaders as leaders who also (a) define a set of goals that if achieved will improve organizational fitness, (b) create conditions of "flow" for themselves and others, and (c) create a sequence of resources that support the desired activity sequences. First, managerial leaders look out for the whole of the organization so as to sustain the organization and provide return to its owners. Managerial leaders have long-term perspective, recognizing that short-term benefits are of not value if they decrease the organization's long-term survivability. The computational managerial leader is both visionary and transformational, helping create a sequence of goals that will improve organizational fitness over time. These goals map the intangible (fitness) to the tangible (objectives and deadlines).

Second, if leading concerns influencing others' activity sequences, then de facto it concerns influencing how others "pay attention". Managerial leaders help create environments whereby others can "pay attention" in organizationally productive ways; this comes from creating opportunities for "flow". Flow is a psychological state which people can attain where their attention is completely absorbed in the task at hand (Csikszentmihalyi, 1991). While in a state of flow, a person can achieve very high levels of both performance and personal satisfaction. The state of flow can be invoked through innumerable means, and it may or may not involve interpersonal interaction. In a work environment, flow may be induced because of the type of work being done, how the work is being done, or from interaction with the environment the work is being done in.

Third, managerial leaders secure and nurture a sequence of human and technological resources that support the required activity sequences of the organization (Lichtenstein & Brush, 2001). In doing so, a managerial leader in the computational organization understands the role and quantity of different resources that are required, acts so as to secure them in a timed manner, and works to help improve the computational efficiency of those resources.

Conclusion

In this chapter I have explored leadership from the perspective of a metaphor – the computational organization. As a model, it only attempts to mirror some portion of reality and is not complete (Dooley, 2004). Organizations exist to do work which creates benefit to members and owners of the organization; the computational metaphor emphasizes the capacity for that work and how that work may or may not impact organizational fitness.

A computational perspective is humanizing, not de-humanizing. Human resources are not secured to provide physical labor, but rather computational labor. While some of that computation may be aimed at controlling physical actions, an emphasis on computational highlights the contribution that every person can make with their thoughts and creativity. Additionally, the computational metaphor recognizes that leadership is common, local, and reciprocal, thus moving us away from a definition of leadership that depends on position, authority, or power. As such, leadership is an asset that is distributed richly throughout the organization. The computational model also precludes the concept of an "evil" leader – there is no such thing. Any worker or manager who acts influences others in a way that reduces the survivability of the organization is a not a leader.

Finally, the computational metaphor highlights the importance of two issues that are not commonly discussed – time and attention. It is common to view managerial leaders as those who secure resources, influence action, and create goals which enhance organizational fitness – what is missing from this view is the dimension of time. Because computation is a dynamic process, time becomes the critical dimension in understanding computational capacity. Leaders and managerial leaders recognize that the allocation of human or technological capacity is a matter of attention. While ineffective leaders compete with one another for a resource's attention, effective leaders work towards improving attention through creating conditions of flow, and delineate priorities so that people have a better sense of how to allocate their attentional resources.

CHAPTER EIGHTEEN
LEADERSHIP AS THE PROMISE OF SIMPLIFICATION

Nathan Harter

Leadership can be understood as the promise of simplification in response to complexity, with simplicity and complexity expressing the bounds of an inescapable tension. As subjective complexity increases, human systems experience pressure to simplify. Five strategies for simplification can be delineated, namely leadership as focal point, as reversion to compactness, as transformation to a new order, as disintegration of the system, and as pragmatic adaptation. Leaders would be advised to use some combination of each strategy to help systems cope with their strains.

Nathan Harter, J.D., left the practice of law in 1989 to join the Department of Organizational Leadership at Purdue University, where he was tenured in 1995 and promoted to Associate Professor. At his location, Harter teaches in an undergraduate degree program for non-traditional students. *Clearings in the Forest*, his first book, was published in 2006 by the Purdue University Press. He has authored or coauthored articles in *The Encyclopedia of Leadership, Integral Review, Leadership, Journal of Information Communication and Ethics in Society, Journal of Leadership Education, Journal of Management Systems, Philosophy of Management, Journal of Management Inquiry, APA Newsletter on Philosophy and Teaching, Philosophy for Business, Leadership Review, Proteus, Modern Age,* and *Journal of Individual Employment Rights*.

Moving Within the Tension Between Simplicity and Complexity

Not only do the terms "simple" and "complex" represent a polarity, with a continuum between them, there is also a crucial difference between *subjective* and *objective* complexity[1]. Thus, Dietrich Dörner (1996) claims that complexity is not an objective attribute of the system but rather a *subjective* assessment. With increased familiarity and understanding of any system, its complexity decreases, just as the complexity of driving an automobile decreases with practice. To an outsider, the system can seem more complex than it would to a participant within it (p. 39). For Dörner, complexity, like beauty, is in the eye of the beholder.

Luhmann (1995) disagrees. He asserts that complexity is indeed an attribute of systems that reach a certain stage or level, regardless of how people react to that system. Their experience of the system is irrelevant. For Luhmann, "complexity" means that not every element in the system can connect with every other element, which in turn permits multiple different configurations (pp. 24ff). In other words, once a system becomes complex, it must order itself in some fashion in order to persist. After a certain point, a system becomes too complex to continue without the simplifying contribution of order, just as we simplify a stack of papers by sorting them into piles. Once the piles proliferate and become confusing, we might categorize the piles and put them into separate desk drawers. The process can go on and on.

For purposes of this paper, both meanings are pertinent. Complexity can be both subjective *and* objective. We need to include both meanings. An integrated understanding of human systems, as characterized by Ken Wilber (2000), shows how the same basic phenomenon has both an interior and an exterior, a subjective and an objective correlate.

Simplicity and complexity are not two bare alternatives, an either/or. Rather, they are two directions, between which we constantly operate in a state of tension[2]. Plato referred to this state or condition of being in-between as the

---

1 Daniel Born once complained, "False dichotomies abound in leadership studies, as in many demagogic movements [becoming] facile tools for many undergraduates to oversimplify the political and social complications of their world" (1996: 64). Leadership studies do abound in dichotomies; this much is true. Kenneth Thompson argues that leadership is essentially dichotomous (1984). And to the extent one can say that leadership is a sociological form, in the terminology of the eminent sociologist Georg Simmel, then it is comprised of dichotomies. These are what give it shape (1971). G.E.R. Lloyd asserts as a matter of basic logic that one cannot classify without first describing basic contrasts (1992: 80). Dichotomies help to define limits or boundaries. They serve to orient a person. Whether a dichotomy is false or not remains a separate and legitimate inquiry. Nevertheless, this paper – like leadership studies generally – abounds in dichotomies: tensions, contrasts, polarities, opposites, contraries, and contradictions.
2 Lloyd explains that dualism or the antithesis into two groups (in this case, simple and complex) "is an element in any classification" (1992: 80). Once made, the pair of opposites stand in a certain relation to each other. Some opposites such as Odd and Even exclude intermediate terms. They are exhaustive. It is our contention that simple and complex do admit intermediates, in the middle ground (ibid.: 95).

Metaxy (Webb, 1981). Humans and their organizations experience a tug in each direction, so that the nearer we get to one pole the further we seem to get from the other. The two directions are in this sense incompatible. This bipolar model – the *metaxy* – is a static model, depicting the situation at any given moment in time.

Simplicity ◆————————◆ **Complexity**

I must add another model already implicit in an earlier reference to Luhmann, because it illustrates a process within the *metaxy*. In other words, we must complement the static model with a dynamic model that depicts a process from compactness through differentiation toward order, a model elaborated in the last century by the philosopher Eric Voegelin (Harter, 2006). Here is one way to explain it:

- The first phase, referred to as "compactness" by Voegelin, is a state or condition of fusion, complete undifferentiated mass, the confusion and pulp of immediate experience. Psychologist James Hillman characterizes it as twilight, seemingly without form and void of things or parts (1971/2005). Webb calls compactness an "experience having distinguishable features yet to be noticed as distinct."[3]

- Differentiation would be "consciousness in which the distinguishable features of a previously 'compact' field of experience are noticed as distinct" (Webb, 1981: 279). That is, the seemingly solid and amorphous breaks apart – not so much in physical reality, like vinegar and oil, but *to the mind* it breaks apart. The mind sees different aspects as different. Hillman draws attention to the experience of walking into a dimly lit room and flicking on the light, so that you can make out the shapes and colors. The furniture was there all along; the table and chair did not suddenly separate. It is just that you can say now, because you notice it, that "this" is not "that" – the table is here and the chair is over there. Subjective complexity arises as the process of differentiation reaches a critical point where the various parts or aspects have proliferated so far that in the aggregate they make no sense. They begin to blur, becoming confused and resembling their previously blended state, a hodge-podge. You can't keep them straight.

- At that point, in order to take advantage of the differentiation and not succumb by letting separate items slip back into twilight, you must organize that which has become differentiated. You need order, a way of configuring them in the mind, a schema, based on their relations with each other[4]. In

---

3 A surprising number of adults continue to experience the sensory world as a compact reality. For instance, many experience synesthesia, "the evocation of one kind of sense impression when another sense is stimulated, e.g., the sensation of color when a sound is heard" (Encarta® World English Dictionary [North American Edition] 2005 Microsoft Corporation).

4 Aquinas put it succinctly: *ordo est relatio* (Grimley-Kuntz, 1991: 158). To illustrate how this works, in perception you might find yourself organizing stimuli according to

other words, you progress from compactness, through differentiation, toward order[5]. In so doing, you initially increase complexity by adding elements, which in turn creates pressure to simplify as the opposite pole pulls you back.

Compactness ➡ Differentiation ➡ Order

One might be tempted to revert, to renounce the differentiations and pretend they do not exist, to return to compactness, like pulling the blanket over your head and hoping the rest of the world goes away. But we cannot do that indefinitely. We shall have lost our innocence. The bell cannot be unrung. What we can do is reach greater simplification by embracing the differentiation and discerning or creating a sense of order. Instead of going back, we can push ahead. Simplification also lies on the other side of complexity. This distinction is important.

What we find is that with regard to subjective complexity, simplicity is not the contrary attribute, as Ugly is to Beautiful. Rather, it is the absence of complexity, a privation, as Dark is to Light (Lloyd, 1992: 146, 161). Consider that physicians once contrasted the visible agitation of Parkinson's disease with the absence of such agitation, in a simple either/or, only to discover that the visible agitation (the shaking and trembling we commonly associate with the disease) could be missing for one of two reasons: the person might not be suffering from the condition or the person might be experiencing such intense agitation as to be clenched, locked into immobility. Both physical states contrast visibly with the familiar tremors of Parkinson's, but they lie at opposite ends of the spectrum.

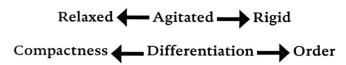

Relaxed ⬅ Agitated ➡ Rigid

Compactness ⬅ Differentiation ➡ Order

Leadership Promises Simplification

This paper contends that leadership can be conceived as the promise of simplification. With this, the central question emerges: Does leadership reduce complexity by restoring compactness or by achieving a new order? In which direction does it go? As we said, there are two stereotypical ways to simplify. One is to remove the elements that make a system complex, to return to the compact relationships, by shrinkage, getting smaller (in a sense), more intimate. Organizations do this sometimes by splintering, for example, whether voluntarily or involuntarily. In a cluttered home, it might occur to someone that

---

any combination of several principles, including proximity, similarity, common fate, and closure – determining the nature of the various relationships among discrete elements (Rock, 1995: Chap. 5).

5 Wilber made the same observation using different words, when he wrote that one of the great "Kosmic patterns" is that evolution has increasing differentiation and then integration (2000: 115, 314).

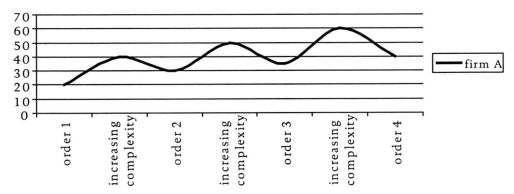

Figure 1 *Magnitudes of order*

the time has come to throw things away. The other way to simplify is to order the system in such a manner as to make it easier to conceive and easier to use. Neither direction is inherently right or wrong. One can conceive of instances where each would be appropriate. There is no reason to take sides.

It is my contention that leadership could go in *either* direction, which is why it is important to know which is going on. But first, this paper had to make the distinction clear.

Pressures Associated With Increasing Complexity

We are all inescapably held within the *metaxy*, between simplicity and complexity, experiencing the tug or pull in each direction. As we move toward complexity, the pressure to simplify increases, in the way that a rubber band pulls with greater elastic tension the further it is extended, or in the way that a pendulum builds gravitational potential energy as it swings toward its apex. Now, granted, human systems are not exactly the same as physical objects[6], but we can use the analogy.

The analogy does not work, however, when we notice that the rubber band pulls directly back and the pendulum's bob swings directly back (all other things being equal), for as noted earlier the pressure to simplify does not have to mean simple reversion to the state or condition we left before, back to compactness. Simplicity can lie on the *other side* of complexity, in a state or condition referred to as order. Compactness and order might resemble each other in their contrast to complexity, just as relaxation and rigidity resemble each other in their contrast to motion.

Magnitudes of Order

This is not to say that once a human system achieves some kind of order it has escaped the *metaxy* once and for all, as though order is the destination and promised land. For the order itself – whatever it turns out to be – will go through the same process of increasing complexity such that the whole process begins again, on its way to a new order – what one might call a comprehending order. We can

---

6 For one thing, the evolution of an organization is "directed... in which selection pressures are exerted by individual human beings" (Gell-Mann, 1994: 298).

speak in terms of *orders* that are more and less complex. We see this for example in the difference between (i) an interpersonal relationship between two people and (ii) any form of relationship among three. *Adding* a person *multiplies* the confusion (e.g., Simmel, 1950: Chap. 3, § 9[a]). There is in other words a kind of progression through *magnitudes* of order, illustrated in Figure 1, and with each stage moving through complexity, the orders themselves become more and more complex[7].

One of the reasons for describing these magnitudes of order is to show the same basic pattern at work, no matter at what level you conduct your analysis. There is still the tension between simplicity and complexity. For example, when a conglomerate divests itself of a subsidiary, it is moving toward simplification, even though the subsidiary is in its own right a global, multimillion-dollar corporation with layer upon layer of hierarchy. We operate forever, together and alone, in the *metaxy*.

Order < > Disorder

Just as the terms "simplicity" and "complexity" represent polarities, so too do the terms "order" and "disorder". The polarity between order and disorder is similar in structure to any other polarity: it is a *metaxy* between two poles, each pulling from a different direction. There is pressure to order what seems disordered, as for example when you look around at a dirty kitchen, just as there is pressure to disorder what seems ordered, as for example when you play a practical joke.

Probably the most famous analysis of this tension occurs in Friedrich Nietzsche's early work known as *The Birth of Tragedy*, in which he contrasts the Apollonian energy toward structure, light, linear logic, rhythm, discipline, and stability, with the Dionysian energy toward uncertainty, freedom, shadow, surprise, and indulgence (1872/1995)[8]. Both tendencies are real, present at any given moment reflecting our full humanity. Apollo would drive us toward bureaucracy and a depersonalized uniformity, routine. Dionysus would tempt us toward carnival, toward pleasure, spastic self-assertion, drunkenness, and humor. Apollo represents the ambition to order; Dionysus, the allure of disorder. There is never one without the other. Go too far in either direction, and you suffer. Neglect Apollo, and your life tumbles toward disarray, even squalor and regret. Neglect Dionysus, on the other hand, and your life clenches, sanitizes, losing its savor and grinding you into a soul-crushing flatness – or a sudden burst of bodily rebellion known as a heart attack. In either case, the unpropitiated gods come back to haunt you[9].

7 One could argue that we already possess a term for the highest level of complexity in human systems, namely bureaucracy.

8 Nietzsche's rhetorical device has indeed found its way into the literature on management. For similar applications of these and other pagan gods to organizational management, see Handy (1995) and Hillman (1995).

9 For readers uncomfortable giving equal status to the two deities, who distrust any valorization of Dionysus as a pagan myth, we can characterize the tension differently. We can break them out as Form and Content, or Transcendence and the *Apeiron*, or Spirit and Matter, or God and Creation. The abstract distinction is more important here,

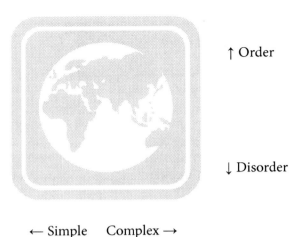

↑ Order

↓ Disorder

← Simple   Complex →

Figure 2 *Two-dimensional orientation*

What is the significance of this new polarity? How is it related to the earlier polarity between simplicity and complexity? They are not the same polarity. One could confuse simplicity with order, for example, but that would be a mistake. Simplicity can be found in order, but it can also be found in compactness, a kind of pre-order, the chaos associated with the book of Genesis. Chaos as such looks simple. By the same token, order is not always simpler than what it replaces. Sometimes, the new order makes the situation even more complicated, not simpler. One cannot equate order with simplicity. These are distinct, yet related polarities.

Imagine, if you will, an organization reaching the critical moment on the path toward complexity when it must simplify or disintegrate[10]. What happens to that organization? The rubber band stretches too far. The pendulum nears its apex. It can revert, as we said earlier, or it can achieve a new magnitude of order – in either case, it aspires to resolve the tension of complexity by reaching simplicity. But that does not exhaust the alternatives. The organization can break under the stress – shudder, shatter, and fail. The elements and all of their intricate relationships can fly apart, in chunks and pieces, destroying the organization as we know it, as they search for new relationships, new orders, or as they drift unaligned in the void. In short, the organization can experience disintegration and die[11].

I would urge caution, however, because the way we have described the situation, order and disorder would appear to be alternatives, one or the other, a simple choice. Either you are ordered or you are not. And to the extent that you are not ordered, you do not exist, period. But in truth order and disorder (just like simplicity and complexity) are a matter of degree. They are the boundaries of a continuum. Any entity (which for our purposes is a human system such as

---

whatever names we give it.

10 We are presupposing at least a minimal degree of order for us to call it an organization to begin with.

11 As we explain below, some organizations probably *should* shatter and die. Disintegration is not always a bad thing.

a business or tribe) would be more or less ordered, which is to say more or less *dis*ordered, somewhere en route across the *metaxy*.

Disorder  **Order**

At any given time, therefore, a human system struggles between simplicity and complexity and also between order and disorder, just as a seagoing vessel always finds itself at a precise longitude and latitude, between north and south and between east and west, heading somewhere perhaps, but always oriented within these compass points, as indicated in Figure 2.

Strategies to Cope With the Tension

The experience of complexity, as a subjective state or condition, accompanies pressure to simplify. Resistance to this pressure can be referred to as dissociation (Wilber, 2000: 115). We can sustain the tension only so long before we go in search of some kind of relief[12]. In the short term, however, sometimes the complexity can persist, especially if the participants in human systems are not yet fully aware of their plight. They might feel a vague sense of unease. They might even believe things are fine. It is not uncommon for those in positions of authority to extend this situation for as long as possible. Indeed, many managers assume this to be their job, to preserve the existing order[13,14]. What often happens is that the system experiences what Axelrod and Cohen refer to as "eternal boiling… when the level of mutation, temperature, or noise is so high that the system remains permanently disorderly" (2000: 43).

One strategy is to revert back to compactness, to simplify by pretending the differentiation never happened. We go into denial. We repress. Or we revert by dismantling the organization, returning to fewer elements, moving down in magnitudes of order, uncluttering by shrinking. Another strategy is to seek some kind of order, to put the elements together in some configuration that helps us categorize and understand the differentiations. These two strategies are not the only options, however.

12 The same basic experience occurs when we entertain doubt. Roughly speaking, doubt is to belief what complexity is to simplicity. The logician Charles Sanders Peirce put it this way: "Doubt is an uneasy and dissatisfied state from which we struggle to free ourselves and pass into the state of belief; while the latter is a calm and satisfactory state which we do not wish to avoid, or to change to a belief in anything else. On the contrary, we cling tenaciously, not merely to believing, but to believing just what we do believe. Doubt… stimulates us to action until it is destroyed" (1877/1992: 114). In the same manner, it is my proposition that humans become agitated by complexity.

13 For example, Northouse cites Kotter (1990) for the following contrast between management and leadership: "The overriding function of management is to provide order and consistency to organizations, whereas the primary function of leadership is to produce change and movement. Management is about seeking order and stability; leadership is about seeking adaptive and constructive change" (2001: 8).

14 Not surprisingly, Nietzsche regarded such tenacity as pathological, evidence of "stagnation, paralysis, and decline, [s]ick, pale, unhealthy and weak" (Reinert & Reinert, 2006). For him, health consists in overcoming "the *vis inertiae*, the forces of status quo" (ibid.).

We have not yet mentioned a fairly common strategy – a hybrid, really – in which a person or group of people arrive at some kind of order only by occluding *some* of what had been differentiated. It is not a complete retreat to compactness, but then neither is it a complete embracing of the differentiations. It might come across as a deformation, a monstrosity or freak, frequently difficult to detect. It is our purpose in the penultimate section to elaborate a bit on these dis-orders, because one of our hypotheses is that all human systems are, to one extent or another, similarly "deformed." This is not a minor point.

That is why this paper takes the position, which some may view as controversial, that leadership's promise of simplification will likely result in deformation. Almost by definition, it has to. And at the risk of getting ahead of ourselves, we might hold that the creating of deformation consciously – choosing our deformations – is actually a more practical long-term strategy than either (a) complete reversion, sticking one's head in the sand, or (b) some utopian fantasy that presumes to represent the highest order fully and completely. We should be fine using this hybrid strategy described in a subsequent section of this paper so long as we:

- Remember that we do in fact live with a deformation of some sort;
- Remember what it is we are choosing to occlude, and;
- Realize that we may reorder ourselves later in response to changing circumstances[15].

It must be emphasized that all orders, whether orders in the mind, on paper, or in practice, are incomplete, inexact, less than perfect. Humans will always have reason to restore or refine whatever order they find themselves in, holding it together and making it better. One reason for this need to monitor and respond to the emergence of disorder is the tendency of reality to change and otherwise resist order, in a kind of undomesticated wildness. Another reason is our own limitation: we can never completely empty the compactness of reality. There is always more to learn, notice, unearth, and otherwise consider. In every order, there lurks some disorder. When referring to deformations, however, I intend a specific kind of disorder, an order that often passes itself off as genuine, complete, and whole, but that includes mechanisms to block and otherwise suppress disturbing facets of reality. It is my paradoxical contention that deformation (ill order) can be a conscious choice – and a prudent choice, at that.

Leadership Studies

Leadership scholarship supports five alternatives for how leadership involves a simplification of complexity:

- The leader as unifying symbol;
- Reverting to compactness;

---

15 We are reminded here of Alfred North Whitehead's aphorism, "Seek simplicity, then distrust it" (quoted by Warren Bennis, 1989: 102).

- Achieving a new order;
- Shattering order and releasing its energies;
- Pragmatic rhythms as we tolerate our deformations.

The Leader as Unifying Symbol

Concerning the first on this list, James MacGregor Burns (1978) made an interesting observation:

"Every person, group, and society has latent tension and hostility, forming a variety of psychological and political patterns across social situations. Leadership acts as an inciting and triggering force in the conversion of conflicting demands, values, and goals into significant behavior" (p. 38).

He added that "conflict… is necessary for leadership and, indeed, for higher levels of coherence, in a kind of dialectical and synthesis response" (p. 45). So far, this sounds much like the promise of simplification. As complexity increases, people respond in different ways, finding themselves in conflict with each other, and often within themselves, torn about what to do next. Then, Burns inserts a telling comment, citing William Whyte, that a "leader is a focal point for the organization of the group… In the absence of the leader its cohesion disintegrates and the group becomes a collection of smaller groups" (p. 80). In other words, in the complexity of the moment, a leader promises simplification partly by serving as a "focal point" – a lode star, if you will, or a symbol for the whole, embodying in his or her person the identity of the group. The leader serves as figure to the ground of complexity.

Burns goes on to characterize this leadership role as heroic and even idolatrous, in which leaders personalize movements and symbolize ideas: "The halo surrounding Number One bathes the political landscape in a glow of harmony and consent" (p. 248). Unfortunately, such leadership has no shared purpose, no direction, so that it draws attention away from the complexity, subsuming it (in a manner of speaking), presenting a surface simplicity that obscures the complexity underneath. In recent history, we might categorize Saddam Hussein as one such leader: so long as he was in power, the various conflicts between Western and Muslim values, for instance, and among Sunnis, Shiites, and Kurds, persisted and perhaps even intensified, without breaking out completely into civil war. It was a simplicity bought with corruption and violence, to preserve the charade that probably fooled outsiders more than it did the people of Iraq.

None of which is to suggest that such leadership is always blameworthy. It is neither inherently good nor evil, neither wise nor stupid. Not only are there occasions when people enmeshed in complexity need to rally around a single person before taking meaningful action, but we hold that some of the most praiseworthy leadership is nothing more than drawing attention, modeling, serving as an example, being singled out as representative: "Look at him!" This alone might not resolve a system's tension, but it can galvanize and inspire the participants, or even serve as catharsis, creating distance for everyone else from the press of perplexing circumstance, either to envision a new way of being (St.

Francis) or to recognize in one person's predicament that something is dread-fully, dreadfully wrong (Rosa Parks)[16].

Reverting to Compactness

The second way leaders can simplify is described by John Gardner (1990) in re-gard to the US, where a rhetoric about unity and being a melting pot has not pre-vented Americans from finding themselves suffering "the mischiefs of faction" (quoting James Madison). According to Gardner: "The war of the parts against the whole is the central problem of pluralism today" (p. 95). Nevertheless, we have no choice but to accept the idea of pluralism while at the same time work-ing to achieve some level of unity, a unity within diversity.

In reaction against pluralism, some leaders promise to restore a more tra-ditional community that is homogenous, unchanging, conformist, and relatively small. Thus, Gardner refers to the "trance of nonrenewal [in which] individuals can look straight at a flaw in the system and not see it as a flaw" (p. 126). Revert-ing is simply not realistic. Neither is it, in his opinion, desirable. Just as Burns had reservations about heroic leadership, so also Gardner had reservations about leadership under the trance of nonrenewal.

Webb (1981) depicts what happens when we choose to revert. In our quest to revert, we might neglect fresh, contrary evidence or stop listening to critics or in some other way cling to our beliefs beyond reason. In doing so, how-ever, reverting condemns us to create in our imagination a distorted view of re-ality that conveniently omits what we don't want to remember. At some point, to preserve our compact consciousness, we might have to destroy reality and remake it in our false image, even claiming moral superiority[17].

People often want a leader to turn back the clock – not so much to re-claim a heritage or recover lost virtues, which is often praiseworthy, but simply to escape harsh realities, stuffing the genie back into the bottle. The primary rea-son we should worry about this approach to simplification is that truth – how-ever one hopes to define it –is movement in participation with reality (Webb, 1981).

---

16 Barry Schlenker refers to this as a view in psychology known as cognitive prototypes (1985: 11f, citing Kuiper, 1981).

17 Going back to John Gardner's concerns about pluralism, let us consider for a moment how reversion might work. A leader who promises simplification might seek to impose an ethic that he or she knows to offend certain factions. The leader might evict or isolate individuals who do not conform. The leader might dismantle groups and agencies within the organization that foster pluralism. The leader might also try to unify the people by rallying against a common foe. But beware! Any order worthy of the name will take equivalent measures in extreme cases. At some point, to preserve itself an organization has to adopt common values, confront members who work counter to its purpose, release segments that no longer fit the mission, and help everyone identify the risks of failure. Jeffrey Hart was credited in a book review recently for confronting this realization in the American political conservative movement's opposition to abortion. He asks, to what extent is it a distorting reversion for conservatives today to seek abolition (Nash, 2006: 48f)?

Voegelin, however, wrote of achieving a "maximum of differentiation" – in response to which receding and rebelling lead to nihilism and power doctrines, neither of which sounds very wholesome (Grimley-Kuntz, 1991: 169, citing *The New Science of Politics*).

Achieving a New Order

Ron Heifetz (1994) draws attention to the third way of simplification, leadership as adaptive work. In particular, adaptive work responds to conflict by examining both (a) existing values and (b) the reality of the situation. By clarifying values and testing reality, a human system learns how to advance together toward a resolution that brings values and reality into alignment. Sometimes, however, values are in conflict with one another, and sometimes the implications and nuances of values are insufficiently understood. At such times, it can help to bring about some sort of clarification.

But Heifetz emphasizes another scenario. Sometimes values prevent people from adapting successfully to pressures from their environment. At such times, certain values increase the likelihood of stress and disintegration. Are people in these situations aware of this? Are they willing to hold on to their values at such a cost? Will they persist and, by persisting, perish?

The values themselves might be internally consistent after years of debate and reflection. They might be a model of coherence, elegance, and thoroughness. Nonetheless, over the course of time certain stresses appear, and the value system itself may be preventing a resolution of those stresses. Heifetz argues that in such situations, the values preventing adaptation pose a threat. The leader then may question those values because they endanger the well being of the group or community. People will have to give up values for something presumably they value more, up to and including their survival.

The first step toward doing adaptive work is to develop the capacity for it. Heifetz identifies the first step as "improving [the] ability to reflect, strengthening [the] tolerance for frustration, and understanding... blind spots and patterns of resistance to facing problems...." (p. 5). Adaptive work is a response to pressures brought about by increasing complexity. In human systems, the increase of complexity accompanies stress. Something has to be done in such a situation and that "something" is to revisit people's values, so that they can adapt without trying to hold contradictory positions.

Heifetz admits that adaptive work can be difficult and demand much of the participants. The cost can be high. It is therefore a fair question to ask, in advance of any proposal to make extraordinary sacrifices, whether the sacrifice will have been for naught. Is the push for this particular solution (whatever it is) a "premature convergence" (Axelrod & Cohen, 2000: 44)?

Shattering Order and Releasing Its Energies

The fourth approach to simplicity by means of leadership concerns freeing oneself from the dominating order itself, thereby letting all of the elements reattach and reorder in new and better ways. To the naked eye, freedom often resembles disorder, but they are not the same thing. Just as both "relaxed" and "rigid" contrast with "motion," so also freedom and disorder might seem to contrast with order. However, there are two relevant distinctions. First, relaxed and rigid are contrary. Freedom and disorder are not contrary – not necessarily. Second, it is my contention that at a certain level order and freedom coincide. The right order embodies freedom – a proposition we will have reason to elaborate in the next section.

For the most part leadership studies rarely contemplate dismantling the system itself or splitting off its parts, although in reality such an eventuality frequently occurs. Employees are laid off. Work teams are disbanded. Corporations are sometimes sold off piecemeal. The phenomenon has been studied formally in economics as "creative destruction" – a concept that has been traced back to Friedrich Nietzsche, but that has been associated most with economist Joseph Schumpeter (Reinert & Reinert, 2006; Diamond, 2004).

The root of creative destruction is the finding that existing structures sometimes impede innovation, and thus require dismantling, a process, according to Schumpeter, that is the *sine qua non* of capitalism (Diamond, 2004).

Luhmann (1995) contends that from a systems perspective, long-term viability depends on an interdependence of disintegration and reproduction. For one reason, as elements vanish, the system must replenish the supply, and to do that it must pass through a phase of disintegration. Vilfredo Pareto (1901/1991) detected a similar dynamic inherent in larger social systems – a dynamic that he named "the circulation of elites" – in which the status quo required some displacement of those at the top of society's hierarchies by fresh leadership of one kind or another.

In his work on the concept of order in political organization, the philosopher Eric Voegelin recognized that any order is precarious (Grimley-Kuntz, 1991: 160). A wise ruler will confront this fact, finding the right balance for a community, knowing which destructive forces to resist and which to integrate into the dynamics of that community's development. Certain failure lies in thinking that one's community can escape the *metaxy*, resolving the tension inherent in human life and securing permanent concord by means of designing and implementing any one particular political order (see generally Franz, 1992).

Pragmatic Rhythms As We Tolerate Our Deformations

Finally, the fifth aspect of simplicity has to do with establishing pragmatic rhythms as the system tolerates deformations. The word "deformation" connotes misbegotten, a monstrosity or freak, some sad or loathsome departure from that which we regard as healthy and beautiful. The use of such a word prejudices the case to be made for leadership dedicated precisely to tending a system's deformations.

Writing in 1940 for an Argentine newspaper, José Ortega y Gasset (1946), a renowned Spanish philosopher, published an apt study on *Del Imperio Romano*. In that essay, Ortega illustrated the historical work of a social system to preserve and prolong itself by means of adaptation, or what he refers to as makeshift. So long as the system shares a common purpose, without which the system will disintegrate, it will inevitably squabble over this and that. Participants are motivated to belong and to cooperate, but they also bear independent desires and different opinions. Ortega firmly believed in the inherent tensions of collective life. He wrote, in echoes of Nietzsche's Apollonian/Dionysian image:

"*Society, by its own nature, provides the place for social and antisocial doings alike, crime occurring as normally as love of one's neighbor. Major criminal elements may at best be kept at bay temporarily. But even so they only lie concealed in the underworld of the social body ready at any moment to break loose de profundis*" (1940/1946: 25).

For this reason, every order worthy of the name holds things in check, or in constraint, for the sake of something else. No order could completely release everything to its unencumbered nature. As vital preferences shift, they pose a problem that cannot be "solved" so much as it is remedied, alleviated, accommodated. The perduring system (as in this case the Roman Republic) "fits the growing complexity of society with new institutions," rather like an engineer faced with an original, concrete predicament (p. 40). These innovations respond to the moment, ingenious and unforeseeable. They can be said to build on the deep strata of belief that the participants share, yet change as the accumulating struggles dictate, trying this and inventing that.

    And why does it proceed in this way? Why cannot a system's order be submitted to rational theories in the abstract, disconnected in the mind from circumstance and fashioned in a vacuum to be perfect? Ortega answered as a pragmatist: no system exists in isolation from a network of interlocking forces and institutions. One does not introduce a factory-made heart into the patient without watching how it integrates into the organism that is to be its environment. Thus, each system – however it turns out to be ordered – is in Ortega's word "untransferable"; that is, uniquely adapted to its history and its context (p. 47). Every existing order is in reality a deformation of some sort, something impure with regard to concept, but ruggedly responsive to human experience at a particular moment. And that is the genius of perduring systems.

    Since Ortega chose not to write about the pragmatic kind of leadership required in this context, we can turn to what another philosopher, Isaiah Berlin, had to say about this. On the way toward a celebrated academic career, Berlin spent a considerable amount of time analyzing and working alongside statesmen in Great Britain and the United States. Berlin also participated in the deliberations that led to the creation of the state of Israel, so he knew the Zionist leadership intimately. In addition, he devoted years of study to Russian intellectuals leading up to the Revolution of 1917[18]. This combination of interests and experiences gave Berlin a valuable perspective on leadership as it is actually practiced.

    In 1954, while attempting to describe the Zionist statesman Chaim Weizmann, Isaiah Berlin (2001) described what he called a "realist" leader. Re-

---

18 For biographical information, see Ignatieff, 1998.

alists can seem pessimistic, if not boring. They certainly accept far less from a situation. Nonetheless, in the long run realists get more of what they want. They piece together more information. They constantly shift in response to circumstances. They can admit mistakes quickly, without losing face. What they are doing, in the words of Berlin, is improvisation:

"[T]here is an element of improvisation, of playing by ear, of being able to size up the situation, of knowing when to leap and when to remain still, for which no formulae, no nostrums, no general recipes, no skill in identifying specific situations as instances of general laws can substitute" (Berlin, 1996: 33).

From a systems perspective, the realist knows that he cannot revert, has no desire to disintegrate *tout court*, yet he turns out to be wary of grand, unproven schemes promising new orders, so he makes a series of little adjustments: responding to stresses in subtle fashion, progressing by nearly imperceptible stages toward novel makeshifts. The order emerging as a result of a thousand experiments is likely to appear to the uninitiated as hopelessly (and needlessly) complex, with countless exceptions produced by the unique history of an institution within a unique environment. Yet, to participants who live through reforms, the regime seems admirably adapted to their freedom, like a physical body, so that ordinarily they hardly notice the complexity.

Conclusion: The Promise of Leadership

It is not the purpose of this paper to recommend one method for simplification, to the exclusion of all the rest. Each has its merits. As pressures mount to resolve complexity, a leader might be advised to adopt a "population of strategies," each of which promises ultimately to simplify the lives of participants[19]. It is also incumbent on leaders to appreciate the limits of each method, to act with humility toward the scale of complexity for which they assume responsibility when they step forward to lead.

For Voegelin, "the whole human enterprise in history is the search for order," yet that search never ends because we live within a variety of polarities. There are natural polarities, such as light and dark; moral polarities, such as justice and injustice; intellectual polarities, such as delusion and truth; and spiritual polarities, such as time and eternity (Grimley-Kuntz, 1991). We move about within these various polarities, and one of the central tasks we have set for ourselves is achieving right order in our lives as individuals and in our relationships with other people, although because we cannot ever finally reach that goal, what we end up with is a variety of orders, approximations that are tentative and incomplete. And that's okay. That is the human condition. The challenge lies in how we live within it, in the choices we make day after day.

---

19 For an explanation of the phrase "population of strategies," see Axelrod and Cohen (2000: 5).

Acknowledgment

The author thanks Dr. Terry Price of the University of Richmond for valuable comments on sections of this paper.

CHAPTER NINETEEN
GENERATIVE LEADERSHIP: NURTURING INNOVATION IN COMPLEX SYSTEMS

Gita Surie & James K. Hazy

This chapter contributes a theoretical framework for generative leadership, a form of leadership that creates a context to stimulate innovation in complex systems. Our framework links theories of leadership with perspectives on innovation and complex systems to suggest that generative leadership involves balancing connectivity and interaction among individuals and groups in complex systems by managing complexity and institutionalizing innovation. By focusing on how generative leaders create conditions that nurture innovation rather than individual traits or creativity, our framework provides new directions for leadership research and policy implications for managers.

Gita Surie (Senior Fellow, Wharton School, University of Pennsylvania; Assistant Professor, Adelphi University) researches technology and innovation, entrepreneurship, and multinational corporations. She has worked for Control Data Corporation, the United Nations, and the Economist Group, and has been a consultant to Educational Testing Services and Indian Oil Corporation. She received her M.A. (Economics) from Columbia University and her Ph.D. from the Wharton School of the University of Pennsylvania.

James Hazy (Associate Professor, Adelphi University) researches organizational leadership, leadership effectiveness metrics, complex systems in social science, computational organization theory, and organizational capabilities. With over 25 years of business experience, including senior positions at AT&T Corp. and Ernst &Young, LLP, he received his Ed.D. from The George Washington University and an MBA from the Wharton School of the University of Pennsylvania.

Introduction

"If man is not to do more harm than good in his efforts to improve the social order, he will have to learn that in this, as in all other fields where essential complexity of an organized kind prevails, he cannot acquire the full knowledge which would make mastery of the events possible" (Friedrich August von Hayek).

It is clear from the pervasive impact of distant events, both natural and man made, that we inhabit a complex and interdependent world. Havoc wreaked by disasters such as floods in New Orleans, tsunamis in Southern Asia, the spread of bird flu, oil shocks, or stock market crashes have far-reaching effects. The impact of good fortune is also widespread, as exemplified by stock market and real estate booms and productivity gains from using internet and other new technologies. Action is local, yet likely to have global effects. Firms, organizations, and nations are not isolated, but, rather, interdependent parts of a complex system. Moreover, a complex systems worldview highlights that *interactions* between parts of the system and the behavior of the system as a *whole* are critical. Yet how interactions are managed by agents to influence the behavior of the whole system is not well understood.

Research from a complexity perspective suggests that organizations are complex systems composed of interacting agents that learn, adapt, and co-evolve. Moreover, fostering innovation to facilitate adaptation to a changing environment necessitates understanding the dynamics and evolution of complexity in natural systems (Levinthal, 1997). While this view has largely been applied to the design of complex systems, (Levinthal & Warglien, 1999; Rivkin, 2001; Siggelkow & Rivkin, 2005), the critical issue of *how* leadership can be exercised to nurture innovation, adaptation, and high performance over time is insufficiently emphasized. Hence, we investigate the following research question in this chapter: "How can leadership be exercised in a complex, interdependent world to foster problem solving and innovation?"

We contribute new insights by linking research on complexity and leadership to develop a framework for *generative leadership*, defined as those aspects of leadership that foster innovation, organizational adaptation, and high performance *over time*. A critical element of generative leadership is the ability to seek out, foster, and sustain generative relationships (Lane & Maxfield, 1996) that yield new learning relevant for innovation. This, in turn, requires a nuanced understanding of the environment and an ability to structure situations and manage interactions. Although other aspects of leadership may also be important to system sustainability, they are not the subject of this analysis. Here we focus on the role of generative leadership as a catalyst for innovative adaptation from a theoretical perspective as applied to a case study of an Indian automotive manufacturer.

Theoretical Background
Leadership Research

Earlier perspectives on leadership focus largely on individual traits and be-haviors to elicit super-ordinate performance, whether via transactional, instrumental (House, 1971; Luthans & Kreitner, 1975; Podsakoff, *et al.*, 1982), charismatic, transformational (Shamir, *et al.*, 1993; Burns, 1978; Bass, 1985; Bennis & Nanus, 1985; Kouzes & Posner, 1987; Judge & Piccolo, 2004), or value-based approaches (House & Aditya, 1997; Conger &Kanungo, 1987; Shamir, *et al.*, 1993). While team-oriented leadership theories like leader–member exchange theory (Graen & Cashman, 1975; Graen, *et al.*, 1982; Waka-bayashi & Graen, 1984; Graen & Uhl-Bien, 1995) highlight the importance of role-based exchanges between leaders and team members, they do not empha-size how a rapidly changing context alters roles dynamically. In contrast, entre-preneurial leadership (Gupta, *et al.*, 2004) emphasizes innovation and problem solving and notes that context is an important element of leadership.

Yet, previous perspectives focus on leaders' individual characteristics rather than on the dynamics of interactions between leaders, group members, and the context in complex organizational systems over time; nor do they eluci-date sufficiently how leaders create conditions that allow their organizations to evolve.

Innovation Research

It has been shown that innovation in organizations may stem from technical or administrative systems (Damanpour, 1991), and may be incremental or radical (Henderson & Clark, 1990; Kuhn, 1970). Research suggests that promoting in-novation requires:

- A diversity of experience, expertise, and affect to allow pooling of relevant knowledge from various sources (Ancona & Caldwell, 1992; Dougherty & Hardy, 1996; Cohen & Levinthal, 1990);

- Repeated practice (Pisano, 2000) or cognitive search (Gavetti & Levinthal, 2000);

- Champions that insulate the group from everyday pressures, and provide re-sources to permit sustained and focused activity on specific projects (Shane, *et al.*, 1995; Dougherty & Hardy, 1996; Leonard-Barton, 1995);

- Presenting a challenge on which organizational survival depends (Dough-erty & Hardy, 1996);

- Exploiting innovations through rapid market testing to gain feedback, make modifications, and determine whether to continue pursuing specific inno-vation trajectories (Clark & Fujimoto, 1991; March, 1991).

Studies have examined innovation in the context of technology adop-tion (Van de Ven, 1986; Van de Ven, *et al.*, 1989; Rogers, 1983), culture (Shane, *et al.*, 1995), creativity (Amabile, *et al.*, 1996), learning, capability building, ex-ploration and exploitation (Winter & Szulanski, 2001; March, 1991), performance (Lawless & Anderson, 1996), sources of innovation (Wade, 1996; von Hippel, 1988), and characteristics of innovation adopters (Greve, *et al.*, 1995). However, few studies link innovation with leadership and complex systems.

Complex Adaptive Systems

We consider complex adaptive systems here since they are suitable for modeling problems in a variety of domains, including leadership (Carley & Prietula, 1994; Anderson, 1999; Hazy, 2007a; Marion & Uhl-Bien, 2001), to yield insights into the dynamics of evolution (Arthur, 1997, 1999; Hage, 1999; Simon 1965). In general, models of complex adaptive systems (CASs) highlight the relational aspect of complexity. Four elements of CASs are relevant for organizational theorists:

- First, outcomes emerge from actions of agents at a lower level of aggregation (Holland & Miller, 1991);

- Second, self-organization in the system is emergent as a result of the interdependent behavior of agents who act on local information (Anderson, 1999). These interactions need to remain within a delicate range to prevent stagnation and decay on the one hand, and unpredictable, random dynamics on the other (Kaufmann, 1993; Carroll & Burton, 2000);

- Third, since agents coevolve with one another (Holland & Miller, 1991; Levinthal, 1997), the processes and structures that emerge from their interactions are dynamic and not static (Anderson, 1999);

- Fourth, complex adaptive systems evolve over time through the entry, exit, and transformation of agents. Continuous evolution ensures that CASs operate far from the equilibrium of what may otherwise be thought of as globally optimal system performance (Holland & Miller, 1991; Kauffman, 1995). Nevertheless, this sub-optimality is not necessarily disadvantageous.

Studies using Kauffman's NK adaptive landscape model (McKelvey, 1999; Rivkin, 2000; Levinthal, 1997; Siggelkow & Rivkin, 2005; Carroll and Burton, 2000; Levinthal & Warglien, 1999; Brown & Eisenhardt, 1997), cellular automata models (Lomi & Larsen, 1997), neural networks (Heydebrand, 1989), and genetic algorithms (Bruderer & Singh, 1996) suggest that for any level of differentiation, moderate levels of integration will outperform low or high levels of integration. However, with some notable exceptions (Hazy, 2004), computational models do not apply a complexity perspective to leadership and innovation. Similarly, despite noting cognitive and behavioral complexity (Weick, 1979; Denison, *et al.*, 1995), with only a few exceptions (Marion & Uhl-Bien, 2001), leadership research does not emphasize interactions in complex systems. Hence, in the following section we apply a complexity science approach and present a framework for generative leadership that stimulates innovation in complex organizations.

A Framework for Fostering Innovation Via Generative Leadership

For adaptation to occur, effective leadership creates a system in which appropriate collections of knowledgeable individuals can be brought together and allowed to interact with minimal friction and under conditions that catalyze innovation. Since such interactions generate new understanding, knowledge, and meaning, an important element of generative leadership is the ability to seek out, foster, and sustain generative relationships (Lane & Maxfield, 1996). Generative leadership is particularly relevant in situations of complexity when uncertainty and rapid change are dominant; since outcomes are not certain, the focus must be on the process. In a complexity science context, this type of leadership, or any leadership for that matter, must be implemented in the context of how it affects the simple, local rules that govern agent-to-agent interactions.

Our model of generative leadership uses a complexity science perspective to yield fresh insights on dynamic processes underlying innovation and departs somewhat from prior research, in that it suggests that it is not simply the composition of the team or the ability to increase interactions but *how* interactions are managed and regulated that leads to innovation. It focuses on the management of complexity itself as an enabler of innovation and explores the role of leadership as the catalyst that creates an effective context for innovation to occur. It emphasizes ways in which complexity can be reduced and absorbed structurally in the system without limiting the richness of interaction that is critical to innovation.

Thus, our generative leadership model explores what steps can be taken to manage interactions even in highly complex environments to focus and direct the team's attention. For example, attention can be focused by partitioning tasks to allow effort to be concentrated and structured within a confined, often specialized context, rather than allowing attention to be continually distracted in unstructured interactions that, because of their diffuse nature, do not allow for the accumulation of knowledge and capabilities. Moreover, generative leaders promote information flow and feedback seeking. A consequence is that exploitation and exploration can be managed concurrently (March, 1991). Similarly, exercising generative leadership involves problem-solving and innovation, and suggests that these can be distributed on a wider scale rather than limited to a few organization members at the top of the hierarchy or within a specialized group. It also suggests that innovation can be institutionalized and that novelty and system evolution are generated from simple rules that operate locally. While rules are necessary at various stages for all innovation processes, in this chapter we focus specifically on rules for interaction to aid problem solving and innovation. Table 1 situates generative leadership in the context of other studies on leadership.

Facilitating Innovation via Generative Leadership

Successful innovations link a genuine purpose or need with an effect that can be exploited to satisfy it. The ability to solve problems collaboratively is thus

Perspective on leadership	Characterization of environment	Characterization of innovation
Charismatic/Transformational Leadership	Effective in situations of ambiguity; environment not emphasized.	Catalyzes organizational change through leader's ability to elicit extraordinary effort from followers. Primary focus on individual leader characteristics. Innovation not emphasized.
Value based/Team-oriented Leadership	Effective in stable environments; environment not emphasized.	Organizational change through leader-member exchange. Focus on values and leader-member exchange in teams. Innovation not emphasized.
Entrepreneurial Leadership (Gupta, *et al.*, 2004)	Effective in turbulent environments.	Entrepreneurial leadership involves helping to bring innovation to market by ensuring adherence to vision, emphasizing problem solving, and providing resources. Focus on characteristics of individual entrepreneur/leader necessary to elicit creativity, problem solving, effort, and achievement of aspirations and goals.
Generative Leadership, based on complexity theory, complex adaptive systems (Surie & Hazy, 2006); other research from complex systems perspective (Thompson, 1967, Lawrence & Lorsch, 1969; Damanpour, 1991; Kauffman, 1993; Anderson, 1999; Hage, 1999; Brown & Eisenhardt, 1997; Siggelkow & Rivkin, 2005; Levinthal, 1997; Levinthal & Warglien, 1999)	Effectiveness contingent on match between system design and environment. Environment is a key factor in overall system performance.	Change and innovation necessitate manipulating organization design and interactions within and between sub-systems as well as between different systems. Innovation may be technical or organizational. Focus on organization as a complex system of interacting elements including individual agents, groups, and organizations. Leadership involves tuning the system for innovation, growth, and high performance via manipulation of interactions. Innovation involves changing the system-environment model.

Table 1 *Linking leadership, innovation, and complexity*

critical, since innovations often result from the recombination of existing and unfamiliar technologies and knowledge from diverse sources (Fleming, 2001; Cohen & Levinthal, 1990). Systems evolve to handle more complexity over time by matching internally generated variations with the variety of the environments they encounter, thus enhancing their survival chances and improving reproductive fitness (Boisot & Child, 1999). Survival and evolution, in turn, are predicated on the ability to solve problems and innovate.

We view innovation as a social process rather than a purely technical one; innovation emerges in the context of interactions to solve problems (Wenger, 1998). Therefore, we posit that generative leadership can catalyze innovation by structuring the overall context in which agents operate to sustain positive and powerful interactions while managing complexity. Various types of agents include individuals, organizational sub-units, the organization as a whole, and the community in which organizations coevolve. Generative leadership focuses on managing interactions within the entire organizational ecology by institutionalizing rules for collaboration.

Successful innovation teams require clear, stable rules and objectives to regulate action, while collaborative efforts yielding innovation require learning how to interact effectively (Lynn & Reilly, 2002). However, as more information is gathered about the need in the environment and the system's set of potential approaches to exploit it, a complex system such as this carries the risk that its own complexity can overwhelm it (Anderson, 1999). Hence, internal interactions must be regulated to prevent a "complexity catastrophe" – the break point where the interdependence between actors (or elements of the system) overwhelms the system's ability to digest all that interaction (Kauffman, 1993). Thus, while bringing together the right combination of interactions to create innovation, generative leadership must also limit the number of interactions so that each individual's ability to perceive, interpret, and synthesize knowledge is challenged but not overloaded.

Boisot and Child (1999) note that complexity can be managed either through complexity reduction or complexity absorption. Complexity reduction involves using routines and standards to articulate and codify knowledge, while complexity absorption involves building relationships to gain access to information available to those perceived as clan members. In the next two sections we outline five processes that generative leaders follow to regulate complexity while enhancing interactions, and three processes that help to institutionalize innovation.

Regulating Complexity

Generative leadership induces a continued focus on problem solving and innovation by facilitating interactions while regulating complexity. As shown in Figure 1 later, this necessitates managing the *context for innovation* to structure various aspects of interactions in support of evolutionary processes. Consequently, generative leaders focus on processes that influence five aspects of interactions: experience, alignment, speed, partitioning, and leveraging.

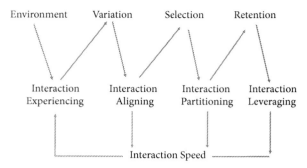

Figure 1 *The evolution of innovation and organizational capabilities: Leadership regulates complexity as interactions generate, select and retain variations*

Interaction experience

Since innovation occurs largely within one-to-one interactions, one idea building on another in untested variations, fostering system-wide innovation necessitates regulating interactions to ensure that all or most interactions are *experienced* by participants as dyadic even if they are one-to-many or many-to-one. By using symbolic language or interpreting events in a meaningful way, generative leaders can communicate to groups in ways that allow individuals to experience the communication as personalized.

For example, visionary and charismatic leaders make personalized appeals to establish purpose through symbolic language (Burns, 1978; Bass, 1985; House & Aditya, 1997; Sashkin & Sashkin, 2003). This reduces complexity by enabling individuals to share cogent ideas about the opportunity within a common language while less important informational elements, such as irrelevant facts and spurious speculations, are repressed and therefore do not add complexity to the exchange. A clear implication for successful innovation projects is that observation, sensemaking, and sensegiving (Weick, 1979) skills are critical aspects of generative leadership.

Likewise, generative leaders set the stage for interactions and promote clear and effective communication between groups and individuals that reduce and absorb complexity. The use of whiteboards, "War Rooms," and brainstorming technologies are all means to foster clarity in one-to-many and many-to-one communication interactions while limiting signal noise in complex interaction environments to reduce complexity (Davila, *et al.*, 2006). For such interactions to lead to fruitful results, they must absorb complexity and involve messages that simplify and synthesize details to signify value to relevant agents. Thus, communication must evolve to the point that agents use the same language; often a new language or code must be adopted or invented for this purpose (Lane & Maxfield, 1996). Therefore, generative leaders focus on helping to evolve a language that evokes meanings that are well understood in the organizational context. As a result, because the number of people able to understand the context is increased, the capacity of the organization to absorb complexity is enhanced (Boisot & Child, 1999). Consequently, even lower-level members of the organization can contribute to innovation, corroborating Burgelman's (1983) contention that successful bottom-up innovation depends on promoting such interactions.

Interaction Alignment

Interactions must also be aligned toward the achievement of system goals so that knowledge gained through interactions can be selected and applied to problem solving. Generative leaders ensure that goals are specified in advance to ensure that all group members participating in the innovation project are aware of them. For example, a system-wide or firm-level goal may be to attain the technological frontier and achieve the identity of leading innovator; goals of individual organizational units or sub-systems could include improving the speed of project implementation, reducing costs, or enhancing safety. By making these parameters explicit early in the project, project teams can incorporate these goals into the overall innovation solution.

Interaction Speed

Generative leaders are open to collaboration and emphasize the use of technological tools that enhance the effectiveness of connections and interactions. Increasing the speed of interactions raises the amount of information available within a given period to enhance problem solving and task performance. However, the risk of overloading the system presents a design problem in complex systems that are tightly integrated (Rivkin, 2001), since bottlenecks in information processing can cascade throughout the system. A solution is to upgrade system capabilities to enable speedier information processing via the adoption of new communication technologies.

For example, multinational corporations have adopted enterprise resource planning (ERP) systems to connect and coordinate various sub-systems worldwide via technology. Such technologies not only increase interaction speed but reduce complexity by standardizing processes, while disseminating information more rapidly to relevant parts of the system and maintaining a high degree of connectivity between various system components. Technology facilitates real-time interactions between sub-systems, including those that are geographically distant. Wal-Mart's state-of-the-art information-processing systems provide the company with superior operational capabilities that competitors find difficult to match. New technologies thus enhance complexity absorption and permit rapid interactions.

Interaction Partitioning

Generative leaders focus on allocating resources dynamically across sub-systems and manage the interfaces between them. By adopting modular organizational systems (Baldwin & Clark, 2000) that are loosely coupled (Weick, 1976), generative leaders help to limit the impact of interactions to a subset of the system when conducting experiments, and thus limit the consequences of mistakes or underdeveloped ideas that may result in complexity catastrophes. Modular systems thus allow the system to develop and retain more variations that may prove useful in future innovation and problem-solving exercises. Generative leaders also recognize that complex tasks must be sub-divided into simpler tasks and performed in independent modules to enable collaborative interactions without overloading the system. Therefore, they encourage parallel experiments to be carried out independently without adversely affecting the system while ensuring adherence to quality and other relevant parameters for sub-system output.

However, partitioning interactions may constrain communication and inhibit opportunities for further novelty. Generative leaders guard against these constraints on innovation by ensuring that evolving needs inform partitioning decisions and that partitioned sub-systems remain linked to the information flow through periodic information exchange. Modular systems of this type are prevalent in automotive manufacturing firms and software firms (Baldwin & Clark, 2000).

Interaction Leveraging

Interactions that yield significant information or insights leading to innovation are a scarce resource. Generative leaders ensure that this resource is leveraged effectively by retaining and reusing knowledge or ideas generated through such interactions in other interactions in a wide variety of contexts. Examples of methods to leverage knowledge include re-using team experience in different projects or sub-units (Surie, 1996), embedding knowledge from interactions in methodologies, tools, and other artifacts that can be used by others (Wenger, 1998), and disseminating knowledge wherever required in the system via training (Surie, 1996).

As described above, generative leaders manage complexity by encouraging innovation-inducing interactions while simultaneously reducing and absorbing the resulting complexity. Partitioning and leveraging interactions and using technology to speed interactions are mechanisms for reducing complexity by codifying and replicating knowledge. On the other hand, establishing centers of excellence, accumulating pockets of expert knowledge, and encouraging relationships that make this knowledge accessible to others are ways of absorbing complexity. Generative leaders focus on both to leverage resources generated from each set of interactions by diffusing and re-using them in as many new projects as possible. Figure 1 provides a schematic view of how the various dimensions of interactions help innovation and the evolution of capabilities.

Institutionalizing Innovation

In addition to setting the stage to enable and regulate interactions, generative leadership also enhances problem-solving capabilities by institutionalizing innovation both in sub-systems and in the system as a whole. Hence, generative leaders must evolve and enforce rules that govern the system's dynamic use of information generated through interactions to facilitate problem solving. We outline three rules followed by generative leaders to help create routines for innovation.

First, interactions *per se* do not facilitate problem solving unless they reveal information relevant to the task or make salient certain features of the problem. Hence, interactions must be structured so as to yield a representation of the problem to be solved by enabling group participants to parse the problem into its component features (Holland, 1995); in other words, the rules must serve to bracket relevant experience for the participants (Weick, 1979).

Traditional perspectives on leadership focus how leaders' behaviors help to establish and articulate vision, strategy, or objectives and mobilize followers. Generative leadership, in contrast, focuses on structuring the context and system to enable organizational or group members to analyze or represent problems accurately from multiple perspectives, while avoiding the risks inherent in insular, self-referential environments. At a system level, generative leaders are catalysts who help capture diverse perspectives and focus attention on salient features of the environment and multiple dimensions of a problem. At a sub-system level, new product generation requires that innovation teams seek to identify and conceive the problem in new ways by focusing on key outcomes and constraints. Generative leadership is thus exercised at all levels of the organization to catalyze this process. Consequently, generative leaders help to change the system–environment model by focusing attention on the constraints and possibilities of the market and context.

For example, by focusing on constraints in developing countries such as the need to conserve fuel, coupled with poor roads and lack of space, small cars suitable for crowded conditions were developed. Similarly, recognizing the potential of a market for consumers with low discretionary income led to a focus on making cheaper computers and cell phones; this involved representing the problem of creating novel products differently. Rather than focusing solely on technology, generative leaders are sensitive to the nuances of social conditions and the needs of the context.

Second, since group interactions must culminate in action based on a match between the model or representation of the problem and the environment, generative leaders focus on gaining rapid feedback through action. In contrast to traditional perspectives that conceive of leaders as the gatherers, interpreters, and synthesizers of feedback and as those who heroically convert the information into a strategy or vision, generative leadership channels feedback through the organization's members who are in the best position to interpret and synthesize the new information into ever more useable models of the environment. The accuracy of representations thus formed can be judged by acting on the basis of their predictions and determining whether the predictions match the state of the world (Holland, 1995). In fast-changing environments, frequent action is necessary to check whether a representation is accurate (Eisenhardt & Martin, 2000). Subjecting product or service prototypes to market tests at different stages of the innovation life cycle helps gain rapid feedback and update the organizational representation of the problem. These rapid iteration and feedback dynamics based on insight drawn from both internal and external interactions are shown in Figure 2.

Third, generative leaders emphasize using a disciplined procedure for continuing or stopping innovation projects depending on the likelihood of success or failure. Consequently, they focus on tracking outcomes via milestones that evaluate the progress of the innovation project on its own terms. This is in contrast to traditional approaches that evaluate a project based on its perceived contribution to a predetermined strategy. Besides relying on exit strategies such as divestment in case of failure at the end of a project, generative leaders use these interim milestones to reconfigure and reallocate resources rapidly and minimize waste in case an innovation project is unlikely to succeed. In contrast to traditional models of leadership, generative leadership emphasizes rapid learning to evolve rules for proceeding at different stages of an innovation project, thus helping to mitigate the uncertainty inherent in innovation.

A key feature of any evaluation process is evolutionary selection: the ability to learn continuously and implement learning in action as the project proceeds. Thus, generative leadership explicitly encompasses learning and evolution. A case study of generative leadership in an Indian automotive and farm equipment company is presented below. Figures 2 and 3 present an outline of innovation and institutionalization processes.

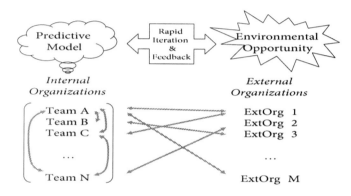

Figure 2 *Innovation dynamics leverage internal and external interactions to match predictive models to opportunities via rapid interaction and feedback*

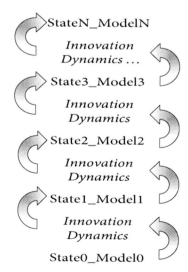

Figure 3 *Institutionalizing innovation: Capability configurations are improved to sustain fitness-enhancing innovations*

A Case Study of Generative Leadership in an Indian Automotive Manufacturer

This case study was conducted by the first author as part of a larger study on capability building and innovation in the context of foreign technology adoption by Indian firms. Interviews were conducted between 1993 and 1996 with senior executives involved in technology transfer at the corporate headquarters, and at the engine manufacturing plant with manufacturing and R&D heads and other managers. Subsequent details are obtained from published sources (annual reports from 1996 onwards, and websites; the name of the organization has been disguised for confidentiality).

Liberalization of the Indian economy in the wake of India's financial crisis in 1991 led to the abandonment of post-independence economic policies of import substitution and infant industry protection, in favor of policies focused on exports and reducing barriers to entry to foreign firms (Jalan, 1991). Competition from multinationals led domestic firms to seek a solution to the problem of how to compete globally and participate in world markets. Interactions with foreign firms supplying technology can thus be viewed as learning experiments situated within an environmental context of transition from a closed to an open economy. External circumstances prompted many leading domestic firms to exercise generative leadership by emphasizing system-wide innovation and problem solving in response to external challenges.

IndiaMotors, a manufacturer of utility vehicles and farm equipment, had entered a technical collaboration with a French company in the mid-1980s to manufacture automotive engines in India. Project leaders exercised generative leadership by ensuring that the relationship between the French supplier of technology and the Indian recipient was structured to nurture collaboration and foster capability building in the Indian firm.

Regulating Complexity

Interaction Experience

The environment in IndiaMotors was structured to achieve both complexity reduction and absorption by codifying tacit knowledge and standardizing information flow in relationships between different internal and external subsystems. Managers in IndiaMotors reported that their relationship with the Japanese technology supplier was open and supportive; the French supplier provided technical information and process know-how on a timely basis, and adopted a mentoring stance toward the Indian collaborator, even helping with testing components and processes in India to ensure that the product met international quality standards.

Within IndiaMotors, top management, departmental heads, and project leaders exercised generative leadership by ensuring that inter-departmental relations followed protocols of cordiality. Managers collaborated during a labor strike to study internal processes and improved the layout of the factory to enhance efficiency. Managers also understood the value of using mechanisms such as cross-functional teams and had adopted such practices by the mid-1990s. By including members of all departments at the outset of a new project, the company was able to pool expertise and rapidly disseminate information relevant for accomplishing the task of manufacturing equipment based on new technology. Top management also reduced complexity by using symbolic communication to help the organization survive and compete by emphasizing goals such as the need to achieve international quality standards.

Interaction Alignment

Interactions between the manufacturing plant and other departments such as R&D and corporate were aligned to promote information flow at every stage of work; this reduced complexity and enabled the company to increase responsibility at each stage of the hierarchy, so that even workers on the shop floor were aware of the need to improve quality and productivity. Moreover, because objectives were clear, each department was responsible for monitoring its own actions and seeking feedback by benchmarking performance against agreed standards. Standard tools used by companies worldwide were employed to align goals. Although the idea of a hierarchy was not abandoned, complexity was absorbed as junior engineers could gain access to top levels of management and thus expert knowledge sources in order to address problems that could not be handled at lower levels.

Interaction Speed

New communication technologies were widely adopted to speed interactions and communication. Since communication by telephone and facsimile machines was the only option during the early phases of technology adoption, face-to-face interactions were necessary. Later, the adoption of email, intranets, and other technologies permitted the firm to standardize information and speed interactions between organizational sub-units, international partners, and local suppliers. Also, computer-aided manufacturing systems allowed all parts of the organization to be linked instantaneously and sped up interactions with overseas technology suppliers. Despite the potential for overwhelming the system by increasing interactions, complexity was managed by substituting face-to-face communication with asynchronous communication. This permitted large amounts of data to be processed offline and enhanced the efficiency of communication.

Interaction Partitioning

In 1999-2000, the company adopted a new business model that leveraged the internet to improve connectivity and provide interfaces between all modules involving different stakeholders of the organization, such as dealers, vendors, and customers. Computerized systems were also installed in the late 1990s to ensure smooth integration across marketing, design and production sub-systems and intranets were used to manage knowledge more efficiently in the different independent projects embarked on. As more resources were generated, new projects could be pursued concurrently in new markets by diversifying into engineering services, automotive components, information technology, trade- and finance-related services, and infrastructure development.

Interaction Leveraging

Learning from interactions with technology suppliers and in other implementation and technology-adaptation situations was fostered through practice, participation, and training both in India and France. Selected employees were sent for training in France and some Indian suppliers were also provided with training in France by the suppliers of the French partner. French experts provided assistance in tools, component validation, and testing.

When production began in India, all components were sent to France for validation and testing. The French also helped develop systems and approaches in relevant areas of manufacturing. This knowledge was diffused within the organization and shared with suppliers. Similarly, in design, R&D engineers leveraged their learning from suppliers' designs and drawings and worked with design consultants in modifying designs to suit local conditions. At the system or organizational level, quality control and benchmarking programs were implemented to achieve international standards and diffused to local suppliers.

Institutionalizing Innovation

By focusing on adopting new technology and new practices to manufacture engines indigenously, members of the organization developed a new representation of the problem of innovating to compete in world markets. This involved tapping knowledge from a variety of sources, including workers, customers, and suppliers, rather than limiting innovation and new product development to in-house R&D engineers. As a result of reconfiguring the organizational system through interactions with French experts, a problem-solving lens emerged. Testing, diagnosis, and evaluation were applied to manufacturing, and dominated every sphere of activity including planning, prototype construction, quality, materials, and supplier development. A quality orientation also emerged and design changes were triggered by monitoring the performance of excavators in use. By 1995 business process reengineering was introduced in the division and the engine plant obtained ISO 9002 certification from TUV of Germany, signaling the firm's intent to be regarded as a world-class manufacturer.

Organizational leaders exercised generative leadership by testing this emerging representation of a world-class manufacturer through initiating other projects and forging other alliances. In 1996 a light commercial vehicle was launched; all engines types were approved for new emission norms; and an integrated design and manufacturing center was established to design an entirely new vehicle with the help of internationally renowned consultants. In 1997, the firm entered a manufacturing alliance with a leading American automotive manufacturer and a technical alliance with a Japanese one. By 2002, a new-generation sports utility vehicle was launched, and in 2004 exports of these vehicles commenced to Latin America, the Middle East, and South Africa.

Successes in domestic and export markets led the firm to enter joint ventures with another French collaborator to manufacture a mid-sized sedan, and with an American company to manufacture trucks and buses in India. The company is currently one of the leading manufacturers of utility vehicles and farm equipment in India, with revenues of $2.59 billion in 2005.

The emergence of system-wide innovation at various levels in this organization suggests that promoting innovation need not be a top-down exercise. Rather, exercising generative leadership requires wider diffusion of problem-solving efforts through enhancing connectivity and interactions by regulating the environment in which innovation occurs.

Conclusion

This chapter uses a complexity science perspective to posit a framework for generative leadership that helps to foster innovation. Our view of generative leadership contributes a new perspective on leadership by drawing attention to structuring the overall context of innovation and suggesting how system-wide innovation is stimulated. Our framework outlines how generative leaders can influence five aspects of interactions to enhance system capabilities for innovation and three processes for institutionalizing innovation. In addition, our view of generative leadership suggests that the capacity to solve problems and innovate is widely distributed in organization systems and can be harnessed only through concerted efforts that both increase and regulate interactions to facilitate knowledge recombination. Moreover, rather than focusing on individual interactions between leaders and followers, our perspective on generative leadership emphasizes the *organizational* capacity to enhance connectivity, and thereby promote innovation by synthesis and recombination of ideas from different parts of the system and adaptation to a dynamic context.

Our framework is supported by evidence from a case study of new technology adoption and innovation in an Indian automotive manufacturing firm. Despite the limitations of a case study of one organization, details from the case and examples provided for each element of the framework support our perspective. March, *et al.* (1991) note that organizations often learn despite very limited experience – a sample of one – because they augment the experience by attending to different aspects of it. In addition, they argue that the richness of history can be enhanced by focusing on critical events; three aspects of events render an event critical. First, events located at important points in history that change the world are critical. Second, events that change what is believed about the world are critical. Third, the metaphorical power of an event makes it critical – events that evoke meaning, interest, and attention are critical. Based on these criteria, we argue that innovation and capability building in the context of technology adoption by the automotive manufacturing company via interactions with foreign technology suppliers is a critical event, since it evoked a change in the organization's representation of itself, aroused widespread interest and meaning, and was located at a critical juncture in the history of the firm and the nation. By analogy, we can learn from details yielded by a sample of one, just as organizations do.

Nevertheless, our understanding of generative leadership can be enhanced by further testing this framework through more case studies, large-sample studies of innovation, computer simulation models, and laboratory experiments. The concept of generative leadership and its effect on innovation via the management of complexity raises new research questions for investigation:

- Are all mechanisms for regulating complexity through structuring interactions essential to facilitate innovation or is there a minimum set?

- What is the impact of each mechanism and how can it be measured?

- Is there a variation in the types of larger systems that emerge from structuring interactions? What are the competitive attributes of these different emergent forms?

- Does eliminating interactions and connectivity lead to cessation of innovation?

- Do simple rules for institutionalizing innovation lead to the emergence of complex structures over time? What are these rules? How do rules evolve? What kinds of trajectories can we anticipate based on these interventions?

These questions can be best answered through a combination of historical studies of the evolution of organizations (Surie, 1996, 2003); laboratory experiments that generate detailed information on interaction strategies and rules to yield insights on generative leadership; and studies that use computational techniques such as variants of Kauffman's *NK* model, system dynamics, or agent-based modeling techniques (Hazy, 2007a), to simulate the impact of interaction management and complexity on innovation.

CHAPTER TWENTY
TOWARDS SOCIAL COMPLEXITY VIEW ON CONFLICT, COMMUNICATION, AND LEADERSHIP

Pekka Aula[1] & Kalle Siira

Research on conflict management has made it evident that conflict is a complex phenomenon. However, the characteristics of the complexity have not yet been examined thoroughly. A majority of the previous research has concentrated on the examination of linear cause-and-effect relationship in conflict interaction; however, some of the latest developments in the scientific paradigm suggest that it might be useful to examine the phenomenon from a different theoretical perspective. The purpose of this article is to provide a social complexity view on organizational conflict management. We argue that to be both conceptually and practically useful, social complexity view should approach conflict with a framework of an interpretative view on organization and organizational communication. In particular, we propose a concept of dual function of communication as a tool for understanding and explaining the complex nature of conflict management. From the social complexity perspective, leadership is seen as dialogue that emphasizes a co-constructive and contested nature of meaning making as opposed to the monologic view that treats leaders as the primary architects of meaning. In addition, the social complexity view is compared to the traditional view of conflict management on four counts: purpose, control, styles, and outcomes. The comparison indicates that the two views differ considerably from each other on each count. These views, in turn, are argued to have significant effects on day-to-day conflict management. In the article, the conventional assumptions of conflict management are reinterpreted from the complexity perspective, and new insights on conflict management are discussed

Pekka Aula is a professor at the University of Helsinki in the Department of Communication. Professor Aula's research interests are in the problematics of formation and reformation, construction and reconstruction of communicative processes in and between complex organizational networks. His approach to organizational communication is based on the notion of communication as a core process in the social construction of reality. In organization studies this approach can be related to the interpretive school of thought in which the deep structures and communicative actions are explored as ontological primaries. On the practical/methodological front his point of reference is to explore and to develop new methodological views for organizational communication research based on his former work in the area of nonlinear dynamical communication, organizational networks and reputation.

---

1 Both authors have contributed equally to this chapter

Kalle Siira is a researcher and doctoral candidate at the University of Helsinki, Department of Communication. Siira's research is focused on conflict and communication processes in complex organizational environments. In particular his research stresses a systems analytical approach which refers to a comprehensive view on organizational processes. His current research explores and develops theories of conflict management and leadership employing principles from complexity sciences. He has also published in the area of intercultural conflict and communication.

Introduction

Organizational conflict management is receiving increasing attention by top managers and policy makers across major corporations and non-profit organizations. Conflicts resulting from misunderstandings, incompatible goals, and different working habits may cause problems on an individual level, but may also inhibit the greater organization from functioning effectively. On the other hand, conflicts are essential to modern organizations, in that they are often the key source of ground-breaking ideas and inventions. According to Ruben (1978), "...conflict is not only essential to the growth, change, and evolution of living systems, but it is, as well, a system's primary defense against stagnation, detachment, entropy, and eventual extinction" (206). Accordingly, Aula (1999; 2000) maintains that conflicts bring forth the differences between the agents' opinions, logics, and worldviews, which, in turn, lead to more creative and novel outcomes. Also in business negotiations solutions are often found through conflicts (Shockley-Zalabak, 1990).

It has been noted that managers may spend up to 20 percent of their time dealing with conflicts (Thomas & Schmidt, 1976). In a more recent study, Watson and Hoffman (1996) noted that 42 percent of managers' time is spent on conflict related negotiations. Especially during the past 25 years, a major paradigm shift has occurred in the practice of conflict management (Lipsky & Seeber, 2006). In particular, organizations are more inclined to adopt "a proactive, strategic approach to managing organizational conflicts" (Lipsky & Seeber, 2006: 360). This approach, employed in practice as a "conflict management system," draws from the general systems theory and refers to "a comprehensive set of policies designed to manage workplace conflict" (Lipsky & Seeber, 2006: 371). Thus, similar to the "systems-interactional" approach to leadership, organizational conflict management has taken steps towards "emphasizing the properties of wholeness and interdependence" (Fairhurst, 2001: 383) in theory and practice.

However, the systems-interactional approach, unlike the systems perspective in conflict management, breaks away from the traditions of determinism and reductionism in viewing leadership as "an emergent property of group interaction," where "[t]he locus of leadership is not the individual, but in the patterned sequential behavior of leaders and constituents who form an interactional system" (Fairhurst, 2001: 383). This perspective, in turn, is consistent with complexity theory's drawing attention to aggregate behaviors and interdependence of organizational agents. In particular, "...complex leaders understand that the best innovations, structures, and solutions to problems are not necessarily those that they, with their limited wisdom, ordain, but those that emerge when interacting aggregates work through issues" (Marion & Uhl-Bien, 2001: 394). In sum, even though there have been developments towards a more holistic view on organizational conflict, there is a need for approaches that challenge the dominant views that are based on determinism, individualism, and managerially focused assumptions (Nicotera & Dorsey, 2006).

Conventional View on Conflict Management

According to various scholars (e.g., Hughes, 2004; Lewicki, *et al.*, 1992: Nicotera & Dorsey, 2006: Putnam, 2006), conflict management research has followed paths that are based on a limited set of assumptions. The predominant worldview of linearity, reductionism, objectivism, determinism, prediction and rationality restricts the way we are thinking about conflict and conflict management (Hughes, 2004; Nicotera & Dorsey, 2006); conflict is considered as something that can be managed with the right tools and careful analyses. In relation to everyday conflict management, these notions are important, because they are the roads and landscapes of mental maps managers are using, when they make decisions and act as leaders.

The term conflict is typically perceived as a negative aspect of human life. Disputes over trivial matters have potential to deteriorate relationships in families, between friends, workmates, and even nations. In organizations, conflicts may inflict resignations, absenteeism, accidents, and overtime (Meyer, 2004), which, in turn, have an effect on the organizational efficiency and results. In addition, it has been noted that poorly managed conflicts may also have long-term consequences on individual health and well-being (De Dreu, *et al.*, 2004). Even though the functional aspects of conflict have been widely noted, most of the conflict research has concentrated primarily on preventing destructive conflicts rather than on understanding productive ones (Putnam, 2006).

There is no one clear definition of conflict. However, scholars generally agree that "conflict centers on incompatibilities, an expressed struggle, and interdependence among two or more parties" (Putnam, 2006: 5). According to Putnam (2006), the definition by Mortensen (1972) has served as basis for many conflict scholars' definition for conflict: "conflict is an expressed struggle over incompatible interests in the distribution of limited resources" (93). In organizations, conflicts can be caused by "any friction that produces a mismatch in expectations of the proper course of action for an employee or group of employees" (Lipsky, *et al.*, 2003: 8), such as interpersonal differences, inadequate communication, group dynamics, status and power, external pressures, or structural issues. Also, the movement of conflicts contributes to the ambiguousness of the phenomenon. That is, according to Smith (1989), conflicts may be manifested in totally different location than where it was originated; yet, this movement is rarely taken into account in research or in practice. All in all, despite the apparent complexity of the conflict, research and practice have not, in general, matched with the sophistication of the phenomenon itself.

Conflict Management Models

Organizational conflict management is based on few dominant models (Putnam, 2006; Lewicki, *et al.*, 1992). Within the field of communication, three models have dominated (Putnam, 2006). Formal approaches have generally been viewed through (1) the integrative and distributive negotiation model and (2) the role of a third party through the mediation competency model, and informal, individual level conflict management through (3) the dual concern model. The first model is based on Walton and McKersie's

(1965) work on labor negotiations, where the integrative approach tends to follow a joint problem-solving format in order to benefit all parties whereas the distributive approach treats bargaining as a fixed-sum situation where parties try to maximize their own payoffs (Lewicki, *et al.*, 1992). The mediation competency model refers to situations where a third-party intervenes to assist the parties in managing conflict. As opposed to the more formal approaches, such as arbitration, mediation leaves the final resolution in the hands of the disputants (Lewicki, *et al*, 1992). However, of most significance to this article is the dual concern model, which focuses on the individual-level informal conflicts that managers are mostly faced with.

According to the dual concern model, organizational agents are expected to behave according to certain patterns and to handle conflicts in generally consistent ways regardless of the situation and context. Conflict management behavior is typically reduced to two to five styles, though most contemporary researchers use a five-style approach (Nicotera & Dorsey, 2006). Blake and Mouton (1964) were among the first researchers to propose a five-category scheme to assess behavior in organizational conflict. They built their model based on the way managers would handle conflicts in organizations. The five styles represented two dimensions, concern for self and concern for others, and included forcing, confronting, smoothing, avoiding, and compromising. Most of the research on conflict management styles examines the relationship between superiors and subordinates (Nicotera & Dorsey, 2006). Superiors are typically reported to use collaborative conflict style, whereas avoidance and competitive styles are used less. It is a general belief that conflict outcomes are straightforwardly dependent on the way conflicts are managed; collaborative management leads to positive outcomes and avoidance and competitive approaches lead to negative outcomes (e.g., Wilmot & Hocker, 2001). Although it has been noted that there is no one best way to handle conflict situations (Putnam, 1987), there is a considerable amount of data stating that collaborative behavior is strongly desirable way to manage and resolve conflict situations (Lewicki, *et al.*, 1992; Nicotera & Dorsey, 2006).

Communication and conflict

Communication is argued to be the means through which conflicts are expressed, managed and addressed (Oetzel & Ting-Toomey, 2006). Particularly, "communication constitutes the essence of conflict in that it undergirds the formation of opposing issues, frames perceptions of the felt conflict, translates emotions and perceptions into conflict behaviors, and sets the stage for future conflicts" (Putnam & Poole, 1987: 552). As such, communication is the medium that both directs the conflict process and connects the conflict parties to each other. Putnam (2006) examined the relationship of conflict and communication and identified four categories of the role of communication in conflict research: communication as a variable, as a process, as interpretative, and as a dialectical pattern. Regardless of the approach, the link between conflict and communication has been confirmed to be vital.

Ruben (1978) argued that assumptions about the nature of communication lead to different conceptualizations of conflict. Typically, conflict research carries either explicitly or implicitly the communication notion based on the central ideas of the mathematical information theory (Shannon & Weaver, 1948), according to which communication is sending and receiving information between agents. The dual concern model, for example, treats communication predominantly "as a variable that shapes conflict styles in particular ways" (Putnam, 2006: 13). Following a typical textbook definition embedded in the traditional systems perspective (e.g., von Bertalanffy, 1975; Katz & Kahn, 1966; Monge, 1977), organizational communication is two-way information exchange that ought to make possible, in different situations, the realization of the goals of the organization and its members. From this perspective, the presence of conflict is often presumed to be "a consequence – or at least evidence – of a stoppage, breakdown, error, or deterioration in communication" (Ruben, 1978: 205). This linear view of the relationship between communication and conflict was prevalent especially in the early work on conflict; however, the assumption that ineffective communication causes all conflict has influenced organizational conflict research to date (Nicotera & Dorsey, 2006). From our perspective, the conventional view of communication and conflict is in line with the process paradigm of human communication, which we will discuss later in the article.

Conventions

All in all, four specific notions are highlighted here to illustrate the divergence of the two views on conflict management: purpose, control, outcomes, and styles. The notions of purpose, control, and outcomes are identified as they are often explicitly articulated in the complexity literature of management (and result from few central concepts, such as unpredictability, nonlinearity, and unorder), whereas the corresponding notions (i.e., predictability, linearity, and order) in conflict management literature are typically ignored or taken for granted. The notion of styles, on the other hand, is the dominant concept in the traditional conflict management literature and, thus, it is essential to examine the phenomenon from the social complexity perspective.

Purpose

The purpose of conflict management is to prevent future conflicts and to terminate existing conflicts. This assumption draws support from the linear perspective on communication and the nature of conflict. Organizational conflict is viewed as friction that needs to be sanded down. Ultimately, it is the purpose of conflict management to avoid these impurities and wipe them away once they appear.

Control

Conflicts can be controlled by a neutral authority. This assumption is based on the notion that conflict is out there; managers are detached from the conflict interaction and can objectively assess, determine outcomes, and implement proper actions to achieve the outcomes. From this point of view, conflict is assessed and acted on by its manifest part only.

Style

Individual styles are considered stagnant; that is, one is likely to maintain one's style across different conflicts and contexts. Of the various predispositions, collaboration is the best way to manage conflicts. This assumption is embedded in the Western ideal of individualism and linear cause-and-effect relationship.

Outcomes

Conflict outcomes are predictable and proportionate to the size of conflict. According to the traditional view, conflicts follow a predictable course or pattern and linear cause-and-effect model. Outcomes are predictable, because people behave in "typical" ways. Conflict is considered as a closed system that has no effects beyond the active participants.

In sum, most of conflict research has followed paths that are based on a limited set of assumptions and a determinist worldview. The leadership model embedded in these notions is in accordance with Fairhurst's (2001) "a traditional view of the world" where "in a figure-ground arrangement the individual is figure, the system is background, and communication is incidental or, at best, intervening." (383). Naturally, other views exist as well; however, the assumptions that are brought forward here have been of the most interest to the conflict researchers to date.

Social Complexity View

Mortensen (1972) and Ruben (1978) were among the earliest scholars to challenge the mechanistic approach to conflict interaction (Putnam, 2006). Mortensen (1972) introduced a transactional model of conflict that emphasized a developmental view of conflict, the purpose of which was to capture the whole process as well as the unfolding and contingent aspects of it. A few years later, Ruben (1978) presented a system-theoretic framework that emphasized the interrelationship between conflict and a system's environmental adaptation. Lately, there have been few efforts to implement the principles of complexity theory in conflict research (e.g. Sword, 2007) as well as in organizational communication research in general (e.g. Contractor, 1994, 1999; Houston, 1999; Hawes, 1999). In fact, Putnam and Boys (2006) noted that, in organizational communication, there has been a significant paradigm change from linear towards nonlinear communication within the last decade. However, within conflict research, this interpretive approach, the systems-based approach in particular, has not gained much ground. The interpretative systemic perspective that we advocate needs, however, clarification.

Organizational Communication

We, along with several other scholars (e.g., Dolan, *et al.*, 2003; Goldspink & Kay, 2003; Lansing, 2003; Stacey, 2003), argue that human systems can be distinguished from all other natural complex systems because of the highly sophisticated level of communication. That is, the elementary process that constitutes the social domain as a special reality is the process of communication (Luhmann, 1995), and all social action can be defined as communication (Maturana & Varela, 1988).

There are broadly speaking two genres of paradigm of human communication. These can be illustrated by looking at the root of the English word "communication". The word comes from the Latin word "communicare", which means doing things together, sharing, participating. On the one hand, it means belonging, a connection, socializing, brotherhood ("communis: community"). On the other hand, the Latin word for "communication", "communicatio", denotes sending or distributing. Traditionally the communications of organizations has been seen primarily as an exchange of information and as a framework supporting this, and not as a form of organizational operations or community.

We can make a clear distinction between the two views. The process view ("communicatio") sees human communication as a mechanistic process and the interpretative view ("communicare") sees communication as a negotiation and exchange of meaning (see O'Sullivan, *et al.*, 1994; Fiske, 1990). The process view is closely connected to the traditional organizational communication process models, which, in turn, have their roots in traditional information theory. The Mathematical Theory of Communication of Shannon and Weaver (1949) is an early attempt to extend the applicability of information theory into human communication and it has been one of the most important and authoritative in the development of later communication process models and theories. It models communication on a process in which a source encodes and then transmits a message along a channel. Message is received and decoded at its destination upon which it produces an effect. Regardless of the model's omissions and deficiencies in relation to human communication, it has remained as perhaps the longest-lasting description of the communication process (Bowman & Targowski, 1987).

The information theory has had notable contributions to the study of communications including the measurement of the quantity of information by bits and the understanding of entropy as applied to communication. However, the model is, by nature, a reductionistic sender-centered model and a straight derivative of the so-called linear main paradigm of human communication: A -> B = X, or in other words A communicates something to B, with X resulting. Thayer (1978) stated almost 30 years ago that "...several Western communication models and theories are based on this model, when first we strip from it surface understanding and development whose purpose is to differentiate the models from each other. No matter what type of communication we talk about, this model directs - whether in its appearance or by its support - a large part of research and literature. It also determines how we relate to everyday communication - the model is linear, mechanical, atomic, reminiscent of algebraic formulas and appears official" (18).

Furthermore, information theory is associated with the balancing and strengthening of a system's structure. Accordingly, new information is also in the first place centered on the strengthening of already existing information structures. The amount of information is taken as given; due to inevitable disturbances it can only diminish (Jantsch, 1980). Communication process models are linear, predictable, rational, and part of the framework of positivistic organizational framework. Stochastic errors and human irrational actions are abstract explanations of deviations from the linear model and most often they seem to be the receiver's mistake. The process view of communication treats leadership as monologue that "conceives of members as largely surrendering their right to make meanings by virtue of their employment contract within a hierarchical organization" (Fairhurst, 2001: 387). From this view, leaders are "the primary architects of meaning through such vehicles as an organizational vision, mission, and statement of values" (387).

Interpretative View on Communication

The interpretative view of human communication concentrates on the relationship between fundamental components necessary for meaning to emerge. Messages, people as members of cultures, and reality interacts so as meaning can be produced. Accordingly, the interpretative view of organizational communications is based on the assumption that communication is a prerequisite for all social life, and that human socialness is a prerequisite for communications. No one can be without communicating. The point of it is the formation and preservation of a common, well-framed, and agreeable cultural entity. Communication is not directed toward the extension of messages in space but toward the maintenance of society in time; not the act of imparting information but the representation of shared beliefs. From the interpretive view, communication can be defined as a process, in which a common meaning structure is created, reformed and regenerated. Communication portrays the core of culture, renews or represents it, and strengthens cultural unity (Carey, 1975). Communications is unity and community; what is central is maintaining this community over time and renewing shared beliefs. Communication is a symbolic process that produces, maintains, repairs and transforms reality. It should be noted that, in addition to strengthening community, communications can also destroy it.

Organizational communication differs from general notions of communication in terms of the complexity of the context and human dimensions (Conrad, 1994). An organization's communications relations are at the same time similar to and different from other social relations. People communicate with others within organizations because they like each other, but also because goals require communications relations. This notion of communications emphasizes how communications is a question of relations between people. Organization's members interact with messages and realities that are constantly being interpreted in such a way that enables the production of meanings and thus common understanding.

Organizational communication can, thus, be defined as a process through which people, acting together, create, sustain, and manage meanings through the use of verbal and nonverbal signs and symbols within a particular organizational context (Aula, 1996, 1999, 2000). This definition follows the interpretive view of human communication (Carey, 1975) and is based on the fundamentals of the social construction of reality (Berger & Luckmann, 1966) according to which an organization is socially constructed among its members and this construction takes place, not just with, but also within communication

(Deetz, 1986). Meaning factors of organizational communication need to be considered to be able to understand organization as a human community (Weick, 1995). Communication is used to create shared realities about an organization that reflect its members' interpretations about the organization itself and its environment. For example, an organization's culture reflects the organization's shared realities and how these realities create and transform the organization's events. Communication essentially includes the subjective and appraising reactions of an organization's members to the organization's communicational events (Aula, 2000). For example, from the conflict point of view, work units are likely to develop unique conflict cultures, in which people have common beliefs about appropriate conflict behavior (De Dreu, *et al.*, 2004). Aula (1999, 2000) has argued that those beliefs are dictated by human communication, and thus, the central task of conflict management is to figure out the underlying interaction processes of communication and cultural structures in these units. Encoding and decoding messages is not possible until the sender and receiver share a common language and culture.

Our definition accepts that communication is a process, but the outcome is not the transmission of messages but production of meaning. In general, people communicate in order to share information and experiences. "Sharing" implies that we want to convey something that we know or think we know to others. We strive to convey information. In addition, our communications strive to make information and its experience something communal, something that is shared. In addition to conveying information, we build knowledge. To be precise, no kind of sense can be made of anything without sufficiently shared meanings. The general forms taken by human communication are language, speech, writing, gestures and expressions. According to its definition, communication can be interactive, purposeful or purposeless. It can also be verbal or non-verbal, bilateral or multilateral. Sharing information and experiences within organizations can also be a reason to communicate.

As we can see, our interpretative definition borrows elements from the process view. In fact, the interpretative approach of organizational communication does not contradict the notion of communication as a process (Smith, 1972). At one level, communication is a physical activity (Buder, 1996), but it always includes the idea of meaning making and -processing (Carey, 1975).

The Dual Function of Organizational Communication

An organization is not a static monolith system of cultures, but a constitution of multiple segmented and often overlapping culture structures (e.g., Boje, *et al.*, 1996) and its communications are a diverse, dynamic series of overlapping interactions in which meanings are created, changed, and exchanged. The communication processes are determined by the premise of the parties that concerns communication, which is based on Goffman's (1983) idea of "interaction order." According to Kovačić's (1994) interpretation of the Goffman's concept, the social interaction is a mixture between customary verbal and nonverbal communication routines, which on one hand reproduces the cultural, financial and political aspects of social order and on the other, produces new unexpected consequences and interpretations. Interaction is a micro level world, where strategic, instrumental, and spontaneous as well as unconventional communicative actions occur. In addition, interaction is order without rules. Local contextually situated language games or communication practices are based on heterogeneous systems of rules. These rules produce separate, incommensurable and/or loosely interrelated social realms as well as constant transfer of discourses – movement from one language game to another.

It is important to note, that especially in organizational settings, communication can be argued to carry a dual function (Aula, 1996, 1999, 2000), which, in turn, has a meaning for social complexity view on conflict management. To justify this argument, we explicate a novel conception about dual function of communication. In general, the central purpose of communication is to keep the organization up-to-date, to renew the common beliefs, and to make sense of the complex, unordered meaning structures (e.g., Weick, 1995). Nevertheless, communication can also break the existing meaning-making structures and create intentional disintegration, which can foster organization emergent properties. Thus, communication includes both integrating and dissipative elements, with which one can create or reduce the diversity of the existing meaning structures, and, consequently, increase the chance of emergence of new meanings in the unfolding interaction (Aula, 1996, 1999). When defining dual function, we build on the conceptual ideas of Aula's (1996, 1999, 2000) development of the theory of dynamic organizational communication.

In relation to organizational transformation, the theory follows the idea of dissipative systems (Prigogine, 1976; Jantsch, 1980) and dissipative structure model on organizational transformation (Leifer, 1989) according to which change emerges when internal or external conditions of the system are unstable enough to throw the system from its balance. In transformation, the existing form and structure of the system break and seek new forms and constructions.

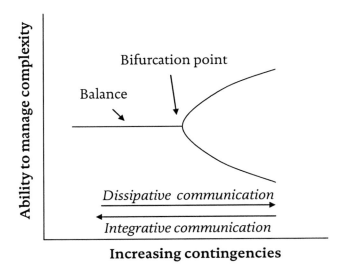

Figure 1 *The Emergence of Dissipative Systems (Leifer, 1989) Complemented with the Dual Function of Organizational Communication (Aula, 1999).*

Despite this seemingly disordered condition, the system retains its internal capacity to be restructured and this restructuring will take place after change periods when it is faced with far-from-equilibrium conditions (Leifer, 1989).

According to the dissipative structure model, the growing structural instabilities of the system caused by the turbulence of the environment, the loss of control, or the lack of resources creates a critical state or condition that could be characterized as the breaking of the symmetry or the bifurcation point of the system. Prigogine and Stengers (1984) argue that the bifurcation point gives the system an opportunity to adapt itself to the new demands of the environment. The conditions of the bifurcation point provide the opportunity for the creation of the new dynamic order, which makes the dealing of the growing uncertainty potentially successful. The behavior of the organization is directed by the human operation, which makes it possible to rise to the challenge caused by bifurcation instabilities (Leifer, 1989). From our point of view, this "human operation" is synonymous to "human communication," which, in turn is the essence of leadership.

The core idea of the dual function of organization's communications is that communication is characterized by two simultaneous counter forces (Figure 1). On the one hand, communication integrates organization's forms and structures by reducing contingencies and thus increasing organizations ability to manage complexity. On the other hand, communications destroy existing forms and structures, breaking old and creating new ones. This communication's dissipative quality increases contingencies and decrease organization's abilities to control complexity. If an organization's goal is, for example, shared understanding (e.g., "balance in meaning structure"), effective integrated communications are a tool that the organization can use to handle outside pressure for transformation. Following the idea of organization as meaning structures this could be achieved, for example, by aiming at literal, intentional, controlled, and monophonic communication. Dissipative communications work the other way, deliberately increasing organizational disorder by breaking down the existing meaning structures. The ways of doing this is diffusing rich, metaphoric, impulsive, and polyphonic communication content. This can work favorably for an organization, but also harmfully, leading the organization down the wrong path of development at the bifurcation point. However, controlled disorder can sometimes be the objective. Order in itself is not necessarily advantageous for organizations, nor disorder disadvantageous. Thus, according to dual function, communications can be used to control an organization's structuring, as well as its diversity, and we argue that human communication plays a vital role in both determining and maintaining the complexity of the organization (Aula, 1996, 1999).

In sum, our conceptualization about the nature of communication and the concept of dual structure stems from the social complexity view on organizational communication. Instead of a mechanistic process, communication is conceptualized as a negotiation and an exchange of meaning (see Fiske, 1990; O'Sullivan, et al., 1994). Similar to Ruben's (1978) notions, communication is viewed as "a systemic or transactional process involving the transformation of symbols as a means by which living things organize with one another and their environment" (Ruben, 1978: 203). This definition does concur in part with the notion that communication is a process, yet the "outcome" is not the linear transmission of information, but the nonlinear production of interpretations (Aula, 1999). From this perspective, the management of organizational conflict is closely interconnected with the conceptualization of an organization's communication systems and meaning structures. In particular, communication can be either integrating or dissipative and it can be used to create or reduce the diversity of the meaning structures. Leadership, from the interpretative view, is dialogic. That is, meanings are co-constructed: "[t]here is no leader or constituent, only individuals engaged in a dialogue of conversing and listening" (Fairhurst, 2001: 388). As opposed to the deterministic and positivistic process view, "the individual takes an active, constructive role in creating knowledge through language and communication. Individuals are neither passive not reactive, but intentional and reflexively self-aware" (385).

Social Complexity, Communication and Conflict

From the social complexity perspective, conflict is considered as a natural phenomenon of complex human systems. Needs and desires of organizational agents "are not homogeneous and, therefore, their goals and behaviors are likely to conflict" (Rouse, 2000: 144). The social complexity view on conflict and communication opposes the idea that conflict situations are about false, wrong, or errors in communication, and, instead posits that they are, by definition, communicative events. The meaning of a conflict is co-developed by the members of the organization; the social domain of conflict is created, maintained, and changed through communicative action. From the interpretive perspective, conflict and communication are co-developed, "thus communication is not an input, moderator, or mediator of outcomes; it becomes the conflict itself" (Putnam, 2006: 18). Conflict is critical in renewing organizations, as it is an antecedent and an outcome of diversity in organizations. From this perspective, local interactions and communication processes have significant effects on the management of the organization; conflicts emerge from micro diversity in organizations and bring forth the differences between the agents' opinions, logics, and worldviews (Aula, 1999).

Essentially, the social complexity view highlights the role of communication in conflict management, as well as the role of conflict management in the survival and success of the whole organization; conflict management is not merely a mandatory subtask of the organizational leadership, but rather, an integral part of the overall management of an organization. As opposed to the monologic view on leadership that prohibits treating meaning as "contested or problematic," leadership as dialogue emphasizes co-construction, according to which "talk is essentially contested where contestation is not just about what exists, but includes competing perspectives, future possibilities, and prescriptions for action" (Fairhurst, 2001: 387). In other words, the aim of leadership is not simply keeping peace or providing answers, but to create the conditions "in which followers' behaviors can produce structure and innovation" (Marion &

	Complexity view	**Conventional view**
Purpose	Creation of suitable conditions	Reduction of conflicts
Control	Total control not possible	Conflicts can be controlled by a neutral authority
Styles	Fluctuating	Stable
Outcomes	Unpredictable; Disproportionate	Predictable; Proportionate
Nature of communication	Meaning construction	Sending and Receiving messages
Direction of communication	Towards order and disorder	Towards order
Leadership	Leadership as dialogue	Leadership as monologue

Table 1 *Comparison of complexity and conventional views on conflict management, communication, and leadership*

Uhl-Bien, 2001: 394). In the following, the traditional conventions of purpose, control, outcomes, and styles are reinterpreted from the social complexity perspective.

Conventions Reinterpreted

Purpose. The purpose of conflict management in complex human organization is a creation of suitable conditions, instead of the traditional view of direct and systematic reduction of the existing conflicts. This perspective does not deny the need for conflict resolution function, but instead, promotes conditions where the forces that are causing conflicts and forces that are enforcing harmony are in balance.

Control

No one is in charge of conflict interaction and outcomes. In other words, all organizational agents and not just those whose official capacity labels them as "leaders" are components of the system and, consequently, parts of the whole. One cannot step outside conflict interaction and directly influence it; it is only possible to change something and wait for the consequences.

Styles

In contrast to the conventional view, there is no superior management approach to conflicts, because organizations and its agents go through a dynamic change due to constant variations in internal and environmental conditions. From this perspective, conflict style should be considered as a flexible and dynamic approach that should vary according to the situational demands, rather than being a predetermined constant.

Outcomes

Conflict outcomes are unpredictable and disproportionate to the initial conditions. Initial conditions, in turn, cannot be determined to the accuracy that permits the prediction, nor production of desired outcomes. Conflicts are not viewed merely as isolated events that have consequences for only the active conflict participants, but instead, as complex systems that have potential to have an effect on the organization as a whole.

All in all, the assumptions rooted in the traditional views on conflict management and the assumptions rooted in the social complexity view differ drastically from each other (see Table 1 for comparison). These assumptions, in turn, are argued to have a fundamental effect on day-to-day management of conflicts in organizations.

Practical Implications

Assumptions about organizational behavior and conflict dynamics play a big role when leaders make decisions about their actions. The above notions about purpose, control, styles, and outcomes of conflict may seem frustrating in their ambiguousness, and to a certain degree they are. They require rethinking of one's assumptions about almost every aspect of organizational life. As opposed to the traditional approach, one cannot impose solutions on conflicts and get desired outcomes. Yet, as the formal leaders of organizations, managers need to, and are obliged to, do something to keep the organization running. In effect, from the social complexity perspective, one cannot not have an impact on organizational life. That is, organizational agents exercise control continually, because "[i]n our interaction with each other we constrain and enable each other, and that is control" (Stacey, 2003: 37). Yet, the control cannot be forced directly to get planned outcomes, but instead, one needs to funnel the energy indirectly to facilitate the creation of suitable conditions. Keeping this in mind, we offer a few suggestions on how managers can put these ideas in use.

Start From Within

Managers play a key role in the creation of emergent conditions in organizations, as they are responsible for the creation and translation of symbols in organizations (Deetz, 1986; Weick, 1995) and the flows of information (Choo, 1998; Nonaka, 1985, 1988). Thus, it is essential for managers to start from themselves, carefully examining one's own assumptions and perceptions of organizational dynamics, especially the beliefs concerning conflict management, i.e., purpose, control, styles, and outcomes. On floor level, this could mean a shift away from the reliance on "best practices", total control, and conflict resolution to embracing exploration, trial-and-error, and self-organizing properties of human life.

Look Beyond the Surface

Social complexity perspective considers conflict as a continuous and polymorphic phenomenon, as opposed to the traditional view of conflict as episodic and isolated event, of which the manifest part is only a small portion. From this perspective, managers should pay attention to organizational conflicts beyond the visible and try to answer questions, such as what issues are in play; who are the other stakeholders in addition to the active disputants; what benefits and/ or damages could this incident have for the larger whole; where and what is the origin of this conflict; and how deeply am I involved in the mesh of events? Questions like these help getting a deeper and more critical understanding of the phenomenon than approaching the issue with the habitual, standard way. One should be especially cautious if one thinks of a conflict as a repetition of the old, which, from social complexity view, is not feasible. In fact, signs of conflict ought to raise the level of consciousness every time; however, managers operating from the conventional perspective, which emphasizes proportionality and linear causality, feel the need to be alert only in conflicts that appear big and significant on the surface, thus not paying much attention to the smaller conflicts. Our notion is consistent with Langer's (1989) concept of mindfulness, which emphasizes the importance of "alertness and activity that relies on information from current situation to determine behavior" (Canary & Lakey, 2006: 189) instead of relying on past experiences and precedents in conflict interaction.

Pay Attention to Communication

Good communication skills cannot be defined unequivocally. That is, from the interpretive approach, conflict and communication are co-developed (Putnam, 2006); thus, there is no a set of best practices with which one could excel under all conditions. Yet, there are certain factors of human behavior that can be developed in order to become a better facilitator of favorable conflict contexts. In particular, we stress the importance of realizing the dual function of communication. From our view, conflict management is essentially the act of communication by balancing dissipative and integrative qualities of communication. Traditionally, conflict management has promoted the use of integrative qualities of communication, such as reactivity, control, and monophony. Conflicts have been viewed as negative aspects of organizational functioning that need to be resolved with reason and careful planning. Accordingly, we recognize the crucial role of integrative communication in keeping organizations in their preferred path, especially during crises. However, to keep the organization in move, one should not forget the dissipative aspects of communication. Dissipative communication is effective when the conflict situation is stuck and there is a need for innovative and creative problem solving. According to Stacey (2003), "... novelty and creativity come about through the amplification of difference" (31). In their study of brainstorming techniques, Nemeth, *et al.* (2004) found that instructions that encouraged criticizing stimulated more creative ideas. They concluded that "normative environment that permits - even encourages - debate, dissent and criticism may liberate people to freely generate ideas" (367). In an ideal scenario, all members of the system cultivate positive criticism, debate, diversity, and a free flow of information and conflicts are perceived as a source of innovation, creativity, and development (Nemeth, *et al.*, 2004).

Influence Indirectly

Managers often find it difficult to decide when to intervene in conflict inter-action. From social complexity perspective, habitual intervention should not, however, be the main concern of organizational leadership. Self-organizing sys-tems, such as individual conflict interactions, possess self-correcting proper-ties and managers have a tendency to get in the way of that process (Anderson, 1999). For conflict managers, this means giving up the belief of being in com-mand of organizational conflicts and, instead, paying attention to the contextual factors that funnel the conflict interaction, such as maintenance of relationships, and facilitation of interaction. For example, in a conflict between two employ-ees, instead of imposing a solution, the manager can serve as a facilitator: intro-ducing a set of simple rules that promotes open dialogue, respect for the other party, confidentiality, and active listening. Essentially, this requires managers to rethink their role in organizations: a person who sees oneself as a coach or a facilitator approaches difficult situations quite differently from one that sees oneself as an officer or a judge.

Empower Employees

As opposed to a traditional systems perspective, leaders may not impose con-trolled change on an organization. Instead of implementing comprehensive change programs, the suitable conditions emerge through the interaction of various agents in the organization. Leaders can help in the process by actively in-volving employees in change processes, not merely as followers of orders, but as creators of the new order. Anderson, *et al.* (2003) examined the relationship be-tween emergence-facilitating nursing home management practices and resident outcomes and found that increases in communication openness, participation in decision-making, and relationship-oriented leadership, as well as decreases in formalization in nursing homes contributed to better outcomes. Empowering employees is important especially in the movement towards a suitable conflict culture. Employees should be involved in the creation of new symbols and sto-ries, and encouraged to voice their dissent and opposing opinions in the process. This perspective stresses a shift away from the formal and managerially focused approach, considers conflict management as a joint venture, and encourages training and learning. Ultimately, this means a more comprehensive, proactive management of conflicts than the conventional view on conflict management entails.

Conclusion

Conflicts pose a realistic challenge and a threat to modern organizations in many ways. A conflict that seems as a minor, isolated incident may grow out of proportion and have major effects in terms of legal expenses, lost of workforce, and decline in organization's reputation. So far, few approaches have taken into account the growing complexity and the nonlinear nature of or-ganizational conflict in communication research. The same applies also to prac-tice. Nicotera and Dorsey (2006) note that majority of the conflict management training is relying heavily on the conflict styles approach. Our purpose is not to devalue the body of knowledge that has dominated and accumulated during the past few decades; however, it is our intention to challenge some of the assumptions that have had a strong influence in the past research and, consequently, the practice of every-day conflict management in organizations.

Specifically, our aim was to further the nonlinear view on organizational conflict communication by examining the phenomenon through the lenses of social complexity. We argued that conflict management is, essentially, communicative action that appreciates the integrative and dissipative qualities of communication. As a result, we proposed a set of implications to conflict management. The purpose was not to present a detailed set of practices, but, instead, to provide tentative ideas on what the complexity view on conflict and communication has to offer to the management of organizational conflicts. In particular, the management of organizations can employ these views by challenging one's own assumptions, being more attentive and thorough in the examination of organizational conflicts, paying attention to the constructive aspects of conflict, intervening in conflicts indirectly, and empowering employees to transform the conflict culture.

All in all, our take on conflict management is in accordance with the dialogic view on leadership that emphasizes holism and interdependence as opposed to the monologic view that accentuates the role of leaders in affecting organizational outcomes. In fact, we would like to regard this approach more as "conflict leadership" rather than "conflict management," where "management" refers to "the nuts and bolts of detailed operations" and "leadership" to "the fitness, innovation, and the future of organizations" (Marion & Uhl-Bien, 2001: 406). Also, our intention is to shift away from the individually and managerially focused tradition of conflict management (Nicotera & Dorsey, 2006) by drawing attention to "the often indirect, catalytic process within organizations – which might be performed by people in rotation or in tandem" instead of falsely signaling that "there are individual and positional factors that strictly distinguish leaders from others" (Schneider & Somers, 2006: 356). The social complexity view does not ignore the micro-level processes; on the contrary, recognizes the importance of actively involved leadership, "for such leadership can help enable complex behavior" (Marion & Uhl-Bien, 2001: 396). So far, organizational conflict has been examined on the systemic level mainly by scholars of law and business, however, we maintain that the terrain is favorable to, and could benefit greatly from, communication perspectives.

Finally, social complexity offers various intriguing paths for the scholars of conflict and communication. So far, the literature on theory and practice is very scarce, which leaves the doors open in many directions. One of the strengths of this approach is the potential for multilevel examination of conflict. According to Oetzel, *et al.* (2006), one of the biggest challenges of future conflict scholars is to find and develop theories that integrate the research of different conflict contexts in which conflict occurs: interpersonal, organizational, community, and intercultural/international. The focus of this paper is on organizational conflict; however, the framework implemented here is argued to be useful on various contexts.

CHAPTER TWENTY-ONE
LEADERS' DETECTION OF PROBLEMATIC SELF-ORGANIZED PATTERNS IN THE WORKPLACE

Pamela Buckle Henning & Sloane Dugan

Organizational leaders have been charged to remove constraints to productivity, innovation, and creativity in their workplaces. One such constraint can be self-organized patterns of organizational behavior: an unconscious, emergent dynamic occurring in complex systems. Self-organized patterns can deplete organizations by diverting human functioning away from organizational behaviors that create and sustain the productivity, innovation, and creativity possible in complex systems. The organizational literature has been silent on an important matter with respect to such patterns: how leaders can become aware of the self-organized patterns that emerge in corporate settings. This research investigated how a group of leaders detect self-organized patterns in their workplaces. Using early stage grounded theory research methods, the study identified conceptual categories and propositions pertaining to the self-organized pattern detection process. Leaders' openness to surprise emerged as a welcoming cognitive condition creating a readiness to explore the identity of unanticipated, autonomous workplace dynamics. To discern such dynamics as coherent (i.e., patterned), leaders employed an action strategy of bracketing intended coherence. They then sought to detect patterns in their organizations' behaviors with a cognitive action strategy of suspending normative appraisal and a verbal strategy of non-evaluative description. Leader entrainment emerged as an intervening condition that influenced leaders' capacity to discern self-organized workplace patterns.

Pamela Buckle Henning, who received her Ph.D. from the University of Calgary, is Assistant Professor, Department of Management, Marketing, and Decision Sciences in the School of Business at Adelphi University, Garden City, NY. Her research examines tacit dimensions of organizational life: in particular, how individuals, corporations, professions, and industries operate under the influence of complex, unrecognized patterns of behavior; and how managers can become aware of such patterns in order to more effectively lead their corporations and serve their stakeholders. She has published both conceptual and empirical aspects of this work in *Systems Research and Behavioral Science*, the *International Journal of Project Management*, the *Journal of Organizational Transformation and Social Change*, and various conference proceedings.

Sloane Dugan, Ph.D, is an Associate Professor of Human Resources and Organizational Dynamics at Haskayne School of Business, University of Calgary in Calgary, Alberta Canada. For over three decades, Sloane Dugan's activities have focused on refining an action research process with persons, teams, organizations, and communities in North America, Asia and Europe. This action research approach enables them to create a vision of a good quality of life for themselves, marshal the resources necessary to pursue this vision, and develop the attitudes and skills necessary to move toward their vision. He is a Diploma candidate at the International School of Analytical Psychology in Switzerland, examining how persons' mental models influence their personal and professional lives and learning how to assist persons to more consciously make informed decisions.

Introduction

The research presented in this article investigates how a group of leaders detected self-organized behavioral patterns in their workplaces. To understand why detecting such patterns is both challenging and useful to leaders, we begin with Marion and Uhl-Bien's (2001) examination of "complex leadership." We extend their discussion by highlighting the unconscious dimension of self-organized "correlation," and the human needs that motivate its emergence. We take the controversial position that rather than always signifying a positive event for an organization, self-organized behavioral patterns can also act to constrain organizational creativity and innovation. Hence, we argue that self-organized pattern detection is an imperative skill for complex leaders wishing to enable employees to work through such constraints.

A note about our use of the term "self-organization" is in order, since we are going against the grain of the positive bias associated with this term in organizational literature that has been inspired by complexity theory. There is nothing inherent in the idea of self-organizing processes which mandates that such processes lead to a beneficial result in workplaces. Indeed, within the scientific context of the study of complex system where the idea of self-organization originates, self-organization is a neutral valued concept. Here, though, we are positing spontaneously arising, self-organizing processes which have the deleterious effect of stultifying innovation, creativity, and productivity – hallmarks of effective corporate functioning.

We label such processes as "self-organizing" according to typical definitions from complexity theory, such as Goldstein's (2001) definition: "A process in a complex system whereby new emergent structures, patterns, and properties arise without being externally imposed on the system. Not controlled by a centralized, hierarchical 'command and control' center..." (p. 270). Although the use of the term in organizational literature is customarily biased towards the positive, we hold that such a meaning is just that: "biased," since in research domains like the Benard System, the Belousov-Zhabotinsky reaction, or artificial life, self-organizing processes do not hold either a positive or negative value judgement but are an indexical way of pointing to novel patterns that emerge without seemingly being programmed into the system ahead of time.

There are no theories currently existing that either explain or demonstrate how leaders may identify self-organized patterns emerging in workplace behavior which may be serving as hindrances to organizational success. To begin theory development on this topic, we used early stage grounded theory methods to identify conceptual categories and propositions regarding the self-organized pattern detection processes used by leaders who participated in this research.

Unconscious Correlation: Self-Organized Patterns in the Workplace

Complexity research offers this insight: amidst the fast pace and myriad details inherent in daily organizational life, unplanned patterns of organizational behavior arise in systems (e.g., departments, corporations, and industries). When a system "self-organizes" (Jantsch, 1980), system participants coalesce into repetitive patterns of interaction (Lorenz, 1962; Ruelle, 1991), a correlated sharing of particular behaviors (Marion, 1999). Marion and Uhl-Bien (2001) define the complex dynamic of "correlation... as the emergence of common understanding in interacting social systems" (p. 396). In a complex organizational system, the presence of "common understanding" may not be as straightforward as it initially seems.

Letiche (2000) has made the provocative observation that neither theoretical nor empirical reasons exist to support a belief "that consciousness precedes self-organization" (p. 550). Letiche's assertion suggests that shared, yet *non*-conscious (i.e., unconscious) understanding is one dimension of complexity's correlation dynamic[1]. Marion and Uhl-Bien (2001) explain another dimension: human needs. They posit that human desires and needs provide motivation for correlation to emerge. Considerable research (which we will survey below) suggests that, both individually and collectively, people possess desires of which they are unaware. Such research suggests that it is quite possible for groups of individuals to unconsciously share a "common understanding" of their unconsciously held needs. Correlated behavior in complex systems can be motivated by commonly shared, yet unrecognized, human needs and desires.

Arguments for the influence of unconscious factors on group behavior come from several streams of research. Freudian psychologists argue that people, individually and collectively, possess drives and emotions that they seek to repress (Laplanche & Pontalis, 1973). Such repressed energies affect human behavior in identifiable, patterned ways. This Freudian perspective suggests that self-organized patterns can be difficult to detect because neither pattern participants nor observers want to acknowledge the instinctual, emotional content they may contain. Some Jungian psychologists (e.g., Conforti, 1999; Mattoon, 1984) argue that unconscious dimensions of human psychology actively seek expression through individual and group behavior. This Jungian perspective suggests that the particular ways an organization self-organizes is a sophisticated systems language expressing that organization's unconscious desires and needs. Systems scholars have argued that self-organized patterns may express an organization's deeply-held (perhaps barely conscious) perceptions about itself. For instance, Maturana and Varela (1980) have argued that such patterns reflect a system's beliefs about its identity, including how and to what extent that identity may be under threat. Identity is born of past experience. Cilliers's

---

1 In self-organization, non-consciousness is present, in that none of the individual system members are necessarily aware of macro-level self-organized patterns in which they are participating. In self-organization, understanding is also present, in that the system exhibits a unified, "collective intelligence" (Sulis, 1997) or "mind" (Jantsch, 1980) capable of coordinating system members in intricate ways.

(1998) claim that self-organized patterns reflect a system's collective memory suggests that these patterns reflect ways in which the failures, successes, and struggles of a workplace's distant past may continue to exert unrecognized influence on present-day behavior. What these various perspectives hold in common is a view that self-organization works autonomously in relation to leaders' plans. Self-organized behavior patterns emerge and maintain themselves without permission, intention, or reflection (Bella, 1997; Forrester, 1968; Kim, 1992; Senge, 1990; Stacey, 1993; 1995).

In the workplace, there's no doubt that unconscious human needs may operate autonomously of corporate vision statements and strategies. Such needs can produce interaction patterns yielding unexpected organizational behaviors, events, and outcomes (Mathews, *et al.*, 1999). Researchers and practitioners have long used human guile (Williamson, 1973) and human error (Perrow, 1999) to explain unplanned organizational outcomes. Both explanations locate the cause of unexpected workplace behavior in individuals. Both explanations fuel leaders' interest in getting to the bottom of unexpected corporate events by locating blame at the level of individual actors. Self-organization offers an alternative explanation. Individual people do not initiate or cause self-organization; systems do. The organized patterns of behavior that emerge in self-organization are properties of systems, not individuals (Stacey, 1995). When self-organized patterns drive unexpected workplace behavior, the search for individual culprits, covert plots, or human effort will fail to account for past organizational difficulties and fail to prevent their happening again.

The phenomenon of correlated human interaction that occurs naturally in complex systems creates spontaneously self-organized patterns of organizational behavior. These patterns are a product of shared understandings, including unconsciously shared understandings about emotions, drives, needs, and self-perceptions that comprise an organization's unrecognized liabilities and strengths.

Unconscious Correlation: Constraints to Organizational Innovation and Creativity

Why should leaders be concerned with self-organized workplace dynamics motivated by unconscious human needs? To begin, the "new science" of complexity itself compels new thinking about the role of leaders in organizations. Marion and Uhl-Bien (2001; 2003) have argued that leaders should refocus traditional efforts to control organizations in favour of indirect leadership behaviors, such as "learning to capitalize on interactive dynamics" and "foster[ing] interactive conditions that enable a productive future" (2001: 394), "creating the conditions that enable productive... future states" (2001: 319). Authors such as Thietart and Forgues (1995) suggest that "the greatest creativity, productivity, and innovation comes out of people who are provided opportunities to innovate and network" (Marion & Uhl-Bien, 2001:410). Opportunities to create new network structures can act as transformational catalysts for organizations. However, regardless of the opportunities leaders provide for employees to innovate and network, when self-organized behavioral patterns are driven by unconscious factors, such patterns may serve to constrain employees' abilities to interact in novel and productive ways.

Even well-educated, contemporary knowledge workers can be "imprisoned" (Morgan, 1997) by human needs that compel people to enact behaviors originating in childhood or even more primitive stages of human development. Morgan argues that people in organizations share certain basic human needs and ways of coping with them[2] through "common unconscious consent" (p. 233). This unconscious consent can manifest itself through the emergence of self-organized groups of people collectively expressing unrecognized or unwanted drives, emotions, and desires that oppose the expected rationality of organizational life (Denhardt, 1981). People's efforts to hide or deny unconscious human needs consume considerable human energies (Singer, 1994) that remain unavailable to leadership initiatives aimed at fostering creativity, innovation, and the achievement of organizational objectives.

The kind of self-organized patterns we are examining, then, can deplete organizations by diverting human functioning away from organizational behaviors that create and sustain the corporate productivity possible in complex systems. The genesis of such patterns in deeply human needs may well explain the observations of complexity scholars (e.g., Thietart & Forgues, 1995; Cilliers, 1998), that self-organized patterns can persist, stubbornly resisting changes in the organization's external or internal environment, including leaders' active attempts to alter groups' behaviors. The desire people have to keep certain drives and desires hidden may well explain why self-organized patterns manifest indirectly, through symptoms such as task-related conflicts (Jehn, 1997) or seemingly anomalous events that are unrelated to an organization's espoused goals (Kim, 1992; Senge, 1990). Meanwhile, the longer leaders fail to recognize that such behaviors and events are patterned – the longer people remain unaware of the unconscious content unifying self-organized behaviors and events – the stronger the pattern may become (Bella, 1997), drawing increasing numbers of unwitting participants like "sleepwalking actors" (Lichtenstein, 1995) into self-organized configurations of behavior.

Numerous theories offer suggestions about the role of leaders. Among them is the view that leaders should help individuals and groups to work through the conflicting demands and constraints of organizational life (Greenleaf, 1977). We propose that one important category of constraint in complex organizations is the self-organized behavioral pattern in which we are interested. As we have seen, such a pattern can be motivated by needs of which the pattern's own participants are unaware, and can absorb employees' collective energies, rendering them inaccessible to organizations and their leaders. It stands to reason that leaders and employees alike would find it easier to work through self-organized constraints to organizational productivity if they could detect the patterns inhibiting this productivity. Just as physicians can more effectively prescribe a

---

2 Examples of unconscious content that can imprison groups in counterproductive behavior patterns include unconsciously held views toward gender and sexuality (Foucault, 1979; Freud, 1962), concerns about death (Becker, 1973), and defenses against fear or anxiety (Bion, 1959).

Construction	Financial markets	Natural resources
Counselling	Health care	Pharmaceuticals
Education	Insurance	Social services
Executive recruiting	International diplomacy	Software design

Table 1 *Industries Represented by Study Participants*

medical intervention when they know with some precision the health situation a patient is facing, leaders can better support work groups in working through the constraints of a counterproductive pattern when they can detect with some clarity the self-organized dynamics driving that behavior.

A central dilemma of the unconscious correlation of behaviors in complex systems is managers' ability to detect the self-organized patterns that result. The dilemma is one of awareness and understanding. It is an epistemological dilemma, since it is about a capacity for *knowing*[3]. Pragmatically, the unconsciousness of some organizational correlation constrains leaders' ability to create conditions for corporate creativity and innovation. No theories exist to explain how organizational leaders might detect the self-organized patterns of behavior that result from unconscious correlation in complex systems (Jackson, 2000; Stacey, 1993). If we are to heed Marion and Uhl-Bien's urging to "develop leaders' abilities to influence organizational behavior in ways that enhance the odds of productive futures" (2001: 403), research is needed to explain how leaders can detect unrecognized self-organized patterns in workplaces.

Research Question and Method

How can people in leadership roles detect self-organized patterns amidst the complexity of organizational dynamics? Complexity literature discusses the presence of self-organization as a dynamic that emerges in complex organizational systems. However, awareness of the existence of self-organized patterns is of little use to a leader who does not understand how to detect them when they emerge. Up to this point, scant organizational research has addressed self-organized pattern detection; when a phenomenon has rarely been explored, grounded theory offers a means to generate theory that is both original and accurate (Brown & Eisenhardt, 1997). To advance the usefulness of self-organization theory for leaders, this grounded theory study examined processes used by leaders to perceive self-organized patterns operating in workplace settings.

Sampling and Data Collection Strategies

Our objective was to identify conceptual categories underlying the self-organized pattern detection processes of a variety of leaders. Thus, our research activities were governed by the search for sources of data that would exemplify and illustrate those processes. Patton (1990) describes such

---

3 Members of the complexity community have argued that epistemological concerns are among the "least well-represented" schools of thought in the current complexity literature (Richardson & Cilliers, 2001: 7).

an approach as "operational construct sampling." To aid in clarifying the conceptual categories that emerged, we employed "confirming and disconfirming cases" sampling (ibid.) in later data analysis stages of the study. To locate study participants who could provide examples of pattern detection, we employed criterion sampling in conjunction with snowball sampling. Together, operational construct sampling, sampling for confirming and disconfirming cases, criterion sampling, and snowball sampling were the four purposive sampling strategies (Miles & Huberman 1994; Patton 1990) used in this research.

Four criteria informed the selection of study participants. First, participants must have carried either formal or informal leadership roles within their organizations. Second, participants needed to have an awareness of self-organization as a dynamic that emerges in workplaces. The third criterion required study participants to have the ability to detect patterns in unplanned organizational behavior or events. Several considerations informed the researchers' assessments of who met this criterion. We eliminated from the study individuals who attributed unplanned organizational occurrences to human guile or mistakes. We sought leaders whose pattern detection abilities had enabled them to predict future organizational events with greater accuracy than others[4]. We sought leaders who had used pattern detection to resolve persistent organizational difficulties with greater success than previous attempts where an understanding of an underlying self-organized pattern was absent. Fourth, participants needed to be able to articulate processes they used to detect self-organized patterns. When prospective respondents could not articulate how they discerned workplace patterns, or could speak only in generalities (rather than offering specific, concrete examples), they were not included. Prospective study participants who did not meet all of these four criteria were not selected to participate in this research. Some of the initial study participants (who did meet all criteria) were identified at systems conferences, through their roles as keynote speakers. Others were observed discussing workplace pattern identification by the researchers at seminars (described below), and were then invited to participate in this study. At the end of every interview, we asked each study participant for recommendations of others who might have experiences of pattern identification to share with us – a "snowball sampling" technique (Patton 1990). We subjected each recommended study participant to these same selection criteria.

In total, the researchers identified 23 leaders who satisfied the criteria for participation in this study. Several study participants had varying degrees of affiliation with a US-based organization, Assisi Conferences and Seminars (ACS). This organization explores the use of complexity science and Jungian psychology to understand self-organized patterning in both physical and human systems. Several ACS members work actively, as leaders or consultants, detecting self-organized dynamics in therapeutic, organizational, and international set-

---

4 While Marion and Uhl-Bien (2001) have noted that the complex dynamic of correlation offers "a level of predictability on which leadership can operate" (p. 397), we suspect that, when a leader is unaware that a series of organizational behaviors and/or incidents are correlated, such powers of prediction are lessened.

Data Source	
Interviews with ACS-affiliated study participants	17 (74% of research subjects)
Interviews with non-ACS-affiliated study participants	6 (26% of research subjects)
Pattern Analysis Incidents	
Pattern analysis incidents (gathered in interviews)	40
Pattern analysis incidents (gathered by observation)	20

Table 2 *Study Data Summary*

tings. Of the people participating in this study, 74% had some affiliation with ACS. Another 26% had no affiliation or knowledge of that community. The snowball technique, conferences, and keynote speakers at business luncheons were sources of non-ACS-affiliated study participants meeting the four criteria. The 23 participants selected for inclusion in this study lived, worked, and identified self-organized workplace patterns in Australia, Canada, Italy, South America, and the United States. The industries in which they worked and used pattern detection varied widely, as indicated in Table 1.

Participants had diverse educational backgrounds. Most participants had one or more master's degrees. Five of them had doctoral degrees. Many participants held formal leadership roles within their organizations, in positions such as partner/owner, CEO, and vice president. Other participants held informal leadership roles as entrepreneurs, intrepreneurs, industry analysts, and consultants. Various Fortune 200 companies employed the participants of this study, as did the public sector and not-for-profit organizations.

Often, researchers sample a wide variety of research participants to minimize a study's limitations due to bias and to maximize the strength of generalizability claims. This study involved a variety of research participants for a different purpose: to collect a diverse array of pattern detection examples for the purpose of identifying theoretically robust conceptual categories about leaders' pattern detection processes. We wished to understand how certain leaders we had met were able to identify self-organized dynamics in the workplace. Thus, this research follows Weick's recommendation that researchers utilize "compelling exemplars" in management research (1999). Strictly speaking, this study's findings are substantive only to the population of workplace pattern analysts who participated in this research, as is typical with grounded theory studies (Goulding, 2002; Parry, 1998). However, the conceptual categories and propositions generated by this study emerged from a wide variety of leaders working in diverse organizations and industries, suggesting that the findings generated by this study would prove fruitful for future research.

Two forms of data yielded the pattern detection incidents required for this study: interviews and observation data. Semi-structured interviews were conducted in person and by telephone. In them, researchers sought to understand the contexts in which individual leaders attempted to identify self-organized dynamics, and the challenges they faced in doing so. Interview questions focused on eliciting narratives about incidents of workplace pattern detection in which study participants had engaged. For this study, a "pattern detection incident" was defined as the thought processes occurring between the moment when a participant noticed unexpected behaviors[5] and the moment when that participant perceived a pattern that accounted for those behaviors.

The researchers also secured opportunities to observe groups of participants engaged in pattern detection work. During this research, ACS seminars convened each year in the Pacific Northwest United States, the north-eastern United States, and Assisi, Italy. Several leaders involved in this study attended these meetings to discuss self-organized dynamics in their workplaces and enlist one another's help in understanding what patterns might account for cases of particularly perplexing organizational dynamics. The researchers attended eleven of these meetings, taking extensive field notes of participants' discussions and drafting analytical memos, as Miles and Huberman (1994) have recommended. The researchers' field notes recorded the questions that participants asked themselves and one another to understand what occurred in the cases, identifying which lines of analysis proved fruitful to participants and which did not. As the study progressed, the researchers' memos noted which pattern detection processes seemed similar to those identified earlier in the study, and which seemed new. Table 2 presents a summary of this study's data sources.

Data collection ran from November 2001 to August 2004, yielding 60 incidents of pattern detection. Together, interview transcripts, analytical memos, and field notes generated 21,560 lines of text for data analysis.

Data Analysis Strategies

The grounded theory method prescribes that data collection and analysis run concurrently (Glaser & Strauss, 1967). This "constant comparison" (ibid.) guided the identification of conceptual categories pertaining to leaders' identification of self-organized workplace patterns.

Shortly after beginning interviews and case observation, open coding (Strauss & Corbin, 1998) began. A researcher read interview transcripts and field notes, labelling passages with provisional concept names that described the processes study participants used (Swanson, 1986). The central question guiding this open coding phase was: "What category or property of a category does this incident indicate?" (Glaser, 1992: 39). Repeatedly answering this question surfaced new concepts and confirmed concept names identified in earlier transcripts. The qualitative data analysis software, Atlas.ti, assisted in tracking transcript and field data, and the growing list of category names.

The constant comparison of each new incident to previous ones surfaced converging lines of evidence (Yin, 1998) early in the process. Two data reduction strategies (Miles & Huberman, 1994) assisted the converging process. The first involved rewriting pattern detection incidents, distilling leaders' accounts

---

5 We discuss the importance of unexpected behaviors in the pattern detection process below.

into brief outlines of what occurred. The second involved drafting flow charts of each leader's pattern-detection processes. Both data reduction strategies provided new insights and refined the pattern-detection conceptual framework. After each round of data reduction, a return to the full-text versions of study participants' stories confirmed or disconfirmed the similarities detected.

Eisenhardt (1989) has observed that, while "convergent perceptions add to the empirical grounding" of a study, "conflicting perceptions keep [researchers] from premature closure" (p. 538). In the open coding phase of this study, data that contradicted categories (on the list) emerged from various sources. Some processes used by leaders associated with the ACS community differed from processes used by leaders outside that community. A single leader sometimes used different pattern-detection processes in different incidents. Sources of divergent data like these clarified limitations in existing conceptual categories and informed the continued search for additional, more broadly explanatory categories. As the study progressed, the researchers actively sought study participants who could offer diverging perspectives on pattern identification – a purposive sampling strategy Patton terms "confirming and disconfirming cases" sampling (1990). This sampling effort also included soliciting and analyzing examples of times when participants failed to successfully identify self-organized patterns in their places of work.

Numerous grounded theory paradigms exist that suggest possible relationships among the conceptual categories researchers might identify during the open coding process (Glaser, 1978). Locke (2001) has cautioned researchers against forcing their data into any such paradigm: "data has to earn its way into the framework rather than being predetermined [into it]" (p. 74). For the conceptual categories that emerged during this study, Strauss and Corbin's (1998) coding scheme that highlights "conditions", "strategic actions" and "intervening context" appeared most informative. Our readings of Kruglanski's "lay epistemics" research (1989) led us to refine Strauss and Corbin's generic concept of "conditions." Kruglanski argues that "welcoming cognitive conditions" are a structural feature of lay epistemics. Such conditions are necessary for people to make sense of circumstances; particular attitudes are conducive to a person's capacity to understand circumstances. Said differently, Kruglanski asserts that certain mental stances create a "welcoming" mindset wherein perplexing information can begin to make sense to a person. Refining Strauss and Corbin's "conditions" template with Kruglanski's "welcoming cognitive conditions was, we felt, an adaptation of a standard grounded theory paradigm that more accurately represented the interior, cognitive nature of a certain conceptual category this study generated[6]. Strauss and Corbin's coding template also includes "action strategies." In this study, certain conceptual categories representing particular leader decisions, thought processes, and verbalizations had emerged. We framed these as action strategies leaders used in self-organized pattern identification. Finally, Strauss and Corbin's coding scheme suggests that researchers may surface conceptual categories that act as "intervening conditions." Among the categories generated by data gathering, a certain condition involved dynam-

---

6 See section on "Openness to Surprise" below.

ics intrinsic to the phenomenon of self-organization itself which could either help or hinder leaders in identifying self-organized patterns[7]. Thus, we found Strauss and Corbin's "intervening conditions" to be an informative template for this study. Together, the generic coding templates of welcoming cognitive conditions, strategic actions, and intervening context offered a way to understand how the categories identified in this research relate to one another.

The researchers assessed the emerging framework for relevance in two ways. First, we ensured that the pattern-detection processes in all 60 incidents could be explained by the conceptual categories generated by this study. The goal was to build a framework sufficiently robust to account for all of the data. At times, the relevance of a particular concept was strengthened by revising its title to narrow or broaden its focus. At times, scant evidence for a category or a sparse understanding of its properties informed ongoing data collection. The second strategy for confirming relevance of the framework involved enlisting participant readers (Maxwell, 1998; Yin, 1998) twice in the data analysis process to offer comments and critique on the emerging pattern-detection framework. This strategy ensured that researchers' understanding of study participants' processes made sense to the participants themselves.

Data collection and analysis proceeded past the point when it appeared that each conceptual category was theoretically saturated, i.e., the point at which no new or different data were being found (Glaser & Strauss, 1967). At this stage, subsequent interviews and case observations became experiments in confirming the conceptual categories and proposed relationships among them. This stage of framework-testing follows Hyde's advice that research requires "an inductive stage followed by a deductive one" (2000: 84). It also confirmed that the study had yielded a "realistic range of topics that might be considered a complete description of what [was] studied" (Yin, 1998: 236).

Findings
Welcoming Cognitive Condition for Self-Organized Pattern Detection: Openness to Surprise

For the leaders who participated in this study, unexpected behaviors triggered the attempt to detect self-organized patterns. Unexpected behaviors in their workplaces caught leaders by surprise, attracting attention (Louis, 1980), producing cognitive dissonance (Festinger, 1957), and destabilizing the usefulness of previous frames of understanding and expectation. Such frame-breaking opened the potential for enlarging leaders' existing mental models about organizational behavior. The unexpected triggered leaders to try identifying self-organized dimensions of the workplaces they led.

Leaders' stories of self-organized pattern detection typically began with descriptions of ordinary corporate situations. In the first column of *Table 3*, we present paraphrased synopses of three such situations. One example involved a health care service provider whose work had earned the organization an excellent reputation. Another leader described a regularly-scheduled team-building

---

7 See section on "Entrainment" below.

Situation	Leader Responses
A service provider with a reputation for high quality health service delivery suddenly learns that certain clients have long deemed their relationship with this provider completely unsatisfactory. The provider, proud of its exceptional work in satisfying clients' needs, is shocked to learn that the services it considered top-notch "completely missed the mark" in satisfying this group's needs.	"I expected something else to happen. I catch myself saying, 'Who'd have expected them to behave that way!' And then I'm realizing that I'd had them locked into some kind of an expectation that they'd respond [to the services] in a particular way. So now I say, 'Oh! Isn't this curious!'"
A routine executive team building retreat erupts into conflict early on the first day. This is not the kind of conflict typical of creative and capable managers, but full-scale warfare. "If these people had had bazookas, they would have been killing each other."	"There's more going on here than I initially thought."
An oil and gas firm hired a new vice president of exploration for his clear vision and experience with dwindling global oil reserves. His initial strategy had been clear: "We're not going to go for the big mother lode strikes because the odds of finding them are narrowing, and the risks of losing substantial capital are increasing." In two years, "he reversed that position entirely, always speaking now about hitting jackpot reserves like in the early days."	"Isn't that remarkable? I see a person saying *this* and doing *that*, but there's not congruence between the pieces that they say and what they do. So I say, 'Hmmm, something interesting is happening here.'"

Table 3 *Openness to Surprise: Examples of Unexpected Organizational Events and Leaders' Responses*

retreat for a management group. A third leader discussed the hiring of an oil and gas executive whose exploration strategy made sense given the current stage of that industry's life cycle. In each of these unremarkable situations, study participants describe the emergence of something unexpected. The health care provider, reputation notwithstanding, discovered it had "completely missed the mark" for a long time in serving certain clients. The team-building session revealed co-workers bent on "killing each other." The energy executive reversed an initial, well-reasoned strategy in favour of one more appropriate for the industry in its earlier years. For the leaders participating in this study, the dissonance between the expected and the unexpected sat squarely at the entry point into self-organized pattern detection. Such moments represented a transition point wherein the predictable became unpredictable, and the expected failed to materialize. Unexpected organizational occurrences confronted leaders involved in this study with their unmet assumptions about how their organizational stakeholders should behave.

Central to this confrontation was the experience of surprise. Surprise was a valuable cue to leaders that their intentions were misaligned with observable reality. In the second column of *Table 3*, we present participants' responses to the three situations described above. Responses contained the recognition that leaders' initial expectations were not being met: "I'd had them locked into some kind of an expectation they'd respond to us in a particular way," and "There's more going on here than I initially thought." The gap between study participants' expectations of the circumstances they described and what actually occurred took them aback, as in the comment, "Who'd have expected them to behave that way!?" And, contained within study participants' responses was a curiosity and interest in the behaviors they had not expected to see, evidenced in comments such as "Isn't that remarkable?" Embedded within leaders' responses to these organizational circumstances was an attitude we term *openness to surprise.*

Openness to surprise was an attitudinal stance of receptivity to unexpected behaviors that predisposed leaders to treat such behaviors as informative indicators of previously unrecognized patterns in the workplace. Such a stance was a condition that facilitated leaders' ability to detect patterns that could be present in initially perplexing organizational events. Openness to surprise is an attitudinal orientation that contrasts with factors that create an unwelcoming orientation toward the unexpected. Collectively, members of organizations develop purposes and norms that create a realm of expectable reality (Ashforth, Saks, and Lee, 1998), leading many organizational members to shrug off unexpected behaviors as inconsequential flukes. Bateson (1987) has written about how this phenomenon operates in individuals' minds:

"... people are self-corrective systems. They are self-corrective against disturbance, and if the obvious is not of a kind that they can easily assimilate without internal disturbance, their self-corrective mechanisms work to sidetrack it, to hide it... Disturbing information can be framed like a pearl so that it doesn't make a nuisance of itself; and this will be done, according to the understanding of the system itself, of what would be a nuisance" (p. 435).

One possible response to unexpected workplace behavior involves mentally framing it "like a pearl" so it "doesn't make a nuisance of itself." One study participant recounted a conversation with a firm's long-term human resources staff member that illustrates Bateson's point. Speaking about the large percentage of leaders who had left the company "broken people," this staff member "saw it as a curious fact, a number of isolated incidents." Her understanding of her company's purposes and norms left no room for other interpretations. Organizational norms and the tendency to overlook information that fails to confirm or conform to such norms make openness to surprise a difficult attitudinal stance to cultivate in corporate life.

Remaining open and curious toward surprise is also a radical cognitive stance in organizational life. That skilled knowledge workers would permit themselves an honest encounter with surprise runs counter to what management literature would leave us to expect. A survey of this literature uniformly portrays surprises as unwelcome disruptions (Ansoff, 1975; Erlenkotter, *et al.*, 1989) to be shielded against (Lampel & Shapira, 2001). This literature paints a picture of managers who are, or should be, positioned against surprise. Surprise implies failure. Organizations design sophisticated forecasting techniques to eliminate surprise (Watkins & Bazerman, 2003). Surprise indicates that forecasting techniques have failed (Ansoff, 1975). Accordingly, much management writing recommends that managers and theorists have a responsibility to help organizations avoid surprise (King, 1995; Weick & Sutcliffe, 2001). In short, surprises have a reputation as bad news. While some exceptions do emerge in the literature (e.g., Louis, 1980), rarely do they treat surprise as a helpful or even neutral emotion resulting simply from the discovery that a difference exists between anticipated and actual experiences in workplace settings.

Leaders who do view surprise as a helpful emotion appeared unusual to others. One study participant reported:

A client of mine just the other day said, *"It always amazes me how you don't get all upset about something going wrong."* Well, that's the issue, she thinks of it in terms of something "going wrong." Instead of speaking that way, I ask myself, *"What's the real pattern here? Have I really been honest about what's going on here? Am I really paying attention to what's actually happening or am I stuck in my romance about it?"*

People become attached to their expectations about how people in organizations should behave (Ashforth, *et al.*, 1998). When study participants recognized and released such attachments, they could reorient their perceptions in greater alignment with observable reality.

Detecting self-organized patterns begins with the ability to notice the unexpected. A leader's observational capacity must be decoupled from a confirmative, surprise-resisting mode of engaging with organizational events. Leaders operating in a confirmative mode explain unexpected workplace behavior using existing organizational explanatory schemes. Such schemes variously dismiss unexpected organizational behaviors as insignificant, or label them plans "gone wrong." By contrast, openness to surprise is a cognitive stance that leaves room for releasing one's "romance" with existing explanations. This stance enables leaders to recognize when they do not understand what is causing unexpected workplace behavior. In one CEO's words, "It's a good idea to develop a friendship with the experience of not knowing." Such "friendship" is a welcoming cognitive condition for the detection of self-organized dynamics.

Proposition 1: Being open to surprise is a welcoming cognitive condition conducive to a leader's decision to initiate a process of self-organized pattern identification.

Action Strategy for Self-Organized Pattern Detection: Bracketing Intended Coherence

An action strategy ensuing from openness to surprise involves articulating and *bracketing intended coherence* – leaders named, and then mentally set aside, their expectations about how members of their organization ought to behave.

Study participants caught in the surprise of unusual organizational behavior responded by articulating the coherence they expected to see in their firm's behavior, i.e., intended coherence. They named the behaviors that "should have" occurred. Contained in leaders' stories of "what should be happening" were perceptions of how observed behavior departed from intended behavior. For example, a study participant remarked, "The customers should be loving this service." One leader mused, "He pushed so hard to recruit that manager. They should be getting along but they just can't seem to work together." Another commented, "It makes no sense – sales performance for a car like this should be much higher [than it is]." At times, leaders' perceptions about what should have occurred was couched implicitly, in statements about what should not have occurred, such as: "An experienced interview candidate oughtta know not to act that way." At times, leaders' articulation of how the workplace behaviors they observed differed from the behavior they expected to see included perceptions of why that difference occurred. For instance, one leader explained, "Since wages haven't increased along with responsibilities, employee resentment is growing and jeopardizing the very staff satisfaction that this empowerment program was supposed to improve." Contained in each of these brief comments about what was happening in their companies, leaders voiced the intended coherence they had expected to see.

To discern the coherence at the centre of a self-organized pattern, these leaders then set aside – or bracketed – these explanations. By articulating and bracketing intended organizational coherence, study participants acknowledged a familiar dichotomy. Researchers have long studied the differences between what organizational participants intend to happen (i.e., intended coherence) and what actually does happen. Argyris and Schön (1976) have noted the gap between organizational participants' espoused theories and their theories-in-use. Policy capture studies (e.g., Graves & Karren, 1992) have identified people's unrecognized policies affecting organizational decision making. Phenomenology scholars (e.g., Giddens, 1977; Schutz, 1967) have advised researchers to "bracket" their personal perspectives to more clearly discern research subjects' experiences of lived phenomena. Similarly, study participants recognized that loyalty to their initial explanations of what had gone awry obstructed their capacity to discern the logical coherence at the core of unexpected workplace behaviors. "I have to figure out how to take each of these moments I'm seeing as being perfectly logical, perfectly understandable, perfectly right," stated one study participant. This sentiment was echoed widely, even among study participants who had never met: "You want to understand the situation and *why it's logical*" (our emphasis). Bracketing their own stories about the ways they had intended their companies to behave freed leaders to search for self-organized coherence.

Study Participants' Questions	Evidence Source
"Just forget what the executive team wanted for a minute. What needs or feelings are being expressed by these employees here?"	Group observation
"What if all of this actually makes perfect sense? What are these behaviours telling me about where we're really at?"	Interview
"What is needed or wanted here that we haven't really admitted?"	Interview
"What's been going on that would create results like this?	Interview
"What is trying to happen here that I can't yet see or acknowledge?"	Group observation
"What results are being achieved by this behaviour?"	Group observation
"In what archetypal storyline would these behaviours fit?"	Interview
"What is it telling us that these results are occurring?	Group observation

Table 4 *Language Expressive of Suspending Normative Appraisal*

Why take this approach? Both interview and case observation data illustrated that loyalty to initial explanations of what went awry obstructed leaders' capacity to recognize the inherent coherence of unexpected, repetitive configurations of workplace behavior. As a study participant who consulted to management teams remarked, "the problem that an organization reports to a consultant is invariably not the problem. As long as you're stuck in their definition of the problem, you'll get nowhere." Such loyalty to an organization's explanations for its behavior obstructed an observer's ability to "transcend the system's definition of the situation" (McCormick & White, 2000). Therefore, leaders deliberately articulated – and then bracketed – their initial understanding of what was going (or "going wrong") in their companies.

Proposition 2: To understand unanticipated organizational behaviors or events as indicators of a self-organized pattern, a leader must bracket normative expectations of organizational behavior based on espoused corporate visions or strategies.

Proposition 3: Too much loyalty to established explanatory schemes to explain organizational behavior can hinder a leaders' capacity to understand unexpected behaviors as potentially indicating the presence of a self-organized pattern.

Action Strategies for Self-Organized Pattern Detection: Suspending Normative Appraisal and Non-Evaluative Description

Suspending Normative Appraisal

Articulating and bracketing intended coherence acknowledges leaders' initial expectations for the behavior of their companies. Leaders participating in this study used two further action strategies to perceive coherence in their companies' actual self-organized behavior. One action strategy aimed at discovering the coherence of self-organized dynamics was cognitive. Study participants *suspended normative appraisal* about perplexing organizational behaviors – temporarily deferring an assessment of the situation that judges its appropriateness or acceptability. Another action strategy involved in discovering self-organized coherence was verbal. Leaders used *non-evaluative description* to examine unexpected workplace behaviors – they sought language to describe the behaviors they observed which avoided expressing a value judgment about those behaviors.

Suspending normative appraisal was a strategy both counterintuitive and difficult for business leaders. Why? Aspiring leaders pay business schools tens of thousands of dollars in tuition to learn to evaluate better from worse, effective from ineffective, and appropriate from inappropriate courses of managerial action. Normative judgement is, perhaps, the central skill that management and leadership training programs transmit. Employers prize this expertise, as reflected in the increased salaries of MBA graduates (Page, 2003). Many organizational studies (e.g., Burt, 1987; DiMaggio & Powell, 1983; Mizruchi, 1990) describe people's deeply ingrained tendency to behave as they believe people in their positions should behave. People working in business settings do their best to act like business experts.

Why is suspending normative appraisal useful for corporate leaders? A confident ability to apply normative appraisal to business problems may reassure corporate shareholders. However, study participants found that it impeded their ability to understand self-organized patterns in workplaces. Business logic belongs to the language and rationality of business. For leaders participating in this study, understanding a pattern that operates according to logic running autonomously from business logic required that their "expert thinking mode" be temporarily suspended. Self-imposed suspension of normative appraisal[8] required these leaders to take the counterintuitive position that every unintended action, decision, emotion, or behavior displayed within their organization be understood as entirely appropriate to whatever self-organized dynamic was operating in that system (Kaufmann, 2004). By "appropriate," we do not mean to suggest that self-organized behaviors were considered acceptable to these leaders. Such behaviors were often damaging to the health of organizations and employees alike, and the leaders knew it. Rather, leaders who participated in this study suspended normative appraisal of self-organized behavior as an analytical strategy. Those leaders who could view organizational behaviors as appropriate and accurate expressions of some unrecognized, autonomous pattern demon-

---

8 – called simply "suspension" by Senge, *et al.* (2005).

strated an ability to discern coherence in those behaviors.

Evidence that leaders sought to suspend normative judgment appeared in both interviews and group observation data. Repeatedly, when leaders discussed workplace behaviors that they hadn't expected and couldn't understand, they reported asking themselves some variation of the question, "How does this behavior make sense?" Table 4 illustrates the many forms this question took for study participants.

Each question contained these leaders' assumption that, although unintended, patterned behaviors were counterproductive, in some way they were coherent. Study participants assumed that, at some level, perplexing behaviors or events in their workplace were reasonable if understood in a self-organized context that might initially have been unrecognized for its significance. Leaders' questions revealed the presumption that some collectively held goals, values, needs, or feelings were being expressed through perplexing behaviors. Even apparently sudden behavior could be viewed as an understandable outgrowth of an organization's history. Suspending normative appraisal about how behaviors failed to meet leaders' expectations or corporate objectives enabled leaders to consider how those behaviors might be offering useful insight into previously unrecognized dimensions of the companies they led.

Proposition 4: Suspending normative appraisal of unplanned organizational occurrences is an action strategy that aids leaders in perceiving such events as coherent.

Non-Evaluative Description

In this study, leaders coupled the cognitive action strategy of suspending normative appraisal with often laborious efforts to neutrally describe the unexpected behaviors they observed in their workplaces. *Non-evaluative description* was a verbal action strategy aimed at understanding the coherence in self-organized behaviors.

Study participants carried out non-evaluative description by asking questions of themselves and others (such as those in Table 4 above) to understand the defining features of the relationship among participants in a perplexing organizational dynamic. These questioning strategies served a goal of describing, as accurately as possible, how pattern participants interacted together using language stripped of as much subjective influence as possible. How could concern for neutralized description contribute to an understanding of self-organized system dynamics?

To illustrate, a senior administrator in social services described her work in one of several agencies charged with serving high-risk children. These agencies, staffed with highly trained and capable professionals, struggled for years with their frustrating and largely ineffective interaction with a county's growing population of truant children. Their evaluative assessment of the situation during this time was this:

H_1 *(evaluative): "One hypothesis was, 'Ah, they're bad kids and they're bad families... [The] kids are intentionally disturbed, they intentionally go rob stores, there is intent behind it.'"*

A second hypothesis was more descriptive of the systemic situation facing truant children. It began a significantly more successful stage in their work with this population:

H_2 *(descriptive): "We entered this new chapter with [a] second hypothesis: 'Hey, there's trouble brewing in that home, that's why these things are happening. Look, he doesn't want to fail. He wants to succeed; but we need to understand that nobody, neither you nor I, could survive in that morass."*

The assessment, "They're bad kids" evaluated the children involved in recurring truancy and crime. By contrast, the leaders of these agencies found "There's trouble brewing in that home" to be descriptive language that reframed their thinking about the familiar relationships experienced by truant children, enabling the agencies to generate successful, systemic solutions in a way they previously could not. No longer did the agencies view the children as causing trouble because of their inherent badness. Rather, these children's behavior now appeared to accurately reflect the state of the families falling within these agencies' jurisdiction. The fundamental essence of this situation was no longer misbehaving children. Rather, truancy made perfect sense within a self-organized pattern of families in crisis.

Proposition 5: Searching for non-evaluative language to describe unplanned organizational occurrences is an action strategy that assists leaders in perceiving such events as coherent.

The leaders participating in this study were seasoned managers. However, when they began trying to understand the dynamics of unplanned, autonomous organizational dynamics, they suspended the ready store of managerial judgement ingrained by their training and experience in favour of often painstaking attempts to neutrally describe the unexpected behaviors they observed. Like most professionals, these leaders' educational training and the fast pace of corporate life pressured them to generate quick explanations for self-organized work behaviors. The search for non-evaluative description was a discipline that slowed their thinking. One vice president alluded to this issue of pacing with the remark, "The shortcoming of reading patterns is that you sometimes start reading before you really know the pattern." The action strategy of non-evaluative description created a deliberately methodical pace. This pacing appeared to help delay cognitive closure or a premature sense of having mastered the reasons underlying the complexities of self-organized workplace patterns. In the words of one participant, the rush to fix undesirable circumstances got deferred in favour of taking time for "discovering and acknowledging [an organizational] reality – and bowing to it." This stance was a challenging one for leaders accustomed to exercising authority and influence over their corporations. And at times, even those leaders most practiced in identifying self-organized dynamics found their concerted efforts to suspend normative judgment and describe workplace patterns neutrally would fail. For instance, a study participant admitted he once felt an intense pull to critically label a particular pattern: "you guys made naïve decisions." A substantial obstacle to suspending normative appraisal is the siren's call to demonstrate managerial expertise by making evaluative comments about companies' self-organized behaviors.

Intervening Condition for Self-Organized Pattern Detection: Entrainment
To a degree, people's individuality becomes subsumed in the maintenance of a self-organized pattern when it emerges. When members of a workplace become involved in such a pattern, their speech, behavior, and reasoning styles express the pattern in which they are entrained. *Entrainment* refers to the ways in which the behavior of individuals and organizations become pulled into correlation with one another. It "serves as a powerful coordination mechanism.... Entrained organizational rhythms... dominate many organizational activities" (Ancona & Chong, 1996: 253).

Organizational theorists (e.g., Ancona, *et al.*, 2001) borrow the term entrainment from the natural sciences. However, when adopting this term for management usage, these theorists assume that in organizations, entrainment is intentional. The management entrainment literature has assumed that firms can choose when, how, and to what they should be entrained. These entrainment theorists believe that if organizational behaviors "are *coincidentally* synchronized... *just happen to be* at a phase that meshes with [another]   [if] the cycles are not mutually adjusted, [but they *simply evolve*"], this constitutes "*pseudo*-entrainment" (our emphases – Ancona & Chong, 1996: 259). However, theorists of self-organization (e.g., Bella, 1997; Jantsch, 1980) argue that intention is entirely unnecessary for corporations to fall into entrainment with self-organized patterns.

Recognizing the entrainment of others can alert one to the presence of self-organized patterns. For example, consider the observation made by a researcher speaking to executives in the tobacco industry: "I felt the presence of the company within them.... I felt that I was speaking with more company than person, or perhaps a person who could no longer distinguish between the two" (Rosenblatt, 1995, cited in Bella, 1997). The image of people's individuality subsumed by a larger emergent dynamic is an apt description of self-organization at work. It is, perhaps, comparatively easy to detect entrainment in others. However, entrainment is not merely a phenomenon that happens to others. As we discussed pattern detection with leaders and watched their pattern-detection processes in action, it became apparent that many leaders understood that they were integrally part of the organizations they led, and integrally connected to the self-organized patterns they sought to understand.

The phenomenon of entrainment demanded that leaders have considerable capacities for introspection. When that capacity was present, leaders could recognize their own entrainment with a problematic self-organized pattern.

Moments of such recognition were potent clues to leaders attempting to investigate self-organized dynamics in their workplaces. When leaders detected that their inner experience was congruent with an organization's outer behavior, they perceived themselves as resonating with a self-organized dynamic. This recognized resonance could become a valuable data source. One leader working in the financial sector described his experiences with such resonance:

The best investments I've ever made for myself is when I've been the most fearful, most afraid. And you say, "Why is that?" Well, because I have absorbed the fear that surrounds investing in that particular item, or that particular stock, or whatever, from the investing public. And because the public is so fearful about it, they've driven the prices way down.

When a self-organized workplace (or in this case, industry) entrained this leader's own personal psychology – when he could accurately name the character of the entrainment (in this case, fear) – he could often understand the pattern in a way that enabled him to take fruitful action on it.

Proposition 6: Leaders themselves may be entrained in the very self-organized pattern they are seeking to understand.

Proposition 7: Recognizing how one is entrained in a self-organized pattern is a tool that can help one understand the pattern under investigation.

Discovering one's personal resonance with autonomous, self-organized dynamics was often humbling to study participants. Many of the incidents of self-organized patterns reported by leaders in this study focused on ineffective interpersonal relationships in the workplace. In the process of identifying a particular pattern, study participants often discovered their own personal involvement in that same ineffective dynamic. Certain study participants familiar with psychological jargon described this experience as falling into a "complex" – a term defined by Mattoon (1981) as a largely uncontrollable, strongly emotional reaction to an issue that we do not realize is significant to us. For instance, one study participant's job responsibilities included consulting to work groups within her firm. She described incidents when she recognized that she had become entrained in self-organized dynamics operating within some of those groups. She described her experience of entrainment this way:

I almost become blinded to anything except my reaction to what's going on...... I can see it. At that point I am no longer the observer, I'm the participant. I do have a sense of when I drop in and out of [the observer] role.... I can feel when I do that... and I've got to fight to get back in [my role]. When I step out of that role, as leader or whatever, then I've lost my ability to read patterns because I'm only reading my own complexes.

When this study participant recognized that she had lost her sense of objectivity, she perceived that her internal experience was operating under the influence of a self-organized pattern. People involved in human systems (through participation or observation) are not inert actors. Rather, their own personal psychology has considerable influence on whether and how systemic self-organization takes hold[9].

Both interview and case observation surfaced many examples of leaders discovering that they had unwittingly adopted roles, moods, or decision-making habits belonging to a self-organized pattern they were seeking to understand. Each time, the leaders experienced such revelations as both destabilizing and intensely revealing, reporting that their sense of personal autonomy and clarity about their organizational role was overtaken by discovery that they had become entrained, for a time at least, in a self-organized pattern. The ability for self-organized dynamics to entrain even leaders is the antithesis of self-affirming, confirmatory news. (It may well be a delusion of "narcissistic isolation" [Fiumara, 1990: 163] for any leader to expect that a self-organized dynamic "won't entrain me".) To understand any particular pattern dynamic that has beset an organization, the recognition of one's own personal entrainment may well be a necessary admission price.

The tendency for self-organized dynamics to entrain even leaders suggests that those wishing to detect self-organization must direct their observational capacities in both inward and outward directions. To one study participant, this was the essence of self-organized pattern detection itself: "I have to pay attention both to the various data I'm getting from them... as well as paying attention to the inner response that I'm having... If I understand what's going on with me it helps me understand better what's going on with them." Failing to recognize how one's own thoughts, emotions, and behaviors may have become entrained in a self-organized pattern makes detecting such patterns difficult.

Proposition 8: Leaders' own entrainment can be an intervening condition affecting their ability to perceive self-organized dynamics as coherent.

Discussion: The Nature of Complex Leadership

Complexity makes a difficult demand of leaders: foster conditions in which your company can achieve a vision of creativity and innovation. Self-organization demands leaders to understand that amidst the complex behaviors observed in organizations, patterns entirely unrelated to this leadership vision may interfere with its attainment. Complexity demands that leaders recognize and reckon with unintended, autonomous, complex organizational dynamics.

---

9 The argument that personal complexes and entrainment are linked comes from a view of psychology positing that people's outward behavior is often a result of inward complexes that lay latent until an outer circumstance (such as a self-organizing pattern) activates that behavior (e.g., Conforti, 1999; Mattoon, 1981). Implicit in this perspective is the argument that systems have their power, in part, because of their capacity to activate tendencies already latent in us.

In this study, we sought to understand how leaders try to detect some such dynamics. We were guided by Kruglanski's lay epistemic research that postulates the importance of welcoming cognitive conditions, and Glaser and Strauss' counsel to identify action strategies and intervening conditions. Taken together, the welcoming cognitive condition, action strategies, and intervening condition used by study participants offers some useful perspectives on the leadership endeavour.

This study highlights how some leaders acknowledge the complexity of their organizations by actively seeking to detect and respond to emergent behavioral patterns that constrain corporate productivity. This validates Jackson's (2000) claims that if people could detect and understand a self-organized pattern, such understanding could inform leaders' decision making. The detection of self-organized patterns uncovered in this study is perhaps most accurately framed as a process of recognizing and juxtaposing two types of pattern: one intended and one unintended. We might then frame complex leadership as the acknowledgement that multiple intended and unintended forces have an active presence in organizational life. Whether recognized or not, alongside "leadership vision," "self-organized patterns" are active stakeholders (Mitroff, 1983) around the boardroom table. The leaders participating in this study sought to identify and deal skilfully with these boardroom visitors. This study paints a picture of complex leadership as a necessary dialogue between intended visions and emergent dynamics.

This study also highlights an uncomfortable dimension of the difference between leadership vision and observed corporate behavior. Complex leadership involves more than the recognition that a leader's intentions and a company's self-organized behavior differ. Self-organization involves entrainment; it involves often disturbing revelations that a leader's own behavior has become entrained in counterproductive self-organized dynamics. Complex leadership requires leaders to acknowledge their own complicity in self-organized dynamics that may contradict their espoused leadership vision. This study suggests that the leadership of complex systems demands considerable courage and capacity for self-confrontation.

Our research ties in closely with the leadership development framework research of Fisher, Rooke, and Torbert (2000), Fisher and Torbert (1995), and Torbert and Associates (2004). These researchers have found that leaders at more complex (i.e., postconventional) levels of development become increasingly aware of differences (and dissonances) between the leadership intentions and actual behaviors of themselves and others. Postconventional leaders actively seek out and explore these differences. Such leaders become comfortable with the tensions among these differences. The results of such reflection are more than fodder for personal growth for an elite stratum of the business world (only 15% of managers fall into postconventional stages of development - Rooke & Torbert, 2005). People operating at these developmental levels are the only ones demonstrating consistent success in the complex challenge of leading organizational innovation and change (ibid.).

The argument emerging from this study is this: despite the catalyzing impact of a powerful leader's vision, complex organizations never have such single-minded focus. Complex organizations demand leaders with the capacity to detect emergent, unintended dynamics and create dialogue between corporate objectives and these autonomous forces. The dialogue we observed in study participants differed substantially from the efforts to re-exert vision-driven control advocated by traditional leadership theories. For those who participated in this study, leadership involves negotiating a company's way forward through the tensions between leaders' plans and self-organized emergence. These tensions, themselves, become a valued vehicle for questioning and revising leadership strategies that fail to appropriately reflect the complexities of the organization seeking to achieve them.

An increasing number of leaders have come into contact with information about complex system dynamics. This study explores how several leaders are applying that information in their leadership roles. This study suggests that leaders are developing particular cognitive conditions and action strategies in order to relate effectively with the complexities of their firms. A lay epistemic perspective on complexity and leadership will help researchers to identify, evaluate, and refine these conditions and strategies.

Conclusions

We aimed to address an important question: how can leaders comprehend and relate to obstructive self-organized patterns of behavior in complex organizations? This study suggests that behavioral patterns generated by self-organization become a useful entry point for leaders wishing to engage fruitfully with the complexity of organizations. Conceptually, "self-organized pattern" is a theoretical construct with intelligibility and practicality to leaders wanting to relate effectively to organizational complexity. At the core of self-organization is patterned behavior. By nature, patterns involve elements correlated in a particular, repetitive configuration or logic. We might consider self-organized behavior as a symbolic language operating in workplaces, expressing how members subconsciously perceive the organization at a given point in time. Self-organization is self-expressive, then, offering informative, real-time data about the state of an organization. "Learning to see the systemic whole can be revelatory" (Marion & Uhl-Bien, 2001:406). Leaders who learn the language of self-organization which may be hindering corporate productivity may gain access to a wealth of information about complex forces threatening the achievement of corporate objectives.

Understanding such forces is important. Complexity research may well have revealed that self-organizing systems are more coherent – more patterned – than most of us ever understood (Jantsch, 1980; Marion & Uhl-Bien, 2001). But for twenty-first century leaders, scientific findings that unexpected organizational behavior is actually coherent are insufficient (Buckle, 2003; Osborn, et al., 2002). When an organization's coherence departs from that which leaders expect (i.e., when it shifts instead into self-organized coherence) the leadership challenge becomes discerning the identity of that particular coherence and working through any constraining effects it has on the development of organizational creativity and innovation. Before they try pre-empting or changing self-organized dynamics, leaders need to know how to discern them.

REFERENCES

Abraham, R. (1987). "Dynamics and self-organization," in F. E. Yates, A. Garfinkel, D. Walter and G. Yates (eds.), Self-Organizing Systems: The Emergence of Order, ISBN 9780306421457, pp. 599-613.

Ackoff, R. L. (1989). "The circular organization: An update," *Academy of Management Executive*, ISSN 0896-3789, 3(1): 11-16.

Adami, C. (1998). *An Introduction to Artificial Life*, ISBN 0387946462.

Adams, J.S. (1965). "Inequity in social exchange," *Advances in Experimental Social Psychology*, ISSN 0065-2601, 2: 267-299.

Adams, R.N. (1988). *The Eighth Day: Social Evolution as the Self-Organization of Energy*, ISBN 0292720602.

Agle, B.R., Nagarajan, N.J., Sonnenfeld, J.A. and Srinivasan, D. (2006). "Does CEO charisma matter? An empirical analysis of the relationships among organizational performance, environmental uncertainty, and top management teams perceptions of charisma," *Academy of Management Journal*, ISSN 0001-4273, 49: 161-174.

Albanese, R. and Van Fleet, D.D. (1985). "Rational behavior in groups: The free riding tendency," *Academy of Management Review*, ISSN 0363-7425, 10: 244-255.

Albrecht, T.L. and Adelman, M.B. (1984). "Social support and life stress: New directions for communication research," *Human Communication Research*, ISSN 0360-3989 ,11(1): 3-32.

Allen, P.M. and McGlade, J. (1987). "Evolutionary drive: The effect of microscopic diversity, error making, and noise," *Foundations of Physics*, ISSN 0015-9018 17: 723-738.

Allen, P.M. and Strathern, M. (2003). "Evolution, emergence, and learning in complex systems," *Emergence*, ISSN 1521-3250, 5(4): 8-33.

Allport, F.H. (1954). "The structuring of events: Outline of a general theory with applications to psychology," *Psychological Review*, ISSN 0033-295X, 61: 281-303.

Allport, F.H. (1962). "A structuronomic conception of behavior: Individual and collective," *Journal of Abnormal and Social Psychology*, ISSN 0096-851X, 64: 3-30.

Allport, F.H. (1967). "A theory of enestruence (event-structure theory): Report of progress," *American Psychologist*, ISSN 0003-066X, 22: 1-24.

Amabile, T., Barsade, S., Mueller, J. and B. Staw (2005). "Affect and creativity at work," *Administrative Science Quarterly*, ISSN 0001-8392, 50(3): 367-403.

Amabile, T.M., Conti, R., Coon, H., Lazenby, J. and Herron, M. (1996). "Assessing the work environment for creativity," *The Academy of Management Journal*, ISSN 0001-4273, 39(5): 1154-1184.

Ancona, D.G. and Caldwell, D.F. (1992). "Bridging the boundary: External activity and performance in organizational teams," *Administrative Science Quarterly*, ISSN 0001-8392, 37(4): 634-665.

Ancona, D.G. and Chong, C.-L. (1996). "Entrainment: Pace, cycle, and rhythm in organizational behavior," *Research in Organizational Behavior*, ISSN 0747-5632, pp. 251-284.

Ancona, D.G., Goodman, P., Lawrence, B. and Tushman, M. (2001). "Time: A new research lens," *Academy of Management Review*, ISSN 0363-7425, 26(Oct): 645-663.

Anderson, P. (1972). "More is different: Broken symmetry and the nature of the hierarchical structure of science," *Science*, 177(4047): 393-396.

Anderson, P. (1999). "Complexity theory and organization science," *Organization Science*, ISSN 1047-7039, 10(3): 216-232.

Anderson, P. and Stein, D. (1987). "Broken symmetry, emergent properties, dissipative structures, life: Are they related?" in F. Eugene Yates (ed.), *Self-Organizing Systems: The Emergence of Order*, ISBN 9780306421457, pp. 445-457.

Anderson, P., Meyer, A., Eisenhardt, K., Carley, K. and Pettigrew, A. (1999). "Introduction to the special issue: Applications of complexity theory to organization science," *Organization Science*, ISSN 1047-7039, 10: 233-236.

Anderson, R.A., Issel, L.M. and McDaniel, Jr., R.R. (2003). "Nursing homes as complex adaptive systems: Relationship between management practice and resident outcomes," *Nursing Research*, ISSN 0029-6562, 52(1): 12-21.

Andrade, L., Plowman, D.A. and Duchon, D. (2007). "Getting past conflict reduction: A complexity view of conflict," unpublished manuscript, San Antonio.

Anghel, M., Toroczkai, Z., Bassler, K.E. and Korniss, G. (2004). "Competition driven network dynamics: Emergence of a scale-free leadership structure and collective efficiency," *Physical Review Letters*, ISSN 0031-9007, 92(5): 058701.

Ansoff, H.I. (1975). "Managing strategic surprise by response to weak signals," *California Management Review*, ISSN 0008-1256, 18(Winter): 21-33.

Anthony, W.P. (1978). *Participative Management*, ISBN 0201002531.

Archer, M. (1988). Culture and Agency: The Place of Culture in Social Theory, ISBN 0521564417.

Argyris, C. (1953). "Some characteristics of successful executives," *Personnel Journal*, ISSN 0031-5745, 32(3): 50-55.

Argyris, C. and Schön, D. (1976). *Theory in Practice: Increasing Professional Effectiveness*, ISBN 1555424465.

Arikan, A.T. (2007). "Regional entrepreneurial transformation: A complex systems perspective," presented at the Academy of Management Conference, Atlanta, GA.

Arthur, B. (1997). "Process and emergence in the economy," in B. Arthur, S.N. Durlauf and D.A. Lane (eds), *The Economy as an Evolving Complex System II*, ISBN 0201959887.

Arthur, B. (1999). "Complexity and the economy," Science, ISSN 0036-8075, 284(2 April): 107-109.

Artigiani, R. (1987). "Revolution and evolution: Applying Prigogine's dissipative structures model," *Journal of Social and Psychological Structures*, 10: 249-264.

Ashby, W.R. (1956). *Introduction to Cybernetics*, ISBN 0412056704

Ashby, W.R. (1960). *Design for a Brain*, 2nd edition, New York, NY: Wiley.

Ashby, W.R. (1962). "Principles of the self-organizing system," in H. Von Foerster and G. Zopf (eds.). *Principles of Self-organization: Transactions of the University of Illinois Symposium*, London, England: Pergamon Press, pp. 255-278.

Ashforth, B.E., Saks, A.M. and Lee, R.T. (1998). "Socialization and newcomer adjustment: The role of organizational context," *Human Relations*, ISSN 0018-7267, 51(7): 897-925.

Ashmos, D.P. and Huber, G. (1987). "The systems paradigm in organizational theory: Correcting the record and suggesting the future," *Academy of Management Review*, ISSN 0363-7425, 12(4), 607-621.

Aula, P. (1996). "Chaos and the double function of communication," *Studies of Nonlinear Phenomena in Life Science*, ISSN 1793-1428, 5: 191-206.

Aula, P. (1999). *Organisaation Kaaos vai Kaaoksen Organisaatio? Dynaamisen Organisaatioviestinnän Teoria*, ISBN 952964678X.

Aula, P. (2000). *Johtamisen Kaaos vai Kaaoksen Johtaminen? Juva*, ISBN 9510240117.

Austin, J. (1978). *Chase, Chance, and Creativity: The Lucky Art of Novelty*, ISBN

0231042949

Axelrod, R. (1984). *The Evolution of Cooperation*, ISBN 0465021220.

Axelrod, R. (1997). *The Complexity of Cooperation*, ISBN 0691015686.

Axelrod, R. and Bennett, D.S. (1993). "A landscape theory of aggregation," *British Journal of Political Science*, ISSN 0007-1234, 23: 211-233.

Axelrod, R. and Cohen, M.D. (2000). *Harnessing Complexity: Organizational Implications of a Scientific Frontier*, ISBN 0465005500.

Babbage, C. (1832). *On the Economy of Machinery and Manufactures*, London, England: Charles Knight.

Baert, P. (1998). *Social Theory in the Twentieth Century*, ISBN 0745613861.

Bailey, K.D. (1994). *Sociology and the New Systems Theory*, ISBN 0791417433.

Bak, P. (1996). *How Nature Works: The Science of Self-Organized Criticality*, ISBN 0387947914.

Bak, P. and Chen, K. (1991). "Self-organized criticality," *Scientific American*, ISSN 0036-8733, 264: 46-53.

Baker, G. and Gollub, J. (1996). *Chaotic Dynamics: An Introduction*, ISBN 0521382580

Baker, W.E. (1992). "The network organization in theory and practice," in R.C. Eccles (ed.), *Networks and Organizations: Structure, Form and Action*, ISBN 0875843247, pp. 397-429.

Baldwin, C.Y. and Clark, K.B. (2000). *Design Rules*, ISBN 0262024667.

Bandura, A. (1989). "Human agency in social cognition theory," *American Psychologist*, ISSN 0003-066X, 44(9): 1175-1184.

Bantel, K. and Jackson, S. (1989). "Top management and innovations in banking: Does composition of the top teams make a difference?" *Strategic Management Journal*, ISSN 0143-2095, 10: 107-124.

Barabási, A. (2002). *Linked: The New Science of Networks*, ISBN 9780738206677.

Barker, R. (2001). "The nature of leadership," *Human Relations*, ISSN 0018-7267, 54: 469-494.

Barley, S. R. and Kunda, G. (1992). "Design and devotion: Surges of rational and normative ideologies of control in managerial discourse," *Administrative Science Quarterly*, ISSN 0001-8392, 37: 363-399.

Barley, S.R. (1986). "Technology as an occasion for structuring: Evidence from observations of CT scanners and the social order of radiology departments," *Administration Science Quarterly*, ISSN 0001-8392, 31(1): 78-109.

Barnard, C.I. (1938). *The Functions of the Executive*, ISBN 9780674328037 (2007).

Barnard, C.I. (1968). *The Functions of the Executive*, ISBN 9780674328037 (2007).

Barnes, L.P. and Kriger, M.P. (1986). "The hidden side of leadership," *MIT Sloan Management Review*, ISSN 1532-9194, 28(1): 15-26.

Barney, J.B. (1991). "Firm resources and sustained competitive advantage," *Journal of Management*, ISSN 0149-2063, 17(1): 99-120.

Bartlett, C.A. and Ghoshal, S. (1998). *Managing Across Boarders: The Transnational Solution*, ISBN 0585232520.

Barton, S. (1994). "Chaos, self-organization, and psychology," *American Psychologist*, ISSN 0003-066X, 49(1): 5-14.

Bartunek, J., Gordon, J. and Weathersby, R. (1983). "Developing 'complicated' understanding in administrators," *Academy of Management Review*, ISSN 0363-7425, 8(2): 273-284.

Bar-Yam, Y. (2004). "Multi-scale variety in complex systems," *Complexity*, ISSN 1076-2787, 9: 37-45.

Bass, B.M. (1973). *Leadership, Psychology, and Organizational Behavior*, ISBN

0837166314.

Bass, B.M. (1985). *Leadership and Performance Beyond Expectations*, ISBN 0029018102.

Bass, B.M. (1990). *Bass and Stogdill's Handbook of Leadership: Theory, Research and Managerial Applications*, ISBN 0029015006.

Bass, B.M. and Avolio, B.J. (2004). *Multifactor Leadership Questionnaire*, 3rd edition, Manual and Sampler Set, Palo Alto, CA: Mind Garden Inc.

Bateson, G. (1969). Letter from Gregory Bateson to George Sarant dated 6/25/1969.

Bateson, G. (1987). "Conscious purpose versus nature," in G. Bateson (ed.), *Steps to an Ecology of Mind*, ISBN 9780226039053 (2000), pp. 432-445.

Baughman, W.A. and Mumford, M.D. (1995). "Process-analytic models of creative capacities: Operations influencing the combination-and-reorganization process," *Creativity Research Journal*, 8: 37-62.

Baum, J. and Singh, J. (eds.) (1994). *Evolutionary Dynamics of Organizations*, ISBN 0195077369.

Baum, J.A.C. (1999). "Whole-part coevolutionary competition in organizations," in J.A.C. Baum and B. McKelvey (eds.), *Variations in Organization Science: In Honor of Donald T. Campbell*, ISBN 0761911251, pp 113-135.

Bechtel, W. and Richardson, R. (1992). "Emergent phenomena and complex systems," in A. Beckermann, H. Flohr and J. Kim (eds.), *Emergence or Reduction? Essays on the Prospects of Nonreductive Physicalism*, ISBN 3110128802, pp. 257-288.

Bechtel, W. and Richardson, R. (1993). *Discovering Complexity: Decomposition and Localization as Strategies in Scientific Research*, ISBN 9780691087627.

Becker, E. (1973). *The Denial of Death*, ISBN 0684832402.

Becker, G.S. (1975). *Human Capital: A Theoretical and Empirical Analysis, With Special Reference to Education*, ISBN 0870145134.

Bedeau, M. (1997). "Weak emergence," *Philosophical Perspectives*, ISSN 1520-8583, 11: 375-399.

Bedeian, A.G. and Hunt, J.G. (2006). "Academic amnesia and vestigial assumptions of our forefathers," *The Leadership Quarterly*, ISSN 1047-7039, 17(2): 190.

Bella, D. (1997). "Organized complexity in human affairs: The tobacco industry," *Journal of Business Ethics*, ISSN 1573-0697, 16(Jul): 977-999.

Bénard, H. (1901). "Les tourbillons cellulaires dans une nappe liquide transportant de la chaleur par convection en régime permanent," *Annales de Chimie et de Physique*, 23: 62-114.

Bennett, C. (1986). "On the nature and origin of complexity in discrete, homogeneous, locally-interacting systems," *Foundations of Physics*, ISSN 0015-9018, 16(6): 585-592.

Bennett, C. (1988). "Dissipation, information, computational complexity, and the definition of organization," in D. Pines (ed.), *Emerging Syntheses in Science*, ISBN 9780201156867, pp. 215-231.

Bennis, W.G. (1959). "Leadership theory and administrative behavior: The problem of authority," *Administrative Science Quarterly*, ISSN 0001-8392, 4(3): 259-301.

Bennis, W.G. (1989). *On Becoming a Leader*, ISBN 0201409291.

Bennis, W.G. (1989). *Why Leaders Can't Lead*, ISBN 1555421520.

Bennis, W.G. (1996). "Becoming a Leader of Leaders," in R. Gibson (ed.), *Rethinking the Future*, ISBN 1857881036.

Bennis, W.G. (1997). "Cultivating creative genius," Industry Week, ISSN 0039-0895, 18(August): 84-88.

Bennis, W.G. and Biederman, P.W. (1997). *Organizing Genius: The Secrets of Creative Collaboration*, ISBN 0201570513.

Bennis, W.G. and Nanus, B. (1985). *Leaders: Strategies for Taking Charge*, ISBN 0887308392.

Bennis, W.G. and O'Toole, J. (2005). "How business schools lost their way," *Harvard Business Review*, ISSN 0017-8012, 83(5): 96-104.

Bennis, W.G. and Townsend, R. (1995). *Reinventing Leadership*, ISBN 0060820527.

Berge, P., Pomeau, V. and Vidal, C. (1984). *Order Within Chaos: Towards a Deterministic Approach to Turbulence*, L. Tuckerman (trans.), ISBN 9780471849674.

Berger, P.L. and Luckmann, T. (1966). *The Social Construction of Reality*, ISBN 0385058985.

Bergson, H. (1911). *Creative Evolution*, A. Mitchell (trans.), Lanham, MD: University Press of America.

Berlin, I. (1996). *The Sense of Reality*, ISBN 0374525692.

Berlin, I. (2001). *The Power of Ideas*, ISBN 069105018X.

Bernstein, F. and DeCroix, G. (2004). "Decentralized pricing and capacity decisions in a multi-tier system with modular assembly," *Management Science*, ISSN 0025-1909, 50(9), 1293-1308.

Bernstein, F. and Federgruen, A. (2003). "Pricing and replenishment strategies in a distribution system with competing retailers," *Operations Research*, ISSN 0030-364X, 51(3): 409-426.

Bernstein, F. and Federgruen, A. (2005). "Decentralized supply chains with competing retailers under demand uncertainty," *Management Science*, ISSN 0025-1909, 51(1): 18-29.

Berrien, F.K. (1961). "Homeostasis theory of groups: Implications for leadership," in L. Petrullo and B. Bass (eds.), *Leadership and Interpersonal Behavior*, New York, NY: Holt, Rinehart & Winston.

Berson, Y. and Avolio, B. J. (2004). "Transformational leadership and the dissemination of organizational goals: A case study of a telecommunication firm," *The Leadership Quarterly*, ISSN 1047-7039, 15(5): 625-646.

Bettis, R. and Prahalad, C.K. (1995). "The dominant logic: Retrospective and extention," *Strategic Management Journal*, ISSN 0143-2095, 16: 5-14.

Bettis, R.A. and Hitt, M.A. (1995). "The new competitive landscape," *Strategic Management Journal*, ISSN 0143-2095, 7(13): 7-19.

Beyer, J.M. (1999a). "Taming and promoting charisma to change organizations," *The Leadership Quarterly*, ISSN 1048-9848, 10(2): 307-330.

Beyer, J.M. (1999b). "Two approaches to studying charismatic leadership: Competing or complementary," *The Leadership Quarterly*, ISSN 1048-9843, 10(4): 575-588.

Bienhocker, E. (1999). "Robust adaptive strategies," *Sloan Management Review*, ISSN 0019-848X, Spring: 95-106.

Bigelow, J. (1982). "A catastrophe model of organizational change," *Behavioral Science*, ISSN 0005-7940, 27: 26-42.

Binks, M. and Vale, P. (1990). *Entrepreneurship and Economic Change*, ISBN 0077072189

Bion, W. (1959). Experiences in Groups, ISBN 0415040205 (1968).

Bion, W. (1961). Experiences in Groups and Other Papers, ISBN 0415040205 (1968)

Black, J.A. and Oliver, R. (2004). "Proactive versus passive leader behavior and style influences on the group level context-for-learning," paper presented at the *Proceeding for the Irish Academy of Management*.

Black, J.A., King, J.P. and Oliver, R.L. (2005). "Simulation of emergence of context for learning," *Advances in Applied Business Strategy*, ISSN 0749-6826, 3(3): 275-304.

Black, J.A., Oliver, R.L., Howell, J.P., and King J.P. (2006). "A dynamic system simulation of leader and group effects on context for learning," *The Leadership Quarterly*, ISSN 1048-9843, 17(1): 39.

Blake, R.R. and Mouton, J.S. (1964). *The Managerial Grid: Key Orientations for Achieving Production Through People*, ISBN 0872014746.

Blake, R.R. and Mouton, J.S. (1994). *The Managerial Grid*, ISBN 0884152529.

Blitz, D. (1992). *Emergent Evolution: Qualitative Novelty and the Levels of Reality*, ISBN 9780792316589.

Bluedorn, A. (2002). "Images of planning, performance, and other theory," in F. Yammarino and F. Dansereau (eds.), *Multi-Level Issues in Organizational Behavior and Processes*, ISBN 0762311061, pp. 67-72.

Boal, K. and Schultz, P.L. (in press). "Strategic leadership in complex adaptive systems, storytelling, time and evolution: The role of strategic leadership in complex adaptive systems," *The Leadership Quarterly*, ISSN 1048-9843.

Boden, D. (1997). "Temporal frames: Time and talk in organizations," *Time and Society*, ISSN 0961-463X, 6(1): 5-33.

Boedeker, R.R. and Hughes, S.B. (2005). "How Intel finance uses business partnerships to supercharge results," *Strategic Finance*, ISSN 1524833X, 87(4): 26-33.

Bogardus, E.S. (1934). *Leaders and Leadership*, New York, NY: Appleton-Century-Crofts.

Bohr, N. (1934). *Atomic Theory and the Description of Nature*, ISBN 0-918024-51-X.

Boisot, M. (1998). *Knowledge Assets: Securing Competitive Advantage in the Information Economy*, ISBN 0198290861.

Boisot, M. and Child, J. (1999). "Organizations as adaptive systems in complex environments," *Organization Science*, ISSN 1047-7039, 10(3): 237-252.

Boje, D.M., Gephart Jr., R.P. and Thatchenkery, T.J. (1996). *Postmodern Management and Organization Theory*, ISBN 0803970056.

Boles, H.W. and Davenport, J.A. (1975). *Introduction to Educational Leadership*, ISBN 0060408561.

Boman, M. (1999). "Norms in artificial decision making," *Artificial Intelligence and Law*, ISSN 0924-8463, 7(1): 17-35.

Bonabeau, E. and Meyer, C. (2001). "Swarm intelligence: A whole new way to think about business," *Harvard Business Review*, ISSN 0017-8012, 79(5): 106-114.

Bono, J.E. and Judge, T. (2003). "Self-concordance at work: Toward understanding the motivational effects of transformational leaders," *Academy of Management Journal*, ISSN 0001-4273, 46: 554-571.

Born, D. (1996). "Leadership studies: A critical appraisal," in P. Temes (ed.), *Teaching Leadership*, ISBN 0820428620, Chap. 3.

Boulding, K.E. (1956). "General systems theory: The skeleton of science," *Management Science*, ISSN 0025-1909, 2(3): 197-208.

Boulding, K.E. (1978). *Ecodynamics: A New Theory of Societal Evolution*, ISBN 0803909454

Bowman, J. and Targowski, A. (1987). "Modeling the communication process: The map is not the territory," *Journal of Business Communication*, ISSN 0021-9436, (Fall): 21-34.

Bradbury, H. and Lichtenstein, B. (2000). "Relationality in organizational research: Exploring the space between," *Organization Science*, ISSN 10477039, 11: 551-564.

Breed, W. (1955). "Social control in the newsroom: A functional analysis," *Social Forces*, ISSN 0037-7732, 33: 326-335.

Broad, C.D. (1925). *The Mind and its Place in Nature*, London, England: Routledge and Kegan Paul.

Brock, W.A. (2000). "Some Santa Fe scenery," in D. Colander (ed.), *The Complexity Vi-*

sion and the Teaching of Economics, Cheltenham, UK: Edward Elgar, ISBN, pp, 29-49.

Brooks, R.A. (1990). "Elephants don't play chess," *Robotics and Autonomous Systems*, ISSN 0921-8890, 6: 3-15.

Brown, B.L. (2002). "CTE Organizations," *ERIC Digest*, ISSN 0889-8049, 235, http://SearchERIC.org/ericdc/ED467238.htm.

Brown, C. (1995). *Chaos and Catastrophe Theories*, ISBN 0803958471.

Brown, M.E. and Gioia, D.A. (2002). "Making things click: Distributive leadership in an online division of an offline organization," *Leadership Quarterly*, ISSN 1048-9843, 13(4): 397-420.

Brown, S.L. and Eisenhardt, K.M. (1997). "The art of continuous change: Linking complexity theory and time-paced evolution in relentlessly shifting organizations," *Administrative Science Quarterly*, ISSN 0001-8392, 42(Mar): 1-34.

Brown, S.L. and Eisenhardt, K.M. (1997). *Competing on the Edge: Strategy as Structured Chaos*, ISBN 0875847544.

Brown, S.L. and Eisenhardt, K.M. (1998). *Competing on the Edge: Strategy as Structured Chaos*, ISBN 0585236690.

Browning, L., Beyer, J. and Shetler, J. (1995). "Building cooperation in a competitive industry: Sematech and the semiconductor industry," *Academy of Management Journal*, ISSN 0001-4273, 38: 113-151.

Bruderer, E. and Singh, J.V. (1996). "Organizational evolution, learning and selection: A genetic-algorithm-based model," *Academy of Management Journal*, ISSN 0001-4273, 39: 1322-1349.

Bryman, A. (1996). "Leadership in organizations," in S.R. Clegg, C. Hardy and W. Nord (eds.), *Handbook of Organization Studies*, ISBN 0585323321, pp. 276-292.

Buber, M. (1970). *I and Thou*, ISBN 0684717255.

Buckle, P. (2003). "Uncovering system teleology: A case for reading unconscious patterns of purposive intent in organizations," *Systems Research and Behavioral Science*, ISSN 1092-7026, 20: 435-444.

Buckle-Hennings, P. and Dugan, S. (2007, this volume). "Leaders' detection of problematic self-organized patterns in the workplace," in J. Hazy, J. Goldstein and B. Lichtenstein (eds.), *Complex Systems Leadership Theory*, ISBN 9780979168864.

Buckley, W. (1967). *Sociology and Modern Systems Theory*, ISBN 9780138213305.

Buckley, W. (1968). "Society as a complex adaptive system," in W. Buckley (ed.), *Modern Systems Research for the Behavioral Scientist*, Chicago: Aldine, ISBN 9780202300115, pp. 490-513.

Buder, E.H. (1996). "Dynamics of speech processes in dyadic interaction," in J.H. Watt and C.A. VanLear (eds.), *Dynamic Patterns in Communication Processes*, ISBN 0803956193, pp. 301-326.

Bundel, C.M. (1930). "Is leadership losing its importance?" *Infantry Journal*, 36: 339-349.

Bunge, M. (2003). *Emergence and Convergence: Qualitative Novelty and the Unity of Knowledge*, ISBN 9780802088604.

Burgelman, R.A. (1983). "A process model of internal, corporate venturing in the diversified major firm," *Administrative Science Quarterly*, ISSN 0001-8392, 28(2): 223-244.

Burgelman, R.A. (1983). "Corporate entrepreneurship and strategic management: Insights from a process study," *Management Science*, ISSN 0025-1909, 29: 1349-1364.

Burns, J.M. (1978). *Leadership*, ISBN 0061319759.

Burns, J.M. (2003). *Transforming Leadership: A Pursuit of Happiness*, ISBN

0871138662.

Burrell, G. and Morgan, G. (1979). *Sociological Paradigms and Organizational Analysis: Elements of the Sociology of Corporate Life*, ISBN 1857421140.

Burt, R.S. (1987). "Social contagion and innovation: Cohesion versus structural equivalence," *American Journal of Sociology*, ISSN 0002-9602, 92(May): 1287-1335.

Burton, R.M. (2003). "Computational laboratories for organization science: Questions, validity and docking," *Computational and Mathematical Organization Theory*, ISSN 1381-298X, 9(2): 91-108.

Burton, R.M. and Obel, B. (2002). *Strategic Organizational Diagnosis and Design: The Dynamics of Fit*, ISBN 1402076843.

Bushev, M. (1994). *Synergetics: Chaos, Order, Self-Organization*, ISBN 9810212860

Calvert, R.L. (1992). "Leadership and its basis in problems of social coordination," *International Political Science Review*, ISSN 0192-5121, 13(1): 7-24.

Canary, D.J. and Lakey, S.G. (2006). "Managing conflict in a competent manner: A mindful look at events that matter," in J.G. Oetzel and S. Ting-Toomey (eds.), *The Sage Handbook of Conflict Communication: Integrating Theory, Research, and Practice*, ISBN 0761930450, pp. 185-210.

Canella, A.A. and Monroe, M.J. (1997). "Contrasting perspectives on strategic leaders: Toward a more realistic view of top managers," *Journal of Management*, ISSN 0149-2063, 23(3): 213-230.

Cano, J. and Bankston, J. (1992). "Factors which influence participation and non-participation of ethnic minority youth in Ohio 4-H programs," *Journal of Agricultural Education*, ISSN 1042-0541, 33(1): 23-29.

Capra, F. (1996). *The Web of Life*, ISBN 0385476760.

Capra, F. (2005). "Complexity and life," *Theory, Culture and Society*, ISSN 0263-2764, 22(5): 33-44.

Carey, J.W. (1975). "A cultural approach to communication," *Communication*, ISSN 0882-4088, 2: 1-22.

Carley, K.M, and Svoboda, D. (1996). "Modeling organizational adaptation as a simulated annealing process," *Sociological Methods and Research*, ISSN 0049-1241, 25(1): 138-168.

Carley, K.M. (1990). "Group stability: A socio-cognitive approach," in H. Walker (ed.), *Advances in Group Processes: Theory and Research*, ISSN 0882-6145, Vol. VII, pp. 1-44.

Carley, K.M. (1991). "A theory of group stability," *American Sociological Review*, ISSN 0003-1224, 56(3): 331-354.

Carley, K.M. (1992). "Organizational learning and personnel turnover," *Organization Science*, ISSN 1047-7039, 3(1): 20-46.

Carley, K.M. (1995). "Computational and mathematical organization theory: Perspective and directions," *Computational and Mathematical Organization Theory*, ISSN 1381-298X, 1: 39-56.

Carley, K.M. (1996). "A comparison of artificial and human organizations," *Journal of Economic Behavior and Organization*, ISSN 0167-2681, 31: 175-191.

Carley, K.M. (1997). "Organizational adaptation," *Annals of Operations Research*, ISSN 0254-5330, 75: 25-47.

Carley, K.M. (1999a). "Organizational change and the digital economy: A computational organization science perspective," in B. Kahin (ed.), *Understanding the Digital Economy: Data, Tools, Research*, ISBN 0262024748.

Carley, K.M. (1999b). "On the evolution of social and organizational networks," in D. Knoke (ed.), special issue of *Research in the Sociology of Organizations on Networks in and around Organizations*, ISBN 0762304731, 16: 3-30.

Carley, K.M. (1999c). "Learning within and among organizations," *Advances in Strategic Management*, ISSN 0742-3322, 16: 33-53.

Carley, K.M. (2002a). "Intra-organizational computation and complexity," in J.A.C. Baum (ed.), *Companion to Organizations*, ISBN 0631216952, pp. 208-232.

Carley, K.M. (2002b). "Smart agents and organizations of the future," in S. Livingstone (ed.), *The Handbook of New Media*, ISBN 0761965106, pp. 206-220.

Carley, K.M. (2003). "Dynamic network analysis," in P. Pattison (ed.), *Dynamic Social Network Analysis: Workshop Summary and Papers*, ISBN 0309519160, 133-145.

Carley, K.M. and Gasser, L. (1999). "Computational organization theory," in G. Weiss (ed.), *Multiagent Systems: A Modern Approach to Distributed Artificial Intelligence*, ISBN 0262232030, pp. 299-330.

Carley, K.M. and Hill, V. (2001). "Structural change and learning within organizations," in E.R. Larsen (ed.), *Dynamics of Organizations: Computational Modeling and Organization Theories*, ISBN 0262621525, pp. 63-92.

Carley, K.M. and Kamneva, N. (2004). "A network optimization approach for improving organizational design," Carnegie Mellon University, School of Computer Science, Institute for Software Research, International, Technical Report, CMU-ISRI-04-102.

Carley, K.M. and Krackhardt, D. (1999, June). "A typology for C2 measures," presented at the 1999 International Symposium on Command and Control Research and Technology, Newport, RI.

Carley, K.M. and Lee, J.-S. (1998). "Dynamic organizations: Organizational adaptation in a changing environment," *Advances in Strategic Management*, ISSN 0742-3322, 15: 269-297.

Carley, K.M. and Prietula, M.J. (1994). "ACTS Theory: Extending the model of bounded rationality," in K.M. Carley and M.J. Prietula (eds.), *Computational Organizational Theory*, ISBN 080581406X, pp. 55-88.

Carley, K.M. and Prietula, M.J. (1994). *Computational Organization Theory*, ISBN 080581406X

Carley, K.M. and Reminga, J. (2004). "ORA: Organizational risk analyzer," Carnegie Mellon University, School of Computer Science, Institute for Software Research, International, Technical Report, CMU-ISRI-04-101.

Carley, K.M. and Ren, Y. (2001). "Tradeoffs between performance and adaptability for C3I architectures," presented at the Command and Control Research and Technology Symposium, Annapolis, MD.

Carley, K.M. and Svoboda, D.M. (1996). "Modeling organizational adaptation as a simulated annealing process," *Sociological Methods and Research*, ISSN 0049-1241, 25(1): 138-168.

Carley, K.M., Ren, Y. and Krackhardt, D. (2000a, June). "Measuring and modeling change in C3I architecture," presented at the 2000 Command and Control Research and Technology Symposium, Annapolis, MD.

Carley, K.M., Ren, Y. and Krackhardt, D. (2000b, June). "Measuring and modeling change in C3I architectures," presented at the 2000 Command and Control Research Symposium, Naval Postgraduate School, Monterey, CA.

Carlyle, T. (1907). *Heroes and Hero Worship*, Boston, MA: Adams. (Original work published 1841)

Carniero, R. (1970). "A theory of the origin of the state," *Science*, ISSN 0036-8075, 169: 733-738.

Carniero, R. (1987). "The evolution of complexity in human societies and it mathematical expression," *International Journal of Comparative Sociology*, ISSN 0020-7152, 28: 111-128.

Carroll, T. and Burton, R.M. (2000). "Organizations and complexity: Searching for the edge of chaos," *Computational and Mathematical Organization Theory*, ISSN 1381298X, 6(4): 319-337.

Cartwright, D. and Zander, A. (1953). *Group Dynamics: Research and Theory*, New York, NY: Harper and Row.

Casti, J. (1994). *Complexification: Explaining a Paradoxical World through the Science of Surprise*, ISBN 978-006168889

Cattell, R.B. (1951). "New concepts of measuring leadership in terms of group syntality," *Human Relations*, ISSN 0018-7267, 4: 161-184.

Chaisson, E. (2001). *Cosmic Evolution: The Rise of Complexity in Nature*, ISBN 067400342X.

Chaitin, G. (2001). *Exploring Randomness*, ISBN 978-1852334178.

Chandler, G. and Lyon, D. (2001). "Issues of research design and construct measurement in entrepreneurship research: The past decade," *Entrepreneurship Theory and Practice*, ISSN 1042-2587, 25(4-Summer): 101-113.

Chang, M.-H. and Harrington, J.E. (2006). "Agent-based models of organizations," in L. Tesfatsion and K.L. Judd (eds.), *Handbook of Computational Economics II: Agent-Based Computational Economics*, ISBN 0444512535, pp. 1273-1337.

Chemers, M.M. (1997). *An Integrative Theory of Leadership*, ISBN 0805826785.

Cheng, Y. and A. Van de Ven, (1996). "The innovation journey: Order out of chaos?" *Organization Science*, ISSN 1047-7039, 6: 593-614.

Child, J. and McGrath, R.G. (2001). "Organizations unfettered: Organizational form in an information-intensive economy," *Academy of Management Journal*, ISSN 0001-4273, 44(6): 1135-1148.

Chiles, T., Meyer, A. and Hench, T. (2004). "Organizational emergence: The origin and transformation of Branson, Missouri's musical theaters," *Organization Science*, ISSN 1047-3039, 15(5): 499-519.

Choi, T., Dooley, K., and Rungtusanatham, M. (2001). "Supply networks and complex adaptive systems: Control versus emergence," *Journal of Operations Management*, ISSN 0272-6963, 19:351-366.

Choo, W.C. (1998). *The Knowing Organization: How Organizations Use Information to Construct Meaning, Create Knowledge, and Make Decisions*, ISBN 0195110129.

Cilliers, P. (1998). *Complexity and Postmodernism: Understanding Complex Systems*, ISBN 0415152860

Clark, A. (1996). "Happy couplings: Emergence and explanatory interlock," in M. Boden (ed.), *The Philosophy of Artificial Life*, ISBN 0198751559, pp. 262-281.

Clark, K.B. and Fujimoto, T. (1991). *Product Development Performance*, ISBN 0875842453.

Cohen, J. and Stewart, I. (1994). *The Collapse of Chaos: Discovering Simplicity in a Complex World*, ISBN 9780140178746.

Cohen, M. (1999). "Commentary on the Organization Science Special Issue on Complexity," *Organization Science*, ISSN 1047-7039, 10: 373-376.

Cohen, M. D., March, J. G. and Olsen, J. P. (1972). "A garbage can model of organizational choice," *Administrative Science Quarterly*, ISSN 0001-8392, 17: 1-25.

Cohen, W. and Levinthal, D.A. (1990). "Absorptive capacity: A new perspective on learning and innovation," *Administrative Science Quarterly*, ISSN 00018392, 35:128-152.

Colbert, B. (2004). "The complex resource-based view: Implications for theory and practice in strategic human resource management," *Academy of Management Review*, ISSN 0363-7425, 29: 341-358.

Cole, G.A. (1996). *Management: Theory and Practice*, ISBN 1844800881.

Collinson, D. (2006). "Rethinking followership: A post-structuralist analysis of follower identities," *The Leadership Quarterly*, ISSN 1048-9843, 17: 179-189.

Colomer, J. M. (1995). "Leadership games in collective action," *Rationality and Society*, ISSN 1043-4631, 7(2): 225-246.

Computational and Mathematical Organization Theory. Volumes 1 through 10, ISBN 080581406

Conforti, M. (1999). *Field, Form, and Fate: Patterns in Mind, Nature, and Psyche*, ISBN 188267040X.

Conger, J.A. (1999). "Charismatic and transformational leadership in organizations: An insider's perspective on these developing streams of research," *The Leadership Quarterly*, ISSN 1048-9843, 10(2): 145-179.

Conger, J.A. and Kanungo, R.N. (1987). "Toward a behavioral theory of charismatic leadership in organizational settings," *Academy of Management Review*, ISSN 0363-7425, 12: 637-647.

Conger, J.A. and Kanungo, R.N. (1994). "Charismatic leadership in organizations: Perceived behavioral attributes and their measurement," *Journal of Organizational Behavior*, ISSN 0160-8061, 15, 439-452.

Conrad, C. (1994). *Strategic Organizational Communication: Toward the Twenty-First Century*, ISBN 0155007866.

Conte, R. and Castelfranchi, C. (1995). *Cognitive and Social Action*, ISBN 1857281861.

Contractor, N.S. (1994). "Self-organizing systems perspective in the study of organizational communication," in B. Kovačić (ed.), *New Approaches to Organizational Communication*, ISBN 0791419185, pp. 39-65.

Contractor, N.S. (1999). "Self-organizing systems research in social sciences: Reconciling metaphors and the models," *Management Communication Quarterly*, ISSN 0893-3189, (13)1: 154-166.

Copeland, N. (1942). *Psychology and the Soldier*, Harrisburg, PA: Military Service Publications.

Coren, R. (1998). *The Evolutionary Trajectory: The Growth of Information in the History and Future of the Earth*, ISBN 9056996010.

Corman, S. and Dooley, K. (2006). "Crawdad Text Analysis System 2.0," Chandler, Arizona: Crawdad Technologies, LLC.

Corman, S. R., Dooley, K.J., Kuhn, R. and McPhee, R.D. (2002). "Studying complex discursive systems: Centering resonance analysis of communication," *Human Communication Research*, ISSN 0360-3989, 28(2): 157-206.

Cowan, G., Pines, D. and Meltzer, D. (eds.) (1994). *Complexity: Metaphors, Models, and Reality*, ISBN 0201626055.

Cowley, W.H. (1928). "Three distinctions in the study of leaders," *Journal of Abnormal and Social Psychology*, 23: 144-157.

Croom, D.B. and Flowers, J.L. (2001). "A question of relevance: FFA programs and services as perceived by FFA members and non-members," *Journal of Southern Agricultural Education Research*, 51: 1-13.

Crossan, M.M., Lane, H.W. and White, R.E. (1999). "An organizational learning framework: From intuition to institution," *Academy of Management Review*, ISSN 0363-7425, 24(3): 522-537.

Crowston, K. (1996). "An approach to evolving novel organizational forms," *Computational and Mathematical Organization Theory*, ISBN 080581406, 2: 29-47.

Crutchfield, J. (1993). "The calculi of emergence: Computation, dynamics, and induction," SantaFe Institute working paper # 94-03-016, Santa Fe, NM: Santa Fe Institute.

Crutchfield, J. (1994). "Is anything ever new? Considering emergence," in G. Cowan, D. Pines and D. Meltzer (eds.), *Complexity: Metaphors, Models, and Realty*, ISBN 0201626055, pp. 515-537.

Csanyi, V. and Kampis, G. (1985). "Autogenesis: Evolution of replicative systems," *Journal of Theoretical Biology*, ISSN 0022-5193, 114: 303-321.

Csikszentmihalyi, M. (1991), *Flow: The Psychology of Optimal Experience*, ISBN 0060920432.

Cyert, R. and March, J. (1963). *A Behavioral Theory of the Firm*, ISBN 0631174516 (1992).

Daft, R.L. and Weick, K.E. (1984). "Toward a model of organizations as interpretation systems," *Academy of Management Review*, ISSN 0363-7425, 9(2): 284-295.

Dal Forno, A. and Merlone U. (2001). "Incentive policy and optimal effort: Equilibria in heterogeneous agents populations," Quaderni del Dipartimento di Statistica e Matematica Applicata, n. 10, Università di Torino, working paper.

Dal Forno, A. and Merlone U. (2005). "Network dynamics when selecting work team members: A comparison between experimental and computational results," paper presented at the 2005 North American Association for Computational Social and Organizational Science, Notre Dame, IN.

Dal Forno, A. and Merlone, U. (2004). "From classroom experiments to computer code," *Journal of Artificial Societies and Social Simulation*, ISSN 1460-7425, 7(3), http://jasss.soc.surrey.ac.uk /7/3/2.html.

Dal Forno, A. and Merlone, U. (2006). "The emergence of effective leaders: A experimental and computational approach," *Emergence: Complexity and Organization*, ISSN 1521-3250, 8(4): 36-51.

Damanpour, F. (1991). "Organizational innovation: A meta-analysis of effects of determinant and moderators," *Academy of Management Journal*, ISSN 0001-4273, 34: 555-590.

Dansereau, F., Yammarino, F. and Kohles, J. (1999). "Multiple levels of analysis from a longitudinal perspective: Some implications for theory building," *Academy of Management Review*, ISSN 0363-7425, 24: 346-357.

Davenport, T.H. (2001). "Knowledge work and the future of management," in W.G. Bennis, G.M. Spreitzer and T.G. Cummings (eds), *The Future of Leadership: Today's Top Leadership Thinkers Speak to Tomorrow's Leaders*, ISBN 0787955671, pp. 41-58.

Davidsson, P. and Wiklund, J. (2001). "Levels of analysis in entrepreneurship research: Current research practice and suggestions for the future," *Entrepreneurship Theory and Practice*, ISSN 1042-2587, 25(4): 81-100.

Davila, T., Epstein, M.J., and Shelton, R. (2006). *Making Innovation Work: How to Manage It, Measure It, and Profit from It, Upper Saddle River*, ISBN 0536122326.

Davis, J.N. (2005). How is charisma routinized? A new look at an old question. Unpublished Dissertation, Texas Tech University, Lubbock.

Davis, J.P., Eisenhardt, K. and Bingham, C. (2007). "Developing theory through simulation methods," *Academy of Management Review*, ISSN 0363-7425, 32: 480-499.

Davis-Blake, A. and Pfeffer, J. (1989). "Just a mirage: The search for dispositional effects in organizational research," *Academy of Management Review*, ISSN 0363-7425, 14(3): 385-400.

De Dreu, C.K.W., van Dierendonck, D. and Dijkstra, M.T.M. (2004). "Conflict at work and individual well-being," *International Journal of Conflict Management*, ISSN 1044-4068, 15(1): 6-26.

De Vany, A. (1996). "Information, chance, and evolution: Alchian and the economics of self-organization," *Economic Inquiry*, ISSN 0095-2583, 34: 427-442.

Deetz, S. (1986). "Metaphors and the discursive production and reproduction of organization," in L. Thayer (ed.), *Organizations-Communication: Emerging Perspectives*, ISBN 0893912743, pp. 168-182.

Denhardt, R. (1981). *In the Shadow of Organization*, ISBN 0700602100.

Denison, D.R., Hooijberg, R., and Quinn, R.E. (1995). "Paradox and performance: Toward a theory of behavioral complexity in managerial leadership," *Organization Science*, ISSN 10477039, 6(5): 524-540.

Dent, E. (1999). "Complexity science: A worldview shift," *Emergence*, ISSN 1521-3250, 1(4): 5-19.

Depew, D. and Weber, B. (1995). *Darwinism Evolving*, ISBN 0262041456

Depew, D. and Weber, B. (eds.) (1985). *Evolution at a Crossroads: The New Biology and the New Philosophy of Science*, ISBN 0262040794

Dhillon, G. and Fabian, F. (2005). "A fractal perspective on competencies necessary for managing information systems," *International Journal of Technology Management*, ISSN 0267-5730, 31(1/2): 129-139.

Diamond, A., Jr. (2004). "Schumpeter's central message," Milan Conference of the International Schumpeter Society.

DiMaggio, P.J. and Powell, W.W. (1983). "The iron cage revisited: Institutional isomorphism and collective rationality in organizational fields," *American Sociological Review*, ISSN 0003-1224, 48(Apr): 147-160.

Diner, S., Fargue, D. and Lochak, G. (eds.) (1986). *Dynamical Systems: A Renewal of Mechanism*, ISBN 978-9971501501.

Dolan, S.I., Garcia, S. and Auerbach, A. (2003). "Understanding and managing chaos in organizations," *International Journal of Management*, ISSN 0813-0183, 20(1): 23-35.

Donaldson, G. and Lorsch, J.W. (1983). *Decision-Making At the Top: The Shaping of Strategic Direction*, ISBN 0465015840.

Dooley, K.J. (1997). "A complex adaptive systems model of organization change," *Nonlinear Dynamics, Psychology and Life Sciences*, ISSN 1573-6652, 1(1): 69-97.

Dooley, K.J. (2004). "Complexity science models of organizational change," in S. Poole and A. Van De Ven (eds.), *Handbook of Organizational Change and Development*, ISBN 0195135008, pp. 354-373.

Dooley, K.J. (in press). "Organizational psychology," in S. Gaustello, D. Pincus and M. Koopmans (eds.), *Chaos and Complexity: Recent Advances and Future Directions in the Theory of Nonlinear Dynamical Systems Psychology*, Cambridge, MA: Cambridge University Press.

Dooley, K.J. and Lichtenstein, B. (in press). "Research methods for studying the complexity dynamics of leadership," in M. Uhl-Bien and R. Marion (eds.), *Complexity and Leadership Volume I: Conceptual Foundations*, Charlotte, NC: Information Age Publishing.

Dooley, K.J. and Van de Ven, A. (1999). "Explaining complex organizational dynamics," *Organization Science*, ISSN 1047-7039, 10(3): 358-372.

Dooley, K.J., Bush, D. and Johnson, T. (1995). "TQM, chaos, and complexity," *Human Systems Management*, ISSN 0167-2533, 14(4): 1-16.

Dooley, K.J., Corman, S. R., McPhee, R. D. and Kuhn, T. (2003). "Modeling high-resolution broadband discourse in complex adaptive systems," *Nonlinear Dynamics, Psychology and Life Sciences*, ISSN 1090-0578, 7(1): 61-86.

Dörner, D. (1996). *The Logic of Failure*, ISBN 0201479486.

Dosi, G. and Fagiolo, G. (1998). "Exploring the unknown: On entrepreneurship, coordination and innovation-driven growth," in J. Lesourne and A. Orlean (eds.), *Advances in Self-Organization and Evolutionary Economics*, ISBN 1902282000, pp.

308-352.

Dosi, G., Nelson, R. R. and Winter, S. G. (eds.) (2000). *The Nature and Dynamics of Organizational Capabilities*, ISBN 0199248540.

Dougherty, D. and Hardy, C. (1996). "Sustained product innovation in large, mature organizations: Overcoming innovation-to-organization problems," *The Academy of Management Journal*, ISSN 0001-4273, 39(5): 1120-1153.

Drath, W. (2001). *The Deep Blue Sea: Rethinking the Source of Leadership*, ISBN 0787949329.

Drazin, R. and Sandelands, L. (1992). "Autogenesis: A perspective on the process of organizing," *Organizational Science*, ISSN 1047-7039, 3: 230-249.

Dubinskas, F. (1994). "On the edge of chaos: A metaphor for transformative change," *Journal of Management Inquiry*, ISSN 1056-4926, 3: 355-366.

Dumont, L. (1966). *Homo Hiérarchicus Essai sur le Système des Castes*, Paris: Gallimard: Bibliothèque des Sciences Humaines.

Dupuy, J.P. (1992). *Introduction aux Sciences Sociales, Logique des Phénomènes Collectifs*, ISBN 2729892265

Dupuy, J.P. (2000). *The Mechanization of Mind*, ISBN 9780691025742

Dvir, T., Eden, D., Avolio, B.J. and Shamir, B. (2002). "Impact of transformational leadership on follower development and performance: A field experiment," *Academy of Management Journal*, ISSN 0001-4273, 45: 735-74.

Eastman, W. and Bailey, J.R. (1998). "Mediating the fact-value antinomy: Patterns in managerial and legal rhetoric, 1890-1990," *Organization Science*, ISSN 1047-7039, 9(2): 232-245.

Eisenhardt, K.M. (1989). "Agency theory: An assessment and review," *The Academy of Management Review*, ISSN 0363-7425, 14(1): 57-74.

Eisenhardt, K.M. (1989). "Building theories from case study research," *The Academy of Management Review*, ISSN 0363-7425, 14(4): 532-550.

Eisenhardt, K.M. and Bhatia, M. (2002). "Organizational complexity and computation," in J. Baum (ed.), *Companion to Organizations*, ISBN 0631216944

Eisenhardt, K.M. and Martin, J.A. (2000). "Dynamic capabilities: What are they?" *Strategic Management Journal*, ISSN 0143-2095, 21: 1105-1121.

Elliott, E. and Kiel, D. (eds.) (1996). *Chaos Theory in the Social Sciences: Foundations and Applications*, ISBN 0472106384

Emmech, C., Koppe, S., and Stjernfelt, F. (1998). "Explaining emergence: Towards an ontology of levels," *Journal for General Philosophy of Science*, 28: 83-119.

Epstein, J. M. and Axtell, R. (1996). *Growing Artificial Societies: Social Science from the Bottom Up*, ISBN 0585033579

Erlenkotter, D., Sethi, S., and Okada, N. (1989). "Planning for surprise: Water resources development under demand and supply uncertainty," *Management Science*, ISSN 1526-5501, 35(Feb): 149-163.

Etzioni, A. (1964). *Modern Organizations*, ISSN 9901336384.

Eve, R., Horsfall, S. and Lee, M. (eds.) (1997). *Chaos, Complexity, and Sociology*, ISBN 0761908897.

Fairhurst, G.T. (2001). "Dualism in leadership research," in F.M. Jablin and L.L. Putnam (eds.), *The New Handbook of Organizational Communication: Advances in Theory, Research, and Methods*, ISBN 0803955030, pp. 379-439.

Fama, E.F. (1980). "Agency problems and the theory of the firm," *The Journal of Political Economy*, ISSN 0022-3808, 88(2): 288-307.

Fauconnier, G. and Turner, M. (2002). *The Way We Think: Conceptual Blending and the Mind's Hidden Complexities*, ISBN 9780465087860.

Fayol, H. (1949). *General and Industrial Management*, C. Storrs (trans.), London: Pitman.

Ferber, J. (1999). Multi-Agent Systems: An Introduction to Distributed Artificial Intelligence, ISBN 0201360489.

Festinger, L. (1950). "Informal social communication," *Psychology Review*, ISSN 1354-1129, 57: 271-282.

Festinger, L. (1957). *A Theory of Cognitive Dissonance*, ISBN 0804709114.

Fiedler, F.E. (1967). *A Theory of Leadership Effectiveness*, ISBN 0070206759.

Finke, R., Ward, T. and Smith, S. (1996). *Creative Cognition: Theory, Research, and Applications*, ISBN 9780262560962

Finkelstein, S. (2002). "Planning in organizations: One vote for complexity," in F. Yammarino and F. Dansereua (eds.), *Multi-level Issues in Organizational Behavior and Processes*, ISBN 0762311061, pp. 73-80.

Fiol, C.M., Harris, D. and House, R. (1999). "Charismatic leadership: Strategies for effecting social change," *The Leadership Quarterly*, ISSN 1047-7039, 10: 449-482.

Fioretti, G. and Visser, B. (2004). "A cognitive interpretation of organizational complexity," *Emergence, Complexity & Organization*, ISSN 1521-3250, 6(1/2): 11-23.

Fishbein, M. and Ajzen I. (1975). *Belief, Attitude, Intention, and Behavior: An Introduction to Theory and Research*, ISBN 0201020890.

Fishbein, M. and Ajzen, I. (1981). "Acceptance, yielding, and impact: Cognitive processes in persuasion," in R.E. Petty, T.M. Ostrom, and T.C. Brock (eds), *Cognitive Responses in Persuasion*, ISBN 0898590256.

Fisher, D. and Torbert, W. (1995). *Personal and Organizational Transformations: The True Challenge of Continual Quality Improvement*, ISBN 0077078349.

Fisher, D., Rooke, D. and Torbert, B. (2003). *Personal and Organizational Transformations through Action Inquiry*, ISBN 0953818403

Fisher, R.A. (1930). *The Genetical Theory of Natural Selection*, Oxford, UK: Clarendon.

Fiske, J. (1990). *Introduction to Communication Studies*, ISBN 0415046726.

Fiumara, G.C. (1990). "Midwifery and philosophy," in G. C. Fiumara (ed.), *The Other Side of Language: A Philosophy of Listening*, ISBN 0415026210, pp. 143-168.

Fleishman, E.A. (1953). "Leadership climate, human relations training, and supervisory behavior," *Personnel Psychology*, ISSN 0031-5826, 6: 205-222.

Fleishman, E.A. (1953). "The description of supervisory behavior," *Personnel Psychology*, ISSN 0031-5826, 37: 1-6.

Fleming, L. (2001). "Recombinant uncertainty in technological search," *Management Science*, ISSN 0025-1909, 47(1): 117-132.

Fleming, L. and Sorenson, O. (2001). "Technology as a complex adaptive system," *Research Policy*, ISSN 0048-7333, 30: 1019-1039.

Fontana, W. and Buss, L. (1996). "The Barrier of objects: From dynamical systems to bounded organizations," in J. Casti and A. Karlqvist (eds.), *Boundaries and Barriers: On the Limits to Scientific Knowledge*, ISBN 978-0201555707, pp 55-115.

Forrester, J.W. (1961). *Industrial Dynamics*, Cambridge, MA, MIT Press, ISBN 9781883823368.

Forrester, J.W. (1968). *Principles of Systems: Text and Workbook*, ISBN 0262560178.

Forrester, J.W. (1987). "Nonlinearity of high-order models of social systems," *European Journal of Operational Research*, ISSN 0377-2217, 30: 211-221.

Forrester, J.W. (1996). "Leadership in a changing society," paper presented at the Cultural leadership forum, Center for American studies at Concord, Concord, MA.

Foster, J. (2000). "Competitive selection, self-organization and Joseph A. Schumpeter," *Journal of Evolutionary Economics*, ISSN 0936-9937, 10: 311-328.

Foucault, M. (1979). *The History of Sexuality*, ISBN 0713910941.

Franz, M. (1992). *Eric Voegelin and the Politics of Spiritual Revolt*, ISBN 0807117404.

Fredericks, E. (2005). "Cross-functional involvement in new product development: A resource dependency and human capital perspective," *Qualitative Market Research*, ISSN 1352-2752, 8(3): 327-341.

French, J. P. R. and Raven, B. (1960). "The bases of social power," in D. Cartwright and A. Zander (eds.), *Group Dynamics*, ISBN 9780060412012 (1998), pp. 607-623

Freud, S. (1962). *Three Essays on the Theory of Sexuality*, ISBN 0465086063.

Frost, C.H., Wakely, J.H. and Ruh, R.A. (1974). *The Scanlon Plan for Organizational Development: Identity Participation, and Equity*, ISBN 0870131842.

Fudenberg, D. and Tirole, J. (1991). *Game Theory*, ISBN 0262061414.

Gale, D. (1993). "Mathematical entertainments," *Mathematical Intelligencer*, ISSN 0343-6993, 15: 54-55.

Galton, F. (1871). *Hereditary Genius: An Inquiry Into Its Laws and Consequences*, London, England: Macmillan.

Gantt, H.L. (1919). *Organizing for Work*, New York, NY: Harcourt, Brace, and Howe.

Gardner, J. (1990). *On Leadership*, ISBN 0029113121.

Garud, R. and Karnøe, P. (2003). "Bricolage versus breakthrough: distributed and embedded agency in technology entrepreneurship," *Research Policy*, ISSN 0048-7333, 32: 277-301.

Garud, R. and Van de Ven, A. (2002). "Strategic organizational change processes," in H. Pettigrew, H. Thomas and R. Whittington (eds.), *Handbook of Strategy and Management*, ISBN 0761958932, pp. 206-231.

Garud, R., Kumaraswamy, A. and Sambamurthy, V. (2006). "Emergent by design: Performance and transformation at Infosys Technologies," *Organization Science*, ISSN 1047-7039, 17: 277-286.

Gavetti, G. and Levinthal, D.A. (2000). "Looking forward and looking backward: Cognitive and experiential search," *Administrative Science Quarterly*, ISSN 0001-8392, 45(1): 113-137.

Gavetti, G., Levinthal, D. and Rivkin, J. (2005). "Strategy making in novel and complex worlds: The power of analogy," *Strategic Management Journal*, ISSN 0143-2095, 26: 691-712.

Gell-Mann, M. (1994). *The Quark and the Jaguar*, ISBN 0716727250.

Gemmill, G. and Oakley, J. (1992). "Leadership: An alienating social myth," *Human Relations*, ISSN 0018-7267, 45:113-129.

George, J.M. (1991). "State or trait: Effects of positive mood in pro-social behavior," *Journal of Applied Psychology*, ISSN 0021-9010, 76: 299-307.

Georgescu-Roegen, N. (1971). *The Entropy Law and the Economic Process*, ISBN 9781583486009 (1999).

Gersick, C. (1994). "Pacing strategic change: The case of a new venture," *Academy of Management Journal*, ISSN 0001-4273, 37(1): 9-45.

Gibb, C.A. (1954). "Leadership," in G. Linzey (ed.), *Handbook of Social Psychology*, Vol. 2, Reading, MA: Addison-Wesley, pp. 877-920.

Giddens, A. (1977). *New Rules of Sociological Method: A Positive Critique of Interpretative Sociologies*, ISBN 0091275210.

Giddens, A. (1979). *Central Problems in Social Theory: Action, Structure and Contradiction in Social Analysis*, ISBN 0520039750.

Giddens, A. (1984). *The Constitution of Society: Outline of the Theory of Structuration*, ISBN 0520052927.

Giddens, A. (1993). *New Rules of Sociological Method*, ISBN 0804722269.

Gilbert, N. and Troitzsch, K.G. (1999). *Simulation for the Social Scientist*, ISBN 0335197450

Gillett, C. (1998). "Back to the cosmological future? Samuel Alexander's emergentism, non-reductive physicalism, and Kim's challenge," presented at the eighth annual international conference, Society for Chaos Theory in Psychology and the Life Sciences, Boston, MA, August 2.

Gioia, D., Schultz, M. and Corley, K. (2000). "Organizational identity, image, and adaptive instability," *Academy of Management Review*, ISSN 0363-7425, 25: 63-81.

Glaser, B. (1978). *Theoretical Sensitivity: Advances in the Methodology of Grounded Theory*, ISBN 1884156010.

Glaser, B. (1992). *Emergence vs. Forcing: Basics of Grounded Theory and Analysis*, ISBN 1884156002.

Glaser, B. and Strauss, A. (1967). *The Discovery of Grounded Theory: Strategies for Qualitative Research*, ISBN 0202302601.

Gleick, J. (1987). *Chaos: Making a New Science*, ISBN 9780140092509 (1988).

Gödel, K. (1962). *On Formally Undecidable Propositions of Principia Mathematica and Related Systems*, ISBN 0486669807

Goerner, S. (1994). *Chaos and the Evolving Ecological Universe*, Gordon and Breach, ISBN 9782881246357.

Goffman, E. (1983). "The interaction order," *American Sociological Review*, ISSN 0003-1224, 48(1): 1-17.

Goldspink, C. and Kay, R. (2003). "Organizations as self-organizing and sustaining systems: A complex and autopoietic systems perspective," *International Journal of General Systems*, ISSN 03081079, 32(5): 459-474.

Goldstein, J.A. (1986). "A far-from-equilibrium systems approach to resistance to change," *Organizational Dynamics*, ISSN 0090-2616, 15(1): 5-20.

Goldstein, J.A. (1994). *The Unshackled Organization*, ISBN 156327048X.

Goldstein, J.A. (1996). "Causality and emergence in chaos and complexity theories," in W. Sulis and A. Combs (eds.), *Nonlinear Dynamics in Human Behavior*, ISBN 9781586030209, pp. 161-190.

Goldstein, J.A. (1997a). "Riding the waves of emergence: Leadership innovations in complex systems," in C. Lindberg, P. Plsek and B. Zimmerman (eds.), *Edgeware: Complexity Resources for Health Care Leaders*, ISBN 9780966782806 (1998), pp. IX17-IX36.

Goldstein, J.A. (1997b). "Map-makers, explorers, and tricksters: New roles for planning and prediction in nonlinear, complex systems," in C. Lindberg, P. Plsek and B. Zimmerman (eds.), *Edgeware: Complexity Resources for Health Care Leaders*, pp. V3-V31.

Goldstein, J.A. (1999). "Emergence as a construct: History and issues," *Emergence*, ISSN 1521-3250, 1(1): 49-72.

Goldstein, J.A. (2000). "Emergence: A concept amid a thicket of conceptual snares," *Emergence*, ISSN 1521-3250, 2 (1): 5-22.

Goldstein, J.A. (2000). "Psychology and corporations: A complex systems perspective," in Y. Bar-Yam (ed.), Unifying Themes in Complex Systems, ISBN 9780813341231, pp. 239-247.

Goldstein, J.A. (2001a). "Glossary," in B. Zimmerman, C. Lindberg, P. Plsek (eds.) *Edgeware: Insights from Complexity Science for Health Care Leaders*, ISBN 9780966782806, pp. 257-272.

Goldstein, J.A. (2001b). "Emergence, radical novelty, and the philosophy of mathematics," in W. Sulis and I. Trofimova (eds.), *Nonlinear Dynamics in the Life and Social Sciences*, ISBN 9784274904080, pp. 133-152.

Goldstein, J.A. (2002). "The singular nature of emergent levels: Suggestions for a theory of emergence," *Nonlinear Dynamics, Psychology, and Life Sciences*, ISSN 1090-0578, 6 (4): 293-309.

Goldstein, J.A. (2003). "The construction of emergence order, or how to resist the temptation of hylozoism," *Nonlinear Dynamics, Psychology, and Life Sciences*, ISSN 1090-0578, 7 (4), 295-314.

Goldstein, J.A. (2006). "Emergence, creative process, and self-transcending constructions," in K. Richardson (ed.), *Managing Organizational Complexity: Philosophy, Theory, and Application*, ISBN 9781593113186, pp. 63-78.

Goldstein, J.A. (2007, this volume). "A new model for emergence and its leadership implications," in J. Hazy, J. Goldstein and B. Lichtenstein (eds), *Complex Systems Leadership Theory*, ISBN 9780979168864.

Goldstein, J.A. (Forthcoming). *Flirting with Paradox: Emergence and Creative Process in Complex Systems*, Mansfield, MA: ISCE Publishing.

Goldstein, J.A. (in press). "Conceptual foundations of complexity science: Development and main constructs," in M. Uhl-Bien and R. Marion (eds), *Complexity and Leadership Volume I: Conceptual Foundations*, Charlotte, NC: Information Age Publishing.

Golembiewski, R.T. (1961). "Toward the new organization theories: Some notes on 'staff'," *Midwest Journal of Political Science*, ISSN 0026-3397, 5: 237-246.

Goodwin, B. (1994). *How the Leopard Changed its Spots: The Evolution of Complexity*, ISBN 9780691088099.

Gopal, G., Viniak, V. and Caltagirone, J. (2004). "A team approach to global sourcing," *Supply Chain Management Review*, ISSN 0972-3900, 8(8): 54-59.

Gordon, W. (1961). *Synectics: The Development of Creative Capacity*, New York, NY: Harper Collins.

Goulding, C. (2002). *Grounded Theory: A Practical Guide for Management, Business, and Market Researchers*, ISBN 0761966838.

Gouldner, A.W. (1954). *Patterns in Industrial Bureaucracy*, Glencoe, IL: Free Press.

Graen, G.B. (2003). "Role making onto the starting work team using LMX leadership: Diversity as an asset," in G.B. Graen (ed.), *Dealing with Diversity: LMX Leadership: The Series*, ISBN 1930608497, 1: 1-28.

Graen, G.B. and Cashman, J.F. (1975). "A role-making model of leadership in formal organizations: A developmental approach," in J.G. Hunt and L.L. Larson (eds.), *Leadership Frontiers*, Kent, OH: Kent State University Press.

Graen, G.B. and Scandura, T. (1987). "Toward a psychology of dyadic organizing," *Research in Organizational Behavior*, ISSN 0191-3085, 9: 175-208.

Graen, G.B. and Uhl-Bien, M. (1995). "Relationship-based approach to leadership: Development of leader-member exchange (LMX) theory of leadership over 25 years: Applying a multi-level multi-domain perspective," *The Leadership Quarterly*, ISSN 1047-7039, 6(2): 219-247.

Graen, G.B., Novak, M. and Sommerkamp, P. (1982). "The effects of leader-member exchange and job design on productivity and satisfaction: Testing a dual attachment model," *Organization Behavior and Human Performance*, ISSN 0030-5073, 30: 109-131.

Granovetter, M. (1973). "The strength of weak ties," *American Journal of Sociology*, ISSN 0002-9602, 78(6): 1360-1380.

Grathoff, R. (ed). (1978). The Theory of Social Action: The Correspondence of Alfred Schutz and Talcott Parsons, ISBN 0253359570.

Graves, L. and Karren, R. (1992). "Interviewer decision processes and effectiveness: An experimental policy-capturing investigation," *Personnel Psychology*, ISSN 0031-5826, 45(Summer): 313-332.

Greenleaf, R. (1977). *Servant-Leadership: A Journey Into the Nature of Legitimate Power and Greatness*, ISBN 080910220X.

Gresov, C., Haveman, H. and Oliva, T. (1993). "Organizational design, inertia and the dynamics of competetive response," *Organization Science*, ISSN 1047-7039, 4: 181-208.

Greve, H.R., Strang, D., and Tuma, N.B. (1995). "Specification and estimation of heterogeneous diffusion models," *Sociological Methodology*, ISSN 0081-1750, 25: 377-420.

Griffin, D. (2002). *The Emergence of Leadership*, ISBN 0415249171.

Grimley-Kuntz, P. (1991). "Voegelin's experiences of disorder out of order and vision of order out of disorder," in E. Sandoz (ed.), *Eric Voegelin's Significance for the Modern Mind*, ISBN 0807115886, pp. 111-173.

Gronn, P.C. (1983). "Talk as the work: The accomplishment of school administration," *Administrative Science Quarterly*, ISSN 0001-8392, 28: 1-21.

Gronn, P.C. (2002). "Distributed leadership as a unit of analysis," *Leadership Quarterly*, ISSN 1048-9843, 13: 423-451.

Gronn, P.C. (2003). *New Work of Educational Leaders: Changing Leadership Practice in an Era of School Reform*, ISBN 0761947485.

Gross, E. (1953). "Some functional consequences of primary controls in formal work organizations," *American Sociological Review*, ISSN 0003-1224, 18: 368-373.

Grosz, B.J., Weisntein, S. and Joshi, A.K. (1995). "Centering: A framework for modeling the local coherence of a discourse," *Computational Linguistics*, ISSN 0891-2017, 21: 203-225.

Guastello, S.J. (1995). *Chaos, Catastrophe, and Human Affairs: Applications of Nonlinear Dynamics to Work, Organizations, and Social Evolution*, ISBN 9780805816341.

Guastello, S.J. (1998). "Self-organization and leadership emergence," *Nonlinear Dynamics, Psychology, and Life Sciences*, ISSN 1090-0578,2: 301-315.

Guastello, S.J. (2002). *Managing Emergent Phenomena: Nonlinear Dynamics in Work Organizations*, ISBN 9780805831634.

Guastello, S.J., Craven, J., Zygowicz, K.M. and Bock, B.R. (2005). "A rugged landscape model for self-organization and emergent leadership in creative problem solving and production groups," *Nonlinear Dynamics, Psychology and Life Sciences*, ISSN 1090-0578, 9(3):297-333.

Guerin, S. and Kunkle, D. (2004). "Emergence of constraint in self-organizing systems," *Nonlinear Dynamics, Psychology, and Life sciences*, ISSN 1090-0578, 8(2): 131-146.

Gunz, H., Lichtenstein, B. and Long, R. (2002). "Self-organization in career systems: A view from complexity science," *M@n@gement*, ISSN 1286-4892, 5(1): 63-88.

Gupta, V., MacMillan, I.C., and Surie, G. (2004). "Entrepreneurial leadership: Developing and measuring a cross-cultural construct," *Journal of Business Venturing*, ISSN 08839026, 19(2): 241-260.

Habermas, J. (1987). *Lifeworld and System: A Critique of Functionalist Reason*, ISBN 0807014001.

Hage, J. (1999). "Organizational innovation and organizational change," *Annual Review of Sociology*, ISSN 0360-0572, 25: 597-622.

Haken, H. (1981). *The Science of Structure: Synergetics*, ISBN 9780442237035.

Haken, H. (1984). "Can synergetics be of use to management theory?" in H. Ulrich and J. B. Probst (eds.), *Self-Organization and the Management of Social Systems*, Berlin, Springer-Verlag, ISBN 9780387134598.

Haken, H. (1987). "Synergetics," in F. E. Yates, A. Garfinkel, D. Walter, and G. Yates (eds.), *Self-organizing Systems: The Emergence of Order*, ISBN 9780306421457, pp. 599-613

Hall, A.D. and Fagen, R.E. (1956). "Definition of systems," *General Systems*, (1): 18-

28.

Hall, R. (1976). "A system pathology of an organization: The rise and fall of the old Saturday Evening Post," *Administrative Science Quarterly*, ISSN 0001-8392, 21: 185-211.

Hambrick, D.C. and Mason, P.A. (1984). "Upper echelons: The organization as a reflection of its top managers," *Academy of Management Review*, ISSN 0363-7425, 9(2): 193-206.

Handy, C. (1995). *Gods of Management*, ISBN 0195096169.

Harkema, S. (2003). "A complex adaptive perspective on learning within innovation projects," *The Learning Organization*, ISSN 0969-6474, 10(6): 340-346.

Hart, O. and Moore, J. (2005). "On the design of hierarchies: Coordination versus specialization," *Journal of Political Economy*, ISSN 0022-3808, 113(4), 675-702.

Harter, N. (2006). *Clearings in the Forest*, ISBN 1557533814.

Hawes, L.C. (1999). "Dialogics, posthumanist theory, and self-organizing systems," *Management Communication Quarterly*, ISSN 0893-3189, (13)1: 146 - 153.

Hazy, J.K. (2003). "Successful adaptation in the absence of a top-down change initiative: Reconsidering Intel's shift to microprocessors in the 1970s and 1980s," in K. Carley (ed.), *Proceedings of the 2003 NAACSOS Conference*, Pittsburgh, PA: Carnegie Mellon University.

Hazy, J.K. (2004a). *A Leadership and Capabilities Framework for Organizational Change: Simulating the Emergence of Leadership as an Organizational Meta-Capability*, ISBN 0496167804.

Hazy, J.K. (2004b). "Organizational transformation as strategic resonance between leadership initiatives and dynamic capabilities development," *Proceedings of the 3rd International Conference on Systems Thinking in Management*, Philadelphia, PA: University of Pennsylvania.

Hazy, J.K. (2004c). "Organizational transformation as strategic resonance between leadership initiatives and dynamic capabilities development," *Proceeding of the 3rd International Conference on Systems Thinking in Management*, Philadelphia, PA: University of Pennsylvania.

Hazy, J.K. (2004d). "Leadership in complex systems: A meta-level information processing capabilities that bias exploration and exploitation," in K. Carley (ed.), *Proceedings of the 2004 NAACSOS Conference*, Pittsburgh, PA: Carnegie Mellon University.

Hazy, J.K. (2004e). "A leadership and capabilities framework for organizational change: Simulating the emergence of leadership as an organizational meta-capability," unpublished dissertation, Washington, D.C.: The George Washington University.

Hazy, J.K. (2005). "A leadership and capabilities framework for organizational change: Simulating the emergence of leadership as an organizational meta-capability," unpublished Doctorate, The George Washington University, Washington, DC.

Hazy, J.K. (2005, August). "Leadership, dynamic organizational capabilities and sustainability: The leadership and capabilities model (LCM) of performance and adaptation," presented at the Academy of Management, Honolulu, HI.

Hazy, J.K. (2006a). "Measuring leadership effectiveness in complex socio-technical systems," *Emergence: Complexity & Organization*, ISSN 1521-3250, 8(3): 58-77.

Hazy, J.K. (2006b). "Emergent signaling networks in complex socio-technical systems: How cooperative interactions among agents contribute to system sustainability," North American Association of Computational Social and Organization Science. South Bend, Indiana: University of Notre Dame.

Hazy, J.K. (2007a). "Computer models of leadership: Foundation for a new discipline or meaningless diversion?" *The Leadership Quarterly*, ISSN 1048-9843, 18:391-410.

Hazy, J.K. (2007b). "Parsing the 'influential increment' in the language of complexity: Uncovering the systemic mechanisms of leadership influence," paper presented at the Academy of Management Annual Conference, Philadelphia, PA.

Hazy, J.K. (in press-a). "Patterns of leadership: A case study of influence signaling in an entrepreneurial firm," in M. Uhl-Bien and R. Marion (eds), *Complexity and Leadership Volume I: Conceptual Foundations*, Charlotte, NC: Information Age Publishing.

Hazy, J.K. (in press-b). "Leadership or luck? The system dynamics of Intel's shift to microprocessors in the 1970s and 1980s," in M. Uhl-Bien and R. Marion (eds), *Complexity and Leadership Volume I: Conceptual Foundations*, Charlotte, NC: Information Age Publishing.

Hazy, J.K. and Tivnan, B.F. (2004). "On building an organizationally realistic agent-based model of local interaction and emergent network structure," paper presented at the 2004 Winter Simulation Conference, Washington D.C., December 5-8.

Hazy, J.K., Millhister, P. and Solow, D. (2007, this volume). "Mathematical and computational models of leadership," in J. Hazy, J. Goldstein and B. Lichtenstein (eds.), *Complex Systems Leadership Theory*, Mansfield, MA: ISCE Publishing.

Heckscher, C. (1994). "Defining the post-bureaucratic type," in A. Donnellon and C. Heckscher (eds.), *The Post-Bureaucratic Organization: New Perspectives on Organizational Change*, ISBN 0803957173, pp. 14-63.

Heifetz, R.A. (1994). *Leadership Without Easy Answers*, ISBN 0674518586.

Heifetz, R.A. and Laurie, D.L. (2001). "The work of leadership," *Harvard Business Review*, ISSN 1047-7039, 79(11): 131-141.

Hempel, C.G. and Oppenheim, P. (1948). "Studies in the logic of explanation," *Philosophy of Science*, 15: 135-175.

Henderson, R. and Clark, K. (1990). "Architectural innovation: The reconfiguration of existing product technologies and the failure of established firms," *Administrative Science Quarterly*, ISSN 0001-8392, 35: 9-30.

Henle, P. (1942). "The status of emergence," *Journal of Philosophy*, ISSN 0022-362X, 39, 486-493.

Hernes, G. (1998). "Real virtuality," in P. Hedström and R. Swedberg (eds.), *Social Mechanisms: An Analytical Approach to Social Theory*, ISBN 0521593190, pp. 74-101.

Hersey, P. and Blanchard, K.H. (1977). *Management of Organizational Behavior: Utilizing Human Resources*, ISBN 0135488753.

Heydebrand, W.V. (1989). "New organizational forms," *Work and Occupations*, ISSN 0730-8884, 16: 323-357.

Hillman, J. (1995). *Kinds of Power*, ISBN 0385469640.

Hillman, J. (2005). *Senex and Puer*, ISBN 0882145819.

Hitt, M.A. (1998). "Twenty-first-century organizations: Business firms, business schools and the academy," *Academy of Management Review*, ISSN 0363-7425, 23(2): 218-224.

Hitt, M.A., Keats, B.W., and DeMarie, S.M. (1998). "Navigating in the new competitive landscape: Building strategic flexibility and competitive advantage in the 21st century," *Academy of Management Executive*, ISSN 0869-3789, 12(4): 22-42.

Hofstadter, D. (1979). *Gödel, Escher, Bach: An Eternal Golden Braid*, ISBN 9780855277574.

Hogg, M. (1992). *The Social Psychology of Group Cohesiveness: From Attraction to Social Identity*, ISBN 9780814734995.

Holland, J.H. (1975). *Adaptation in Natural and Artificial Systems*, ISBN 0262581116.

Holland, J.H. (1994). "Echoing emergence: Objectives, rough definitions, and speculations of ECHO-class models." in G. Cowen, D. Pines and D. Meltzer, (eds.), *Complexity: Metaphors, Models, and Reality*, ISBN 9780738202327 (1999).

Holland, J.H. (1994). *Hidden Order: How Adaptation Builds Complexity*, ISBN 9780201442304.

Holland, J.H. (1995). *Hidden Order: How Adaptation Builds Complexity*, ISBN 0201442302.

Holland, J.H. (1998). *Emergence: From Chaos to Order*, ISBN 073820142

Holland, J.H. (2001). "Exploring the evolution of complexity in signaling networks," http://www.santafe.edu/sfi/publications/wplist/2001.

Holland, J.H. and Miller, J. (1991). "Artificial adaptive agents in economic theory," *American Economic Review, Papers and Proceedings*, ISSN 0002-8282, 81: 365-370.

Hollander, E.P. (1961). "Emergent Leadership and social influence," in L. Petrullo and B. M. Bass (eds.), *Leadership and Interpersonal Behavior*, New York, NY: Holt-Rinehart-Winston, pp. 30-47.

Hollander, E.P. (1978). *Leadership Dynamics*, ISBN 0029148200.

Hollander, E.P. and Julian, J.W. (1969). "Contemporary trends in the analysis of leadership processes," *Psychological Bulletin*, ISSN 0033-2909, 5: 387-397.

Homans, G.C. (1950). *The Human Group*, New York, NY: Harcourt.

Homans, G.C. (1958). "Social behavior as exchange," *American Journal of Sociology*, ISSN 0002-9602, 63: 597-606.

Hoover, T.S. and Scanlon, D.C. (1991). "Enrollment issues in agricultural education programs and FFA membership," *Journal of Agricultural Education*, ISSN 1042-0541, 32(4): 2-10.

House, R.J. (1971). "A path goal theory of leader effectiveness," *Administrative Science Quarterly*, ISSN 0001-8392, 16: 321-338.

House, R.J. and Aditya, R.N. (1997). "The social scientific study of leadership: Quo vadis?" *Journal of Management*, ISSN 0149-2063, 23(3): 409-473.

House, R.J. and Mitchell, T.R. (1974). "Path-goal theory of leadership," *Journal of Contemporary Business*, ISSN 0194-0430, 3: 81-97.

Houston, R. (1999). "Self-organizing systems theory: Historical challenges to new sciences," *Management Communication Quarterly*, ISSN 0893-3189, (13)1: 119-134.

Howell, J.M. and Boies, K. (2004). "Champions of technological innovation: The influence of contextual knowledge, role orientation, idea generation, and idea promotion on champion emergence," *The Leadership Quarterly*, ISSN 1047-7039, 15(1): 123-143.

Hoy, W.K. and Miskel, G. (1987). *Educational Administration: Theory, Research, and Practice*, ISBN 0394340892.

Hubler, A. and Pines, D. (1994). "Prediction and adaptation in an evolving chaotic environment," in G. Cowan, D. Pines and D. Meltzer (eds), *Complexity: Metaphors, Models and Reality*, ISBN 0201626055, pp. 343-382.

Hubler, A.W. (2005). "Predicting complex systems with a holistic approach," *Complexity*, ISSN 1076-2787, 10: 11-16.

Hughes, S. H. (2004). "Understanding conflict in a postmodern world," *Marquette Law Review*, ISSN 0025-3987, 4: 681-690.

Hunt, J. G. (1999). "Transformational/charismatic leadership's transformation of the field: an historical essay," *The Leadership Quarterly*, ISSN 1048-9843, 10(2): 129-144.

Hyde, K. (2000). "Recognizing deductive processes in qualitative research," *Qualitative Market Research*, ISSN 1352-2752, 3(2): 82-90.

Ibarra, H., Kilduff, M., and Tsai, W. (2005). "Zooming in and out: Connecting individuals and collectivities at the frontiers of organizational network research," *Organization Science*, ISSN 1047-7039, 16: 359-371.

Ignatieff, M. (1998). *Isaiah Berlin: A Life*, ISBN 0805055207.

Ilgen, D.R. and Hulin, C.L. (2000). *Computational Modeling of Behavior in Organizations: The Third Scientific Discipline*, ISBN 1557986398.

Ireland, R.D. and Hitt, M.A. (1999). "Achieving and maintaining strategic competitiveness in the 21st century: The role of strategic leadership," *Academy of Management Executive*, ISSN 0869-3789, 13(1): 43-57.

Jackson, M. (2000). *Systems Approaches to Management*, ISBN 030646506X.

Jackson, S., May, K. and Whitney, K. (1995). "Understanding the dynamics of diversity in decision-making teams," in R. Guzzo and E. Salas (eds.), *Team Effectiveness and Decision Making in Organizations*, ISBN 978-1555426415, pp. 204-261.

Jacobs, T.O. (1970). *Leadership and Exchange in Formal Organizations*, Alexandria, VA: Human Resources Research Organization.

Jacobs, T.O. and Jaques, E. (1990). "Military executive leadership," in K.E. Clark and M.B. Clark (eds.), *Measures of Leadership*, ISBN 1878435000, pp. 281-295.

Jacobsen, C. and House, R.J. (2001). "Dynamics of charismatic leadership: A process theory, simulation model, and tests," *The Leadership Quarterly*, ISSN 1048-9843, 12(1): 75-112.

Jacques, E. (1989). *Requisite Organization*, ISBN 096210700X

Jacques, E. and Clement, S.D. (1990). *Executive Leadership: A Practical Guide to Managing Complexity*, ISBN 9780631193135 (1994).

Jalan, B. (1991). *India's Economic Crisis: The Way Ahead*, ISBN 0195632036.

Jamshidi, M. (1997). *Large-Scale Systems: Modeling, Control and Fuzzy Logic*, ISBN 0131256831.

Janis, I.L. (1972). *Victims of Groupthink*, ISBN 0395317045 (1982)

Jantsch, E. (1980). *The Self-Organizing Universe: Scientific and Human Implications of the Emerging Paradigm of Evolution*, ISBN 0080243118.

Jaworski, J. (1998). *Synchronicity: The Inner Path of Leadership*, ISBN 9781576750315 (1996).

Jehn, K.A. (1997). "A qualitative analysis of conflict types and dimensions in organizational groups," *Administrative Science Quarterly*, ISSN 0001-8392, 42(Sep): 530-557.

Jennings, H.H. (1944). "Leadership: A dynamic redefinition," *Journal of Educational Psychology*, ISSN 0022-0663, 17: 431-433.

Jennings, J. and Haughton, L. (2001). *It's Not the Big That Eat the Small... It's the Fast That Eat the Slow: How to Use Speed as a Competitive Tool in Business*, ISBN 0066620538

Jensen, D. and Lesser, V. (2002). "Social pathologies of adaptive agents," in M. Barley and H. Guesgen (eds.), *Safe Learning Agents: Papers from the 2002 AAAI Spring Symposium*, Menlo Park, CA: AAAI Press, pp. 13-19.

Jensen, M. and Meckling, W. (1976). "Theory of the firm: Managerial behavior, agency costs, and ownership structure," *Journal of Financial Economics*, ISSN 0304-405X, 3(4): 305-360.

Jiang, L. and Burton, R. (2002). "Internal fit between team structure, communication methods and leader's expertise," Computational Analysis of Social and Organizational Systems, Pittsburgh, PA: Carnegie Mellon University, http://www.casos.cs.cmu.edu/events/conferences/2002/pdf/day2.pdf.

Juarrero, A. (1999). *Dynamics in Action: Intentional Behavior as a Complex System*, ISBN 9780262100816.

Judge, T.A. and Piccolo, R.F. (2004). "Transformational and transactional leadership: A meta-analytic test of their relative validity," *Journal of Applied Psychology*, ISSN 0021-9010, 89(5): 755-768.

Jun, J.K. and Hubler, A.W. (2005). "Formation and structure of ramified charge transportation networks in an electromechanical system," *Proceedings of the National Academy of Sciences*, ISSN 1091-6490, 102: 536-540.

Jung, D.I. and Avolio, B.J (1999). "Effects of leadership style and followers' cultural orientation on performance in group and individual task conditions," *Academy of Management Journal*, ISSN 0001-4273, 42: 208-218

Kaeter, M. (1993). "The age of the specialized generalist," *Training*, ISSN 0095-5892, 30(12): 48-53.

Kahneman, D. and Tversky, A. (1972). "Subjective probability: A judgment of representativeness," *Cognitive Psychology*, ISSN 0010-0285, 3: 430-454.

Kandel, E. and Lazear, E.P. (1992). "Peer pressure and partnerships," *Journal of Political Economy*, ISSN 0022-3808, 100(4): 801-817.

Kast, D. and Rosenzweig, J. (1972). "General systems theory: Applications for organization and management," *Academy of Management Journal*, 15: 447-465.

Katz, D. and Kahn, R. L. (1978). *The Social Psychology of Organizations*, 2nd edition, ISBN 0471023558.

Katz, D. and Kahn, R.L. (1966). *The Social Psychology of Organizations*, ISBN 0471023558 (1978).

Kauffman, S.A. (1969). "Metabolic stability and epigenesis in randomly connected nets," *Journal of Theoretical Biology*, ISSN 0022-5193, 22: 437.

Kauffman, S.A. (1993). *The Origins of Order: Self-Organization and Selection in Evolution*, ISBN 0195058119.

Kauffman, S.A. (1995). *At Home in the Universe: The Search for Laws of Self-Organization and Complexity*, ISBN 0195111303.

Kauffman, S.A. and Levin, S. (1987). "Towards a general theory of adaptive walks on rugged landscapes," *Journal of Theoretical Biology*, ISSN 00225193, 128(1): 11-45.

Kauffman, S.A. and Macready, W. (1995). "Search strategies for applied molecular evolution," *Journal of Theoretical Biology*, ISSN 0022-5193, 173: 427-440.

Kaufman, F. (1978). *The Infinite in Mathematics*, ISBN 9789027708472.

Kaufmann, Y. (2004). *The Way of the Image: The Orientational Approach to the Psyche*, Brattleboro: Assisi Foundation.

Kellert, S. (1993). *In the Wake of Chaos*, ISBN 9780226429748.

Kelly, R.E. (1988). "In praise of followers," *Harvard Business Review*, ISSN 0017-8012, Nov-Dec: 142-148.

Kelso, S. (1995). *Dynamic Patterns: The Self-Organization of Brain and Behavior*, ISBN 9780262112000.

Keren, M. and Levhari, D. (1979). "The optimum span of control in a pure hierarchy," *Management Science*, ISSN 0025-1909 , 25(11): 1162-1172.

Kerr, S. and Jermier, J. M. (1978). "Substitutes for leadership: Their meaning and measurement," *Organizational Behavior and Human Performance*, ISSN 0749-5978, 22: 375-403.

Kickert, W. (1993). "Autopoiesis and the science of (public) administration: Essence, sense and nonsense," *Organization Studies*, ISSN 0170-8406, 14 : 261-278.

Kickul, J. and Neuman, G. (2000). "Emergent leadership behaviors: The function of personality and cognitive ability in determining teamwork performance and KSAS," *Journal of Business and Psychology*, ISSN 0889-3268, 15(1): 27-51.

Kiel, D. (1994). *Managing Chaos and Complexity in Government*, ISBN

9780787900236.

Kilduff, M. and Tsai, W. (2003). *Social Networks and Organizations*, ISBN 9780761969563.

Kilduff, M., Crossland, C. and Tsai, W. (in press). "Pathways of opportunity in dynamic organizational networks," in M. Uhl-Bien and R. Marion (eds), *Complexity and Leadership Volume I: Conceptual Foundations*, Charlotte, NC: Information Age Publishing.

Kim, D. (1992). "Systems archetypes: Diagnosing systemic issues and designing high-leverage interventions," in D. Kim (ed.), *Toolbox Reprint Series: Systems Archetypes*, ISBN 1883823005, pp. 3-26.

King, A. (1995). "Avoiding ecological surprise: Lessons from long-standing communities," *Academy of Management Review*, ISSN 0363-7425, 20(Oct): 961-985.

Klee, R. (1984). "Micro-determinism and concepts of emergence," *Philosophy of Science*, ISSN 0031-8248, 51: 44-63.

Klein, K.J., Tosi, H. and Cannella, A.A. (1999). "Multilevel theory building: Benefits, barriers, and new developments," *Academy of Management Review*, ISSN 0363-7425, 24(2): 243-249.

Klimontovich, Y.L. (2001). "Entropy, information and ordering criteria," in W. Sulis and I. Trofimova (eds.), *Nonlinear Dynamics in the Life and Social Sciences*, ISBN 9784274904080, pp. 13-32.

Klir, G. J. (1969). *An Approach to General Systems Theory*, New York, NY: Van Nostrand Reinhold.

Kogut, B. and Zander, U. (1996). "What firms do? Coordination, identity, and learning," *Organization Science*, ISSN 1047-7039, 7(5): 502-518.

Kolay, S., Shaffer, G. and Ordover, J.A. (2004). "All units discounts in retail contracts," *Journal of Economics and Management Strategy*, ISSN 1058-6407, 13(3): 429-459.

Kolb, J. (1997). "Are we still stereotyping leadership? A look at gender and other predictors of leader emergence," *Small Group Research*, ISSN 1046-4964, 28(3): 370-393.

Kotter, J. (1982). *The General Managers*, ISBN 0029182301.

Kotter, J. P. (1996). *Leading Change*, ISBN 0875847471.

Kouzes, J.M. and Posner, B.Z. (1987). *The Leadership Challenge: How to Get Extraordinary Things Done in Prganizations*, ISBN 0608216542.

Kouzes, J.M. and Posner, B.Z. (1989). "Leadership is in the eye of the follower," in J.W. Pfeiffer (ed.), *The 1989 Annual: Developing Human Resources*, ISBN 0883900203.

Kovačič, B. (1994) "New perspectives on organizational communication," in B. Kovačič, *New Approaches to Organizational Communication*, ISBN 0791419185, pp. 1-39.

Kracke, W. H. (1978). *Force and Persuasion: Leadership in an Amazonian Society*, ISBN 0226452107.

Krackhardt, D. (1994). "Graph theoretical dimensions of informal organizations," in K. Carley and M. Prietula (eds.), *Computational Organization Theory*, ISBN 9780805814064 , pp. 89-111.

Krackhardt, D. and Carley, K.M. (1998). "A PCANS model of structure in organization," paper presented at the International Symposium on Command and Control Research and Technology, Monterrey, CA.

Krackhardt, D. and Carley, K.M. (1998, June). A PCANS model structure in organization. Paper presented at the 1998 International Symposium on Command and Control Research and Technology, Monterey, CA.

Kruglanski, A. (1989). *Lay Epistemics and Human Knowledge: Cognitive and Motivational Bases*, ISBN 0306430789.

Krugman, P. (1996). *The Self-Organizing Economy*, ISBN 1557866996

Kuhn, T.S. (1961). *The Structure of Scientific Revolutions*, ISBN 0226458040.

Kuhn, T.S. (1970). *The Structure of Scientific Revolutions*, 2nd Edition, ISBN 0226458040.

Kurzwel, R. (2005). *The Singularity Is Near: When Humans Transcend Biology*, ISBN 0670033847.

Lampel, J. and Shapira, Z. (2001). "Judgemental errors, interactive norms, and the difficulty of detecting strategic surprises," *Organization Science*, ISSN 1526-5455, 12(Sep/Oct): 599-611.

Lane, D. and Maxfield, R. (1996). "Strategy under complexity: Fostering generative relationships," *Long Range Planning*, 29(April): 215-231.

Langer, E.J. (1989). *Mindfulness*, ISBN 0201523418.

Langton, C.G. (1985). *Artificial Life: An Overview*, ISBN 0585036152

Langton, C.G. (1986). "Studying artificial life with cellular automata," in D. Farmer, A. Lapedes, N. Packard and B. Wendroff (eds.), *Evolution, Games, and Learning: Models for Adaptation in Machines and Nature, Proceedings of the Fifth Annual Conference of the Center for Nonlinear Studies*, ISBN 9780444870315 (1987), pp. 120-149

Langton, C.G. (1996). "Artificial life," in M Boden (ed.), *The Philosophy of Artificial Life*, ISBN 0198751559, pp. 39-94

Lansing, J.S. (2003). "Complex adaptive systems," *Annual Review of Anthropology*, ISSN 0084-6570, 32: 183-204.

Laplanche, J. and Pontalis, J.-B. (1973). *The Language of Psychoanalysis*, ISBN 0946439494.

Larson, R.W. and Seepersad, S. (2003). "Adolescents' leisure time in the United States: Partying, sports, and the American experiment," *New Directions for Youth Development*, ISSN 1533-8916, 99: 53-64.

Lasdon, L. and Schoeffler, J. (1966). "Decentralized plant control," *ISA Transactions*, ISSN 0019-0578, 5: 175-183.

Laszlo, E. (1987). *Evolution: The Grand Synthesis*, ISBN 978-0877733898.

Laughlin, R. (2005). *A Different Universe: Reinventing Physics from the Bottom Down*, ISBN 9780465038282.

Lave, J. and Wenger, E. (1991). *Situated Learning: Legitimate Peripheral Participation*, ISBN 0521413087.

Lawless, M.W. and Anderson, P.C. (1996). "Generational technological change: Effects of innovation and local rivalry on performance," *The Academy of Management Journal*, ISSN 0001-4273, 39(5): 1185-1217.

Lawrence, P.R. and Lorsch, J. (1969). *Organization and Environment: Managing Differentiation and Integration*, ISBN 0256003149.

Lazarsfeld, P. and Merton, R. (1978). "Friendship as a social process: A substantive and methodological analysis," in C. Page (ed.), *Freedom and Control in Modern Society*, ISBN 0374906084.

Lee, C.H. (2001). "Coordinated stocking, clearance sales, and return policies for a supply chain," *European Journal of Operational Research*, ISSN 0377-2217, 131(3): 491-513.

Lees, M. (2002). *A History of the Tileworld Agent Testbed*, Computer Science Technical Report No. NOTTCS-WP-2002-1.

Lehman, B.H. (1928). *Carlyle's Theory of the Hero: Its Sources, Development, History and Influence on Carlyle's Work*, New York: AMS Press.

Leifer, R. (1989). "Understanding organizational transformation using a dissipative structure model," *Human Relations*, ISSN 0018-7267, 42(10): 899-916.

Leonard-Barton, D. (1995). *Wellsprings of Knowledge: Building and Sustaining Sources of Innovation*, ISBN 9780875848594 (1998).

Letiche, H. (2000). "Phenomenal complexity theory as informed by Bergson," *Journal of Organizational Change Management*, ISSN 0953-4814, 13(6): 545-557.

Levinson, H. and Rosenthal, S. (1984). *CEO: Corporate Leadership in Action*, ISBN 0465007902.

Levinthal, D.A. (1997). "Adaptation on rugged landscapes," *Management Science*, ISSN 0025-1909, 43: 934-950.

Levinthal, D.A. (2001). "Organizational adaptation and environmental selection: Interrelated processes of change," *Organization Science*, ISSN 1047-7039, 2: 140-144.

Levinthal, D.A. and Warglien, M. (1999). "Landscape design: Designing for local action in complex worlds," *Organization Science*, ISSN 1047-7039, 10(3): 342-357.

Lewes, G.H. (1875). *Problems of Life and Mind*, Vol. 2, London, England: Kegan Paul, Trench, Turbner.

Lewicki, R.J., Weiss, S.E. and Lewin, D. (1992). "Models of conflict, negotiation and third party intervention: a review and synthesis," *Journal of Organizational Behavior*, ISSN 0894-3796, 13(3): 209-252.

Lewin, K. and Lippitt, R. (1938). "An experimental approach to the study of autocracy and democracy: A preliminary note," *Sociometry*, ISSN 0038-0431, 1: 292-300.

Lewin, R. (1992). *Complexity: Life at the Edge of Chaos*, ISBN 9780753812709.

Lewin, R. and Regine, B. (2003). "The core of adaptive organizations," in E. Mitleton-Kelly (ed.), *Complex Systems and Evolutionary Perspectives on Organizations: The Application of Complexity Theory to Organizations*, ISBN 0080439578, pp. 167-184.

Lichtenstein, B.B. (1995). "Evolution or transformation: A critique and alternative to punctuated equilibrium," *Academy of Management Journal*, ISSN 1535-3990, (Best Papers Proceedings): 291-295.

Lichtenstein, B.B. (2000a). "Self-organized transitions: A pattern amid the 'chaos' of transformative change," *Academy of Management Executive*, ISSN 1079-5545, 14(4): 128-141.

Lichtenstein, B.B. (2000b). "Emergence as a process of self-organizing: New assumptions and insights from the study of nonlinear dynamic systems," *Journal of Organizational Change Management*, ISSN 0953-4814, 13: 526-544.

Lichtenstein, B.B. (2000c). "Valid or vacuous: A definition and assessment of New Paradigm research in management," *American Behavioral Scientist*, ISSN 0002-7642, 43: 1334-1366.

Lichtenstein, B.B. (2000d). "Dynamics of rapid growth and change: A complexity theory of entrepreneurial transitions," in G. Liebcap (ed.), *Advances in the Study of Entrepreneurship, Innovation, and Economic Growth*, ISBN 9781559383738, pp. 161-192.

Lichtenstein, B.B. (2007, this volume). "A matrix of complexity for leadership: 14 disciplines of complex systems leadership theory," in J. Hazy, J. Goldstein and B. Lichtenstein (eds), *Complex Systems Leadership Theory*, Mansfield, MA: ISCE Publishing, ISBN 9780979168864.

Lichtenstein, B.B. and Brush, C. (2001), "How do 'resource bundles' develop and change in new ventures? A dynamic model and longitudinal exploration," *Entrepreneurship Theory and Practice*, ISSN 1042-2587, 25(3): 37-58.

Lichtenstein, B.B. and Jones, C. (2004). "A self-organization theory of radical entrepreneurship," Best Papers Proceedings, National Academy of Management, New Orleans, LA. OMT Division, CD Format.

Lichtenstein, B.B. and McKelvey, B. (2005). "Toward a theory of emergence by stages: Complexity dynamics, self-organization, and power laws in firms," presented at the

Academy of Management Conference, OMT division, New Orleans, LA.

Lichtenstein, B.B., Carter, N., Dooley, K. and Gartner, W. (2007). "Complexity dynamics of nascent entrepreneurship," *Journal of Business Venturing*, ISSN 0883-9026, 22: 236-261.

Lichtenstein, B.B., Dooley, K., and Lumpkin, G.T. (2006). "Measuring emergence in the dynamics of new venture creation," *Journal of Business Venturing*, ISSN 0883-9026, 21: 153-175.

Lichtenstein, B.B., Uhl-Bien, M., Marion, R., Seers, A., Orton, J. D. and Schreiber, C. (2006). "Complexity leadership theory: An interactive perspective on leading in complex adaptive systems," *Emergence: Complexity and Organization*, ISSN 15217000, 8(4): 2-12.

Likert, R. (1961b). *New Patterns of Management*, ISBN 0824082141 (1987).

Likert, R. (1961a). "The nature of highly effective work groups," in D.A. Kolb, I. M. Rubin and J.M. McIntyre (eds.), *Organizational Psychology*,4th edition, Princeton, NJ: McGraw-Hill, ISBN 9780136411420 .

Lin, F. and Pai, Y. (2000). "Using multi-agent simulation and learning to design new business processes," *IEEE Transactions on Systems, Man, and Cybernetics - Part A: Systems and Humans*, ISSN 0018-9472, 30(3): 380-384.

Lindblom, C.E. (1959). "The science of 'muddling through'," *Public Administration Review*, ISSN 0033-3352, 19: 79-88,

Linsky, M. and Heifetz, R.A. (2002). *Leadership on the Line: Staying Alive through the Dangers of Leading*, ISBN 1578514371.

Lipsky, D.B. and Seeber, R.L. (2006). "Managing organizational conflicts," in J.G. Oetzel and S. Ting-Toomey (eds.), *The Sage Handbook of Conflict Communication: Integrating Theory, Research, and Practice*, ISBN 0761930450, pp. 359-390.

Lipsky, D.B., Seeber, R.L. and Fincher, R.D. (2003). *Emerging Systems for Managing Workplace Conflict: Lessons from American Corporations for Managers and Dispute Resolution Professionals*, ISBN 0787964344.

Lissack, M. (2000). Private conversation with Prigogine communicated to the author of this article.

Lissack, M. and Roos, J. (1999). *The Next Common Sense*, ISBN 9781857882407.

Lloyd, G.E.R. (1992). *Polarity and Analogy*, ISBN 0872201406.

Locke, K. (2001). *Grounded Theory in Management Research*, ISBN 0761964282.

Lomi, A. and Larsen, E.R. (1997). "Density delay and organizational survival: Compuational models and empirical comparisons," *Computational Mathematical Organizational Theory*, ISSN 1381-298X, 3(4): 219-247.

Lord, R.G. (in press). "Beyond transactional and transformational leadership: Can leaders still lead when they don't know what to do?" in M. Uhl-Bien and R. Marion (eds.), *Complexity and Leadership Volume I: Conceptual Foundations*, Charlotte, NC: Information Age Publishing.

Lorenz, E. (1962). "The statistical prediction of solutions of dynamic equations," paper presented at the International Symposium on Numerical Weather Prediction, Tokyo, Japan.

Louis, M.R. (1980). "Surprise and sensemaking: What newcomers experience in entering unfamiliar organizational settings," *Administrative Science Quarterly*, ISSN 0001-8392, 25(Jun): 226-251.

Luce, R.D. and Raiffa, H. (1957). *Games and Decisions: Introduction and Critical Survey*, ISBN 0486659437.

Luhmann, N. (1984). *Soziale Systeme*, ISBN 3518282662 (2001)

Luhmann, N. (1995). *Social Systems*, ISBN 0804726256.

Luksha, P. (2005). Self-reproduction of the enterprise: Von Neumann's model applied.

in K. Richardson (ed.), *Managing Organizational Complexity: Philosophy, Theory, Application*, ISBN 1593113196.

Luthans, F. and Kreitner, R. (1975). Organizational Behavior Modification, Chicago, IL: Scott, Foresman, ISBN 067307966X.

Luthans, F., Hodgetts, R.M. and Rosenkrantz, S.A. (1988). *Real Managers*, ISBN 0887301037.

Lynn, G.S. and Reilly, R.R. (2002). *Blockbusters: The Five Keys to Developing GREAT New Products*, ISBN 006008474X.

MacIntosh, R. and MacLean, D. (1999). "Conditioned emergence: A dissipative structures approach to transformation," *Strategic Management Journal*, ISSN 0143-2095, 20: 297-316.

Mackey, A., McKelvey, B. and Kiousis, P.K. (2006). "Can the CEO churning problem be fixed? Lessons from complexity science, Jack Welch and AIDS," presented at the Academy of Management Annual Meeting, Atlanta.

Macready, W. and C. Meyer, (1999). "Adaptive operations: Creating business processes that evolve." in J.H. Clippinger (ed.), *The Biology of Business*, ISBN 078794324X.

Macy, M. and Skvoretz, J. (1998). "The evolution of trust and cooperration between strangers: A computational model," *American Sociological Review*, ISSN 0003-1224, 63: 683-660.

Maguire, S. (1999). "Strategy is design: A fitness landscape framework," in M. Lissack and H. Gunz (eds.), *Managing Complexity in Organizations: A View in Many Directions*, ISBN 9781567202854, pp. 67-104

Maguire, S. and McKelvey, B. (1999). "Complexity and management: Moving from fad to firm foundations," *Emergence*, 1521-3250, 1(2): 19-61.

Maguire, S., Hardy, C. and Lawrence, T. (2004). "Institutional entrepreneurship in emerging fields: HIV/AIDS treatment advocacy in Canada," *Academy of Management Journal*, ISSN 00014273, 47(5): 657-679.

Maguire, S., McKelvey, B., Mirabeau, L. and Oztas, N. (2006). "Complexity science and organization studies," in S. Clegg, C. Hardy, T. Lawrence and W. Nord (eds.), *Handbook of Organization Studies*, ISBN 0761949968, pp. 165-214.

Mainzer, K. (1997). *Thinking in Complexity*, 3rd edition, ISBN 3540625550.

Makadok, R. (2001). "Toward a synthesis of the resource-based and dynamic-capability views of rent creation," *Strategic Management Journal*, ISSN 0143-2095, 22: 387-401.

Malerba, F., Nelson, R., Orsenigo, L. and Winter, S. (1999). "'History-friendly' models of industry evolution: The computer industry," *Industrial and Corporate Change*, ISSN 0960-6491, 8: 3-40.

Malone, T. (1987). "Modeling coordination in organizations and markets," *Management Science*, ISSN 0025-1909, 33(10): 1317-1333.

Malone, T. and Smith, S. (1988). "Modeling the performance of organizational structures," *Operations Research*, ISSN 0030-364X, 36(3): 421-436.

Mandelbrot, B.B. (1983). *The Fractal Geometry of Nature*, ISBN 0716711869

Mandelbrot, B.B. and Hudson, R. L. (2004). *The (Mis)Behavior of Markets: A Fractal View of Risk, Ruin, and Reward*, ISBN 0465043550

Mantrala, M.K. and Raman, K. (1999). "Demand uncertainty and supplier's return policies for a multi-store style-good retailer," *European Journal of Operational Research*, ISSN 03772217, 115(2): 270-284.

Manz, C.C. and Neck, C. (2004). *Mastering Self-Leadership: Empowering Yourself for Personal Excellence*, ISBN 013-1400460.

Manz, C.C. and Sims, H.P. (1989). *Superleadership*, ISBN 0425123561.

Manz, C.C., and Sims, H. P. (1980). "Self management as a substitute for leadership: A social learning perspective," *Academy of Management Review*, ISSN 0363-7425, 5: 361-367.

March, J.G. (1991). "Exploration and exploitation in organizational learning," *Organization Science*, ISSN 1047-7039, 2(1): 71-87.

March, J.G. and Coutu, D. (2006). "The HBR interview: Ideas as art," *Harvard Business Review*, ISSN 0017-8012, 84(10): 82-89.

March, J.G. and Olsen, J.P. (1976). *Ambiguity and Choice in Organizations*, ISBN 8200014789.

March, J.G. and Simon, H.A. (1958). *Organizations*, ISBN 063118631X.

March, J.G. and Simon, H.A. (1961). "The theory of organizational equilibrium," in A. Etzioni (ed.), *Complex Organizations: A Sociological Reader*, ISBN 225500111, pp. 61-71.

March, J.G., Sproull, L.S. and Tamuz, M. (1991). "Learning from samples of one or fewer," *Organization Science*, ISSN 1047-7039, 2(1): 1-13.

Marinaro, M. and Tagliaferri, R. (2002). *Neural Nets*, ISBN 978-3540442653.

Marion, R. (1999). *The Edge of Organization: Chaos and Complexity Theories of Formal Social Organization*, ISBN 0761912657.

Marion, R. and Uhl-Bien, M. (2001). "Leadership in complex organizations," *Leadership Quarterly*, ISSN 1048-9843, 12: 389-418.

Marion, R. and Uhl-Bien, M. (2003). "Complexity theory and Al-Qaeda: Examining complex leadership," *Emergence*, ISSN 1521-3250, 5(1): 54-76.

Marion, R. and Uhl-Bien, M. (2007). "Complexity and strategic leadership," in R. Hooijberg, J. Hunt, J. Antonakis, K. Boal and N. Lane (eds.), *Being There Even When You Are Not: Leading through Structures, Systems, and Processes*, ISBN 019513530X, pp. 273-287.

Marion, R. and Uhl-Bien, M. (2007, this volume). "Paradigmatic influence and leadership: The perspective of complexity theory and bureaucracy rheory," in J.K. Hazy, J. Goldstein and B.B. Lichtenstein (eds.), *Complex Systems Leadership Theory*, ISBN 9780979168864.

Marion, R. and Uhl-Bien, M. (eds.) (in press). *Complexity Theory and Leadership: Social Dynamics in the Knowledge Era*, Greenwich: CT, Information Age Publishing

Markose, S.M. (2005). "Computability and evolutionary complexity: Markets as complex adaptive systems (CAS)," *The Economic Journal*, ISSN 0013-0133, 115(504): F159-F192.

Martelli, M. (1999). *Introduction to Discrete Dynamical Systems and Chaos*, ISBN 9780471319757.

Maruyama, M. (1963). "The second cybernetics: Deviation-amplifying mutual causal processes," *American Scientist*, ISSN 0003-0996, 51: 164-179.

Massie, J.L. (1965). "Management theory," in J.G. March (ed.), *Handbook of Organizations*, Chicago, IL: Rand McNally, pp. 387-422.

Masuch, M. (ed.) (1990). *Organization, Management, and Expert Systems*, ISBN 3110119420.

Mathews, K., White, M., Long, R. (1999). "The problem of prediction and control in theoretical diversity and the promise of the complexity sciences," *Journal of Management Inquiry*, ISSN 1552-6542, 8(Mar): 17-31.

Mattoon, M. (1981). *Jungian Psychology in Perspective*, ISBN 0029204402.

Mattoon, M. (1984). *Understanding Dreams*, ISBN 0882143263.

Maturana, H.R. (1988). "Reality: The search for objectivity or the quest for a compelling argument," *The Irish Journal of Psychology*, ISSN 0303-3910, 9(1): 25-82,

Maturana, H.R. and Varela, F.J. (1980). *Autopoiesis and Cognition: The Realization of the Living*, ISBN 9027710163.

Maturana, H.R. and Varela, F.J. (1988). *The Tree of Knowledge: The Biological Roots of Human Understanding*, ISBN 0877736421 (1992).

Maxwell, J. (1998). "Designing a qualitative study," in L. Bickman and D. Rog (eds.), *Handbook of Applied Social Research Methods*, ISBN 076190672X, pp. 69-100.

May, R. (1976). "Simple mathematical models with very complicated dynamics," *Nature*, ISSN 0028-0836, 26: 455-467.

Mayo, E. (1933). *The Human Problems of an Industrial Civilization*, New York, NY: Macmillan.

McClelland, D.C. (1961). *The Achieving Society*, ISBN 9780029205105 (1967).

McCormick, D. and White, J. (2000). "Using one's self as an instrument for organizational diagnosis," *Organizational Development Journal*, ISSN 0143-7739, 18(Fall): 49-62.

McCurdy, H.E. (2001). *Faster, Better, Cheaper: Low-Cost Innovation in the U.S. Space Program*, ISBN 0801867207.

McGrath, R.G. (2001). "Exploratory learning, innovative capacity, and managerial oversight," *Academy of Management Journal*, ISSN 0001-4273, 44(1): 118-131.

McKelvey, B. (1997). "Quasi-natural organization science," *Organization Science*, ISSN 1047-7039, 8: 351-381.

McKelvey, B. (1999a). "Avoiding complexity catastrophe in coevolutionary pockets: Strategies for rugged landscapes," *Organization Science*, ISSN 1047-7039, 10(3): 294-321.

McKelvey, B. (1999b). "Toward a Campbellian Realist Organization Science," in J. Baum and B. McKelvey (eds.), *Variations in Organization Science*, ISBN 0761911251, pp. 383-412.

McKelvey, B. (1999c). "Complexity theory in organization science: Seizing the promise or becoming a fad?" *Emergence*, ISSN 1521-3250, 1: 5-32.

McKelvey, B. (2001a). "Energizing order-creating networks of distributed intelligence," *International Journal of Innovation Management*, ISSN 1363-9196, 5: 181-212.

McKelvey, B. (2001b). "What is complexity science? It is really order creation science," *Emergence*, ISSN 1521-3250, 3(1): 137-157.

McKelvey, B. (2002a). "Managing coevolutionary dynamics," presented at the 18th EGOS Conference, Barcelona, Spain.

McKelvey, B. (2002b). "Model-centered organization science epistemology," in J. Baum (ed.), *Blackwell Companion to Organizations*, ISBN 0631216944, pp. 752-780.

McKelvey, B. (2003). "Emergent order in firms: Complexity science vs. the entanglement trap," in E. Mitleton-Kelly (ed.), *Complex Systems and Evolutionary Perspectives on Organizations: The Application of Complexity Theory to Organizations*, ISBN 9780080439570, pp. 99-125.

McKelvey, B. (2004a). "Toward a 0th Law of Thermodynamics: Order creation complexity dynamics from physics and biology to bioeconomics," *Journal of Bioeconomics*, ISSN 1387-6996, 6: 65-96.

McKelvey, B. (2004b). "Toward a complexity science of entrepreneurship," *Journal of Business Venturing*, ISSN 0883-9026, 19: 313-342.

McKelvey, B. (2004c). "Complexity science as order-creating science: New theory, new method," *Emergence, Complexity and Organization*, ISSN 1521-3250, 6(4): 2-27.

McKelvey, B. (2004d). "1st Principles of efficacious adaptation," working paper, Anderson School of Management, UCLA, Los Angeles, CA.

McKelvey, B. (2006). "Van de Ven and Johnson's 'Engaged Scholarship': Nice try, but...," *Academy of Management Review*, ISSN 0363-7425, 31: 822-829.

McKelvey, B. (2007). "Emergent strategy via complexity leadership: Using complexity science and adaptive tension to build distributed intelligence," in M. Uhl-Bien and R. Marion (eds.), *Complexity and Leadership Volume I: Conceptual Foundations*, Charlotte, NC: Information Age Publishing.

McKelvey, B. (under review). "MicroStrategy from MacroLeadership: Distributed intelligence via new science," in A.Y. Lewin (ed.), *Mobilizing the Self-Renewing Organization*, Armonk, NY: M.E. Sharp.

McKelvey, B. and Andriani, P. (2005). "Why Gaussian statistics are mostly wrong for strategic organization," *Strategic Organization*, ISSN 1476-1270, 3: 219-228.

McKelvey, B. and Boisot, M. (forthcoming). "Redefining strategic foresight: 'Fast' and 'far' sight via complexity science," in L. Costanzo and B. Mackay (eds.), *Handbook of Research on Strategy and Foresight*, Cheltenham, UK: Edward Elgar.

McKelvey, B. and Lichtenstein, B. B. (2007, this volume). "Leadership in the Four Stages of Emergence," in J. Hazy, J. Goldstein and B. Lichtenstein (eds), *Complex Systems Leadership Theory*, ISBN 9780979168864.

McKenzie, J. and van Winkelen, C. (2003). *Understanding the Knowledgeable Organization: Nurturing Knowledge Competence*, ISBN 1861528957.

McMaster, M. (1995). *The Intelligence Advantage: Organizing for Complexity (sic)*, ISBN 095255240X

McShea, D. (2000). "A hypothesis about hierarchies," in Y. Bar-Yam (ed.), *Unifying Themes in Complex systems: Proceedings of the International Conference on Complex Systems*, ISBN 9780813341231, pp. 45-52.

Mead, G. H. (1938). *The Philosophy of the Act*, ISBN 0226516695 (1972)

Mead, G.H. (1932). *The Philosophy of the Present*, Chicago, IL: Open Court Publishing Company.

Mead, G.H. (1934). *Mind, Self, and Society*, ISBN 0226516679.

Meindl, J., Ehrlich, S. and Dukerich, J. (1985). "The romance of leadership," *Administrative Science Quarterly*, ISSN 0001-4273, 30: 78-102.

Mélèse, J. (1991). *L'Analyse Modulaire des Systèmes*, ISBN 9782708112473.

Meyer, A., Gaba, V. and Colwell, K. (2005). "Organizing far from equilibrium: Nonlinear change in organizational fields," *Organization Science*, ISSN 1047-7039, 16: 456-473.

Meyer, S. (2004). "Organizational response to conflict: Future conflict and work outcomes," *Social Work Research*, ISSN 1070-5309, 28(3): 183-190.

Mihata, K. (1997). "The persistence of emergence," in S.H.R. Eve, M. Lee (eds.), *Chaos, Complexity, and Sociology*, ISBN 0761908897

Miles, M. and Huberman, M. (1994). *Qualitative Data Analysis: An Expanded Sourcebook*, ISBN 0803955405.

Miles, R.E. and Snow, C.C. (1986). "Network organizations: New concepts for new forms," *California Management Review*, ISSN 0008-1256, 28: 62-73.

Milgram, S. (1974). *Obedience to Authority*, ISBN 006131983X.

Miller, J.G. (1978). *Living Systems*, ISBN 0070420157.

Miller, K.I. and Monge, P.R. (1986). "Participation, satisfaction and productivity: A meta-analytic review," *Acadamy of Management Journal*, ISSN 0001-4273, 29: 727-753.

Millhiser, W.P. and Solow, D. (2007). "How large should a complex system be? An application in organizational teams," *Complexity*, ISSN 1076-2787, 12(4): 54-70.

Mingers, J. (1989). "An introduction to autopoeisis: Implications and applications," *Systems Practice*, ISSN 0894-9859, 2: 159-180.

Mintzberg, H. (1973). *The Nature of Managerial Work*, ISBN 0060445564.

Mitchell, S. (2004). "Why integrative pluralism?" *Emergence: Complexity and Organization*, ISSN 1521-3250, 6(1,2): 81-91.

Mitroff, I. (1983). *Stakeholders of the Organizational Mind: Toward a New View of Orga-*

nizational Policy Making, ISBN 0875895808.

Mizruchi, M. (1990). "Cohesion, structural equivalence and similarity of behavior: An approach to the study of corporate political power," *Sociological Theory*, ISSN 0735-2751, 8(Spring): 16-32.

Mohamed, M., Stankosky, M. and Murray, A. (2004). "Applying knowledge management principles to enhance cross-functional team performance," *Journal of Knowledge Management*, ISSN 17059232, 8(3): 127-142.

Moldoveanu, M. (2004). "A subjective measure of organizational complexity: A new approach to the study of complexity in organizations," *Emergence: Complexity and Organization*, ISSN 1521-3250, 6(3): 9-26.

Monge, P. R. (1977). "The system perspective as a theoretical basis for the study of human communication," *Communication Quarterly*, ISSN 0146-3373, (25): 19-29.

Moore, B.V. (1927). "The May conference on leadership," *Personnel Journal*, ISSN 0031-5745, 6: 124-128.

Morel, B. and Ramanujam, R. (1999). "Through the looking glass of complexity: The dynamics of organizations as adaptive and evolving systems," *Organization Science*, ISSN 1047-7039, 10(3): 278-294.

Morgan, C.L. (1923). *Emergent Evolution: The Gifford Lectures Delivered in the University of St. Andrews in the Year 1922*, New York, NY: Henry Holt.

Morgan, G. (1997). *Images of Organization*, ISBN 1412939798.

Mortensen, C.D. (1972). *Communication: The Study of Human Interaction*, ISBN 007043395X.

Mosey, S. (2005). "Understanding new-to-market product development in SMEs," *International Journal of Operations and Production Management*, ISSN 01443577, 25(2): 114-130.

Moss, L. (2003). *What Genes Can't Do*, ISBN 978-0262632973.

Mumford, M., Bedell-Avers, K.E. and Hunter, S.T. (in press). "Planning for innovation: A multi-level perspective," in M. D. Mumford, S.T. Hunter and K.E. Bedell (eds.), *Research in Multi-Level Issues*, Oxford, England: Elsevier.

Munson, C.L. and Rosenblatt, M.J. (2001). "Coordinating a three-level supply chain with quantity discounts," *IIE Transactions*, ISSN 0740817X, 33(5): 371-384.

Murnigan, J. and Conlon, D. (1991). "The dynamics of intense work groups: A study of Britishstring quartets," *Administrative Science Quarterly*, 36: 165-186.

Nash, G. (2006). "Re: Us," *National Review*, ISSN 0028-0038, LVIII:(1, January 30):48-49.

Nelson, R.R. and Winter, S.G. (1982). *An Evolutionary Theory of Economic Change*, ISBN 0674272285 (2006).

Nemeth, C.J., Personnaz, B., Personnaz, M. and Goncalo, J.A. (2004). "The liberating role of conflict in group creativity: A study in two countries," *European Journal of Social Psychology*, ISSN 0046-2772, 34: 365-374.

Neumann, J. von (1966). *Theory of Self-Reproducing Automata*, Champaign, IL: University of Illinois Press.

Newman, D. (1996). "Emergence and strange attractors," *Philosophy of Science*, ISSN 0031-8248, 63: 245-261.

Nichols-Nixon, C.L. (2005). "Rapid growth and high performance: The entrepreneur's 'Impossible Dream?'" *Academy of Management Executive*, ISSN 1079-5545, 19(1): 77-89.

Nicolis, G. and Prigogine, I. (1989). *Exploring Complexity: An Introduction*, ISBN 0716718596.

Nicotera, A.M. and Dorsey, L.K. (2006). "Individual and interactive processes in organizational conflict," in J.G. Oetzel and S. Ting-Toomey (eds.), *The Sage Hand-*

book of Conflict Communication: Integrating Theory, Research, and Practice, ISBN 0761930450, pp. 293-325.

Nietzsche, F. (1995). The Birth of Tragedy, C. Fadiman (trans.), ISBN 0486285154, original work published 1872.

Nohria, N. (1992). "Is a network perspective a useful way of studying organizations?" in R.G. Eccles (ed.), *Networks and Organizations: Structure, Form and Action*, ISBN 0875843247, pp. 1-22.

Nohria, N. and Gulati, R. (1996). "Is slack good or bad for innovation?" *Academy of Management Journal*, ISSN 0001-4273, 39(5): 1245-1264.

Nonaka, I. (1985). "Toward a self-organization paradigm: Managing the creation of information," working paper, Institute of Business Research, Hitotsubashi University.

Nonaka, I. (1988). "Creating organizational order out of chaos: Self-renewal in Japanese firms," *California Management Review*, ISSN 0008-1256, 30(3): 57-73.

Nonaka, I. (1994). "A dynamic theory of organizational knowledge creation," *Organization Science*, ISSN 1047-7039, 5(1): 14-37.

Nonaka, I. and Takeuchi, H. (1995). *The Knowledge Creating Company: How Japanese Companies Create the Dynamics of Innovation*, ISBN 0195092694.

Northouse, P.G. (2001). *Leadership: Theory and Practice*, ISBN 0761919260.

Northouse, P.G. (2007). *Leadership: Theory and Practice*, ISBN 9781412941617.

Nowak, M.A. (2006). "Five rules for the evolution of cooperation," *Science*, ISSN 0036-8075, 314(Dec.): 1560-1563,

Nowak, M.A., May, R.M. and Sigmund, K. (1995). "The arithmetics of mutual help," *Scientific American*, ISSN 0036-8733, 272(6): 76-81.

O'Neill, R. V., DeAngelis, D., Waide, J. and Allen, T. (1986). *A Hierarchical Concept of Ecosystems*, ISBN 978-0691084367.

O'Sullivan, T., Hartley, J., Saunders, D., Montgomery, M. and Fiske, J. (1994). *Key Concepts in Communication and Cultural Studies*, ISBN 0415061733.

O'Toole, J. (1999). *Leadership A to Z: A Guide for the Appropriately Ambitious*, ISBN 0787946583.

Odling-Smee, F. J., Laland, K. and Feldman, M. (2003). *Niche Construction*, ISBN 9780691044378.

Oetzel, J.G. and Ting-Toomey, S. (2006). *The Sage Handbook of Conflict Communication: Integrating Theory, Research, and Practice*, ISBN 0761930450.

Oetzel, J.G., Ting-Toomey, S. and Rinderle, S. (2006). "Conflict communication in contexts: A social ecological perspective," in J.G. Oetzel and S. Ting-Toomey (eds.), *The Sage Handbook of Conflict Communication: Integrating Theory, Research, and Practice*, ISBN 0761930450, pp. 727-739.

Olson, M. (1965). *The Logic of Collective Action*, ISBN 0674537505.

Ortega y Gasset, J. (1946). *Concord and Liberty*, H. Weyl (trans.), ISBN 0393001245, original work published 1940.

Osborn, R.N. and Hunt, H.G. (1975). "An adaptive-reactive theory of leadership: The role of macro variables in leadership research," *Organizational and Administrative Sciences*, 6(2-3): 27-44.

Osborn, R.N., Hunt, J.G. (in press). "Leadership and the choice of order: Complexity and hierarchical perspectives near the edge of chaos," *The Leadership Quarterly*, ISSN 1048-9843.

Osborn, R.N., Hunt, J.G., and Jauch, L.R. (2002). "Toward a contextual theory of leadership," *The Leadership Quarterly*, ISSN 1048-9843, 13: 797-837.

Ouchi, W.G. (1981). *Theory Z*, ISBN 038059451X (1983).

Page, D. (2003). "MBA guide 2003," *Canadian Business*, ISSN 0008-3100, 76(Oct/

Nov): 41-47.

Page, S. (2007). *The Difference: How the Power of Diversity Creates Better Groups, Firms, Schools, and Societies*, ISBN 9780691128382.

Paige, G.D. (1977). The Scientific Study of Political Leadership, ISBN 0029236304.

Pantzar, M. and Csanyi, V. (1991). "The replicative model of the evolution of the business organization," *Journal of Social and Biological Structures*, 14: 149-163.

Panzar, C., Hazy, J. K., McKelvey, B. and Schwandt, D.R. (2007, this volume). "The paradox of complex organizations: Leadership as multiplexed influence," in J.K. Hazy, J. Goldstein and B.B. Lichtenstein (eds.), *Complex Systems Leadership Theory*, ISBN 9780979168864.

Pareto, V. (1991). *The Rise and Fall of Elites*, H. Zetterberg (trans.), ISBN 0887388728, original work published 1901.

Parry, K. (1998). "Grounded theory and social process: A new direction for leadership research," *Leadership Quarterly*, ISSN 1048-9843, 9(1): 85-105.

Parsons, T. (1937). *The Structure of Social Action*, New York, NY: McGraw-Hill.

Parsons, T. (1951). *The Social System*, New York, NY: The Free Press.

Parsons, T. and Shils, E.A. (1952). *Toward a General Theory of Action*, ISBN 0674896556.

Pascale, R.T. (1999). "Surfing the edge of chaos," *MIT Sloan Management Review*, ISSN 1532-9194, 40(3): 83-94.

Pascale, R.T., Millemann, M. and Gioja, L. (2000). *Surfing the Edge of Chaos*, ISBN 0609808834.

Patton, M. (1990). *Qualitative Evaluation and Research Methods*, ISBN 0803937792.

Paul, D.L., Butler, J.C., Pearlson, K.E. and Whinston, A.B. (1996). "Computationally modeling organizational learning and adaptability as resource allocation," *Computational and Mathematical Organization Theory*, ISSN 1381-298X, 2: 301-324

Pearce, C.L. and Conger, J.A. (2003). *Shared Leadership*, ISBN 0761926232.

Pearce, C.L. and Conger, J.A. (2003). *Shared Leadership: Reframing the Hows and Whys of Leadership*, ISBN 0761926232.

Pearce, C.L. and Sims, H.P.J. (2000). "Shared leadership. Toward a multi level theory of leadership," in M.M. Beyerlein, D.A. Johnson and S.T. Beyerlein (eds.), Advances in Interdisciplinary Studies of Work Teams, ISBN 0762309814 (2003), pp. 115-139.

Peirce, C.S. (1992). "The fixation of belief," in N. houser and C. Kloesel (eds.), *The Essential Peirce*, ISBN 0253328497, Chapter 7.

Pentland, B. (1992). "Organizing moves in software support hot lines," *Administrative Science Quarterly*, ISSN 0001-8392, 37: 527-549.

Pepper, S. (1926). "*Emergence*," Journal of Philosophy, 23: 241-250.

Perrow, C. (1970). *Organizational Analysis: A Sociological View*, ISBN 0818502878.

Perrow, C. (1999). *Normal Accidents: Living with High-Risk Technologies*, ISBN 0691004129.

Pertrullo, L. and Bass, B.M. (eds.) (1961). *Leadership and Interpersonal Behavior*, New York, NY: Holt, Rinehart and Winston, pp. 82-99.

Peteraf, M.A. (1993). "The cornerstones of competitive advantage: A resource-based view," *Strategic Management Journal*, ISSN 0143-2095, 14(3): 179-191.

Peterson, R. (1997). "A directive leadership style in group decision making can be both virtue and vice: Evidence from elite and experimental groups," *American Journal of Personality and Social Psychology*, ISSN 0022-3514, 72: 1107-1121.

Petty, R.E. and Cacioppo, J.T. (1996). *Attitudes and Persuasion: Classic and Contemporary Approaches*, ISBN 081333005X.

Petzinger, T. (1999). *The New Pioneers*, ISBN 0684846365

Pfeffer, J. (1977). "The ambiguity of leadership," *The Academy of Management Review*, ISSN 03637425, 2(1): 104-112.

Pfeffer, J. (2005). "Producing sustainable competitive advantage through the effective management of people," *The Academy of Management Executive*, ISSN 1079-5545, 19(4): 95-108.

Phelps, K.C. and Hubler, A.W. (2006). "Towards an understanding of membership and leadership in youth organizations: Sudden changes in average participation due to the behavior of one individual," *Emergence: Complexity and Organization*, ISSN 1521-3250, 8(4): 28-35.

Phelps, K.C. and Hubler, A.W. (2007, this volume). "Towards an understanding of membership and leadership in youth organizations: Sudden changes in average participation due to the behavior of one individual," in J.K. Hazy, J.A. Goldstein and B.B. Lichtenstein (eds.), *Complex Systems Leadership Theory*, ISBN 9780979168864.

Piccolo, R.F. and Colquitt, J.A. (2006). "Transformational leadership and job behaviors: The mediating role of core job characteristics," *Academy of Management Journal*, ISSN 0001-4273, 49: 327-340.

Pierce, C.L. and Conger, J.A. (2003). "All those years ago: The historical underpinnings of shared leadership," in C.L. Pierce and J.A. Conger (eds), *Shared Leadership: Reframing the Hows and Whys of Leadership*, ISBN 0761926240, pp. 1-18.

Pigors, P. (1935). *Leadership and Domination*. Boston, MA: Houghton Mifflin.

Pillai, R. (1996). "Crisis and the emergence of charismatic leadership in groups," *Journal of Applied Social Psychology*, ISSN 0021-9029, 26: 543-562.

Pisano, G. (2000). "In search of dynamic capabilities: The origins of R&D competence in biopharmaceuticals," in G. Dosi, R.R. Nelson, and S.G. Winter (eds.), *The Nature and Dynamics of Organizational Capabilities*, ISBN 0199248540, pp. 129-154.

Plowman, D.A, and Duchon, D. (in press). "Dispelling the myths about leadership: From cybernetics to emergence," in M. Uhl-Bien and R. Marion (eds), *Complexity and Leadership Volume I: Conceptual Foundations*, Charlotte, NC: Information Age Publishing.

Plowman, D.A. and Duchon, D. (2007, this volume). "Emergent leadership: Getting beyond heros and scapegoats," in J.K. Hazy, J.A. Goldstein and B.B. Lichtenstein (eds.), *Complex Systems Leadership Theory*, ISBN 9780979168864.

Plowman, D.A., Baker, L.T., Beck, T.E., Kulkarni, M., Solansky, S.T. and Travis, D.V. (2007a). "Radical change accidentally: The emergence and amplification of small change," *Academy of Management Journal*, ISSN 0001-4273, 50(3): 515-543.

Plowman, D.A., Solansky, S., Beck, T., Baker, L., Kulkarni, M. and Travis, D. (2007b). "The role of leadership in emergent, self-organization," *The Leadership Quarterly*, ISSN 1048-9843, 18: 341-356.

Podsakoff, P.M., Todor, W.D. and Skov, R. (1982). "Effect of leader contingent and non contingent reward and punishment behaviors on subordinate performance and satisfaction," *Academy of Management Journal*, ISSN 0001-4273, 5: 810-821.

Poole, M., Dooley, K., Holmes, M., Van de Ven, A. (2000). *Organizational Change and Innovation Processes: Theory and Methods for Research*, ISBN 0195131983

Popper, K. (1966). *The Open Society and its Enemies*, ISBN 0691019681.

Popper, S. (1926). "Emergence," *Journal of Philosophy*, ISSN 0022-362X, 23: 241-245.

Potts, M. and Behr, P. (1987). *The Leading Edge*, ISBN 9780070505995.

Poundstone, W. (1985). The Recursive Universe: Cosmic Complexity and the Limits of Scientific Knowledge, ISBN 9780688039752.

Powell, W.W. (1990). "Neither market nor hierarchy: Network forms of organization," *Research in Organizational Behavior*, ISSN 0191-3085, 12: 295-336.

Prietula, M. J., Carley, K. M. and Gasser, L. (eds.) (1998). *Simulating Organizations: Computational Models of Institutions and Groups*, ISBN 026266108X.

Prigogine, I. (1955). *Introduction to the Thermodynamics of Irreversible Processes*, ISBN 0470699280

Prigogine, I. (1976). "Order through fluctuations: Self-organization and social system," in E. Jantsch and C.H. Waddington (eds.), *Evolution and Consciousness: Human Systems in Transition*, ISBN 0201034387, pp. 95-133.

Prigogine, I. and Glansdorff, P. (1971). *Thermodynamic Theory of Structure, Stability, and Fluctuations*, ISBN 0471302805.

Prigogine, I. and Stengers, I. (1984). *Order Out of Chaos: Man's New Dialogue with Nature*, ISBN 0553340824.

Prusak, L. (1996). "The knowledge advantage," *Strategy and Leadership*, ISSN 1087-8572, 24: 6-8.

Putnam, L.L. (1987). "Leadership and conflict management," *Association for Communication Administration Bulletin*, ISSN 0360-0939, 61: 42-49.

Putnam, L.L. (2006). "Definitions and approaches to conflict and communication," in J.G. Oetzel and S. Ting-Toomey (eds.), *The Sage Handbook of Conflict Communication: Integrating Theory, Research, and Practice*, ISBN 0761930450, pp. 1-32.

Putnam, L.L. and Boys, S. (2006). "Revisiting metaphors of organizational communication," in S. Clegg, C. Hardy and W. Nord (eds.), *The Sage Handbook of Organizational Studies*, ISBN 9780761949961, pp. 541-576.

Putnam, L.L. and Poole, M.S. (1987). "Conflict and negotiation," in F.M. Jablin, L.L.Putnam, K.H. Roberts, and L.W. Porter (eds.), *Handbook of Organizational Communication: An Interdisciplinary Perspective*, ISBN 0803923872, pp. 549-599.

Qian, Y. (1994). "Incentives and loss of control in an optimal hierarchy," *Review of Economic Studies*, ISSN 0034-6527, 61: 527-544.

Quinn, B. (1992). *Intelligent Enterprise: A Knowledge and Service Based Paradigm for Industry*, ISBN 0029256151.

Radcliffe-Brown, A. (1952). *Structure and Function in Primitive Society*, London, England: Cohen and West.

Rahim, M. (2002). "Toward a theory of managing organizational conflict," *International Journal of Conflict Management*, ISSN 1044-4068, 13: 206-235.

Rapoport, A. (1960). *Fights, Games, and Debates*, Ann Arbor, MI: University of Michigan Press.

Rapoport, A. (1967). "Exploiter, leader, hero, and martyr: Four archetypes of the 2 X 2 game," *Behavioral Science*, ISSN 0005-7940, 12(2): 81-84.

References

Regine, B. and Lewin, R. (2000). "Leading at the edge: How leaders influence complex systems," *Emergence: A Journal of Complexity Issues in Organizations and Management*, ISSN 1521-3250, 2(2): 5-23.

Reinert, H. and Reinert, E.S. (2006). "Creative destruction in economics: Nietzsche, Sombart and Schumpeter," in J. Backhaus and W. Drechsler (eds.), *Friedrich Nietzsche 1844-2000: Economy and Society*, ISBN 038732979X.

Reitman, E. (1993). *Creating Artificial Life: Self-Organization*, ISBN 9780830641505.

Reuter, E.B. (1941). *Handbook of Social Psychology*, New York, NY: Dryden Press.

Rhee, Y.P. (2000). "Complex systems approach to the study of politics," *Systems Research and Behavioral Science*, ISSN 1099-1743, 17(6): 487-491.

Richardson, K.A. (2005). "The hegemony of the physical sciences: An exploration in complexity thinking," *Futures*, ISSN 0746-2468, 37(7): 615-653.

Richardson, K.A. and Cilliers, P. (2001). "What is complexity science? A view from different directions," *Emergence*, ISSN 1521-3250, 3(1): 5-23.

Riggs, N.R. and Greenberg, M.T. (2004). "After-school youth development programs: A developmental-ecological model of current research," *Clinical Child and Family Psychology Review*, ISSN 1096-4037, 7(3): 177-190.

Rivkin, J.W. (2000). "Imitation of complex strategies," *Management Science*, ISSN 0025-1909, 46(6): 824-844.

Rivkin, J.W. (2001). "Reproducing knowledge: Replication without imitation at moderate complexity," *Organization Science*, ISSN 1047-7039, 12(3): 274-293.

Rivkin, J.W. and Siggelkow, N. (2002). "Organizational sticking points on NK landscapes," *Complexity*, ISSN 1076-2787, 7(5): 31-43.

Rivkin, J.W. and Siggelkow, N. (2003). "Balancing search and stability: Interdependencies among elements of organizational design," *Management Science*, ISSN 0025-1909, 49: 290-311.

Rock, I. (1995). *Perception*, ISBN 0716760118.

Roethlisberger, F.J. and Dickson, W.J. (1939). *Management and the Worker: An Account of a Research Program Conducted by the Western Electric Company, Hawthorne Works, Chicago*, ISBN 0674546768.

Roffman, J.G., Pagano, M.E. and Hirsch, B.J. (2001). "Youth functioning and experiences in inner-city after-school programs among age, gender, and race groups," *Journal of Child and Family Studies*, ISSN 1062-1024, 10(1): 85-100.

Rogers, E.M. (1983). *Diffusion of Innovations*, ISBN 0029266505.

Romanelli, E. (1991). "The evolution of new organizational forms," *Annual Review of Sociology*, 17: 79-103.

Romme, A.G.L. (1999). "Domination, self-determination and circular organizing," *Organization Studies*, ISSN 0170-8406, 20(5), 801-831.

Rooke, D. and Torbert, W. (2005). "Seven transformations of leadership," *Harvard Business Review*, ISSN 0017-8012, 83(Apr): 66-76.

Rosen, R. (1974). "On the design of stable and reliable institutions," *International Journal of General Systems*, ISSN 1563-5104, 1: 61-66.

Rosen, R. (1996). "On the limitations of scientific knowledge," in J. Casti and A. Karlqvist (eds.), *Boundaries and Barriers: On the Limits to Scientific Knowledge*, ISBN 9780201555707, pp. 199-214.

Rouse, W. B. (2000). "Managing complexity: Disease control as a complex adaptive system," *Information Knowledge Systems Management*, ISSN 1389-1995, 2: 143-165.

Rousseau, D. (1985). "Issues of level in organizational research: Multi-level and cross-level perspectives," *Research in Organizational Behavior*, ISSN 0191-3085, 7: 1-38.

Rowe, C. (2004). "The effect of accounting report structure and team structure on performance in cross-functional teams," *The Accounting Review*, ISSN 0001-4826, 79(4): 1153-1180.

Rowen, S. (2006). "Redesigning the store experience: New Zealand's farmers trading begins a technology refresh," *Chain Store Age*, ISSN 1087-0601, 82(2): 50-51.

Roy, D. (1954). "Efficiency and 'the fix': Informal intergroup relations in a piecework machine shop," *American Journal of Sociology*, ISSN 0002-9602, 60: 255-266.

Ruben, B.D. (1978). "Communication and conflict: A system-theoretic perspective," *The Quarterly Journal of Speech*, ISSN 0033-5630, 64: 202-210.

Rubin, R.S., Munz, D.C. and Bommer, W.H. (2005). "Leading from within: The effects of emotion recognition and personality on transformational leadership behavior," *Academy of Management Journal*, ISSN 0001-4273, 48: 845-858.

Rudolph, J. and Repenning, N. (2002). "Disaster dynamics: Understanding the role of quantity in organizational collapse," *Administrative Science Quarterly*, ISSN 0001-8392, 47: 1-30.

Ruelle, D. (1991). *Chance and Chaos*, ISBN 0691085749.

Russell, S. and Norvig, P. (1995). *Artificial Intelligence: A Modern Approach*, ISBN 0133601242.

Ruzavin, G. (1994). "Self-organization and organization of the economy and the search for a new paradigm in economic science," *Problems of Economic Transition*, ISSN 10611991, 47(6): 67-81.

Salancik, G.R. and Pfeffer, J. (1978). "A social information processing approach to job attitudes and task design," *Administrative Science Quarterly*, ISSN 0001-8392, 23: 224-253.

Salthe, S.N. (1985). *Evolving Hierarchical Systems: Their Structure and Representation*, ISBN 0231060165

Salthe, S.N. (1993). *Development and Evolution: Complexity and Change in Biology*, ISBN 0262193353

Sandell, N., Varaiya, P., Athans, M. and Safonov, M. (1978). "Survey of decentralized control methods for large scale systems," *IEEE Transactions on Automatic Control*, ISSN 0018-9286, 23(2): 108-128.

Sashkin, M. and Sashkin, M.G. (2003). *Leadership that Matters: The Critical Factors for Making a Difference in People's Lives and Organizations' Success*, ISBN 1576751937

Sastry, A. (1997). "Problems and paradoxes in a model of punctuated organizational change," *Administrative Science Quarterly*, ISSN 0001-8392, 42 (2): 237-275.

Saviotti, P.P. and Mani, G.S. (1998). "Technological evolution, self-organization, and knowledge," *Journal of High Technology Management Research*, ISSN 1047-8310, 9: 255-270.

Sawyer, R.K. (2003). "Artificial societies: Multiagent systems and the micro-macro link in sociological theory," *Sociological Methods and Research*, ISSN 0049-1241, 31(3): 325-363.

Sayles, L.R. (1957). *Research in Industrial Human Relations*, New York, NY: Harper and Row.

Schein, E.H. (1992). *Organizational Culture and Leadership*, ISBN 0783765053.

Schelling, T. (1960). *The Strategy of Conflict*, ISBN 0674840313.

Schelling, T. (1978). *Micromotives and Macrobehavior*, ISBN 0393057011.

Scheutz, M. and Schermerhorn, P. (2003). "Many is more, but not too many: Dimensions of cooperation of agents with and without predicitive capabilities," *Proceeding of the IEEE/WIC International Conference on Intelligent Agent Technology*, pp. 378-384.

Schieve, W. and Allen, P. (eds.) (1982). *Self-Organization and Dissipative Structures: Applications in the Physical and Social Sciences*, ISBN 0292703546.

Schlenker, B.R. (1985). "Introduction: Foundations of the self in social life," in B.R. Schlenker (ed.), *The Self and Social Life*, ISBN 0070553076, Chapter 1.

Schmidt, R. (1933). "Leadership," in E.R.A. Seligman (ed.), *Encyclopaedia of the Social Sciences*, New York, NY: Macmillan, pp. 282-286.

Schneider, M. and Somers, M. (2006). "Organizations as complex adaptive systems: Implications of complexity theory for leadership research," *The Leadership Quarterly*, ISSN 1048-9843, 17(4): 351-365.

Schreiber, C. (2006). "Human and organizational risk modeling: Critical personnel and leadership in network organizations," Carnegie Mellon University, School of Computer Science, Institute for Software Research, International. Technical Report, CMU-ISRI-06-120.

Schreiber, C. and Carley, K.M. (2004a). "Going beyond the data: Empirical validation leading to grounded theory," *Computational and Mathematical Organization Theory*, ISSN 1381298X, 10(2): 155-164.

Schreiber, C. and Carley, K.M. (2004b). "Key personnel: Identification and assessment of turnover risk," paper presented at the NAACSOS Conference Proceedings, Pittsburgh, PA.

Schreiber, C. and Carley, K.M. (2005). "Ineffective organizational practices at NASA: A dynamic network analysis," Carnegie Mellon University, School of Computer Science, Institute for Software Research, International, Technical Report, CMU-ISRI-05-135.

Schreiber, C. and Carley, K.M. (2006). "Leadership style as an enabler of organizational complex functioning," *Emergence: Complexity and Organization*, ISSN 1521-7000, 8(4): 61-76.

Schroder, J. (1998). "Emergence: Non-deducibility or downwards causation?" *Philosophical Quarterly*, 48 (193): 432-452.

Schrodinger, E. (1944). *What is Life?*, ISBN 0521427088 (1992).

Schutz, A. (1967). *The Phenomenology of the Social World*, G. Walsh and F. Lehnert (trans.), ISBN 0810103907.

Schwandt, D.R. (in press). "Individual and collective coevolution: Leadership as emergent social structuring," in M. Uhl-Bien and R. Marion (eds.), *Complexity and Leadership, Volume I: Conceptual Foundations*, Charlotte, NC: Information Age Publishing.

Schwandt, D.R. and Marquardt, M.J. (2000). *Organizational Learning: From World-Class Theories to Global Best Practices*, ISBN 1574442597.

Scott, W.R. (1998). *Organizations: Rational, Natural, and Open Systems*, ISBN 0138990220.

Scott, W.R. (2004). "Reflections on a half-century of organizational sociology," *Annual Review of Sociology*, ISSN 0360-0572, 30: 1-21.

Searle, J. (1994). *The Rediscovery of Mind*, ISBN 978- 0262691543.

Seeman, M. (1960). *Social Status and Leadership*, Columbus: Ohio State University, Bureaus of Business Leadership.

Seers, A. (2004). "Leadership and flexible organizational structures," in G.B. Graen (ed.), *New Frontiers of Leadership*, ISBN 1593112394, pp. 1-31.

Seers, A. and Wilkerson, J.W. (2005). "Toward a model of relational micro-organizing: Social exchange, identity, and structure," unpublished paper.

Selznick, P. (1957). *Leadership in Administration: A Sociological Interpretation*, Evanston, IL: Row, Peterson and Company.

Senge, P.M. (1990). *The Fifth Discipline: The Art and Practice of the Learning Organization*, ISBN 0385517254.

Senge, P.M. (1994). "The leader's new work," *Executive Excellence*, ISSN 8756-2308, 11(11): 8-9.

Senge, P.M. and Sterman, J.D. (1992). "Systems thinking and organizational learning: Acting locally and thinking globally in the organization of the future," in T.A. Kochan and M. Useem (eds.), *Transforming Organizations*, ISBN 0195065042, pp. 353-371.

Senge, P.M., Scharmer, O., Jaworski, J. and Flowers, B. (2005). *Presence: An Exploration of Profound Change in People, Organizations, and Society*, ISBN 038551624X.

Sengupta, A. (2007). "Chaos, nonlinearity, complexity: A unified perspective," in A. Sengupta (ed.), *Chaos, Nonlinearity, Complexity: The Dynamical Paradigm of Nature*, ISBN 9783540317562, pp. 273-355.

Sethi, S.P., Yan, H., Zhang, H. and Zhang, Q. (2002). "Optimal and hierarchical controls in dynamic stochastic manufacturing systems: A survey," *Manufacturing and Service Operations Management*, ISSN 1523-4614, 4(2): 133-170.

Shamir, B., House, R. and Arthur, M. (1993). "The motivational effects of charismatic leadership: A self-concept-based theory," *Organization Science*, ISSN 1047-7039, 4: 577-594.

Shane S.A., Venkataraman, S. and MacMillan, I.C. (1995). "Cultural differences in innovation championing strategies," *Journal of Management*, ISSN 0149-2063, 21: 931-952.

Shannon, C. and Weaver, W. (1949). *The Mathematical Theory of Communication*, ISBN 0252725484.

Shapiro, K. (2001). *The Limits of Attention: Temporal Constraints on Human Information Processing*, ISBN 0198505167.

Shin, S.J. and Zhou, J. (2003). "Transformational leadership, conservation, and creativity: Evidence from Korea," *Academy of Management Journal*, ISSN 0001-4273, 46: 703-714.

Shockley-Zalabak, P. (1990). *Fundamentals of Organizational Communication : Knowledge, Sensitivity, Skills, Values*, ISBN 0205453503 (2005).

Siggelkow N. and Rivkin, J.W. (2006). "When exploration backfires: Unintended consequences of multi-Level organizational search," *Academy of Management Journal*, ISSN 0001-4273, 49: 779-795.

Siggelkow, N. (2001). "Change in the presence of fit: The rise, the fall, and the renascence of Liz Claiborne," *Academy of Management Journal*, ISSN 0001-4273, 44: 838-857.

Siggelkow, N. (2002). "Evolution toward fit," *Administrative Science Quarterly*, ISSN 0001-8392, 47(1): 125-159.

Siggelkow, N. and Rivkin, J.W. (2005). "Speed and search: Designing organizations for turbulence and complexity," *Organization Science*, ISSN 1047-7039, 16(2): 101-122.

Siggelkow, N. and Rivkin, J.W. (2006). "When exploration backfires: Unintended consequences of multilevel organizational search," *Academy of Management Journal*, ISSN 0001-4273, 49(4): 779-796.

Simmel, G. (1950). *The Sociology of Georg Simmel*, K. Wolff (trans.), ISBN 0029289203.

Simmel, G. (1971). *On Individuality and Social Forms*, D. Levine (ed.), ISBN 0226757765.

Simmons, K.(1990). "The diagonal argument and the Liar," *Journal of Philosophical Logic*, ISSN 0022-3611, 19: 277-303.

Simon, H.A. (1947). *Administrative Behavior*, ISBN 9780684835822 (1997).

Simon, H.A. (1955). "A behavioral model of rational choice," *Quarterly Journal of Economics*, ISSN 0033-5533, 69(Feb): 99-118.

Simon, H.A. (1957). *Administrative Behavior*, ISBN 0029289718.

Simon, H.A. (1962). "The architecture of complexity," *Proceedings of the American Philosophical Society*, ISSN 0003-049X, 106(6): 467-482.

Simon, H.A. (1965). "The architecture of complexity," *General Systems*, 10: 63-73, reprinted in *Emergence: Complexity and Organization*, ISSN 1521-3250, 7(3-4): 138-154.

Simon, H.A. (1976). *Administrative Behavior*, ISBN 0684835827.

Simon, H.A. (1981). "Studying human intelligence by creating artificial intelligence," *American Scientist*, ISSN 0003-0996, 69(3): 300-309.

Simon, H.A. (1990). "A mechanism for social selection and successful altruism," *Science*, ISSN 0036-8075, 250: 1665-1668.

Sinclair, A. (1992). "The tyranny of team ideology," *Organization Studies*, ISSN 0170-8406, 13: 611-632.

Singer, J. (1994). *Boundaries of the Soul: The Practice of Jung's Psychology*, ISBN 0385475292.

Smircich, L. and Stubbart, C. (1986). "Strategic management in an enacted world," *Academy of Management Review*, ISSN 0363-7425, 10(4): 724-738.

Smith, A. (2000). *The Wealth of Nations*, ISBN 0679783369, original work published 1776.

Smith, A.C.T. (2004). "Complexity theory and change management in sports organizations," *Emergence: Complexity & Organization*, ISSN 1521-3250, 6(1-2): 70-79.

Smith, C. (1986). "Transformation and regeneration in social systems: A dissipative structure perspective," *Systems Research*, ISSN 1092-7026, 3: 203-213.

Smith, C. and Comer, D. (1994). "Change in the small group: A dissipative structure perspective," *Human Relations*, ISSN 0018-7267, 47: 553-581.

Smith, C. and Gemmill, G. (1991). "Self-Organization in small groups: A study of group effectivenss within non-equilibrium conditions," *Human Relations*, ISSN 0018-7267, 44: 697-716.

Smith, D.H. (1972). "Communication research and the idea of process," *Speech Monograph*, ISSN 0038-7169, 39, 174-182.

Smith, K.K. (1989). "The movement of conflict in organizations: The joint dynamics of splitting and triangulation," *Administrative Science Quarterly*, ISSN 0001-8392, (34)1: 1-20.

Smith, M.R. (2005). "Team approach to ergo dolly cuts injuries and saves money," *Plant Engineering*, ISSN 0032-082X, 59(9): 66, 70.

Solow, D. and Leenawong, C. (2003). "Mathematical models for studying the value of cooperational leadership in team replacement," *Computational and Mathematical Organization Theory*, ISSN 1381-298X, 9(1): 61-81.

Solow, D. and Szmerekovsky J.G. (2006). "How much central control is best for a complex system? Insights from a mathematical model," working paper.

Solow, D. and Szmerekovsky, J.G. (2005). "Mathematical models for explaining the emergence of specialization in performing tasks," *Complexity*, ISSN 1076-2787, 10(1): 37-48.

Solow, D. and Szmerekovsky, J.G. (2006). "The role of leadership: What management science can give back to the study of complex systems," *Emergence: Complexity & Organization*, ISSN 1521-7000, 8(4): 52-60.

Solow, D. and Szmerekovsky, J.G. (2007). "How much central control is best for a complex system? Insights from a mathematical model," unpublished manuscript.

Solow, D., Burnetas, A.N., Piderit, S.K. and Leenawong, C. (2005). "Mathematical models for studying the value of motivational leadership in team replacement," *Computational and Mathematical Organization Theory*, ISSN 1381-298X, 11(1): 5-36.

Solow, D., Burnetas, A.N., Roeder, T. and Greenspan, N.S. (1999a). "Evolutionary consequences of selected locus-specific variations in epistasis and fitness contribution in Kauffman's NK model," *Journal of Theoretical Biology*, ISSN 0022-5193, 196: 181-196.

Solow, D., Burnetas, A.N., Tsai, M. and Greenspan, N.S. (1999b). "Understanding and attenuating the complexity catastrophe in Kauffman's NK model of genome evolution," *Complexity*, ISSN 1076-2787, 5(1): 53-66.

Solow, D., Burnetas, A.N., Tsai, M. and Greenspan, N.S. (2000). "On the expected performance of systems with complex interactions among components," *Complex Systems*, ISSN 08912513, 12(4): 423-456.

Solow, D., Piderit, S., Burnetas, A. and Leenawong, C. (2005). "Mathematical models for studying the value of motivational leadership in teams," *Computational and Mathematical Organization Theory*, ISSN 1381-298X, 11(1): 5-36.

Solow, D., Vairaktarakis, D., Piderit, S. K. and Tsai, M. (2002). "Managerial insights into the effects of interactions on replacing members of a team," *Management Science*, ISSN 0025-1909, 48(8): 1060-1073.

Sorenson, O.J. (1997). "The complexity catastrophe: Interdependence and adaptability in organizational evolution," unpublished Unpublished Ph.D. dissertation, Stanford University, Palo Alto, CA.

Sorenson, O.J. (2002). "Interorganizational complexity and computation," in J. Baum (ed.), *Companion to Organizations*, ISBN 0631216952, pp. 664-685.

Sorenson, O.J. and Audia, P. (2000). "The social structure of entrepreneurial activity: Geographic concentration of footwear production in the U.S., 1940-1989," *American Journal of Sociology*, ISSN 0002-9602, 106: 424-461.

Sorenson, O.J., Rivkin, J.W. and Fleming, L. (2006). "Complexity, networks and knowledge flow," *Research Policy*, ISSN 0048-7333, 35: 994-1017.

Souder, W. (1987). *Managing New Product Innovations*, ISBN 066910809X.

Spada, C. (2007, this volume). "Bureaucratic agents: Simulating organizational behavior and hierarchical decision-making," in J.K. Hazy, J.A. Goldstein and B.B. Lichtenstein (eds.), *Complex Systems Leadership Theory*, ISBN 9780979168864.

Sperry, R.W. (1986). "Discussion: Macro- versus micro-determinism," *Philosophy of Science*, 53: 265-270.

Stacey, R.D. (1992). *Managing the Unknowable*, ISBN 1555424635.

Stacey, R.D. (1993). *Strategic Management and Organizational Dynamics*, ISBN 0273708112.

Stacey, R.D. (1995). "The science of complexity: An alternative perspective for strategic change processes," *Strategic Management Journal*, ISSN 0143-2095, 16(Sep): 477-495.

Stacey, R.D. (1996). *Complexity and Creativity in Organizations*, ISBN 9781881052890.

Stacey, R.D. (2003a). "Research perspective: organizations as complex responsive processes of relating," *Journal of Innovative Management*, ISSN 1081-0714, 8(2): 27-39.

Stacey, R.D. (2003b). *Strategic Management and Organizational Dynamics: The Challenge of Complexity*, ISBN 0273658980.

Stacey, R.D., Griffin, D. and Shaw, P. (2000). *Complexity and Management: Fad or Radical Challenge to Systems Thinking*, ISBN 0203190157.

Stanley, M., Amaral, L., Buldyrev, S. (1996). "Scaling behavior in the growth of companies," *Nature*, ISSN 0028-0836, 379: 804-806.

Stephan, A. (1992). "Emergence: A systematic view on its historical facets," in A. Beckermann, H. Flohr and J. Kim (eds.), *Emergence or Reduction: Essays on the Prospects of Nonreductive Physicalism*, ISBN 978-3110128802, pp. 24-48.

Sterman, J.D. (2000). *Business Dynamics. System Thinking and Modeling for a Complex World*, ISBN 007238915X.

Stevenson, H.H. and Harmeling, S. (1990). "Entrepreneurial management's need for a more 'chaotic' theory," *Journal of Business Venturing*, ISSN 0883-9026, 5: 1-14.

Stewart, T.A. (1997). *Intellectual Capital: The New Wealth of Organizations*, ISBN 0385482280.

Stogdill, R.M. (1948). "Personal factors associated with leadership: A survey of the literature," *Journal of Psychology*, ISSN 0022-3980, 25: 35-71.

Stogdill, R.M. (1950). "Leadership, membership, and organization," *Psychological Bulletin*, ISSN 0033-2909, 47: 1-14.

Stogdill, R.M. (1955). *Methods in the Study of Administrative Leadership*, ISBN 0877760802.

Stogdill, R.M. (1974). *Handbook of Leadership: A Survey of the Literature*, ISBN 002901820X.

Stoller, A.W. and Knobloch, N.A. (2005). "Students' participation and self perceived impact of extracurricular activities on developing leadership skills," paper presented at the meeting of the AAAE North Central Agricultural Education Conference at Columbus, OH.

Strauss, A. and Corbin, J. (1998). *Basics of Qualitative Research: Grounded Theory Procedures and Techniques*, ISBN 0803932502.

Streatfield, P.J. (2001). *The Paradox of Control in Organizations*, ISBN 0415250315.

Strogatz, S. (2003). *Sync: The Emerging Science of Spontaneous Order*, ISBN 9780786868445.

Sulis, W. (1997). "Fundamental concepts of collective intelligence," *Nonlinear Dynamics, Psychology, and Life Sciences*, ISSN 1090-0578, 1(Jan): 35-53.

Sulis, W. and Combs, A. (eds.) (1996). *Nonlinear Dynamics in Human Behavior*, ISBN 9810227426

Surie, G. (1996). "The creation of organizational capabilities through international transfers of technology," Ph.D. dissertation, The Wharton School, University of Pennsylvania.

Surie, G. (2003). "Knowledge transfer, identity, and internationalization through communities-of-practice," paper presented at the Academy of Management, Seattle, August.

Surie, G. and Hazy, J.K. (2007). "Generative leadership: Nurturing innovation in complex systems," *Emergence: Complexity & Organization*, ISSN 1521-3250, 8(4): 13-28.

Swanson, J. (1986). "Analyzing data for categories and description," in C. Chenitz and J. Swanson (eds.), *From Practice to Grounded Theory: Qualitative Research in Nursing*, ISBN 0201129604, pp. 121-132.

Swenson, R. (1989). "Emergent attractor and the law of maximum entropy production: Foundations to a theory of general evolution," *Systems Research*, ISSN 1092-7026, 6(3): 187-197.

Swenson, R. (1991). "End-directed physics and evolutionary ordering," in F. Geyr (ed.), *Cybernetics of Complex Systems*, Salinas, CA: Intersystems Press.

Swenson, R. (1992). "Order, evolution, and natural law: Fundamental relations in complex system theory," in C. Negoita (ed.), *Cybernetics and Applied Systems*, ISBN 0824786777, pp. 125-147.

Swenson, R. (1997). "Thermodynamics and evolution," in G. Greenberg and M. Haraway (eds.), *Comparative Psychology: A Handbook*, ISBN 0815312814, pp. 207-219.

Sword, L.D. (2007). "Complexity science conflict analysis of power and protest," *Emergence: Complexity & Organization*, ISSN 1521-3250, 9(3), accepted for publication.

Talbert, B.A. and Balschweid, M.A. (2004). "Engaging students in the agricultural education model: Factors affecting student participation in the national FFA organization," *Journal of Agricultural Education*, ISSN 1042-0541, 45(1): 29-41.

Tannenbaum, R. and Schmidt, W.H. (1958). "How to choose a leadership pattern," *Harvard Business Review*, ISSN 0017-8012, 36(2): 95-101.

Tannenbaum, R., Weschler, I. R. and Massarik, F. (1961). *Leadership and Organization: A Behavioral Science Approach*, New York, NY: McGraw-Hill.

Taylor, E.I. (1998). "William James' prophecy on the demise of positivism in American

Psychology," in R. Rieber and K. Salzinger (eds.), *Psychology: Theoretical-Historical Perspectives*, ISBN 9781557985248 .

Taylor, F.W. (1911). *Principles of Scientific Management*, 1st edition, ISBN 9781434638205 (2007).

Taylor, J.R., and Van Every, E.J. (2000). *The Emergent Organization*, ISBN 0805821945

Tead, O. (1935). *The Art of Leadership*, New York, NY: McGraw-Hill.

Teece, D.J. (2005). "Dynamic capabilities: The causes, consequences and challenges of change," in J. Hazy (ed.), Comment at a Symposium at the Academy of Management Annual Conference, Tuesday, August 8, 2005, Honolulu, HI.

Teece, D.J. and Pisano, G. (1994). "The dynamic capabilities of firms: An introduction," *Industrial and Corporate Change*, ISSN 0960-6491, 3(3): 537-556.

Teece, D.J., Pisano, G., and Shuen, A. (1997). "Dynamic capabilities and strategic management," *Strategic Management Journal*, ISSN 01432095, 18(7): 509-533.

Thayer, L. (1978). "Viestinnän tutkimus: kritiikki ja kehitysnäkymät," in E. Erholm and L. Åberg (eds.), *Viestinnän Virtauksia*, ISBN 9511046780, pp. 15-43.

Thiétart, R.A. and Forgues, B. (1995). "Chaos theory and organization," *Organization Science*, ISSN 0263-2136, 6(1): 19-31.

Thom, R. (1975). *Structural Stability and Morphogenesis*, ISBN 0805392769.

Thomas, C., Kaminska-Labbé, R. and McKelvey, B. (2005). "Managing the MNC and exploitation / exploration dilemma: From static balance to irregular oscillation," in G. Szulanski, Y. Doz and J. Porac (eds.), *Advances in Strategic Management: Expanding Perspectives on the Strategy Process*, ISBN 0762312009, pp. 213-247.

Thomas, K. and Schmidt, W. (1976). "A survey of managerial interest with respect to conflict," *Academy of Management Journal*, ISSN 0001-4273, 19: 315-318.

Thompson, D. J. (1967). *Organizations in Action*, ISBN 070643806.

Thompson, K. (1984) "The dilemmas and antinomies of leadership," in R.S. Khare and D. Little (eds.). *Leadership: Interdisciplinary Reflections*, ISBN 081913970X, pp. 9-20, 131-133.

Tichy, N. and Devanna, M. A. (1986). *The Transformational Leader*, ISBN 0471822590.

Tiles, M. (1989). *The Philosophy of Set Theory: An Introduction to Cantor's Paradise*, ISBN 9780486435206.

Torbert, B., and Associates. (2004). *Action Inquiry: The Secret of Timely and Transforming Leadership*, ISBN 157675264X.

Torbert, W. (1991). *The Power of Balance*, ISBN 080394067X

Trice, H.M. and Beyer, J.M. (1993). "Leadership and organizational cultures," in H.M. Trice and J.M. Beyer, *The Cultures of Work Organizations*, ISBN 9780131914384, pp. 254-298.

Trist, E.L. and Bamforth, K.W. (1951). "Social and psychological consequences of the Longwall method of coal-getting," *Human Relations*, ISSN 0018-7267, 4: 3-28.

Tsoukas, H. and Chia, R. (2002). "On organizational becoming: Rethinking organizational change," *Organization Science*, ISSN 1047-7039, 13: 567-583.

Tsvetovat, M., Reminga, J. and Carley, K.M. (2004). "DyNetML: Interchange format for rich social network data," Carnegie Mellon University, School of Computer Science, Institute for Software Research International, Technical Report CMU-ISRI-04-105.

Turing, A. (1937). "On computable numbers, with an application to the Entscheidungsproblem," *Proceedings of the London Mathematical Society*, ISSN 0024-6115, 2(42): 230-265.

Turing, A.(1952). "The chemical basis of morphogenesis," *Philosophical Transactions of the Royal Society*, Series B, ISSN 0264-3839, 237(641): 37-72.

U.S. Census Bureau (2002). "Census 2000 urban and rural classification," http://www.census.gov/geo/www/ua/ua_2k.html.

Uhl-Bien, M. (2007). "Relational leadership theory: Exploring the social processes of leadership and -organizing," *The Leadership Quarterly*, ISSN 1048-9843, 18: 298-318.

Uhl-Bien, M. and Marion, R. (2007). "The mechanisms of emergence in complexity leadership theory: A meso-model of adaptive dynamics in organizations," University of Nebraska-Lincoln, Lincoln, NE and Clemson University, Clemson, SC.

Uhl-Bien, M. and Marion, R. (in press). *Complexity and Leadership, Volume I: Conceptual Foundations*, Charlotte, NC: Information Age Publishers.

Uhl-Bien, M., Marion, R. and McKelvey, B. (2004). "Complexity leadership theory: Shifting leadership from the industrial age to the knowledge era," presented at the Academy of Management, New Orleans, LA.

Uhl-Bien, M., Marion, R., and McKelvey, B. (2007). "Complexity leadership theory: Shifting leadership from the industrial age to the knowledge era," *The Leadership Quarterly*, ISSN 1048-9843, 18(4): 298-318.

Ulrich, H. and Probst, J. B. (eds.) (1984). *Self-Organization and Management of Social Systems*, ISBN 038713459X.

Van de Ven, A.H. (1986). "Central problems in the management of innovation," *Management Science*, ISSN 0025-1909, 32: 590-607.

Van de Ven, A.H. (1992). "Suggestions for studying strategy process: a research note," *Strategic Management Journal*, ISSN 0143-2095, 13: 169-188.

Van de Ven, A.H. and Poole, M.S. (1990). "Methods for studying innovation development in the Minnesota Innovation Research Program," *Organization Science*, ISSN 1047-7039, 1(3): 313-335.

Van de Ven, A.H., Angle, H.L. and Poole, M.S. (1989). *Research on the Management of Innovation*, ISBN 0887303331.

Van Dyne, L. and Saavedra, R. (1996). "A naturalistic minority influence experiment: Effects on divergent thinking, conflict, and originality in work groups," *British Journal of Social Psychology*, ISSN 0144-6665, 35: 151-167.

Verhagen, H.J.E. (2000a). *Norm Autonomous Agents*, ISBN 9172656737, http://citeseer.ist.psu.edu/cache/papers/cs/29908/ftp:zSzzSzftp.dsv.su.sezSzuserszSzverhagenzSzphdthesis.pdf/verhagen00norm.pdf.

Verhagen, H.J.E. (2000b). "Simulation of the learning of norms," *Proceedings of the Workshop on Simulation of Social Agents: Architectures and Institutions*, pp. 95-107.

Vincent, A., Decker, B. and Mumford, M. (2002). "Divergent, thinking, intelligence, and expertise," *Creativity Research Journal*, ISSN 1040-0419, 14(2): 163-178.

von Bertalanffy, L. (1950). "The theory of open systems in physics and biology," *Science*, ISSN 0036-8075, 3: 23-29.

Von Bertalanffy, L. (1956). "General systems theory," *General Systems*, 1: 1-10.

von Bertalanffy, L. (1968). *General System Theory: Foundations, Development, Applications*, ISBN 9780807604533 (1976).

von Bertalanffy, L. (1975). *Perspectives on General System Theory: Scientific-Philosophical Studies*, ISBN 0807607975.

von Bertalanfy, L. (1969). *General System Theory: Foundations, Development, Applications*, ISBN 0807604534.

von Clausewitz, C. (2004). *On War*, ISBN 0415350387.

von Hippel, E. (1988). *The Sources of Innovation*, ISBN 0195040856.

von Neumann, J. and Burks, A. (1966). *Theory of Self-Reproducing Automata*, ISBN

9780598377982 (2002).

Vroom, V.H. (2000). "Leadership and the decision making process." *Organizational Dynamics*, ISSN 0090-2616, 28(4): 82-94.

Vroom, V.H. and Jago, A.G. (1988). *The New Leadership*, ISBN 0136150306.

Vroom, V.H. and Yetton, P.W. (1973). *Leadership and Decision-Making*, ISBN 0822932660.

Wade, J. (1996) "A community-level analysis of sources and rates of technological variation in the micro-processor market," *Academy of Management Journal*, ISSN 0001-4273, 39(5): 1218-1244.

Wakabayashi, M. and Graen, G. (1984). "The Japanese career study progress: A seven-year follow up," *Journal of Applied Psychology*, ISSN 0021-9010, 69: 603-614.

Wakefield, D. (2003). "Factors influencing minority enrollment in agricultural education: A qualitative study in an urban School in Illinois," Agricultural Education Research Summary Report, October.

Waldman, D., Ramirez, G., House, R. and Puraham, P. (2001). "Does leadership matter? CEO leadership attributes and profitability under conditions of perceived environmental uncertainty," *Academy of Management Journal*, ISSN 0001-4273, 44(1): 134-143.

Waldrop, M. (1992). *Complexity*, ISBN 0671767895.

Wall, S.D. (1999). "Reinventing the design process: Teams and models," NASA Jet Propulsion Lab, Technical Report 99-0379.

Walton, R. E. and McKersie, R.B. (1965). *A Behavioral Theory of Labor Negotiation*, ISBN 0070680493.

Warglien, M. and Masuch, M. (eds.) (1996). *The Logic of Organizational Disorder*, ISBN 3110137070, pp. 1-34.

Watkins, M., and Bazerman, M. (2003). "Predictable surprises: The disasters you should have seen coming," *Harvard Business Review*, ISSN 0017-8012, 81(Mar): 72-80.

Watson, C. and Hoffman, R. (1996). "Managers as negotiators: A test of power versus gender as predictors of feelings, behavior, and outcomes," *Leadership Quarterly*, ISSN 1048-9843, 7(1): 63-85.

Webb, E. (1981). *Eric Voegelin*, ISBN 0295964111.

Webber, S.S. (2002). "Leadership and trust facilitating cross-functional team success," *The Journal of Management Development*, ISSN 02621711, 21(3-4): 201-214.

Weber, B.H., Depew, D.J. and Smith, J.D. (eds.) (1990). *Entropy, Information, and Evolution*, ISBN 0262231328

Weber, M. (1924). *Gesammelte Aufsätze zur Sozial- und Wirtschaftsgeschichte*, Tübingen: Mohr (Siebeck), republished as *The Theory of Social and Economic Organization*, A. H. Henderson and T. Parsons (trans.), Glencoe, IL: Free Press, 1947.

Weber, M. (1930). *The Protestant Ethic and the Spirit of Capitalism*, T. Parsons (trans.), ISBN 9780486427034 (2003).

Weber, M. (1947). *The Theory of Social and Economic Organization*, A. M. Henderson and T. Parsons (trans.), ISBN 0684836408.

Weber, M. (1958). "Bureaucracy," in H. H. Gerth and C. W. Mills (eds.), H.H. Gerth (trans.), *From Max Weber: Essays in Sociology*, ISBN 0195004620, pp. 196-244.

Weber, R., Camerer, C., Rottenstreich, Y. and Knez, M. (2001). "The illusion of leadership: Misattribution of cause and effect in coordination games," *Organization Science*, ISSN 1047-7039, 12(5): 582-598.

Weick, K.E. (1969). *The Social Psychology of Organizing*, ISBN 0075548089 (1979).

Weick, K.E. (1976). "Educational organizations as loosely coupled systems," *Administrative Science Quarterly*, ISSN 0001-8392, 21: 1-19.

Weick, K.E. (1977). "Organization design: Organizations as self-designing systems,"

Organizational Dynamics, ISSN 0090-2616, 6(2): 30-46.

Weick, K.E. (1979). *The Social Psychology of Organizing*, ISBN 0075548089.

Weick, K.E. (1985). *Sensemaking in Organizations*, ISBN 0803971761 (1995)

Weick, K.E. (1995). *Sensemaking in Organizations*, ISBN 0803971761.

Weick, K.E. (1999). "Theory construction as disciplined reflexivity: Tradeoffs in the 90s," *Academy of Management Review*, ISSN 0363-7425, 24(Oct): 797-806.

Weick, K.E. (2001). *Making Sense of the Organization*, ISBN 0631223177.

Weick, K.E. and Quinn, R. (1999). "Organizational change and development," *American Review of Psychology*, ISBN 0824302508, 50: 361-386.

Weick, K.E. and Roberts, K. (1993). "Collective mind in organizations: Heedful interrelating on flight decks," *Administrative Science Quarterly*, ISSN 0001-8392, 38: 357-381.

Weick, K.E. and Sutcliffe, K. (2001). *Managing the Unexpected: Assuring High Performance in an Age of Complexity*, ISBN 0787956279.

Weick, K.E., Sutcliffe, K. and Obstfeld, D. (2005). "Organizing and the process of sensemaking," *Organization Science*, ISSN 1047-7039, 16: 409-421.

Weisbord, M. R. (1990). *Productive Workplaces: Organizing and Managing for Dignity, Meaning, and Community*, ISBN 1555423701.

Weiss, N. (1987). "Dynamics of convection," in M. Berry, I. Percival and N. Weiss (eds.), *Dynamical Chaos: Proceedings of the Royal Society of London*, ISBN 9780691085197, pp. 71-85.

Wenger, E. (1998). *Communities-of-Practice: Learning, Meaning and Identity*, ISBN 0521663636.

Wheatley, M.J. (1999). *Leadership and the New Science*, ISBN 1576750558.

Wheatley, M.J. and Kellner-Rogers, M. (1996). *A Simpler Way*, ISBN 1881052958

Wheelan, S. A. and Johnston, F. (1996). "The role of informal member leaders in a system containing formal leaders," *Small Group Research*, ISSN 1046-4964, 27: 33-55.

Wicken, J. (1986). "Evolutionary self-organization and entropic dissipation in biological and socioeconomic systems," *Journal of Social and Biological Structures*, 9: 261-273.

Wiener, N. (1948). *Cybernetics*, ISBN 9781432594442 (2007).

Wiener, N. (1954). *The Human Use of Human Beings*, Boston, MA: Houghton Mifflin, ISBN 9780306803208 (1988).

Wilber, K. (1995). *Sex, Ecology, Spirituality*, ISBN 1457620725

Wilber, K. (1998). *The Marriage of Sense and Soul*, ISBN 0375500545

Wilber, K. (2000). *A Brief History of Everything*, ISBN 1570627401.

Wilber, K. (2001). *A Theory of Everything*, ISBN 1570628556

Wiley, N. (1988). "The micro-macro problem in social theory," *Sociological Theory*, ISSN 0735-2751, 6(Fall): 254-261.

Williamson, O.E. (1973). "Markets and hierarchies: Some elementary considerations," *The American Economic Review*, ISSN 0002-8282, 63(May): 316-325.

Williamson, O.E. (1975). *Markets and Hierarchies*, ISBN 0029347807.

Wilmot, W.W. and Hocker J.L. (2001). *Interpersonal Conflict*, ISBN 007231253X.

Wimsatt, W.C. (1972). "Complexity and organization," in K. Schaffner and R.S. Cohen (eds.), *PSA 1972: Proceedings of the 1972 Biennial Meeting of the Philosophy of Science Association*, Dordrecht: D. Reidel, pp. 67-82.

Wimsatt, W.C. (1976). "Reductionism, levels of organization and the mind-body problem," in G. Globus, G. Maxwell and I. Sabodnik (eds.), *Consciousness and the Brain*, ISBN 9780306308789.

Wimsatt, W.C. (1994). "The ontology of complex systems: Levels of organization, perspectives, and causal thickets," *Canadian Journal of Philosophy*, ISSN 0045-5091, 20: 207-274.

Wimsatt, W.C. (1997). "Aggregativity: Reductive heuristics for finding emergence," *Philosophy of Science*, ISSN 0031-8248, S372-S384.

Winter, S. (2005). "Developing evolutionary theory for economics and management," in M. Hitt and K. Smith (eds.), *Oxford Handbook of Management Theory*, ISBN 0199275254

Winter, S. and Szulanski, G. (2001). "Replication as strategy," *Organization Science*, ISSN 1047-7039, 12 (6, Nov-Dec): 730-743.

Wolfram, S. (1983). "Statistical mechanics of cellular automata," *Reviews of Modern Physics*, ISSN 0034-6861, 55: 601-644.

Wolfram, S. (1994). *Cellular Automata and Complexity*, ISBN 0201627167.

Wolfram, S. (2002), *A New Kind of Science*, ISBN 0814703259.

Wolpert, D. and Macready, W. (2000). "Self-dissimilarity: An empirically observable complexity measure," in Y. Bar-Yam (ed.), Unifying Themes in Complex Systems: Proceedings of the International Conference on Complex Systems, ISBN 9780813341231, pp. 625-643.

Wood, R. (2000). *Managing Complexity: How Businesses Can Adapt and Prosper in the Connected Economy*, ISBN 1861971125.

Woodward, J. (2003). *Making Things Happen: A Theory of Causal Explanation*, ISBN 0195155270.

Wooldridge, M. (2002). *An Introduction to Multi-Agent Systems*, ISBN 9780471496915.

Yammarino, F.J. (1994). "Indirect leadership: Transformational leadership at a distance," in B.M. Bass and B.J. Avolio (eds.), *Improving Organizational Effectiveness through Transformational Leadership*, ISBN 0803952368, pp. 26-47.

Yammarino, F.J., Dubinsky, A.J., Comer, L.B. and Jolson, M.A. (1997). "Women and transformational and contingent reward leadership: A multiple-levels-of-analysis," *Academy of Management Journal*, ISSN 0001-4273, 40: 205-232.

Yin, R. (1998). "The abridged version of case study research: Design and method," in L. Bickman and D. Rog (eds.), *Handbook of Applied Social Research Methods*, ISBN 076190672X, pp. 229-259.

Yukl, G. (1999a). "An evaluative essay on current conceptions of effective leadership," *European Journal of Work and Organizational Psychology*, ISSN 1464-0643, 8(1): 33-48.

Yukl, G. (1999b). "An evaluation of conceptual weaknesses in transformational and charismatic leadership theories," *The Leadership Quarterly*, ISSN 1048-9843, 10(2): 285-305.

Yukl, G. (2006). *Leadership in Organizations*, ISBN 0131494848.

Zaccaro, S.J. and Klimoski, R.J. (2001). "The nature of organizational leadership: An introduction," in S.J. Zaccaro and R.J. Klimoski (eds.), *The Nature of Organizational Leadership: Understanding the Performance Imperatives Confronting Today's Leaders*, ISBN 0787952907, pp. 3-41.

Zaror, G. and Guastello, S. (2000). "Self-organization and leadership emergence: A cross-cultural replication," *Nonlinear Dynamics, Psychology, and Life Sciences*, ISSN 1090-0578, 4: 113-120.

Zeeman, E. (1977). *Catastrophe Theory: Selected Papers*, ISBN 0201090147.

Zeleny, M. (ed.) (1981). *Autopoiesis, Dissipative Structures, and Spontaneous Social Orders*, ISBN 0865310351

Zimmerman, B. and Hurst, D. (1993). "Breaking the boundaries: The fractal organization," *Journal of Management Inquiry*, ISSN 1056-4926, 2: 334-354.

Zohar, A. and Borkman, T. (1997). "Emergent order and self-organization: A case study of alcoholics anonymous," *Nonprofit and Voluntary Sector Quarterly*, ISSN 0899-7640, 26: 527-552.

INDEX

A

Actors 26, 39, 43, 53, 55, 129, 135, 139-40, 248, 314, 355, 391
Adaptability 4, 31, 83, 90-1, 94, 122, 133, 139, 143-4, 148, 150-1, 153-7, 229, 243, 299
Adaptation 5, 21-2, 24, 27, 34, 51, 81, 90, 111-2, 115, 124, 175, 187-8, 232-3, 243-4, 350
  organizational 228, 237, 291, 308-9, 350
Adaptive
  change 24, 136, 141, 231-2, 295, 298, 312
  leaders 233, 235, 239, 242-4, 312
  leadership 129, 134-6, 139, 143, 149, 151-3, 155-6, 158, 232-3, 237, 242-3, 311-2
  tensions 63, 102, 105-6, 112, 125, 152, 155, 307-8, 311, 315, 318, 320, 322
Agent
  behavior 101-2, 258-60, 300
  interactions 5, 7, 11, 27, 57, 99, 135-6, 175-6, 264-5, 273, 294-5, 298, 317, 321
Agent-based
  modeling 34, 102, 138, 169-70, 177, 184, 254, 293, 295, 298, 300
  models 5, 89, 170-2, 175, 181, 197, 205
Agents, contribution of 192
Assumptions 18-9, 36, 59, 80, 110, 114, 119, 132-3, 144-5, 148, 176, 178, 292-3, 372-3, 381, 384
Attraction, basins of 290, 322-4
Attractors 64, 77, 82, 86-8, 167, 290, 314, 317, 319-20
Authority 19, 38, 49, 111, 113, 115, 123, 134, 144-7, 156, 247, 250-1, 275, 316, 318, 332
Automata, cellular 5, 77, 97, 288, 291, 293-4, 298
Autonomy 55, 118, 154-5, 305, 307, 316, 323
Autopoiesis 291, 293, 301-2

B

Behaviors 5-8, 44-5, 48-52, 100-2, 115, 119-20, 138-40, 145-7, 152-4, 169-70, 205-9, 213-7, 272-3, 390-3, 402-5, 407-11
  human 119-20, 314, 382, 390
  self-organized 105, 392, 404-5, 407, 410-1
Biases 25, 34, 67-8, 302, 304, 395
Bureaucracy 27, 95, 145-7, 150, 152, 155, 158, 171, 178, 190, 247, 250-3, 255-8, 260-6, 268, 338

Equilibrium 6, 22, 43, 48-51, 59, 112, 123, 222, 267, 312, 352
Evolution 13, 31, 35-7, 48, 53, 57-9, 66, 77, 86-7, 93, 158, 197, 228, 291, 336-7, 355-6
Experiments 35, 88, 206-9, 211-3, 215, 218-25, 254, 256, 266, 270, 302, 306, 347, 357, 398

F

Fair leaders 177, 216, 218-23
Feedback 23, 48, 52-3, 58, 64, 74, 112-3, 255, 289, 296, 351, 353, 359-60, 362
Fitness 7, 154, 291, 307, 328-31, 384
Fluctuations, random 87, 89, 90, 197, 202
Folklore 61, 65-7, 69, 70, 85, 94
Formal leaders 9, 95, 135-6, 139, 141, 176, 206, 229, 233-4, 237, 243, 308, 310-3, 317, 319-21, 323-4
Free choice 43, 47-8, 52, 55, 313
Functions 11, 13, 37, 47, 50, 59, 65, 73, 125-6, 146-7, 150-1, 158-9, 197, 256-7, 272-3, 320-2

G

Generative
  leaders 106, 349, 353, 355-9, 364
  leadership 32, 34, 312, 349-61, 363-5
Genetic algorithms 5, 87, 98, 100, 172, 255, 291, 294, 298-300, 352
Goals 38-9, 43, 45, 47-50, 90, 120, 147-9, 151-2, 168-9, 252-4, 259-60, 262, 289, 292, 329-32, 357
Group
  dynamics 50, 82, 146, 302, 310, 370
  norms 95-6, 100, 104, 300, 323
Groups 10, 36, 38-9, 44-7, 50, 53-5, 64, 99-104, 111-3, 176, 178-83, 201-2, 207-16, 300-1, 319-22, 341-2
Growth 27, 103, 124-5, 158, 182, 185, 197, 201-2, 328, 354, 369

H

Heterogeneity 106, 141, 144, 147-8, 151-2, 155-6, 175, 251, 314-5, 322
Heterogeneous agents 94-5, 97, 104, 133-4, 175-6, 216, 313, 325
Hierarchical
  levels 104-5, 147, 257, 260, 310, 316
  structures 43, 185, 190, 230, 267-8, 315
Hierarchy 10, 64, 84, 95-7, 104-5, 151, 177-8, 184-5, 247, 250-2, 257, 260, 262-3, 267-9, 319, 362
Homogeneity 67, 82-3, 154

Leadership
  definition of 3, 7, 23, 317, 330, 332
  activities 95, 187-8, 289
  administrative 143, 149, 151-3, 156
  behaviors 51, 57, 141, 146, 218
  directive 24, 229, 240, 242
  discourse 37, 43-6, 50-1, 53, 55, 57-8
  distributed 55, 133-4, 155, 309
  effective 2, 7, 10, 54, 132, 185, 325, 353
  emergence 31, 34, 96, 111, 190, 223
  formal 65, 104, 230, 313-4, 317, 319-20, 322
  managerial 106, 149, 153, 232, 311-2, 330
  mechanisms 28, 307-9, 312
  model 31, 172, 184, 305, 307, 311, 373
  nature of 36, 58, 113, 129, 229
  participative 25, 229, 234, 240, 242-3
  processes 11, 24-5, 118-9, 151, 171, 178, 187-8, 232, 300, 307, 314
  research 3, 12, 17, 19, 21, 23, 25-7, 29, 31, 33, 140-1, 158, 163, 165,
      172-3, 295-6
  roles 3, 31-2, 34, 38, 57, 64-5, 75, 103, 115, 132, 195, 201, 217, 273-5,
      279, 310
  skills 197, 199, 202
  studies 2, 3, 61-2, 73, 89, 133, 334, 341, 345
  style 32, 34, 106, 216-7, 223, 227, 229, 231-5, 237-9, 241-5, 255, 270
    participative 176, 237, 240, 242
  theory 9, 19, 29, 35-6, 51, 95, 129, 133-4, 158, 174, 206, 227, 243, 289,
      305, 324
    conventional 17-9, 27-8
Learning 9, 21-2, 52, 114-5, 122-5, 127, 139-40, 144, 150-1, 153-5, 171,
      182, 229, 231-3, 242-4, 321
Levels 5, 6, 39, 78-9, 83-5, 94-7, 99-107, 178, 180, 185-6, 201-2, 242-4,
      253, 258-60, 292-7, 299-302, 308-9
  of analysis 36-7, 163, 175, 294, 324
Lower levels 27, 70, 72, 77-8, 83-4, 86, 113, 125, 147, 243, 251, 258, 265,
      352, 362

M

Macro-level events 248
Management 1-3, 17-8, 22, 27-8, 93-4, 117-8, 129-30, 143-4, 146, 148-9,
      152-3, 158-9, 163, 271, 285, 340
  supply chain 17, 182, 271, 273, 327
Managers 1, 2, 4, 8, 9, 26-7, 54, 93-4, 104-5, 111-2, 117-8, 123-6, 150,
      331-2, 361, 371-2, 381-3, 401-2
Mathematical and Computational Modeling of Leadership 164, 166, 168,
      170, 172, 174, 176, 178, 180, 182, 184, 186, 188, 190, 192, 196

Organizations
  computational 328, 330-2
  postmodern 227, 229, 231, 243-4

P
Paradigm 18, 24, 58, 94, 149, 158, 163, 230-1, 243, 374, 397
Paradox 27, 30, 124-5, 229, 232, 305, 309, 324
Participants 55, 82, 135, 138, 207, 249, 285, 319, 334, 340, 342, 344,
    346-7, 356, 394-8, 405-6
Participation 43, 49, 58, 109, 155, 187, 197-203, 247, 252, 316, 343, 363,
    383, 394, 409
  levels 197, 199, 200, 202
  limiting 198-9, 201, 203
Pathologies, social 27, 249-50, 268
Patterns 6, 11, 59, 67, 70, 77-8, 88, 126-7, 157, 289, 294-5, 297-302, 387,
    389-92, 396, 406-11
Peer pressure 11, 174, 195, 197-203, 211
Performance 18, 102, 117, 120, 139, 144-5, 156, 168-9, 171, 177-81,
    190-3, 211-2, 239-40, 262, 272-5, 277-80
  optimal 175, 273, 275, 279
  organizational 114, 116, 131, 227, 273
Power
  laws 97, 100, 177, 290, 297-8
  utilitarian 251-2, 260, 267
Problem solving 126, 350-1, 354-5, 357-8, 361
Processes 3, 4, 43-7, 72-3, 85-7, 89, 90, 93-5, 136-7, 146-7, 187-9, 244,
    307-10, 315-8, 321-4, 334-5, 373-6, 396-8
  dynamic 134, 308, 313-4, 318, 324, 332, 353
  organizational 90, 150, 290, 324, 368

R
Random numbers 168, 179-81, 191-2, 202
Randomness 39, 64, 70, 74, 87-9, 91
Reductionism 49, 51-3, 55, 57, 59, 62, 79, 369-70
Relationships 8, 9, 35-9, 41-3, 48, 55, 57-9, 115-6, 141, 152, 175-6, 179-
    81, 297-8, 309-10, 361, 371-2, 397-9
Resources 4, 5, 9, 45, 53, 63, 91, 102, 104-5, 150, 152, 175, 187, 235-6,
    307, 317-8, 332
Rules 5, 9, 66-8, 83, 100, 111, 118, 135-6, 146-7, 250-1, 268, 291, 299-
    301, 358-60, 365, 377
  adaptive 152, 154, 156
  biased 68, 74

S

Systems
  discourse, social 37-8, 43, 49, 52, 55, 59
  theory 9, 36-8, 42-3, 48, 58, 288, 293, 369

T

Tasks 51, 119, 175-7, 208-10, 235-6, 238-9, 247, 255-6, 262, 264-5,
    268-9, 308, 310-1, 314-5, 317-21, 358
Team
  members 179-81, 206-7, 211, 308-9, 311-2, 316-24, 351
  performance 178-81, 207, 274, 309
Teams 83, 125, 130, 164, 169-71, 176, 178-80, 182-3, 215-6, 237-40, 242,
    307-8, 311, 313-25, 353-4, 360
  cross-functional 124, 273, 279, 361
Technology 34, 106, 130, 143, 328-9, 350, 357-9, 361-3
Tension 23-4, 27, 49, 53, 124-7, 129, 133, 136, 141, 156, 233, 244, 334,
    338-40, 345-6, 410-1
  sustaining 109, 119, 121, 124-5
Top-down 17, 22, 27-8, 104-7, 144, 147-9, 153, 157-8, 230-1, 307
Top management teams 103, 115, 171, 182-4, 305
Traditional leadership 25, 143-4, 146, 148, 152-4, 156-8, 305, 310
  theories 22, 24, 144, 146, 155, 227, 229-30, 232, 411
Traits 5, 22, 44, 47-8, 114, 138, 230, 294, 298-9, 315, 349, 351
Transactional leadership 19, 54, 116, 188-9, 319
Transformational leadership 19, 30, 54, 111, 114, 116-7

U

Unexpected behaviors 290, 396, 398, 400, 403, 405-6
Unpredictability 3, 87-9, 112, 144, 372

V

Values 19, 37, 40, 48, 54, 58-9, 92, 121-3, 168-9, 180-3, 192-3, 275-7,
    279-80, 290-1, 344, 354
Visions, indeterminate 149, 154-6, 159

W

Work teams 307, 311, 313, 324, 345
Workplaces 29, 89, 387, 389-91, 393-401, 403-5, 407-9, 411

Y

Youth organizations 31, 34, 195-9, 201-3

Printed in the United States
101378LV00002B/1/A

119
126